FROM PATRIOTS TO UNIONISTS

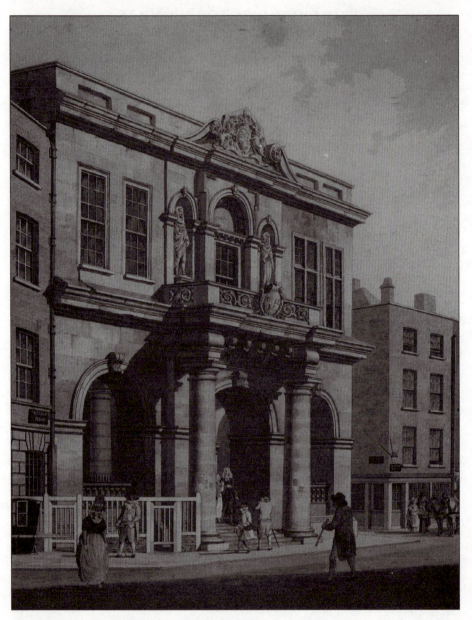

The Tholsel, Skinner's Row (now demolished), by James Malton, 1792.
Reproduced by courtesy of the National Gallery of Ireland.

FROM PATRIOTS TO UNIONISTS

*Dublin Civic Politics
and Irish Protestant Patriotism,
1660–1840*

JACQUELINE HILL

CLARENDON PRESS · OXFORD
1997

Oxford University Press, Great Clarendon Street, Oxford OX2 6DP

Oxford New York

Athens Auckland Bangkok Bogota Bombay
Buenos Aires Calcutta Cape Town Dar es Salaam
Delhi Florence Hong Kong Istanbul Karachi
Kuala Lumpur Madras Madrid Melbourne
Mexico City Nairobi Paris Singapore
Taipei Tokyo Toronto
and associated companies in
Berlin Ibadan

Oxford is a trade mark of Oxford University Press

Published in the United States
by Oxford University Press Inc., New York

British Library Cataloguing in Publication Data
Data applied for

Library of Congress Cataloging in Publication Data
Data available
ISBN 0–19–820635–6

1 3 5 7 9 10 8 6 4 2

Typeset by Cambrian Typesetters Frimley, Surrey
Printed in Great Britain
on acid-free paper by
Bookcraft Ltd., Midsomer Norton
Nr. Bath, Somerset

To Jennifer and Edwin

and in memory of my parents

Surely we should, with the utmost Gratitude and Exultation, call to our Minds that critical . . . Period, in which the glorious Spirit of Liberty first took its Rise in this great Metropolis . . . Do we forget that all the Inhabitants of the Land fell in with the Citizens of *Dublin*? That those Citizens became the Admiration and the Envy of the surrounding Nations? That *Rome* herself, in all her meridian Glory, could not boast more noble, more disinterested, or more zealous Patriots?

Anon., *A Letter to the Citizens of Dublin. By a Farmer* (Dublin, 1766), 9–10.

Acknowledgements

This book has taken a long time to write, and I have incurred many debts in the course of its preparation. I wish first to thank St Patrick's College, Maynooth for granting me spells of study leave in 1986 when the research was begun and in 1994 when the first draft had been completed.

For permission to quote from manuscript sources in their care I am grateful to the Board of Trinity College, Dublin; Dublin Corporation Archives; the Trustees of the Harrowby MSS Trust; Keele University Library; the National Archives; the Council of Trustees of the National Library of Ireland; the Public Record Office of Northern Ireland; the Representative Church Body Library, and the Royal Irish Academy. I also wish to thank the staffs of the British Library; Cambridge University Library; the Guinness Museum; Marsh's Library; the National Archives; the National Library of Ireland; the Public Record Office, London; the Public Record Office of Northern Ireland; the Representative Church Body Library; the Royal Irish Academy; the Royal Society of Antiquaries of Ireland, and Trinity College, Dublin. For archival help and advice I am grateful to Douglas Bennett of the Assay Office; Paula Howard of the Gilbert Library; Dr Malachy Powell of Apothecaries' Hall; Brendan Teeling of the Dublin Heritage Group, and Penny Woods of the Russell Library, St Patrick's College. Along with all who study the history of this great city, I owe an enormous debt to Mary Clark, who is doing so much, under difficult conditions, to transform Dublin Corporation's archives into a major scholarly resource. Her courteous co-operation and advice on all occasions greatly facilitated the work. Thanks are also due to Jim Keenan for preparing the maps, and to Helen Litton for making the index.

To my departmental colleagues, and especially Vincent Comerford and the former professor of modern history, Monsignor Patrick Corish, I wish to record my gratitude for their unfailing friendship, kindness, and support; to David Steele of the University of Leeds for inspiring my interest in Irish history, and to Kevin B. Nowlan and the late Theo Moody for cultivating it. As the ideas in the book were taking shape, I was fortunate to be able to work some of them out in the pages of *Irish Historical Studies* and *Past & Present*, as well as to have the benefit of comments from international seminar groups such as the Folger Institute Seminar on the British Union of 1707, conducted in 1991 by John Robertson. At home, I have benefited greatly from discussions with many scholars, and particularly with my former student, Cadoc Leighton. He, together with David Dickson, Ray Gillespie, James Kelly, Colm Lennon, James McGuire, Sean Murphy, and Kevin Nowlan generously read all or part of the text at different stages of its evolution. To James Kelly are due special thanks for his considered advice and comments on the entire work. Not all their suggestions could be adopted, but I am grateful to them all for saving me from errors and for their encouragement. My greatest debt is to my sister and brother-in-law, and this book is dedicated to them.

Dublin   J.H.
August 1996

Contents

List of Maps

List of Tables

Abbreviations and Conventions

AHR	*American Historical Review*
Anal. Hib.	*Analecta Hibernica*
Arch. Hib.	*Archivium Hibernicum*
Cal. SP Dom.	*Calendar of State Papers, Domestic Series*
Cal. SP Ire.	*Calendar of State Papers Relating to Ireland*
CARD	*Calendar of Ancient Records of Dublin*, ed. John T. and R. M. Gilbert (19 vols.; Dublin, 1889–1944)
CHR	*Canadian Historical Review*
Commons Jn. Ire.	*Journals of the House of Commons of the Kingdom of Ireland*
CULBC	Cambridge University Library, Bradshaw Collection
DCA	Dublin Corporation Archives
DEP	*Dublin Evening Post*
DHDG	*Directory of Historic Dublin Guilds*, ed. Mary Clark and Raymond Refaussé (Dublin, 1993)
DPLGC	Dublin Public Libraries, Gilbert Collection
Dublin Hist. Rec.	*Dublin Historical Record*
ECI	*Eighteenth Century Ireland*
Econ. Hist. Rev.	*Economic History Review*
EHR	*English Historical Review*
FDJ	*Faulkner's Dublin Journal*
FJ	*Freeman's Journal*
Friends' Hist. Soc. Jn.	*Journal of the Friends' Historical Society*
Hib. Jn.	*Hibernian Journal*
Hist. Jn.	*Historical Journal*
Hist. Pol. Thought	*History of Political Thought*
HMC	*Historical Manuscripts Commission*
Hug. Soc. Proc.	*Proceedings of the Huguenot Society of London*
IER	*Irish Ecclesiastical Record*
IHS	*Irish Historical Studies*
JMH	*Journal of Modern History*
Jn. Ecc. Hist.	*Journal of Ecclesiastical History*
Jn. Hist. Ideas	*Journal of the History of Ideas*
JRSAI	*Journal of the Royal Society of Antiquaries of Ireland*
MLD	Marsh's Library (Dublin)
NA	National Archives (Dublin)

NHI	*A New History of Ireland*
NLI	National Library of Ireland
NUI	National University of Ireland
P. & P.	*Past & Present*
Parl. Hist.	*Parliamentary History*
Parl. Hist. Eng.	*Parliamentary History of England*
PRO	Public Record Office (London)
PRONI	Public Record Office of Northern Ireland
RIA	Royal Irish Academy
RSAI	Royal Society of Antiquaries of Ireland
Studia Hib.	*Studia Hibernica*
TCD	Trinity College, Dublin
UCD	University College, Dublin
VJ	*Volunteer's Journal*

Dates are given in old style, as used in Ireland and England until the calendar change of 1751, except that the year has been taken to begin on 1 January. Original spelling and punctuation have been retained.

The following contemporary terms are used in the text:

acts of assembly	decisions taken by both houses of Dublin corporation at quarter-assembly or post-assembly meetings
the board	board of aldermen, the upper house of Dublin corporation, chaired by the lord mayor
the commons (or city commons)	lower house of Dublin corporation, chaired by the sheriffs
the common council	both houses of Dublin corporation
post assembly	extraordinary meeting of Dublin corporation.

Maps

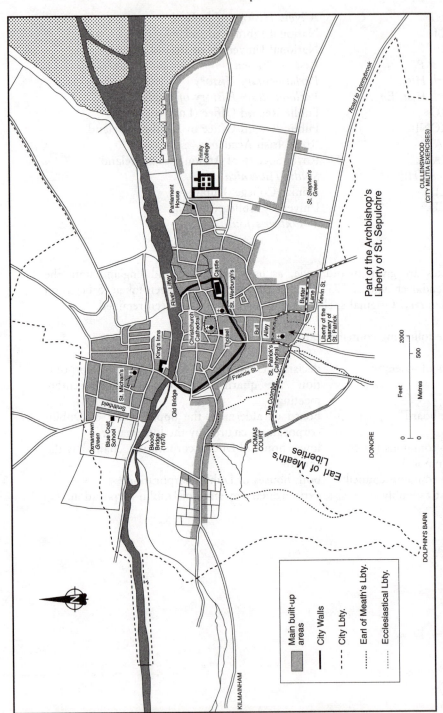

Oxmantown Green

Blue Coat School

Smithfield

St. Michan's

King's Inns

Bloody Bridge (1670)

Old Bridge

River Liffey

Castle

St. Werburgh's

Christchurch Cathedral

Tholsel

Bull Alley

Francis St.

THOMAS COURT

Earl of Meath's Liberties

The Coombe

St. Patrick's Cathedral

Liberty of the Deanery of St. Patrick

Butter Lane

Kevin St.

Parliament House

Trinity College

St. Stephen's Green

Road to Donnybrook

Part of the Archbishop's Liberty of St. Sepulchre

CULLENSWOOD (CITY MILITIA EXERCISES)

DONORE

DOLPHIN'S BARN

Feet   0   500   2000

Metres 0

Main built-up areas

—— City Walls

- - - City Lbty.

······· Earl of Meath's Lbty.

········ Ecclesiastical Lbty.

N

Map 1. Dublin, *c.* 1673 (after Bernard de Gomme)

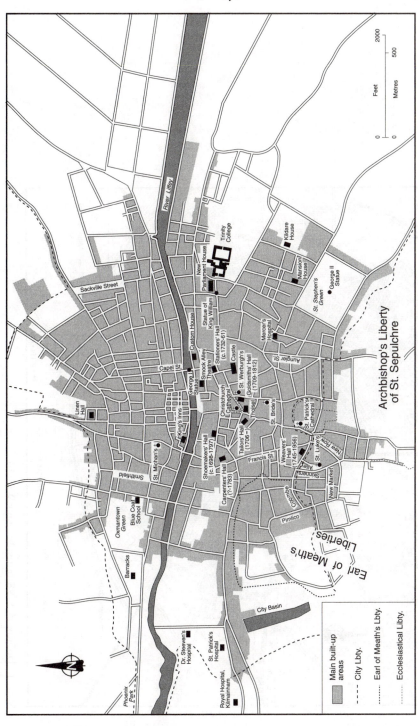

River Liffey

Trinity College

Kildare House

New ——
Parliament House

Mansion House

George II Statue

St. Stephen's Green

Sackville Street

Custom House

Statue of King William

Mercer's Hospital

Capel St

George's Statue

Snock Alley Theatre

Stationers' Hall (c. 1732–61)

Castle

St. Werburgh's

Goldsmiths' Hall (1709–1812)

Aungier St

Linen Hall

King's Inns

Christchurch Cathedral

Tholsel

St. Bride's

St. Patrick's Cathedral

Archbishop's Liberty of St. Sepulchre

St. Michan's

Tailors' Hall (1706–)

St. Luke's (1745–1956)

New Row

Shoemakers' Hall (c. 1698–1797)

Weavers' Hall

Smithfield

Carpenters' Hall (?–1783)

Francis St

Skinners' Alley

Ormantown Green

Blue Coat School

Cole St

New Market

Barracks

Pimlico

Earl of Meath's Liberties

City Basin

Phoenix Park

Dr. Steeven's Hospital

St. Patrick's Hospital

Royal Hospital, Kilmainham

Main built-up areas

– – – City Lbty.

········· Earl of Meath's Lbty.

········· Ecclesiastical Libty.

MAP 2. Dublin, *c.* 1756 (after John Rocque)

Feet 2000
500
0
Metres 0

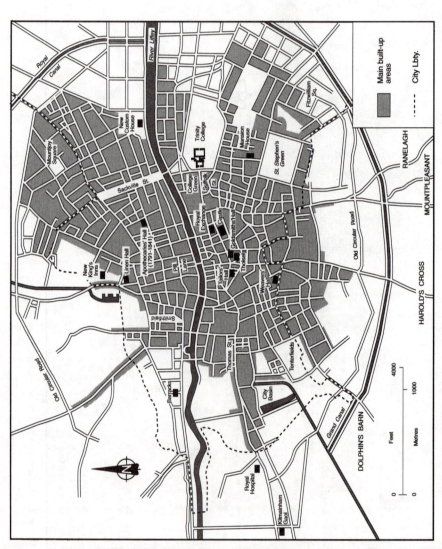

MAP 3. Dublin, *c.* 1798 (after William Wilson)

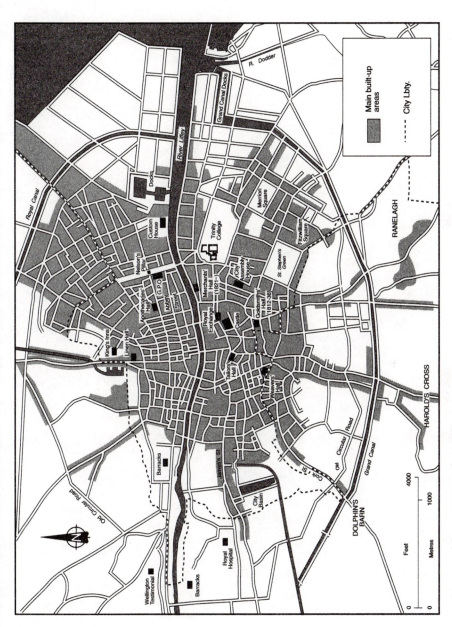

Map 4. Dublin, *c.* 1821 (after William Duncan)

Introduction

The rise of a Protestant Patriot movement has long formed a standard theme in histories of eighteenth-century Ireland. With glances at the contributions of Molyneux in the 1690s and then of Swift, accounts typically reach their apex with the Volunteers and the winning of legislative independence in 1782–3. Not that 1782 by any means marked the end of Protestant involvement; but with the United Irishmen of the 1790s Patriotism fractured, and was eclipsed by the act of union with Britain in 1800. Thereafter most Protestants quickly embraced what would turn out to be a lasting unionist position.[1] Little has appeared to challenge this well-known motif in Irish history; an attempt to cast doubt on the continuity of a Protestant Patriot tradition has not attracted support.[2]

If the phenomenon itself is a familiar one, coverage by historians has been decidedly uneven. The official mouthpiece of the landed élite, the Irish parliament, has received a good deal of attention, while outside the élite many studies have been made of what might be termed unofficial or voluntary vehicles of opinion, such as the Volunteers themselves.[3] The views of official organs of the urban Protestant citizenry, however, the corporations and guilds, have been largely ignored.

In Dublin, townsmen who were active on the national political stage were traditionally drawn from a small mercantile body with strong ties to the landed class. But by the mid-eighteenth century a political role was being embraced by a wider section of the civic community, especially the lower house of the corporation, and the guilds. Political resolutions were passed more frequently, and new emphasis was placed on the importance of the corporate dimension both in civic and in national political life.

These developments may be regarded as part of a wider movement of corporate self-assertion, analagous in some respects to the aristocratic resurgence that took place in western Europe towards the end of the *ancien régime*. Commercial and industrial expansion, which helped to make Dublin one of the ten largest cities in Europe by 1800, increased the confidence of its citizenry. Ideologically, the example of London was influential. London's role in resisting 'arbitrary' monarchy under Charles II

---

[1] An early example is W. E. H. Lecky, *A History of Ireland in the Eighteenth Century*, abridged edn. (Chicago, 1972) (all refs. to this edn.); more recent accounts are T. W. Moody and W. E. Vaughan (eds.), *A New History of Ireland*, iv. *Eighteenth Century Ireland 1691–1800* (Oxford, 1986) (hereafter *NHI* iv.), chs. 1, 5, 8, 10–13; Roy Foster, *Modern Ireland 1600–1972* (London, 1988), chs. 7–12.

[2] Gerard O'Brien, 'The Grattan Mystique', *ECI* 1 (1986), 177–94.

[3] See bibliography in Moody and Vaughan (eds.), *NHI* iv. 753–9, 763–6.

lent weight to claims concerning the need for corporate independence and integrity: claims that seemed to be vindicated by the revolution of 1688–9. Dublin could not boast of having played an advanced role in resisting arbitrary monarchy during the restoration period; but passive resistance during the Jacobite era, followed up by defiance of a Tory lord chancellor during Queen Anne's reign, provided the city with somewhat similar credentials. Thereafter, the corporation took a Patriot stand on a range of issues, including Wood's halfpence in the 1720s, free trade and Irish parliamentary rights in the 1770s and 1780s, and legislative union in 1800. Hostility to union actually persisted in Dublin corporate circles and among freemen of the guilds long after most of the landed élite had become reconciled to it.

Support for such causes, however, should not obscure the fact that, like other corporations during the seventeenth and eighteenth centuries, Dublin corporation and even its guilds were arms of the state; their officials acting as intermediaries between the state and the citizens. This, however, merely adds interest to the evolution of civic Patriotism. What also adds interest is the fact that from the restoration of the monarchy in 1660 down to municipal reform in 1840, Dublin in its corporate capacity was predominantly, if not always exclusively, Protestant.

With the exception of the mayoral controversy in Queen Anne's reign, and the politicization of the Dublin freemen in the 1740s, few of these developments have received much attention from historians;[4] and where studies have been made, they have often been carried out with little reference to each other. The reasons for this are not immediately apparent. There is no lack of sources. The records of Dublin corporation's quarterly meetings were published long ago by Sir John and Lady Gilbert.[5] Surviving guild records, although patchy, contain information on political attitudes as well as trading matters. Official sources make at least occasional reference to Dublin civic politics. Regular newspapers were appearing in Dublin by the 1690s, and together with pamphlets, were to become ever more numerous in the following century. Besides, several of the leading Patriots, including Molyneux, Swift, Lucas, and Grattan had Dublin backgrounds or connections.[6] If we turn to England, there is no shortage of studies of London politics in the eighteenth century, or of biographies of prominent

---

[4] Some notable exceptions are Catherine M. Flanagan, ' "A Merely Local Dispute"? Partisan Politics and the Dublin Mayoral Dispute of 1709–1715', Ph.D. thesis (Notre Dame, Ind., 1983); Sean Murphy, 'The Lucas Affair: A Study of Municipal and Electoral Politics in Dublin, 1742–9', MA thesis (NUI (UCD), 1981); id., 'Charles Lucas and the Dublin Election of 1748–1749', *Parl. Hist.* 2 (1983), 93–111.

[5] John T. and R. M. Gilbert (eds.), *Calendar of Ancient Records of Dublin, in Possession of the Municipal Corporation of that City* (*CARD*) (19 vols.; Dublin, 1889–1944).

[6] For Molyneux, see n. 21 below; for Swift and Lucas, see Ch. 3; for Grattan, see below, App. B.

London politicians such as John Wilkes.[7] Yet so far there is no biography of the apothecary Charles Lucas, who was easily the most important of the Irish Patriots in the middle decades of the century, and whose political career was firmly grounded in the Dublin corporate world.[8]

The neglect of Dublin, however, is not accidental. There is, for instance, the traditional bias that favours the rural dweller over the townsman as being somehow more authentically Irish and worthy of attention. This bias has been compounded by the tendency to regard the Protestant population as a monolithic, landed class, while the rising middle class (outside Ulster, at any rate) is thought of as being largely Catholic. Yet according to Sir William Petty, writing in the late seventeenth century, half the Protestants in Ireland were townsfolk.[9] Irish Protestantism, then, was as much an urban as a landed phenomenon, and the implications of this for Irish history are only beginning to be explored.[10]

A further reason for the neglect of Dublin city politics is bound up with the nature of contemporary political culture. Since civic Patriotism was robustly confessional, it has proved generally repellent. Far more attention has been paid to such figures as Grattan and Tone[11]—who in the 1790s found ways to incorporate Catholics within their definition of the political nation—than to Lucas, who remained convinced that Catholics must be excluded from political life.[12] Yet any study of Irish Patriotism remains unsatisfactory which fails to do justice to the importance of Protestantism in the outlook of Lucas and his supporters among the Dublin freemen. And it is here that the would-be student of Patriot politics encounters a serious difficulty. For, according to the nationalist model that historians have used for the past

[7] See the bibliographies in Gary Stuart de Krey, *A Fractured Society: The Politics of London in the First Age of Party, 1688–1715* (Oxford, 1985) and John Stevenson (ed.), *London in the Age of Reform* (Oxford, 1977); for Wilkes, see George Rudé, *Wilkes and Liberty* (Oxford, 1965); Ian R. Christie, *Wilkes, Wyvill and Reform* (London, 1962).

[8] But see Murphy, 'The Lucas Affair'.

[9] T. W. Moody, F. X. Martin, F. J. Byrne (eds.), *A New History of Ireland*, iii. *Early Modern Ireland 1534–1691* (Oxford, 1976), 474.

[10] David Dickson, ' "Centres of Motion": Irish Cities and the Origins of Popular Politics', in *Culture et pratiques politiques en France et en Irlande xvie–xviiie siècle. Actes du Colloque de Marseille 28 Sept.–2 Oct. 1988* (Paris, 1990), 101–22; Eamon O'Flaherty, 'Urban Politics and Municipal Reform in Limerick, 1723–62', *ECI* 6 (1991), 105–20; Kenneth Milne, 'The Corporation of Waterford in the Eighteenth Century', in W. Nolan and T. P. Power (eds.), *Waterford: History and Society* (Dublin, 1992), 331–50.

[11] See e.g. Henry Grattan (jun.), *Memoirs of the Life and Times of the Rt. Hon. Henry Grattan, by his Son* (5 vols.; London, 1839–46); Stephen Gwynn, *Henry Grattan and his Times* (Dublin, 1939). For Theobald Wolfe Tone (1763–98), (b. Dublin, educated TCD, founder member of United Irishmen), see Marianne Elliott, *Wolfe Tone: Prophet of Irish Independence* (New Haven, 1989).

[12] Sean Murphy contends that Lucas developed a more benign attitude towards Catholics: 'Charles Lucas, Catholicism and Nationalism', *ECI* 8 (1993), 83–102; but see C. D. A. Leighton, *Catholicism in a Protestant Kingdom: A Study of the Irish Ancien Régime* (Dublin, 1994), 77–83.

century to characterize Irish Patriotism, Lucas does appear to be more
marginal than a Grattan or a Tone. Accordingly, if any progress is to be
made in evaluating Dublin's role in Patriot politics, the model itself will
have to be reviewed.

The present study does not set out to provide a comprehensive political
history of the city in this period, which still remains to be written. Rather, it
investigates the evolution of Dublin civic Patriotism and its relationship
(particularly of an ideological kind) with Protestant Patriotism in general,
and considers how ideas influenced actions. Our understanding of the
languages of political argument, and the importance of relating them to the
values and goals of the societies that used them, has been transformed in
recent decades thanks to the work of scholars such as Quentin Skinner and
J. G. A. Pocock.[13]

I. The Historiographical Context

Eighteenth-century Ireland is still dominated by a historiographical
consensus which, in its essential features, derives from Lecky's *History of
Ireland in the Eighteenth Century*, and in certain respects reaches back still
further to Burke's *Tracts on the Popery Laws* (unpublished during Burke's
lifetime, but composed in the 1760s).[14] Both Burke and Lecky were
preoccupied with the problem of religious divisions in Ireland, divisions that
for many Irish people apparently took precedence over ties of country or
'nationality' (the term favoured by Lecky). Both writers considered such a
condition to be backward and unnatural, and they were all the more critical
because the penal laws, which had fostered such attitudes, had been directed
against a majority of the population. However, with the Patriot movement
Lecky believed that a sense of nationality was emerging among Protestants;
and he saw this reflected in the progressive repeal of the penal laws from the
1770s onwards. Being natural and forward-looking, this development
required little elaboration. But when in the 1790s there was an apparent
reversal in these trends, Lecky (again following Burke) introduced an
extraneous (unnatural) factor to account for the fact: government. First
Dublin Castle was charged with inciting opposition to proposals for
granting political rights to Catholics in 1792; and subsequently the British
government was indicted for thwarting the viceroy's policy of removing the
remaining penal laws, at a time when such a policy would (in Lecky's view)
have been generally acceptable to all denominations in Ireland. The results

---

[13] See e.g. Quentin Skinner, *The Foundations of Modern Political Thought* (2 vols.;
Cambridge, 1978), i, pp. ix–xv; J. G. A. Pocock, 'The Concept of a Language and the *Métier
d'Historien*', in Anthony Pagden (ed.), *The Languages of Political Theory in Early-Modern
Europe* (Cambridge, 1987), 19–38.

[14] This consensus is beginning to be challenged: T. C. Barnard, 'Farewell to Old Ireland',
Hist. Jn. 36 (1993), 909–28.

of this intervention, and specifically the recall of Lord Fitzwilliam, were described by Lecky as 'a fatal turning point', leading on to the revival of sectarian hostility, the rebellion of 1798, and the act of union.[15]

The events of the 1790s will be considered in more detail below. For the moment, it is worth noting the extent to which these assumptions continue to inform modern histories of eighteenth-century Ireland. In the twentieth century, historians pursued Lecky's use of the term 'nationality' to its logical conclusion, and Patriotism began to be depicted as a form of nationalism— albeit usually in qualified form, as 'colonial' or 'settler' nationalism. Moreover, it has been taken for granted that support for Patriotism went together with a growth of religious toleration, so that by the 1770s even Catholics were coming to be regarded as loyal citizens.[16]

Clearly this interpretation of Irish politics has enjoyed an extended appeal. Yet it raises problems. One is that Burke and Lecky's critique of the elevation of religious ties above those of nationality scarcely does justice to the nature of contemporary European political thought. Admittedly, the rising importance of natural law in the 1600s and 1700s reflected a search for principles that would marginalize those religious zealots (Protestant or Catholic) whose belief in universal moral obligations seemed to be responsible for the destructive wars of religion in early modern Europe. But on the Protestant side, even those who rejected the view that rulers had a duty to impose 'true' religion on their subjects, nevertheless (from Harrington to Locke and even to Hegel) continued to hold as an ideal the reconciliation of the sacred and the secular—most commonly through some form of civil religion, which may be regarded as a further working out of the reformed (Protestant) tradition.[17]

A related difficulty concerns the nature of nationalism. Studies in the last thirty years have produced general agreement about some basic features of modern nationalism. First, modern nationalism depends on the idea that individuals (not institutions or orders such as the aristocracy, the church, or corporations) constitute the 'nation', a term which, like many others, has changed its meaning since the eighteenth century. Second, the rights of those individuals are understood to spring from the natural rights of man, rather than from inherited privileges deriving from God, the monarch, custom, etc. Third, nationalism is bound up with the idea of the all-powerful sovereign

---

[15] Edmund Burke, *The Works of the Rt. Hon. Edmund Burke* (6 vols.; London, 1884–99), vi. 20, 26–7; Lecky, *History of Ireland in the Eighteenth Century*, 41–2, 87, 103–8, 114, 137–8, 160–1, 194, 241–2, 282–9.

[16] See e.g. Denis Gwynn, *The Struggle for Catholic Emancipation 1750–1829* (London, 1928), 58; J. G. Simms, *Colonial Nationalism, 1698–1776* (Cork, 1976); Moody and Vaughan (eds.), *NHI* iv. pp. liv, 233.

[17] Richard Tuck, 'The "Modern" Theory of Natural Law', in Pagden (ed.), *The Languages of Political Theory*, 99–119, at 117–18; Mark Goldie, 'The Civil Religion of James Harrington', ibid. 197–222, at 201–2.

state; and fourth, although precursors of nationalism may certainly be found in earlier periods, these elements only came together in the context of the upheavals associated with the French revolution at the end of the eighteenth century (the term 'nationalism' itself was first used in 1798). The idea that nation-states formed the natural political units of mankind only took hold during the nineteenth century.[18] By contrast, despite the emergence of romanticism, the main intellectual currents of the eighteenth century assumed the underlying unity of mankind, and promoted cosmopolitan ideals.

Of course, it can be argued that Irish Patriotism represented, if not a fully fledged, still an embryonic form of nationalism. But like the Whig interpretation of English history—with which it has much in common—such a teleological approach risks obscuring what the characteristic values and goals of the Patriots actually were.[19] And some acquaintance with the pantheon of eighteenth-century Irish Patriots provided by Lecky (including Molyneux, Swift, and Lucas) suggests that a nationalist model may have limitations when it comes to explaining their political outlook. Lucas, for instance, was on occasion prepared to adopt the pseudonym 'Britannicus', in preference to the apparently more obvious 'Hibernicus'. And his essentially moral and confessional perception of the constitution and his insistence that the state was constrained by fundamental laws also suggest that if the Patriots are to be understood an effort has to be made to reconstruct the world as they saw it.[20]

It has also been noted that both Burke and Lecky contended that the Irish penal laws were peculiarly unnatural because they were employed against a majority of the population. This sounds eminently reasonable to modern ears. But how important were majorities in politics before the end of the eighteenth century? Until then, in Ireland as elsewhere, ownership of land—and in towns, membership of corporations—meant far more, in political terms, than sheer weight of numbers. If judged by those criteria, it becomes easier to understand how Molyneux, first in the pantheon of Protestant Patriots, could argue that in his own day there remained but a 'meer handful' of the ancient Irish.[21]

Finally, it seems worth looking again at the rise of 'nationality', the

[18] Anthony D. Smith, *Theories of Nationalism*, 2nd edn. (London, 1983), 190–1; K. R. Minogue, *Nationalism* (London, 1969), 10–11, 33–52; Eugene Kamenka, 'Political Nationalism—the Evolution of the Idea' in E. Kamenka (ed.), *Nationalism: The Nature and Evolution of an Idea* (Canberra, 1973), 3–20, at 8.
[19] Cf. J. T. Leerssen, 'Anglo-Irish Patriotism and its European Context: Notes Towards a Reassessment', *ECI* 3 (1988), 7–24.   [20] See below, Ch. 3.
[21] William Molyneux, *The Case of Ireland's Being Bound by Acts of Parliament in England, Stated* (Dublin, 1698), 35. All refs. are to the reprint, ed. J. G. Simms (Dublin, 1977). Molyneux (1656–98), b. Dublin, educated TCD; first secretary, Dublin Philosophical Society (J. G. Simms, *William Molyneux of Dublin, 1656–98*, ed. P. H. Kelly (Dublin, 1982)).

decline of sectarian animosity, and the repeal of the penal laws: all of which Lecky took to be closely related. It has been assumed that the relaxation of the penal laws against Catholics was part of a continuous process which, once begun, would lead inexorably on to the repeal of all such laws. But it is doubtful whether contemporaries regarded the matter in this light,[22] and hence the whole question of the extension of political rights to Catholics in the 1790s requires reassessment. These are just some of the issues that seem to justify re-examining common assumptions about Patriot ideology and politics.

II. Patriotism and Contemporary Political Thought

It may be noted at the outset that the term 'Patriot' was rooted in contemporary usage. As early as the 1670s an Anglo-Irish magnate was described by the English parliamentary opposition as 'an excellent patriot'.[23] This, of course, does not necessarily make understanding any easier. On the contrary, the very continuity of terminology can mislead, because of changes in meaning over time. Irish Protestant Patriotism drew on a number of ideologies or political languages that informed the contemporary debate about authority and rights. Some of these are familiar, if not always well understood (the divine right of kings, natural rights), but others have received less attention in the Irish context. Particularly important for Patriot thought were the ideas and idioms associated with the ancient constitution, civic republicanism, and conquest theory. In the case of Dublin, corporatism and Anglican political theory also figured prominently. None of these languages was exclusive to Ireland. They were for the most part European in origin (though Anglicanism and the ancient constitution were peculiarly English); and in general the form they took in Ireland had frequently been modified by or mediated through Irish, English, Scottish, or American, writers. Until the 1790s, it can be said of them that they provided the means for contemporaries to discuss what was the most important political question of the age in Ireland, Britain, and Europe: whether (and if so how, and how far) the liberties of the subject could or should be protected from absolutism.

Although some of these languages contained justification for opposing oligarchy, none of them were democratic in the modern sense. Natural rights theorists might stress the universal right to self-defence or protection of property, but even radicals such as Locke regarded the franchise as a civil

---

[22] Recent writing stresses how slight was the decline of anti-Catholicism in Ireland: see e.g. Jacqueline Hill, 'Religious Toleration and the Relaxation of the Penal Laws: An Imperial Perspective, 1763–1780', *Arch. Hib.* 44 (1989), 98–109; Thomas Bartlett, *The Fall and Rise of the Irish Nation: The Catholic Question 1690–1830* (Dublin, 1992), ch. 7; Leighton, *Catholicism in a Protestant Kingdom*, ch. 3.

[23] Quoted in T. C. Barnard, 'Land and the Limits of Loyalty', in Toby Barnard and Jane Clark (eds.), *Lord Burlington: Architecture, Art and Life* (London, 1995), 167–99, at 178.

matter for governments to determine. Locke was prepared to exclude
Catholics from political rights because they were deemed to hold views
(such as that oaths need not be kept—or not kept with heretics) that were
contrary to the preservation of civil society. Corporatism, too, had its own
built-in élitism in the basic distinction between the freeman (the sworn
citizen and member of the body corporate of the city) and the unfree: a view
that still had echoes in Rousseau. Only towards the end of the eighteenth
century did reformers begin to articulate what was in effect a new political
creed: that there was an intimate connection between personal liberty and
the political participatory power of citizens, regardless of corporate,
confessional, or ancient rights.[24] That language then took its place in the
political debate of the revolutionary era, and was to develop in the
nineteenth and twentieth centuries into liberalism and democracy: it was
also to be an important ingredient in the ideology of modern nationalism.

The political assumptions of the period before the 1790s were thus
specific to the *ancien régime*. In Ireland as elsewhere, issues of rights and
liberties were discussed, in general, with little reference to the bulk of the
population. Viewed from this perspective, it hardly signified that the
majority was of a different religion and culture from the dominant élite. For
in Ireland as elsewhere, politics was mainly the preserve of an aristocracy
(using this term in its wider sense to denote a landed gentry as well as a titled
nobility), claiming rights that derived, in part at least, from conquest.[25]
There was nothing unusual, by contemporary standards, about that.
Aristocratic pre-eminence was to be observed all over Europe, and it was
frequently explained in terms of conquest. Many countries had their local
variant of the 'two races' theory, here illustrated by Goubert with reference
to France:

The nobility is defined by its antonym, the commonalty. In the contemporary view,
the commoner, non-noble or ignoble . . . bears a stain, blot, or leavening of impurity
. . . and it will not be long before the nobility is echoing the tradition articulated by
Boulainvilliers (in works appearing in 1727 and 1732) and claiming descent from a
special race of conquerors, the Franks, who enslaved the Gallic peasants and whose
'blue blood' attested to their racial individuality.[26]

In England, such ideas found expression in discussion of 'Saxon' liberty
and 'Norman' conquest. As Goubert's example shows, myths explaining the

---

[24] David Rosenfeld, 'Rousseau's Unanimous Contract and the Doctrine of Popular
Sovereignty', *Hist. Pol. Thought*, 8 (1987), 83–110; J. A. W. Gunn, *Beyond Liberty and
Property: The Process of Self-Recognition in Eighteenth Century Political Thought* (Kingston,
1983), ch. 6.
[25] For a discussion of this point, see Leighton, *Catholicism in a Protestant Kingdom*, 36–7,
67–8, 77–9.
[26] Pierre Goubert, *The Ancien Régime: French Society, 1600–1750* (1969: Eng. trans.,
London, 1973), 160.

origins and transmission of aristocratic qualities were still being developed and refined during the eighteenth century. For, while aristocratic conquest and its attendant privileges were often resented, aristocracies as such had not yet become redundant. Feudalism might have declined, but the dynastic state required bureaucrats, and commanders for its armies; and social order, it was widely believed, still depended on the preservation of aristocratic dignity and privilege. Aristocrats also moved into commanding positions in the fields of banking, commerce, and agricultural innovation: they promoted improvement, which so powerfully took hold of the eighteenth-century imagination. Moreover, no other order in society could act so effectively as a check on the royal absolutism that was so marked a feature of the European *ancien régime*. Historians have described an aristocratic resurgence, which arguably reached its peak in the third quarter of the eighteenth century. One sign of this was the near universal adoption in Europe of a standard court dress (originally French, and featuring a lavishly decorated silk or velvet coat and waistcoat) which served to draw a clear visual distinction between the aristocratic élite and the rest of society. Subsequently the élite began to favour military or monarchical uniforms;[27] and this fashion was quickly copied by those who aspired to an 'aristocratic' role in society, such as the Irish Volunteers of the 1770s and 1780s.

If Ireland's domination by a conquering aristocracy was not exceptional in itself, it must nevertheless be acknowledged that the conquests that underscored the position of the Protestant élite after 1660 were of very recent date. True, for William Molyneux, writing in the 1690s, the focus of debate about conquest concerned the medieval Norman conquest; but in practice it was the Cromwellian and Williamite conquests that had produced the characteristic 'Protestant ascendancy'[28] (a term not apparently in use before the 1780s, but which serves to describe the political reality in Ireland from the mid-seventeenth to the nineteenth century). It was these conquests that were largely responsible for the dispossession of Catholics so that by the early 1700s Catholics formed only a small minority of the landed class.

It was these conquests, too, that served to tie the Protestant aristocracy to the monarchy and to England. In part, this represented a simple insurance policy. Both the Cromwellian and Williamite conquests had depended for success on English intervention; and given that they had resulted in the substantial dispossession of a former landed class whose descendants remained in Ireland, it was no more than prudence to cling to a connection

---

[27] Philip Mansel, 'Monarchy, Uniform and the Rise of the *Frac* 1760–1830', *P. & P.* 96 (1982), 103–32; Linda Colley, *Britons: Forging the Nation 1707–1837* (New Haven, 1992), 165, 183–7.
[28] James Kelly reviews studies on the origins of this term in 'Eighteenth-Century Ascendancy: A Commentary', *ECI* 5 (1990), 173–87.

that might deter any future challenge to the status quo. This was particularly important during the era of a strong Jacobite claim to the throne (from the 1690s to the 1760s), a claim that was legitimized by indefeasible hereditary divine right, upheld by the pope, and backed from time to time by the Catholic powers of Europe. Most Irish Protestants after 1690 rejected divine right of this kind; but not necessarily the principle itself. After all, divine right had originated in medieval times in efforts to carve out a sphere for the civil power independent of the church's authority. In England the principle was typically invoked not in defence of absolutism but against the authority of the papacy, and against a right of resistance claimed by Catholics and Calvinists. Divine right in this sense was not incompatible with mixed monarchy.[29]

The questions of law and legitimacy also loomed large. For the Protestant (mainly Anglican) élite of Molyneux's day did not see their ancestors as mere adventurers, but as loyalists whose role in the civil wars of the 1640s and 1650s had been to uphold monarchical rights in the face of (Catholic and Presbyterian) rebellion, and more recently to assist William of Orange in a just war against an unjust ruler.[30] Clearly this represented a highly one-sided interpretation of the complex seventeenth-century upheavals in Ireland. Catholic spokesmen claimed that in the 1640s they had risen in support of Charles I, and that during the Williamite wars they had merely fought on behalf of their lawful king. But Protestants contended that in both periods Catholics had aimed at separating the kingdom of Ireland from that of England, and that they, or their leaders, had looked for support to foreign powers (to the pope in the 1640s and to Louis XIV during the Williamite wars). The justice of Protestant victory—which quickly acquired providential significance—was copper-fastened in Protestant eyes by reference to the massacres allegedly perpetrated by Catholics on Protestants in 1641, which appeared to mark out Irish Catholics as religious fanatics who would never rest until Protestants had been extirpated from Ireland.[31]

The result of all this was to forge a close link between the (Protestant) aristocracy, the Protestant dynasty, and the established church. Following Molyneux, some Irish Protestants might deny that there had been a royal conquest of Ireland; but the idea of an aristocratic conquest, accomplished by those who had been commissioned by the crown to intervene in Ireland, served to define the rights of the aristocracy both in relation to the crown

---

[29] Glenn Burgess, 'The Divine Right of Kings Reconsidered', *EHR* 107 (1992), 837–61.

[30] For the significance of law in Irish Protestant values see S. J. Connolly, *Religion, Law and Power: The Making of Protestant Ireland, 1660–1760* (Oxford, 1992), ch. 6; T. C. Barnard, 'Lawyers and the Law in Later Seventeenth Century Ireland', *IHS* 28 (1993), 256–82.

[31] Sir John Temple's *The Irish Rebellion: Or, an History . . . of the General Rebellion Raised Within the Kingdom of Ireland . . . Together with the Barbarous Cruelties and Bloody Massacres which Ensued Thereupon* (London, 1646), formed a classic record of the rebellion for Protestants.

and to the native Irish. Conquest in this sense had preceded Molyneux's twelfth-century 'compact' that gave Ireland a constitution, with a parliament consisting of king, lords, and commons, English common law, and (later) a reformed episcopal church. Without a (Protestant) kingdom, none of these privileges would exist.[32] And as long as a Jacobite restoration was something to be dreaded in Britain, Irish Protestants could rest assured that their role as bastions against Jacobitism and popery would be endorsed by government. Thus spokesmen for Irish Protestants never tired of reiterating their loyalty to the crown; this was not mere rhetoric but was fundamental to the Protestant self-image. Accordingly, too, Dublin was studded with statues of Protestant monarchs,[33] while anniversary sermons stressed the goodness of providence in preserving Protestant Ireland from the loss of life, liberty, and estates at the hands of popish rebels.[34]

Given such views, it may seem hard to account for the rise of a Patriot movement among Irish Protestants at all, much less one that would by 1782 demand and obtain legislative independence. A leading difficulty here concerns our perception of what Patriots aimed at. Thanks to the nationalist model, it has been taken for granted that the essence of the Patriot position was the defence of Irish rights (especially parliamentary rights) against English legislative encroachment. In fact, the evidence suggests that at the end of the seventeenth century Irish Protestants were anxious to obtain closer, not weaker, links with England. This was the era of negotiation that led to legislative union between England and Scotland (1707); that Irish Protestants wished for something similar appears in contemporary correspondence as well as in resolutions of the Irish parliament in 1703 and 1709.[35] Unionist sentiment in this period has been little studied,[36] but it is

[32] Molyneux, *The Case of Ireland*, 115–16; Jacqueline Hill, 'Ireland Without Union: Molyneux and his Legacy', in John Robertson (ed.), *A Union for Empire: The Union of 1707 in the History of British Political Thought* (Cambridge, 1995), 271–96.

[33] An equestrian statue (1701) of William III by Grinling Gibbons stood on College Green (blown up, 1929); of George I (1717) by John Van Nost the elder on Essex bridge (now in the Barber Institute, Birmingham); of George II, by John Van Nost the younger, in St Stephen's Green (blown up, 1937). An image of George II by Benjamin Rackstraw surmounted the weavers' hall in the Coombe (removed in the 1920s). A bronze statue of George III, by the younger Van Nost, in the Royal Exchange until the 1920s, is now in search of a home (John Gilbert, *A History of the City of Dublin* (3 vols.; Dublin, 1854–5), repr. 1973), i. 21, 40–56; Anne Kelly, 'Van Nost's Equestrian Statue of George I', *Irish Arts Review Yearbook*, 11 (1995), 103–7; Edward McParland, 'A Note on George II, and St Stephen's Green', *ECI* 2 (1987), 187–95).

[34] T. C. Barnard, 'The Uses of 23 October 1641 and Irish Protestant Celebrations', *EHR* 106 (1991), 889–920.

[35] *Journals of the House of Commons of the Kingdom of Ireland (1692–1713)* (*Commons Jn. Ire. 1692–1713*), ii. 341–2; *Journals of the House of Lords 1703–1725*, ii. 247; David Dickson, *New Foundations: Ireland 1660–1800* (Dublin, 1987), 53.

[36] But see James Kelly, 'The Origins of the Act of Union: An Examination of Unionist Opinion in Britain and Ireland, 1650–1800', *IHS* 25 (1987), 236–63; Hill, 'Ireland without Union'.

not difficult to see the attractions. Since the restoration, Irish Protestants had been unable to prevent their more powerful English neighbours from reserving the main benefits of the colonial trade, through the navigation acts, to themselves. Worse, in deference to its own agricultural and industrial lobbies, the English parliament had passed laws that discriminated directly against Irish trade. A legislative union could be expected to strengthen Irish Protestants domestically by ending commercial discrimination and by integrating the country more closely with England.

Yet it was the Scots who in 1707 obtained a union, and a comparison of their position with that of the Protestant Irish is instructive.[37] The Scots, too, chafed under commercial restraints, and their most ambitious attempt to launch a colonial policy of their own, the Darien scheme of 1698–9, aroused English susceptibilities, and ended in failure. However, the Scots represented a formidable problem for the English government, particularly in respect of the troublesome question of the succession, which became urgent in the early 1700s. In the bitter aftermath of the Darien débâcle there could be no guarantee that the Scottish parliament would follow the English example and fix the succession on the Protestant Hanoverians; the prospect of greater independence from England under their native Stuart dynasty (with appropriate guarantees for the security of the kirk) was bound to have some appeal. There was a real possibility, therefore, that the Scottish and English kingdoms might drift apart. In other international circumstances these centrifugal forces might have triumphed. But ever since the 1670s there had been a prospect of the establishment of a French 'universal monarchy' in western Europe; and with European Protestantism in full retreat, there was a strong incentive for Protestant states to co-operate against the aggrandizement of a regime which, following the revocation of the Edict of Nantes and Louis XIV's *rapprochement* with the pope in the 1690s, boded ill for Protestantism and the 'liberties of Europe'.[38] Against this background William III consistently supported a union of England and Scotland, and in the event the Scots were admitted to the benefits of English colonial trade for the sake of the security that union would bring.

In the case of Ireland there was no such powerful incentive for the English government to accept a union, and Irish Protestants lacked the political weight of the Scots. Numerically weak, divided among themselves on the church question, and owing their estates to recent conquest, they could not afford even to toy with a Jacobite and Catholic succession. Consequently

[37] Brian P. Levack, *The Formation of the British State: England, Scotland and the Union, 1603–1707* (Oxford, 1987); John Robertson, 'An Elusive Sovereignty: The Course of the Union Debate in Scotland 1698–1707', in Robertson (ed.), *A Union for Empire*, 198–227.
[38] See F. Bosbach, *Monarchia Universalis. Ein Politischer Leitbegriff der Fruhen Neuzeit* (Göttingen, 1986); Steven Pincus, 'The English Debate Over Universal Monarchy', in Robertson (ed.), *A Union for Empire*, 37–62.

the government found no reason to depart from the policy of ruling Ireland through the subordinate Irish parliament. This was the context for the propagation of arguments that might enhance Protestant control over their own affairs,[39] of which the best-known synthesis was Molyneux's *The Case of Ireland, Stated* (1698). Its arguments were not particularly new. Most of them had been devised by Old English parliamentarians earlier in the century, and they were taken up by Molyneux to defend a distinctively Irish 'ancient constitution'. This drew on ideas originally shaped by English common lawyers in the sixteenth and seventeenth centuries, for whom the common law, based on custom and precedent, was superior to rival legal systems because of its supposed antiquity, rationality, and indigenous qualities. Moreover, it embodied the wisdom of ages rather than the edicts of particular rulers. Its origins were taken to be immemorial; and although it was constantly evolving, it had never been decisively changed because successive conquerors had recognized its excellence. According to this view, the common law enshrined the rights (especially those concerning liberty and property) of free-born Englishmen, and rendered those who lived under that law free to transmit their rights to their descendants. Sometimes these rights were expressed as fundamental laws, and efforts were made in the seventeenth century to show that they were beyond the reach of the royal prerogative.[40]

The other main inspiration came from the English anti-absolutist or civic republican tradition.[41] The crown itself had helped to highlight such ideas: Charles I's celebrated *Answer to the Nineteen Propositions* (1642) portrayed the constitution as one in which 'the balance hangs even' between the three estates, monarchy, aristocracy, and democracy. During the commonwealth period, a more Machiavellian form of republicanism was invoked by James Harrington in *The Commonwealth of Oceana* (1656). Fearing the return of the monarchy, Harrington argued that the key to the preservation of liberty lay in the body of armed freeholders, active citizens whose use of arms would discourage tyranny.

After the monarchy was restored, Harrington's ideas were transformed by members of a new political generation who accepted that republican liberty, with safeguards, was compatible with mixed monarchy. They

---

[39] James I. McGuire, 'The Irish Parliament of 1692', in Thomas Bartlett and David Hayton (eds.), *Penal Era and Golden Age: Essays in Irish History, 1690–1800* (Belfast, 1979), 1–31; Isolde Victory, 'Colonial Nationalism in Ireland, 1692–1725: From Common Law to Natural Right', Ph.D. thesis (TCD, 1984), chs. 1–2.

[40] J. W. Gough, *Fundamental Law in English Constitutional History* (Oxford, 1955); J. G. A. Pocock, *The Ancient Constitution and the Feudal Law . . . A Reissue with a Retrospect* (Cambridge, 1987); Glenn Burgess, *The Politics of the Ancient Constitution: An Introduction to English Political Thought, 1603–1642* (London, 1992).

[41] J. G. A. Pocock, *The Machiavellian Moment: Florentine Political Thought and the Atlantic Republican Tradition* (Princeton, 1975); id., 'The Machiavellian Moment Revisited', *JMH* 53 (1981), 49–72.

relocated Harrington's community of armed freeholders in an idealized Gothic past (thus blending their arguments with those of the ancient constitution). Like most contemporary political languages, this was an aristocratic creed, with the bulk of the population debarred from an active political role because they lacked the necessary independence conferred by the ownership of land. 'Virtue', a characteristic Machiavellian term denoting the active pursuit of the good of the commonwealth, was still perceived to lie in a balanced constitution, but for the neo-Harringtonians the stress now lay in maintaining a principled independence of each estate from the others. The loss of such independence, leading to 'corruption', was one danger; another was the rise of a standing army, which threatened to undermine the principle and practice of a citizens' militia.

These ideas were articulated in the 1660s and 1670s by 'Country' critics of the court, also known, as in the 1640s, as Commonwealthmen or Patriots (later, also as Old, Real, or Country Whigs). In these circles 'Patriot'—a term taken up by Molyneux—already formed part of the political vocabulary. Patriots appealed to the idea of a balanced constitution and to natural law, according to which 'the people' had a natural right to defend their liberty and property. Patriotism in this sense also had a unionist dimension; the Commonwealthmen in Ireland and England were foremost among those who considered that civil and religious liberty would be best protected by union. Molyneux, together with Swift, shared this view; but failing a union, the essence of *The Case of Ireland* was that the English parliament should respect Irish parliamentary rights, and stop legislating for Ireland.[42]

The English parliament condemned Molyneux's tract, including his endorsement of union, and in 1720 passed a declaratory act (6 Geo. I, c. 5) affirming its own right to make laws for Ireland. However, this was still an age of personal monarchy—hence the fear of absolutism—and the issue was far from fully resolved. Consequently, it can be argued that in practice the core of Molyneux's argument was conceded. After 1720 the English parliament was cautious in legislating for Ireland: when it did so, the laws in question were mostly of an unexceptional administrative kind.[43] The growth of Irish trade (despite the controversial restrictions) took some of the sting out of Irish resentment over the declaratory act. All this meant that the lack of formal legislative independence was slow to emerge as a major grievance. When it did come to the fore, however, it had no more committed and ardent supporters than the civic Patriots of Dublin.

The study is divided into three parts. Part 1 (1660–1791) traces the

---

[42] Molyneux, *The Case of Ireland*, 84, 130; Jonathan Swift, *The Story of the Injured Lady*, in *The Prose Works of Jonathan Swift, D. D.*, ed. Temple Scott (12 vols.; London, 1902–11), vii. 97–103.
[43] J. C. Beckett, *Confrontations: Studies in Irish History* (London, 1972), 124–5.

origins, values, aims, and achievements of Dublin civic Patriotism. It begins in the restoration period since it was then that the crown formalized its claim to regulate the city's magistracy, a claim that loomed large for the Dublin Patriots of the mid-eighteenth century. Besides, the restoration era witnessed the evolution in England of political vocabularies that were to dominate the language of Irish politics throughout the eighteenth century. Part 2 (1792–1814) examines the challenge to Patriot assumptions in the 1790s, while Part 3 (1815–40) considers how and why the Dublin Patriots of the eighteenth century became the unionists of the Victorian age. Since politics did not take place in a vacuum, Chapters 1, 7, and 11 give some idea of the principal social and economic features of Dublin's experience in the three periods.

PART 1

The Origins and Growth of Dublin Civic Patriotism, 1660–1791

1

Ancien-régime *Dublin:*
The City and the Guilds

Metropolitan cities were one of the wonders of early modern Europe. From the sixteenth to the eighteenth centuries they achieved unprecedented growth and prosperity. Paris quadrupled its population between 1500 and 1650 ... New capitals like Madrid or Berlin increased fivefold in size. ... Most striking of all, London leapt from a modest 50,000 in 1500 to over 600,000 in 1750. Metropolitan increase was all the more remarkable given that in much of Europe during the seventeenth and eighteenth centuries cities and towns generally languished in decay.[1]

I. The Metropolitan City

In common with many other metropolitan cities, Dublin enjoyed an astonishing period of growth in the seventeenth and eighteenth centuries. The population, rising from around 10,000 in 1600 to perhaps 40,000 in the 1660s and to 180,000 by 1800, established the Irish capital by 1700 as the 'second city of the empire', and by 1800 as one of the ten largest cities in Europe.[2] Comparison with the Scottish capital, Edinburgh (83,000 in 1800) only reinforces the point. The key to such prodigious growth, according to de Vries, was that such cities combined a number of important functions, especially those of port and capital.[3] Thanks to the English navigation acts, which required most colonial goods to be imported via England (to the advantage of east-coast Irish ports), Dublin dominated Irish overseas trade, generating nearly 40 per cent of customs revenue. Even linen, although manufactured mainly in the north and west, was mostly exported through Dublin's linen hall, opened in 1728. Accordingly, it was in Dublin that the country's principal banking and insurance services grew up, and it was

---

[1] Peter Clark, 'Metropolitan Mêlées', in *Times Literary Supplement*, 26 Feb.–3 Mar. 1988, p. 210.
[2] David Dickson, 'The Demographic Implications of Dublin's Growth, 1650–1850', in Richard Lawton and Robert Lee (eds.), *Urban Population Development in Western Europe from the Late-Eighteenth to the Early-Twentieth Century* (Liverpool, 1989), 178–89. Dublin's 17th-c. size is reviewed in Louis Cullen, 'The Growth of Dublin 1600–1900: Character and Heritage', in F. H. A. Aalen and Kevin Whelan (eds.), *Dublin City and County: From Prehistory to Present* (Dublin, 1992), 251–78, at 277 n. 2. See also maps 1–4 above.
[3] Jan de Vries, *European Urbanization 1500–1800* (London, 1984), ch. 7.

Dublin merchants who could offer the best credit terms to provincial retailers. It was to Dublin that the aspirant for higher education or professional training had to proceed, to the only university in Ireland (Trinity College), or to the College of Physicians.

On top of this, Dublin was the viceregal and administrative capital, thanks to the presence of Dublin Castle and the Irish parliament; the abolition of the provincial presidencies of Munster and Connaught in 1672 confirmed this ascendancy. Regular sessions of parliament in the eighteenth century made the city a focus for the landed aristocracy and gentry; but Dublin's cultural assets, including theatres, such as Smock Alley and Crow Street, a music hall in Fishamble Street, with visiting artists and performers of international repute, as well as shops and coffee houses, all generated their own appeal, ensuring that the city was thronged even during seasons when parliament was not sitting.[4] The physical growth of the city was rapid from the restoration period onwards; by 1700 considerable expansion had taken place, with new quays, bridges, and residential areas being developed both inside and outside the walls.[5]

In religious terms, the town that in the 1660s is estimated to have had a Protestant majority of over 70 per cent had become by 1800 a great city in which the Protestant proportion had shrunk to around one-third. Recent research has yielded different conclusions on Protestant demographic trends in the city, but there is broad agreement that Protestants still represented a clear majority of the population in the early 1700s, and that subsequently they comprised 40 per cent or more, at any rate until the 1760s. At their peak, Protestant numbers probably exceeded 70,000.[6]

In some respects it is unnecessary to dwell unduly on the question of numbers, since the business world from which the corporation and guilds were drawn was predominantly Protestant: the bulk of Dublin's trade remained in Protestant hands into the nineteenth century.[7] Master craftsmen and merchants were mostly Protestants, though during the eighteenth century the journeymen were becoming a predominantly Catholic body. Members of the established church formed over 80 per cent of the city's Protestants, but there were also (among others) congregations of Presbyterians, Quakers, Baptists, Huguenots, Lutherans, and, from the mid-eighteenth century, Moravians and Methodists.[8]

[4] Tighearnan Mooney and Fiona White, 'The Gentry's Winter Season', in David Dickson (ed.), *The Gorgeous Mask: Dublin 1700–1850* (Dublin, 1987), 1–16.
[5] Maurice Craig, *Dublin 1660–1860* (Dublin, 1969), chs. 2–3.
[6] Patrick Fagan, 'The Population of Dublin in the Eighteenth Century with Particular Reference to the Proportions of Protestants and Catholics', in *ECI* 6 (1991), 121–56, at 147–9; see also below, Ch. 7.
[7] David Dickson, 'Catholics and Trade in Eighteenth-Century Ireland: An Old Debate Revisited', in T. P. Power and Kevin Whelan (eds.), *Endurance and Emergence: Catholics in Ireland in the Eighteenth Century* (Dublin, 1990), 85–100, at 87.
[8] Fagan, 'The Population of Dublin', 134–5; R. Lee Cole, *A History of Methodism in Dublin* (Dublin, 1932), 103.

A wide range of industries operated in the capital, including brewing, distilling, sugar-refining, and leather trades, in which a variety of firms, some large and capital-intensive, produced about half the country's beer, a rather smaller proportion of its (legal) output of whiskey and over two-thirds of its sugar.[9] But it was the textile industries that dominated Dublin in terms of employment, providing the livelihood for a third of the growing population. While certain other cities in Britain and Europe were losing their textile industries to the countryside where labour was cheaper and guild restrictions absent, in Dublin these industries were still capable of expansion in the 1770s.

The oldest of them was the woollen industry, which enjoyed an international reputation as early as the fourteenth century. During the restoration period immigrant clothiers from the west of England introduced the 'new draperies' to Dublin, leasing land in the earl of Meath's Liberty and helping to develop the Coombe and Weavers' Square, which became a highly prosperous area of the city. But the prospect of competition from Ireland aroused the resentment of manufacturers in England, who success-fully lobbied the English government to curb the activities of their rivals in Ireland. As a result, in 1699 both the Irish and the English parliaments passed measures that effectively curbed the export potential of the industry, and it had to fall back on the home market. At a reduced level it continued until the 1760s and 1770s, when the introduction of Spanish wool and encouragement from the Dublin Society provided the basis for another period of growth, especially of fine woollens; by 1792 some 5,000 people were employed in the industry.[10] By then, however, a different problem had arisen. English manufacturers could offer better credit terms than their Irish counterparts, so Dublin retailers had an incentive to stock English-made woollens. The importing of textiles caused a good deal of resentment in Dublin's artisan community, and was responsible for periodic bursts of aggression directed against those who bought or wore foreign materials. The 'cutting weavers', who established themselves in the folk-lore of the period, were so called because they vented their hostility by slashing the garments of people suspected of wearing imported clothing.[11]

The *quid pro quo* proposed by the English government in return for curbing the Irish woollen industry was to be the development of linen manufacture: and that industry did grow spectacularly in the course of the century. But although Dublin was to play a central role in the linen trade,

---

[9] L. M. Cullen, *Princes & Pirates: The Dublin Chamber of Commerce 1783–1983* (Dublin, 1983), 18.

[10] John Warburton, James Whitelaw, Robert Walsh, *A History of the City of Dublin* (2 vols.; London, 1818), ii. 980–4; Nuala T. Burke, 'Dublin 1600–1800: A Study in Urban Morphogenesis', Ph.D. thesis (TCD, 1972), 141.

[11] *CARD* viii. 176–7; J. D. Herbert, *Irish Varieties for the Last Fifty Years* (London, 1836), 86–9.

the manufacture of linen never rivalled the woollen industry there, giving employment at most to around 2,000–3,000 people. Nor did cotton manufacture present a significant challenge, despite its presence in the Liberties, introduced by Robert Brooke and others in the 1780s. Cotton spinning rose and fell dramatically in County Dublin and nearby County Kildare during the 1770s and 1780s, while in the city the weaving side of the industry gave employment to up to 2,000 weavers towards the end of the century. It was the silk industry, however, that was the most distinctive of Dublin's textile industries. Its growth in the late 1600s and early 1700s was expedited by an influx of French Huguenots, many of them coming via London to settle in the earl of Meath's Liberty, where London names (Spitalfields, Pimlico) were reproduced. At its height between the 1760s and 1780s, before changes in fashion occurred, the industry employed perhaps 5,000 people, supplying the home market, notably the aristocracy and gentry, with a variety of silks, tabinets, and poplins.[12]

Socially, Dublin was dominated by the landed class, which, as in other European countries, was looking more and more to an urban expression of its wealth and power. The most obvious sign of the gentry's presence in Dublin was the number of town houses that sprang up in the course of the eighteenth century, complemented by the splendid new parliament building in College Green, which came into operation in 1731. In the heyday of Irish parliamentary independence during the 1780s there were as many as forty-six earls and viscounts alone with town houses in Dublin, and many more gentry besides. It was they who provided most of the demand for the luxury goods and services produced by the Dublin artisans, such as the fine furniture, plasterwork, coaches, gold- and silverware for which the city was renowned. It was their style, their extravagant tastes, their ubiquitous preoccupation with honour, their duels, that caught the attention of contemporary visitors and Victorian essayists alike. Supporting roles were played by Church of Ireland clergy and by lawyers, professions often filled by younger sons of the gentry (though increasingly the sons of successful merchants were entering the field). For these professions, too, architecture reflected a high degree of self-confidence. New or rebuilt parish churches included St Luke's (1708), St Werburgh's (*c.*1715 and 1759), St Mark's (1729), St Thomas's (1758), St Catherine's (1769), St James's (1773), and St Andrew's (1793). On the other hand, the fabric of older churches was often neglected, with the result that several churches were badly in need of repair by the end of the century. The law received its main architectural expression in the imposing Four Courts (built 1786–1802), while the rising profile of

---

[12] Warburton, Whitelaw, Walsh, *History of Dublin*, ii. 971–9; David Dickson, 'Huguenots in the Urban Economy of Eighteenth-Century Dublin and Cork', in C. E. J. Caldicott, H. Gough, J.-P. Pittion (eds.), *The Huguenots and Ireland: Anatomy of an Emigration* (Dun Laoghaire, 1987), 321–32.

the medical profession, which unlike the law was open to Catholics, was reflected in a number of hospitals, founded through the charitable initiative of private individuals, including Dr Steevens' (1733), Mercer's (1734), the Lying-in Hospital (1751–7), and St Patrick's (Swift's), opened in 1757.[13]

Below the landed and professional classes, socially speaking, came the Dublin business community, headed by the wholesale merchants. Compared with their counterparts in London, the position of Dublin merchants *vis-à-vis* the landed class was weak, chiefly because as a group they lacked financial weight. There was no Dublin equivalent of the great financial institutions such as the Bank of England or the East India Company, which were strongly identified with merchant capital, and which strengthened the London merchants in their dealings with the landed interest. Attempts were made in the first half of the century to establish Dublin banks based on merchant capital, but after two of the largest failed in mid-century, legislation was passed to prohibit merchants involved in foreign trade from engaging in banking enterprises. Thereafter landed capital and interests dominated Dublin banking, including the most famous and durable of the eighteenth-century banks, La Touche's, which (after a mercantile start) became identified with landed interests. Dublin also suffered from a poorly developed colonial trade, compared, say, with that of Cork, which cut off one possible source of amassing the kind of capital necessary for mercantile banking ventures.[14]

In these circumstances, the landed gentry and aristocracy were able to impose more than just their social style on Dublin. During the restoration period, the merchant-run Dublin corporation (by far the largest landlord in the city) indicated a desire to keep control of the physical growth of the city in its own hands. The ancient common of St Stephen's Green was laid out as an open space, with the centre planted and the land around leased out in parcels mostly to corporation and guild members. But subsequently individuals such as Sir Humphrey Jervis and Luke Gardiner were to put their stamp on Dublin's development more effectively than the corporation.[15] And by the mid-eighteenth century the Irish parliament was taking an interest in the growth of the metropolis, reflected in the establishment in 1758 of the wide streets commission, originally set up to supervise the construction of a street from Essex Bridge to the Castle. Although the lord mayor was named as a member of the commission, the other members were mostly gentry and politicians. Through the commission, the landed class was able to determine the main outlines of Dublin's physical development in

---

[13] Samuel Lewis, *A History and Topography of Dublin City and County* (Dublin, 1980), 108–9, 127–37, 148–9.

[14] Cullen, *Princes & Pirates*, 19–21; id., 'The Dublin Merchant Community in the Eighteenth Century', in P. Butel and L. M. Cullen (eds.) *Cities and Merchants: French and Irish Perspectives on Urban Development, 1500–1900* (Dublin, 1986), 195–209.

[15] For Jervis, see also below, Ch. 2 n. 63; for Gardiner, Ch. 3 n. 67.

the second half of the century. The most striking demonstration of this occurred in the 1780s when, in the teeth of merchant opposition, a new bridge and custom house were situated well to the east of the commercial heart of the city.[16]

Accordingly, the habit of mercantile deference towards the gentry was slow to decline. However, one of the hallmarks of *ancien régime* society was to be the forging of closer ties between the landed gentry and mercantile élites; a process that was promoted by the gentry's role in urban development, and by the growing wealth of the business classes. Through convivial societies such as the freemasons, through the guilds and municipal corporations, which found it advantageous to have a scattering of gentlemen among their members, through the theatre and musical societies, through the very layout of the larger towns—which included wide malls in which the rich and elegant of all classes could promenade—the breaking down of social barriers between gentlemen and merchants was going on. From the mid-sixteenth century onwards Dublin aldermen—the most wealthy and senior of the merchants—had called themselves 'Master', a title once reserved for sons of gentlemen. By the 1750s the term 'esquire', once confined to sons of knights and baronets, was being applied to those in contention for aldermanic status; and by the 1780s merchants in general were adopting this practice.[17]

II. *The Dublin Guilds: Rights and Functions*

If the Dublin merchants remained deferential in their attitudes towards the landed class, this did not mean that they lacked self-esteem. On the contrary, they had firm convictions about their importance in the social and commercial order of things; and they had their own hierarchies of wealth and seniority.

For hundreds of years guilds were an integral part of Dublin life, regulating trade, administering property, carrying out charitable work, and providing public entertainments. Their early history has attracted some attention, but although they retained an important place in civic life down to 1841 little interest has been shown in their activities after 1700.[18] To some extent, this may simply reflect the influence of English historiography,

---

[16] Craig, *Dublin 1660–1860*, 18–20, 25–7, 102–5; Edward McParland, 'Strategy in the Planning of Dublin, 1750–1800', in Butel and Cullen, *Cities and Merchants*, 97–107.

[17] The Mall in London (1660s) set the pattern; Dublin's Sackville Mall was a striking example of the genre (McParland, 'Strategy in the Planning of Dublin'; Eamon Walsh, 'Sackville Mall, the First One Hundred Years', in Dickson (ed.), *The Gorgeous Mask*, 30–50). On nomenclature, see Colm Lennon, *The Lords of Dublin in the Age of Reformation* (Dublin, 1989), 69; *CARD* x. 480; Cullen, *Princes & Pirates*, 44.

[18] John J. Webb, *The Guilds of Dublin* (1929; repr. London, 1970) is unduly dismissive of the guilds' trading role after 1700. See Maureen Wall, *Catholic Ireland in the Eighteenth Century: Collected Essays of Maureen Wall*, ed. Gerard O'Brien (Dublin, 1989), 61–72; Leighton, *Catholicism in a Protestant Kingdom*, ch. 4.

where interest in guild control over trade in the era of industrialization has only recently revived after decades of neglect.[19] It now appears that evidence from London, which suggested an early (pre-1700) decline in guild regulation (although with some control over the handicraft and retail trades persisting beyond the 1750s)[20] was probably unrepresentative. In provincial English cities manufacturing guild membership and the binding of apprentices remained buoyant until the fourth and fifth decades of the eighteenth century, and in the case of service and construction guilds even later.[21]

Guilds were present in several of the older Irish towns, though (with the exception of Dublin) few records remain. But the quality of the records and the influence of English historiography are only part of the reason for neglect. There has also been a certain reluctance, until recently,[22] to acknowledge the very existence of an urban Protestant middle class (from the restoration period onwards, freedom of guilds was a mainly Protestant preserve). What appears to have happened is that the verdict of the municipal corporation commissioners in the 1830s—that the guilds had largely lost their links with trade—has been accepted as broadly correct for the preceding century or more.[23] Paradoxically, research is now being conducted into the decline of the Protestant middle class in southern Ireland, while the period of its heyday remains decidedly sketchy; and although there are studies of certain small urban denominations, there has been a failure to focus directly on what was by far the most important group, the Church of Ireland or Anglican community.[24]

A southern Protestant business and artisan class grew up in the period *c.*1600–1750, at first mainly through immigration, later supplemented by

---

[19] K. D. M. Snell, *Annals of the Labouring Poor: Social Change and Agrarian England, 1660–1900* (Cambridge, 1985), ch. 5.

[20] J. R. Kellett, 'The Breakdown of Gild and Corporation Control over the Handicraft and Retail Trade in London', *Econ. Hist. Rev.* 2nd ser. 10 (1958), 381–94 at 389–93.

[21] Snell, *Annals of the Labouring Poor*, 238–9.

[22] For recent correctives see Dickson, ' "Centres of Motion" '; id., 'Demographic Implications of Dublin's Growth'. On a formative period in the growth of a Protestant urban population, see T. C. Barnard, *Cromwellian Ireland* (Oxford, 1975), esp. ch. 4.

[23] For the commissioners' report, see below, Ch. 14. For its influence see Webb, *Guilds of Dublin*, 241–50; Mel Doyle, 'The Dublin Guilds and Journeymen's Clubs', *Saothar*, 3 (1977), 6–14, at 6. Cf. William Doyle, 'nearly all the trading community of Ireland were either Presbyterians or Roman Catholics' (*The Old European Order 1660–1800* (Oxford, 1978), 146).

[24] Kerby A. Miller, 'No Middle Ground: The Erosion of the Protestant Middle Class in Southern Ireland During the Pre-Famine Era', in *Huntington Library Quarterly*, 49 (1986), 295–306. Denominational case studies include Olive Goodbody, 'Anthony Sharp, Wool Merchant, 1643–1707, and the Quaker Community in Dublin', *Friends' Hist. Soc. Jn.* 48 (1956), 38–50; Raymond Hylton, 'Dublin's Huguenot Communities: Trials, Development, and Triumph, 1662–1701', *Hug. Soc. Proc.* 24 (1983–8), 221–31. The publication of 'The Church of Ireland: A Critical Bibliography, 1536–1992', *IHS* 112 (1993), 345–84, and A. Ford, J. McGuire, K. Milne (eds.), *As By Law Established* (Dublin, 1995), may encourage research in this field.

recruitment from the younger sons of Anglo-Irish farming and gentry families. Membership of the Dublin guild of merchants, for instance, grew by 50 per cent from about 400 to over 600 between 1680 and 1750, and the total freeman body probably grew by a similar proportion, to reach an estimated 3,000 by the later date.[25] Despite erosion through emigration, notably in the half century before the great famine, there was still a substantial Protestant population in the southern towns in the early nineteenth century. In the 1830s Protestants comprised about one third of the population in city-centre parishes in Cork city. As in Dublin, urban Protestants were over-represented in the business community: in the early 1800s some two-thirds of the merchants in Waterford and Cork were Protestants.[26] And while most of these Protestants had been in Ireland for no more than a few generations, by and large they lacked the wealth and lifestyle that enabled some members of the landed élite to move easily and often between Ireland and England. In respect of domicile, therefore, they should be regarded as Irish.[27]

Failure to engage the phenomenon of a rising Protestant middle class has perpetuated the view that in eighteenth-century Ireland guilds were little more than political and sectarian clubs: instruments by which a few lackeys of a landed ascendancy class harassed a mainly Catholic business community with archaic and oppressive regulations.[28] In fact, in Ireland as in other countries, the primary purpose of the guilds—as outlined in their charters—was to regulate trade, partly in the interests of their members, but also, historically, in the interest of the crown. Recognition by the state of these bodies as the legitimate custodians of the interests of trade and industry meant that they were the natural vehicles for the promotion of commercial goals. Thus, during the 1720s and 1730s the Dublin merchants' guild and the city corporation were active in urging the administration to modify the navigation acts so as to facilitate Irish merchants; in the 1750s the weavers' guild took up the issue of foreign imports with parliament; in the 1760s the brewers guild petitioned parliament on matters concerning the excise. The goldsmiths' guild continued throughout the period (and beyond) to be considered by parliament as the guardian of standards for gold- and silverware.[29]

[25] Charters and documents of the guild of Holy Trinity or merchants' guild of Dublin, 1438–1824, transcribed for J. T. Gilbert, Dublin Public Libraries, Gilbert Collection (DPLGC), MS 78, fo. 164; Murphy, 'The Lucas Affair', 38.
[26] Miller, 'No Middle Ground', 295; Ian d'Alton, *Protestant Society and Politics in Cork 1812–1844* (Cork, 1980), 13, 33–4; Dickson, 'Catholics and Trade', 90; Jacqueline Hill, 'Artisans, Sectarianism and Politics in Dublin, 1829–48', *Saothar*, 7 (1981), 12–27.
[27] Cf. Barnard, 'Crises of Identity among Irish Protestants', 46–7, 80–3.
[28] Webb, *The Guilds of Dublin*, 241–2; T. P. Le Fanu, 'A Note on Two Charters of the Smiths' Guild of Dublin', *JRSAI* 60 (1930), 150–64, at 151; Doyle, 'The Dublin Guilds', 6–7.
[29] DPLGC, MS 79, fos. 192–3, 196; *CARD* vii. 447–8, viii. 1; William Cotter Stubbs, 'The Weavers' Guild, the Guild of the Blessed Virgin Mary, Dublin, 1446–1840', *JRSAI* 49 (1919),

True, in 1768 a Dublin 'committee of merchants' complained of 'the utter inattention of corporate bodies to the interest of trade'; but the historian of this body acknowledges that many of its members were themselves freemen of guilds, and has drawn attention to the political element present in such criticism. Down to the opening of the Royal Exchange in 1779, the Tholsel (or city hall)—the meeting place of the merchants' guild and municipal corporation—was the hub of mercantile life; and it is significant that attempts (from 1783) to set up a Dublin chamber of commerce, as an alternative vehicle for mercantile interests, achieved only spasmodic success until the 1820s.[30] It is significant, too, that down to the 1760s, when the pattern began to change, surviving guild records reveal a low level of interest in purely political matters.[31]

On the question of guild regulation of trade, at the beginning of this period, in the 1660s, the modern division between manufacturers and retailers still lay in the future. Producers and distributors were, for the most part, one and the same. Of course, there were merchants who imported and exported goods, and some of them also acted as retailers; but in an age before mass production, such goods were mostly luxuries, sold to a small and select clientele, or ingredients for manufacturers. Thus guild control over manufacturing—involving regulation of the number of apprentices, hours of work, wages, inspection of goods, and quality of materials—also extended to control over retailing. Later, as distributors began to lose their manufacturing links, they no longer had the same interest in maintaining strict controls over many aspects of trade.[32]

But for how long did the Dublin guilds continue to regulate manufacturing and retailing? Regrettably, surviving guild records provide no direct answers to this question. Sensibly enough from their own point of view, the guilds were more anxious to preserve charters, lists of members, records of leases, charitable payments and so on rather than the hall books that contained more ephemeral day-to-day regulations, such as hours of work and prices.[33] Even so, and accepting that detailed investigation will doubtless reveal many variations, there are strong indications that the guilds

---

60–88, at 70; brewers' guild, minute book 1750–1802 (Guinness Museum, Dublin (GMD), 198). The goldsmiths' guild's powers to regulate goldware quality were confirmed by 23 & 24 Geo. III, c. 23 and 9 & 10 Vict., c. 76.

[30] Cullen, *Princes & Pirates*, 35, 45–68.

[31] Cf. Leighton, *Catholicism in a Protestant Kingdom*, 72; also below, Ch. 4.

[32] In London, merchants were gaining predominance in the handicraft guilds by the early 1600s: Charles Wilson, *England's Apprenticeship 1603–1763* (London, 1971 edn.), 49–50; P. J. Corfield, *The Impact of English Towns* (Oxford, 1982), ch. 6. In Dublin, efforts to limit free merchants to keeping only one shop were still being made in the 1650s. Of the craft guilds, the saddlers were probably exceptional in reaffirming controls over retailing as late as 1769 (DPLGC, MS 78, fo. 127; saddlers' guild, book of by-laws, NLI, MS 81, esp. no. 11, fo. 17).

[33] The weavers' guild records refer to hall books, but none have survived: minute book 1755–1809 (Royal Society of Antiquaries of Ireland (RSAI), entry for 2 July 1792).

continued to exercise some sort of control over the handicraft and retail trades in Dublin at least down to the mid-eighteenth century. Naturally, as the city expanded, hucksters and petty traders multiplied, largely outside guild control; but as far as substantial tradesmen were concerned, it appears that during the 1750s many guilds were still acting on the powers granted in their charters, as in the case of the goldsmiths, brewers, weavers, barber-surgeons, tanners, and chandlers.[34] Also suggestive is the persistence of the quarter brother system into the 1750s (of which more below), and the revision of by-laws. In the 1760s certain guilds, including the smiths and stationers, adopted by-laws that explicitly relaxed guild controls over trade—suggesting that hitherto control had been exercised, or at least aspired to.[35] The process was not uniform; the saddlers introduced new by-laws in 1769 which reaffirmed control over manufacturing as well as retailing.[36]

The guilds' role as regulators of trade awaits further investigation. But that was not their only function. They also enjoyed an intimate link with the municipal corporation or 'common council' which lasted until the municipal reform act of 1840, and was reflected in the frequently reaffirmed by-law that only those who were free of the city should be admitted to full guild freedom and permitted to trade.[37] For the guilds were the means whereby, on the payment of fines, tradesmen of a certain standing could acquire 'freedom' (or citizenship—the concept was originally medieval) through which they assumed the privileges and responsiblities of active citizens, becoming eligible to serve in a range of offices in parish, guild, and common council, to bear arms, to pay certain taxes: in short, to constitute the body corporate of the city. By the mid-eighteenth century, the approximately 3,000 freemen constituted perhaps a quarter of the city's adult male Protestant population—so by contemporary standards the

---

[34] See goldsmiths' guild, minute book 1731–58 (NLI, n 6056 p 6782, pp. 327, 354). In 1750 the brewers' guild summoned 'all Persons concerned in that Trade' to adjust measures and prices (minute book 1750–1802, GMD, p. 72); in 1754 the weavers' guild ruled that all woollen goods must bear a seal with the guild's crest (Stubbs, 'The Weavers' Guild', 69–70); in 1757 the barber-surgeons' guild convened brethren and quarter brothers to regulate journeymen's employment (minute book 1757–92, TCD, MS 1447/8/2, p. 79); in 1763 the tanners' guild sought parliamentary approval for new tanning methods (Edward Evans, 'The Ancient Guilds of Dublin', NLI, MS 738, pp. 36–9); in 1769 the chandlers' guild imposed a fine for fraud in melting grease (ibid. 40). The merchants' guild abandoned controls earlier, although efforts to exclude foreigners' goods were still being made in George I's reign (DPLGC, MS 79, fo. 186).
[35] St Loy's guild, extracts (National Archives (NA), M 2925, fos. 11–13); in 1764 the feltmakers' guild relaxed controls on Catholic tradesmen but obliged them to abide by guild regulations (Transcripts, NA, M 6118 b); in 1767 the stationers' guild described many of its old by-laws as 'nugatory, obsolete and repugnant' and unenforceable at law (St Luke's guild, transactions 1766–85, NLI, MS 12125, p. 10). As late as 1750 government had tried to enlist the guild to control seditious literature (M. Pollard, *Dublin's Trade in Books 1550–1800* (Oxford, 1989), 20, 166).   [36] NLI, MS 81, fos. 7–63.
[37] See e.g. *CARD* iii. 21–2; v. 84, 131. Breaches could be punished: ibid. viii. 143–5.

opportunities for involvement in the process of local government were fairly widely spread.[38] Moreover, on closer examination it can be seen that there was considerable continuity of outlook and ethos between the guilds in their self-consciously Catholic and recusant phase in the late 1500s and early 1600s, and their subsequent manifestation as part of Protestant Ireland. A brief examination of the guilds' origins and links with the municipal corporation will illustrate this continuity.

Most of Dublin's craft guilds were of medieval origin, though none was formally incorporated before the fifteenth century, and new ones were still being formed in the eighteenth century, bringing the total to twenty-five. The last to be incorporated, representing the apothecaries, received its charter from the king in 1747 after separating from the barber-surgeons. (The last French guilds were incorporated in 1767).[39] True to the value that contemporaries attached to antiquity, the Dublin guilds had a strict order of precedence in the city corporation depending on seniority.[40] As in other countries, the Dublin guilds enjoyed the right to regulate the conditions of all who followed particular trades, including masters, journeymen, and apprentices. All guild members were obliged by their oaths to obey the authority of their guild officials (master and wardens).[41] The merchants' guild was the largest and most prestigious, and in medieval times it had established very close ties with the municipal corporation, providing the great majority of aldermen and mayors; little had changed by the mid-eighteenth century. All the guilds had representatives (known as 'numbers') in the corporation's lower house or 'city commons', but it was less usual for members of the craft guilds to rise in the civic hierarchy.[42]

Full guild freedom could be obtained in a variety of ways, but most commonly through birth or service (apprenticeship). Historically, freedom had been open to women as well as men, and in the first half of the seventeenth century women made up just over one-tenth of admissions to freedom. Very occasionally they still featured among admissions in the 1690s, but with the business élite seeking to emulate the lifestyles of the gentry, and with the growing separation between home and workplace, in the eighteenth century women ceased to be made free in their own right (or,

[38] For estimated freemen numbers in the mid-1700s see Murphy, 'The Lucas Affair', 38. Assuming that 1 in 4–5 of the population was an adult male (freemen were not usually sworn before age 21), these figures suggest an adult male population of *c.*12,000–15,000 out of a total Protestant population of 50,000–60,000.
[39] Le Fanu, 'A Note on Two Charters of the Smiths' Guild', 150–1; Henry S. Guinness, 'Dublin Trade Gilds', *JRSAI* 52 (1922), 143–63, at 162; *CARD* ix. 354; David Ogg, *Europe of the Ancien Régime 1715–1783* (London, 1965), 23.
[40] The order is that given in *CARD* x. 500–2: see also below, App. A.
[41] See the freeman's oath (with minutes for 1735), in RSAI, weavers' guild, minute book 1734–60.
[42] Lennon, *Lords of Dublin*, 99; Murphy, 'The Lucas Affair', 34.

perhaps, were not recorded as such)—although it remained common for widows to continue a husband's business and to take apprentices, and for such (male) apprentices to seek freedom in the usual way.[43] Assuming that the candidate was the child of a freeman or had served an apprenticeship to a freeman and had thus come under the recognition of a guild, the applicant approached the municipal corporation for admission to freedom of the city: a procedure known as a 'beseech', from the first word of the application. Provided no objection was raised by the board of aldermen or by the city commons, in which sat the representatives of the guilds, the applicant would proceed to be sworn, to pay the fine (if any) and sign the freeman's bond,[44] which required the keeping of arms in readiness to defend the city and the king. The freeman also promised not to intrude upon the trades of any other guild. To complete the process, in order to become fully free of the guild as well as of the city, more oaths and fines were exacted at guild level.

Freedom brought with it various privileges, including a parliamentary vote, access to local offices, and exemption from certain municipal tolls that the non-free were obliged to pay. The first of these privileges alone, it has been assumed, served to make freedom an object of aspiration for anyone with the remotest claim to it.[45] Guild records, down to the mid-eighteenth century, contain enough complaints about the burdens of freedom, and the failure of tradesmen to apply for it, to suggest that the matter was more complex. Becoming a free brother was a time-consuming and expensive business; indeed, apprenticeship was an expensive business. Filling offices depended in general on seniority, and freemen were obliged to fill posts such as master or wardens, on pain of fines.[46] Office-holding might bring the chance to influence guild or civic affairs; but the posts were for the most part unpaid, and again the occupant would incur expense, such as the cost of putting on a dinner for the brethren. In addition, freemen became liable for certain parochial taxes that were not levied on the non-free. As the barber-surgeons' guild put it in 1715, freemen 'pay Lott and Scott bear offices and undergoe other Charges which Strangers and others not free are not Lyable to nor will perform'.[47]

---

[43] Brendan Fitzpatrick, 'The Municipal Corporation of Dublin 1603–40', Ph.D. thesis, (2 vols.; TCD, 1984), i. 143. Many freedom applications are extant: DCA, Fr/B/1660–1765, 1803–39. See also Imelda Brophy, 'Women in the Workforce', in Dickson (ed.), *The Gorgeous Mask*, 51–63.   [44] See DCA, Fr/Bond/1674–1759.

[45] Webb, *Guilds of Dublin*, 242.

[46] In 1688 Sir Abel Ram was fined £20 for declining the merchants' guild mastership (DPLGC, MS 78, fo. 170). Apprenticeship fees had risen greatly above their 16th-c. level (Fitzpatrick, 'Municipal Corporation of Dublin', i. 70): in 1713 Dublin corporation laid out £10 in fees for a deceased wigmaker's son (*CARD* vi. 471). Merchants' guild fees could run into £100s.

[47] TCD, MS 1447/8/2, fo. 2^v; feltmakers' guild, transcripts, 8 Oct. 1716 (NA, M 6118 a); Charles Lucas's address to merchants' guild, 1768 (DPLGC, MS 79, fo. 230). 'Scot and lot' denoted the liability to pay parochial taxes and fill offices.

Complaints about the numbers of non-free tradesmen had become common a century earlier, when Dublin's rapid growth was just beginning, and when the guilds were still predominantly Catholic in composition. At that time, government policy was unsympathetic towards guild monopolies on trade, and by the mid-1630s the non-free had come to outnumber the freemen.[48] The fall of Strafford marked an end to royal obstruction of guild rights, and following the upheavals of the 1640s and 1650s a new drive to enrol freemen was launched. In the merchants' guild the number of free brothers rose from just over 100 in 1662 to around 400 by 1679. The guilds' determination to retain control of trade despite changing economic circumstances can be illustrated by a case involving the weavers' guild. Faced with an immigrant clothier, the Quaker Anthony Sharpe, who by 1680 was employing some 500 people as outworkers in the Liberties, the guild admitted him to freedom and eventually elected him master in 1688.[49]

By the 1670s, however, a new complication had arisen. Not only were there Protestant tradesmen who, perhaps because of the expense, were unwilling to apply for freedom, but (for reasons to be discussed below) Catholics were no longer eligible for freedom. Although by this time trade in Dublin had largely passed into Protestant hands, the principle of guild control over all tradesmen was still important to the guilds, and—to judge by its willingness to grant guild charters—to the crown.[50] Accordingly, the Dublin guilds followed the example of those in London, which faced similar difficulties consequent upon rapid population growth, and introduced a quarterage system.[51] This involved the payment of a quarterly fee, known, as in London, as quarterage, which entitled the quarter brother to practise his (or her) trade without incurring the steep fines and harassment that might otherwise face the non-free. Since 'quarterers' did not take the oaths of supremacy and allegiance prescribed for freemen in 1678, they were not eligible for guild or civic office or for the parliamentary franchise.[52] In the early years, a good deal of heart-searching went on in the merchants' guild and in the city corporation as to whether quarterers should even be allowed

[48] Fitzpatrick, 'Municipal Corporation of Dublin', i. 42, 120, 126–7; Lennon, *Lords of Dublin*, 289 n. 181.

[49] DPLGC, MS 78, fos. 135, 164; Olive Goodbody, 'Anthony Sharp, a Quaker Merchant of the Liberties', *Dublin Hist. Rec.* 14 (1955–8), 12–19, at 17. The case reflected the good prospects for textiles in the decades before the English ban (1699) on Irish woollen exports.

[50] The coopers (1666), feltmakers (1667), stationers, and bricklayers (both 1670) were all incorporated in this period. See Oliver Snoddy, 'The Charter of the Guild of St Luke, 1670', *JRSAI* 98 (1968), 79–87.

[51] Kellett, 'The Breakdown of Gild Control'. The pioneering work on quarterage in Ireland was done by Maureen Wall (*Catholic Ireland in the Eighteenth Century*, ch. 2). Since she wrote, several more Dublin guild records have come to light: Mary Clark and Raymond Refaussé, *Directory of Historic Dublin Guilds* (DHDG) (Dublin, 1993). Cf. Leighton, *Catholicism in a Protestant Kingdom*, ch. 4.

[52] Wall, *Catholic Ireland in the Eighteenth Century*, 64–5. It was also common for the freemen to pay a quarterly fee.

to trade without being free of the city.[53] But by the early 1700s quarterage had become an entrenched feature of the guild system. It represented a typically eclectic answer to the problems posed by conflicting political and economic goals: to maintain civic freedom as a Protestant monopoly, while also retaining guild control over tradesmen of all denominations. As such, it was recognized in 1707 by the Irish parliament, in a set of resolutions urging the guilds to enforce the apprenticeship laws on quarterers as well as freemen. Where it is possible to trace its development and extent, as in the case of the weavers' guild, the records show that the quarter-brother system was still operating effectively as late as the 1750s. And when the newest guild (the apothecaries) began operating in the late 1740s it was just as keen as older ones to implement the system.[54]

The introduction of the quarterage system is thus best regarded not as a means of excluding Catholics from trade, rather the contrary: it was designed to facilitate some degree of guild control over all substantial tradesmen, including Catholics, and it reflected the guilds' ability to adapt to changing conditions.

III. The Guilds and the Confessional Question

The confessional dimension of corporate life is not easy to bring into proper focus, but its origins lay in the history of the relations between the crown and the corporate towns. Although in the early 1600s the established Protestant episcopal church enjoyed support from only a minority of the Dublin aldermen, state insistence on civic officials taking the oath of supremacy brought those who were prepared to conform into prominence. Following strong government pressure, by the mid-1630s the mayoralty was consistently in Protestant hands, although there were still Catholics on the common council, and, of course, among the freemen.[55] After the 1641 rising and civil wars, and Cromwell's reconquest of Ireland, government policy towards the Irish corporations went further, seeking to exclude Catholics from both civic government and the guilds. Under a series of Cromwellian mayors, and against a background of heightened millennial expectations, steps were taken towards creating an exclusively Protestant body politic in Dublin. In 1651 the corporation petitioned the parliamentary commissioners to encourage tradesmen from England to come and settle, promising them admission to freedom at low fines, provided they

---

[53] CARD v. 84, 189–90; DPLGC, MS 78, fo. 159.

[54] CARD vi. 379; *Commons Jn. Ire. 1692–1713*, ii. 566; weavers' guild, quarter brethren books, 1747–60, 1756–64 (RSAI); apothecaries' transactions 1747–95 (Apothecaries' Hall), 13, 35. See also DPLGC, MS 80, fo. 91; TCD, MS 1447/8/2, p. 91; NLI, MS 680, ii. 28; goldsmiths' minute book 1731–58, NLI n 6056 p 6782, p. 339. In St Luke's guild income from quarter brothers only fell drastically in the late 1760s (NLI, MS 12130). The saddlers' by-laws still allowed for quarter brothers in 1792 (NLI, MS 81, fo. 92).

[55] Lennon, *Lords of Dublin*, 129; Fitzpatrick, 'Municipal Corporation of Dublin', i. 262.

were 'Englishmen and Protestants'. Eighteen months later, the corporation adopted a new regulation to the effect that only Protestants would be eligible for freedom and admission to apprenticeship. In certain Irish towns, the comparative lack of Protestant merchants and traders meant that such exclusivity led to depopulation and impoverishment; this was not the case in Dublin, where Protestants by this time constituted a majority of the population.[56]

Following the restoration of the monarchy in 1660, spokesmen for the Irish Protestant gentry were convinced of the importance of retaining Protestant control of the corporate towns. The lord president of Munster, Roger Boyle, earl of Orrery, expressed the view that the Catholics 'could never have rebelled, if the corporations had been in the king's hands, and planted with loyal protestants'. In keeping with this spirit, Dublin corporation passed a by-law in January 1661 to bar Catholics from the common council and from civic freedom.[57] For his part, Charles II was grateful to those Catholics who had supported the royalist cause during the upheavals of the previous two decades, and neither he nor his viceroy, the duke of Ormond, shared the gentry's paranoia about popery. Besides, the king wished to be accepted as an arbiter by those who did not conform to the established church. He was therefore prepared to urge (May 1661) that Catholics in Ireland be restored to their former trading privileges.[58]

Difficulties, however, remained. For no solution had yet appeared to the problem that once again faced Catholics: how to testify their loyalty to a Protestant monarch without offending the susceptibilities of Rome and their own clergy. And the Irish parliament, now almost entirely a Protestant preserve, remained anxious at the prospect of the corporate towns, which returned members to parliament, falling into Catholic hands. Unlike Dublin, many of the towns were still predominantly Catholic in composition. To guard against this, the act of explanation of 1665[59] stipulated that Catholics (and anyone not willing to take the oaths of supremacy and allegiance) were not to be permitted to purchase any forfeited lands in corporate towns, and a clause in the act of settlement (1662) empowering the king to restore 'innocent' papists to their former property in such towns was repealed. Down to this point, in compliance with royal wishes, Dublin corporation had continued to admit 'innocent' Catholics to freedom.[60] However, in 1667, the corporation reaffirmed its commitment to exclude

---

[56] *CARD* iv. 3–5, 38; Barnard, *Cromwellian Ireland*, 77–89.

[57] Roger Boyle, *A Collection of the State Letters of the Right Honourable Roger Boyle, the First Earl of Orrery*, ed. Thomas Morrice (2 vols.; Dublin, 1743), i. 93; *CARD* iv. 198 n. 1.

[58] *Letters Written by His Excellency Arthur Capel, Earl of Essex, Lord Lieutenant of Ireland, in the Year 1675* (London, 1770), 185–9; Ronald Hutton, *Charles II King of England, Scotland, and Ireland* (Oxford, 1991), 176.

[59] 17 & 18 Chas II, c. 2.

[60] This at any rate was what the corporation later claimed (petition to Lord Clarendon, *CARD* v. 402–6).

Catholics from the common council. Meanwhile, efforts to find a formula for Catholics to testify their loyalty foundered in the midst of Roman disapproval and clerical divisions.[61]

For some years after the passing of the act of explanation the crown pursued a 'Protestant' policy for Dublin, at least in relation to trading privileges. The royal patent granted to the bricklayers' guild in 1669 required all its members to take the oaths of supremacy and allegiance, while the guild of St Luke's charter of 1670 stipulated that apprentices were to be of the Protestant religion.[62] But from 1670 (when the king made a secret pledge in the Anglo-French treaty of Dover to declare himself, in due course, a Catholic) preparations were under way to relax the penal laws against both Protestant dissenters and Catholics. Suspicions were aroused when, under a new viceroy, Lord Berkeley, a synod of Catholic bishops met openly in Dublin. No Irish parliament was summoned after 1666 until 1689, so there was no national forum in which the gentry could make known their views; but in England both houses of parliament addressed the king in 1671, deploring the 'great insolencies' of the Irish papists. Within weeks of this address Dublin corporation had resolved not to admit Catholics to freedom or apprenticeship.[63]

It was nothing new for Catholics to have to rely on the royal prerogative for any relaxation of the penal laws, but the next fifteen years were to witness marked swings in their fortunes at civic level, depending on the relative strengths of the crown and its parliamentary critics: that is, critics in the English parliament, since the Irish parliament was in abeyance. Dublin corporation was swayed first one way and then the other, depending on whether the crown or the parliamentary opposition held the initiative. Early on, the crown found some allies for its policy of toleration among Dublin's Protestant dissenters, whose roots in the city went back to the Cromwellian era.[64] Although they were not barred from Irish corporations (there being no Irish counterpart of the English corporation act) dissenters resented being excluded from the established church under the restoration church settlement, and there were tensions between them and the Anglicans. In compliance with a viceregal proclamation of 1672 which restored Catholics in corporate towns to their former privileges, a Presbyterian lord mayor duly proposed a dozen Catholic freemen for the lower house or city commons. But by this time royal indulgence to popery was under severe attack in the English parliament, and the government decided against

[61] *CARD* iv. 400; Moody, Martin, Byrne (eds.), *NHI* iii. 429–30.
[62] *Cal. SP Ire. 1666–9*, 782–3; *Cal. SP Ire. 1669–70*, 215–17.
[63] Paul Seaward, *The Restoration, 1660–1688* (London, 1991), 52–3; Moody, Martin, Byrne (eds.), *NHI* iii. 431–2; James McGuire, 'Government Attitudes to Religious Non-Conformity in Ireland 1660–1719', in Caldicott, Gough, Pittion (eds.), *The Huguenots in Ireland*, 255–84; *CARD* iv. 527–8.
[64] Barnard, *Cromwellian Ireland*, 81–8, 99–100.

confirming this proposal.[65] At the time of the 'popish plot' in 1678, when the king's life was believed to be in danger from Catholic assassins, and the English parliamentary opposition began its campaign to exclude the Catholic duke of York from the succession, Dublin corporation reasserted a Protestant policy by requiring freemen to take the oaths of supremacy and allegiance. By 1686, however, James II was strong enough to insist on relaxation, and by April 1687, even before Dublin's charter was challenged by the crown, the corporation had erased the by-laws that drew a distinction between Protestants and Catholics in the city.[66]

The fact that royal policy was from time to time at odds with statute and municipal laws over the question of toleration created a frustrating situation for Dublin Catholics, who down to 1687 repeatedly came close to readmission to full corporate privilege, without actually achieving it. Nevertheless, the admission of Catholics to freedom during the 1660s and again from 1686 to 1689 maintained a Catholic presence among the freemen; and the corporation's somewhat uneven 'Protestant' posture did not rule out some notable instances of co-operation across denominational boundaries.[67]

Even after the Williamite reconquest there were still Catholics among the freemen. This can be explained by the fact that orders excluding Catholics from freedom—the corporation passed another in 1690—do not appear to have been rigorously enforced. Civic records reveal that during the 1690s a few Catholics were picked out by name and disfranchised: these were mostly cases where the individuals concerned had been indicted for high treason, or were flouting regulations that prohibited the taking of Catholic apprentices. All the freemen were required by a civic by-law (1692) to take the new oaths to William and Mary, but the status of those who refused remained ambiguous; the stationers' guild, for instance, retained lists down to the 1710s of 'brothers not sworne'.[68] In an exceptional case, the tailors' guild requested and obtained from the crown a new and explicitly Protestant charter; apparently only seven out of some eighty of the guild's brethren refused to take the new oaths.[69] Not only was there no general

[65] On royal policy, see Peter Gale, *An Inquiry into the Ancient Corporate System of Ireland, and Suggestions for its Immediate Restoration and General Extension* (London, 1834), app. xxii, p. cxlix.

[66] *CARD* v. 164, 389–91, 426. The admission of Catholics to civic freedom (by fines rather than by birth, service, or special grace) stands out for the years 1687–8: Gertrude Thrift, 'Roll of Freemen, City of Dublin, 1468–85, 1575–1774' (4 vols.; NLI, MSS 76–9).

[67] A case in point concerned the religious guild of St Anne. Headed by Protestants from the 1640s, the guild thwarted several state attempts to repossess its property (The booke of St Anne's guild, RIA, MS 12/D/1, pp. 425, 483, 564); Colm Lennon, 'The Chantries in the Irish Reformation: The Case of St Anne's Guild, Dublin, 1550–1630', in R. V. Comerford, Mary Cullen, Jacqueline Hill, Colm Lennon (eds.), *Religion, Conflict and Coexistence in Ireland: Essays Presented to Monsignor Patrick J. Corish* (Dublin, 1990), 6–25.

[68] *CARD* v. 509; *CARD* vi. 7–8, 137–8, 184, 188, 199; St Luke's guild, lists of members 1676–1724, NLI, MS 12122, fos. 66ᵛ, 67, 69ᵛ, 72.

[69] *CARD* vi. 151–2.

expulsion of Catholic freemen, but the corporation was even prepared to countenance the existence of the new hosiers' guild, set up by charter from James II in 1688 (apparently on the initiative of a Catholic). Notwithstanding the terms of an English act of 1690 which restored all cities, towns, and bodies corporate in Ireland to their condition as on 24 June 1683, the guild continued in existence after the revolution, and in 1692 obtained from the corporation the privilege of representation on the city commons. This came to light in 1695, when a group claiming to be stocking knitters of Dublin, Protestants, and freemen (they would have belonged to the tailors' guild, which had hitherto catered for hosiers) complained to the Irish parliament that they were being prevented from trading by the new guild. Three months later the Irish house of commons ruled that the hosiers' charter was illegal.[70]

That the desire to retain corporate privileges took precedence over purely sectarian considerations can further be illustrated by examining the corporation's dealings with certain categories of Protestants. In 1662, and again in 1692, the Irish parliament passed laws to encourage immigrant Protestant tradesmen to settle in Irish towns; under the 1692 Protestant strangers act, such Protestants were to be allowed their customary forms of worship, and tradesmen could obtain their freedom on preferential terms.[71] Many such immigrants settled in Dublin, including French Huguenots, fleeing from persecution at home; and during the 1680s and 1690s the corporation was sympathetic to their plight, admitting them without fines, and waiving certain city taxes in their favour.[72] But by the eighteenth century the corporation considered that the act was being abused. In the 1730s complaints were made that (Protestant) tradesmen, unqualified by birth or service, were resorting to the act in order to avoid applying for freedom 'by grace especial': the usual, and costly, resort for those who sought freedom in these circumstances. The corporation's objection to this procedure was partly financial and partly regulatory; applicants who invoked the Protestant strangers act could bypass guild regulations by obtaining a certificate from a county magistrate.[73] The city's indulgence did

---

[70] 'An Act for the Better Security and Relief of Their Majesties' Protestant Subjects of Ireland', 1 Will. & Mary, sess. 2, c. 9 (Eng.); *CARD* v. 541–2; *Commons' Jn. Ire. 1692–1713*, ii. 64, 136. After this ruling the hosiers ceased for some years to be represented on the city commons: the circumstances of their readmission remain obscure (cf. Monday book 1658–1712, DCA, MR/18, fos. 131ᵇ, 138ᵃ, 174ᵃ).

[71] 14 & 15 Chas II, c. 13; 4 Will. & Mary c. 2; further extended by 2 Anne, c. 14, and made perpetual by 4 Geo. I, c. 9.

[72] *CARD* v. 228–30; vi. 43–4. While 'ffrench refugees' were usually admitted without fines, English Protestant 'strangers' who invoked the act were charged a 20s. fine: presumably they were not deemed to be fleeing religious persecution (see e.g. DCA, Fr/B/1694/3). See also Dickson, 'Huguenots in the Urban Economy'.

[73] *CARD* viii. 143–5, 154–5.

not extend beyond the first generation of strangers, for when the sons or apprentices of those who had obtained their freedom under the act came to apply for freedom, they were made to pay a fine.[74] Quakers posed a special problem; in the late seventeenth century they were still considered to be dangerously radical, and their refusal to swear oaths appeared subversive of political and religious cohesion. The corporation did admit some Quakers to freedom, but charged them steep fines.[75]

All this indicates that the corporation exercised discrimination even in relation to Protestants, and did not simply set out to maximize Protestant membership. In fact, if Dublin's Protestant population is taken as the constituency (50,000–60,000 by 1750), then it emerges that the proportion of adult males who were freemen and enjoyed the parliamentary franchise— about one-quarter—was not very different from the position in the two major English provincial cities, Bristol and Norwich, where the proportion was about one-third.[76]

The fitful nature of Dublin's progress towards a Protestant body corporate meant that guild membership remained quite mixed. Down to the early 1700s there were still some Catholics among the freemen, just as there were some Protestants as well as Catholics among the quarter brothers, and among the non-free. Nevertheless, from the 1660s on (except for a brief period under James II) the guilds' official confessional orientation was towards the established church. The relationship, inheriting much from the pre-reformation past, was a close one. All the guilds had patron saints, and some made regular payments to the parish churches that were dedicated to their saint, as in the case of the stationers (St Luke's) and the tailors (St John's).[77] Church festivals, including Christmas, Easter, and Whitsun, were observed in a corporate capacity. A more distinctly Protestant flavour was reflected in the practice for a newly elected master to pay for a sermon to be preached before the brethren in church on swearing day, and by guild support for particular charities. The merchants' guild subsidized the Blue-Coat charity school; the tailors gave funds to the parish boys of St Nicholas; the carpenters subsidized a charity school in St Paul's parish; the weavers supported a school and almshouse beside their guildhall in the Coombe (the

[74] See e.g. DCA, Fr/B/1725/1; Fr/B/1742/4. Those admitted under these acts were classified 'A.P.' in the civic records.
[75] In 1694 two dissenters 'called Quakers' were admitted to freedom for fines of £10 and £5 respectively (DCA, Fr/B/1694/1). By the 1740s Quakers appear to have been admitted on the same terms as other Protestants (e.g. Fr/B/1742/1A).
[76] Nicholas Rogers, 'Popular Jacobitism in Provincial Context: Eighteenth-Century Bristol and Norwich', in Eveline Cruickshanks and Jeremy Black (eds.), *The Jacobite Challenge* (Edinburgh, 1988), 123–41, at 124. It was rare for more than one-third of the adult male inhabitants to have the vote (Corfield, *Impact of English Towns*, 151). See also n. 38 above.
[77] St Luke's guild, lists, pictures, and accounts 1720–1833, NLI, MS 12130; DPLGC, MS 80, fos. 79, 86.

school, though open to working weavers' children irrespective of religion, no doubt reflected a Protestant ethos).[78]

It is not surprising, therefore, that during the eighteenth century it should have been Catholic tradesmen who found the principle of guild control most irksome; not because quarterage payments were unduly onerous—in general, this does not appear to have been the case—but because as Catholics they were not entitled to enjoy the chief benefits of the guild system. They were also exposed, occasionally, to guild control being used for proselytizing purposes.[79] Moreover, although Catholics might be in a minority among Dublin's tradesmen, they formed majorities in many other towns; and even in Dublin they were over-represented in certain trades, notably the food, drink, and leather trades. In these cases the principle of (Protestant) guild control was naturally irritating—and not just to Catholics. In the late 1690s the Irish parliament, impatient at the effect of guild monopolies on prices in the Dublin baking, butchery, and brewing trades, discussed the desirability of suspending guild charters in these trades.[80]

It was one thing for Catholic tradesmen to put up with these aggravations as long as there was a real possibility of a reversal in their fortunes, such as took place in James II's reign, and which it was not unreasonable to expect would occur through a Jacobite restoration at any time from the 1690s to the 1740s. During that period Catholic resistance to paying quarterage fees was essentially passive. But by the 1750s resistance was becoming more active. And just as the non-free found in England—where chartered rights did not always stand up well at law—the common law courts often ruled against the guilds. Following such a decision in King's Bench in 1759, a campaign backed by several Irish corporations was launched to obtain statutory backing for quarterage fees. In a counter-attack spearheaded by the newly established Catholic Committee, Catholic merchants from several towns, including Dublin, mobilized opposition. The corporations persisted, and as late as 1778 heads of a quarterage bill were introduced into the Irish parliament; but subsequently the bill failed to return from England, where (under Poynings' law) Irish bills were still required to be scrutinized by the English privy council. Catholic opposition had been strong, and government was on the point of granting a measure of Catholic relief; moreover, the climate of informed opinion was turning against guild restrictions on trade.[81] The implications of this failure were considerable. In Dublin as in

[78] DPLGC, MS 78, fos. 158–9; MS 79, fos. 189–90; DPLGC, MS 80, fos. 80–1; Michael Quane, 'The Royal Hibernian Military School', pt. 1, *Dublin Hist. Rec.* 18 (1862–3), 15–23, at 16; Evans, 'The Ancient Guilds of Dublin' (NLI, MS 738, p. 48).
[79] Wall, *Catholic Ireland in the Eighteenth Century*, 63–5, 88; Leighton, *Catholicism in a Protestant Kingdom*, 69–74, 177–8, nn. 13–15.
[80] *Calendar of State Papers, Domestic Series 1699–1700* (*Cal. SP Dom. 1699–1700*) (London, 1937), 82–3; *Commons' Jn. Ire. 1692–1713*, ii. 361.
[81] Wall, *Catholic Ireland in the Eighteenth Century*, 65–72; Leighton, *Catholicism in a Protestant Kingdom*, 69–83.

other towns the guilds were forced at last to abandon hope of fulfilling their principal function, control over all the tradesmen of the city.[82]

IV. The Guilds in an Age of Aristocracy and Capitalism

During this period the guilds contained a small number of freemen who were not tradesmen, a phenomenon for which there were precedents in the early seventeenth century.[83] Such freemen fell into a number of categories. Some were members of the nobility or gentry, in cases where the guild wished to confer a distinction, or hoped to enlist support in the guild's interest; their presence was a reflection of the breaking down of boundaries between the landed and urban élites. Members of the Fitzgerald family, for instance, headed by the earls of Kildare, later dukes of Leinster, were free of several Dublin guilds. Their ties with the city were both political (two sons of the first duke represented the city in parliament)[84] and economic: the building and furnishing of Leinster House in the 1740s gave much employment to the guilds' craftsmen. Others might seek freedom in order to practice as attorneys in the civic courts. All such applications for freedom had to be sought 'by grace especial'—a category that also covered those working tradesmen who did not qualify for freedom by birth or service. Applicants for freedom by grace were always liable to have their 'beseeches' turned down.[85] Except for the gentry who were being granted freedom as a distinction, or converts from Catholicism from the 1760s on, most had to pay the city corporation an entry fine (those applying by birth or service were normally exempt). This usually amounted to one or two pounds, but could be up to ten pounds or more, in addition to fines levied at guild level.[86]

By the mid-eighteenth century the guilds were faced with a comparatively new category of non-trading applicants for freedom: sons of freemen who had entered the professions, or had otherwise moved out of their trading backgrounds. In the period when the guilds could still claim to be regulating the handicraft trades, such candidates might apply for admission by special grace, rather than by birth (an indication that freedom was not regarded as

---

[82] In view of Leighton's claim that the Catholic campaign destroyed the guilds (*Catholicism in a Protestant Kingdom*, 90), it may be noted that certain guilds (the goldsmiths, saddlers) were not seriously damaged by the defection of the quarter brothers in the 1760s. In some other cases, decline was gradual. In St Luke's guild the enrolment of apprentices—an important sign of guild control of trade—was falling in the 1770s, but did not tail off until the 1820s (Doyle, 'The Dublin Guilds', 12 n. 6); also below, Ch. 7.

[83] Fitzpatrick, 'Municipal Corporation of Dublin', i. 16–17. Some names of honorary freemen are given in Stubbs, 'The Weavers' Guild', 78.

[84] William Robert Fitzgerald; Lord Henry Fitzgerald (below, App. B).

[85] In 1772 the corporation reminded the guilds that (with certain exceptions) freedom was reserved for practising tradesmen (*CARD* xii. 556).

[86] See e.g. DCA, Fr/B/1762/2. The corporation was ready to extend freedom by grace to converts ('conformists') even when they were not practising tradesmen (*CARD* xii. 556).

a *right* for any but working tradesmen). The most easily identifiable applicants in this category were clergymen, who, whether they applied by birth or grace, were usually admitted without fines, out of deference to their calling.[87]

To complete this survey of the Dublin guilds it is necessary to say something about relations between masters and journeymen. Eighteenth-century Dublin witnessed considerable economic growth. As in London, this produced internal tensions in the guilds, manifested in attempts by the journeymen to combine, or establish organizations for themselves. Before this period, those journeymen who had completed their apprenticeship could reasonably expect to become masters and perhaps employers in their own right. But as demand grew and the scale of business operations increased, more and more journeymen found that they were failing to move out of the class of employees. For a tradesman in this position, there was the option of becoming a quarter brother, rather than incurring the expense of freedom. But quarter brothers received few guild benefits, although the occasional reference can be found to their dependants receiving charitable payments. Hence the formation of friendly societies, or clubs, usually (in the early days) for charitable purposes, and usually dependent on the guilds' goodwill.[88] They rarely endured more than a few years. But by the 1720s and 1730s other journeymen's societies were being formed where the main emphasis was on protection of working conditions: keeping up wages, regulating the number of apprentices, and so on. Their formation was a sign that at least some of the masters were quietly abandoning traditional guild restrictions on trade; in other words, they were not unresponsive to economic opportunities.

These journeymen's societies almost invariably incurred the hostility of the masters, but they too were mostly ephemeral bodies. To judge by the sporadic nature of the masters' complaints, they did not constitute a serious threat to the guild system before the 1770s. Anti-combination acts were passed by parliament from the 1720s on, directed for the most part at specific trades, and not notably effective. But even where a particular trade showed a high degree of organization (the journeymen hosiers, for instance, conducted a long-running battle with the masters over wages in the 1730s and 1740s) the emphasis was on winning over the guild to accommodate the men's demands, rather than ignoring it as irrelevant. The hosiery trade, in fact, is a good illustration of the success of the journeymen in putting pressure on the guild masters during the peak period of Dublin's prosperity in the 1750s and 1760s. Following the labour unrest of the earlier decades, and after arbitration by the corporation, the hosiers' guild accepted

---

[87] For the admission by grace of a clergyman, son of a freeman, see Fr/B/1742/1A.

[88] Doyle, 'The Dublin Guilds', 8–9. For relief payments to a quarter brother's widow see St Loy's guild, extracts, NA, M 2925, fo. 14.

restrictions on the number of apprentices. As for wages, by 1780 the hosiers' wages were one-third higher than those of their counterparts in England.[89] In cases of labour unrest, masters did not shrink from prosecutions; but it was not until 1780 that they had general statutory backing,[90] which signalled the demise of the guild spirit of confraternity, at least as between masters and men.

To sum up, the evidence suggests that down to about the 1750s there was still some degree of guild control over the handicraft trades in Dublin. However, the campaign against quarterage fees in the 1760s effectively undermined the guilds' claim to regulate the work of all the city's tradesmen. Moreover, in the context of rapid economic growth employers increasingly ignored traditional guild restraints on employment, while retailers, gradually losing their links with manufacturing, were ready to sell imported goods as well as those produced at home. Protests on the part of what contemporaries called 'the mob' about the sale of imported cloth were made as early as the 1720s, but it was not until the 1770s that matters had gone so far as to induce artisans to mount sustained campaigns to persuade the public to buy Irish goods,[91] suggesting that the balance between producers and distributors had shifted in favour of the latter. Market forces were becoming more important, and manufacturers now looked to parliament and protective duties rather than to guild regulations to limit competition from English goods.

Although guild representation on the city commons continued to reflect a close connection with trade well into the nineteenth century, under the circumstances it is not surprising that the failure of the last quarterage bill was followed by some loss of guild morale. In the smiths' guild the records were poorly kept during the mid-1780s, and the fraternity was said to be in a declining state. In the weavers' guild—their products under pressure from English competition—the number of freemen dropped by over one-fifth to around 300 between 1759 and 1789.[92] However, if trading matters had become less important, the guilds had not lost all sense of purpose. For they also had political functions, and these had expanded in importance in the course of the century.

[89] Doyle, 'The Dublin Guilds', 9; Andrew Boyd, *The Rise of the Irish Trade Unions 1729–1970* (Tralee, 1972), chs. 1–2. [90] See below, Ch. 7.
[91] *CARD* viii. 137–8; Dickson, *New Foundations*, 149–50, 164–5.
[92] St Loy's guild, extracts, NA, M 2925, fo. 50; weavers' guild, book of brothers, 1746–64; book of brothers, 1767–92 (RSAI).

2

Dublin Corporation and the State, 1660–1714

I. The Origins of the Corporation

Like many towns all over Europe, Dublin's origins as a corporate entity go back to medieval times. Under the first Anglo-Norman ruler of Ireland (Henry II), the Hiberno-Norse inhabitants of Dublin (Duvelina), who had opposed the new regime, were forced to resettle outside the walls and the city was turned over to newcomers from Bristol and other English towns. For some years Dublin functioned as a dependency of Bristol. However, a charter of 1192 recognized the citizens as a self-contained body, and by 1229 they had obtained the right to elect their own mayor. The process of excluding royal officials was completed in 1548 when the city was incorporated as a county in its own right. From the citizens' point of view, incorporation was desirable because it guaranteed a degree of self-government. For the monarchy, corporations were a means of urban control, and served to channel taxes towards the royal exchequer.[1]

Dublin corporation's power of self-government, outlined in charters and by-laws, was at its peak in the early 1600s before royal and statutory encroachment began to be felt. The corporation possessed extensive criminal jurisdiction through a series of local courts; it ran prisons, supervised markets and levied tolls on those coming into the city to trade, checked weights and measures, administered property, appointed to certain church livings, and imposed building regulations. It also superintended Dublin port. In 1669 the corporation helped to establish, and to maintain, a charity school for boys, the King's Hospital, or Blue-Coat school. Its paternalistic ethos was reflected in the mayor's power to regulate the price of foodstuffs, of vital importance during shortages. On top of this, the aldermen (aided by members of the watch, appointed by the parishes) had police functions; while at times of unrest or in wartime the freemen were expected to take responsibility for the city's safety and to contribute to national defence. Military functions were particularly important in a city whose Anglo-Norman settlers had remained racially distinct from the Irish population. A massacre of some hundreds of Dublin citizens by the native

---

[1] R. Dudley Edwards, 'The Beginnings of Municipal Government in Dublin', *Dublin Hist. Rec.* 1 (1938–9), 2–10; Howard B. Clarke, 'The 1192 Charter of Liberties and the Beginnings of Dublin's Municipal Life', ibid. 46 (1993), 5–14.

Irish on Easter Monday 1209 at Cullenswood, a mile or two south of the city, was still commemorated in the 1660s with military exercises in the area, on what had been known ever since the event as Black Monday. A more recent 'massacre' tradition—that of 1641—took time to emerge as one of the city's chief anniversaries, though it was well established by the early Hanoverian era.[2]

Municipal institutions in Dublin evolved in line with those in other Anglo-Norman towns and especially those in southern England. They grew in importance over time, subsuming earlier organs of royal government such as the hundred court, constituted by the 'free men' of the district. The charter of 1229 recognized only a mayor and citizens (meaning property owners and burgage tenants rather than residents at large); in practice the city was dominated by the mayor and leading merchants, later known as *jurés* or aldermen. By the fourteenth century, paralleling developments in other European towns,[3] a guild element had succeeded in establishing a place in the common council of the city, with the formal recognition of a body of forty-eight *demi-jurés* (later, sheriffs' peers), and a body of ninety-six, or 'numbers'. For a time, these bodies were, up to a point, self-selecting, and they apparently enjoyed some share in the government of the city, and in the election of officials. But their status in city government declined during the 1400s. How representative they were of the guilds (which by the fifteenth century included craft guilds) is not clear. It was thought that until 1574 the forty-eight and the ninety-six were drawn exclusively from the merchants' guild; but craft guild presence has recently been identified among the forty-eight in 1500.[4] Certainly, in 1574 craft as well as merchant guild members were given the formal right to be selected for the forty-eight and the ninety-six;[5] subsequently, each guild obtained a fixed number of representatives among the ninety-six, with the merchants receiving the largest share. From the late 1400s the forty-eight were selected by aldermanic committee; it is not clear how the ninety-six were chosen, but there is some indication that they were selected, or at least nominated, by the master and wardens of their guilds, and that they served for life.[6]

The dominance of the (self-selecting) mayor and aldermen in the city government was reflected in the evolution, by the late sixteenth century, of a two-tier system in the municipality. The mayor and twenty-four aldermen met weekly to run the day-to-day city business; they began keeping records

[2] *CARD* iv. 293; DPLGC, MS 80, fo. 81.
[3] Antony Black, *Guilds and Civil Society in European Political Thought From the Twelfth Century to the Present* (London, 1984), ch. 5 and ch. 7 on corporatist thought.
[4] Edwards, 'Beginnings of Municipal Government', 10; Lennon, *Lords of Dublin*, 53, 99. Sheriffs' peers were those who had served as sheriff, or had paid a fine to be excused from doing so.   [5] *CARD* ii. 97.
[6] Edwards, 'Beginnings of Municipal Government', 9; Fitzpatrick, 'Municipal Corporation of Dublin', i. 6.

of their own proceedings in 1567. Municipal by-laws and appointments were made at the quarterly general assembly meetings, attended by the entire common council. The forty eight and the ninety-six, who together were known as the 'commons' ('city commons' to distinguish them from the parliamentary body), sat apart in an upper room in the Tholsel, the city assembly house in Skinner's Row. They also met before the quarterly assemblies to draw up petitions; the guilds held similar meetings. The process of excluding the citizens at large from the quarterly meetings was completed in 1573 with the passing of a resolution that stipulated that the only voices to be heard in the assembly were those of the mayor, aldermen, sheriffs, the forty-eight, and the ninety-six.[7]

A variety of ceremonies took place during the civic year, designed to give public expression to the corporation's privileges, dignity, and authority. By the 1700s, the most spectacular was 'riding the franchises', which occurred on a triennial basis in the month of August. The lord mayor and civic officials, accompanied by the masters and wardens of the guilds (mounted), with rank-and-file guild members (on foot), perambulated the city boundaries to reassert the corporation's immunity from royal, ecclesiastical, and seigneurial authorities.[8] Halts were made at particular points on the route, where ancient and modern rituals, reflective of corporate authority, were carried out. The guilds' main contribution to the procession—a series of what would now be called floats—was a mixture of entertainment and self-advertisement, which blended classical, biblical, and folk themes, and drew on the tradition of the mystery plays which the guilds had acted down to Elizabethan times.[9]

On the political front, with the accession of James I and the ending of the nine years war, the government embarked on a series of moves designed to improve its own finances and increase royal control in Ireland. By 1613 Dublin had lost its entitlement to customs revenues, and soon afterwards the right to levy poundage was abolished. At the same time the crown was encouraging the immigration and settlement of Protestants by plantation and the establishment of new urban corporations (particularly in Ulster) which were given an explicitly Protestant complexion. In Dublin, immigration gradually helped to swell the small Protestant community that dated

[7] For the aldermen at this period see Lennon, *Lords of Dublin*, ch. 2; Fitzpatrick, 'Municipal Corporation of Dublin', i. 7–8, 28.

[8] Several ecclesiastical and seigneurial Liberties were located around the city, still in 1600 mostly beyond the built-up area, except for those around the two cathedrals: Burke, 'Dublin 1600–1800', 61–3. See also map 1 above.

[9] Lennox Barrow, 'Riding the Franchises', *Dublin Hist. Rec.* 33 (1979–80), 135–8; id., 'The Franchises of Dublin', ibid. 36 (1982–3), 68–80. For an 18th-c. account see John Swift, *History of the Dublin Bakers and Others* (Dublin, 1948), 134–42. Processions were also held on guilds' saints' days. See Henry Nelson, *Poem on the Procession of Journeymen Smiths, on May the First, 1729* (Dublin, 1729), in Cambridge University Library, Bradshaw Collection (CULBC), Hib. 3. 730. 1 (98).

from Elizabeth I's reign, and this afforded the basis for a challenge to the Old English (and still largely Catholic) élite. In 1604 the lord deputy took the unprecedented step of ordering a new election for mayor of Dublin, because the candidate chosen by the aldermen was a Catholic; in the course of the next thirty years the corporation bowed to royal pressure and confined the mayoralty to Protestants. But the promotion of Protestantism was merely one aspect of royal policy: it also served as a pretext for government intervention in corporate affairs.[10]

II. The Restoration and Jacobite Eras

For the Dublin civic Patriots of the mid-eighteenth century, the restoration period held special significance. For it was under Charles II that, according to Charles Lucas, the rights of Dublin citizens had been overturned, leaving them with a 'distempered, broken Constitution . . . endless Slavery, of the most dangerous Kind'.[11] Lucas was referring here to the introduction of the new rules in 1672, by which the Irish privy council formally obtained certain rights concerning the affairs of urban corporations.[12] In order to understand what those rules meant to Lucas and his contemporaries, it will be useful to consider why they were originally introduced, and what reaction they produced in their own day.

Historians of the restoration period in England have laid much emphasis recently on the deep sense of insecurity that persisted after 1660. Following the traumatic upheavals of the two previous decades, many placed their faith in a strong monarchy, bolstered by divine right principles; others feared that such a system would jeopardize the rights of the subject.[13] Moreover, the restoration church settlement was controversial. Down to the 1640s the established church had comprehended virtually the entire Protestant community; now significant groups of Protestant dissenters, notably the Presbyterians, found themselves outside it. Since it was still generally held that only conformity to 'the national church' was compatible with harmony and order, the marked lack of religious conformity was a matter of much concern. In this climate, rumours abounded; of revolts, conspiracies, and planned assassinations. Some of these rumours materialized, as in the rising of the Fifth Monarchy Men in 1661, and Monmouth's rebellion in 1685; Ireland witnessed a plot to seize Dublin Castle in 1663, and there were risings in Scotland in 1666 and 1679.

Signs of insecurity on the part of the crown and its chief supporters during

---

[10] Fitzpatrick, 'Municipal Corporation of Dublin', i. 93, 132, 259–62; Lennon, *Lords of Dublin*, 176–7. Bristol also suffered encroachment on its liberties: David Harris Sacks, 'The Corporate Town and the English State: Bristol's "Little Businesses" 1625–1641', in *P. & P.* 110 (1986), 69–105.

[11] Charles Lucas, *Divelina Libera: An Apology for the Civil Rights and Liberties of the Commons and Citizens of Dublin* (Dublin, 1744), 21.

[12] *CARD* i. 56–67.　　　　[13] See e.g. Seaward, *The Restoration*, chs. 1–2.

this period were apparent in policy towards the corporate towns. These had frequently shown themselves to be bastions of parliament and the commonwealth during the 1640s and 1650s. Hence the restoration government was anxious to see control of towns in friendly (especially Anglican) hands, particularly in view of their national political significance: both in England and in Ireland some four-fifths of MPs represented parliamentary boroughs, elected, in most cases, by very few people. The key to control lay in the selection of municipal officials, especially mayors, sheriffs (who were responsible for conducting parliamentary elections and empanelling juries), town clerks, and recorders (who kept the civic records and acted as law officers). The lessons of the 1640s seemed to suggest that order and stability—the prime concern for the political élite—could only be guaranteed by rallying behind the established church, which now more than ever could claim to avoid both the perceived errors of Rome (in particular, the pope's claim to possess a deposing power), and the anti-episcopal systems of the Protestant dissenters ('fanaticks' to their critics), who were held responsible for the execution of Charles I and suspected of harbouring republican tendencies.

It was the conviction that only members of the established church could safely be entrusted with municipal office that lay behind the corporation act for England (1661), which required civic officials to be in communion with the Church of England, and to take other oaths designed to exclude those with allegedly subversive principles.[14] The act was followed up by some piecemeal challenges by the crown to borough charters, through writs of quo warranto, whereby on a technicality a town could be induced to forfeit its charter. When new charters were issued in return, they frequently gave the crown a right of veto over key appointments.[15] There has been some disagreement among historians as to whether such actions amounted to a consciously 'absolutist' policy on Charles II's part, or whether they sprang from simple insecurity, shared by monarch and local élites alike: whatever the answer, the effect—to increase the power of the crown and its Anglican adherents—was much the same.[16]

As the threads of royal government were picked up again in Ireland, how had Dublin been affected by the events of the 1640s and 1650s? The main change concerned religion. Thanks to the thwarting of a plan to seize Dublin Castle at the outbreak of the Irish rebellion in 1641, the city had remained in Protestant hands throughout these decades, and this had

---

[14] 13 Chas II, st. 2, c. 1.

[15] J. H. Sacret, 'The Restoration Government and Municipal Corporations', *EHR* 45 (1930), 232–59, at 247–58. Quo warranto was a writ directed against anyone who usurped any franchise against the crown.

[16] Sacret believed there was a systematic policy to increase royal control over the corporate towns. For a different view, see John Miller, 'The Crown and the Borough Charters in the Reign of Charles II', *EHR* 100 (1985), 53–84. See also Seaward, *The Restoration*, 35–6.

fostered the consolidation of a Protestant mercantile and trading community, helped by immigration from England and elsewhere. The commonwealth period had witnessed the emergence of a small number of Presbyterians and other Protestant radicals;[17] from the 1660s on, they formed the nucleus of Protestant dissent in the city. Catholics, by contrast, had been reduced by war and expulsion to about one-third of the city's population, living mainly outside the walls. The commonwealth authorities had toyed in the early 1650s with reducing guild privileges, but had come to support the guild system. The leading merchants were an important source of loans for the war, and they had benefited by being allowed to monopolize a large share of Ireland's trade with England.

The commonwealth period had also witnessed some assertiveness on the part of the city commons. They had contended for a share in the election of officials (1649), and in particular that of mayor (1653), on the grounds of ancient custom. But little had come of this. In 1653 the sheriffs and sixteen members of the city commons participated in the election of mayor, but in 1657 it was agreed to revert to the practice whereby the most senior alderman filled the office.[18] There was to be a strong element of continuity in the transfer not merely from the Cromwellian to the restoration regime, but even from the pre-Cromwellian regime; at least eight aldermen in the 1660s had held civic office or were free of the city before Cromwell came to Ireland in 1649.[19]

In the dying days of the commonwealth the corporation threw its weight behind the efforts of Sir Charles Coote, lord president of Connaught, in support of a restoration of the monarchy. That the corporation saw its fate as intimately bound up with that of England was apparent from its statement that 'a full and free parliament in England is the birthright of the people of England, and in whose prosperitie or adversitie the saide Maior, Sheriffs, commons and cittizens are sure to bee sharers'.[20] This statement also makes it clear that the corporation's range of political concepts included 'the rights of Englishmen'.[21]

---

[17] Barnard, *Cromwellian Ireland*, ch. 4.

[18] Ibid. 71–3; *CARD* iii. 473; iv. 37, 46–7, 113. Black has noted that in this period both guild traditions and natural rights theories (inspired by the Levellers) were invoked in support of greater internal democracy in the London companies (*Guilds and Civil Society*, 126–7).

[19] William Smith (below, App. B); Raphael Hunt, mayor 1650–1; Richard Tighe, mayor 1651–2, 1655–6; Daniel Hutchinson, mayor 1652–3; Robert Deey, mayor 1659–60, lord mayor 1672–3; Daniel Bellingham, lord mayor 1665–6; John Desmynieres, lord mayor 1666–7; Lewis Desmynieres, lord mayor 1669–70 (*CARD* iii. 457, 462, 466, 471). The dominance of pre-Cromwellian settlers in restoration Irish politics has been noted by Karl S. Bottigheimer, 'The Restoration Land Settlement in Ireland', *IHS* 18 (1972), 1–21. A full list of mayors is given in T. W. Moody, F. X. Martin, F. J. Byrne (eds.), *A New History of Ireland*, ix. *Maps, Genealogies, Lists* (Oxford, 1984), 547–62.

[20] *CARD* iv. 180.

[21] Bristol corporation was appealing to 'the rights of Englishmen' in the 1620s: Sacks, 'The Corporate Town', 99–100.

A 'free parliament' would in effect mean the return of the monarchy, and in May 1660 the corporation fulsomely greeted Charles II's restoration, following this up in 1661 by endorsing the return to the established episcopal church. Relations between the crown and the municipality began well; the resumption of normal relations was highlighted in 1662 by the appointment as viceroy of James Butler, duke of Ormond, and Ireland's premier peer. He had previously been appointed viceroy by Charles I in 1643, and had actually handed the city over to the parliamentary forces in 1647. Under the strongly pro-Anglican Ormond, and his son the earl of Ossory, who between them headed the Irish administration from 1662 to 1669, the corporation was anxious to co-operate with government for mutual benefit. In 1664 overtures were made for the confirmation of charters, and for a share of forfeited land. What the corporation obtained was an annual grant from the crown of £500 to be paid in perpetuity, in recognition of the city's support for the crown at the restoration. Moreover, in 1665 the viceroy recommended that Alderman Sir Daniel Bellingham should take the title 'lord mayor' (authorized by Charles I in 1641, but not then implemented).[22] On top of these benefits, Ormond was anxious to promote the interests of Irish trade and industry. Individual aldermen were commissioned to carry out government business (such as the import of arms in the 1670s), and Alderman Bellingham, a silversmith, served for a time in the 1660s as the crown's deputy vice-treasurer in Ireland. Against this background, the aldermen were prepared to comply with Ormond's wishes in respect of the mayoralty.[23] That he was rather less severe in his attitudes to Catholics than the earl of Orrery and some of the Anglo-Irish gentry (many of the Butlers were Catholic) apparently did him no harm in Dublin; on the contrary, the city marked its appreciation of and loyalty to Ormond's family by placing the Butler arms over the newly rebuilt Tholsel in 1683.[24]

For their part, the Protestant gentry shared many of their English counterparts' concerns about urban corporations. Influential figures, such as Orrery, were anxious to see the towns as the preserve of loyalists and members of the established church. As noted in Chapter 1, the act of explanation (1665) sought to calm the gentry's fears about Catholics by preventing those who refused the oaths of supremacy and allegiance from purchasing houses in corporate towns. But the numerical weakness of the Anglicans in Ireland ensured that there was no Irish equivalent of the English corporation act to exclude Protestant dissenters from civic office:

[22] Aidan Clarke, '1659 and the Road to Restoration', in Jane Ohlmeyer (ed.), *Ireland from Independence to Occupation 1641–1660* (Cambridge, 1995), 241–64, at 250; *CARD* iv. pp. xvi, 308–9, 359.

[23] J. C. Beckett, *The Cavalier Duke: A Life of James Butler—1st Duke of Ormond* (Belfast, 1990), 93–4; *CARD* iv. 261, 373, 381.

[24] Beckett, *The Cavalier Duke*, 144. For the corporation and the Butlers, see *CARD* iv. pp. xxi–xxiii, v, 324–5.

the gentry had to rely on their own influence to keep non-Anglicans out.[25] This gave the crown more freedom of action than in England; and in 1665 the crown formally obtained the right to review the government of the corporate towns. The act of explanation empowered the viceroy and Irish privy council, within seven years, to make rules for better regulating cities, towns, and corporations in Ireland. Accordingly, in August 1670 the English privy council instructed the new viceroy, Lord Berkeley, to commence a thorough review of Irish municipal charters, with a view to reducing the extensive privileges of the larger corporations and securing for the crown a power of veto over key civic appointments. This advice was repeated a year later, and the viceroy was told to challenge by quo warranto any corporation that failed to apply for a new charter.[26]

Lord Berkeley had his own reasons for wishing to obtain greater control over Dublin corporation. Plans for a new bridge over the Liffey (with government support) had recently been obstructed by members of the corporation, who had vested interests in ferry revenues, and who in general had no desire to improve access to the city for country tradesmen, or to promote development north of the river.[27] 'Lord Berkeley's rules', issued in November 1671, were designed to increase state control, and to concentrate civic power in fewer hands. They soon proved contentious. The vesting of the election of the lord mayor, recorder, sheriffs, town clerk and auditors in the lord mayor and aldermen formally abolished any vestigial rights of the city commons in such elections. The provision that all freemen were to take the oath of supremacy effectively excluded Catholics, whose hopes of toleration had been raised by the dismissal of Ormond in 1669, and by Berkeley's pro-Catholic sympathies. The non-resistance oath (denying that it was lawful to take up arms against the king) was aimed at excluding any Catholics or Protestant dissenters who might feel inclined to justify revolt against a ruler who did not uphold the true faith. In addition, the rules represented a significant step towards oligarchy and state control. Elections of the lord mayor, recorder and sheriffs were in future to be subject to viceregal approval, formalizing an earlier *ad hoc* exercise of influence; and the guild representatives, or 'numbers' on the common council were to be selected annually by the lord mayor, with the advice and consent of the aldermen, from double returns supplied by the guilds. Guild representation itself was regularized; each craft guild was to have just two representatives, and the merchants ten: for the older guilds, this meant a reduction in their

[25] 'Instructions to MPs', 30 July 1661, *Commons' Jn. Ire. 1613–1661/2*, i. 442; Boyle, *Collection of the State Letters of Roger Boyle*, i. 93, ii. 18, 302–5. See also McGuire, 'Government Attitudes to Religious Non-Conformity', 256.
[26] *Cal. SP Ire. 1669–70*, 224–5; *Cal. SP Dom. 1671*, 432.
[27] 'A True and Impartial Narrative of the Late Disorders in Dublin', *Cal. SP Dom. 1672*, 127–31; Craig, *Dublin 1660–1800*, 25.

representation. Other procedural innovations restricted the role of the city commons; no debate on a petition was to be considered by that body until it had first been considered by the aldermanic board.[28]

The corporation submitted to these rules, but they were unpopular among the guilds, and there was disquiet lest they should operate to the advantage of powerful individuals, rather than to the city in general. Such suspicions were particularly directed towards the city's recorder and clerk of the Tholsel, Sir William Davies, who was believed to be seeking a concessionary lease in relation to the city's water supply. He had influential connections, being a son of the secretary of state, Sir Paul Davies, and son-in-law of the chancellor, Archbishop Michael Boyle of Dublin, who was Orrery's cousin and one of Berkeley's strongest critics in the Irish privy council. As criticism of the rules continued, Sir William emerged as a probable scapegoat, for he had been charged with drawing them up, and the viceroy hinted that it was he who was responsible for their unpopular features (a charge strongly denied by Sir William).[29] On 2 March 1672, the Irish privy council announced that the rules would remain in operation only until the end of the year (at that time, 24 March). To further complicate matters, the king now openly embarked on a policy of indulgence towards the Irish Catholics; a viceregal proclamation of 8 March 1672 lifted the statutory ban on Catholics purchasing forfeited property in Irish corporate towns and restored them to the corporate privileges they had enjoyed in Charles I's reign.[30]

The rescinding of Lord Berkeley's rules encouraged certain members of the city commons to seek the dismissal of Sir William Davies. For his part, the viceroy, though he had distanced himself from the rules, had not abandoned his intention of regulating Dublin corporation, a goal that he proceeded to pursue through the complicity of the lord mayor, Sir John Totty (whom he later urged the corporation to re-elect for a second year). At the end of March 1672 Berkeley wrote to the corporation, indicating which members of the city commons he would like to see chosen to fill two vacancies on the aldermanic board.[31] One of his nominees was an acting sheriff. The aldermen pointed out with some spirit that by virtue of the recent royal proclamation, one of the positions belonged to 'old Alderman Kennedy' (a Catholic), and that it was contrary to their practice to promote

---

[28] *CARD* v. 548–54. The non-resistance oath had been included in the provisions of the English corporation act (1661).

[29] *CARD* v. pp. vi–vii; DCA, Monday Book 1658–1712, MR/18, fo. 61ª; *Cal. SP Dom. 1672*, 127–31. Davies (below, App. B) had been recommended as clerk by Lord Ossory (*CARD* iv. 333–4).

[30] *CARD* v. 558; DCA, MR/18, f. 63ᵇ; *Cal. SP Dom. 1671–2*, 185. Lord Berkeley and his predecessor, Lord Robartes, had instructions to divide the Irish Catholics by favouring those prepared to take the supremacy oath (Hutton, *Charles II*, 268).

[31] *Cal. SP Dom. 1671–2*, 257–8, 344.

a sheriff while he was in office. They also protested against the bid to have Sir William dismissed. Lord Mayor Totty reacted by invoking Dublin's chartered rights. He summoned some members of the city commons to the aldermen's chamber, and with their support[32] he proceeded to dismiss Sir William, on the grounds of his alleged responsibility for the rules, replacing him by the viceroy's secretary, Sir Ellis Leighton, a Catholic. When seven of the aldermen, including two old Cromwellian Independents, protested, the lord mayor proceeded to appoint members of the city commons in their places, and to obtain for himself the post of clerk of the Tholsel.[33] This marked the beginning of disruption in the corporation which lasted for several years.

There is much about this controversy that remains obscure, for everyone concerned was anxious to justify themselves with the government in England, and accusations and counter-accusations flew about. However, the leading protagonists held views of civic government that paralleled contemporary debates in England—where talk of 'Court' and 'Country' parties became common in the later 1660s and 1670s—about the nature of the polity.[34] The ousted Sir William's political views had something in common with English Country sentiment. On presenting the mayor to the duke of Ormond in 1663, Davies had made a speech praising the nature of corporate government in Dublin, in which he blended the language of ancient constitution, corporatism, and classical mixed government:

For it appears that all these perfections which may bee gathered from all these three severall kinds of government, monarchical, aristocraticall and democraticall, doe most happily concurre in the making up and compleating the present and ancient government of this citty. For have you not the prudent Maior, the prime magistrate, answering monarchy; the grave senators, the aldermen, answering aristocracy; and the understanding commons answering democracy, which, being thus composed, twisted and knitt together, are as a three fould corde not easily broken and . . . resembled to the body of a man united in all its severall members, from heade to foote, by such a strict conjunction, mutuall assistance and admirable sympathy under and with the government of the head, as they are all carried on with one voluntary consent to supply the defects of each other?[35]

The new recorder, Sir Ellis Leighton, by contrast, took an absolutist line. He considered corporations to be 'creatures of the monarchy', which were

---

[32] The point was that Dublin's charters granted rights to the mayor, bailiffs (sheriffs), commons and citizens; mention of aldermen was a comparatively late development. See *CARD* i. 1–56.

[33] The posts of mayor and clerk were in principle incompatible (*CARD* iii. 503). See also *Cal. SP Dom. 1671–2*, 257–8, 349; *Cal. SP Dom. 1672*, 126–7, 153–4. The old Cromwellians were Richard Tighe (MP Dublin city in the Cromwellian parliament) and Daniel Hutchinson, chandler (Barnard, *Cromwellian Ireland*, 81).

[34] Tim Harris, *Politics Under the Later Stuarts: Party Conflict in a Divided Society 1660–1715* (London, 1993), ch. 3.   [35] *CARD* iv. p. xx n. 3.

bound to leave affairs of state to the king and his ministers. The aldermen 'ought to have no politick maximes of their own'. He went so far as to recommend to Dublin corporation that 'if any body could find out a shape of government, or devise any rules that would make you more subject to the will and personal power of the prince, you would petition the king for that model, and for those rules'.[36] The two men's political contacts were consistent with such differences in outlook. Leighton had been secretary[37] to James, duke of York, the king's brother and heir to the throne, shortly to reveal himself as a Catholic by his refusal to comply with the test act of 1673. But Davies too had friends in high places. He and the dismissed aldermen (all but two of them former mayors or lord mayors) took their case to the royal court in London, where they complained that the lord mayor was acting from motives of personal ambition, and that their own dismissal had been engineered in the absence of most of the aldermen. Lord Berkeley's rules, it was insinuated, would reduce Dublin 'to more monarchical principles than their present constitution allowed of'. They obtained the support of the Presbyterian peer, Lord Ashley (a former colleague of Oliver Cromwell) recently raised to the rank of the earl of Shaftesbury, who was to emerge in 1673 as a leading spokesman for the Country opposition.[38]

In the meantime, Lord Berkeley's administration had come under attack in the English parliament for its indulgence to Catholics, and early in 1672 the king decided to replace him. The Dublin dismissals were accordingly referred to the new viceroy, the earl of Essex, and the Irish privy council. In September 1672 the privy council unanimously agreed that the dismissals had been irregular, and ordered that Davies and his colleagues be reinstated. But the principle of government regulation was not abandoned: in the same month Essex issued new rules, which were to be in force 'for ever'. In Dublin's case they set out the composition of the corporation: the lord mayor and twenty-four aldermen to form one chamber, and the two sheriffs, up to forty-eight sheriffs' peers, and ninety-six guild representatives, the other. This merely confirmed the existing two-tier system. But some of the most controversial points of Lord Berkeley's rules were retained, and new ones added. Elections of the chief office-holders were to be sanctioned by the viceroy, and, as prescribed in the English corporation act, such officials, along with the entire common council, were to take the oaths of supremacy, allegiance, and non-resistance (though in keeping with the royal policy of indulgence to Catholics the viceroy was empowered to dispense

---

[36] 'Speech of Sir Ellis Leighton, recorder of Dublin, on the 4th of April, at the Tholsel' (1672), *CARD* v. 558–62.

[37] See *DNB*. Leighton was arrested in 1678 after being named by Oates in the alleged popish plot (*HMC Ormond MSS*, NS iv. 464).

[38] *Cal. SP Dom. 1672*, 127–31; *CARD* v. p. x.

with the supremacy oath). The guild representatives were still to be selected from double returns by the lord mayor in the presence of the aldermen, although they were henceforth to serve for three years rather than one. Sheriffs and the lord mayor were to be chosen only by the lord mayor and aldermen, and the lord mayor was empowered to alter the number of any guild's representatives on the city commons. Moreover, 'foreign' tradesmen, including non-Anglicans, residing in or moving to Dublin, were to be entitled to freedom of the city and guilds at low fines, provided they took the oath of allegiance and other freemen's oaths.[39]

The new rules turned out to be as contentious as the earlier ones. They were criticized as being subversive of Dublin's chartered rights: an Irish judge, Dr Dudley Loftus of the prerogative court, thought they were illegal, and contrary to the principles of the English constitution.[40] Several Presbyterians and other Protestant dissenters among the freemen objected strongly to the non-resistance oath on the grounds that it enjoined a species of 'passive obedience'; while Catholics were disappointed at the merely discretionary scope of their own toleration. The selection of the city commons at the end of 1672 only made things worse, for the Presbyterian lord mayor, Robert Deey, caused controversy by selecting up to a dozen Catholics (though he subsequently lost his nerve and chose Protestants in their place).[41] Charles II was duly gratified at the choice of Catholics, but he had already decided to suspend the new rules until Essex answered criticisms that they were unfair to Catholics. By this time, however, the king was coming under pressure from landed opinion in both Ireland and England to abandon indulgence to Catholics, and in 1673 he was forced to accept the first English test act.[42]

Meanwhile, in Dublin, Anglican, Presbyterian, and Catholic guild representatives boycotted the quarterly corporation meetings, in an impressive show of solidarity in defence of traditional guild privileges.[43] However, the new rules were reaffirmed in July 1673, and Essex confirmed the lord mayor's second set of returns for the city commons, which contained no Catholics. The upshot was that for several years civic life remained

---

[39] *Cal. SP Dom. 1671–2*, 418–19; *Cal. SP Dom. 1672*, 644; DCA, MR/18, fos. 78ᵇ–80ᵃ; CARD i. 56–67; v. 12–18.

[40] CARD v. p. xii. Dr Dudley Loftus (1619–95), Master in Chancery and oriental scholar; educated TCD; from 1651 held Irish government posts. His capacity for indiscretion (see *DNB*) appeared in his opposition to the new rules, leading to a spell of imprisonment (*Cal. SP Dom. 1673*, 527).

[41] CARD v. p. xii; *Cal. SP Dom. 1672–3*, 64–5. See also enclosure in [Essex] to Lord Arlington, 19 July 1673, *Cal. SP Dom. 1673*, 444–6. As mayor, 1659–60, Deey's support for the restoration had won him command of a foot company, to be vested in successive mayors after his death (CARD i. 44–6).

[42] 25 Chas. II, c. 2; *Cal. SP Dom. 1672–3*, 431–2; Hutton, *Charles II*, 300.

[43] Certain guild representatives refused to be sworn, alleging that the oaths had not been administered in time, or in keeping with the new rules (*Cal. SP Dom. 1673*, 444–6, 528; DCA, MR/18, fos. 67ᵃ–67ᵇ, 68ᵃ–70ᵃ).

unsettled. Petitions, attacking the rules, were drawn up and circulated among the citizens; and at guild level the part played by the city commons in the ousting of Davies (who continued to be held responsible for inspiring the rules) and his aldermanic colleagues remained a source of pride. Evidence from guild representatives reveals that at this level criticism was couched in traditional corporate and legalistic terms. Opposition to the rules was equated with 'the good of the city', 'the good of the whole city'; the rules were described as 'destructive to many charters and priviledges thereby granted to this city and the several Guilds and Corporations therein', and incompatible with the acts of settlement and explanation (presumably the objection here was the obligation to accept 'foreign' artisans).[44] Doubtless this stand had been encouraged by Dr Loftus's condemnation of the rules.[45] There was no attempt to suggest that the city had been the victim of 'arbitrary power': on the contrary, willingness to obey the king and viceroy was constantly stressed. Nor was there any denunciation of popery; in so far as there was sectarian sparring among the guild representatives it was conducted between Anglicans and Protestant dissenters.[46] Lord Mayor Totty in fact chose as one of his counsel Sir Nicholas Plunkett, a leading spokesman for Irish Catholics. Moreover, opposition was expressed, for the most part, very properly, in guildhalls and through petitions; the boycott of the city assembly was perhaps the nearest the commons came to non-cooperation.[47]

Notwithstanding such apparent moderation, this defence of corporatist values caused the administration some anxiety. One petition from Anglican guild representatives pleaded that to attend the city assembly would be to overthrow their charters and injure their respective guilds 'by whom only we are bound in conscience to be regulated in matters of this nature'. Against this statement, an official noted in the margin, 'by this they declare themselves to be free states'.[48] And it was an appeal to religious conscience that lay behind the resistance to the new oaths (acceptable to the Anglican guild members, but not, apparently, to the Presbyterians or Catholics).[49] Attitudes of this kind, in the light of what had been justified in the name of

---

[44] DPLGC, MS 78, fos. 151–4; statement by Anglican guild representatives, *Cal. SP Dom. 1673*, 444–6, 456–7, 475. Such language echoed earlier opposition to royal encroachment (Lennon, *Lords of Dublin*, 195). London too resisted naturalization of immigrants (Daniel Statt, 'The City of London and the Controversy over Immigration, 1660–1722', *Hist. Jn.* 33 (1990), 45–61).
[45] Dr Loftus was said to have predicted that none of the 7 dismissed aldermen would ever again serve as lord mayor (*Cal. SP Dom. 1673*, p. 527). But Sir Joshua Allen served in 1673–4, Sir Francis Brewster in 1674–5.
[46] *Cal. SP Dom. 1673*, 444–6. The bitterness of relations between Anglicans and Presbyterians is noted by McGuire, 'Government Attitudes to Religious Non-Conformity', 257.   [47] CARD v. 15.   [48] *Cal. SP Dom. 1673*, 444–6.
[49] Presbyterian representatives singled out the 'new [non-resistance] oath' as being too great a burden for their consciences; Catholics were also critical (*Cal. SP Dom. 1673*, 444–6).

conscience during the 1640s and 1650s, were clearly subversive of the established order, and the viceroy made strenuous efforts to bring the guilds to heel. In a public speech to the city in March 1674, Essex insisted that the new rules, which had the same force of law as the act of settlement, were for the city's benefit. Proceedings would be taken against anyone resisting them. But a year later, details of the irregular dismissals had still not been erased from the corporation's records. The lord mayor and aldermen indicated their willingness to comply with the viceroy's wishes, but the meeting summoned for the purpose of expunging the record was disrupted by members of the city commons.[50] It was these proceedings that led Essex to reflect

nothing will reduce this city to a due composure unless it be the avoiding their charter by a *Quo Warranto* and granting them a new one; for the body of the commons are so numerous . . . [and] . . . being extreme poor men, are continually mutinous and fractious; whereas, if they had a new charter, and the number reduced to be fewer, and those named out of the most substantial chief trading men of the city, whose interest it is to be quiet, I am confident it would be the only way to bring them into order and peace.[51]

These remarks were prophetic, but twelve years were to elapse before Dublin lost its charter. What precipitated a more systematic assault by the crown on corporate charters in England and Ireland was the exclusion crisis of 1678–81: an episode that shook English politics from top to bottom.

The exclusion crisis highlighted, in a particularly stark way, a recurring constitutional problem. It was still generally accepted that monarchical rule formed part of the God-centred universe that most contemporaries took for granted. But in 1673 the duke of York's public admission of his conversion, and the consequent prospect of a Catholic succession, once again focused attention on the gap between constitutional theory, which stressed harmony of interests between the king and his subjects, and reality. With the Counter-Reformation in the ascendant on the Continent, it was not fanciful to fear for the future of English Protestantism. Anxieties were the more intense because of concerns about the narrow nature of the restoration church settlement and harassment of Protestant dissenters: to some, the Church of England was still too much tainted with popery. The climate of insecurity was compounded by Charles II's foreign policy at this time, and especially his support for France during the Dutch crises of the 1670s. As in 1640 and 1641 rumours of popish plots began to circulate.

The most specific of these rumours was Titus Oates's tale in 1678 of a Jesuit conspiracy (backed by the French) to assassinate the king and the duke of Ormond, put James on the throne and restore England to

[50] *CARD* v. pp. xiv–xv.
[51] *Letters Written by . . . Arthur Capel, Earl of Essex*, 113–15. Essex did not apparently blame the Dublin disorders on any wish to challenge monarchy (*CARD* x. 511–14).

Catholicism. Some unfortunate coincidences lent credibility to the allegation of a plot, and the upshot was a campaign—which to some extent cut across former Court and Country positions—to exclude the duke of York from the succession. The climate of alarm was such that, despite royal hostility, the campaign's prospects looked good, and a series of general elections in England afforded widespread coverage for the issues.[52]

In their propaganda the exclusionists gave prominence to the claim that popery and arbitrary power went together by drawing attention to the military expansion of Catholic France with its standing army and allegedly boundless royal prerogative. Although they did not create popular anxiety about popery, which had a long history in England—sharpened by exaggerated reports of massacres perpetrated by Catholics in Ireland in 1641—they did play on such fears and give them focus. However, by appealing to popular elements in the electorate, especially in London, by encouraging their supporters there to instruct their MPs how to vote, and by publishing proposals to extend the franchise in parliamentary boroughs (strongholds of Protestant dissent), the exclusionists appeared ready to risk the sort of challenge to the established order that figured in memories of the civil wars of the 1640s. Accordingly, they were labelled 'Whigs' (Scottish Presbyterian rebels) by their opponents. To many members of the landed élite, leaving the succession intact seemed preferable to such a prospect; and the ensuing 'Tory' reaction not only preserved James's place as heir to the throne but produced a flood of pamphlets in which the indefeasible hereditary divine right of kings, the historical primacy of the royal prerogative over common and statute law, and 'passive obedience' were strongly reaffirmed.[53] Evidently, fear of popery had by no means cancelled out fear of radical Protestant dissent. But before it had run its course, the exclusion crisis had given new life to another term, 'Patriot'.

Traditionally, a Patriot simply meant a fellow countryman. But during the seventeenth century the term was drawn into constitutional debate. In the 1640s those who used civic republican language to present the monarch, parliament, and people 'as forming a polity in which any part might be resisted and restrained in the name of the whole' were sometimes called 'Commonwealthmen', or 'Patriots'.[54] In the 1670s Country politicians again sought to defend the rights of the subject by invoking a balanced constitution. Kings, lords, and commons had distinct roles, and the

[52] J. R. Jones, *The First Whigs; The Politics of the Exclusion Crisis, 1678–1683* (London, 1961); Hutton, *Charles II*, 358–60; Harris, *Politics Under the Later Stuarts*, 89.

[53] 'Tories' were Irish Catholic outlaws (Robert Willman, 'The Origins of "Whig" and "Tory" in English Political Language', *Hist. Jn.* 17 (1974), 247–64. See also Seaward, *The Restoration*, ch. 5; Jones, *The First Whigs*, 95, 180.

[54] J. G. A. Pocock, *The Machiavellian Moment: Florentine Political Thought and the Atlantic Republican Tradition*, (Princeton, 1975), 371–2.

independence of the commons ought to be defended by regular elections. Champions of this position were described as 'Patriots'.[55]

This term therefore had already come back into circulation when it was employed in two of the better-known publications to emerge from the exclusion crisis. One was Elkanah Settle's *The Character of a Popish Successour*, published before the meeting of parliament at Oxford (1681). Settle's point was that a popish king would set aside England's ancient constitution and overturn '*Religion, Liberty,* and *Property*'. The author described himself as a 'Commonwealths-man', and welcomed signs that 'true *English* Patriots' were exerting themselves to prevent 'approaching Destruction'.[56] The term was taken up later in the year by Settle's rival poet and the crown's most articulate defender during this period, John Dryden. In his famous satire *Absalom and Achitophel* Dryden put into the mouth of King David (Charles II) a denunciation of 'Patriots' who sought to displace the real heir in favour of Absalom (the king's illegitimate but Protestant son, the duke of Monmouth). For Dryden, 'Patriot' was another name for faction, and Absalom merely a tool in the hands of designing politicians: 'Gull'd with a Patriots name, whose Modern sense is one that would by Law supplant his Prince'.[57] Later, after the revolution of 1688–9 had accomplished what the exclusionists had been unable to do, 'Patriot' was to become a more acceptable label even to Tories, some of whom were prompted by the unexpected turn of events to adopt Country positions. Dryden himself wrote in 1699, 'A patriot both the King and Country serves, Prerogative and privilege preserves'; and Pope, a little later, made the same point: 'An honest Courtier, yet a Patriot too, Just to his Prince, and to his Country true'.[58] Such examples suggest the supra-party potential of the 'Patriot' tag that would be realized in George II's reign.

The reaction that followed the exclusion crisis had serious consequences for the English parliamentary boroughs. In London, where the Whigs had attempted to use the common council as a substitute forum after the king had dissolved parliament in 1681, the corporation's charter was successfully challenged by a writ of quo warranto in 1683, overturning the city's claims of indefeasible corporate rights derived from prescription and statute. Whig aldermen were relieved of their posts, the guilds had to surrender their charters, and the common council disappeared. The loss of London's independence was widely interpreted as another manifestation of popish designs against the Protestant religion and constitution: the house of

---

[55] See e.g. Anon., *Two Seasonable Discourses Concerning the Present Parliament* (1675), in *State Tracts; Being a Collection of Several Treatises Relating to the Government* (London, 1693), 66–8.

[56] Settle, *The Character of a Popish Successour* (State Tracts, 148).

[57] *The Poems of John Dryden*, ed. John Sargeaunt (Oxford, 1910), 61. Cf. Ormond's strictures on the Rye House plotters as 'the chief patriots for the liberty of their country' (*HMC Ormond MSS*, ns vii. 169).   [58] See *Oxford English Dictionary*.

commons would be targeted next.[59] Other parliamentary boroughs where Whigs and Protestant dissenters had made a strong showing also found their charters challenged.

Although Ireland could scarcely avoid being dragged in to the popish plot controversy, there was no direct Irish parallel to the exclusion crisis, chiefly because, with buoyant hereditary revenues, it was possible for the crown to avoid calling a parliament there (thus reinforcing English suspicions about the arbitrary tendencies of royal policy).[60] English exclusionists sought to find evidence of Irish involvement in the plot, but with little success. In 1680–1, witnesses before the English house of lords alleged that certain Irish Catholics had accepted commissions from Louis XIV, and were planning to facilitate a French invasion; the house concluded that there was a plot in Ireland to massacre Protestants and subvert the Protestant religion. (In fact, Louis XIV was preoccupied with consolidating his control over France's eastern approaches, and there was apparently no French plan to invade Ireland).[61] As the Tory reaction gathered strength, the invasion scare blew over.

Meanwhile, in Dublin, by 1675 Essex had at last secured compliance from the corporation in the matter of expunging the order for the controversial dismissals from the civic records. The dispute had begun to have adverse effects on the corporation, and the aldermen at length decided to order the erasure; this was accomplished by the simple, if irregular, expedient of dealing with the matter at a meeting to which the city commons was not summoned. Although the popish plot prompted the corporation to limit civic freedom to those who were willing to take the oaths of allegiance and supremacy,[62] the city was persuaded by Ormond (reinstated as viceroy, 1677–85) to keep a low profile so as to avoid adding to the crown's difficulties; and in general the city's conduct during the last years of Charles II's reign reflected Ormond's Anglicanism and moderation.[63]

Thus in 1681, when Charles II dissolved the Oxford parliament in controversial circumstances, Dublin corporation offered to address the king. Even though the proposed address would have endorsed royal policy (to reject exclusion, but to offer safeguards for Protestant interests),

---

[59] Jennifer Levin, *The Charter Controversy in the City of London, 1660–1688, and its Consequences* (London, 1969); De Krey, *A Fractured Society*, 11–14; Miller, 'The Crown and the Borough Charters', 75.

[60] Plans were made to hold an Irish parliament in the 1670s, but the popish plot intervened (*HMC Ormond MSS*, NS iv. pp. vii–viii).

[61] Hutton, *Charles II*, 391–2, 397; Moody, Martin, Byrne (eds.), *NHI* iii. 432–3.

[62] *CARD* v. pp. xvi–xvii, 19, 73–6.

[63] Ormond did not demand an exclusively Anglican mayoralty: he urged the retention in office of Sir Humphrey Jervis (Presbyterian) for a second year in 1682 (TCD, Hutchison MSS 8556–8/74, 75). Jervis was about to build the bridge that he named after the viceroy (Craig, *Dublin 1660–1860*, 27).

Ormond urged his son Arran to consult the king concerning the propriety of such an address. He was told that it should not be encouraged, lest government critics seize the chance to put their stamp on it, as the Whigs had done in London. When shortly afterwards English Whigs tried to embarrass the government on the grounds of alleged abuses in the Irish administration, Dublin corporation condemned the attack, and strongly vindicated Ormond's conduct of affairs.[64] In 1682 the city did address the king, praising Ormond, deploring recent attempts to alienate the affections of the king's subjects, and affirming its own commitment to defend the monarch and the established church against 'either Papists or fanaticks, or other disturbers of the publick peace'.[65] The corporation's willingness to follow Ormond's lead rested, no doubt, largely on deference to a peer who was a towering figure in England as well as Ireland; but the duke was able to reinforce his authority by using his good offices to secure regular payment of the corporation's royal grant. In this way, Dublin corporation played its part in the campaign to defeat the Whigs in England; and on Charles II's death in 1685 the city promptly addressed James as the true and lawful sovereign.[66]

Emboldened by the accession of a Catholic monarch, certain Catholic merchants in Dublin petitioned the Irish privy council to uphold their applications for admission to civic freedom. Such admissions would contravene the 1678 civic by-laws; and the corporation decided to mobilize a fund to oppose such applications in the courts. But in 1686 the king ordered qualified Catholics to be admitted to freedom and civic office, on condition merely that they take the oath of allegiance, and the customary freeman's oath. The corporation temporized, pleading its good record in the matter of Catholic admissions: up to 500 Catholics (it was claimed) who qualified as 'innocent' under the terms of the act of settlement had been admitted to freedom. This plea failed to move the government, and the corporation backed down and passed an act of assembly to admit Catholics without taking the supremacy oath. The following spring, the corporation complied with the royal wish that 'there be no difference made betweene his Protestant and Roman Catholick subjects in this citty': the relevant acts of assembly were erased. Attempting to stave off a challenge to its charter, the corporation stressed its own complete loyalty to the monarchy ever since 'the first conquest of this kingdome by your royall auncestors'.[67] This spirit of submission and compliance, however, did not save the city's charter; nor

---

[64] *HMC Ormond MSS*, NS vi. 57, 61–2, 64, 68; *CARD* v. 216–17.

[65] *CARD* v. 233. By this time the exclusion campaign had failed, and an address from a place so 'out of the road' as Dublin caused only merriment when read to the king (*HMC Hastings MSS*, ii. 392).

[66] *CARD* v. 355–7; *HMC Ormond MSS*, NS vi. 57.

[67] *CARD* v. 389–95, 401–6, 423, 426. The corporation had made an earlier reference (1647) to a royal conquest of Ireland (ibid. iii. 392, 450).

did a desperate appeal to Ormond, once again serving as lord steward at court in London. In May 1687 the lord deputy (the Catholic earl of Tyrconnell) disallowed the aldermen's choice of lord mayor and sheriffs for the ensuing year. In June, the king authorized the lord deputy to issue new charters for corporate towns and cities in Ireland, and Dublin's charter was duly challenged by a writ of quo warranto.[68]

The new charter, issued in November, contained several striking differences from the old one. The number of the city commons was cut by half (Essex's wish had been acted on) to forty-eight; the key officials, as well as members of the two houses, were named; and the chief governor was empowered to remove officials, and even members of the common council. The guilds, too, were deemed to have been dissolved in consequence of the recall of the city's charter. The new charter of November 1687 authorized the establishment of a merchant's guild, and during the following year thirteen of the twenty craft guilds were granted new charters—the process was not complete before the Williamite invasion of England in November 1688. As in the case of the corporation, guild officials were named, with Catholics figuring prominently among them.[69]

In comparison with London's experience, Dublin's corporate bodies had escaped fairly lightly: but then, London had been a stronghold of the court's critics, while Dublin corporation—despite the difficulties over the new rules—had tended rather to the government side. But the new Dublin charter highlighted a dimension of royal policy that had even more far-reaching implications for Ireland than for England. Fifteen of the twenty-four aldermen named in the charter, and thirty-three of the forty-eight city commons, were Catholics. Manifestly the corporation was being brought into line with James II's Catholic appointments in the army, the judiciary, and the administration. In England, quite small numbers of Catholic appointments had been sufficient to unsettle the crown's traditional supporters; in Ireland, large Catholic numbers and the existence of a class of ex-landowners bent on the reversal of the restoration land settlement made the Protestant position much more delicate. Even in Dublin, where Protestants outnumbered Catholics by two to one, and where tensions between Presbyterians and Anglicans had been more apparent than those between Protestants and Catholics, news of the appointment of a Catholic lord deputy early in 1687 prompted some families to leave for England. Further alarm greeted the attack on corporate charters, since this was a clear signal that the crown intended to obtain the means of influencing parliamentary elections: and the calling of a parliament signalled that the

[68] DCA, MR/18, fos. 112ᵈ, 114ᵃ⁻ᵇ; *CARD* v. 613–14.
[69] *CARD* i. 73–6; William King, *The State of the Protestants of Ireland Under the Late King James's Government*, 4th edn. (London, 1692), 91–2; Le Fanu, 'A Note on Two Charters of the Smiths' Guild', 152.

land settlement would come under attack (as, indeed, it did, though the Williamite victory in 1690 rendered acts of James II's Irish parliament abortive).[70]

The new, predominantly Catholic Dublin corporation took office towards the end of 1687 under a Catholic lord mayor, the merchant Sir Thomas Hackett. Although some Protestants had been nominated to the new body, corporation records show a high rate of absenteeism on their part, especially for the city commons: eleven of the fifteen Protestant commons failed to take their seats. Among the nine Protestant aldermen, Anthony Sharpe,[71] one of the two Quakers nominated to the aldermanic board, took part in its affairs, as did John Otrington.[72] But the new corporation had been in operation for little more than a year when William of Orange staged his dramatic intervention in English affairs.

In the immediate aftermath of the Williamite revolution in England Irish Protestants in general showed no signs of abandoning their loyalty to James II.[73] It was not clear whether William would immediately follow up his advantage by attacking Ireland; in the event he did not send troops until the summer of 1689. Meanwhile, however, Protestant insecurity grew, and 'massacre' fears began to spread. In Dublin, where there were sufficient Protestants to constitute a large armed force—a contemporary estimate put the figures at around 12,000 Protestants and some 5,600 Catholics capable of bearing arms—armed associations of Protestants were formed in the Liberties and at Trinity College. Until this point (mid-1689), the number of Protestants leaving Ireland had been small; now many more began to leave, especially women and children.[74]

By this time James II himself had arrived in Dublin (March 1689), where he was welcomed by the corporation, and granted the freedom of the city. With one eye on public opinion in England (as he admitted himself, for he hoped to win back his English and Scottish kingdoms) he proceeded to issue a proclamation of religious freedom for all, provided they were loyal, and offered protection to those who had fled to England, if they would return.[75]

---

[70] J. G. Simms, *Jacobite Ireland 1685–91* (London, 1969), 32–5.

[71] Above, Ch. 1.

[72] Patrick Monks claimed that Otrington did not serve ('The Aldermen of Skinner's Alley', *Dublin Hist. Rec.* 19 (1963–4), 45–63, at 52–3), but see DCA, MR/18, fo. 115ᵃ. Monks identified 25 Protestant nominees in the Jacobite charter, but at least one (Alderman Sir Michael Creagh) was then a Catholic (R. B. McDowell, *Ireland in the Age of Imperialism and Revolution 1760–1801* (Oxford, 1979), 180). For the charter, see *CARD* i. 75.

[73] Raymond Gillespie, 'The Irish Protestants and James II, 1688–90', *IHS* 28 (1992), 124–33, at 128–9.

[74] Marsh's Library, Dublin (MLD), 'An Abstract of the Numbers of Protestants, and Papists, Able to Bear Arms in the City of Dublin, and Liberties Thereof' (n.d. [c.1690]), Z 2.1.7 (39); Simms, *Jacobite Ireland*, 49.

[75] *Cobbett's Parliamentary History of England*, v (1688–1702), cols. 303–5. Because of these concerns James gave only reluctant assent to a bill of his Irish parliament declaring that the English parliament had no right to bind Ireland (Simms, *Jacobite Ireland*, 80).

However, the Dublin Protestant associations were disarmed, and during the summer and autumn, as news arrived of James's reverses in the field, a number of prominent Protestants were arrested and imprisoned in Trinity College, now taken over by Jacobite soldiers. For a time, some Protestant churches were taken over by Catholics, but on James's return to the capital they were handed back, except for Christ Church.[76] Six months later, on 1 July 1690, the king's forces suffered a defeat at the battle of the Boyne, and three days later James left Dublin with his army for France, directing the release of Protestant prisoners, and the surrender of the city to William. With him departed most of his civilian administration.[77]

In the confusion that followed (which included looting of Catholic houses) Robert Fitzgerald, a son of the earl of Kildare, took charge and formed a provisional government. On 6 July, William entered Dublin, and was presented on the following day with a petition bearing eleven signatures, from those calling themselves 'the Protestant Aldermen' of the city of Dublin. The petitioners informed William that they were all former aldermen of the city, who had served until set aside under the terms of James II's charter. They welcomed William's 'victorious Arms [which] have by the providence of God miraculously restored us to the exercise of our Religion and the Enjoyment of our Auncient rights and Liberties'. The aldermen explained that in order to keep the peace they had revived the magistracy, and they obtained William's endorsement for this course of action, proposing that Walter Motley (most senior alderman, but passed over for lord mayor in 1687) should serve as lord mayor for the time being.[78]

III. The Significance of the Williamite Revolution

The Williamite victories at the Boyne and at Aughrim a year later coloured all subsequent Irish history, though this was by no means immediately obvious. The main effect was to bring Ireland into line with England, where William and Mary had already been crowned as joint monarchs in 1689, following the introduction of new coronation oaths by which they promised to uphold the Protestant reformed religion established by law. Moreover, the English bill of rights (1689) at last made good the exclusionists' goal by barring those in communion with Rome, or those married to a papist, from the royal succession.[79] These new, if limited, restrictions on the royal prerogative reflected the now widespread view that popery and arbitrary power were inextricably linked. Events abroad as well as at home contributed to this perception. In France, where James had taken refuge, Louis XIV's centralizing policies had been accompanied by a drive for

---

[76] Simms, *Jacobite Ireland*, 55, 88.
[77] *Cal. SP Dom. 1690–1*, 59.
[78] DCA, MR/18, fo. 117ᵃ; Walter Harris, *The History of the Life and Reign of William-Henry . . . King of England, Scotland, France and Ireland* (Dublin, 1749), 271–7.
[79] 1 Will. & Mary, sess. 2, c. 2.

religious uniformity, culminating in 1685 in the revocation of the Edict of Nantes, which ushered in a new phase of persecution for French Protestants, many of whom subsequently fled abroad. Accounts written by English travellers on the Continent in the 1680s highlighted the twin dangers of popery and tyranny if the French threat of universal monarchy were realized. All this encouraged a tendency to see Protestantism as the natural ally of those who championed the liberties of the subject, at home and abroad. Slogans such as 'the Protestant religion and the liberties of Europe' began to proliferate. (Use of the term 'Europe' in this context was itself a political statement; the Stuarts and the French spoke not of Europe but of Christendom).[80]

Yet the 'glorious revolution' in England remained highly conservative. Although some were anxious to use the opportunity to introduce more radical changes, they were overruled. In a disingenuous but pragmatic formula James was officially deemed to have 'abdicated the government', leaving the throne 'vacant'; by contrast with the formula in Scotland, no hint was given that he had forfeited the crown through misgovernment. The bill of rights did little more than rehearse what its framers took to be the rights of Englishmen; several of James II's policies were denounced, but, apart from excluding Catholics from the succession, procedures for ensuring that similar abuses would not arise again were lacking. After all, the revolution had been accomplished through the intervention of a foreign prince, who had no wish to see his own powers as monarch curbed. Divine right assumptions about monarchy did not disappear, as was shown in the readiness of certain Tories, and even Whigs, to designate William's accession to the throne a 'conquest'; and legitimism retained a strong appeal, to judge by the correspondence kept up between certain English politicians and the exiled dynasty.[81]

In the Irish context, the proposition that James II had abdicated, and that no resistance had been offered to a legitimate king, was scarcely tenable; though once the new regime was in place, the myths of the English revolution were soon incorporated into local use. Irish Protestants, facing imminent dispossession in Jacobite Ireland, had even stronger incentives than their English counterparts to accept the new monarchs. Nevertheless, even in Ireland the legitimacy of the new regime was a pressing issue. This explains the remarkable success of a work, first published in London in

---

[80] J. R. Western, *Monarchy and Revolution: The English State in the 1680s* (London, 1972), 383; Pincus, 'The English Debate over Universal Monarchy'. The treaty of Utrecht (1713) was the last to use the concept of Christendom (M. Sheehan, 'The Development of British Theory and Practice of the Balance of Power Before 1714', *History*, 73 (1988), 24–37, at 36). Dublin corporation last used the term in 1697 (*CARD* vi. 187): thereafter 'Europe' was used.

[81] J. C. D. Clark, *English Society 1688–1832* (Cambridge, 1985), 124–6; Eveline Cruickshanks and Jeremy Black (eds.), *The Jacobite Challenge* (Edinburgh, 1988), 1–3.

1691, which went into four editions within a year, and which has been called the most important vindication of William in the period after the Boyne. *The State of the Protestants of Ireland Under the Late King James's Government* was written by William King, formerly dean of St Patrick's in Dublin and recently promoted to the see of Derry. The subtitle continued, 'in which their Carriage towards him is justified, and the absolute Necessity of their endeavouring to be freed from his Government, and of submitting to Their Present Majesties, is demonstrated'.

As the title suggested, the work was not so much a dispassionate account of Jacobite Ireland as an indictment of James II, written with all the fervour of one who had been imprisoned in Dublin by the Jacobite regime in 1689, and even sentenced to death.[82] These experiences enabled King to write about imputed Jacobite intentions to extirpate Protestantism with more than ordinary conviction. What was particularly striking about his case, however, was the argument that not only James, but 'every Roman Catholick King, if he throughly [*sic*] understand his Religion . . . is obliged, if he be able, to destroy his Protestant Subjects', thus placing the debate in a broad European context.[83] The charge was illustrated with reference to Catholic teachings, and the alleged practice of Continental Catholic rulers. King admitted that James had promised protection to his Protestant subjects in Ireland. But, even had he been disposed to keep that promise, King argued, the 'Papists of Ireland'—who had openly declared their resolve to make the king 'absolute', along French lines—had made no secret of their intention to take over Protestant churches and lands, and to make the Protestants 'hewers of wood and drawers of water'. This plan was well on the way to realization when 'God's Providence' raised up a 'Deliverer', at which point (i.e., only *in extremis*) Protestants took the opportunity to save themselves by transferring their allegiance to William.[84] Of course, this account included much special pleading. However, the cumulative effect of the catalogue of Jacobite crimes towards Protestants, crimes that were presented as inherent in the very nature of popery and popish monarchy, served to vindicate King's rejection of his own earlier 'passive obedience' stand, and gave the transfer of allegiance to William an air of inevitability.

---

[82] Walter Harris, 'William King, D.D.', in Walter Harris (ed.), *The Works of Sir James Ware Concerning Ireland, Revised and Improved*, (3 vols.; Dublin, 1739), i. 363–9, at 365; Patrick Kelly, 'Ireland and the Glorious Revolution: From Kingdom to Colony', in Robert Beddard (ed.), *The Revolutions of 1688* (Oxford, 1991), 163–90, at 178.

[83] *State of the Protestants*, 4th edn., 15. King's tract has been called the most important vindication of William after the Boyne (Mark Goldie, 'The Political Thought of the Anglican Revolution', in Beddard (ed.), *The Revolutions of 1688*, 102–3, at 128 n. 74).

[84] *State of the Protestants of Ireland*, 19–20, 253–6. It has been suggested that King's 'providential' interpretation was a much later formulation: James I. McGuire, 'The Church of Ireland and the "Glorious Revolution" of 1688', in Art Cosgrove and Donal McCartney (eds.), *Studies in Irish History Presented to R. Dudley Edwards* (Dublin, 1979), 137–49, at 143, 146–7, but it is present in the 4th edn. ('with additions': London, 1692), 253–5.

Bishop King's influential tract also provided an eloquent defence of the conduct of Irish corporations during the two previous reigns. Dublin corporation, he argued, had gone as far as it reasonably could in complying with royal wishes. The new rules had been accepted. But the policy of admitting Catholics to freedom and to corporate offices tended 'to alter the very Nature of the Government': in other words, Protestant control of the corporations was not merely contingent on royal policy, but enjoyed the status of fundamental law, as a guarantee against arbitrary power. When the aldermen had protested, their charter had been challenged. Certain guild officers, according to King, had been imprisoned rather than accept the new charters.[85] The corporation and the guilds thus emerged from King's account as pillars of constitutional rectitude. Their resistance to now-discredited royal policies had been judicious and restrained, in contrast to the position in London, where opposition was widely considered to have gone too far. Moreover, in Dublin the former aldermen had been ready in the wings to take over civic government and restore order as soon as the Jacobite administration had left. Later accounts held that during the Jacobite period these aldermen had constituted an alternative corporation, holding meetings in an alehouse in Skinner's Alley, off the Coombe, in the earl of Meath's Liberty.[86] Certainly, seven former aldermen and sheriffs acted in concert in early 1690, when, trusting to an ultimate Williamite victory, they petitioned the English government to make over to the city any property of Dublin papists deemed to be in rebellion against William and Mary.[87] And to commemorate this era, a prestigious political and convivial club, the Aldermen of Skinner's Alley, was set up, which lasted well into the Victorian age.

It was all very well for Bishop King to eulogize the corporation, but where had the revolution left it? In July 1690 William himself confirmed the Protestant aldermen's resumption of office, but in any case the legal position of Irish corporations had already been ruled on by an English act designed to relieve Irish Protestants under the Jacobite regime. Among other things, this act restored all cities, boroughs, and bodies corporate in Ireland to their position as on 24 June 1683, notwithstanding any quo warranto proceedings against them or any new charters, which were declared void.[88] As a measure designed to cope with an emergency in Ireland, it does not

---

[85] King, *State of the Protestants*, 57, 82–93, 177, 181, 188, 217–56.

[86] Monks accepted that an anti-Jacobite group may have met in Skinner's Alley, but doubted whether it was very active ('Aldermen of Skinner's Alley', 60). See also Warburton, Whitelaw, Walsh, *History of the City of Dublin*, ii. 1068; Jonah Barrington, *Recollections of Jonah Barrington*, Every Irishman's Library edn. (Dublin, n.d.), 154–60; map 2 above.

[87] *Cal. Treasury Papers, 1556/7–1696*, 96. Dublin corporation later endorsed the request, but only obtained the restoration of the £500 annual grant awarded by Charles II (*CARD* v. 506–8, 529, 531).

[88] 'An Act for the Better Security and Relief of their Majesties Protestant Subjects of Ireland', 1 Will. & Mary, sess. 2, c. 9.

appear to have been contentious. In practice, its status turned out to be uncertain; and this was at least partly due to the fate of a related measure for England. While the Irish bill was passing through parliament, a parallel measure in the form of a corporation bill for England was also under discussion.[89] That bill passed the house of commons, but got bogged down in the lords; whereupon the king, who feared that the bill would lead to permanent Whig control of the English corporations and thence of parliament, stepped in and brought the session to a premature end.

The effect of the corporation bill's failure was to leave English cities and boroughs in the confused situation that James II's abrupt volte-face had brought about. For in his panic to forestall the Williamite challenge, James had restored those borough charters whose surrenders had been enrolled, but had failed to cancel new ones. This meant that certain towns were left with two charters (some were left with three) containing different prescriptions for the composition of the common council, eligibility for the franchise, and so on.[90] Yet, intolerable as such a situation might seem to be, from the point of view of the landed élite the matter was not without its advantages. The salient point was that it was the house of commons that determined disputed elections.[91] If disputes arose (as, in the circumstances, they were bound to do) over which candidate had been returned, and who was qualified to vote, then the house could decide on the individual merits of the case. In other words, parliament retained control in this vital area, and this presumably helped to reconcile MPs to the loss of the corporation bill.

None of these difficulties should have arisen in Ireland, for the English statute 1 Will & Mary, sess. 2, c. 9 had apparently made matters perfectly clear. But perhaps because the failure of the English corporation bill had cast doubt on the constitutional propriety of attempting to put the clock back—perhaps even more because of a general mood of self-assertion[92]— Irish parliaments in the 1690s placed little weight on the English act, and moved to introduce Irish statutes to cover those provisions (such as the nullifying of the acts of James II's Irish parliament) which were regarded as really important.[93] As for the Irish corporations, which had, in any case, returned to Protestant control, if there was any doubt about their legal

---

[89] The English bill would have restored the urban corporations in England, Wales and the American colonies to their condition in 1675 (Western, *Monarchy and Revolution*, 344).

[90] J. P. Kenyon, *Stuart England* (Harmondsworth, 1978), 264–5; John Miller, 'Proto-Jacobitism? The Tories and the Revolution of 1688–9', in Cruickshanks and Black (eds.), *The Jacobite Challenge*, 7–23, at 10.

[91] This right had effectively been conceded by the early 1600s: F. W. Maitland, *The Constitutional History of England* (Cambridge, 1908), 247–8.

[92] See McGuire, 'The Irish Parliament of 1692'.

[93] 'An Act Declaring All Attainders, and All Other Acts Made in the Late Pretended Parliament, to be Void' (7 Will. III, c. 3 (Ire.)).

position—disputed elections, or queries about whether certain boroughs had the right to return MPs at all—then the Irish house of commons, like its English counterpart, had the power to settle individual cases.

Paradoxically, then, the post-revolutionary status of charters granted by James II to Irish corporations was not much clearer than that of those in England; a situation well illustrated by the case of the Dublin hosiers' guild mentioned in Chapter 1. Strictly speaking, as a new Jacobite creation, its charter had been consigned to oblivion by the English act of 1690; but when in 1692 the guild applied to Dublin corporation for representation on the city commons, the act was ignored (or snubbed) and the request was granted on the grounds that the charter had been issued before James II's 'abdication'.[94]

In view of all this, what stands out is that Dublin corporation had survived the upheavals of the restoration era with its privileges substantially intact. With the setting aside of the Jacobite charter, the city returned to the position as set out in the new rules, so the chief civic officials still had to be approved by the viceroy and privy council. But in 1690 the guild representatives returned to their full strength, if not to their former weight in the common council before the introduction of the new rules. The aldermen had survived even more successfully. The attempt on the part of the lord mayor (with viceregal backing) to dislodge seven of them in 1672, in a clear breach of civic privilege, had failed, and the seven had been restored (two of them were still active on the board after the Boyne).[95] The Jacobite charter had set most of them aside, but, displaced or not, the majority returned after the Williamite victory as if nothing had happened.[96] Walter Motley, due to take office as lord mayor at Michaelmas 1687, and Anthony Percy, one of the sheriffs elect (both had been rejected by Tyrconnell before the Jacobite charter was issued) were duly reinstated by their colleagues in July 1690 to serve until new elections could be held.[97]

What then, were the lessons of this era for the corporation? One of the most important concerned religion. In the early part of the century royal pressure had been required to bring about a Protestant magistracy. Even during the restoration period, by which time Dublin had become a predominantly Protestant city, the corporation's commitment to a Protestant common council was essentially pragmatic, and there was little sign of the anti-popery phobia that was typical of London. (It is worth noting here that

[94] CARD v. 541–2.
[95] Sir Joshua Allen and Sir Francis Brewster (MLD, Roll of numbers 'Before November 1690', MS Z 2.1.7 (40)).
[96] Ibid. At least 16 of the 18 aldermen identified on the Roll of numbers had been in office before the Jacobite period.
[97] DCA, MR/18, fos. 112[d], 117[a]. Moreover, (Protestant) aldermen who had served on the Jacobite corporation were not barred from the mayoral office: Alderman John Otrington was lord mayor in 1690–1.

Dublin's Catholics were well integrated with the Protestant community; there were no Catholic ghettos).[98] But experience during the Jacobite period had suggested that assaults on corporate privilege went hand in hand with indulgence to popery; and by 1690 the corporation could speak of the city reverting to its 'auncient Protestant government'.[99] Following Bishop King, Protestantism was now being presented as something fundamental to the constitution, not as merely contingent.

Even so, there was little by way of a backlash against Catholic freemen after the Williamite revolution. In October 1690 a municipal by-law disfranchised Catholic freemen on the grounds that they had connived at the assault on corporate privileges. But, as noted in Chapter 1, it seems that there was little force in this measure, for later in the decade individual Catholics who had been indicted on charges of high treason were singled out by the corporation for disfranchisement.[100] More serious in its implications for a Catholic presence among the freemen was the reassertion in 1692 of the 1678 by-law requiring freemen to take the supremacy and allegiance oaths. Under an English act of 1692 these oaths had been reframed, and included the notorious declaration affirming that the sacrifice of the mass was superstitious and idolatrous.[101] Charitable relief for Catholic freemen did not cease, but stringent conditions might be attached; the three sons of a Catholic freeman who applied to the corporation for relief in 1709 were awarded the amount of their apprenticeship fees, but on condition that they were Protestants and apprenticed to Protestants.[102] Another blow for Dublin Catholics was signified by sporadic requests in the 1690s (apparently emanating from a poorer class of Protestants) to have Catholics dismissed from civic posts, in order to give employment to Protestants, and improve city security: in the nervous climate during the last months of the Jacobite regime, and again following Queen Mary's death in 1694, there were echoes of London's paranoia about the danger of papists setting the city on fire.[103]

---

[98] For residence patterns, see 1659 census of Dublin (*CARD* iv. 560–70).

[99] *CARD* v. 507. An Irish act of 1704 (2 Anne c. 6) recited the ban in the act of explanation on Catholics buying houses in corporate towns, and added 'which law, if it had been duly observed, would in great measure have prevented the late rebellion in this kingdom' (*The Statutes at Large*, iv (Dublin, 1765), 27).

[100] *CARD* v. 509. Two such were Simon Archbold, tailor, and John Moore, merchant, whom the corporation described as having borne arms against King William 'after the abdication'—another case of the tendency to adopt English norms (ibid. vi. 188, 199).

[101] Ibid. vi. 7–8; 3 & 4 Will. & Mary, c. 2 (Eng.).

[102] *CARD* vi. 411.

[103] Ibid. vi. 132, 224; Anon., *A True Account of a Plot Lately Discovered in Ireland, for Fireing the City of Dublin, and Putting All the Protestants to the Sword* (Dublin, 2 Dec. 1690), NLI, Thorpe P12 (24): probably designed for English consumption. During the exclusion crisis an inscription had been added to the London monument commemorating the great fire of 1666, blaming 'the treachery and malice of the Popish faction'. It was removed under James II, restored under William III, and remained until 1830 (J. P. Kenyon, *The Stuart Constitution*

The other significant lesson for the corporation was not new. It was the need to preserve and defend the city's charters, which still provided the authority for municipal rights. In 1668 the corporation had requested the recorder to enter Dublin's various charters into a single book. After the revolution it was agreed to petition the Irish parliament to have Dublin's charters confirmed by statute as London's had been in 1690.[104] Nothing came of this, but the corporation tried to ensure that anything of interest concerning the city was preserved. In 1706 a Dublin bookseller, Matthew Gunne, petitioned the quarterly assembly for support for an edition he had brought out in English of Sir James Ware's *Antiquities of Ireland*, which contained details of early foundations in Dublin, lists of mayors, and so on. The corporation granted him £60, stipulating that copies were to be furnished to the lord mayor and others.[105]

In the last resort, municipal privileges were still perceived to depend on royal goodwill, and the corporation showed no sign of ignoring that. William and Mary, no less than James II, were 'their sacred majesties'; William was described as 'the fountain of all power', and his intervention was deemed providential, even miraculous.[106] Indeed, the corporation followed the example of London and elevated the king into something of a folk hero. His birthday (4 November) was celebrated in 1690 with a procession and a dinner in Dublin Castle for leading citizens. Ten years later, the corporation commissioned a large equestrian statue, by the sculptor Grinling Gibbons, which stood in College Green as the focus for the great state and civic processions that were to mark William's birthday down to the early 1800s.[107] Clad as a victorious Roman general, William was invested with all the majesty and power once accorded to James II.[108] For that very reason, and regardless of which monarch or dynasty was on the throne, the danger of royal encroachment on local liberties had not vanished. There was little the corporation could do to guard against this

(Cambridge, 1969), 466). There was still fear of popish incendiarism in England in the mid-18th c. (Colin Haydon, 'Anti-Catholicism in Eighteenth Century England, *c*.1714–*c*.1780', D.Phil. thesis (Oxford, 1985), 208).

[104] *CARD* iv. 433; vi. 180; DCA, Recorder's book, MR/25.

[105] *CARD* vi. 411; *The Antiquities and History of Ireland, by the Right Honourable Sir James Ware, Knt. Now First Published in One Volume in English* (Dublin, 1705).

[106] *CARD* v. 529, 635. The aldermen's views were close to those of Bishop King: William King, *Europe's Deliverance from France and Slavery: A Sermon Preached at St Patrick's Church, Dublin, 16 Nov. 1690* (Dublin, 1691), 13, 21.

[107] *CARD* vi. pp. viii–xi. According to Harris (*Life and Reign of William-Henry*, 500), Irish Protestants celebrated four days in William's memory; 4 Nov. (birthday, 1650); 5 Nov. (gunpowder plot, 1605; William's landing in England, 1688); 1 July (battle of the Boyne, 1690), and 12 July (battle of Aughrim, 1691). See also James Kelly, ' "The Glorious and Immortal Memory": Commemoration and Protestant Identity in Ireland 1660–1800', *RIA Proc.* 94, C (1994), 25–52.

[108] These qualities were enhanced by the equestrian form; classical Roman statues usually showed the subject on foot.

danger, except to ensure that among the aldermen there remained some whose political horizons stretched beyond civic politics. In the 1670s, aldermanic privileges had been successfully defended thanks to the privy council contacts of the recorder, Sir William Davies; these contacts reached as far as the English house of lords. The absence of any meetings of the Irish parliament between 1666 and 1689 meant that no help had been forthcoming from that quarter, but the 1690s saw the start of more regular sessions. One of the leaders of the Irish parliamentary opposition in 1692 was the Kerry landlord and Dublin alderman, Sir Francis Brewster, who had been among the seven dismissed aldermen in 1672. In the absence of Irish parliamentary sessions it appears that valuable political experience could be obtained through the medium of civic politics.[109]

IV. *Corporate Rights Vindicated, 1690–1714*

For many years after the revolution, relations between Dublin corporation and successive privy councils were relatively smooth. Corporate interests were routinely protected by 'treateing the government and nobility' (a mansion house was to be acquired for this purpose in 1715, some two decades before London followed suit), and by extending honorary freedoms to influential individuals.[110] The corporation's agent also maintained a watching brief on the city's behalf during the parliamentary sessions. At the same time, an eye was kept on corporate life in England (especially in London) to make sure that Dublin was not falling behind in status or rights.[111]

In political terms, during the 1690s and early 1700s the corporation moved in a mildly Whiggish direction. There was enthusiasm for the European wars in which William had involved his new dominions; wars regarded in Dublin civic circles as designed to defend the Protestant interest and the liberties of Europe against the encroachments of France. Ireland's own Jacobite era was portrayed as a 'French usurpation' or invasion.[112] The Anglican sacramental test, introduced for Irish urban corporations in 1704, came in for some restrained criticism; hints were dropped that there was no

---

[109] McGuire, 'The Irish Parliament of 1692', 11, 14, 25. Brewster, d. 1704; MP Tuam, 1692–1703, Doneraile, 1703–4, writer on commercial issues; a parliamentary manager for Lord Deputy Capell (*HMC Buccleuch & Queensberry MSS*, ii, pt. 1, 283–4); commissioner of forfeited estates, 1698 (*DNB*).

[110] *CARD* vi. 268, 276, 534–5; Craig, *Dublin 1660–1860*, 110–11. For examples of honorary freedoms, see *CARD* v. 535–6. Certain guilds also granted such freedoms (Stubbs, 'The Weavers' Guild', 68, 78).

[111] In 1697 confirmation of charters was sought ('the same has been done in England for the citty of London severall tymes'); in 1698 new gowns were authorized for officers at mace 'such as are usually worne by the Lord Mayor and Sherriffes officers at London' (*CARD* vi. 180, 189).

[112] *CARD* vi. 262, 312–13, 381–2. Bishop King had led the way here (*Europe's Deliverance*, 8–12).

danger to the church from Protestant dissenters, and that the test might prevent the crown from calling on the services of all its Protestant subjects.[113] Any doubts about the propriety of addressing the monarch were swept away in the post-revolutionary era, and royal addresses became quite frequent from the 1690s onwards.[114] The corporation made no formal reaction to the publication of William Molyneux's *The Case of Ireland* (1698), in which the author spoke for many of the Protestant élite in calling for Ireland's constitutional position, with its commercial and other disadvantages, to be regularized—if not by a legislative union (such as Scotland was to obtain in 1707) then by recognition of Ireland's 'ancient constitution'. There were, however, signs that the corporation shared this concern. In October 1703 honorary freedom was granted to Ireland's leading Commonwealthman, Robert Molesworth: in the same month he was a prime mover in the events that led to the Irish house of commons adopting resolutions in favour of 'a full enjoyment of our constitution, or ... a more firm and strict union with your majesty's subjects of England'.[115]

Down to the later years of Queen Anne's reign (1702–14) the corporation's moderately Whiggish tendencies were kept within bounds by a number of other considerations. One was that the queen herself had strong Tory sympathies, and made some notable Tory appointments for Ireland, such as that of Sir Constantine Phipps as lord chancellor in 1711; it was obviously in the corporation's interests to maintain good relations with such officials.[116] Civic enthusiasm for another of the queen's Tory appointments went beyond mere prudence. James Butler, second duke of Ormond, grandson of the first duke, was renowned for his high church principles; and his family ties with Dublin (he had been born in Dublin Castle), his record as a soldier in the anti-French coalitions of the 1690s and early 1700s, and his eminence as a statesman from 1688 onwards, all ensured a rapturous reception for his appointment as viceroy in 1703. Although the duke was to throw in his lot with the Stuarts soon after George I's accession in 1714, there was no hint of this in his conduct of the Irish administration; rather, his firm adherence to the Williamite cause since the revolution suggested that he would abide by the Hanoverian succession. For its part, Dublin corporation denounced the 'Popish Pretender', and stressed its own commitment to the Protestant interest and the Protestant religion.[117] Again, it was in the corporation's interest to support the Hanoverian succession; in the event, a protracted dispute between the

---

[113] *CARD* vi. 355–6, 382.
[114] The period was exceptional; the deaths of Queen Mary (1694), King James II (1701), and King William (1702) all gave rise to addresses (*CARD* vi. 89–90, 254–5, 262–3).
[115] *Commons Jn. Ire. 1692–1713*, ii. 341–2; *CARD* vi. 297.
[116] Phipps was granted the freedom of the city (*CARD* vi. 427).
[117] Ibid. vi, pp. xii, 186, 262, 382, 396.

aldermen and the Irish administration towards the end of Anne's reign served to intensify the city's Hanoverian and Whig proclivities.

The dispute erupted on to the public stage in 1711, with an apparently trivial disagreement concerning the election of a lord mayor.[118] One Robert Constantine complained to the privy council that he had been passed over for the office, even though he had been the most senior alderman since 1709.[119] Mayoral elections were regulated by the new rules of 1672, which stipulated that a quorum must be present on such occasions, but in other respects left the choice to the lord mayor and aldermen, subject to government approval. During the sixteenth century, in circumstances where aldermen showed little enthusiasm for filling the mayoral office, it had been the custom, embodied in an Elizabethan by-law, for the most senior alderman (unless excused) to be elected mayor.[120] Subsequently, increases in the lord mayor's salary and status had rendered the office more desirable. Seniority remained the underlying principle, but the practice had arisen of balloting the aldermen for one of three candidates.

Constantine had served as sheriff in 1696–7 and as an alderman from 1700. In 1709, on the occasion of Alderman Charles Forrest's election as lord mayor, he was admitted 'to pass above the cushion' (to be excused the mayoralty and be entitled to wear the scarlet gown worn by mayors and ex-mayors). He was not present at that meeting, but was later said to have personally requested to be excused, following a poor showing in the ballot for lord mayor. However, he complained (without success) to the privy council about being passed over. Two years went by, for most of which Constantine remained absent from the aldermanic board, though he continued to complain. He resumed attendance in July 1710, and the following April he again protested to the privy council.[121] The circumstances were now quite different. In August 1710 the queen had replaced a Whig ministry in England with one that was mainly Tory; Tory appointments to Irish posts followed. With Phipps as lord chancellor, the Irish privy council began, almost routinely, to set aside Whig candidates for local office in favour of anyone who 'set up for a Church man'. Since Constantine was a Tory, his prospects of becoming lord mayor had suddenly improved. At any rate, the council upheld his complaint, refusing to approve the name sent down by the aldermen, or several other nominations submitted over the

[118] The most detailed study is Catherine M. Flanagan, ' "A Merely Local Dispute?" Partisan Politics and the Dublin Mayoral Dispute of 1709–1715', Ph.D. thesis, (University of Notre Dame, Ind., 1983). See also Gerard McNamara, 'Crown Versus Municipality: The Struggle for Dublin 1713', *Dublin Hist. Rec.* 39 (1986), 108–17; David Hayton, 'The Crisis in Ireland and the Disintegration of Queen Anne's Last Ministry', *IHS* 22 (1981), 193–215; *CARD* vii. 521–64; viii. 519–58.
[119] DCA, MR/18, fo. 180ᵃ.
[120] Lennon, *Lords of Dublin*, 47–8.
[121] For Constantine's civic career see *CARD* vi. 147; DCA, MR/18, fos. 175ᵃ, 179ᵃ, 180ᵇ.

following months.[122] For their part, the aldermen promptly engineered the repeal of the Elizabethan by-law embodying the seniority rule.[123]

It was the attitude adopted by the privy council that turned the dispute into a matter of principle: in taking up Constantine's case, and rejecting repeated alternative nominations from the aldermen, the council apparently came to regard the outcome of the case as reflecting on its own dignity.[124] Beyond this, however, lay other issues: the right of the aldermen to the lord mayor of their choice, and the extent of the privy council's powers under the new rules. But what really heightened the dispute's significance was the precedent of James II's interference in corporations, and the parallel between the principle of strict succession (according to seniority) in the corporation and the question of the royal succession, which—together with the future of the established church—was once again the cause of much apprehension. With none of the queen's children surviving, the English act of settlement of 1701 had fixed the succession on the house of Hanover, bypassing more than fifty Catholic claimants in favour of the Lutheran descendants of James I.[125] The act had been supported by both Tories and Whigs, but for many Tories this new departure from indefeasible hereditary right had only been accepted with much reluctance, and with the stipulation that the Hanoverians must conform to the established church. In the circumstances, there was a strong possibility of a reaction in favour of the Stuarts on Anne's death.

The parties to the Dublin dispute were well aware of the wider reverberations of the issue. The aldermen maintained that, apart from the Jacobite precedent of 1687, the privy council had invariably accepted their choice, regardless of the seniority principle. Suddenly, however, 'so Sacred was the Law of Succession that in Five Months . . . seven Elected Mayors, and Sixteen Sheriffs, all Members of the Established Church, were all Disproved, in order to oblige the Aldermen to elect Alderman Constantine'.[126] They also complained of interference in civic affairs, claiming that when at last the privy council had approved Alderman Ralph Gore as lord mayor for 1711–12, attempts had been made to bribe him to select guild representatives for the city commons according to lists made out

---

[122] David Hayton (ed.), 'An Irish Parliamentary Diary from the Reign of Queen Anne', *Anal. Hib.* 30 (1982), 99–149, at 121; id., 'The Crisis in Ireland', 197–8; DCA, MR/18, fos. 181ᵇ–183ᵇ.

[123] *CARD* vi. 437–9. According to the (Tory) lords justices, the by-law was repealed on the pretext that (despite its Elizabethan provenance) it was popish; many of the commons were not summoned to the meeting in question (ibid. vii. 543).

[124] Flanagan, ' "A Merely Local Dispute?" ', 89.

[125] 12 & 13 Will. III, c. 2. The Hanoverian succession was quickly endorsed by the Irish parliament (Hill, 'Ireland Without Union', 289).

[126] *The Case of the City of Dublin, in Relation to the Election of Magistrates in the Said City*, CULBC, Hib. 1. 679. 1 (32), p. 2. The aldermen were boasting of compliance with the 1704 sacramental test for civic office.

by government. Meanwhile, the corporation ostentatiously pledged its commitment to the Hanoverian succession, as the only security for the free exercise of 'our holy religion, as by law established in this kingdom'.[127]

Taking a different view, Dr John Clayton, dean of Kildare, who offered to mediate between the government and the city (but who was too much inclined to the Tory view to be properly impartial) urged the aldermen to follow the example of London, where, he claimed, Tory aldermen had recently elected a Whig as lord mayor on the seniority principle. London was, perhaps, an unfortunate example to invoke. The corporation there had been locked in party strife since the revolution, and the most senior aldermen had frequently been passed over for lord mayor, especially during the 1690s. More recently, however, Whig aldermen had begun to acquiesce in the election of Tory lord mayors.[128] Clayton painted a grim picture of the consequences of departing from the principle of strict seniority:

> the *Justice, Peace* and *Freedom* of every Alderman and Commoner, cannot be settled on any *Solid Foundation*, the *Liberty* of the Citizens will be precarious, and it will be in the Power of the *Recorder* and some *few* of the *Aldermen* to *Enslave all the rest*. For no one will ever be chosen *Lord Mayor, Alderman, Master of a Company*, or *Wardens*, but such as shall be subservient to them, and observe their Dictates and Commands.[129]

Thus (according to the aldermanic viewpoint) the strict law of succession undermined 'the freedom of elections in this city'; for their critics it represented the only secure basis for social and political order. Because of the queen's poor health, and uncertainty over the royal succession, the issues raised could not be brushed aside. Within months of the start of the dispute, members of the powerful Whig opposition in the Irish parliament had become involved. They heartily disliked the lord chancellor, Phipps, who was an Englishman with (so it was said) not merely Tory but Jacobite leanings.[130] In the absence of an Irish parliamentary session in 1712, some of the heat evaporated, and a compromise candidate, Alderman Samuel Cooke, was inaugurated as lord mayor at Michaelmas 1712. But once installed in office, Cooke 'threw off the Masque', as his Whig critics put it, revealing unsuspected Tory tendencies. The following Easter, he insisted on his right to nominate the three candidates from whom the aldermen must choose the lord mayor elect, and he was backed in this stand by the privy council (his nominees included Constantine). As a result, he found himself

---

[127] CULBC, Hib. 1. 679. 1 (32), p. 2; *CARD* vi. 463–4; *Commons Jn. Ire. 1692–1713*, ii. 775.   [128] De Krey, *A Fractured Society*, 194–6, 200–4.

[129] *Dean Clayton's Letter, to One of the Common-Council of the City of Dublin, Relating to the Means of Reconciling the Present Differences of the Said City* (Dublin, 6 Oct. 1713), CULBC, Hib. 1. 679. 1 (34), p. 2.

[130] *CARD* vi. 437; David Hayton, 'The Crisis in Ireland', 194–6. Phipps had been counsel for Dr Sacheverell during the latter's impeachment (1710) for attacking 'revolution principles'.

at odds with the aldermen, who refused to participate in the election on his terms.[131] The matter was referred to the attorney general in London, who stressed the essentially negative nature of the privy council's powers in the matter: the council had no authority to force a settlement on the aldermen. Irish judges were also consulted, coming down on Cooke's side. But English and Irish ministers were divided on the issue, and with Michaelmas 1713 approaching, no agreement had been reached. The Irish judges argued that, in the absence of any officially approved lord mayor elect, Cooke could stay on in office, and to the outrage of most of the aldermen, that is what happened.[132]

By this time, the prospect of a general election had once again brought the dispute to the forefront of politics. The Dublin city election, which the Tories, with support from government and from Catholic voters, had been confident of winning, was marked by a good deal of violence—one man died—and the Tory candidates were defeated.[133] Their defeat, however, owed much to the tactics of the sheriffs, who delayed the poll, altered venues, and generally acted in the interests of the Whig candidates.[134] Down to this point, Dublin (and Ireland in general) had largely escaped English party strife; now party labels were widely deployed as weapons in the electoral struggle. Supporters of the government were labelled 'Tories', 'Jacobites', and 'Papists'; supporters of the aldermen were denounced as 'Whigs' and 'Patriots'.[135] The latter was a natural consequence of the tendency for the parliamentary opposition at this time to call themselves 'the Country party'.

Since opposition to the queen's government was contrary to the constitutional ideal, neither side was anxious to embrace party labels. (The attraction for the opposition of 'Country party', was that it implied, paradoxically, a non-partisan position, which might attract Tory defectors.)[136] Supporters of the government saw themselves as defenders of 'Monarchy' and as 'honest Churchmen', committed to the test act; supporters of the aldermen saw themselves as upholders of local liberties,

---

[131] *The Case of the City of Dublin*, CULBC, Hib. 1. 679. 1 (32), pp. 2–3.

[132] Flanagan, ' "A Merely Local Dispute?" ', 136–7. Up to 20 of the 24 aldermen took the opposition side: *To the . . . Lord Mayor [etc.] The Humble Petition of Certain of the Commons, 21 Jan. 1714/15*, CULBC, Hib. O. 714. 16; CARD vii. 551.

[133] Alderman Sir William Fownes (d. 1735), banker, Co. Wicklow landowner, lord mayor of Dublin, 1708–9; Martin Tucker, collector of customs, member of the city commons. The (sitting) Whig candidates were Recorder John Forster and Alderman Benjamin Burton (below, App. B). Catholics were not formally excluded from the electorate until 1728.

[134] McNamara, 'Crown Versus Municipality', 113–14 (where Sheriff Surdevill has been mistaken for his fellow corporation member Somervill). A popular ballad taunted the Tories with keeping the lord mayor but losing the sheriffs: *The Dublin Ballad*, CULBC, Hib. 1. 679. 1 (40).

[135] See e.g. *Sir William Fownes's and Tucker's Friends Vindication*, CULBC, Hib. O. 713. 16; *Queries to the Electors of the City of Dublin*, Hib. O. 713. 13.

[136] Hayton, 'The Crisis in Ireland', 204–5.

denying that they were 'Foes to the Church' or to the royal prerogative. Both sides affirmed their commitment to the Hanoverian succession.[137] After the poll, a Tory petition against the Dublin result was heard in parliament in an atmosphere of panic, with Catholics being forbidden to observe from the galleries, and neighbouring householders instructed to allow no access to their roofs while parliament was sitting.[138]

Throughout the winter and spring of 1713–14 the two sides in the dispute remained in a state of confrontation; neither the lord chancellor nor the aldermen would give way, and meanwhile civic life deteriorated. The courts ceased to function; the markets were not supervised; routine cleaning and repair of the streets was suspended. Only the death of the queen in August 1714, the accession of the Hanoverian George I, and the subsequent eclipse of the Tory ministers in England and Ireland enabled the dispute to be brought to an end. In September 1714 a newly constituted and Whiggish Irish privy council was ordered by the lords justices to approve the choice of the majority of the aldermen, and Alderman James Barlow (duly approved) was inaugurated at Michaelmas. The following spring, the privy council accepted without demur the aldermen's choice of a lord mayor elect.[139]

Although the dispute had been resolved without precise clarification of the respective powers of the aldermen and the privy council in disputed elections—the new privy council took the pragmatic view that the important thing was a solution that worked—certain broad principles had emerged as a result. The seniority principle, for instance, had been shown to be a flexible one. More important, the outcome of the dispute confirmed that the privy council, for all its prerogative powers, was not above the law; and that corporate rights were a real guarantee of the liberties of the subject. Thus the intransigence of the aldermen—who were described by an Irish judge in 1713 as being 'as stiff as if they had taken the Solemn League Covenant [sic]'—was finally vindicated.[140] Moreover, the way in which the Whig opposition in the Irish parliament had moved to support the aldermen was in part a measure of the importance attached to the integrity of urban corporations, following the defeat of efforts by the crown to manipulate them in James II's reign. For as long as corporations retained some degree of local autonomy they constituted a barrier to the re-emergence of such policies. Their constitutional importance was all the greater because the role of parliament remained uncertain; both in Ireland and England, regular parliamentary sessions were very much a novelty of the wartime conditions of the 1690s, and might disappear with the coming of peace. Urban

[137] *Queries to the Electors of Dublin*, CULBC, Hib. O. 713. 13; *The Dublin Ballad*, Hib 1. 679. 1 (40).

[138] Hayton, 'The Crisis in Ireland', 205. Protestant fears had been aroused by the presence of French recruiting officers in Ireland (id., 'An Irish Parliamentary Diary', 138).

[139] Flanagan, ' "A Merely Local Dispute?" ', 258, 305–6, 314–16, 337–42.

[140] Ibid. 266, 337–9.

corporations, by contrast, enjoyed chartered rights which, in principle, went on for ever.[141]

After it was all over, it was of course the Whig version of events that went on record. The Irish house of commons found that soon after Phipps' arrival in Ireland, 'a Design was formed . . . to subvert the Constitution and Freedom of Elections of Magistrates of Corporations . . . in order to procure Persons to be returned Members of Parliament disaffected to the Settlement of the Crown on his Majesty and his Royal Issue'.[142] The house agreed to recommend George I to show the corporation some mark of royal favour 'to perpetuate the Virtue and faithful Services of the said Aldermen and Sheriffs, as an Encouragement to those who shall succeed them to imitate their example'. And the ensuing royal grant to Dublin corporation of £300 per annum was a reflection of the real contribution the corporation had made to the smooth transition to the Hanoverians.[143]

Two postscripts may be added. Throughout the dispute, the initiative in maintaining the corporation's rights had remained with the aldermen, reflecting the fact that the lower house had no direct role in mayoral elections. But the latter took a keen interest in the dispute, most members, apparently, backing the aldermen;[144] and their role was not an entirely passive one. In 1713 the city commons resolved to resist any attempt by Lord Mayor Cooke's agent to inspect the city charters for laws concerning elections, arguing that this was *ultra vires*, and that freedom of elections concerned all members of the corporation. This stand provoked some internal disapproval: a minority took the (Tory) view that the resolution denied the queen's right to inspect the charters, and reminded the majority that 'we are Subjects as well as Citizens'.[145] After the dispute was over, aldermen and commons approved a petition (couched, in customary terms, as emanating from the commons) to have Cooke disfranchised for having 'endeavoured the subversion of the constitution of this city'. To guard against any repetition of these events, attention was drawn to the duty of 'every citizen' to uphold the free and regular election of civic magistrates.[146]

---

[141] After 1688 the monarch's formal power to revoke a municipal charter remained, but fell into disuse (Levin, *The Charter Controversy of the City of London*, 65–8; Corfield, *The Impact of English Towns*, 150).

[142] *Commons' Jn. Ire. 1715–30*, iii. 102–3. See also the house of commons' report on the dispute, drawn up by the recorder of Dublin, John Rogerson (below, App. C), ibid., App., pp. lxxviii–ciii.

[143] *Commons' Jn. Ire. 1715–30*, iii. 103; Hayton, 'The Crisis in Ireland', 203, 212–13.

[144] Although the (Tory) privy council later alleged that 36 (around one-third) of the commons had protested at the repeal of the seniority by-law in 1711 (*CARD* vii. 543).

[145] *The Resolutions of the Common Council of the City of Dublin, for Maintaining the Freedom of Elections in the Said City*; *The Answer of Several of the Commons of the City of Dublin, to a Scandalous Libel, Entituled, The Resolutions of the Common-Council of the City of Dublin* (NLI, Thorpe P12 (73), (74)).

[146] *To the . . . Lord Mayor [etc.]*, CULBC, Hib. O. 714. 16; *CARD* vi. 506–9.

But there was no challenge here to oligarchy. Under aldermanic leadership, the corporation was behaving just like its Catholic predecessor in upholding an important corporate right.[147]

Finally, it is worth noting that, for all the studied commitment to the Hanoverian succession, certain elements in Dublin corporate circles were hedging their bets. It was not until April 1715 that the smiths' guild, citing the English act of 1690, passed a resolution declaring its 1688 charter from James II to be null and void, and warning that any member who invoked it was liable to be disfranchised. Later that year, the barber-surgeons' guild, which also had a 1688 charter, brought a document embodying its fifteenth-century charter to Chancery for enrolment.[148] The volatility of high politics in both England and Ireland in the last years of Queen Anne's reign, and especially the strength of the Tories in the administration, meant that it made perfect sense not to count on the Hanoverian succession until George I had actually been crowned.

[147] Lennon, *Lords of Dublin*, 207.
[148] Le Fanu, 'A Note on Two Charters of the Smiths' Guild', 153–4.

3

The Challenge to Oligarchy:
The Political Context, 1714–1749

I. The Early Hanoverian Years, 1714–1741

The Lord Mayor and aldermen next to those at London are the grandest in the 3 Kingdoms.[1]

From an ideological perspective these were quiet years for Dublin civic politics. The language of Patriotism, though it was to become more broadly diffused in this period, had already been deployed during the mayoral dispute of Queen Anne's reign. Likewise, Dublin corporation's Whiggish and Hanoverian stance had been signalled well before the accession of George I. The next major development was to be the challenge to oligarchy associated with Charles Lucas in the 1740s. But the intervening period was not without interest. The first signs of a demand for reform of the corporation were appearing, and Dublin's aldermen were beginning to come under pressure from a number of different directions.

The period began well for the aldermen. Thanks to their stand in the mayoral dispute they were able to bask in the glow of Whig approval emanating from the Irish house of commons and the executive. The aldermen had much to be complacent about. With the backing of the 1672 new rules, this self-selecting group, only twenty-five in number, dominated civic life. Mostly merchants, though with a scattering of lawyers, they could expect to fill a number of lucrative offices, and many others were within their gift. They chose all the important officials and selected the guild representatives for the corporation's lower house. They also monopolized the city's representation in parliament: between 1715 and 1749 all but one of the seven MPs who held city seats were aldermen.[2]

Under the circumstances it followed that, besides cultivating the memory of King William, the corporation should warmly embrace the new dynasty. The civic calendar witnessed a proliferation of royal occasions and anniversaries, all of which, as has been pointed out, helped to foster attachment to the monarchy.[3] However, this was not monarchical

---

[1] Journal of George Pakenham, a London merchant, on a visit to Dublin, 1737, quoted in Edward MacLysaght, 'Longford Papers', *Anal. Hib.* 15 (1944), 111–27, at 120.

[2] The exception was William Howard, KC (below, App. B).

[3] Kelly, ' "The Glorious and Immortal Memory" ', 35–6.

sentiment simply for its own sake. Civic addresses on such occasions rarely failed to link the Hanoverians with support for Protestantism, and sometimes took the chance to commend a Protestant strategy both in marriage alliances and foreign policy. The point was made that 'the preservation of our civil rights and liberties ... do wholly under God depend upon the safety of your majesty's person and the succession in your royal house'. And the idea of rights and liberties was at times expressed in broader constitutional terms. Looking back to the mayoral dispute, in 1737 the corporation boasted of the citizens' 'steady adherence ... to the constitution of their country'. In addition to these themes, and in tandem with developments in London, by the end of George I's reign the monarch was also being praised for his pursuit of commercial objectives.[4]

In promoting the cult of the Protestant dynasty, the corporation was as zealous as any of the landed élite. Another interest promoted by certain gentry, clergy, and merchants, was the 'reformation of manners' that flourished spasmodically in the early decades of the century. The years following George I's accession saw efforts to tighten up Sunday observance by the issuing of civic proclamations, and in 1719 the corporation subscribed to a new edition of the Bible, in a project approved by the archbishop of Dublin. One thousand copies were ordered 'for the use of the city'. Two decades later, when interest had begun to switch away from trying to effect change within the Protestant community towards the conversion of Catholics, the corporation awarded an annual grant to the Incorporated Society in Dublin for Promoting English Protestant Schools.[5]

But if these developments revealed the corporation in harmony with at least some sections of the élite, in other respects relations with the Irish executive and parliament showed signs of strain. The 1720s brought several bad harvests and high levels of unemployment; trade languished, and the city finances suffered. Emigration to the American colonies increased, and in Dublin there was sporadic unrest. Mobs formed, some mainly Catholic in composition, others Protestant. Sometimes they had particular targets or grievances, such as bread shortages; occasionally they fought each other, in great pitched battles.[6] Rival Protestant mobs also clashed. Parish watchmen had little success in curbing the disturbances. In the spring and summer of 1729 rioting was so severe that the lords justices as well as the corporation, which was ultimately responsible for law and order in the city, offered rewards for apprehending the rioters. The house of commons was so dissatisfied with the Dublin magistrates' response that a committee was set up to investigate their conduct. Four aldermen were detained and severely

---

[4] *CARD* vii. 331, 377–8; viii. 128–9, 210–11, 261–2, 367.
[5] Ibid. vii. 25, 85; T. C. Barnard, 'Reforming Irish Manners: The Religious Societies in Dublin during the 1690s', *Hist. Jn.* 35 (1992), 805–38.
[6] See Patrick Fagan, 'The Dublin Catholic Mob (1700–1750)', *ECI* 4 (1989), 133–42.

censured for failing to perform their chartered duties and for charging extortionate fees. In 1730 legislation was drawn up by the privy council to prevent riots in the city (it only failed to pass, allegedly, because the house of commons objected to the fact that it had not been initiated by parliament).[7]

The corporation recorded no reaction to the declaratory act (1720), which asserted the right of the British parliament to legislate for Ireland and denied the appellate jurisdiction of the Irish house of lords. However, the disadvantages of the measure became apparent almost at once when a dispute concerning civic property was appealed to the British house of lords.[8] The other great constitutional issue of the decade arose when in 1722 William Wood of Wolverhampton obtained from the king exclusive rights to manufacture halfpence and farthings for Ireland. The corporation—which shared the general opposition to the scheme—became involved when Dean Jonathan Swift brought out his *Drapier's Letters* attacking the project, and the government decided to prosecute the printer of the fourth *Letter*. The failure of two city grand juries to allow the prosecution to proceed could ultimately be laid at the corporation's door; it was the sheriffs who were responsible for selecting grand juries. Caught between its antipathy for the scheme and reluctance to upset the executive, for some years the corporation resisted hints from Swift and his supporters that he should be awarded honorary freedom of the city. In any case, the corporation did not share Swift's views on how best to remedy Ireland's shortage of silver coin.[9] His freedom only came in 1730, during the period of cool relations between the aldermen and the privy council that followed the Dublin riots, and during the mayoralty of a merchant who had been disappointed of a seat in parliament at a recent by-election.[10] The granting of freedom to Swift occasioned more criticism by government of the aldermen.[11]

Swift's importance went beyond creating difficulties between the aldermen and the executive. In the course of his attacks on abuses of the royal prerogative such as Wood's patent he endorsed Molyneux's rejection of Ireland's 'dependency' on England. He also deployed (besides arguments from common and statute law, and Scripture) a civic republican critique of power and placemen. Appeals to 'virtue' stemmed naturally from this, and

---

[7] Ibid. 141–2; *CARD* vii. 465, 472, 481–2; *Commons Jn. Ire. 1715–30*, iii. 606, 615–19, 650.

[8] 6 Geo. I, c. 5 (GB); *CARD* vii. 123–4, 143.

[9] J. A. Downie, *Jonathan Swift, Political Writer* (London, 1984), 243; James Kelly, 'Jonathan Swift and the Irish Economy in the 1720s', *ECI* 6 (1991), 7–36, at 26–8; *CARD* vii. 268–9, 460–1.

[10] Sir Peter Verdoen, sheriff 1714–15, alderman 1724, lord mayor 1729–30. See *Commons Jn. Ire. 1715–30*, iii. 592.

[11] *CARD* vii. 476; Downie, *Jonathan Swift*, 243.

soon became familiar in Dublin electoral politics.[12] And like English critics of the court, Swift occasionally extended his targeted audience beyond the gentry to citizens and shopkeepers. In response, members of the grand jury aligned themselves openly with those 'Patriots' who, in opposing 'the fraudulent impositions of Wood' had shown themselves zealous for the interests of both king and country.[13]

All this gave point to certain subthemes in Dublin politics during this period: civic reform, and the reassertion of rights on the part of the lower house of the corporation. Although grievances over the new rules had been eclipsed by the upheavals of James II's reign, they had never entirely disappeared. Following the establishment of the Dublin ballast office in 1707, the city commons had reminded the aldermen that successive charters had included the commons and citizens among those with rights over Dublin port; and the conduct of that office continued to create friction between the two chambers.[14] At the time of the general election of 1727 a lawyer, William Howard, KC, successfully contested Dublin city against aldermanic candidates. Although it was not unknown for a lawyer to obtain a Dublin seat, Howard was not even on the first rung of a career likely to lead to ministerial office. However, according to a later account, he offered to bring in a bill for the recovery of rights lost by the commons through the new rules, but died before he could do so.[15] Another lawyer took up the cause at the 1737 by-election, but was defeated.[16] In any case, in the 1720s and 1730s the aldermen were still capable of fielding popular parliamentary candidates, such as Alderman Humphrey French, who won the 1733 by-election. His integrity, independence of government (his rivals were, or had been, placemen) and paternalist conduct as lord mayor (1732–3), plus the endorsement of Dr Swift, were all qualities that earned him the title 'Patriot' in the tributes paid to him during and after the election.[17]

The reforming impulse only quickened again in the late 1730s, when, with civic indebtedness increasing, a corporation committee was set up to consider the city's constitution and recommend improvements (here too Swift had urged action). In 1739 a wide-ranging report was drawn up, calling for the introduction of wards on the London model, new powers to

[12] *The Works of J[onathan] S[wift], DD, SPD, in Four Volumes* (Dublin, 1735), iv. 103–22; *Advice to the Freemen of the City of Dublin*, in Jonathan Swift, *Prose Works*, ed. Temple Scott (London, 1905), vii. 311–16; Anon, *Advice to the Freemen and Freeholders of the City of Dublin; in their Choice of a Representative* (1733), CULBC, Hib. 3. 730. 1 (23), pp. 1–2.
[13] *A Letter to the Shop-Keepers, Tradesmen, [etc.]; The Presentment of the Grand Jury of the County of the City of Dublin*, in *Works of J[onathan] S[wift]*, iv. 51–62, 123–4.
[14] *CARD* vi. 383; viii. 482–4.
[15] A. Briton, *The History of the Dublin Election* (London, 1753), 15, 103–4, 142. For Howard (who did, however, have influential connections, inheriting part of Lord Chancellor Richard West's library in 1726 ('Hugh Howard', *DNB*)), see App. B below.
[16] Sir Simon Bradstreet, father of Sir Samuel Bradstreet (below, App. B).
[17] *A Little More Advice to the People of Dublin* (1733); *Astrea's Congratulation. An Ode upon Alderman Humphry French Being Elected Representative for the City of Dublin* (1733), CULBC, Hib. 3. 730. 1 (108), (118). For French, see App. B below.

curb rioters, improvements to the watch, and other reforms. The committee continued to sit into 1740, when it discussed ways in which lord mayors and sheriffs could be dissuaded from treating city employments as matters for personal disposal or sale.[18]

Reform was therefore already under discussion when the apothecary Charles Lucas was selected by the aldermen to represent his guild on the city commons.[19] The onset of his career as a public representative coincided with the termination of the mayoralty of Alderman Sir Samuel Cooke, son of the Tory lord mayor whose career had caused such controversy at the end of Queen Anne's reign. If Cooke's elevation to the mayoral office could be seen as a sign that the aldermen had put the old partisan disputes behind them, and relaxed their self-appointed role as watchdogs of the constitution, it soon became clear that under the leadership of Lucas, the city commons and freemen were prepared to step into their shoes, with momentous consequences for Irish politics.

It was to be Lucas's achievement during the 1740s to transform a purely municipal struggle for the restoration of 'ancient rights' into a campaign of national (and, in the eyes of some supporters, international) significance, aiming at nothing less than the regeneration of the ancient 'free' constitution as a whole. In the course of the campaign, Lucas identified his fellow-Protestant freemen, most of them members of the Church of Ireland, as the key to this goal.[20] His candidacy for a city seat in 1748–9 not only raised issues about how Dublin was governed, but gave the freemen the chance to elect a tradesman who was one of themselves. Despite Lucas's condemnation in autumn 1749 by virtually the entire political establishment, and his flight to avoid arrest, the election demonstrated that the freemen were capable of breaking loose from deference in their voting behaviour;[21] and by 1750 the first local constituency organization in Ireland with more than a temporary existence, the Free Citizens of Dublin, had been formed. This marked the beginning of an enduring challenge to the oligarchic nature of Irish politics.

II. Lucas's Political Philosophy

> the Board of Aldermen ... assuming any other *powers* ... not warranted by Charter, by *National* or *Municipal* Laws, is ... a manifest Tendency to a kind of *Aristocracy*, or rather an *Oligarchy* ... inconsistent with the Constitution of this *City*.[22]

---

[18] *An Examination of Certain Abuses, Corruptions, and Enormities, in the City of Dublin* (1732), in *Works of J[onathan] S[wift]*, iv. 263–80; CARD viii. 354–60, 371–4; ix. 7.

[19] CARD ix. 449. For Lucas, see below, App. B; Murphy, 'The Lucas Affair'.

[20] Charles Lucas, *The Complaints of Dublin: Humbly Offered to His Excellency William, Earl of Harrington, Lord Lieutenant General ... of Ireland* (Dublin, 1747), 22.

[21] Murphy, 'Charles Lucas and the Dublin Election'.

[22] Charles Lucas, *A Remonstrance Against Certain Infringements on the Rights and Liberties of the Commons and Citizens of Dublin* (Dublin, 1743), 36.

For a man who openly confessed that his preferred legacy to his children would be fame and reputation rather than wealth,[23] Lucas has been singularly unfortunate. Overshadowed by the figure of John Wilkes in London—where oligarchy had been challenged long before Wilkes came on the scene—and by Henry Grattan and Wolfe Tone in Ireland (both of whom stood on foundations that Lucas had helped to build), it may be that where Lucas went wrong, paradoxically, was in failing to grasp that the key to a lasting reputation might lie with the next generation.[24] It is impossible, for instance, to avoid comparisons with Grattan and Tone, whose historical reputations have owed, if not everything, then a very great deal to the filial *Lives* produced or completed by their sons.[25] Both Grattan and Tone stand much higher in the modern pantheon of Irish Patriots than Lucas, whose real political achievements were arguably greater than either of theirs. No full assessment of Lucas's political contribution can be attempted here; nevertheless, some consideration of his civic career and political ideology is essential to the theme of the present study.

Lucas was born in County Clare in 1713, but owing (it was claimed) to the improvidence of his father and elder brother the family moved to Dublin and he was apprenticed to an apothecary. In his professional capacity he soon distinguished himself by producing a pamphlet on preventing fraud in drugs (1735) which formed the basis for an act of parliament.[26] He came to the attention of his guild (St Mary Magdalene, the barber-surgeons: the apothecaries' guild was not founded until 1747) and was selected for the city commons in 1741. His fellow representative James Digges La Touche[27] (merchants' guild) was already active in defence of the rights of the commons, especially the right to initiate business and to strike its own committees.

Lucas was nominated to the corporation's pipe-water committee, where he soon found himself at odds with one of the powerful aldermanic cliques, the Rose Club, over the perennial issue of the development of Dublin's water supply. Like others before him, Lucas suspected the aldermen of being

---

[23] Charles Lucas, *A Second Address to the Right Hon. the Lord Mayor, the Aldermen, Sheriffs, [etc.] of the City of Dublin* (Dublin, 1766), 5.

[24] Lucas was married three times, and reputedly left children by all three marriages, but only Henry is known to have attended his father's funeral. No biography was produced by any of the Lucas children (see *DNB*), but Sean Murphy is currently at work on one.

[25] Henry Grattan (ed.), *Memoirs of the Life and Times of the Rt. Hon. Henry Grattan, By his Son* (5 vols.; London, 1839–46); W. T. W. Tone (ed.), *Life of Theobald Wolfe Tone . . . Written by Himself and Continued by his Son; With his Political Writings and Fragments of his Diary* (2 vols.; Washington, 1826).

[26] 9 Geo. II, c. 10; 'The Life of Dr Charles Lucas', *Dublin Penny Journal*, 1 (1832), 389–91; Murphy, 'The Lucas Affair' 49.

[27] James Digges La Touche (d. 1763); younger son of David Digues La Touche. Took over his father's cloth business; entered municipal life in the 1730s. See David Dickson and Richard English, 'The La Touche Dynasty', in Dickson (ed.), *The Gorgeous Mask*, 17–29, at 17–20.

more interested in personal gain than the good of the city, and he quickly became a thorn in the side of the city fathers. Defeated in the corporation at large over the water supply question, Lucas joined forces with La Touche. They secured the appointment of a committee to inspect the city charters; both of them served on it.[28] La Touche later conceded that it was Lucas who, as a result of these investigations, came to the conclusion—which subsequently became so contentious—that down to the introduction of the new rules in 1672 the city commons had enjoyed rights in the selection of aldermen and civic officials.[29] The articulation of this claim led to a breach between the two houses of the corporation. In 1743 Lucas published a *Remonstrance*, addressed to the lord mayor, aldermen, sheriffs, commons and citizens, in which he argued that the only written authority for the aldermen's powers of selection was contained in the new rules, which had been imposed 'without the consent of the People'.[30] This heralded the beginning of a campaign, which lasted for nearly twenty years, to overturn the aldermanic monopoly.

In the early stages, Lucas maintained a persuasive tone in his writings, portraying the aldermen as upholders of 'Liberty, Freedom and Truth', who, when they recognized that the rights of the commons and citizens had been usurped, would see the need to restore them.[31] Neither the persuasive tone nor the committee's labours had the desired effect on the aldermen, but the impact on the commons was marked. From 1742 a journal was kept to record the commons' business; in 1743 the commons claimed a right to participate in elections of aldermen and in the government of the Blue-Coat school; citizens were encouraged to attend on quarter-assembly days to witness the commons' proceedings, in the spirit of the old hundred court; and there was a generally enhanced air of self-esteem.[32] When in 1744 the aldermen exercised their customary powers to select a new alderman, Lucas and La Touche organized a fund to take the aldermen to court. The case, however, was stopped by the judge, and when, shortly afterwards, the triennial selection of guild representatives for the common council took place, the names of Lucas and La Touche were struck out by the aldermen from the double returns furnished by their respective guilds. In 1747, Lucas

---

[28] *CARD* ix. 504–625; Murphy, 'The Lucas Affair', 56–80.
[29] Hibernicus [J. D. La Touche], *A Freeholder's Address to the Merchants, Traders and Others, the Citizens and Freemen of the City of Dublin* (Dublin, 1748), 14–15. The aldermen defended the new rules, deploring the 'inconvenience, and confusion of popular elections' (*CARD* ix. 560–1). [30] Charles Lucas, *A Remonstrance*, 21.
[31] Ibid. 37.
[32] Murphy, 'The Lucas Affair', 35–6, 56–65; Lucas, *Divelina Libera*, 87–8; *CARD* ix. 576–9. In certain towns, including Cork, Kinsale, and Ardee, assemblies of freemen (courts of d'oyer hundred) had survived the new rules (Kenneth Milne, 'The Irish Municipal Corporations in the Eighteenth Century', Ph.D. thesis (TCD, 1962), 12–13, 41); but in Dublin only vestiges of the court of darein hundred remained. See A Citizen, *A Letter to the Lord Mayor, [etc.] of the City of Dublin* (Dublin, 1740).

tried and failed to get the lord lieutenant to take up the case. The following August, 1748, a vacancy occurred in the parliamentary representation of Dublin city, which ushered in a protracted period of electioneering between an aldermanic candidate, and Lucas and La Touche, standing for the restoration of the commons' and citizens' chartered rights. At first Lucas and La Touche were in competition for the seat, with Lucas contending that La Touche's notions of liberty were too limited; but soon the other city seat also fell vacant. The election thereupon developed into a straight fight between Lucas and La Touche and two aldermen. In the course of this campaign, Lucas alone was to produce over 200,000 words in published addresses and letters to the Dublin electorate.[33] He also set up a newpaper, the *Censor* (1749–50), the better to convey his message to the freemen.

Lucas's prolific printed output makes it possible, at the risk of some oversimplification and the suggestion of consistency where none existed, to reconstruct the main outlines of his political philosophy in the 1740s. The role of free men was to cherish and preserve 'liberty', a condition that Lucas regarded as a legal inheritance, a natural right, and a gift from God. Liberty (more commonly, 'liberties') included security of property, the right to consent to laws, and freedom for 'true religion' to flourish: it also fostered the arts, sciences, and trade. Such a condition was believed to have been present in Saxon or Gothic times, and to have been transmitted through the common law tradition. Even more important, it had been prescribed by 'the Great CHARTER of civil and religious *Liberty*, the *Christian Dispensation*'; and the obligation to uphold it, which was binding even on the monarch and the established church, was legal, moral, and religious. Crucially, liberty was maintained by keeping a proper balance between the rights and functions of the monarchy, the aristocracy, and the people (the classic Patriot position). Like Molyneux, Lucas rejected the claims of the English parliament to make laws binding on Ireland, and denied that there had been a royal conquest of Ireland, for that might mean an unfettered royal prerogative. He also stressed the rights of other local bodies such as urban corporations: the vindication of their rights was equally important to the maintenance of liberty.[34]

Although Lucas occasionally used the term 'compact' to describe the relations between ruler and ruled, and sometimes appealed to natural rights, his programme for constitutional action was shaped primarily by ancient rights and liberties embodied in the common law and confirmed by historic

---

[33] *CARD* ix. 200; Murphy, 'Charles Lucas and the Dublin Election', 99.
[34] Lucas, *Divelina Libera*, 5–11; id., *Address VII* (17 Nov. 1748) in [Charles Lucas], *The Political Constitutions of Great Britain and Ireland, Asserted and Vindicated; The Connection and Common Interest of Both Kingdoms, Demonstrated* (2 vols.; London, 1751) i. 63–78; *A Tenth Address to the Free Citizens, and Free-Holders, of the City of Dublin* (Dublin, 1748); *The Censor: or, The Citizens Journal*, 22 (7–14 Oct. 1749): all references to the first and only volume.

royal charters. These, thanks to his professional knowledge of Latin, he was able to read. It would be hard to exaggerate the significance for contemporaries of what has been called the 'mobilizing capacity' of written documents: Lucas himself compared the rediscovery of the city's historic constitution with the vernacular translations of Scripture that became available with the Reformation.[35] At one time, it seemed, the ancient free constitution had existed over much of Europe and elsewhere, but in many countries the representative institutions and common law that were its main features had fallen victim to arbitrary monarchs, sometimes aided and abetted by the church (which had previously yielded up its freedom to the papal imperium). Indeed, although the constitution had been preserved—even perfected—in Britain and Ireland, thanks to a Protestant monarchy ('the *Bulwark* of *Europe's* Peace and Liberties'),[36] it had often come under threat, only to be saved by the virtue of the citizens, or by 'providential' agents such as William of Orange. It was therefore essential for all parties to the constitution to be vigilant, for at any time the precious inheritance could fall prey to rapacious monarchs, corrupt ministers, or the decay of public spirit or 'virtue'. Even the Hanoverian monarchs had to be constantly reassured that in forgoing arbitrary rule they really had chosen the better way:

YOUR MAJESTY is, by divine Providence, called to the most exalted Station that is known in any Part of the Earth. You preside over the GREATEST, because the FREEST PEOPLE, in the World. You are, in Comparison of [*sic*] those, who *rule Slaves*, by *despotic Sway*; a *King* of *Kings*. YOUR subjects *assent* and *consent* to Your Sovereignty.[37]

Given that the constitution depended on consent, the virtuous citizen should be ready to participate in activities calculated to preserve freedom; filling unpaid offices in local and national government, and maintaining a principled independence of government patronage, which had an inherent tendency to corrupt the recipient and dull his virtue.[38] In his preoccupation with virtue, dislike of standing armies (expressed most fully in the 1760s after the Jacobite threat had receded) and hostility to a heavy national

---

[35] See Lucas, *Divelina Libera*, 9; id., *A Tenth Address*, 11. Cf. Colin Lucas, 'The Crowd and Politics between *Ancien Régime* and Revolution in France', *JMH* 60 (1988), 421–57, at 422.
[36] Lucas, *Divelina Libera*, 6–8; *A Letter, Etc.* (18 Aug. 1749), in *The Political Constitutions*, ii. 424–8, at 443.
[37] Charles Lucas, *The Great Charter of the Liberties of the City of Dublin. . . . Translated into English . . . Addressed to His Majesty and Presented to his Lords Justices of Ireland* (Dublin, 1749), p. iii.
[38] A. F. Barber and Citizen [C. Lucas], *A Second Letter to the Free Citizens of Dublin* (Dublin, 1747), 15; Charles Lucas, *The British Free-Holder's Political Catechism* (Dublin, 1748), 9, 13–14; 'To the People of Ireland' (*Censor*, 5 (24 June–1 July 1749)).

debt,[39] Lucas's views were compatible with mainstream opposition thinking in the English-speaking world: 'From 1688 to 1776 (and after) the central question in Anglophone political theory was not whether a ruler could be cashiered for misconduct, but whether a regime founded on patronage, public debt, and professionalization of the armed forces did not corrupt both governors and governed.'[40] However, Lucas's corporatism, his reverence for ancient rights, and insistence that the church must nurture civil as well as religious freedom indicate that there were many dimensions to his thought, which cannot be comprehended under any single label.

There was also an anti-Catholic dimension in his outlook. Since the constitution was always precarious, it was necessary to restrict the rights of those who might endanger it. The long-standing association in Protestant minds between popery and arbitrary power had been reinforced by the Vatican's continued recognition of the Pretender as king of Great Britain and Ireland; and consequently Catholics were still without any means of testifying their loyalty to the state. Lucas did express some doubt as to whether all the penal laws were really necessary;[41] but the principle of the state's right to defend itself against those with dangerous tendencies was taken for granted. In common with his enlightened Protestant contemporaries Lucas drew a clear distinction between persecution on purely religious grounds (a 'popish' practice), and the need for laws to protect civil and religious liberty:

It is one of the distinguishing marks of true Protestants to quarrel with no man for barely differing in opinion or in religious matters. And it is well known, to the honour of our constitution, that all religious sects among us are tollerated or winked at, unless they profess or propagate a doctrine dangerous to the state ... But if any man can be so weak, as to carry this enthusiasm into temporalities, I must think it my duty, not only to differ from him, but, in just defence of my property, my life, and, what I hold more dear, the PUBLIC LIBERTY, to oppose him. If any, among us, can be so mad, as to assert, that any power in the universe can authorise *Tyranny, Persecution of Consciences, Rebellion, Murder, Oppression, Treachery*, or the like, This, and this only, is the man whom I call a *Papist*; that is, not a follower of the bishop of *Rome*, for that does not concern me, but a *Subject* of the *Pope* of *Rome*, who claims a *temporal* power inconsistent with the liberties to which man is heir. If the *native Irish* had reformed themselves, by throwing off that *Romish* yoke of *Papacy*, which they had long bravely opposed, let them differ never so much in other religious rites or tenets, from the *Engish*, both would be one powerful people, united

---

[39] Lucas, *A Remonstrance*, 36; id., *The Great Charter*, pp. xvii, xx, xxxviii; id., *A Tenth Address*, 30–1; id., *A Mirror for Courts-Martial*, 3rd edn. (Dublin, 1768); *Censor*, 5 (24 June–1 July 1749).

[40] J. G. A. Pocock, 'Virtues, Rights and Manners', in Pocock, *Virtue, Commerce and History* (Cambridge, 1985), 37–50, at 48.

[41] Lucas, *The Great Charter*, pp. xvii–xviii.

in one common bond of peace and liberty. From this you may see it is *foreign, papal, temporal Tyranny*, not *Religion*, I oppose.[42]

Lucas's own religious views are of interest here. He hinted, in one of his *Letters*, that his own inclinations were towards Presbyterianism. He conformed to the Anglican church, out of respect for the church established by 'human Law, which is ever to be observed and obeyed in all things, that are not contradictory to the DIVINE LAW'. This did not prevent him from occasionally denouncing 'priestcraft' in the church, for its tendency to undermine liberty; and this probably made his message more acceptable to Protestants outside as well as inside the established church.[43]

There was nothing in this political philosophy that was new, or even new to Dublin. Lucas was an eclectic rather than an original thinker, and many of his ideas were the common ingredients of contemporary Country thinking in the Hanoverian dominions, looking back to the 1670s or even earlier.[44] Molyneux had already invoked charters and statutes to show that Ireland and England enjoyed the same free constitution; he had also made some reference to natural rights, and occasionally spoke of the constitution as a 'compact'. However, by this he meant not a decision to create a government but an agreement between Henry II and 'the people' (lords, prelates, etc.) to implement in Ireland the existing English constitution. Lucas went somewhat further in a Lockian direction when he imagined the origins of Dublin's civic government, envisaging the 'Men of Bristol' ('as is common to People left in a sort of a state of Nature'), deciding to choose 'a Chief Magistrate to preside over them'. Lucas also went beyond Molyneux— though not beyond some of Molyneux's antecedents—in his willingness to criticize Poynings' law as a symbol of the 'dependent' status of the Irish parliament.[45]

However, the view that Lucas was particularly radical in his outlook should not be pressed too far. His condemnation of the oppressive role of 'the English' in Ireland, and justification of past Irish rebellions, was indebted to Sir John Davies's attack (1612) on 'great English Lords [who] coulde not endure that any Kings should raigne in Ireland, but themselves'. In both cases the main purpose was to highlight failings in aristocratic

---

[42] A. F. Barber and Citizen [C. Lucas], *A Third Letter to the Free-Citizens of Dublin* (Dublin, 1747), 19. See also Leighton, *Catholicism in a Protestant Kingdom*, ch. 4.

[43] Lucas, *A Letter, Etc.*, in *The Political Constitutions*, ii. 442; id., *A Sixteenth Address to the Free Citizens [etc.]* (Dublin, 1748), 4–8. This hint may have misled Froude into calling Lucas a Presbyterian: *The English in Ireland in the Eighteenth Century* (3 vols.; London, 1872–4), i. 606–8.

[44] Above, Ch. 2. Even Court Whigs accepted the idea of constitutional balance: Reed Browning, *Political and Constitutional Ideas of the Court Whigs* (Baton Rouge, La., 1982), 180–1.

[45] Molyneux, *Case of Ireland*, 45–8, 50–2, 55–7, 61–2, 67, 103–4, 119–24. Cf. Lucas, *Divelina Libera*, 14, and on Poynings' law, Britannicus [C. Lucas], *A Free-Man's Answer to the Free-Holder's Address* (n.p., 1748), 8–9.

government, rather than to display sympathy for the native Irish.[46] (Of course, it was one thing for an attorney-general to make such comments, and another for a tradesman to do so: Lucas's critics in the administration and in parliament labelled him seditious in 1749.)[47] Although Lucas condemned 'that infernal Prince', Walpole, for passing the declaratory act, the attack was inspired not by anti-English feeling, rather by concern for ancient rights. And in his corporatism and his championing of guild values (which he regarded as an integral part of the liberties brought to Ireland by the Anglo-Normans) Lucas revealed himself to be a traditional rather than a forward-looking thinker.[48]

The idea that the free constitution had its origins in ancient Germanic (Gothic) traditions had been popular in sixteenth- and seventeenth-century England, though Lucas had also been influenced by more recent writers who considered that the essential features of the Gothic constitution were not merely Germanic but more widely spread.[49] John Toland had insisted that liberty and not absolutism was the source of trade and commerce;[50] and together with Locke and the Commonwealthmen[51] he had inveighed against persecution on purely religious grounds (while acknowledging that Catholics represented a danger to the state and must be restrained). Lucas's own pantheon of heroes ('great and immortal PATRIOTS') reflected the rich variety of influences on him. Besides the predictable figures of Molyneux, Swift,[52] and Archbishop King, there appeared John Hampden, who had defied Charles I over ship-money; John Pym, the parliamentary leader who had challenged Strafford's claim that, Ireland being a conquered country, the king could have a free hand there (Cromwell, by contrast, was an 'arbitrary tyrant'); and the now-forgotten English Tory orator William Shippen, whose virulent attacks on Walpole in the English house of commons proved immensely popular when translated into print.[53] This list

---

[46] Davies, *A Discoverie of the True Causes Why Ireland was Never Entirely Subdued*, in John Davies, *The Complete Prose Works*, ed. Alexander B. Grosart, (2 vols.; n.p., 1876), ii. 85. Cf. Lucas's *Address XI*, in *The Political Constitutions*, i. 132–7. Lucas's radicalism is asserted in Murphy, 'Charles Lucas, Catholicism and Nationalism', 87–8.

[47] Murphy, 'Charles Lucas and the Dublin Election', 104.

[48] Lucas, *Address XI*, in *The Political Constitutions*, i. 144; id. *Divelina Libera*, 13–15.

[49] J. G. A. Pocock, *The Ancient Constitution and the Feudal Law* (Cambridge, 1957), 19–20; R. J. Smith, *The Gothic Bequest. Medieval Institutions in British Thought, 1688–1863* (Cambridge, 1987), 12–13, 40–1.

[50] James Harrington, *The Oceana and Other Works*, ed. John Toland (London, 1700), editor's preface, p. ii.

[51] On the Commonwealthmen see Caroline Robbins, *The Eighteenth-Century Commonwealthman* (Cambridge, Mass., 1959).

[52] It is worth stressing the presence of Molyneux and Swift among Lucas's heroes, since doubt has been cast on the existence of a 'Patriot tradition' in the 18th c. (O'Brien, 'The Grattan Mystique', 190–4).

[53] *Censor*, 9 (22–9 July 1749); [Charles Lucas], *An Eighteenth Address to the Free-Citizens and Free-Holders of the City of Dublin* (Dublin, 1749), 8–9. For Shippen (whose name appeared as 'Sheppin' in the *Censor*), see Gough, *Fundamental Law*, 181; Linda Colley, *In Defiance of Oligarchy, the Tory Party 1714–60* (Cambridge, 1985), 59–60.

confirms for Ireland what historians of English politics have argued recently, that opposition politics under the first two Georges drew its inspiration from diverse sources,[54] though it is worth stressing that Lucas, an avowed Hanoverian, would have had no time for Shippen's Jacobite tendencies.

How closely Lucas had read the works of his heroes is not known. However, even if he had read nothing, the Dublin of his youth was already familiar with the main opposition issues and arguments, and particularly with the defence of local rights. An edition of Swift's works was published in Dublin in 1735; significantly, it included the author's call for the introduction of something like the censor's office in ancient Rome to monitor 'the Conduct . . . of Men in Office'.[55]

III. *Dublin's Response to Lucas*

The warmth of the popular response in the capital to Lucas's campaign was striking. During the early stages of the electoral contest, he and La Touche were granted honorary freedom of several guilds other than their own. Some criticism of Lucas was voiced in the city commons in the summer of 1749,[56] but during the autumn there were street demonstrations in his support. He retained a following even after he had fled the country, following his condemnation by the Irish parliament and by Dublin corporation (October 1749) as an enemy to his country. At the long-awaited poll, not even the spectacle of the Dublin Anglican clergy and a bevy of MPs voting for the aldermen deterred the freemen from voting in considerable numbers for La Touche, who accordingly won a seat.[57]

If Lucas was not an original thinker, then what was the key to his popularity with the Dublin freemen? His own energy, courage, and confidence are part of the answer, but so was the fact that he was inviting the freemen to take on a challenging constitutional role at a time when conditions in Dublin made them willing to respond. Behind the chronic dissatisfaction over the aldermanic monopoly lay social and economic changes that were making Dublin a more divided city. The population (112,000 by the 1740s) had more than doubled since the revolution; the numbers of freemen (*c*.3,000 by 1749) had also increased, and they were becoming more literate, to judge by the signatures on the freemen's bonds.[58]

[54] Colley, *In Defiance of Oligarchy*, ch. 6; Pocock, 'The Machiavellian Moment Revisited', 63.

[55] *A Project for the Advancement of Religion, and the Reformation of Manners* (1709), in *The Works of J[onathan] S[wift]*, i. 130–54, at 137.

[56] Journal of the sheriffs and commons of Dublin, DCA, C1/JSC/1, p. 242. The merchants' guild criticized Lucas earlier; Anon., *A Fuller Account of the Proceedings at Guild-hall on . . . the 2d of April 1744* (Dublin, 1744).

[57] *CARD* ix. 316; Murphy, 'Charles Lucas and the Dublin Election', 95–9, 103–6.

[58] Murphy, 'The Lucas Affair', 38; DCA, Fr/Bond/1674–1759.

Some of them, at least, were also becoming better off. But the decades of greatest prosperity still lay ahead; the 1740s witnessed famine in the countryside and urban distress. The corporation itself was still financially constrained, and had to borrow money to pay for the militia that represented Dublin's contribution to the defence of Ireland during the Jacobite and French invasion scares of 1744–5. Moreover, the landed gentry were by now well established in the capital, reinforcing their ties with the mercantile and moneyed élite from which the aldermen were drawn.[59] The corporation found itself having to respond to unprecedented demands from government and the gentry, as well as from tradesmen, demands that were not always easy to reconcile. In these circumstances, it was inevitable that attention should focus on the oligarchical nature of the corporation. De Krey's description of London applies equally well to Dublin: 'The corporation's working constitution was ... a chronic political irritant ... because it concentrated power in the hands of a few while extending the right of political participation to many.'[60]

Some resentment against the rich and powerful aldermen, then, was to be expected. But what the campaign of the 1740s also revealed, particularly in the columns of Lucas's *Censor*, was a certain antagonism towards the landed class. The phenomenon was not entirely new. A strong and self-conscious defence of 'citizens', whose wealth had originated in 'Merchandize', as distinct from those (i.e. the aristocracy) whose wealth was only 'Plunderer's Booty', had appeared in the Dublin press as long ago as 1727, when the rights of the city commons had first become an election issue.[61] It seems likely therefore that by the 1740s Dubliners had already acquired some of the sensibilities of their counterparts in London, where 'cit' (or 'citizen') was a derogatory term for a tradesman. At any rate, there was a reaction from Dublin artisans and shopkeepers to what they perceived as arrogance or pride of caste on the part of their landed clientele. One correspondent, signing himself Urbanus Vigil, criticized the gentry for their lack of civic spirit. Their carriages dashed through the streets, heedless of the public's safety. The pavements outside their houses remained unrepaired and uncleaned, to the annoyance of passers-by. They had no respect for members of the parish watch, and if a citizen complained, he would be obstructed by 'some privileged Man'—a relation or client, perhaps, of a lord, a judge, or an alderman: even the sheriffs, it seemed, were apt to side with a gentleman in any dispute with a mere citizen. The writer continued

[59] *CARD* ix. pp. v, 137–40. Such contacts were made through convivial clubs such as the Boyne Society, which met in the Tholsel on 4 Nov. (King William's birthday) in the 1730s (*Stopford-Sackville MSS, HMC 9th Rep.*, App., pt. iii. p. 40).
[60] De Krey, *A Fractured Society*, 9.
[61] Letter signed 'J.S.' (Alderman John Stoyte?), *Faulkner's Dublin Journal* (*FDJ*), 10–14 Oct. 1727.

I have known a Country 'Squire horse-whip a Citizen in his own Shop; because he would not trust his Taylor. And he could obtain no Satisfaction: the Sherifs were his *bottle Companions*, the Sub-Sherif was his *Fosterer*,[62] or *Pander*,[63] and if we go to *higher Offices*, it will be found, he had an *Interest* there, that no Shop-Keeper could shake.[64]

Civic and aristocratic values also clashed in the case of the theatre. The manager of Smock-Alley, Tom Sheridan, tried to impose 'polite' standards of behaviour on playgoers, a move that in 1747 led to a confrontation with certain gentlemen in the audience. Lucas took up Sheridan's cause, condemning the gentlemen for using casual violence against their inferiors. Lucas's remedy for such abuses, in true civic republican tradition, was to encourage virtuous citizens to enrol as constables in the (unpaid) watch.[65]

But it was not just the day-to-day conduct of the gentry and their apparent immunity from civic justice that gave offence. Against a background of rural starvation (in the early 1740s) there was concern about recent economic developments, which, it was feared, might not be in the real public interest. The rise of banking, for instance, was looked on with suspicion: the *Censor* reprinted an attack by Swift on bankers for their tendency to drain money out of the country.[66] Resentments like these could coalesce around the spectacle of the *nouveaux riches*, of which Dublin displayed some striking examples. Such figures often had connections with government rather than with the corporation; and, in cases where they set out to put their own stamp on the city's development they were liable to become particularly obnoxious to the freemen. Such a figure was Luke Gardiner (a former banker), whose combined possession of government office and extensive land holdings on the north side of Dublin gave him great influence in matters relating to the city.[67] In a heavily sarcastic account of a civic entertainment held after the quarter sessions at the Tholsel in the run-up to the 1749 election, the *Censor* picked out

the Right Honorable LUKE GARDINER, Esq; Deputee-Vice-Treasurer of *Ireland*, Surveyor general of the Customs of *Ireland*; one of the Keepers of His Majesty's Park, the Phoenix . . . one of the Governors of the Work House; one of the Governors of the Blue-Coat Hospital, and one of the Governors of *Dr Stevens's* Hospital; one of the Trustees of the Linen Manufacture of *Ireland* . . . and one of his Majesty's most honorable Privy Council, etc. etc. etc. who has, of the Redundance of his public Spirit, and abundant Regard for this poor City, long labored to erect a

---

[62] Patron, protector.   [63] Pimp.

[64] *Censor*, 3 (10–17 June 1749).

[65] A. F. Barber [C. Lucas], *A Second Letter to the Free Citizens of Dublin* (Dublin, 1747), 10–15.

[66] *Censor*, 23 (28 Oct.– 4 Nov. 1749).

[67] Luke Gardiner, banker (d. 1755); leased land from Dublin corporation and laid it out on a grand scale, particularly Henrietta St. and Sackville Mall. Retired from business, was made a privy councillor, and obtained several government posts (Craig, *Dublin 1660–1860*, 101–5).

Manor-Court in *Oxman-Town*, to ease the over burdened Magistrates of the City of a principal part of their *antient jurisdiction.*[68]

Gardiner, evidently, was resented not merely as an upstart but for enjoying extensive government patronage; for his presence on the governing bodies of so many civic institutions, and for his imputed desire to encroach on corporate jurisdiction. His declared intention of voting for the aldermen at the coming election simply confirmed his oligarchical qualities. But the really telling blow in this survey of the fruits of Gardiner's connections with the powerful was the reference to the 'Blue-Coat Hospital', the free school run by the corporation. The hospital's charter (1671) had been granted to the mayor and corporation, but for some time the gentry had been active on the governing body, with the result, it was claimed, that a mere tradesman could scarcely get a son admitted to the school. That the aldermen recognized the intensity of feeling on this issue is reflected in the promise made shortly before the election that in future the sons of freemen would receive preference over others.[69]

The manners and mores of the *nouveaux riches* were also suspect. 'Publicola' contrasted the pleasing, 'natural' garden of an acquaintance in the country with the garden of a suburban city friend—everything laid out in straight lines, stiff rows of trees, animals all in cages or on chains. This was repugnant enough on aesthetic grounds, but it raised more fundamental political questions. Publicola asked his suburban friend to free a caged squirrel, thinking that it would delight in its freedom; but all it did was to run round in circles. Lest readers miss the point, Publicola gave the solemn warning that those who lost their liberty might in future never choose to accept freedom.[70]

How far did any of this resentment against 'the great' add up to a critique of a society dominated by an aristocratic élite? The answer would seem to be, not very far. Certainly, aristocratic pretensions were ridiculed. One correspondent in the *Censor* managed to turn the fashionable idea of racial superiority against the aristocracy, by hinting at degeneracy. The opportunity had arisen, he wrote, to compare the blood of a nobleman with that of a tradesman: whereupon his lordship's blood turned out to be 'frothy and full of Bubbles', and 'of a blackish colour', while the tradesman's was 'a bright and florid Red'.[71] But the *Censor* praised the society of orders,[72] and the

---

[68] *Censor*, 7 (8–15 July 1749). The possibility of Gardiner being granted the right to set up a manor court reflects how little had been done since the revolution to put formal limits on the royal prerogative (Maitland, *Constitutional History of England*, 419–21).

[69] A Briton, *History of the Dublin Election*, 32; Lesley Whiteside, *A History of the King's Hospital*, 2nd edn. (Dublin, 1985).

[70] *Censor*, 11 (5–12 Aug. 1749). In England by the 1730s 'natural' gardens were being celebrated as expressions of the spirit of liberty (Rudolf Wittkower, *Palladio and English Palladianism*, paperback edn. (London, 1983), ch. 12).

[71] *Censor*, 22 (21–8 Oct. 1749).

[72] See Georges Duby, *The Three Orders: Feudal Society Imagined* (Chicago, 1980).

Dublin tradesmen for whom Lucas was the spokesman showed little sign of contemplating a society that was not dominated by some sort of landed aristocracy (preferably, of course, a virtuous one). Nor was this an archaic view: in Hanoverian Ireland, as in Britain, political liberties, as well as support for the development of agriculture, trade, and industry, depended very much on the landed class.[73]

This needs to be borne in mind when considering the populist rhetoric that appeared from time to time in the *Censor* and other pro-Lucas literature. Such rhetoric may seem very radical: the author of a set of queries addressed to 'the Wise and Just Patriots of Ireland', asked, 'Do not the King, Lords and Commons and all other Parts of the Administration, *derive* all their *Prerogatives, Powers* and *Privileges* from the People, and *hold* them, in *Trust,* for them?' And in June 1749 the *Censor* gave what sounded to be a very inclusive definition of the term 'freeman', which meant, apparently, every subject of every class, since there were now no 'bondsmen', 'but those, that become such, voluntarily'.[74] The qualification, however, included Catholics, whose willingness to submit to popish usurpations was taken to reflect their lack of and unfitness for constitutional freedom. For while Lucas deplored the exclusion in medieval times of the 'native Irish' from the constitution, he considered that by James I's reign matters had changed; 'the ORIGINAL COMPACT was restored', and the '*Benefit of the Laws,* universally diffused throughout the whole kingdom'.[75] When it is recalled that Catholics represented the great bulk of the Irish population, and the poorest section at that, it is clear that the *Censor*'s understanding of what constituted the political nation was not as novel or as inclusive as might at first appear. Popery, in fact, was still seen primarily in political terms; Catholicism was not taken seriously as a religion, although advertisements for books containing highly coloured and often salacious accounts of monastic life, or the secrets of the confessional, testified to an enduring fascination with the subject.[76]

Despite these qualifications, it is important not to underestimate the challenge posed by the freemen to oligarchy. The fact that this challenge rested on largely traditional assumptions did not mean that it was harmless or could be easily ignored. In effect, Lucas and his supporters were claiming that the (Protestant) freemen could step into the breach left by a corrupt

---

[73] *Censor*, 27 (28 Apr.–5 May 1750); Nicholas Rogers, *Whigs and Cities: Popular Politics in the Age of Walpole and Pitt* (Oxford, 1989), 405.

[74] Anon., *Queries Humbly Offered to the Consideration of the Wise and Just Patriots of Ireland* (1749), CULBC, Hib. 3. 748. 1 (27); *Censor*, 4 (17–24 June 1749).

[75] C. Lucas, *Address XI*, 31 Jan. 1749 (*The Political Constitutions*, i. 130–53, at 132–42). The statement was a typically eclectic blend of Sir John Davies, *A Discoverie of the True Causes*, in *Prose Works*, ii. 71, and Molyneux's *The Case of Ireland*, 46.

[76] Titles advertised in 1749 included *The Amorous Abbess*, and *A Compleat History of the Intrigues of Priests and Nuns*.

aristocratic and mercantile élite, and bring about the regeneration of the ancient constitution. These aspirations were none the less effective for being couched, occasionally, in the traditional apocalyptic language of the poor. What alderman or gentleman could remain wholly unperturbed by the sentiments of 'Jacobus Libertates', who deplored 'the keeping up of spiritual Wickedness in many high Places of Trust in this poor City', and promised his readers that 'the Time will come, when Happiness and Glory, will shine upon them [the people], like the Rays of Phoebus . . . the Cry of the Poor will be heared [*sic*] and the Distress of the Oppressed, will be made known'?[77] Such language could not fail to conjure up images of popular rebellions, and it is no coincidence that at the time of Lucas's flight, his name was satirically linked with the old peasants' revolt invocation:

> When *Adam* delved, and *Eve* Span,
> Who was then the Gentleman?[78]

IV. The Example of London

It was not simply social and economic forces that were responsible for the challenge to oligarchy in Dublin during the 1740s. Developments taking place in English politics, especially in London, were also crucial. It will be worth examining these developments briefly, since they demonstrate how artificial it is to treat Ireland in isolation. The Dublin civic Patriots saw themselves as engaged in an identical campaign with their London counterparts.

Greater London in the early eighteenth century had a population of around 600,000, nearly six times that of Dublin. London corporation, however, was responsible for only a small part of the entire city area, within which it was the supreme authority. The corporation consisted of the lord mayor, a board of twenty-five aldermen, a common council of 210 members, and common hall, the representative body of the city's eighty-nine guilds and livery companies. In contrast to the case in Dublin both aldermen and common councillors were elected on a freeman franchise, comprising 80 per cent of the resident householders in the incorporated wards. The city was an 'open' parliamentary constituency, with four MPs elected by some 12,000–15,000 freemen, including the 8,000 liverymen of the city companies. The freemen thus enjoyed extensive privileges and were the most dedicated of all Londoners in defence of traditional liberties.[79]

The city of London's intervention in national politics dated back at least as far as the civil war period. Although its notorious radicalism was suspect

---

[77] *Censor*, 22 (21–8 Oct. 1749).
[78] *Censor Extraordinary*, 21 (14–16 Oct. 1749).
[79] Stevenson, 'Introduction', in Stevenson (ed.), *London in the Age of Reform*, pp. xiv–xvi; De Krey, *A Fractured Society*, 42.

to some, its prestige was confirmed when the corporation was invited to help frame the revolution settlement of 1688–9. Within a few years of the revolution, a process of realignment was going on, as Tories and disillusioned Country Whigs began to coalesce in opposition to the Court Whigs' monopoly of civic offices, and their failure to pursue a civic 'Commonwealth' reform programme. Progress towards full coalition was, however, hampered by tensions between the champions of the church (usually the Tories) and those who favoured further concessions to Protestant dissent (the Whigs); and by fears for the security of the Protestant succession.[80]

During the 1720s the single most important target for opposition groups was the emergence of Sir Robert Walpole as 'prime minister'. The very label was pejorative—it smacked of monopolizing the royal prerogative and unbalancing the constitution—and the extensive patronage that found its way into Walpole's hands compounded his unpopularity in opposition circles.[81] For their part, Tories detested Walpole for keeping them out of office (on account of alleged Jacobite sympathies), and for his conciliatory views on Protestant dissent. Among Londoners, he was execrated for pushing through the city elections act (1725) which defined the freeman franchise narrowly and confirmed an aldermanic veto over acts of the common council. Whigs as well as Tories were alienated by this partisan measure, and the decade 1725–35 saw the growth in London of a broadly based anti-ministerial coalition, known as the Country or Patriot party, which had both civic and national reform objectives. At the local level, with much looking back to supposed Saxon freedoms, the aim was to secure the restoration of a broader electorate, and to repeal the aldermanic veto (a goal achieved in 1746); at the national level, to end the Tories' proscription from office and to reduce the power of the moneyed interest (the bankers and financiers who had superseded the corporation and guilds as the government's chief creditors).[82]

The Patriots drew much of their inspiration from the Tory Henry St John, Lord Bolingbroke, the leading English opposition ideologue of his age. In his newspaper the *Craftsman* (founded 1726), Bolingbroke helped to propagate the civic republican tradition, insisting that the king was not above the law and that each of the legislative branches must preserve its independence of the others. It was he who popularized the umbrella term 'Patriot' for what was a supra-party opposition of discontented Whigs and Tories. In 1733–4, at a time of intense opposition to Walpole's excise proposals, a series of articles appeared in the *Craftsman*, reprinted in 1735 under the title *A Dissertation on Parties*. Here Bolingbroke drew a

---

[80] De Krey, *A Fractured Society*, 17–18, 39, 190–2; Rogers, *Whigs and Cities*, 14.
[81] Lucas, *The Great Charter*, p. xxxviii.
[82] Rogers, *Whigs and Cities*, 35–42; Smith, *The Gothic Bequest*, 99.

distinction between 'factions' and 'parties': while the former were to be deplored, the latter were legitimate, because they had the true interests of the nation at heart. Besides, they would disappear once corruption had been vanquished.[83]

Against this background, Patriotism increased its appeal in London, especially between 1738 and 1742, when a popular campaign for war with Spain (for commercial ends) helped undermine confidence in Walpole's ministry, and eventually forced him from office. By this time, opposition politicians were looking to Frederick, prince of Wales, as their patron; in 1738 Bolingbroke wrote his celebrated *The Idea of a Patriot King* (published 1749) in which he invoked the prospect of a monarch who would rule without regard to party distinctions, and would thus, like Elizabeth I, embody the true harmonious spirit of the nation.[84] The 1741 election saw the opposition win all four city seats. Moreover, in neighbouring Westminster, an opposition constituency party, the Independent Electors of Westminster, was set up in 1741.

London's example made some impact outside the capital. Because it was perceived to be independent of the court and of the aristocracy, the city had come to be regarded as a barometer of public opinion. During the period 1739–42 the London opposition claimed to speak for the country at large, and began to co-ordinate opposition in the provinces, especially in areas where the Tories were strong. In 1739 the liverymen's instructions to their MPs to support a place bill were echoed by twelve boroughs and five counties. The following year common council resolutions were taken up at local assizes in several parts of the country. And as the opposition to Walpole reached its peak in 1741, the London opposition's instructions to MPs became the model for dozens of constituencies.[85]

Contacts between opposition politicians in London and Dublin were already present during the 1720s and early 1730s: Swift, an old friend of Bolingbroke, at one time contributed to the *Craftsman*.[86] In the late 1730s the Irish writer Henry Brooke spent time in London and was introduced to the prince of Wales by William Pitt (then a member of the prince's household). Brooke's play, *Gustavus Vasa, the Deliverer of his Country* (1738) was probably written with the prince in mind.[87] Although the play

[83] Quentin Skinner, 'The Principles and Practice of Opposition', in Neil McKenrick (ed.), *Historical Perspectives. Studies in English Thought . . . in Honour of J. H. Plumb* (London, 1974), 93–128, at 113–24; J. C. D. Clark, 'A General Theory of Party, Opposition and Government, 1688–1832', *Hist. Jn.* 23 (1980), 295–325, at 317–18.

[84] Colley, *In Defiance of Oligarchy*, 116.

[85] Nicholas Rogers, 'Resistance to Oligarchy: The City Opposition to Walpole, 1725–47', in Stevenson (ed.), *London in the Age of Reform*, 1–29, at 9–12; id., 'Aristocratic Clientage, Trade and Independency: Popular Politics in Pre-Radical Westminster', in *P. & P.* 61 (1973), 70–106, at 73–5.   [86] Downie, *Jonathan Swift*, ch. 14.

[87] Clark, *English Society*, 179–80.

was banned in London at short notice—its theme could plausibly be seen as Jacobite—it was successfully performed in Dublin, under the title *The Patriot*. Besides these personal contacts, literature reflecting both Court and opposition viewpoints circulated in Dublin at this period.[88] Through such channels, the rise of a London opposition party, bent on countering oligarchy at local and national level, and invoking ancient rights and a civic republican tradition, was already well known in Dublin by the 1730s. An anonymous ode, composed to celebrate the election of Alderman French for Dublin city in 1733, praised the Dublin voters for displaying 'Something like the Patriot's Zeal', and went on to compare London and Dublin's respective contributions to the 'Patriot Cause':

> Your Love of Glory is the same
> You've both maintained the Patriot Cause
> Both in one Year, one Year of Fame,
> Gave Life to Liberty and Laws.
> While you oppos'd the *Grand Excise*,
> Here did a French and Stannard rise.[89]

Once established, the tendency to look for inspiration to England persisted. When the election campaign got under way in Dublin in 1748, the exploits of the English opposition were relayed to the Dublin electorate.[90] Although the fall of Walpole had not been followed by any significant reforms—the Jacobite rising of 1745 had forced the opposition on to the defensive—there were local triumphs to celebrate. The election of an independent candidate in Derby in 1748 was hailed in the *Censor* with the words 'Derby has lived to see the day of her deliverance'.[91]

One of the advantages of being informed about London opposition politics was that the Dublin campaigners of the 1740s could invoke Bolingbroke's *Dissertation on Parties* to counter the charge that they represented a 'faction' whose very existence was illegitimate. La Touche quoted this work in one of his early pamphlets in the reform campaign. He revealed that the city commons were apt to be abused by their critics as 'factious' and 'disturbers of the peace', and that they were labelled 'Patriots' and 'Tories'. La Touche was happy to accept the label 'Patriot', though not

---

[88] See e.g. *A Letter from Sir Robert Walpole to the Lord Bolingbroke* (Dublin, 1737), CULBC, Hib. 3. 730. 1 (12); on the opposition side, Henry Fielding's satire, *The Vernoniad* (1741) was printed in a Dublin edition.

[89] *Astrea's Congratulation*, CULBC, Hib. 3. 730. 1 (118). For French, see App. B below; for Stannard, see App. C below.

[90] Some items were published in Dublin editions: see e.g. *A Speech . . . by Sir John Bernard [recte Barnard] . . . in Support of a Bill for Repealing the Aldermens' Negative* (Dublin, 1749). Others were adapted. Lucas simply changed the title and added a preface to Bolingbroke's *The Freeholder's Political Catechism* (1733) for his *The British Free-Holder's Political Catechism* (Dublin, 1748).

[91] *Censor*, 24 (26 Aug.–2 Sept. 1749).

the 'Tory' one: he thought of himself as a Whig, and failed to see how it was possible for a Whig to be other than a Patriot. As for faction, he informed his readers that Bolingbroke had distinguished parties from faction, and that the former represented a national body of opinion with distinctive views about the form and method of governing, for the benefit of the whole community. If there was any 'faction' in existence, it was the aldermen, who consulted together to agree on policy before corporation meetings.[92]

Besides the term Patriot, the party tags of Whig and Tory were still routinely invoked in Dublin politics: all three formed part of the common political language shared with Britain. What was the significance of these party labels in Dublin during the 1740s, and how did they relate to the campaign led by Lucas and La Touche? Ever since the Hanoverian succession political power at ministerial level in both countries had been monopolized by those who, however much they disliked party labels on account of their factious connotations, were the political heirs of the Whig exclusionists. The Whig triumph had been even more complete in Ireland— where few Protestants were prepared to risk flirting with Jacobitism—than in England or Scotland, and by the 1730s little remained of the two-party configuration that had emerged in Queen Anne's reign. However, ideological conflict had not disappeared. On the church question, for instance, the Whigs were thought to be too ready to make concessions to Protestant dissenters who lacked the proper reverence for the church, and whose 'levelling' and republican associations had not been forgotten. (The execution of Charles I by Protestant extremists could still evoke bitter memories in Dublin as well as in England.)[93]

The first three decades of the eighteenth century had seen lively debates in Ireland over the issue of religious toleration for Irish Presbyterians, the introduction of a sacramental test for office-holders (1704), and the regium donum (the royal grant towards the maintenance of Presbyterian ministers). While the Tories were in office in the last years of Queen Anne's reign, Irish Presbyterians who refused to abjure the Stuarts were liable to persecution by hostile local authorities; it was not until several years after George I's accession that they obtained a toleration act, and even then the test was retained.[94] Apparently the test made little difference to those in the public service, but it did tend to exclude Presbyterians from commissions in the

---

[92] A Citizen [J. D. La Touche], *A Second Letter to the Commons of the City of Dublin* (Dublin, 1743).

[93] See *Fanatical Doctrine in a Sermon Preached in D——* (30 Jan. 1728), CULBC, Hib. 3. 730. 1 (63). On the demise of a two-party system in Ireland, see David Hayton, 'Walpole and Ireland', in Jeremy Black (ed.), *Britain in the Age of Walpole* (London, 1984), 95–119, at 99–100.

[94] J. C. Beckett, *Protestant Dissent in Ireland 1687–1780* (London, 1948), 65–71. The 1719 toleration act (6 Geo. I, c. 5) exempted Protestant dissenters from the obligation to attend established church services.

regular army and militia. In 1719 an indemnity act was passed to relieve those who had taken office without complying with the test requirements, but only a handful of Presbyterians sat in the Irish house of commons during the later part of George I's reign. At local level, the test initially operated to remove them from corporations in most parts of the country. But Dublin may well have retained a few Presbyterians on the common council through Anne's reign, and certainly by the 1740s even the board of aldermen included at least two dissenters. Among the freemen, the proportion was in the region of 15–20 per cent.[95]

It may seem strange that Anglicans and dissenters should quarrel over the church question, given the mutual interest of different denominations of Protestants in preventing the return of the Pretender and maintaining 'the Protestant interest' in Ireland. But however logical such a juncture might seem to be, that was not how the question appeared to many Anglican contemporaries. Popery was a danger, certainly; but for some, the immediate task was the preservation of the integrity and privileges of the Anglican church, which seemed to be particularly at risk from Protestant dissenters. This, at any rate, was the belief of Archbishop King, and of Dean Swift, and their views were upheld by the Irish house of commons, which showed no disposition to abolish the test. But although the test remained, Presbyterians could take some comfort in the defeat of the High Church party in the debate over tithe on pasture land in 1736.[96]

Accordingly, therefore, despite the absence of anything like a modern party system, some of the issues raised by the original Whig and Tory strife persisted. Moreover, the Jacobite threat had not receded. In these circumstances, political debate in Ireland as in Britain remained tied to a party rhetoric that dated back to the exclusion crisis, which in turn was overshadowed by memories of the execution of the king and the overthrow of the church in the 1640s.[97] Accordingly, reformers could still be forced on to the defensive by the charge that their programme, or their tactics, would endanger church and state. La Touche himself warned the city commons in 1743 to beware of those who pretended to love liberty, but who claimed a right 'to *dissent* from the *Established Church*, who constantly Drink in *Public* the *Rights* and *Liberties* of the City of *Dublin*, and in *private* the Memory of *Oliver Cromell* [*sic*]'.[98] Whether these 'Tory' sentiments

---

[95] Ibid. 48–9, 80–1; Murphy, 'Charles Lucas and the Dublin Election', 106. Of the 2,304 freemen who voted in the 1749 election, 83.1% were members of the established church, 2.7% were Quakers, and 14.2% were other Protestant dissenters (id., 'The Lucas Affair', 37).

[96] Beckett, *Protestant Dissent in Ireland*, 47, 62, 77–9, 92, 139; *A Letter from a Presbyterian in Dublin to his Friend in Scotland* (Dublin, 1735), 5–9.

[97] For the enduring vitality of Whig and Tory party labels in England, see Marie Peters, ' "Names and Cant": Party Labels in English Political Propaganda, *c*.1755–1765', in *Parl. Hist.* 3 (1984), 103–27; also Reed Browning, *Court Whigs*, 10–11.

[98] A Citizen [J. D. La Touche], *A Letter to the Commons of the City of Dublin*, 2nd edn. (Dublin, 1743), 3–4.

reflected La Touche's genuine fears for the church, whether he was trying to embarrass Lucas, or whether he was simply protecting himself against similar charges—he was, after all, the son of a Huguenot immigrant, albeit a conformist—is not clear. What is clear is that by 1749 Lucas's electioneering had aroused concern among the Dublin Anglican clergy, who accordingly rallied behind the aldermen.

What gave point to their anxiety, following Lucas's condemnation and flight, was the fielding by his supporters of a 'new light' Presbyterian merchant, Thomas Read, in his place.[99] In the crucial weeks between Lucas's departure and the poll, spokesmen for the church seized the initiative and brought out a publication called *The Church Monitor* (October–November 1749). The burden of its message was very similar to La Touche's in 1743: that Lucas's supporters were using the cry of 'Liberty' to promote the interests of 'Independents' (heterodox dissenters) in Dublin, who aimed to take over the management of the city, and pull down the church. Readers were reminded that such people had been responsible for the execution of Charles I. The aldermen, by contrast, could be supported with confidence, since they had the backing of the 'chief personages' and rulers of the kingdom. To vote for them was to support our now 'tottering CHURCH'.[100] This publication, however, was promptly challenged by *The Whigg Monitor*. Its first number appeared on 30 October 1749 ('Being the Birth-Day of his most sacred Majesty King George the 2ᵈ'). Its theme was that the question of who would rule Dublin was not between 'Churchmen and Independents' but between aldermen and merchants. London and Cork were cited as examples of cities where the citizens had the power of electing the aldermen: why not Dublin? Since the poll had by this time commenced, *The Whigg Monitor* was able to point out that several dissenters had in fact voted for the aldermen. By contrast, most of the supporters of Lucas and La Touche were 'Whiggs, in the proper Sense of the Word, Lovers of Liberty, of our present Happy Constitution in Church and State, and Enemies to *Usurpation* on the Constitution of this Loyal and Great City'.[101] These exchanges reveal how important the church question remained to politics.

In the light of all this, it is understandable why upholders of the status quo were apt to label opposition tendencies 'Whig' or 'Tory' almost indiscriminately. The most common charge against the supporters of Lucas and La Touche was that they were 'Patriots and Tories' (occasionally, 'Tories and Jacobites': labels earlier applied to Swift), indicating that they were perceived in the same light as the London opposition. Lucas himself

---

[99] 'New light' Presbyterians were opposed to tests for orthodoxy. Read had just completed a year as master of the merchants' guild.

[100] *Church Monitor*, 1 (27 Oct. 1749), CULBC, Hib. 3. 748. 1 (43).

[101] *Whigg Monitor*, 1 (30 Oct. 1749), ibid. (44). Most dissenters voted for the reformers (Murphy, 'The Lucas Affair', 204).

was also variously charged with being '*disaffected*, a *Presbyterian*, a *Low-churchman*, or a *Whig*'; with putting 'the church in danger', and with being a fomentor of 'popish mobs'. The pejorative use of these labels highlighted the tendency to link any challenge to the politics of deference with a desire to undermine the church.[102]

Apart from the continuing vitality of the issues associated with Whig and Tory debate, there was the problem of finding alternative labels for the political divisions in Dublin. It might seem a foregone conclusion that an opposition bent on restoring constitutional balance in the city and the kingdom should embrace the label 'Patriot': after all, its London counterpart was known by that name, and the term had been in use in Dublin for some time. And that label was used of the Dublin opposition, both by supporters and detractors. Yet Lucas himself occasionally preferred other terms.[103] His reservations sprang from his scepticism about certain 'great men', who, having pronounced themselves Patriots, committed to liberty and the public good, had gone on to obstruct Lucas's campaign. Lucas denounced such figures as 'mock-Patriots', or 'pretended Patriots', who lacked any real commitment to the maintenance of the constitution.[104]

Indeed, one of the by-products of the Dublin freemen's adoption of the language of civic Patriotism, and Lucas's questioning of the subordinate status of the Irish parliament, was that his critics were forced to elaborate what has been called a 'Court Patriot' ideology. This involved a complex balancing act. The reaction in Ireland to the Wood's halfpence affair indicated that some acknowledgement of local Irish rights was unavoidable; but Court spokesmen were apt to justify (even glorify) the existing relationship in which the British parliament both claimed and occasionally exercised the right to make laws for Ireland.[105] The justification advanced for accepting a subordinate role for the Irish parliament was 'security'; a pragmatic, if somewhat inglorious reason for forgoing the heady rhetoric of the civic Patriots. To judge by the Irish house of commons' condemnation of

---

[102] A Citizen [J. D. La Touche], *A Second Letter to the Commons of the City of Dublin*, 3; Lucas, *The Complaints of Dublin*, 22; *Censor*, 8 (15–22 July 1749); 11 (22–9 July 1749); 25 (11 Nov. 1749–21 Apr. 1750). On deference, see Frank O'Gorman, 'Electoral Deference in "Unreformed" England: 1760–1832', *JMH* 56 (1984), 391–429.

[103] Samuel Davey, *A View of the Conduct and Writings of Mr Charles Lucas* (Dublin, 1749), 4–5.

[104] [Charles Lucas], *A Miror for a Mock-Patriot: or, the Cork Surgeon Display'd; In a Letter to Himself*, i (Dublin, 1749), 3. As in England (Skinner, 'The Principles and Practice of Opposition', 99, 109), Irish politicians sometimes contested the 'Patriot' label with the opposition (John Gerard McCoy, 'Local Political Culture in the Hanoverian Empire: The Case of Ireland, 1714–1760', D.Phil. thesis (Oxford, 1993), chs. 1–4, 7).

[105] 'we are by our very Constitution, a Kingdom dependant upon *Great Britain*; and . . . asserting the contrary, is the very Doctrine of the Popish *Irish* Rebels, who Massacred our Grandfathers in 1641' (Anon., *An Appeal to the People of Ireland . . . By a Member of the Incorporated Society for Promoting English Protestant Schools in Ireland* (Dublin, 1749), 7–8. For Court Patriots see John G. McCoy, 'Court Ideology in Mid-Eighteenth Century Ireland: An Examination of Political Culture', MA thesis (NUI (Maynooth), 1990).

Lucas in 1749, these views found broad support in parliament.[106] Even James La Touche made use of such arguments. Having won a seat at the election, he was faced with a petition against his return lodged by the defeated Alderman Charles Burton.[107] Speaking in his own defence in the Irish house of commons, La Touche was careful to distance himself from Lucas, and produced the picturesque maxim: 'from this dunghill Dependence we pluck the sweet Flowers of Peace and Security'. (The verdict, however, went against him.)[108]

The willingness of Lucas's critics to accept a subordinate status for the Irish parliament inevitably gave an 'English' complexion to their position, while the opposition's stand suggested the description 'Irish'. Since 'English' was still almost synonymous with 'Protestant', the Court writers were able to attack Lucas on this point, warning his supporters not to become carried away so as to forget their lasting interest, which lay in preserving the affection and protection of Great Britain.[109] This raises the question of whether the opposition might have adopted the description 'Irish' for themselves, in contrast to the 'English' position of the Court. They rarely did so, again because of the associations raised by these terms. As Sir Richard Cox's usage showed, if 'English' and 'Protestant' were still used synonymously, so too were 'Irish' and 'Popish'.[110] But quite apart from this difficulty, there was the fact that Lucas saw himself fighting for constitutional rights that were common to both countries. The cause of the citizens of Dublin was that of the citizens of London, and vice versa; the cause of the Irish parliament was that of the British parliament, and vice versa. There was a common interest in restraining the royal prerogative within its proper bounds, especially now that it was armed with growing powers of patronage; and a common interest in restraining the powers of the aldermen in their respective capital cities. It was consistent with this outlook that Lucas could sign one of his pamphlets 'Britannicus', while La Touche (despite his Court tendencies) used the pseudonym 'Hibernicus'.[111] With so

---

[106] *Commons Jn. Ire. 1749–56*, v. 14; McCoy, 'Local Political Culture in the Hanoverian Empire', 244–5; Robert E. Burns, *Irish Parliamentary Politics in the Eighteenth Century* (2 vols.; Washington, 1990), ii. 103–10.

[107] Sir Charles Burton, below, App. B.

[108] A Briton, *History of the Dublin Election*, 80, 148–50.

[109] Anthony Litten (pseud.: Sir Richard Cox), *The Cork Surgeon's Antidote, Against the Dublin Apothecary's Poyson* (Dublin, 1749), v. 5. Cf. David Hayton, 'Anglo-Irish Attitudes: Changing Perceptions of National Identity Among the Protestant Ascendancy in Ireland, ca. 1690–1750', in John Yolton and Leslie Ellen Brown (eds.), *Studies in Eighteenth Century Culture*, 17 (1987), 145–57, at 147.

[110] Hayton, 'Anglo-Irish Attitudes', 147. The *Censor Extraordinary*, 13 (19–21 Aug. 1749), asserted that Ireland had experienced tyranny from kings, lords, priests and aldermen 'sufficient to make us . . . abjure the Name of Irishmen, or . . . throw off the Yoke'.

[111] Hibernicus [J. D. La Touche], *A Freeholder's Address*; Britannicus [C. Lucas], *A Free-Man's Answer to the Free-Holder's Address*. In the 1720s 'Britannicus' had been the pseudonym of one of the most libertarian of the English Court Whigs, Bishop Benjamin Hoadly of Bangor.

many difficulties in the way of a new two-party nomenclature, it is not surprising that the old one was so often pressed into service.

V. *The Electoral Breakthrough*

Consider, my dear Friends, that you are not a *hidden People*, you are neither placed in a *dark Lanthorn*, nor *put under a Bushel*. You are the Metropolis of a great Nation, a Light set upon our highest Hill, to illustrate your whole Country by the bright Shining of your Example.[112]

Two weeks before Lucas's condemnation by the Irish house of commons on 16 October 1749, a cobbler, Robert Whitty of Patrick Street, published an open letter to the 'Free Citizens' of Dublin. In this letter Whitty likened Lucas to one who had discovered that his fellow citizens, obscure men, were in fact heirs to a great estate. If he, Whitty, had ten thousand votes, the letter continued, Lucas would have them all. The freemen ought to vote for Lucas so that 'Foreign Nations . . . will . . . bless sweet *Dublin* for making so rare a Choice'.[113]

Whitty's enthusiasm was widely shared among the freemen, but it would be wrong to suppose that this popularity could easily be translated into votes for Lucas and La Touche. On the contrary, elections were public occasions for displaying the relationships of deference and paternalism that underpinned the social and political hierarchy. A disparaging description appeared in an early number of the *Censor*:

The usual Method of solliciting [votes] is this: The *Candidate*, attended by several *knowing* young Fellows, who have been bred *Bailifs' Followers*, or *Clerks to Sub-Sherifs*; sometimes, by the *Agents* of *Lords*, and other great Men, parades all the Streets and Lanes in Town. These *Jack-Calls* set the Game; that is, inform the *Candidate* that such, or such a Man is at Home. Then calling with him the *Landlord*, or *Agent*, the *best Customer*, or *principal Creditor* of the Citizen, the *Candidate* makes his Request, which is, by some of his Attendants, powerfully seconded.[114]

When it is further recalled that polling took place openly, it is remarkable that a candidate such as Lucas, who lacked the customary wealth of an alderman, and who had nothing in the way of patronage, influence, connections or custom to offer an elector in return for his vote, could so much as consider standing for parliament. To account for it contemporaries invoked a classical precedent: Cincinnatus, whose name became a feature of campaign literature.[115]

---

[112] Anon. (Henry Brooke), *A Tenth and Last Letter from the Farmer, to the Free and Independent Citizens of Dublin* (Dublin, 1749), 6. Cf. Matt. 5: 14–16.
[113] Robert Whitty, *A Letter to the Free-Citizens of Dublin* (Dublin, 1749), CULBC, Hib. 3. 748. 1 (45).
[114] *Censor*, 2 (3–10 June 1749); O'Gorman, 'Electoral Deference', 396–9.
[115] See *A Free-Briton's Advice to the Free Citizens of Dublin* (Dublin, 1748), 10–11.

How were these obstacles to independent voting to be overcome? Up to a point, sermons (from the occasional sympathetic clergyman) and speeches could help.[116] But the most important means of communicating with the electorate was through printed material: broadsheets, pamphlets, and newspapers. While Lucas's own output of *Letters, Addresses, Advice,* and so on, was prodigious, it was one of his chief propagandists, Henry Brooke, who produced some of the most compelling rhetoric, bearing in mind that he was writing for a relatively unsophisticated audience, the tradesmen and shopkeepers who formed the Dublin electorate. Brooke was already well known in Dublin for his publications, such as his *Farmer's Letters to the Protestants of Ireland* (1745), which in the year of the Jacobite rising in Scotland urged Protestants to be on their guard against the Catholics. (In fact, Irish Catholics made no move to support the rising.) Brooke was also a veteran of the Patriot campaign in London, and was himself solicited by the Dublin citizens to become a candidate in the election. Although he declined to stand, he threw himself into the campaign, again styling himself 'The Farmer'.[117]

Brooke adopted a varied approach in his *Letters* to the citizens, ranging from exhortations to examples, fables, classical and contemporary analogies. His style was occasionally convoluted, but it was undeniably impressive, mainly because he relied, more heavily than any of the opposition writers, on a strong biblical manner, with messianic overtones. (For his readers, the Bible would have represented the single most familiar piece of literature.) Brooke did not scruple to present Lucas as a latter-day prophet: 'Prophecy and Patriotism are Endowments of a Peculiar Nature . . . they are Sparks, which Heaven alone can kindle . . . To what, if not to such a Spirit as this, can we ascribe the *Powers* of your Fellow Citizen? a Man despised for his Trade, his Poverty, his Pretensions!' Claiming that the word 'Patriot' had only recently acquired significance in Ireland, Brooke envisaged a glorious role for Ireland in reviving Patriot values:

Can any Good, I then said, come out of Galilee?[118] I now can answer Yes . . . that it is here, and here alone, where the Life of Essential Liberty seems at length to revive; where VIRTUE seems to prepare her seat . . . That while the *American, African* and *Asian* Worlds groan under universal bondage; while most of Europe hath bowed to the *Yoke* . . . while even in *Britain* the Terms Liberty and Patriotism are secretly

---

[116] When Lucas was sworn in as master of the barber's guild Revd. Moses Magill preached a celebratory sermon in St Mary's church on the text 'Seest thou a Man diligent in his Business? he shall stand before Kings, he shall not stand before mean Men' (Prov. 22: 29): *A Word to the Wise, or . . . Lucas is the Man* (1748), CULBC, Hib. 3. 748. 1 (4).

[117] Henry Brooke (1703–83), writer. Son of Revd. William Brooke, Co. Cavan; educated TCD, active in the London opposition group linked with the prince of Wales. Back in Ireland, Brooke obtained a government post for his *Farmer's Letters* (1745). Took up Lucas's cause in 1749 (see *DNB*).

[118] Cf. John 7: 52: 'for out of Galilee ariseth no prophet'.

ridiculed as *chimerical* . . . it is to *Ireland* alone, as to the *Heart*, where the *Animal Spirits*, the *Vital Heat* of *Political Nature* appear to make their Retreat; from hence I trust to re-expand, to . . . carry Life and Health anew throughout the whole System.[119]

From here it was a short step to exalting the role of the independent and virtuous representative, in terms that contained an echo of Christ's own steadfastness in the face of temptation:

He can gain no Riches by Over-reaching, nor Friends by Fawning. . . . He cannot bend his upright Soul to humour his Patrons by a base Compliance, or to serve his Protectors by Iniquity . . . If Preferment should happen to lie in so very direct a Road, he accepts it with Gratitude, and he dischargeth his Trust with Faith and unwearied Application; but he quits all Preferment rather than shut his Mouth upon the Truth; he is prepared to resign his Post, if he cannot hold it with Honour. Yet all this he does for the Love of Truth alone; for he expects not to find Protection when Persecution is begun, nor Hopes for any Asylum when once obnoxious and forsaken . . . This, my Friends, is the very Extremity of all Evils that can happen to the Virtuous. Even so, he can fall no lower than the Rock of his own Integrity; and God can call Friends to him from the Wildernesses and the Desarts [*sic*], and *command that these Stones may be made Bread for his Servants*.[120]

Brooke also addressed the voters more directly:

You are the Alpha and Omega, the Beginning and the End . . . Insomuch, that there is not a single Permission of Guilt, Injury, Injustice or Insult throughout the Nation, of Encroachment on Possession or Usurpation of Right, for which Electors are not principally and finally answerable . . . It is by the Liberty of Spirit which we now shew, in the Reclaiming of our own Dues, and in the Assertion of our proper Privileges, that we are apt and evidently prepared to defend those Rights, that are still greatly dearer and more interesting unto Us; even the Rights of his sacred Majesty and these his free Dominions, on whom our proper Rights inclusively depend . . . [When you] demonstrate to the World [that] you tread superior to private Influence . . . you will give a singular Example of living Illumination, to all other Counties and Corporations in the Kingdom. You will give a public Testimony and Sanction to Virtue. You will render it fashionable, approved, and applauded . . . You will deliver down the signal Precedent to many Generations; and when you shall have passed away, future Centuries who shall reap the Harvest of your Truth, in all the blessed Enjoyments of Liberty and Prosperity, will recognize the glorious Ancestors by whom the Seed was sown.[121]

[119] Anon. [Henry Brooke], *An Occasional Letter from the Farmer, to the Free-Men of Dublin* (Dublin, 1749), 3–5. There are parallels with American millennialism and 'apocalyptic Whiggism' in the 1760s, which, though not yet revolutionary, contained much provincial patriotism: *America* would witness the start of the millennium and the downfall of tyranny. See Ernest Lee Tuveson, *Redeemer Nation: The Idea of America's Millennial Role* (Chicago, 1968), 23–4; Ruth H. Bloch, *Visionary Republic: Millennial Themes in American Thought, 1756–1800* (Cambridge, 1985), 47–50.

[120] Cf. Matt. 4: 3.

[121] Anon. [Henry Brooke], *A Ninth Letter from the Farmer to the Free and Independent Electors of the City of Dublin* (Dublin, 1749), 4–5, 8, 12, 15.

In taking Reformation images—('the Reclaiming of our own Dues', 'the Assertion of our proper Privileges')—and applying them to the civil sphere, Brooke, like Lucas, was following in the tradition of Harrington and others who saw an intimate link between the liberty of the gospel and civil liberty.[122] Just as Protestants had reasserted the rights of the laity usurped by a corrupt popish oligarchy, the virtuous freeman was urged to reclaim rights withheld by a corrupt civic oligarchy. In fact, contemporary Irish Protestantism was also undergoing a period of renewal. George Whitefield had visited Dublin in 1738 and met an enthusiastic response, as did the Moravian John Cennick in 1746, while the Wesley brothers, John and Charles, both made visits in 1747.[123] These spiritual reformers all carried a similar message: that the laity were capable of a personal relationship with Christ, and could take greater responsibility for their own moral and spiritual welfare. In church as well as state, therefore, the 1740s witnessed a tendency, not so much to challenge the establishment directly, or its right to lead (after all, Brooke himself was a landowner, and John Wesley was an ordained clergyman), as to place greater emphasis on the individual's capacity for effective restorative action.

Already by 1748 the cumulative impact of repeated appeals to their public spirit was having its effect on the Dublin freemen. A satirical pamphleteer, writing as if in support of the aldermen, observed, 'the Commons and Citizens are grown so *Proud*, and so Arrogant, that they must be humbled . . . They now read News Papers, drink *Porter*, Smoke Tobacco, and Talk, as freely of Religion and Politics, as the Londoners'.[124] Yet rhetoric alone, however high-pitched, was unlikely to overturn deferential habits of voting as long as voters continued to act as individuals; for it was as individuals that they were open to all the force of personal influence. It seems likely that some sort of structure was necessary to promote a sense of group solidarity. In Dublin's case, such structures were available in the form of the guilds.

In the early decades of the eighteenth century the guilds as such appear to have played no very important part in parliamentary elections. It was unusual for candidates to attend guild meetings in order to solicit votes from tradesmen *en bloc*. However, an earlier critic of oligarchy, Counsellor Howard, was said to have gone round the guildhalls to canvass in 1727,[125] and his example was followed by Lucas and La Touche. They were welcomed to many guildhalls, and invited to speak. Such was Lucas's support in the guilds that when in July 1749 both the aldermen and the city commons censured Lucas (for querying whether the summons to a

[122] Goldie, 'The Civil Religion of James Harrington'.
[123] R. Lee Cole, *A History of Methodism in Dublin* (Dublin, 1932), 16–23.
[124] Ant. Constitution (pseud.), *A Short and Easy Method*, 23–4.
[125] A Briton, *History of the Dublin Election*, 103–4.

corporation meeting had been properly served) fifteen of the guilds voted to condemn the majority in the commons, in some cases defying their masters and wardens to do so.[126]

The unprecedented level of interest displayed by the guilds in this election prompted even the aldermanic candidates, Burton and Cooke, to make a brief tour of the guildhalls. A report of one of Burton's speeches suggests that he was rather out of his depth in trying to follow opponents who had deployed both oratorical skills and populist sentiments:

He endeavoured to shew ... that Eloquence is in no Sort to be looked on as a Qualification for a Member of Parliament; that it was seldom made Use of, with a Design to persuade, but only with a Design ... to depreciate ... the Characters, or Persons of Rivals ... that, if he cou'd not himself speak in publick, there were a sufficient Number in the House of Commons, who cou'd; and it was well known, that the greatest Part of those were his Relations, or particular Friends ... that most People might mistake their own Talents, but if he knew his own Heart, it was an honest one ...[127]

Burton concluded his speech by exhorting his audience to obey authority, love one another, and avoid faction. That such sentiments could be expressed by one who was regarded by his backers (because of his Old Whig connections) as a strong candidate, likely to draw off votes from the opposition, is a reflection of how exceptional anything like an election address was at this time. Evidently it was quite enough in normal circumstances for an aldermanic candidate to be honest, rich, and have highly placed friends.

There was, however, in the reported version of Burton's speech one concession to the new-style electioneering. Burton reportedly said that 'he had Understanding enough to receive Instructions'.[128] Instructions to parliamentary representatives (as already noted) was a tactic that had been used occasionally in London politics since the exclusion crisis; the practice became common between 1739 and 1742 during the build-up of opposition to Walpole. They were used as an alternative to civic petitions or addresses that might invite the aldermanic veto.[129] In Dublin, it was Lucas's guild, the barber-surgeons, that seems to have pioneered the practice, by issuing formal instructions to its representatives on the city commons in 1744. During the parliamentary election campaign, Lucas indicated that as an MP he would be guided by the instructions of his constituents, and in 1749 certain guilds responded to this invitation by formulating their own.[130]

---

[126] Murphy, 'Charles Lucas and the Dublin Election', 98.

[127] A Briton, *History of the Dublin Election*, 31–2.   [128] Ibid. 32.

[129] Colley, *In Defiance of Oligarchy*, 165–9; Rogers, 'Resistance to Oligarchy', in Stevenson (ed.), *London in the Age of Reform*, 12.

[130] Barber-surgeons' guild minute book, TCD, MS 1447/8/2, fos. 12–17ᵛ; *Censor*, 2 (3–10 June 1749); report of saddlers' guild meeting, *Censor Extraordinary*, 16 (9–15 Sept. 1749).

The idea of the public representative as one who stayed in close touch with his constituents, was guided by their wishes and diligent in his parliamentary attendance, not unnaturally gave rise to the question of payment for MPs, especially because Lucas himself lacked independent means. It was typical of the outlook of the opposition that the proposal for payment should be represented as the revival of a 'good old Custom'.[131] Nothing came of these speculations in the 1740s, but the idea was taken up again in the 1760s, when Lucas had actually achieved a parliamentary seat.

One other constitutional issue discussed in the *Censor* was the freedom of the press. This issue arose after an attempt by the Irish house of commons to make James Esdall, Lucas's printer, identify Lucas as the author of certain publications. As in so many other cases, the British constitution was invoked as embodying the highest state of purity then in existence ('In England, [public writers] are held Sacred'). But even in England, where (according to the *Censor*) such writers enjoyed a parliamentary-type privilege, the freedom of the press had come under attack during Walpole's administration. Irishmen were warned that the same fate lay in store for them: it was all too easy for a people 'lulled in golden Dreams of *Liberty*, to be awaked from the flattering Vision, by the *galling and ratling of their Chains*'. Accordingly, Irishmen should waste no time in discovering whether they were in fact 'Freemen' or 'Slaves'—and, if the former, they should be alert, for 'To the Freedom of the Press, We are indebted for all the Blessings of the *Reformation . . . and [for] the Restoration of Liberty* and Our *Constitution*, in Church and State'.[132]

The first number of the *Censor* had announced the intention of collecting histories of all the Irish cities and corporate towns, in order to see why so many had fallen into a state of 'devastation'—by which was meant political as much as economic decline.[133] It seems appropriate to consider, before leaving the Dublin campaign of the 1740s, what impression (if any) it had made elsewhere. Since the 1749 election was a by-election only, the rest of Ireland had no particular reason to be drawn into the debate. However, in September 1749, Henry Brooke was quizzed by friends in the country with 'What News? . . . nothing I suppose but *Liberty* and *Lucas*'.[134] There does seem to have been some effort to carry news of the campaign beyond the capital. The freemen of Kilkenny were informed of the progress of the election by 'A Tribune of the People of Dublin'; and by 1752, an

---

[131] Philo-Hibernicus, *His Letter of Advice to the Free-Men, and Free-Holders of the City of Dublin* (Dublin, 1748), 8.
[132] *Censor*, 25 (11 Nov. 1749–21 Apr. 1750). A stamp tax had been imposed on the English press in 1712.
[133] *Censor*, 1 (3 June 1749). See also n. 32 above.
[134] The Farmer to the Censor, *Censor*, 18 (23–30 Sept. 1749).

investigation had begun in the city of Waterford into the ancient charters.[135] Even in London, the downfall of Lucas ('the famed Patriot'), and the Dublin election results, were reported in some detail.[136]

[135] Lucius Severus Publicola (pseud.), *To the Freemen and Freeholders of the City of Kilkenny . . . From . . . a Tribune of the People in Dublin* (Dublin, 1748); T. Cunningham (ed.), *Magna Charta Libertatum Civitatis Waterford* (Dublin, 1752); Milne, 'Irish Municipal Corporations', 156, 162.
[136] *The Gentleman's Magazine*, xix (Nov. 1749), 523.

4

Civic Patriotism in Action:
Setbacks and Gains, 1750–1773

> Surely we should, with the utmost Gratitude . . . call to our Minds that
> critical . . . Period, in which the glorious Spirit of Liberty first took its
> Rise in this great Metropolis, as its proper Fountain-head, and spread
> itself through the whole Nation, animating with its genial Heat all
> Ranks and Degrees of People; a People long absorb'd in a deadly
> political Lethargy, and galled with the heavy Chain of slavery![1]

Lucas's unprecedented election campaign of 1748–9 called into being a civic
Patriot movement that was influential down to the French revolutionary era
and, thanks to the survival of the old order in Britain and Ireland into the
nineteenth century, even beyond. When a provincial 'independent' interest
made its appearance in the 1750s, when the Volunteers of the 1770s and
1780s exulted in their rights as 'freemen', when members of the Catholic
Committee in the early 1800s were applauded for conducting themselves
'like freemen', they all owed something to the pioneering anti-oligarchical
efforts of the Dublin freemen.[2] And while the Volunteers were an *ad hoc*
body, the Dublin freemen could look to the corporation and the guilds as
vehicles for a sustained political role. The appearance of an extra-
parliamentary public opinion among tradesmen and shopkeepers was
bound to be controversial; and in the early days hostility was the more
marked because the advent of the freemen into the political arena was
accompanied by an upsurge in street politics in Dublin, which constituted
an intermittent problem for the authorities from the 1750s on.

This chapter will examine the varying fortunes of those who supported
the anti-oligarchical campaign in Dublin during the 1750s and 1760s.
Conventional accounts of the Patriot movement, which focus mainly on the
activities of the Irish parliament, portray this as a relatively quiescent
period, with only the money bill dispute and the campaign for regular

---

[1] Anon., *A Letter to the Citizens of Dublin. By a Farmer* (Dublin, 1766), 9. The author
claimed (p. 3) that he was not 'The Farmer' (Henry Brooke) who had used that pseudonym in
the 1740s.

[2] A. P. W. Malcomson, *John Foster: The Politics of the Anglo-Irish Ascendancy* (Oxford,
1978), 116–17; Grattan, *Memoirs of the Life and Times of Henry Grattan*, ii. 320–1; Brian
MacDermott (ed.), *The Catholic Question in Ireland and England 1798–1822: The Papers of
Denys Scully* (Dublin, 1988), letter 214 (n. 4).

general elections to enliven it. If, however, the broader civic Patriot objectives are taken into account, then the picture that emerges is one of more solid achievement. By the 1760s the oligarchic grip on corporate life in Dublin had been undermined, while the guilds and the city commons component of the corporation were beginning, cautiously, to adopt the part of guardians of the constitution, and were implementing reforms in order to protect and enhance that role. At the same time, the limits to the anti-oligarchical challenge will be noted: city Patriots shared many of the assumptions of those who took a 'Court' or Castle position.

I. *Civic Patriotism Survives, 1750–1760*

The 1750s began badly for the supporters of Lucas. Their champion had been forced to flee (following his condemnation by the Irish house of commons as an enemy to his country), and although La Touche won a seat at the ensuing poll, his return was overruled by the house of commons on the pretext that he and Lucas had used illegitimate means to influence the voters.[3] Even Dublin corporation, despite the strong guild presence in the lower house, joined the chorus of condemnation, agreeing to disfranchise Lucas.[4] There could scarcely have been a stronger demonstration of the hostility of virtually the entire Irish establishment towards those who had challenged the politics of deference. Another decade was to pass before a measure of municipal reform, embodying part of Lucas's programme for the restoration of ancient rights, was finally won.

That decade was spent by Lucas in exile in England and on the Continent. While in England he vigorously pursued the cause of Patriot reforms (both civic and national), attempting, though with limited success, to enlist the support of London corporation,[5] and warning that infringements of the liberties of Ireland and of the American colonies might be only the precursors of similar developments in Britain.

In Dublin, the events of late 1749 gave only a temporary check to the campaign's impetus. Following Lucas's flight, his printer James Esdall also absconded, while Andrew Miller, an engraver who had sold pictures of Lucas entitled 'An Exile for his Country', was detained in prison for nearly two weeks without charge—Ireland, unlike Britain, had no habeas corpus act—and was then freed on conditions that were not made public.[6] This had

---

[3] The result was Samuel Cooke, 1,543; J. D. La Touche, 1,499; Charles Burton, 1,411; Thomas Read, 1,283 (*An Alphabetical List of the Freemen and Freeholders of the City of Dublin Who Polled at the Election for Members of Parliament* (Dublin, 1750), 89). See also Burns, *Irish Parliamentary Politics*, ii. 110.
[4] CARD ix. 315–16; DCA, C1/JSC/2, pp. 74–6.
[5] At least one lord mayor of London failed to present Lucas's case to London corporation (*An Appeal to the Commons and Citizens of London. By Charles Lucas, the Last Free Citizen of Dublin* (London, 1756), 18–21).
[6] Burns, *Irish Parliamentary Politics*, ii. 109; Pollard, *Dublin's Trade in Books*, 20.

a deterrent effect on printers who, it was alleged, became wary of printing anything emanating from the Free Citizens, an apparently *ad hoc* body of freemen who had come together in the confused days surrounding Lucas's condemnation and flight.[7] Furthermore, it was claimed that in the aftermath of the dispute, those who had supported Lucas and La Touche were excluded from any share in civic patronage. But far from cowing the popular party, such tactics merely increased the determination to justify their conduct. When a pamphlet went on sale in London and Dublin claiming that the guilds' endorsement of Lucas and La Touche had been obtained by irregular means, the barber-surgeons' and the hosiers' guilds issued a statement setting the record straight. When this statement in turn was presented by a Dublin grand jury (Easter 1750) the barber-surgeons' guild went to court in a bid to quash the presentment. Emboldened by a legal ruling that the presentment had no legal significance, the Free Citizens decided to go on the offensive by seeking a ruling in King's Bench as to whether acts of the lord mayor and common council were valid without the assent of the citizens at large. It had been Lucas's contention, based on his interpretation of Dublin's charters, that such acts were not valid; and the Free Citizens invoked precedents for wider popular participation in civic government from London, Cork, Limerick, and Galway.[8]

Two aspects of this phase of the campaign are worth noting. First, the sense of self-importance gained as a result of the events of the 1740s. The Free Citizens claimed

That it is of the greatest Consequence to the *Liberty* of a free Country, that the *Spirit* of it should be kept up amongst the Inhabitants; that the Freemen of the several Cities and Corporations do compose the greatest part of the Community of the Kingdom; that the Example of the *Capital* will always have a great Influence on the Minds, Sentiments and Affections of *other* Corporations . . .[9]

They also argued that it was only their rights as citizens 'which . . . distinguishes the Subjects of a free and limited Monarchy, from the Slaves of an arbitrary Prince'. Secondly, the Free Citizens were anxious to attest their Hanoverian credentials and repudiate charges of Tory or Jacobite leanings; they even felt constrained to deny that any supporters of the reform candidates in 1749 had voted for the Tories in 1713 (the last occasion on which Tories had contested a Dublin seat).[10] Clearly they continued to feel vulnerable to charges of disloyalty and disaffection.

---

[7] Anon., *The Case of the Free-Citizens of Dublin*, I (n.p. [1750]), CULBC, Hib. 3. 748. 1 (46), p. 1. In 1750 the Free Citizens, sometimes called the 'Free Electors', or the 'Free and Independent Electors' (*Censor*, 26 (21–8 Apr. 1750) raised funds to defend the guilds for supporting Lucas. In 1754 they congratulated Sir Samuel Cooke on his Patriot stand: see *The Free-Citizens Address to Sir Samuel Cooke, Bart.* (London, 1754), CULBC, Hib. 7. 750. 3. See also below, Ch. 5.   [8] *The Case of the Free-Citizens of Dublin*, I, II.

[9] Ibid. II p. 2.   [10] Ibid. I p. 3.

However, local rights were about to receive a boost from a somewhat unexpected quarter: the Irish parliament. The house of commons' condemnation of Lucas held out little hope that its members would stir themselves in defence of Irish rights. Yet that condemnation had skirted the contentious issue of Ireland's 'dependency' on the British parliament,[11] and where their own privileges were concerned, MPs had from time to time displayed sensitivity. In 1731, for instance, the executive had asked the house to agree to a permanent provision for funding the Irish national debt (which might have freed government from the need to summon parliament regularly). Opposition to the proposal was strong, and the debate was the occasion for a dramatic entrance into the house of commons by Colonel Charles Tottenham, MP for New Ross, who rode through the night to be present. Covered in mud, and still wearing his great jack-boots, he arrived just in time to vote, giving a majority of one against the measure; and the name of Tottenham became one to toast in Patriot circles. Thanks to Lucas, public attention during the late 1740s had been directed towards the rights of local parliaments as well as to those of urban corporations: their independence constituted the '*great Bulwark* of our LIBERTY'.[12] A print of Colonel Tottenham was on sale in Dublin at the time of the by-election of 1749,[13] and when the money bill issue arose in the 1750s there already existed a high degree of awareness about its significance.

It was rare for the Irish treasury to be in surplus, but thanks to a buoyant economy, such a situation arose in 1749, and again in 1751 and 1753. Because it was uncommon, the respective rights of the sovereign and the Irish parliament in disposing of the surplus had not been clarified. It was the lack of trust between the Castle and the leading Irish politicians that brought the differences out into the open. Henry Boyle, speaker of the house of commons and informal 'undertaker' (manager of government business in parliament in return for a share of patronage) suspected, rightly, that the Castle was anxious to reduce his power, and consequently came to view the outcome as reflecting on his own standing and influence.[14] In dealing with the surplus in 1749 he and his allies had inserted into the money bill a formula implying that parliament's rights in this matter took precedence over those of the king. The viceroy, the earl of Harrington, was in no

---

[11] *Commons Jn. Ire.* 1749–56, v. 14; A Briton, *History of the Dublin Election*, p. 44. The unanimity of the vote condemning Lucas was somewhat misleading. A more accurate reflection of MPs' views is to be found in the sizeable minority of over 50 MPs who in 1750 voted that La Touche should keep his seat (Burns, *Irish Parliamentary Politics*, ii. 110).

[12] *Censor*, 5 (24 June–1 July 1749); Burns, *Irish Parliamentary Politics*, ii. 8.

[13] A portrait of Tottenham 'in his boots' by James Latham, dated 1731, hangs in the National Gallery of Ireland.

[14] Henry Boyle (1682–1764), speaker of the Irish house of commons 1733–56, earl of Shannon, 1756 (see *DNB*). See also Declan O'Donovan, 'The Money Bill Dispute of 1753', in Bartlett and Hayton, *Penal Era and Golden Age*, 55–87; Burns, *Irish Parliamentary Politics*, ii, chs. 4, 5.

position to make a stand, for he was indebted to Boyle for his part in orchestrating the parliamentary attack on Lucas, thereby removing a serious political embarrassment. But Harrington was succeeded in 1750 by the duke of Dorset, who was sympathetic to those Castle politicians, led by Primate George Stone, an Englishman, who wished to curb Boyle's power.[15] In 1751 Boyle persuaded the house of commons to modify the viceroy's proposed formula, which indicated the king's 'previous consent' to the disposal of the surplus, but later the house gave way when the original wording was restored by the English privy council under the operation of Poynings' law.

The outcome of this limited confrontation produced considerable dissatisfaction in Dublin, with the politicians who had promoted the persecution of Lucas coming in for particular criticism. Accordingly, when the Irish parliament met for its next session in 1753, at the start of an economic depression, metropolitan opinion was already aroused, and MPs were met with addresses calling on them to stand by Irish rights. Some of these addresses, however, displayed downright cynicism at the prospect of the 'charade' about to be enacted in parliament.[16] Against this background, Boyle, who had become seriously alarmed after his opponents had scored a victory in the house in the case of a disputed election result, decided on a trial of strength. Although there was no disagreement about the use to which the treasury surplus should be put—the reduction of the Irish national debt[17]—Boyle and his supporters sided with opposition MPs in their renewed resistance to the insertion into the money bill of the controversial 'previous consent' formula. Around the city, these politicians did not scruple to hint that if government got its way, Irish wealth would be drained away to benefit the king's dominions in Hanover, and no more parliaments would be held in Ireland. When the 1753 bill returned from England with the formula reinstated, popular hostility was palpable: according to the viceroy's son, it was only with difficulty that 'the mob' was prevented from breaking into the house of commons during the debate.[18] The bill was defeated in the house by 122 votes to 117.

The defeat of the money bill produced great demonstrations of joy in

---

[15] George Stone (?1708–64), son of a London banker; chaplain to the duke of Dorset, viceroy; appointed archbishop of Armagh, 1747, and lord justice, 1747. Stigmatized during the money bill crisis for seeking to destroy Ireland's liberties, he subsequently became something of a Court Patriot (Burns, *Irish Parliamentary Politics*, ii, chs. 3–6, 8).

[16] See e.g. CULBC, Broadsides (Ire.), Hib. 1. 679. 1 (75), (76). For the economic background, see Cullen, *Princes & Pirates*, 20–1; Stubbs, 'The Weavers' Guild', 70.

[17] O'Donovan, 'The Money Bill Dispute', 58.

[18] Lord George Sackville to Pelham, 2 May 1752; same to same, 18 Dec. 1753 (PRONI, Henry Pelham papers, T 2863/1/40, T 2863/1/62). The alleged priority of Hanover was a recurrent complaint in Britain (Jeremy Black, 'The Crown, Hanover and the Shift in British Foreign Policy in the 1760s', in J. Black (ed.), *Knights Errant and True Englishmen* (Edinburgh, 1989), 113–34, at 114–19).

Dublin: celebrations and bonfires went on all night. When Dorset took the drastic step of dismissing Boyle and other leading office-holders for their part in the bill's defeat, he was stigmatized as an opponent of Irish liberties; while Boyle, Sir Richard Cox,[19] and others, hitherto execrated as the scourges of Lucas, were hailed as latter-day converts to genuine Patriot principles. Eulogies on their stand now superseded earlier sceptical comment about the coming meeting of parliament,[20] and government supporters reached for their pens to try to dampen the popular enthusiasm.[21] Following a civic dinner attended by members of the nobility and gentry, the lord mayor and sheriffs were summoned before the privy council to account for the fact that printed copies of the toasts, insulting to the viceroy and Primate Stone, were being hawked around the city.[22] Several Dublin guilds conferred honorary freedoms on the leading opposition figures. Even Sir Samuel Cooke, who had voted against the bill, found himself the object of congratulatory addresses and effusive regrets that his candidature for Dublin city had ever been opposed by the popular party. Sir Samuel appears to have played an active part in orchestrating the expression of metropolitan sentiment, on one occasion presenting an address to Speaker Boyle, accompanied by thirty or forty merchants, and 'two or three hundred mob', who went round the city groaning or cheering, as appropriate, at the homes of the leading politicians.[23]

The presumption that the office-holders had experienced a real change of heart, however, could not be long sustained. The London government decided to recall Dorset, and his successor, the marquess of Hartington, reached a compromise with the dismissed politicians that led to their reinstatement in office. Boyle resigned the speakership, but was created earl of Shannon. By the spring of 1756 it was hard to avoid the conclusion that Boyle and his supporters had simply allied with opposition MPs as a tactic in their tussle with the Castle.[24] If this realization strengthened the tendency to take a cynical view of 'mock-Patriot' politicians, certain individuals

---

[19] Sir Richard Cox, grandson of the lord chancellor of that name in Queen Anne's reign; a prime mover against Lucas in 1749; collector of customs for Cork, 1750; dismissed for his vote on the money bill, 1754 (Burns, *Irish Parliamentary Politics*, ii. 105, 108, 114–15, 178).

[20] See e.g. *Kildare's Welcome to Ireland*; *A New Ballad to be Sung by the C——t Party on the Seventeenth Day of December, 1754*, CULBC, Hib. 1. 679. 1 (77), (87).

[21] Anon. [Archdeacon John Gast], *A Letter to the Tradesmen, Farmers, and the Rest of the Good People of Ireland. by L. B. Haberdasher and Citizen of Dublin*, 2nd edn. (Dublin, 1754); id., *A Second Letter to the Tradesmen, [etc.]* (Dublin, 1754).

[22] Diary of Sir Dudley Ryder, 28 Feb. 1754 (PRONI, Harrowby papers, T 3228/1/65).

[23] *The Free-Citizens Address to Sir Samuel Cooke, Bart.* (London, 1754); Stopford-Sackville MSS, HMC 9th Rep., App., pt. iii, p. 50. The chandlers' guild was one that conferred freedom on Cooke for his opposition to the bill (Evans, 'Ancient Guilds of Dublin', NLI, MS 738, p. 42).

[24] Burns, *Irish Parliamentary Politics*, ii. 200–13. Boyle was burned in effigy in Dublin (J. L. McCracken, 'The Conflict Between the Irish Administration and Parliament, 1753–6', *IHS* 3 (1942), 159–79, at 177).

emerged with enhanced reputations. These included Lord Kildare: his dramatic, though ultimately abortive, self-appointed mission to England to acquaint the king himself with the divisive tactics of Stone and the Castle party earned him great popular acclaim, and did something to restore confidence in the aristocracy as champions of Ireland's interests.[25]

The money bill dispute therefore had a number of important implications for Irish politics. On the eve of the dispute, it looked as if Patriotism in Ireland had become, and might well remain, a purely municipal phenomenon, lacking any significant support among the aristocracy and gentry. One sarcastic pamphleteer suggested that most Irish MPs were wise enough to follow the example of the 'mother country', preferring 'commerce, riches and prosperity' to civil and political liberties.[26] By 1754 it was clear that the issue of Irish parliamentary rights was still capable of mobilizing significant gentry support (as in the case of Wood's halfpence thirty years earlier), even if motives of self-interest were also present. Ministers now began, routinely, to refer to opposition MPs as 'Patriots, as they call themselves'.[27]

Secondly, the dispute shifted attention away from the municipal sphere and focused it on the Irish parliament. Certainly, Lucas had contended for Irish parliamentary rights; but these had remained somewhat in the background, at least until 1749. Moreover, the eventual reconciliation between Boyle, his allies, and the Castle powerfully vindicated Lucas's emphasis on the necessity for the freemen to act as constitutional watchdogs; and from this point onwards MPs came under scrutiny for their public statements and conduct. Parliamentary votes on key issues were published and analysed.[28] At the same time, the degree of popular interest in the subject was an indication to MPs that support for opposition causes could have political and electoral advantages. For this dispute, reflecting as it did divisions within the élite, aroused interest well beyond Dublin; several corporations instructed their MPs to oppose the altered money bill, and in some areas the lesser gentry seized the chance to assert themselves by taking the opposition side.[29] The Castle was forced to take opposition politics in the capital seriously—the Tholsel, or city hall, had been a venue for Patriot meetings—and to set about winning over opposition supporters on the aldermanic board.[30]

---

[25] Anon., *A Vindication of L—— K——e's Memorial* (Dublin, 1753). When Kildare (James Fitzgerald, 1722–73) took office as master-general of ordnance in 1759 it did not seriously damage his Patriot credentials because the appointment was made by the English Patriot, William Pitt.

[26] Anon., *A Letter to the Fool* (n.p. [c.1753]), CULBC, Hib. 1. 679. 1 (74).

[27] *Stopford-Sackville MSS*, HMC 9th Rep., App., pt. iii, p. 52; Archbp. of Tuam to Ryder, 30 Nov. 1754 (PRONI, Harrowby papers, T 3228/1/66).

[28] See e.g. Andrew Freeman [pseud.], *A Letter From a Gentleman in the City, to a Member of Parliament in the North of Ireland* (n.p., 1757), CULBC, Hib. 7. 749. 1 (8).

[29] PRONI, Henry Pelham papers, T 2863/1/62; Malcomson, *John Foster*, 116–17.

[30] *Stopford-Sackville MSS*, HMC 9th Rep., App., pt. iii, 52–4.

Thirdly, the return of Irish parliamentary rights to the centre of Patriot concerns inevitably gave a new significance to the issue of legislative union with Great Britain. It has already been noted that from the 1690s on there had been substantial support among the Protestant élite (mainly on commercial grounds) for a union with England. These sentiments had been boosted by the Scottish union with England in 1707, and for some time afterwards union continued to find support among Irish Protestants, not least among Commonwealthmen, whose concerns were mainly libertarian. Swift's satire *The Injured Lady* (not published until 1746, but written much earlier) reflected the sense of grievance that Scotland, apparently lacking the qualities that made an Irish union so desirable, had stolen a march on her rival. But the London government had shown no interest in an Irish union, and as decades passed, in which the Irish parliament took on a more active legislative role, the issue tended to drop out of sight.[31] As late as 1751, the earl of Hillsborough (the anonymous author of *A Proposal for Uniting the Kingdoms of Great Britain and Ireland*) did not see the issue as a controversial one in Ireland. The earl argued along familiar lines that the two countries already enjoyed common interests—the protection of civil liberty and the Protestant church establishment—and that a union would render them 'one People in Affection, as well as Interest'. Union would also promote Protestant immigration into Ireland, thereby strengthening religion as well as encouraging economic development. For her part, Britain would gain from closer links with Irish Protestants, whose acknowledged zeal for limited monarchy and the house of Hanover would buttress civil and religious liberty at home and abroad, in opposition to the forces of popery, passive obedience, and non-resistance.[32]

That such arguments had not lost all their appeal for opposition politicians may be gauged by a remark made by Lucas, who spent much of the 1750s in exile in England, where he continued to affirm that the British constitution afforded more real liberty than any other. Following the money bill débâcle he was gloomy about the Irish parliament's capacity to achieve any real independence of ministerial direction. It might almost be regarded as a mere register of royal edicts, and as such, a danger to remaining liberties in Ireland and Britain. Consequently, Lucas asked,

Will it not rather be more wise and just, while any Sense of Liberty remanes among the People to intitule them to inroll with the Family of *Britain*, with the same Care to rescue them from domestic as from foreign Destruction, and unite them effectually, as *Scotland* has been, with this Kingdom?[33]

---

[31] Kelly, 'Origins of the Act of Union', 244–5.
[32] *A Proposal for Uniting the Kingdoms of Great Britain and Ireland* (London, 1751), 3–6, 12–13, 38–9.
[33] Lucas, *An Appeal to the Commons and Citizens of London*, 6. By the 1760s Lucas had adopted the popular anti-union view (Kelly, 'Origins of the Act of Union', 248 n. 55).

Such a question makes it particularly plain that Lucas's goal was not a nationalist one of Irish independence from Britain, but the preservation of a particular set of *ancien-régime* liberties.

But if the exiled Lucas was prepared to entertain, in principle, the desirability of a union on libertarian grounds, the idea turned out to be anathema to the artisans of Dublin, who had seen the city grow in size and prosperity during the decades in which the Irish parliament had established itself as a regular part of the legislative process, and who resented even the current levels of commercial control exercised by the London government.[34] From the 1750s on, Dublin was periodically to witness the spectacle of the 'purposive crowd',[35] predominantly local in composition, and (though lacking any formal status) claiming some sort of communal representative function—particularly in opposing the danger, or rumoured danger, of a union. The first outbreak occurred in 1759.[36] Suspicions were aroused by a bill prepared by the administration to enable the crown to summon the Irish parliament in an emergency by proclamation (the country was at war with France, and a similar provision had already been made in respect of the English parliament). On 3 December the inhabitants of the Liberties, the centre of the textile industry, were roused by the beating of a drum. Crowds gathered, and several ministers on their way to parliament, including the lord chancellor and the attorney-general, were threatened and assaulted. Some MPs were stopped and were tendered an oath that they would not vote for a union. Before the disturbances were quelled, a mob broke into the house of lords, and, in parody of parliamentary proceedings, placed an old woman in the chair.

Although William Pitt, secretary of state in the London government, was anxious to be assured that the disturbances could be laid at the door of 'papists' and 'emissaries of France', Dublin Castle was inclined to blame Protestants.[37] Certainly, Protestants in the textile trades had been strong supporters of Lucas and La Touche; the latter's victory at the polls in 1749 owed a great deal to support not merely from the weavers, for whom La Touche was one of their own guild members and a major employer, but from the sheermen and dyers, the feltmakers, and the hosiers (Table 4.1). Moreover, the weavers' guild was, after the merchants, the most numerous in the city: 258 weavers polled in 1749. While it is unlikely that the leading

---

[34] Seamus Cummins, 'Extra-Parliamentary Agitation in Dublin in the 1760s', in Comerford, Cullen, Hill, Lennon (eds.), *Religion, Conflict and Coexistence*, 118–34.

[35] See Lucas, 'The Crowd and Politics', 422.

[36] Sean Murphy, 'The Dublin Anti-Union Riot of 3 December 1759', in O'Brien (ed.), *Parliament, Politics and People*, 49–68; Cummins, 'Extra-Parliamentary Agitation', 122–4.

[37] *Correspondence of John, Fourth Duke of Bedford: With an Introduction by Lord John Russell* (2 vols.; London, 1842–3), ii. 399–401; Murphy, 'The Dublin Anti-Union Riot', 54–5, 57–61.

TABLE 4.1. *Voters by guild casting both votes* for the anti-oligarchical candidates, La Touche and Read, Dublin city by-election, 1749*

75–100%	50–74%	25–49%	0–24%
Sheermen and dyers	Weavers	Carpenters	Bakers
	Curriers	Saddlers	Cooks
	Tanners	Glovers	Apothecaries
	Hosiers	Goldsmiths	Brewers
	Feltmakers	Tailors	
	Chandlers	Shoemakers	
	Joiners	Smiths	
	Barber-surgeons	Merchants	
		Bricklayers	
		Coopers	
		Cutlers	
		Butchers	

* Only 15.6% of the freemen voters split their votes between the anti-oligarchical and aldermanic candidates, thus reflecting how seriously the issues were taken in this election (a further 2.5% of freemen cast just one of their votes).

Source: Calculated from *An Alphabetical List of the Freemen and Freeholders of the City of Dublin, Who Polled at the Election for Members of Parliament* (Dublin, 1750) (RIA, HP vol. 214).

employers themselves took part in the riots,[38] the journeymen weavers still contained a substantial Protestant element, with a lively tradition of parades to commemorate the battle of the Boyne.[39]

However, there were Catholics, too, among the journeymen in the textile trades: the skills were not difficult to acquire, and it was hard to enforce guild regulations that forbade the taking of Catholic apprentices. Thus, while the composition of the crowd was probably mixed, and drawn principally from those who lacked formal political qualifications, the context of action was the political consciousness acquired by the Protestant freemen in the 1740s. The evidence also suggests that in this case, as in other contemporary instances, the crowd demonstration was not spontaneous, but carefully planned in advance, and directed by sections of the élite—who in this case have been identified as students from the college (who had long-standing links with the weavers in the earl of Meath's Liberty), disappointed placemen, and even magistrates.[40] Willingness on the élite's part to

---

[38] The weavers' guild denied involvement (Murphy, 'The Anti-Union Riot', 57). Several of the rioters were textile workers (ibid. 63).

[39] Evans, 'Ancient Guilds of Dublin' (NLI, MS 738, p. 48).

[40] See Murphy, 'The Dublin Anti-Union Riot', 63; Jim Smyth, *The Men of No Property: Irish Radicals and Popular Politics in the Late Eighteenth Century* (Dublin, 1992), 128; *A Letter to the Right Honourable James, Earl of Kildare, on the Present Posture of Affairs*, 2nd edn. (Dublin, 1754), 23–7. On the wider issue of élite leadership or crowd autonomy see Lucas, 'The Crowd and Politics', 430–2; Rogers, *Whigs and Cities*, ch. 10.

encourage street politics suggests that in this period danger from the crown
and executive still appeared more potent than that from 'the mob'.

At civic level, the cause of reform had not dropped out of sight. In 1750, a
group of merchants and traders addressed the king, protesting against the
excessive powers bestowed on the lord mayor and aldermen by the 1672
new rules. Nothing came of this, and again in 1753 a body describing itself
as the 'Merchants, Traders and Citizens of the City of Dublin', expressed
the hope that the king would one day take into consideration the case of
'this great Metropolis' and its administration.[41]

In the corporation itself some of the impetus for reform was lost in the
early 1750s, although a drive to recover lapsed property and other rights
continued unabated. It was not until 1755 that the issue of the respective
rights of the aldermen and city commons came to the fore again, on the
occasion of the election of an alderman who was an acting sheriff. This was
not without precedent, but the commons were now more sensitive to the
prospect of one of their own officials becoming a member of the board, thus
compromising their own independence; and the question proved to be
contentious among the aldermen themselves.[42] The commons petitioned
parliament against the excessive powers of the board, calling for Dublin to
be divided into wards on the London model. In 1756 and again in 1758
heads of bills for reform of the corporation were prepared in parliament,
but on being referred to the viceroy and the English privy council they were
either altered or suppressed.[43] The relative weakness of mercantile interests
was sharply demonstrated when, in response to a number of mercantile
banking failures, the Irish parliament in 1756 passed an act prohibiting
merchants engaged in foreign trade from conducting banking business.[44]
With the corporation demonstrably failing to protect mercantile interests,
the oligarchical nature of city government became still more controversial.
The lord mayor's failure to take effective action to curb the anti-union
rioters in 1759 angered the viceroy and completed the growing isolation of
the city fathers;[45] and the board itself now came round to the view that
some sort of reform was necessary.

At this point, then, the question was not whether city government should
be modified, but how sweeping any changes should be. On the one hand,

[41] *To the King's Most Excellent Majesty. The Most Humble Address of the Merchants,
Traders, and Citizens of the City of Dublin* (Dublin, 1753), CULBC, Hib. 3. 748. 1 (49).

[42] *CARD* x. 33, 101–2, 350–2, 488–99; DCA, MR/19, pp. 265–73.

[43] Murphy, 'The Lucas Affair', 218, 221–2. The 1758 bill would have divided Dublin into
wards, and added 34 members to the lower house: the aldermen disliked the proposed 'popular
manner of electing magistrates and officers': *Commons Jn. Ire.* 1749–56, v. 316, 374, 403; vi.
83, 86–7, 93.

[44] 29 Geo. II, c. 16; Cullen, *Princes & Pirates*, 20–1.

[45] Murphy, 'The Dublin Anti-Union Riot', 60–1. The corporation condemned the
disturbances, but placed their origins outside the city's jurisdiction (i.e., in the Liberties):
CARD x. 395–7.

there was the case Lucas had made out for giving extensive rights to the commons and citizens, including a citizens' veto over corporation measures, through the revival of the old court of darein hundred. This case rested on the authority of ancient charters. On the other hand, there was a minimalist position, supported by those who appealed to custom and patriarchal values. One such was James Grattan, the recorder of Dublin. Although he conceded that changes were needed (he was prepared to see the guilds electing their own city commons' representatives) Grattan deplored 'alterations [that] take away all Pre-eminencies, or, which is the same Thing, spoil them of every Thing that is valuable, leaving only a Name of Distinction, which, in such a Case, would soon become ridiculous'.[46] No one appealed to abstract rights. One pamphleteer did ask whether civic honours shouldn't be 'indiscriminately open to every Claim of Merit',[47] but since he was looking to ancient Rome, it is likely that he still took for granted a distinction between active citizens (freemen) and others.

In January 1760 Grattan and the aldermen obtained the city commons' assent to a very modest set of reform proposals;[48] in the event, the 'Act for the Better Regulating the Corporation of the City of Dublin' (1760) went a little further, ending all vestiges of the aldermen's veto over guild representatives. Sponsored by the city MP Sir Charles Burton, the act gave the guilds the power of direct election of their own city commons representatives. Those so elected were to follow a trade served by their guild—an important restatement of the link between rights and functions. The city commons acquired the right to veto the aldermen's choice of a lord mayor, and also gained a role in the selection of aldermen. On a vacancy occurring, the aldermen would draw up a list of four sheriffs' peers from whom the commons would choose one. Conversely, the two sheriffs would be selected annually by the aldermen, from a list furnished by the commons of eight resident freemen, each possessing property worth £2,000.[49] The act thus vindicated, in part at least, the campaign by the reformers over the two previous decades, and was a tribute to the ability of long-established institutions in Ireland to adapt to changing conditions.

[46] Anon. [James Grattan], *A Second Letter to a Member of the Honourable House of Commons of Ireland. Containing a Scheme for Regulating the Corporation of the City of Dublin* (Dublin, 1760), CULBC, Hib. 7. 749. 1 (14), p. 11. For Grattan, see below, App. B. The Grattans were one of the great Dublin families, whose legendary clannishness was noted by Swift (*Stopford-Sackville MSS, HMC. 9th Rep., App., pt. iii*, 38–9).

[47] Anon., *Queries on the Government of this City, Humbly Offered to Public Impartial Consideration* (Dublin, 1760), CULBC, Hib. 3. 748. 1 (51).

[48] The aldermen would have retained some right of veto over nominees to the city commons (*CARD* x. 404–8; DCA, C1/JSC/1, pp. 394–5).

[49] 'An Act for the Better Regulating the Corporation of the City of Dublin, and for Extending the Power of the Magistrates Thereof, and for Other Purposes Relative to the Said City', 33 Geo. II, c. 16; *Commons Jn. Ire. 1757–60*, vi. 197, 213, 228, 233.

II. *The Dublin Patriots Consolidate their Gains, 1760–1773*

The passing of the Dublin reform act was followed within months by the death of George II in October 1760 and the accession of his grandson, George III. The new king's accession was of no ordinary significance. He was the first of the Hanoverian monarchs to be born in England; the first to speak English as his native tongue; the first to be born into the established church. Moreover, for decades opposition politicians in England had been conjuring up visions of a 'Patriot king', who would unite the country by ending the Whig grip on office and making appointments on merit. Accordingly, the young king (he was 22 when he came to the throne) was greeted with general acclaim. Not only Anglicans but Protestant dissenters and Catholics outdid each other in presenting fulsome addresses of loyalty. Never had the dynasty, or, by extension, the Protestant constitution, looked so secure.[50]

In the euphoria surrounding these events, Lucas received a pardon from the new king,[51] and returned to Dublin in time to be a candidate for the general election (May 1761) following on the accession of the new monarch. The aldermanic interest, hoping to profit from its recent conversion to municipal reform, fielded three candidates.[52] The two strongest came close to taking both seats, a prospect only averted by prompt action during the poll itself. At the request of the two independent candidates (Lucas and one of the sitting MPs, Colonel James Dunn[53]), a meeting of the 'Free Electors' was convened. The state of the poll suggested that it was impossible for both of them to be returned, and that if both continued to poll, Lucas 'whom the Free Electors had invited to return and reside among them, with Intent to choose him one of their Members in Parliament' would fail to be returned. (It is only fair to add that Lucas's candidature was hampered by doubts about his eligibility.)[54] Colonel Dunn acceded, apparently with a good grace, to the request to stand down in Lucas's favour. The final state of the poll bore out Lucas's supporters' assessment of the relative strength of the candidates; the recorder, James

---

[50] Clark, *English Society*, 179–84, 216. The euphoria did not last long (Colley, *Britons*, 401); also below, Ch. 5.

[51] *Charlemont MSS i*, HMC 12th Rep., App., pt. x, 268–9.

[52] James Grattan (recorder), Alderman Sir Charles Burton, one of the sitting MPs (below, App. B), and Perceval Hunt (lord mayor 1755–6).

[53] Dunn (below, App. B) was a Presbyterian who won the seat vacated by Cooke's death in 1758 (Henry Holmes, *An Alphabetical List of the Freeholders and Freemen, Who Voted on the Late Election of a Member to Represent the City of Dublin . . . Also, a Succinct Account of the Elections for Said City from 1749 to 1773 Inclusive* [Dublin, 1774], 38).

[54] *The Free-Electors Address to Colonel Dunn. With his Answer* [1761], CULBC, Hib. 3. 748. 1 (55). The poll was over by 6 May; Lucas was only readmitted to the civic franchises, after seeking legal redress, on 21 May (*CARD* xi. 18–19; *To the Right Honourable the Lord Mayor, Sheriffs [etc.] . . . The Memorial of Charles Lucas, M.D.* (n.p., n.d.), CULBC, Hib. 3. 748. 1 (4)).

TABLE 4.2. *Guilds giving 50% or more of their votes to the independent candidates* at 2 or more of the Dublin city elections of 1749, 1761, and 1773*

1749 and 1761	1749 and 1773	1749, 1761, and 1773
Tanners	Joiners	Weavers
	Feltmakers	Hosiers
	Sheermen and dyers	
	Chandlers	

* La Touche and Read (1749), Lucas and Dunn (1761), Redmond Morres (1773). In the case of the 1749 and 1761 elections '50% or more' means that at least half of those voting cast both votes for the independent candidates. In 1773 voters could choose only one candidate.

Source: 1749 (as Table 4.1); *An Alphabetical List of the Freemen and Freeholders that Polled at the Election of Members to Represent the City of Dublin* (Dublin, 1761) (CULBC, Hib. 8. 761. 1); [Henry Holmes], *An Alphabetical List of the Freeholders and Freemen, Who Voted on the Late Election of a Member to Represent the City of Dublin* (Dublin, 1774).

Grattan, finished well ahead of Lucas, who nevertheless made second place. Alderman Burton, the other sitting MP, polled well, but lost his seat.[55]

A poll book reveals that support for Lucas and Dunn was strong among the textile trades, and, as in 1749, among the trades associated with processing cattle products (Table 4.2). Dunn withdrew days before the poll ended, but he and Lucas still won over half the tanners' votes, and the chandlers were not far behind. All these trades were particularly vulnerable to commercial legislation passed in the British parliament. While some restrictions were being eased—as in the British act of 1759 that removed curbs on the import of Irish cattle into Britain—such measures, like the recurrent wartime embargoes, served as a reminder that control remained in British hands, remote and inaccessible to pressure from Dublin tradesmen. Moreover, in the short term the 1759 act threatened to rob tanners and tallow chandlers of their raw materials, and local resentment was vented on those who came over to Dublin from Britain to buy cattle.[56]

Lucas's election was greeted with acclaim not just in Dublin, but in those localities where an 'independent' interest had emerged during the 1750s. Accordingly, Lucas considered that his representative role should be national as well as local: 'my Care and Regards must extend to the utmost Limits of the Realm, giving Preference to those particular Counties and Cities, who have been pleased to distinguish me with Marks of their Regards and Confidence'.[57] He was to remain in the forefront of opposition politics until his death in 1771. During that period he brought his

[55] *An Alphabetical List of the Freemen and Freeholders that Polled at the Election of Members of Parliament to Represent the City of Dublin* (Dublin, 1761). The result was James Grattan, 1,569; Charles Lucas, 1,302; Charles Burton, 1,210; James Dunn, 1,057; Perceval Hunt, 653; J. D. La Touche, 77.

[56] Cummins, 'Extra-Parliamentary Agitation', 121.

[57] Lucas, *Address to the Free Electors*, CULBC, Hib. 3. 748. 1 (56).

characteristically apocalyptic style[58] to bear on a range of civic republican or Country themes: abuses of the royal prerogative by the king's ministers (facilitated by the operation of Poynings' law); the need for regular general elections; the threat posed by churchmen who failed to uphold liberty, and the evils of a standing army. By the 1760s, opposition MPs in general enjoyed a higher profile, and this phase of Lucas's career has been largely ignored. He appears never to have made much impact in parliament as an orator; this was a period when oratorical skills were much admired. Besides, unlike other Patriot politicians such as the duke of Leinster or Henry Flood, Lucas had no independent fortune, and never built up a nexus of parliamentary supporters. His links with the provinces, too, apparently remained largely rhetorical.

Yet as a point of contact with metropolitan opinion Lucas had no rival. His output of pamphlets on topical issues, many of them directed to his constituents, remained prodigious. And while he was ambivalent in his view of street politics (deploring riots while blaming government for outraging popular feelings), his defence of the right of tradesmen to participate in public affairs through their guilds and corporations, and his championing of equal access to political office, set him apart from contemporary Irish politicians: 'It is the wisdom of our policy . . . to exclude no Man from the highest Offices and Ranks in the State. The Bullock-driver and the Tradesman have alike clamed and obtained the high, the judicial, as well as the Legislative Offices of State in these Kingdoms.'[59] He put his principles into practice by seeking instructions from his constituents as to measures he should support in parliament,[60] and by issuing statements when important matters were under discussion. Together with Henry Brooke, Lucas helped to found the *Freeman's Journal* in 1763, which brought his brand of Patriotism to an even wider audience.

Two main political crises occurred during his parliamentary career which illustrate how closely linked civic and parliamentary Patriotism had become, and how much Irish Patriots in the 1760s still saw themselves as engaged in a common task with the Patriots of Britain and America. Both concerned a perceived abuse of the royal prerogative. The first arose in 1766 over the inclusion in a bill (to prevent the export of corn from Ireland at a time of dearth) of a dispensing power, placed in the hands of the British

---

[58] See e.g. *Address to the Free Electors*.

[59] Charles Lucas, *A Third Address to the Right Honourable the Lord Mayor, the Board of Aldermen, [etc.]* (Dublin, 1766), 38–9. For Lucas's view of street politics, see (id.), *An Answer to the Counter Address of a Pretended Free Citizen, . . . Addressed to Sir James Taylor, Knt.* (Dublin, 1766), 8–9, 17. Bolingbroke had earlier stressed that 'ordinary Men' could contribute to the 'Liberties of their Country' (*The Freeholder's Political Catechism*, in (id.), *A Collection of Political Tracts*, 206).

[60] Lucas, *Address to the Free Electors*. Lucas also returned to the city commons in 1762, representing the barber-surgeons' guild (*CARD* xi. 480).

privy council. Lucas objected to this ostensibly because it relegated the Irish privy council to a subordinate position, but more fundamentally because for him, as for the British opposition, vesting a dispensing power in the crown raised the spectre of Stuart-style despotism. He was horrified at one argument, that the crown had the right to veto or alter any bill, save money bills, of the Irish or the British parliaments. If this were so, he asked, 'in what would an *Irish* or a British Legislature differ from the shattered Remnants of the Gallic Parlements, which are forced to receive, register, or pass . . . the Mandates or Edicts of their mighty Monarch?'[61]

Lucas stayed in close touch with his constituents during the bill's progress, issuing addresses to the lord mayor and citizens outlining the pernicious aspects of the measure. Such a practice was strongly condemned by his critics for its alleged tendency to excite mobs and 'a riotous, illegal Opposition' outside parliament.[62] Others, however, were filled with admiration; one observer urged the Dublin citizens to pay Lucas a stipend ('Wages from the People') so as to enable him to keep up the dignity of an MP. After all, the writer pointed out, it was Lucas's 'Ciceronian Pen' that had awakened the 'Spirit of Liberty', first in Dublin, and subsequently elsewhere: 'The Years 1748, 1749, and 1766 will surely be remembered by yourselves and Your Posterity, to the last Generation, as Years the most auspicious to Liberty, of any that have been, or shall be, recorded in the Annals of your City, or indeed of the whole Kingdom.'[63] (The city commons, under pressure from the guilds, attempted on several occasions to secure a stipend for Lucas out of corporation funds, but the proposal was regularly rejected by the aldermen.)[64]

The other crisis arose at the end of the decade. A new viceroy, Lord Townshend, was anxious for Ireland to contribute to rising imperial defence costs. After rejecting the proposal in 1768, the house of commons agreed to it in 1769, but almost immediately inflicted a defeat on the viceroy by rejecting a money bill on the grounds that it had not originated in the house. The government considered the matter was one of principle, and Townshend prorogued parliament.[65] This action called forth Lucas's last great defence of Irish constitutional liberties, *The Rights and Privileges of Parlements*

---

[61] Charles Lucas, *A Second Address to the Right Honourable the Lord Mayor, the Aldermen, [etc.]* (Dublin, 1766), 13. In a parallel row in England, an English corn act was suspended by order in council.

[62] Anon., *To the Right Honourable the Lord Mayor of the City of Dublin. The Counter Address of a Free Citizen* (Dublin, 1766), 8. Similar charges were directed against Pitt, another populist politician (Richard Pares, *George III and the Politicians* (Oxford, 1967), 54–5.

[63] *A Letter to the Citizens of Dublin. By a Farmer*, 10–12.

[64] *CARD* xi. 472–3; DCA, C1/JSC/3, p. 55; Archbp. of Tuam to Ryder, 27 Jan. 1766 (PRONI, Harrowby papers, T 3228/2/9).

[65] Thomas Bartlett, 'The Townshend Viceroyalty, 1767–72', in Bartlett and Hayton (eds.), *Penal Era and Golden Age*, 88–112, at 96; id., 'The Irish House of Commons' Rejection of the "Privy Council" Money Bill of 1769: A Reassessment', *Studia Hib.* 19 (1979), 63–77.

(1770), and provoked more outbursts of street politics, in which journeymen weavers again figured prominently. On their way to the customary St
Patrick's Day ball at the Castle in 1770, members of the aristocracy and
gentry found their progress barred by crowds in Dame Street, who scrawled
'Wilkes and Liberty' (the current London crowd slogan) on their carriages,
and demanded of the occupants, 'Are you a Patriot?' The city commons
displayed its Patriot credentials by proposing to insert into an address to the
king a request that the Irish parliament be recalled; when this move was
blocked by the aldermen, the commons had its own resolutions on the
matter printed. A meeting of parliament, the resolutions indicated, would
help to remedy the depressed state of agriculture, manufactures, and
trade.[66] When parliament was at last recalled in February 1771, a letter in
the *Freeman's Journal* urged the Dublin city commons to give a lead to
urban corporations everywhere by opposing 'arbitrary Taxation' (American
precedents were by now in mind). As MPs gathered for the new session,
government supporters were given rough treatment by 'a desperate mob,
armed with clubs, cutlasses, etc.', who were convinced, once again, that the
recent political upheavals heralded the approach of legislative union.[67]

For all Lucas's zeal in consulting his constituents, it remains necessary to
stress how little development had taken place in his constitutional thinking
since the 1740s. To the end of his life he remained preoccupied with
preserving a constitutional balance through upholding the independence
and virtue of parliaments, corporations, and guilds. And as a counterweight
to oligarchy and excessive ministerial power, Lucas continued to emphasize
not so much the natural rights of man, as the 'Rights of Christians', or the
'Privileges of Englishmen [which] are hereditary and indefeasable [*sic*]'.[68]

Meanwhile, the 1760s saw the consolidation of gains achieved through
the Dublin corporation act. This can be detected in several areas; a new
willingness by the guilds and city commons to pass resolutions on
constitutional matters (though this practice was at first used sparingly); a
move towards greater internal democracy; and a desire to protect recent
gains by reasserting corporate privileges, and by advancing the civic reform
programme that had been under way for some decades.

One effect of the reform act was to vest in the guilds the right of selecting
their own representatives for the city commons. This did not put an end to
attempts by aldermen and others to influence the outcome, but it did
encourage more democratic procedures in the guilds. As the city commons

[66] DCA, C1/JSC/3, pp. 76, 89.
[67] Evans, 'Ancient Guilds of Dublin', NLI, MS 738, pp. 64–5; *Freeman's Journal (FJ)*, 19–
21 Feb. 1771. Dublin's journeymen weavers were in contact with London weavers in efforts to
keep up wages (Doyle, 'The Dublin Guilds', 8–10; Rudé, *Wilkes & Liberty*, 101).
[68] Charles Lucas, *A Third Address to the . . . Lord Mayor, [etc.]*, 40; id., *The Rights and
Privileges of Parlements Asserted Upon Constitutional Principles; Against the Modern Anti-
Constitutional Clames of Chief Governors* (Dublin, 1770), 68.

had argued in the 1740s, 'liberty ... consists ... in the controul of the many, on the proceedings of the few'.[69] It had been the case in most guilds since Charles II's reign that a minority of the members (the master, wardens, and council) acted for the brethren in making by-laws, admitting freemen, and selecting the lists from which the aldermen chose commons representatives. At the Michaelmas assembly of the prestigious merchants' guild in 1760 a petition for restoring to the whole guild the right of electing guild representatives was carried unanimously. Later in the decade the stationers' guild ruled that a by-law of 1675, which allowed the guild's council to nominate the candidates for master and wardens, was contrary to the spirit of its charter, and that the right should be restored to the whole guild. The saddlers' guild, likewise, decided that for the future the commonalty should have a right to vote in electing or displacing the guild's council.[70]

The city commons reflected this mood. In 1766 (confirmed in 1769) the commons decided that all the corporation's committees should contain two members of craft guilds for every member of the merchants' guild or sheriffs' peer, and in 1772 the commons attempted, unsuccessfully, to increase its own representation on committees at the expense of the aldermen.[71] These tendencies, reinforced by the commons' new role in the selection of civic officials, ultimately witnessed some redistribution of power within the corporation. It would be going too far to say that the balance of power shifted from the merchants' guild to the craft guilds, and from the aldermen to the city commons, but there was a perceptible tilt in that direction. Before the 1760 act it had been rare for members of the craft guilds to reach the aldermanic board and the mayoralty. Over a period of several decades the balance was gradually redressed; whereas during the 1760s only one lord mayor was a member of a craft guild, by the decade 1800–10 the proportion was half and half. The composition of the commons also changed. Down to 1760 when the aldermen alone selected sheriffs and aldermen, the number of sheriffs' peers—those who had served as sheriff but had not been promoted to the board—had been small, rarely exceeding sixteen or seventeen, although the 1672 rules allowed for up to forty-eight. Once the commons obtained a share in selection, their choice for sheriff sometimes fell on those who did not appeal to the aldermen as members of the board, and the numbers of sheriffs' peers soon grew: by the 1780s they had doubled. The presence of such a large, permanent bloc (sheriffs' peers retained their seats for life) gave the commons a greater sense of continuity and experience. The upshot of all this was to heighten the importance of guild representation on the commons, and the triennial elections became objects of much interest to the press.

[69] *CARD* ix. 630; Lucas, *A Third Address to the ... Lord Mayor, [etc.]*, 6–7.
[70] DPLGC, MS 79, fo. 208; NLI, MS 12125, p. 6; NLI, MS 81, fo. 62.
[71] DCA, C1/JSC/3, pp. 5, 136.

The guilds approached the political arena into which they had so suddenly been catapulted with caution and restraint. The conventional picture of bodies that did little but pass political resolutions is wide of the mark. The merchants' guild, doubtless because of its great size and status (there were over 600 members at mid-century), took the most active role, but even the merchants confined their efforts to one or two standard opposition themes, passing several resolutions in favour of a measure for shorter parliaments (1761, 1767, and 1768) and deploring the principle of a standing army (1768). They also asserted their right, even their duty, to instruct their representatives in parliament and on the corporation—a right which, however, they exercised for the most part in a general way, exhorting the representatives in question to support worthy men and measures.[72] The shorter parliaments question was the subject of resolutions in some of the craft guilds, including the barber-surgeons; the stationers passed a resolution on the army issue. The conferring of honorary freedoms on great men whom guilds wished to distinguish—a practice that was not new—continued, with several guilds conferring such freedoms on MPs who had taken the lead in defending parliament's rights during the money bill dispute (though the subsequent acceptance of office by some of those figures must have had a chastening effect).[73] In general, the guilds did not take notice of or encourage the political street demonstrations that had become a feature of the period, but in 1773 the merchants' guild did refer to one of the underlying causes by noting 'the dread of a Union . . . which, if carried into execution must prove destructive to the landed and commercial interests of the Kingdom'.[74]

The third dimension of the guilds' response to corporation reform lay in the efforts made, on a number of different fronts, to confirm or recover corporate privileges, and in particular, to reassert rights in respect of controlling trade. It was noted in Chapter 1 that by the 1750s Catholics were becoming more active in their opposition to the quarterage system (designed to ensure that regulation of the handicraft trades remained in guild hands). The Catholic campaign against quarterage came at a time when, in view of the opportunities afforded by economic growth, the guilds were prepared to relax at least some of their claims to control trade. However, there was as yet no sign of a wish to abandon it altogether, and by the late 1760s a drive to reassert control, through a statutory measure to confirm the quarterage system, was under way. It had the support of the Dublin guilds and corporation, as well as backing from other corporate towns where a guild structure existed.

[72] DPLGC, MS 79, fos. 209, 219, 222–3, 233.
[73] TCD, MS 1447/8/2, p. 112; NLI, MS 12124, p. 306, MS 12125, p. 44; GMD, Brewers' guild, minute book 1750–1802, p. 159; Evans 'The Ancient Guilds of Dublin', NLI, MS 738, p. 42. Regular general elections were conceded in the octennial act, 7 Geo. III, c. 3 (1768).
[74] DPLGC, MS 79, fo. 241.

The case for preserving guild privileges was put most eloquently by Lucas. His position has been described as reactionary and illiberal;[75] and by the standards of the new Scottish economic liberalism it undoubtedly was. But in the rest of Europe there was still much vitality in the corporatism that Lucas articulated, in which rights and functions went together:

As Cities are the Strength and Glory of every Nation, the Nurseries of Literature, Polity and Arts, the Seminaries of Commerce, and the Bulwarks of Liberty; it has been judged good Policy, in all Countries, whether barbarous or civilised, to build . . . Cities . . . and in order to induce Men to inhabit, to cultivate, to improve, and to defend them, it has ever been found necessary to indue a certain Society of Men with certain Franchises, Privileges, Immunities and Pre-eminencies, superior to Foregners or extern Men, to invest them with Powers, distinct from the ordinary Subjects, particularly with a Property in the Soil, and the local Government of the City, and sometimes with an exclusive Right to Trade.[76]

For Lucas, therefore, the freemen's contribution to commerce, the arts, and liberty justified, or rather necessitated, their special privileges. He also stressed the Dublin freemen's quasi-aristocratic and military role 'in defending the City from Traitors and Rebels, and other Enemies of the Crown as well *English*, and *Scotch*, as *Irish*'. It was only reasonable that 'Papists and other Persons', who faced neither these responsibilities nor those of public office, should be required—as in London—to pay the modest quarterage fees charged by the guilds.[77] In 1768 heads of a quarterage bill, introduced by Lucas, passed the Irish house of commons; and despite rejection by the privy council the obvious sympathy of parliament for the principle of protecting guild rights gave cause to hope that a measure would eventually succeed.

The post-reform era also saw the city commons taking up the threads of a civic reform programme, first outlined in the 1740s. Lapsed customs and tolls were to be pursued; admission to honorary freedoms was to be tightened up; the practice of candidates seeking admission to freedom, via guilds other than those in which they qualified by birth or service, was to be discontinued (as enjoined in the corporation act). Above all, in a civic equivalent of a place act, no member of the city commons was to be elected

---

[75] Murphy, 'The Lucas Affair', 229.

[76] Charles Lucas, *The Liberties and Customs of Dublin Asserted and Demonstrated upon the Principles of Law, Justice, and Good Policy; With a Comparative View of the Constitutions of London and Dublin*, 2nd edn. (Dublin, 1768), 7. Cf. Mack Walker, 'Rights and Functions: The Social Categories of Eighteenth-Century German Jurists and Cameralists', *JMH* 50 (1978), 234–51; Black, *Guilds and Civil Society*, chs. 10–11.

[77] Lucas, *The Liberties and Customs of Dublin Asserted*, 28–34, 43, 55; Jacqueline Hill, 'Corporate Values in Hanoverian Edinburgh and Dublin', in S. J. Connolly, R. A. Houston, R. J. Morris (eds.), *Conflict, Identity and Economic Development: Ireland and Scotland, 1600–1939* (Preston, 1995), 114–24.

to any place of profit in the city, or employed in any of the city works.[78] This last regulation was designed to ensure, in accordance with civic republican norms, that the newly acquired rights of the commons and the guilds were not vitiated by the 'corrupting' effects of civic patronage. For their part, the aldermen tried to curb what they saw as one of the abuses of the new system: the practice of canvassing members of the corporation for promotion to the board or shrieval office.[79]

Like the guilds, the city commons took to speaking out on public issues. Not all its political resolutions became acts of assembly, because such acts required the agreement of both chambers, and the aldermen were apt to be closer in outlook to the Castle. But the commons passed its own resolutions on issues such as shorter parliaments.[80] Its members also kept an eye on the progress of the opposition in Britain, with whom they closely identified. In both countries Pitt's reputation as a Patriot had survived his taking office during the 1750s; and in 1757 the Dublin brewers and other guilds followed the example of London and other English corporations by voting freedom to Pitt and Henry Legge, chancellor of the exchequer, after their dismissal by George II. The two ex-ministers were praised, among other things, for making 'the Government of Great Britain belov'd by Britons, Happy to the Subjects united with them, and respected by Foreign Powers'. But when a newspaper suggested that Dublin corporation intended to follow the brewers' example, the printer was summoned before the lord mayor (apparently at the behest of the Castle) and made to retract his statement.[81] However, after prompting from the city commons, Pitt obtained his freedom in 1759. By 1767 Dublin even had a Pitt club, in addition to the older political clubs, the Boyne Society and the Aldermen of Skinner's Alley.[82]

A civic Patriot mentality therefore survived the corporation reform act (which could easily have undermined it by conferring a belated respectability on the freemen's campaign of the 1740s). That is not to deny that many aspects of deference survived. The freemen had never challenged the right of a 'virtuous' aristocracy to lead; and popular susceptibility to the mystique of an aristocratic Patriot was demonstrated in 1767, on the occasion of a by-election caused by the death of James Grattan. It emerged

---

[78] *The Standing Rules and Orders of the Commons of the Common-Council of the City of Dublin* (Dublin, 1772), 25–32; *CARD* xi. 135–9, 140–5, 197–9; TCD, MS 1447/8/2, p. 166; NA, M 2925, fo. 25.

[79] *CARD* xiii. 560–1. Guilds also tried to prevent canvassing for places on the city commons: NA, M 2925, fo. 33.   [80] *CARD* xi. 475–6.

[81] GMD, Brewers' guild, minute book 1750–1802, p. 138; James C. McWalter, *A History of the Worshipful Company of Apothecaries of the City of Dublin* (Dublin, 1916), 24; *Emly MSS, HMC 8th Rep., App., pt. 1*, fos. 182a–b.

[82] *CARD* x. 398; *FJ*, 17–20 Oct. 1767.

that several of the guilds, and a majority of the city commons (though not the aldermen) were disposed to consider the 18-year-old marquis of Kildare,[83] son of the duke of Leinster, as a replacement. This youth's claim to popular support rested entirely on his family name and record. His father, as earl of Kildare, had confirmed his Patriot credentials during the money bill dispute; he was, moreover, rich, and had extensive connections among the aristocracy in Britain and Ireland. The duke also had guild connections as an honorary freeman, and was a considerable employer of craftsmen: his magnificent seat in town, Kildare (Leinster) House, had been built in the 1740s. Such a background placed the young marquis beyond the temptation to become embroiled in aldermanic cliques or place-hunting. In the circumstances, many of the voters were prepared, indeed anxious, to do him the honour of returning him as MP for the city.[84]

Yet doubts were expressed in some quarters. If a candidate worthy of popular support was required to be a Patriot (and the young marquis could only be known as such because of his father's reputation), should he not also be required to know something of trade? The guild of merchants, drawing (consciously or unconsciously) on Bolingbroke's precepts, had earlier hinted that what was required in a representative was 'the promotion of commerce and the support of public liberty'.[85] And was it desirable that candidates who were already in the field should be induced to give way so that the marquis—who was not even in Ireland but travelling on the Continent—could be returned unopposed? Did this not smack of turning Dublin into a pocket borough? As one anonymous critic commented, 'under an Aristocratical government Nobility claims its undenied Rights . . . but it has no right to claim, what the People have a legal Power to deny'.[86] In the event, although one candidate, Thomas Greene,[87] withdrew, despite having previously toured the guildhalls in the independent interest, another (John La Touche, banker, the nephew of Lucas's running mate in 1749) decided to remain in the field. It is possible that La Touche may have had Castle support; if so, he did not advertise the fact.[88] Kildare won by 137 votes; he was also returned at the general election of 1768, on which occasion he was present and dined with several guilds. He held the seat until his elevation to

---

[83] William Robert Fitzgerald (below, App. B).

[84] See e.g. NLI, MS 12125, p. 19; NA, M 2925, fo. 7; DCA, C1/JSC/2, pp. 398–9. All but 7 guilds (merchants, bakers, glovers, weavers, dyers, coopers, and apothecaries) gave Kildare a majority of their votes (*Two Alphabetical Lists of the Freeholders and Freemen who Voted on the Late Election* (Dublin, 1768), 29).

[85] DPLGC, MS 79, fos. 225–6. Bolingbroke, *The Freeholder's Political Catechism*, 210–11. Subsequently the guild expressed satisfaction with Kildare's representation (MS 79, fo. 238).

[86] Anon., *A Short but Interesting Address to the Citizens of Dublin* (Dublin, 1767), CULBC, Hib. 7. 767. 7, p. 3.

[87] Thomas Greene, brewer, d. 1799; alderman 1775, lord mayor 1783–4.

[88] Dickson and English, 'The La Touche Dynasty', 22.

the peerage in 1773. As duke, his prestige in the city was said to be awesome.[89]

III. Patriotism and Protestantism

If the freemen had not entirely managed to shake off habits of deference, neither had they significantly changed their views on the pernicious tendencies of popery. It is important to make this point, because it has been widely assumed that a growth of toleration was under way among Protestants in the second half of the century, usually attributed to the influence of the Enlightenment. In fact, during this period, not only was there no groundswell of support from freemen for the relaxation of penal laws, but in the 1750s and 1760s the civic authorities took several steps that were frankly intended to strengthen Protestant (and specifically Anglican) interests. There was, for instance, the question of education. The corporation had long displayed an interest in this area; its annual grant to the charter schools dated from the 1730s.[90] It was the quite open intention of these schools to teach 'the children of Papists and other poor natives' the English language and instruct them in the established religion. Subsequently other schemes were taken up. In 1767 the merchants' guild agreed to endorse a project, proposed by the governors of the Hibernian Marine School, for the relief of orphans and children of 'reduced sailors'. According to the guild, the scheme would confer several benefits; 'the morals of the children will be rescued from the prevailing vices of the lower class of people, the established religion strengthened, our commerce extended and our country protected'. By the 1770s the corporation was also subsidizing this charity.[91]

The quarterage campaign, too, had the stated aim not merely of securing guild control over trade as a whole but of securing Protestant control.[92] Maintaining Protestant control in all areas of public life was, in fact, a common objective of both houses of Dublin corporation. It can be detected in the reaction to the first statutory relaxation of the penal laws relating to land. The bogland act of 1772 enabled Catholics to take 61-year leases of bogland, a tiny step towards dismantling the penal laws. Without displaying any hostility towards the measure itself, the corporation did make clear its opposition towards any law

---

[89] Evans, 'The Ancient Guilds of Dublin', NLI, MS 738, p. 31; *The Correspondence of the Right Hon. John Beresford*, ed. William Beresford (2 vols.; London, 1854), i. 148–9.

[90] *CARD* viii. 239–40.

[91] *CARD* xii. 158–9, 221; DPLGC, MS 79, fos. 219–20; Michael Quane, 'The Hibernian Marine School, Dublin', *Dublin Hist. Rec.*, 21 (1966–7), 67–78.

[92] Lucas, *The Liberties of Dublin Asserted*, 64; *Commons Jn. Ire. 1765–72*, viii. 78–9, 81–4. Cf. Leighton, *Catholicism in a Protestant Kingdom*, ch. 4, which brings out the crucial importance of confessionalism to the Irish *ancien régime*.

by which the powers of the papists would be increased in the towns Corporate, as it is apprehended there will be an attempt to obtain a law to entitle papists to purchase and take building leases in towns Corporate, which, if obtained, will prove highly prejudicial to the Protestant interest & the independence of Corporations.[93]

Obviously such a stand was self-interested, but it should not be supposed that such attitudes were to be found only among merchants and tradesmen, who (perhaps) lagged behind the better educated and more urbane landed classes. In 1757 the Irish house of lords approved proposals (subsequently dropped by the privy council) to register Catholic priests that would have made unregistered priests liable to transportation or even life imprisonment. A decade later, the Irish parliament was at one with the Dublin tradesmen in welcoming the prospect of a quarterage bill to confirm Protestant control of trade and thus strengthen the Protestant interest.[94] Even in England, where sheer numbers rendered the Protestant establishment far more secure, and where by mid-century the élite was beginning to take a more relaxed attitude towards Catholicism, at a popular level the old prejudices remained powerful, and were always apt to be reinforced during wars with Catholic powers. A notable instance occurred during the alliance with Prussia in the early stages of the seven years war (1756–63), in which for a time the two principal Protestant countries took on the leading Catholic powers, France and Austria. The alliance unleashed much popular enthusiasm in Britain and Protestant Ireland for the charismatic Frederick II of Prussia (Frederick the Great), who promoted the view that he was defending the Protestant cause. The London opposition champion of the 1760s, John Wilkes, portrayed Europe as divided into mutually hostile Protestant and popish camps. For its part, Dublin corporation attributed British victories in the war to the support of 'Divine Providence' for a ruler whose piety and concern for the 'independency of Europe' was pitted against the boundless ambition of the Catholic powers: British aims were benign because they concerned trade and the people's good rather than dynastic power.[95]

The tendency persisted, therefore, to glorify the Protestant prince, and to link religion and politics. As one correspondent in the *Freeman's Journal* put it in 1766, 'our wise forefathers made excellent laws to suppress Popery and establish freedom'.[96] Such sentiments had been reinforced by eulogies

---

[93] *CARD* xii. 173–5, 307–8; DPLGC, MS 79, fo. 238. Catholics were not permitted to buy land in corporate towns until 1793 (33 Geo. III, c. 21).

[94] John Brady, 'Proposals to Register Irish Priests 1756–7', *Irish Ecc. Rec.* 97 (1962), 209–22, at 220; Wall, *Catholic Ireland in the Eighteenth Century*, 68.

[95] Haydon, 'Anti-Catholicism in Eighteenth Century England', ch. 6; Eda Sagarra, 'Frederick II and his Image in Eighteenth Century Dublin', *Hermathena*, 142 (1987), 50–8; John Wilkes (ed.), *The Political Controversy or, Magazine. Of Ministerial and Anti Ministerial Essays* (London, 1762), 20, 24–5: *CARD* x. 330; xi. 21–2, 91–2.

[96] Quoted in John Brady (ed.), *Catholics and Catholicism in the Eighteenth-Century Press* (Maynooth, 1965), 124.

on the British constitution from Montesquieu and other *philosophes*, and
later by the expulsion of the Jesuits from certain Catholic countries in the
1760s. Any disposition towards complacency was counteracted by the
continuing Jacobite claim to the throne. Even after that claim had largely
lost its political significance (from 1766), the conviction that the defence of
liberty depended on Protestant countries standing together persisted for
some time.[97]

On the face of it, then, there was little to challenge the old certainties, and
during the 1750s and 1760s there was great continuity (particularly in
ideological matters) with earlier periods. Yet developments were taking
place at home and abroad that would eventually place great strain on this
conservatism.

One of these developments was philosophical. The works of the Scots
philosopher David Hume (1711–76), especially his *Essays and Treatises on
Several Subjects* (1753–4) and the highly acclaimed *History of England*
(1754–61) revealed ways of thinking about the past and the future that were
to have profound implications for Patriot assumptions. Hume was deeply
impressed by the commercial and industrial growth that had taken place in
his lifetime: he had come to see economic development as the ultimate
reason for every society's existence. He also believed that commercial
growth would eventually make it possible for every individual, not just a
small élite, to satisfy the material and moral requirements of citizenship.
This induced in him a scepticism about the ancient (pre-feudal) past as the
standard of civilization and liberty, for in his view the ancient past meant
slavery, limited commerce, and political instability.

Being a Scot, Hume was more familiar with civil (or Roman) law than
with common law, and he was less suspicious of the idea of absolute
monarchy. He recognized that the growth of European commerce had taken
place under such monarchies, which he regarded in a different light from
ancient and barbarous monarchies. Consequently, he was less concerned
with the evils of arbitrary power and the necessity of representative
institutions than with ensuring that every individual should have the
freedom under the law to pursue material independence and security of
property.[98] Hume's views were drawn on by his fellow Scot, Adam Smith

---

[97] See e.g. Sir John Dalrymple, *Memoirs of Great Britain and Ireland* (4 vols.; Dublin,
1773). Dalrymple recommended an incorporating union between Britain and Ireland, a federal
union with America, and a league offensive and defensive of all three with Holland, so as to
return 'to the condition of the ancient world, in which the nations that were free, commanded
the fate of those that were not free' (ii, app. II, 71–7).

[98] See e.g. 'Of Refinement in the Arts', in David Hume, *Essays and Treatises on Several
Subjects*, new edn. (2 vols.; Dublin, 1779), i, pt. ii, no. ii, 285–98; John Robertson, 'The
Scottish Enlightenment at the Limits of the Civic Tradition', in Istvan Hont and Michael
Ignatieff (eds.), *Wealth and Virtue: The Shaping of Political Economy in the Scottish
Enlightenment* (Cambridge, 1983), 137–78, at 159–60, 168.

(1723–90), in formulating his ideas of economic liberalism, published in *The Wealth of Nations* (1776). Josiah Tucker (1712–99) used the new insights to condemn as reactionary the Patriots of London and elsewhere who upheld restrictions on trade and refused to accept free wage labour.[99] These views were potentially subversive of several of the foundations of the Dublin Patriots' thought: the ancient constitution, civic republicanism, and corporatism. For his part, George III had fulfilled the expectation that he would end the Tories' proscription from office, and this had the effect of giving the political establishment in Britain a more monolithic character: links between (landed) Tories and (urban) Patriots were undermined. Together with the weakening of the Jacobite threat, this facilitated the emergence of a generation of statesmen who were able to break free of old ideological quarrels and think in new imperial ways.[100]

[99] J. G. A. Pocock, 'The Varieties of Whiggism from Exclusion to Reform', in Pocock (ed.), *Virtue, Commerce and History*, 215–310, at 263.
[100] Bartlett, 'The Townshend Viceroyalty, 1767–72'.

5

Dublin Patriots in the American Revolutionary Era, 1774–1782

> Whenever the crown obtains a dominion to *influence* the represent-
> atives of the people, and uses this dominion—representation ceases—
> and our boasted freedom immediately vanishes from our view. For
> some time past, administration has acquired and exerted this power.
> The consequences are now evident. We are equally *slaves* with the
> subjects of Prussia or Sweden—and the monarch, who ought to be
> *limited*, is perfectly ABSOLUTE.[1]

During this period the focus of Irish Patriot politics shifted away from the
Country reforms that had been achieved in the 1760s—Dublin corporation
reform, regular parliamentary elections, and greater legislative control over
the Irish regiments[2]—towards free trade, and then legislative independence.
When these in turn were granted (1779–82), confidence in Ireland's destiny
reached its peak. The context for these developments was Britain's most
serious imperial crisis of the century, the loss of the American colonies. War
with America was responsible for the trade embargo and economic
depression that in turn led to non-importation agreements in Ireland; and
once free trade had been achieved, it was the fall of Lord North's
government, directly as a result of Britain's defeat in the war, that paved the
way for the granting of legislative independence. In Patriot eyes, this should
have given rise to two free and independent parliaments responsible only to
the king. Perhaps if Britain's imperial sun really had been setting—as
appeared, to many, to be the case[3]—the relationship between Ireland and
Britain might actually have developed on those lines. In fact, since the 1760s
a new British imperial policy had been evolving; and although in respect of
the old American colonies its consequences were disastrous, the new
approach undoubtedly preserved some of the newer acquisitions for the
empire. Gradually government was beginning to break free of the
limitations imposed by the Protestant, decentralized empire that had
emerged from the revolution of 1688–9. Since the implications of this shift

---

[1] Letter from 'An Hibernian', *FJ*, 16–19 Feb. 1782.
[2] Dickson, *New Foundations*, 129, 138.
[3] See Stephen Conway, 'Bentham versus Pitt: Jeremy Bentham and British Foreign Policy
1789', *Hist. Jn.* 30 (1987), 791–809, at 791.

were to be so far-reaching, and since at the outset of this period there was still a conviction that the Patriots of Britain, Ireland, and America were engaged in a common cause,[4] it will be worth briefly examining the evolution of British imperial policy in the aftermath of the seven years war (1756–63).

I. British Policy in North America and the Patriot Response

Following the capture of Quebec (1759) the British government set out a policy for the largely Catholic province that would, in effect, have anglicized church and state. But official actions did little to promote this. The see of Quebec, vacant when the British took over, was allowed to be filled: the approved nominee was even permitted to go to Europe to be consecrated, on condition that he did not defy the principle of the royal supremacy over the church by using his title, or maintain links with Rome beyond what was necessary for the exercise of spiritual jurisdiction. Rome's acceptance of these conditions (1766) marked one of the first signs of a thaw in Anglo-Vatican relations following the death of the Old Pretender on 1 January of that year, and the end of Vatican recognition for the Stuart claim to the English throne.[5] Other important concessions were made. Having gauged local opposition to a representative assembly (which, in keeping with British practice, would have had to exclude Catholics), the British governors dropped proposals for such a body.

By the 1770s, however, it was clear that Quebec was in need of a new constitution. There was confusion about whether English or French law was in force, and complaints from English and American settlers about the lack of an elective assembly. Events in the thirteen American colonies were just then demonstrating that representative bodies could be an imperial liability; and in view of the possibility that force might have to be used against the colonists, military and strategic considerations confirmed the wisdom of a conciliatory policy towards the French Canadians. If loyal, they might provide the basis for an army of around 18,000 men.[6] The Quebec act of 1774 accordingly contained no provision for a representative assembly. Instead, the governor was to rule with the aid of a nominated council, on which Catholics would be eligible to serve. The costs of civil government were to be raised by customs duties, licensing fees, and so on, rendering the

---

[4] James Burgh's highly influential *The Political Disquisitions* (3 vols.; London, 1774–5), was dedicated to 'the independent Part of the People of Great Britain, Ireland and the Colonies'.

[5] Ivanhoe Caron, 'La Nomination des évêques Catholiques de Quebec sous le régime anglais', *Mémoires de la Société Royale du Canada*, Sect. 1, 3rd. ser., 26 (1932), 1–44, at 1–6; Hugh J. Somers, 'The Legal Status of the Bishop of Quebec', in *Catholic Historical Review*, 19 (1933–4), 167–89.

[6] John Manning Ward, *Colonial Self-Government: The British Experience 1759–1856* (London, 1976), 6–7.

governor financially independent. The result was that the king's ministers retained virtually complete control in Quebec, beyond anything they enjoyed in respect of the older American colonies. No habeas corpus measure was introduced. The Catholic church was confirmed in its power to levy tithes on Catholics. And while the principle of the royal supremacy over the church was affirmed in the act, the oath of allegiance merely required Catholics to recognize the political, not the ecclesiatical, supremacy of the king.[7] Moreover, the act's scope was to extend far beyond Quebec itself into the north-west territory, a region that the Americans were inclined to regard as within their own sphere of influence.

Given such provisions, it is not surprising that the Quebec measure should have aroused grave suspicion in opposition circles both in North America and in Britain. Here was the clearest indication that arbitrary and popish tendencies were still harboured by government. In Britain, the city of London (especially the liverymen) took a leading part against the bill, and the common council petitioned against it.[8] In the house of commons Charles James Fox deplored the 'despotism' contained in the proposals, while the former William Pitt, now earl of Chatham, denounced the bill in conventional Whig terms:

He deduced the whole series of laws from the supremacy first re-vindicated under Henry VIII, down to this day, as fundamentals constituting a clear compact that all establishments by law are to be Protestant; which compact ought not to be altered, but by the consent of the collective body of the people. He further maintained, that the dangerous innovations of this Bill were at variance with all the safe-guards and barriers against the return of Popery and of Popish influence, so wisely provided against by all the oaths of office and of trust from the constable up to the members of both Houses, and even to the sovereign in his coronation oath. He pathetically expressed his fears that it might shake the affections and confidence of his Majesty's Protestant subjects in England and Ireland; and finally lose the hearts of all his Majesty's American subjects.[9]

Against this view supporters of the bill offered only vague appeals to the decline of 'superstition' and 'dogma'. The really telling consideration was the worsening situation in North America, which had reached such a critical point—with (Protestant) Americans apparently on the point of rebellion— that cultivation of the Quebec Catholics appeared to be imperative if the empire was to be preserved. But if pragmatic considerations helped the bill to pass, opposition continued both inside and outside the legislature, and in

---

[7] Ministers hoped that under state control, and without persecution, the Catholic church in Quebec would wither away (ibid. 8–9, 12).

[8] Paul Langford, 'London and the American Revolution', in Stevenson (ed.), *London in the Age of Reform*, 55–78, at 63–4.

[9] *The Parliamentary History of England from the Earliest Period to the Year 1803* (*Parl. Hist. Eng.*), xvii, col. 1404.

subsequent years repeated attempts were made to obtain the act's repeal.[10]

For the government's critics in the American colonies the Quebec act represented only part of a wider dissatisfaction with recent measures, and especially the imposition by parliament of revenue-raising taxes. Parliamentary sovereignty, soon to be upheld by the leading English legal commentator, Blackstone, was challenged. John Otis made the point in 1764: 'To say that Parliament is absolute and arbitrary is a contradiction. The Parliament cannot make two and two five: omnipotence cannot do it.'[11] Hitherto American discontent might have been exploited by a Tory opposition in Britain. But the Tories were now for the most part reconciled with the court, and only the Patriots and some groups of Whigs were still apt to identify with opposition causes. And for all their sympathy with the Americans, few of them were inclined to contest the principle of British parliamentary sovereignty over the colonies. Similar caution was displayed by the opposition outside parliament.[12] Specific American grievances might gain support, but the issue of parliamentary sovereignty was rarely engaged. This took some of the force out of the popular reaction in support of the colonists, and helps explain the scathing reference in the Declaration of Independence to the failure of 'our British brethren' to support the colonial cause.

Nevertheless, if the parliamentary sovereignty principle was one that the British opposition hesitated to challenge, government moves to relax its anti-Catholic stance at home were to spark off the most serious urban riots ever witnessed in Britain. Research has shown that the government's interest in Catholic relief at this period, formerly attributed to enlightened principles of toleration, had powerful political motives: the recruitment of Catholics from Scotland and Ireland (a hitherto untapped source) into the army.[13] The process began with the passing of a bill for limited relief of English Catholics in 1778. In Ireland, suspicion of government intentions ensured that the only concession the Irish parliament would make was to allow Catholics to take long leases. In Scotland, the prospect of Catholics being deployed against fellow-Protestant Americans provoked riots that forced government to abort its plan for Scottish Catholic relief. Subsequently, disturbances spread to London (the Gordon riots), and were only halted after a week of rioting: over 200 lives were lost.[14]

[10] *Parl. Hist. Eng.*, xvii, cols. 1404–5, 1357–8, 1360–2, 1368, 1393; xviii, cols. 664–5, 679.

[11] Quoted in William Simpson, *Vision & Reality: The Evolution of American Government* (London, 1978), 15.

[12] Langford, 'London and the American Revolution', 63, 74–6; report of address of merchants, etc., of Bristol, *Hib. Jn.*, 16–18 Oct. 1775; Linda Colley, 'Radical Patriotism in Eighteenth-Century England', in Raphael Samuel (ed.), *Patriotism: The Making and Unmaking of English National Identity* (3 vols.; London, 1989), i. 169–87, at 177.

[13] Robert Kent Donovan, 'The Military Origins of the Catholic Relief Programme of 1778', *Hist. Jn.* 28 (1985), 79–102.

[14] Haydon, 'Anti-Catholicism in Eighteenth Century England', ch. 7.

The Gordon riots had far-reaching effects on attitudes among the propertied classes in Britain. The loss of life, the damage to property, and the difficulty in restoring law and order revealed popular anti-popery in a new and alarming light. One result was that some of the leading opposition groups in parliament experienced a change of heart concerning the relations between church and state. The Foxite Whigs began from the 1780s on to commend the separation of religion and politics, and this had the effect of further weakening the links between a plebian and an aristocratic opposition. However, if the Whig opposition had rejected it, anti-popery remained a potent popular sentiment, and a persistent force in British politics.[15]

Dublin reaction to Britain's North American policies followed a similar pattern to that of the opposition in London, Bristol, and other English and Scottish towns. There was widespread sympathy for the colonists, as Benjamin Franklin found on a visit in 1771,[16] and much concern about the effects of these policies, especially on trade. (The Irish provision trade, except for trade with Britain and loyal colonies, was placed under embargo in 1776, and in contrast to earlier embargoes, this one was not quickly relaxed.) Yet the Dublin opposition was little more inclined than its London counterpart to take a stand against the principle of parliamentary sovereignty over the colonies. This may seem surprising, since from time to time British claims to parliamentary sovereignty over Ireland had been contested; and Lucas, at least, shared Otis's view of parliaments when used as instruments of executive sovereignty ('Is an Act of Parliament omnipotent? Can it overturn the established Constitution of the Nation?').[17] But it had long formed part of Irish constitutional thinking that Ireland was a kingdom, with rights and liberties that mere colonies did not possess: in that sense Dublin corporation could recognize 'the imperial crown of these realms'[18] without necessarily admitting the sovereignty of the British parliament over Ireland. Accordingly, despite sympathy for the Americans, the two cases were considered in different lights; and as in London, this was to detract somewhat from the opposition to the government's American policy.

Concern about the American situation was expressed by the Dublin city commons soon after armed hostilities between British troops and the colonists broke out in April 1775. At a post assembly held on 1 June, there was a small majority for a motion to ask the lord mayor to call a special

[15] Clark, *English Society*, 349; Haydon, 'Anti-Catholicism in Eighteenth Century England', 303–5.
    [16] David Noel Doyle, *Ireland, Irishmen and Revolutionary America, 1760–1820* (Dublin, 1981), 154.
    [17] Anon. [Charles Lucas], *An Answer to the Counter Address of a Pretended Free Citizen* (Dublin, 1766), 9.   [18] *CARD* x. 448.

meeting to consider the evils that Ireland and particularly Dublin were likely to suffer 'from the oppression which our Brethren in America labour under', and to petition the king on the subject. When the lord mayor and aldermen demurred, the commons decided to publish their own petition. This avoided discussion of the causes of the conflict, but deplored 'the horrors & calamities of civil war raging in America', which 'must be destructive to the Brittish Empire at large and particularly ... ruinous to the limited Commerce of this Kingdom'. Reconciliation with the colonies would re-establish the 'British Constitution' on a firmer basis, 'with its necessary Attendants, civil Liberty and political Security'. There was unease at the prospect of troops being withdrawn from Ireland 'to enter into an unnatural Conflict with protestant Subjects of the same Empire'. In a pointed reference to the aldermanic board, the commons indicated that those who refused their consent to 'a dutiful petition' tending to undeceive the king and to 'prevent the Effusion of a drop of a Subjects Blood' were no friends to the constitution.[19]

In another move to outflank the more Castle-minded aldermen, the commons resolved to request the sheriffs to call on 'the Aggregate Body of Freemen and Freeholders' to consider the American question: a request endorsed some months later by the merchants' guild. This was a new departure, although in one of his last public pronouncements, Lucas had hinted at the necessity of consulting the 'Aggregate Body of the Citizens' if the aldermen continued to frustrate the wishes of the city commons. In similar circumstances, leaders of the London liverymen were also beginning to speculate about the powers of the 'aggregate Body'. In Dublin, such a meeting took place in October 1775, when some 3,000 freeholders, freemen, and merchants of Dublin city addressed the king to urge reconciliation with the Americans. The city MPs were instructed to oppose any grant for the war,[20] and the merchants' guild prepared an address to those British politicians who had opposed the government's American policy. That guild, and the city commons, copied the example of the London liverymen and passed a vote of thanks to Lord Effingham, who had resigned his commission rather than fight his fellow subjects in America. For their part, the aldermen fell in with government policy: in January 1776 the lord mayor was condemned in the merchants' guild for having signed an address approving the use of force against the Americans.[21] In the same month the

---

[19] DCA, C1/JSC/3, pp. 302–3, 307, 310–15. The comments revealed a sense of the protection afforded by the British 'empire of the sea': cf. Richard Koebner, *Empire* (New York edn., 1965), 244.

[20] DCA, C1/JSC/3, p. 303; *Hib. Jn.* 18–20, 25–7 Oct. 1775. See also Lucas's letter to the sheriffs and commons (*FJ*, 22–4 Oct. 1771); Langford, 'London and the American Revolution', 71.

[21] DPLGC, MS 79, fos. 247–8; DCA, C1/JSC/3, p. 308; J. G. Simms, 'Dublin in 1776', *Dublin Hist. Rec.* 31 (1977–8), 2–13, at 11.

Society of Free Citizens—by now a political and convivial club[22]—toasted the American congress.

All this took place while the British prime minister, Lord North, was still exploring the possibility of conciliation, and before the Declaration of Independence had been drafted. Thereafter, as in London, the Dublin protests died down. In July 1776 the two houses of the corporation found themselves sufficiently in harmony to agree on the granting of honorary freedom to a leading opponent of the Quebec act, and one of Lord North's most vocal critics in the London parliament, the Dublin-born Colonel Isaac Barré.[23] As in Britain, French support for the Americans from 1778 helped to make the war more acceptable: a bid by members of the city commons to ask the king to change his ministers following French entry into the war was withdrawn. Indeed, the government was soon being criticized for not harrying the French strongly enough. When the English opposition scented victory against Lord North's ministry in 1779, following the unsuccessful court martial of Admiral Augustus Keppel (an opposition MP), both houses of Dublin corporation agreed to present freedom of the city to Keppel, for his successful encounter with the French, 'adding security thereby to the commerce of these nations and lustre to the British flag'.[24]

If the Dublin city Patriots failed to identify fully with the American opposition, it was nevertheless true that during the 1770s government policy was anxiously scrutinized for signs that Ireland was to be subjected to the same treatment as the Americans. In 1773 certain guilds took alarm at an impending Irish stamp act; the smiths' guild resolved not to support any future parliamentary candidate who would not pledge himself to work for the repeal of an act that the guild deemed detrimental to trade, and subversive of 'that invaluable blessing, the Constitutional freedom of the Press'.[25] But in general, the government had somewhat better success in pursuing new imperial policies in Ireland than in America. This was partly because of better communications: the Americans had some spokesmen in London to represent the colonial case, but Irishmen could be found in the British parliament itself. Moreover, Ireland was better managed. From the 1770s, when undertaker arrangements were superseded, Ireland was coming in for the same kind of professional, dedicated management in the imperial interest that was being manifested by governors in Quebec. And, just as in the case of Quebec, this development came about through the initiative of governors on the spot, rather than as the result of a blueprint

[22] For the Free Citizens in the 1760s see Eugene A. Coyle, 'Sir Edward Newenham—the 18th Century Dublin Radical', *Dublin Hist. Rec.* 46 (1993), 15–30, at 17.
[23] *CARD* xii. 425; *DNB*. Barré's father, Peter Barré (d. 1776), was a Dublin merchant and alderman.
[24] DCA, C1/JSC/4, fo. 59; *CARD* xiii. 51. A Keppel club was still meeting in Dublin in 1784 (*DEP*, 15 May 1784).
[25] NA, M 2925, fo. 29; DPLGC, MS 79, fos. 243–4. An Irish stamp act (13 & 14 Geo. III, c. 6) was passed in 1774.

laid down for them in London. Through the efforts of Lord Townshend (viceroy 1767–72) and his chief secretary Sir George Macartney, the undertaker system was replaced by a Castle party, based on careful use of patronage and parliamentary management, which was to remain an effective instrument of government business down to the act of union.[26] Faced with this new style of management, the opportunities for an effective parliamentary opposition were limited; and it was only towards the end of the 1770s, through the unforeseen effects of the American war, that the opposition's prospects began to improve.

One of these effects had been to deplete the number of regular army units in Ireland. This encouraged the formation of paramilitary Volunteer groups, which, it has been suggested, represented the first real manifestation of a Protestant middle-class public opinion.[27] However, it is important not to lose sight of the independent interest that had emerged in many counties and towns during the 1750s and 1760s. In at least one county it has been found that the Volunteers were 'broadly synonymous' with the independent interest,[28] and certainly in Dublin that was the case. In the capital, it was the city commons and guilds, urged on by the Free Citizens, that continued to set the pace in Patriot causes.

These bodies were particularly preoccupied with the effect of the war on trade. As early as 1776, resentment against the embargo on the provision trade prompted the Free Citizens, under the leadership of two of Lucas's disciples, James Napper Tandy,[29] and Sir Edward Newenham, to include 'free trade' among their toasts: a slogan that signified opposition to control of trade from London rather than hostility to the principle of protection. When the Irish economy slumped in 1778, owing to poor demand in Britain for Irish linen, Dublin artisans began to press for the exclusive consumption of home manufactures, at first on a selective basis. This was not a new idea. Swift had encouraged it in the 1720s, and more recently Dublin weavers had urged the public to support Irish-made goods during the economic depression of 1771. Well before the Volunteers took up the cause, Dublin corporation had backed it, and Dublin clubs and societies began, ostentatiously, to make a point of drinking Irish porter in preference to English.[30]

[26] Bartlett, 'The Townshend Viceroyalty', 93–6, 101, 111–12.

[27] Maurice R. O'Connell, *Irish Politics and Social Conflict in the Age of the American Revolution* (Philadelphia, 1965), 22, 94.

[28] Malcomson, *John Foster*, 130.

[29] James Napper Tandy (1737?–1803); son of James Tandy, ironmonger; followed father's trade, later an agent for Sir Edward Newenham. Admired Lucas; member of city commons 1777–93. Founder member of the Dublin United Irishmen, 1791; took part in French invasion of Ireland, 1798. See Rupert J. Coughlan, *Napper Tandy* (Dublin, 1976).

[30] The Free Citizens required a pledge from members to wear Irish-made apparel (*FJ*, 19–21 May 1778). See also *CARD* xii. 106; Downie, *Jonathan Swift*, ch. 11; R. B. McDowell, *Irish Public Opinion 1750–1800* (London, 1944), 55–6.

It was in the autumn of 1778, some months after the first Belfast companies had appeared, that Volunteering began in Dublin. It followed the pattern elsewhere, with companies being formed under the leadership of a gentleman or nobleman. Predictably, in view of the status and Dublin connections of the Fitzgeralds, the first Dublin company was formed under the duke of Leinster as colonel. Its members included woollen drapers and others from the textile trades—trades that had a record of supporting Patriot causes (though one cynical observer pointed out that since no corps was complete without uniforms, the participation of drapers reflected the hope of boosting sales). These were not poor wage-earners, but substantial tradesmen, many of them active in the guild of merchants and on Dublin corporation.[31] Later, some of the wealthier branches of trade and the professions, including the merchants, weavers, goldsmiths, and lawyers, organized their own Volunteer companies. Volunteering thus represented one more means by which barriers between the landed and business sectors were being broken down, giving rise to much mockery at the pretensions of shopkeepers who set themselves up as gentlemen.[32]

The Protestant nature of the Volunteers at this time was reflected in Dublin by their periodic attendance at established church services,[33] though later on in different parts of the country certain corps took the significant step of admitting individual Catholics, in small numbers. The failure of government to embody the militia, which on similar occasions in the past would have absorbed groups such as those of 1778 and 1779, meant that the status of the Volunteers remained uncertain. This was reflected in corporation reactions to the movement. While the city commons agreed to show forbearance to any of its own members who were detained on Volunteer duties, in 1779 the aldermanic board shrank from the suggestion that the lord mayor (Sir Anthony King) had encouraged the city's Volunteer corps.[34]

In the meantime, the initiative in the Patriot movement was being maintained by commercial pressure, with Dublin taking a leading part. Although the British government made some trading concessions in 1778—

---

[31] The first Dublin Volunteer corps was formed some time before Oct. 1778 (letter from 'A Dublin Volunteer', *FJ*, 31 Oct.–3 Nov. 1778). In 1779 came the embarrassing charge that owing to a shortage of scarlet cloth many Volunteer uniforms had been made in England. The master of the weavers' guild summoned a meeting of master clothiers, after which he assured the public that supplies were available in Dublin (*FJ*, 7–9, 11–14 Sept. 1779).

[32] Letter from 'A Dublin Volunteer', *FJ*, 31 Oct.–3 Nov. 1778. For details of Dublin corps by late 1779 see *FJ*, 4–6 Nov. 1779. The experience of commanding such 'mobbishly inclined' corps (Lord Charlemont's comment on the goldsmiths' corps) could be educative for the noblemen concerned (*Charlemont MSS i*, HMC 12th Rep., App., pt. x, 97).

[33] Reports of celebration of King William's birthday, *FJ*, 3–5 Nov. 1778; *Faulkner's Dublin Journal* (*FDJ*), 3–6 Nov. 1781.

[34] DCA, C1/JSC/4, fos. 123, 125. The aldermen did thank the duke of Leinster for his encouragement to Volunteer corps (*CARD* xiii. 76–7).

opening up the colonial market to Irish exports—these were limited in scope (textiles were excluded) and were opposed by British manufacturers who feared the effects of Irish competition. Taking its lead from the artisans themselves, early in 1779 a Dublin committee for relieving distressed artisans sought support from retailers for promoting Irish manufactures, particularly textiles. By April corporations and grand juries across the country were following Dublin's lead and adopting non-importation agreements. On 16 April Dublin corporation deplored the 'unjust, illiberal, and impolitic' opposition of many in Great Britain to the proposed encouragement of Irish trade and commerce, and resolved not to import or use any British goods until a more enlightened policy was adopted.[35] Several days later a large meeting 'of the aggregate body of the inhabitants of this city' (summoned, in approved constitutional form, by the high sheriffs)[36] witnessed the adoption of non-importation resolutions: no article of British manufacture was to be imported, purchased or worn as long as the 'illiberal spirit' of English monopoly remained. These resolutions, modelled on American tactics, had been drawn up by a committee whose chief activists were corporation members (including an alderman, James Horan)[37] and barristers.

This initiative met with a fair degree of success, though one of its means of applying pressure—the publication of names of those who imported British goods, with a view to a boycott—proved controversial. Such was the unanimity of the corporation by the autumn of 1779, when the next session of parliament was to begin, that the aldermen agreed to the publication of the city commons' instructions to the city MPs to seek free trade, and to grant supplies for a limited period only. This decision was endorsed by another aggregate meeting of the 'Freeholders and Citizens' of Dublin, convened by the sheriffs.[38] The broad spread of support is suggested by the presence among the activists at the public meeting both of Tandy, the future United Irishman, and John Giffard,[39] the future protagonist of the Orange Order. Both were members of the city commons.

---

[35] Moody and Vaughan (eds.), *NHI* iv. 220–2; *CARD* xiii. 53.

[36] *FJ*, 24–7 Apr. 1779. According to 'Lucas Redivivus', the sheriffs' powers stemmed from their appointment by the 'antient authority of the people', rather than from the crown (*FJ*, 2–5 Oct. 1779); cf. Maitland, *The Constitutional History of England*, 416–17.

[37] Alderman James Horan, indigo merchant (d. 1791), lord mayor 1784–5; non-importation activist; brought a test case over export of woollens; founder member, chamber of commerce (*The Speeches of the Right Hon. Henry Grattan*, ed. D. O. Madden (Dublin, 1853), 44; *Beresford Corr.* i. 86–7).

[38] DCA, C1/JSC/4, fos. 128ᵛ–129; *FJ*, 21–3 Oct., 30 Oct.–2 Nov. 1779.

[39] John Giffard (1746–1819); b. Ireland (son of John Giffard, originally of Great Torrington, Devon, who was disinherited by his grandfather). His mother was a MacMurrough of Co. Wexford. Took apothecary's exam in London; made free of the Dublin apothecaries' guild by grace, 1768; elected to Dublin city commons, 1774. Showed opposition tendencies in 1770s, but obtained a customs post in 1784. Sheriff 1793–4; conducted *FDJ* with Castle

Compared with all this, the Dublin Volunteers' role was much more restricted, though political points could occasionally be made. In October the Volunteers formed an escort for the amended king's speech on its journey from parliament to the Castle, and on 4 November ten Dublin city and county companies turned out to take part in the great annual commemoration of King William's birthday. His statue was hung with placards calling for 'Short Money Bills—a Free Trade—or Else', 'A Glorious Revolution', 'The Relief of Ireland', 'The Loyal Volunteers'.[40] Since the commemoration was customarily attended by the viceroy and other officials, this was an effective way of publicizing opposition issues.

Developments were also taking place at parliamentary level. By 1779 the opposition in Britain had begun to use Irish issues to embarrass the government,[41] with the result that Irish opposition MPs became even more anxious to demonstrate their own standing with the public. They had been flattering Dublin corporate bodies for years, in the hope of ingratiating themselves with these self-appointed guardians of Patriot values;[42] now they also began to heap praises on the Volunteers, who represented the most colourful symbols of public opinion. This enhanced the Volunteers' self-image as the embodiment of a 'citizen's militia', with appropriately exalted constitutional responsibilities of the kind Lucas had described.

The parliamentary opposition, in fact, was dependent on public opinion; lacking other resources, it was obliged to follow popular causes closely. However, not all manifestations of public opinion were equally welcome. Opposition as well as Castle supporters must have felt alarmed at the events of 15 November 1779, when a crowd of several thousand artisans from the Liberties, some armed with swords and pistols, stopped MPs on the way to the house of commons, to persuade them to vote for a short money bill and against new taxes. The attorney-general's house was attacked. (Grattan promptly moved a resolution in the house of commons against new taxes.) The tradition of street politics thus persisted, threatening from time to time to bring the entire opposition, inside and outside parliament, into disrepute—although on this occasion the demonstrations appear to have played a part in inducing Lord North to make further commercial

---

support from 1788; captain in Royal Dublin Militia 1793–8. Most prominent unionist and opponent of Catholic political rights on city commons. Details of his ancestry were fabricated by detractors, and little reliable information on him has been published. But see his obituary in *Gent's Mag.* 89 (1819), 481–4; McWalter, *A History of the Worshipful Company of Apothecaries*, 122; below, Chs. 6, 8–10, 12.

[40] *Beresford Corr.* i. 73–5; *FJ*, 4–6 Nov. 1779. The slogans were mainly Tandy's work (James Kelly, 'Napper Tandy: Radical and Republican', in J. Kelly and U. MacGearailt (eds.), *Dublin and Dubliners: Essays in the History and Literature of Dublin City* (Dublin, 1990), 1–24, at 4).

[41] Grattan, *Memoirs*, i. 281, 285; H. Butterfield, *George III, Lord North and the People* (London, 1949), 72–3, 88.

[42] See e.g. Sir Edward Newenham's letter to the city commons, DCA, C1/JSC/3, pp. 227–8.

concessions. Within three months direct imports from the colonies had been allowed.[43]

Down to this point, the extra-parliamentary opposition had been chiefly preoccupied with commercial matters, reflecting the importance trade and industry had acquired in popular consciousness. Legislative independence was not a priority. Thus, in 1776, the Free Citizens had toasted an 'honest parliament', but not a free parliament.[44] Even when, late in 1779, constitutional reform began to be discussed, this was very much bound up with commercial freedom. As signs appeared that the government would yield on free trade, attention naturally shifted to the question of how such concessions, once granted, might be rendered secure.

This shift began at a time when Britain's international standing had received a severe check. The entry of Spain into the war (June 1779), and French naval successes, culminating in the victory at Chesapeake Bay in 1781, made it seem very likely that the Americans would achieve their independence. The prospect of a British defeat in North America had a disorienting effect in Ireland, as, indeed, it did in Britain.[45] It called in question certain assumptions which, over time, had taken on the nature of eternal verities. British military (and especially naval) superiority; the delinquency of France, and French antipathy to civil and religious liberty; none of these axioms now seemed so incontrovertible. At the same time, Ireland's own sense of consequence was growing, chiefly as a result of the expansion of trade, which, having been very rapid during the 1750s and 1760s, made the recent trade restrictions seem all the more exasperating. The Volunteer movement served to highlight Ireland's military potential.

All this helped to focus attention on Anglo-Irish constitutional relations. One writer, styling himself 'Owen Roe O'Nial',[46] gloomily reviewed the prospects for Ireland's liberties as Britain's fortunes appeared to be waning, and as the famous British constitution seemed to be succumbing to 'corruption'. He floated the possibility of Ireland invoking French assistance to recover legislative independence, arguing that the name of France was no longer synonymous with tyranny, and that, judging by British actions in Quebec, a conqueror was unlikely to change the religion of a state, or interfere with private property. Surely, then, the French would make no change in the established church, or reduce the toleration enjoyed by Protestant dissenters. Irish Catholics would, he conceded, expect some increase in toleration; but any such move would have to be made with great

---

[43] Grattan, *Memoirs*, i. 401; *Beresford Corr.* i. 75–81, 85–91; Smyth, *The Men of No Property*, 131–3.

[44] McDowell, *Irish Public Opinion*, 55.

[45] Colley, 'Radical Patriotism', 179–81.

[46] Joseph Pollock, JP, barrister, Co. Down; active in reform politics, 1780s (Moody and Vaughan (eds.), *NHI* iv. 274, 327–8). Owen Roe O'Neill (d. 1649), a leader of the Gaelic Irish of Ulster in the wars of the 1640s.

care, to avoid offending Protestants. The proximity of Britain would act as a permanent guarantee against oppression on the part of a 'self-created protector'.[47]

The *Letters of Owen Roe O'Nial* represented an extreme case of the unsettling effect produced by the prospect of British defeat. Still, even 'O'Nial' expected that the established church would retain its privileges, and that Ireland would remain loyal to George III.[48] In general, constitutional thinking in opposition circles remained within a framework that Lucas would have recognized: some modification of Poynings' law so as to increase the Irish parliament's control over its own affairs (thus safeguarding any commercial concessions granted by the British government), and a review of the British parliament's claim to make laws binding on Ireland.

Such reforms were canvassed both inside and outside parliament during the winter of 1779–80, with Volunteer companies and electors in many towns and counties instructing their MPs to support legislative independence. Another aggregate meeting was held in Dublin at which the point was pressed home.[49] But the Volunteers' venture into constitutional areas was greeted with indignation and alarm, even among opposition MPs. After all, the Volunteers represented more or less independent armed bodies, whose legal status was still unclear. Parliament had at times thanked them for their exertions, and the opposition had been grateful for their free trade demonstrations. But for such bodies to take up constitutional issues without waiting for a parliamentary lead was another matter altogether, and of the opposition MPs only Grattan was disposed to defend such action; even the duke of Leinster was hostile. The duke's own corps of Dublin Volunteers split on the propriety of addressing Grattan in April 1780, following the latter's unsuccessful bid to move a declaration of Irish legislative rights in the house of commons. The majority agreed that this was not a fit subject for the corps to take up, but Tandy and others seceded and formed their own corps of Independent Volunteers.[50]

For the rest of that parliamentary session the opposition made little headway in parliament. Admittedly, the British government's response to the mutiny bill (to change it into a permanent measure, thus raising the spectre of military rule) provoked some criticism inside and outside parliament during the summer. A meeting of Dublin gentry, clergy, freemen, and freeholders condemned the Irish parliament's acceptance of the bill as a

---

[47] Anon. [Joseph Pollock], *Letters of Owen Roe O'Nial* (Dublin, 1779). Letters 1 and 2 appeared in *FJ*, 30 Sept.–2 Oct., 23–6 Oct. 1779.
[48] Ibid. letter 2, p. 26, letter 3, p. 31.
[49] O'Connell, *Irish Politics and Social Conflict*, 224–6.
[50] P. D. H. Smyth, 'The Volunteers and Parliament, 1779–84', in Bartlett and Hayton (eds.), *Penal Era and Golden Age*, 113–36, at 114–20; 'Independent Volunteers' to H. Grattan, *FJ*, 26–8 Feb. 1782.

subversion of the constitution, a position endorsed by the merchants' corps of Volunteers. But this example was not generally emulated, and no groundswell of opposition developed. A renewed invasion scare during 1781 enhanced the importance of the Volunteers in government eyes, and another wave of respectability and official approval swept over the movement, which served to check its overtly political tendencies.[51]

Nevertheless, during 1781 public interest did return to the issue of legislative independence. The impetus for this, once again, was primarily commercial. In April the Dublin guild of merchants was preoccupied with the question of trade with Portugal, England's oldest trading partner: a country that had so far shown no sign of opening its markets to Irish woollens. The city commons then took up the matter at its midsummer meeting. The difficulties experienced in attempting to open up the Portuguese trade intensified the growing dissatisfaction with Ireland's subordinate legislative status, while the problem of fixing a sugar duty acceptable to Irish as well as British refiners kept up the old irritation about Britain's claim to make laws for Ireland.[52] The *Dublin Evening Post* threw its weight behind legislative independence, but most Volunteer corps confined themselves to pledging their determination to repel invasion.[53] When parliament met in early October, opposition MPs were able to attack the administration over the Portuguese issue and to link it with parliamentary independence, as did Dublin corporation on 19 October. Both houses of the corporation agreed to instruct the city MPs to uphold 'the sole right of the King, Lords, and Commons of Ireland to make laws for the government of this country'. Meanwhile, the Dublin Volunteer corps publicized their support for 'a free trade and a free constitution'. Within weeks of Cornwallis's surrender at Yorktown on 19 October 1781, which effectively marked Britain's defeat in the American war, the Dublin Volunteers again assembled to mark King William's birthday. Once again the statue was hung with placards designed to convey a single message: 'The Volunteers of Ireland', 'Expect a Real Free Trade', 'A Declaration of Rights', 'A Repeal of the Mutiny Bill or Else', 'A Glorious Revolution'.[54]

All this had taken place well before the more celebrated resolutions in favour of legislative independence adopted by the Ulster Volunteer convention at Dungannon in February 1782. The fact that the Dungannon convention was held at all was controversial, for even the Volunteers were divided over whether an armed force had the right to adopt such an open political stance. The point has been aptly made that the effect on parliament

---

[51] Grattan, *Memoirs*, ii. 129; Smyth, 'The Volunteers and Parliament', 121–2.
[52] DPLGC, MS 79, fos. 254–5; DCA, C1/JSC/5, fo. 28; *DEP*, 28 June 1781. See also James Kelly, 'The Irish Trade Dispute with Portugal, 1780–87', *Studia Hib.* 25 (1989–90), 7–48.
[53] *DEP*, 5, 19 May 1781; Smyth, 'The Volunteers and Parliament', 121–2.
[54] *CARD* xiii. 206–7; *DEP*, 9 Oct., 6 Nov. 1781.

was mixed, and that during the following weeks opposition MPs were heavily defeated when they attempted to induce the house of commons to adopt resolutions in favour of legislative rights. Two developments changed the situation: the fall of Lord North's government on 20 March, and the adoption in March and April by corporations and grand juries of resolutions calling for legislative independence (Dublin corporation again passed such resolutions on 12 April).[55] When a new British ministry composed chiefly of opposition Whigs under Lord Rockingham took office, the Irish house of commons could scarcely forbear to endorse the call for change. On 16 April Grattan moved his declaration of rights for a third time, and it received the unanimous support of both houses. The new British ministers, who had been working with the Irish opposition, were in no position to resist; and the summer of 1782 saw the repeal of the declaratory act, and the modification of Poynings' law. Thus the winning of legislative independence came about through a unique combination of events, which could not have been foreseen even a year earlier.

In his speeches calling for Irish legislative independence, Grattan's arguments were of a kind that would have been familiar to Lucas, and before him to Molyneux. Ireland was not a conquered country (i.e. not conquered by the king); she was seeking a restoration of ancient chartered rights and privileges which entitled her to the same constitution as England. The rights of the king and parliament sprang, ultimately, from the people, who through their public pronouncements had made known their wishes for the recovery of ancient rights. In a bid to reassure his landed and aristocratic audience, Grattan emphasized that with this intervention the Volunteers' political involvement would end: 'These associations . . . will perish with the occasion that gave them being, and the gratitude of their country will write their epitaph.'[56]

However, the aftermath of winning parliamentary independence demonstrated how tenuous was the hold of the parliamentary opposition over the Volunteers and other extra-parliamentary forces. Grattan's premature efforts to induce the Volunteers to abandon their political role backfired when in the summer of 1782 certain Volunteers rejected his proposition that simple repeal of the declaratory act constituted a sufficient guarantee for legislative independence. Spurred on by Henry Flood, Volunteers in Belfast, later backed by the Dublin lawyers corps, insisted that the British government must renounce all claims to legislate for Ireland. In April 1783 the British parliament duly acknowledged the exclusive right of

---

[55] Smyth, 'The Volunteers and Parliament', 124; *CARD* xiii. 238.
[56] Grattan, *Speeches*, 49, 61–2, 65, 68–9, 74–6. Whether Grattan actually invoked the names of Molyneux and Swift on 16 April 1782 did not affect the tenor of his argument, which was consistent with theirs (cf. O'Brien, 'The Grattan Mystique', 190–4).

the Irish parliament to legislate for Ireland.[57] Against this background, and with concessions being made to Protestant dissenters, the Irish parliament was even willing to outbid the British government for Catholic support—up to a point. Freedom of worship, the right to conduct schools, and to buy and sell land were all granted to Irish Catholics in 1782.[58] But significantly, these concessions did not extend to the purchase of land in parliamentary boroughs: here the safeguards contained in the 1665 act of explanation remained intact. Nor was there any question of conceding political rights.

II. Ideology and Practice: Dublin's Parliamentary Representation, 1761–1782

By introducing regular general elections, the octennial act of 1768 gave a new character to Irish electoral politics. The effects were marked. During the whole of George II's reign (1727–60) there had been only one general election. During the first twenty-three years of George III's reign (1760–83) there were four general elections. Voters now knew in advance when general elections were coming up, and could plan ahead. Moreover, the octennial act was passed in a decade that had already produced the corporation reform act, giving more power to the Dublin guilds and city commons. Accordingly, it will be appropriate to look back over the two previous decades from the vantage point of the era of legislative independence in 1782, to review the state of political thought, and to assess what practical differences the changes of the 1760s had made.

An examination of statements by candidates and commentators during Dublin parliamentary elections in this period suggests the existence of much underlying agreement about the nature of politics and political values. The celebrated freedom of the constitution was still considered to depend on the preservation of 'that happy Equipoise', or balance, between the powers of the king, nobility, and people.[59] The function of the king's government was to govern, but always under the watchful eye of elected representatives, whose position was a solemn trust.[60] An MP should be a 'Patriot', displaying virtue, or public spirit; and virtue required the candidate to be independent in fortune, so as not to succumb to corruption or undue

---

[57] Grattan, *Memoirs*, ii. 343–70; Smyth, 'The Volunteers and Parliament', 125–7.

[58] 21 & 22 Geo. III, c. 24, c. 62. Dissenters obtained the repeal of the sacramental test (19 & 20 Geo. III, c. 6), and marriages conducted by Presbyterian ministers were declared valid (21 & 22 Geo. III, c. 25).

[59] Election notice of David Ribton, *FJ*, 6–10 Oct. 1767; toast to the 'Freedom and Independency [of the house of commons] from the other two Estates of Parliament' (dinner of the sheermen and dyers' guild, *FJ*, 17–20 Oct. 1767); letters from 'Hambden' ('We are to watch well the three estates' [and act if any arrogate] 'powers that do not belong to them'), 'Hibernicus' (*FJ*, 2–4 Nov. 1773, 28–30 Mar. 1776).

[60] Election notice of John La Touche, *FJ*, 6–10 Oct. 1767.

influence.[61] 'Party' and 'faction' were still pejorative terms: both suggested the pursuit of selfish and sectional interests rather than the public good.[62] Electoral contests should, where possible, be avoided.[63] A *Dublin* MP should work not only for the defence of constitutional liberties but for the city's prosperity.[64] Little had changed since mid-century, save that the language of civic republicanism had become more widely invoked across the political spectrum, and as time went on, virtually all candidates became anxious to appeal for support to the Free and Independent Electors, first conjured up by Lucas.[65]

The existence of broad agreement on these matters, however, did not mean that electoral contests lacked any ideological content. For while few challenged the general principles, there was ample room for differences over their interpretation.[66] Those who tended to a 'Court' or 'Castle' position— and no candidate for Dublin city during this period was prepared to admit outright support for, or backing from, the administration—might see the main danger to a balanced constitution coming from mobs, or self-appointed 'Juntos' acting in the name of the people. One critic in 1782 castigated the 'city Catos' who 'with great modesty style themselves the aggregate body', and who, under the name of the 'Free Citizens', had taken it upon themselves to nominate a parliamentary candidate (Travers Hartley)[67] for the whole city.[68] Those openly on the opposition side (that is, with the exception of James Grattan, all the successful candidates in the 1760s and 1770s) tended to be more mistrustful of royal and ministerial power. They pointed to the recent growth in ministerial patronage—a product of the Townshend viceroyalty—which was denounced as tending to absolute rather than limited monarchy.[69]

---

[61] [Anon.], *The City Spy-Glass: or, Candidates Mirrour. Wherein the Merits and Pretensions of the Several Candidates are Freely Considered, and Impartially Examined. By a Son of Candor* (Dublin, 1767), 6–7; letters from 'A Tanner', *FJ*, 13–17 Oct. 1767; 'Hibernicus', *FJ*, 28–30 Mar. 1776. Bolingbroke had set out the desirable qualities for MPs: see his tract, published by Lucas as *The British Free-Holder's Political Catechism*, 13–14.

[62] The shoemakers' guild referred to the 'malevolence of faction'; 'Hibernicus' to 'the perverted zeal natural to *party*' (*FJ*, 3–7 Nov. 1767, 28–30 Mar. 1776).

[63] *FJ*, 9–12 Nov. 1771; letter from 'Gracchus', ibid. 19–21 Nov. 1771.

[64] Election notices of marquis of Kildare's friends, John La Touche (*FJ*, 6–10 Oct. 1767); Benjamin Geale (*FJ*, 2–4 Dec. 1773).

[65] A Free Citizen [Charles Lucas], *Faction Unmasked: or, A Short Sketch of the History of the Several Parties that Prevailed in the City of Dublin, Since the Year 1748, to the Present Time* (Dublin, 1767), 8. According to *FJ* (16–19 Feb. 1782), both candidates in the current by-election were appealing to the 'independent electors'.

[66] Cf. Reed Browning, *Political and Constitutional Ideas of the Court Whigs*, 180–1.

[67] Travers Hartley, MP Dublin City 1782–90; Presbyterian merchant; active on committee of merchants; founder member, chamber of commerce (*CARD* xi. 466; Cullen, *Princes & Pirates*, 35).

[68] 'An Independent Elector' (*FJ*, 14–16 Feb. 1782). Cf. 'Hibernicus', warning against 'the excess, idleness and riot of the more numerous body of the people' (*FJ*, 28–30 Mar. 1776).

[69] See quotation at the beginning of this chapter. By comparing Ireland with Protestant states whose freedom had (allegedly) lapsed, the point about Ireland's loss of freedom was reinforced.

Occasionally, the aristocracy was seen as posing a danger to liberty. One opponent of the marquis of Kildare's candidacy in 1767 used a cautionary tale to warn the voters that handing over Dublin's representation to the son of a peer would effectively eliminate the 'Democracy or Estate of the People'.[70] Again, while all could agree that parliamentary representation was a solemn trust, the nature of the relationship between MPs and constituents was contentious. Some candidates, following Lucas's example, saw themselves as delegates, duty-bound to seek instructions on how they should vote on particular issues. This practice was endorsed by the Aldermen of Skinner's Alley and the Society of Free Citizens. But not all subscribed to this view; the board of aldermen, for instance, disliked it.[71] The consensus on the desirability of avoiding electoral contests, too, sprang from different premisses. Some appeared to think that the best candidate would emerge through popular acclaim for the most virtuous man: others were more concerned to avoid 'disturbing the peace of the city'.[72] And while churchmen maintained their emphasis on duty and obligation, the opposition continued to invoke divine providence in support of the independent voter. During the 1767 by-election the *Freeman's Journal* carried lengthy extracts from William Penn's address to the electors of England (1679), which urged the voter not to accept bribes, or support those who were in office during the king's pleasure, but only to choose 'sincere Protestants' who had a proper regard for civil and religious liberty.[73]

These differences should not be pressed too far. Even those who identified most strongly with opposition values often revealed latent Court tendencies: toasting the liberty of the press, for instance, but warning against licentiousness or sedition.[74] And from the other side, voices were raised, as in the past, to try to loosen the opposition's grip on the alluring 'Patriot' label:

I have observed that for some Time past, an erroneous Notion has prevailed among certain Ranks in this City and elsewhere, That a Man, in Order to be a PATRIOT and a FAITHFUL Representative, must be in a Constant and Uniform Opposition to every Court Measure and Plan proposed by Government, whether Good or Bad.[75]

[70] 'Aza to Abdullah', inserted by 'A Free Carpenter', *FJ*, 10–13 Oct. 1767.

[71] *CARD* xi. 475–6. Those prepared to accept instructions included Thomas Greene, David Ribton, Redmond Morres (*FJ*, 6–10 Oct. 1767, 7–9 Dec. 1773), Travers Hartley (Cullen, *Princes & Pirates*, 35). 'Gracchus' debated whether MPs were bound by them (*FJ*, 30 Nov.–2 Dec. 1773). In England, Edmund Burke declared his opposition to '*authoritative* instructions' in 1774 (*The Works of Edmund Burke* (6 vols.; London, 1884–99), i. 446–8.) See also Pocock, *The Machiavellian Moment*, 519.

[72] 'Gracchus' argued that the candidate should enjoy public esteem, *FJ*, 19–21 Nov. 1771. But see also ibid., 9–12 Nov. 1771.

[73] *FJ*, 27–31 Oct. 1767.

[74] See toasts nos. 22, 24 at tailors' guild dinner during the 1767 by-election, cited in Dixon, 'The Dublin Tailors and their Hall', 150.

[75] *The City Spy-Glass*, 15. For similar arguments in the 1730s see McCoy, 'Local Political Culture in the Hanoverian Empire', 30–1.

Nevertheless, the strength of 'independent' forces in Dublin during this period ensured that the perceived dangers to liberty were thoroughly aired. Liberty itself was publicly defended in a number of ways. There was the reaffirmation of symbols of the subject's rights, such as Magna Carta;[76] the endorsement of men and measures believed to be virtuous; and, persisting among contemporary political slogans, pointed references to the glorious revolution, and other instances of the downfall of tyrannical rulers. Toasting 'The glorious and immortal memory of King William' in 1776, the Free Citizens added pointedly, 'And may we never have cause to wish for another revolution'. Or again, 'Magna Charta; and Caesar's fate to him that violates it—May we never want a patriotic Brutus'; 'The memory of George the first; and may his descendants ever remember the terms on which his family was elected to the throne of these realms'; 'Oliver Cromwell'.[77] In 1776 the American crisis was at its height, but almost a decade earlier, during the 1767 by-election, among the toasts drunk at guild dinners were 'The Glorious Revolution of 1688 and may we never stand in Need of another', and 'The Exclusioners and Lord Russel [*sic*] at their Head'.[78] Such slogans were hardly indicative of revolutionary intentions; they were repeated too frequently and too openly. Why did they prove so enduring, so far into George III's reign?

One possibility is that the Dublin Patriots were simply echoing their counterparts in London, where the warm welcome given to the accession of George III in 1760 had soon given way to apprehension. The young king's reputed friendship with Catholics; his reconciliation with the Tories and his choice of the Scottish peer, Lord Bute (who lacked a seat in parliament), as chief minister; the controversial Peace of 1763; the ministers' treatment of Wilkes: all this, it has been argued, quite apart from the Quebec and American measures, made the king deeply unpopular during the 1760s and 1770s. And in London this disquiet prompted something of a revival of language and gestures from the English revolutionary era.[79] Since the Dublin Patriots were in the habit, as already noted, of keeping a close eye on city politics in London, it would not be surprising if London's example was influential.[80]

---

[76] Toast proposed by sheermen and dyers' guild, *FJ*, 17–20 Oct. 1767; editorial, *DEP*, 15 June 1779. Vignettes of Magna Carta adorned several of Lucas's works, and in 1782 the *Hibernian Journal* used a figure of Liberty seated beside 'Magna Charta' in its masthead.

[77] *FJ*, 18–20 Jan. 1776. Cromwell's name was rarely invoked before this era (Toby Barnard, 'Irish Images of Cromwell', in R. C. Richardson (ed.), *Images of Cromwell: Essays for and by Roger Howell, Jr.* (Manchester, 1993), 180–206, at 187).

[78] *FJ*, 13–17, 17–20 Oct. 1767. I am grateful to Mary Boydell for access to unpublished notes showing that Russell's name was also toasted in Dublin in 1745.

[79] Colley, *Britons*, 208; Rudé, *Wilkes and Liberty*, 50; John Cannon, *Parliamentary Reform 1640–1832* (Cambridge, 1972), 56–8, 63–4.

[80] Dublin newspapers frequently printed political pronouncements of the lord mayor and corporation of London (see e.g. *FJ*, 26–8 Mar. 1776).

However this may be, the fears expressed about the political tendencies of the new reign also had an Irish dimension. In 1764, one correspondent in the *Freeman's Journal* thought he recognized disturbing parallels between the later years of Queen Anne's reign, and his own day: an anti-war spirit; a villanous Peace; virtuous Whigs (such as Pitt) turned out of office; the nobility drawn towards the Stuarts; and efforts being made by English Tories, discernible even in Ireland, to weaken the memory of the great King William. The writer rehearsed the misdemeanours of Lord Chancellor Phipps in Anne's reign, who had, allegedly,

refused to celebrate the 4th of November, 1713, in the usual Manner, altho' the Nobility and Gentry attended at the Castle for that Purpose; but happily he was frustrated by the spirited Conduct of William Aldrich, Esq., then High Sheriff of the City of Dublin, who quitted the Levee, and being followed by the Nobility and Gentry, headed them in a Cavalcade, marced [*sic*] round the Statue of King William, and left His *Excellency* alone, to meditate on further Schemes for the Destruction of his Country . . .[81]

The letter ended with an exhortation to fellow Protestants not to be the tools of a '*Scotch Favourite*' (Lord Bute) by letting 4 November pass unnoticed. The citizens played their part,[82] but it was not until 1765 that the *Freeman's Journal* was able to report, with evident satisfaction, that King William's birthday had been properly celebrated by the authorities. The viceroy, Lord Hertford, proceeded in state to William's statue in College Green, accompanied by the lord mayor, the lord chancellor, the primate, judges, and 'a levee of the first personages' wearing emblems of the day. The boys from the Blue-Coat school and the orphan children of soldiers, all in new clothes and wearing Orange cockades and ribbons, were drawn up outside the Mansion House in Dawson Street. In the evening, according to custom, a performance of *Tamerlane* was held at the Theatre Royal. Noting that signals had been given from the Castle for the guns in the Phoenix Park to be fired, and for the soldiers in garrison to fire volleys, the report continued, 'This *we have not been able to say before on this Occasion, since a certain Period commenced.*'[83] Such comments, with characteristic coyness about any direct criticism of the king, highlight the symbolic importance for Patriots of 4 November as a touchstone of the authorities' enduring commitment to the revolution. They also explain why William's memory was accorded such prominence among toasts drunk on political and ceremonial occasions, and suggest why 4 November subsequently became 'sacred to the glorious institution of the Volunteers of Ireland', as the

[81] Letter from John Fiens, Oldbridge (*FJ*, 23–7 Oct. 1764). In fact Aldrich (lord mayor, 1741–2), although nominated for sheriff in 1712 and 1713 did not serve until 1714–15 (*CARD* vi. 497; vii. 533, 538).

[82] There was no state procession in 1764 (4 Nov. was a Sunday), but bells were rung, guns fired, and flags flown (*FJ*, 3–6 Nov. 1764).

[83] *FJ*, 2–5 Nov. 1765.

Freeman's Journal put it.[84] For personal monarchy was still intact, and the political tenets of a new king, however impeccable his constitutional credentials, could not be taken for granted.

What emerges from all this is that for the Dublin Patriots the potential for royal absolutism still outweighed the dangers arising from any other source: the mob, the aristocracy, the dissenters—even the Catholics. That did not mean that the Patriots had come to regard the Catholics as fellow citizens deserving of equal rights with themselves. Both houses of Dublin corporation had agreed that safeguards must remain when the penal laws in respect of land were being relaxed. At best it can be said that during the 1770s the Dublin corporate bodies in general abstained from crude attacks on popery,[85] and concentrated instead on defending the Protestant interest by promoting a quarterage measure, and encouraging Catholics to convert to Protestantism (by granting concessionary freedoms to converts).[86]

However, anxiety about popery continued to be expressed. In the aftermath of the Quebec act the Free Citizens made pointed remarks about the English bishops' sympathy for the 'popish interest', and reminded the king of the fate of Charles I. During and after the passage through the Irish parliament in 1778 of the first major Catholic relief bill (inspired by government), even those newspapers that have been described as 'liberal' in this period,[87] such as the *Freeman's Journal*, displayed a near obsession with the subject. Few commentators expressed downright hostility to the actual terms of relief: to allow Catholics to take long leases on land and inherit on the same terms as Protestants. What worried them was the effect on government of a *rapprochement* with Catholics. Popery was a religion founded on 'superstition, bigotry, and usurpation'. Popery and despotism went hand in hand, as demonstrated by the 'infamous Quebec act, by which Popery was rendered the established religion of Canada, and despotism received the sanction of the British legislature'.[88] Another writer was happy to relax the penal laws as long as it was a matter of expediency, not rights; for what rights did Protestants have in Catholic countries? Ultimately, it would be better if Catholics were to emigrate, and thereby cease to pose a threat to Irish Protestants. Thus any shift towards toleration was a limited one.[89]

---

[84] Letter from 'Varro', *FJ*, 2–4 Nov. 1773; report of weavers' guild dinner, *FJ*, 13–17 Oct. 1767; tailors' guild dinner, in Dixon, 'The Dublin Tailors and their Hall', 150; Free Citizens' dinner, *Hib. Jn.*, 20–3 Oct. 1775; *FJ*, 4–6 Nov. 1783.

[85] For the tailors' guild, a fit candidate was one who had voted 'against the Popery bill [of 1772]' (*FJ*, 7–9 Dec. 1773).

[86] *CARD* xii. 188, 241–2; xiii. 59. A clause in the abortive quarterage bill of 1773 would have given converts freedom gratis (Wall, *Catholic Ireland in the Eighteenth Century*, 70).

[87] *Hib. Jn.*, 20–3 Oct. 1775; Brian Inglis, *The Freedom of the Press in Ireland, 1784–1841* (London, 1954), 240.

[88] Article by 'Caractacus' (leader of British resistance to the Romans), *FJ*, 24–6 Sept. 1778.

[89] 'To the members of the house of commons', from L.O., *FJ*, 28–30 May 1778; Hill 'Religious Toleration and the Relaxation of the Penal Laws'.

During the American revolutionary era, therefore, the upheavals of the seventeenth century continued to loom large in political debate. Frequently, the names to conjure with were those of Hampden, Cromwell, and William III on the one hand, and Filmer, Strafford, and Charles I[90] on the other. Nevertheless, certain striking changes did take place in the parliamentary representation of the city during these years. The most obvious one was the complete eclipse of the aldermen. Between 1727 and 1760 nine MPs had represented Dublin city in parliament: eight of them were aldermen. Between 1761 and 1782 seven MPs represented the city: none of them were aldermen.[91] This was not the product of chance, or coincidence—by 1771 supporters of aldermanic candidates were having to refute claims that aldermen were, by their very office, unfit to represent the city.[92] How had this come about?

To begin with, ever since the 1740s the Dublin aldermen had been portrayed as upholders of oligarchy: an image that the 1760 corporation act had not entirely dispelled. On top of that, bankers, whose wealth frequently brought them to the highest civic honours, had received a severe check in the mid-1750s as a result of the act that prohibited merchants engaged in foreign trade from acting as bankers: this was not only a humiliating reminder of the relative weakness of the commercial community, but it forced those who wished to remain in banking to rely on landed capital and hence on ties with the landed class, and (in the public mind) with government. Moreover, in their capacity as magistrates, aldermen could scarcely avoid having contacts with ministers and officials.[93] In an age when Dublin voters set such store by 'independence', this was a disadvantage.

If aldermen failed to get elected—and only a handful were even discussed as serious candidates—what sort of men did succeed with the Dublin voters? Three general types can be identified. There were, first, 'traders', or 'citizens': men such as Lucas himself (MP, 1761–71) or the merchant Travers Hartley (MP, 1782–90) who, while they might have served on the city commons,[94] were not aldermen or bankers. Then there were members of the aristocracy or gentry (the marquis of Kildare, MP, 1767–73, and Redmond Morres, who represented the city from 1773 to 1776). Finally there were professionals, including recorders of Dublin (James Grattan, MP, 1761–6, and Sir Samuel Bradstreet, MP, 1776–84), and the vice-provost of

[90] Sheermen and dyers' guild, *FJ*, 17–20 Oct. 1767; letter from 'Hambden', *FJ*, 2–4 Nov. 1773; Free Citizens' Society, *FJ*, 20–3 Oct. 1775; Free Citizens' Society, *FJ*, 18–20 Jan. 1776; *DEP*, 15 June 1779.
[91] Though James Dunn (MP 1758–60) resigned from the board shortly before election (below, App. B).
[92] Letter from 'A Freeman' (*FJ*, 16–19 Nov. 1771).
[93] For the unfitness of aldermen and bankers see letters from 'Gracchus', 'Menenius' (*FJ*, 21–3 Nov. 1771, 4–7 Dec. 1773); NA, M 2925, fo. 29; goldsmiths' minute book, 1760–79 (NLI, n 6052 p 6782, p. 270).
[94] Hartley had represented the merchants' guild (*CARD* xi. 480).

Trinity College, Dr William Clement, MP for the city from 1771 to 1782. How did this varied set of individuals emerge as candidates?

The first point to note is that the notion cherished in opposition circles that the virtuous candidate would somehow appear, in almost mystical fashion, as a result of popular recognition of his qualities, soon turned out in practice to be flawed.[95] Flattered though individuals were to be informed that they were the object of a call to public service, several of those so distinguished declined the honour, pleading ill-health, pressure of business, or some other impediment. In the lead-up to the general election of 1776 so many names were being publicly canvassed by the Independent Electors, Freemen and Freeholders (a body orchestrated by a group of activists including Tandy) that any idea of a sacred spotlight falling on the one true representative must have been discredited.[96]

In practice, besides possessing the indispensable credentials of independent means and Patriot views, there were several ways in which prospective candidates could come to the notice of the electors. One was by copying Lucas's style and defending the interests of the city commons and citizens. The brewer Thomas Greene, who was a candidate in the early stages of the 1767 by-election, was a case in point; and was, perhaps, unlucky to find himself up against not someone who could be easily dismissed as a Court candidate, but the marquis of Kildare: Greene withdrew from the contest.[97]

Others boasted of having promoted the interests of the corporation and guilds in general. Few were so well placed to distinguish themselves in this respect as those who served as recorder of the city, and both James Grattan and Sir Samuel Bradstreet were able to capitalize on this. The encroachment of the Irish parliament on the city's sphere of influence had begun in earnest with the setting-up of the wide streets commission in 1758 and the paving board in 1774. Moreover, there were statutory measures that the corporation and guilds were anxious to obtain, such as a quarterage act, which necessitated much drafting of heads of bills and liaising with MPs. Bradstreet, who was appointed recorder on Grattan's death in 1766, exploited these opportunities to the full. Within only months of his appointment he had persuaded the corporation that the growing duties of his office warranted a rise in salary.[98] Besides, he seems to have been a consummate politician. At the by-election of 1767 it was allegedly he who, after several lively meetings at Carton, succeeded in persuading the duke of

---

[95] By a contemporary formula, true Patriots did not seek office: it was thrust upon them (Bernard Bailyn, *The Origins of American Politics* (New York, 1968), 143). Those declining the call were apt to be criticized for failing to serve their country ('Gracchus', *FJ*, 19–21 Nov. 1771).

[96] Reports of meetings of the 'Independent Electors, Freemen and Freeholders', *FJ*, 8–10, 13–15 Feb. 1776.

[97] In 1767 Greene had Lucas's support (*Faction Unmasked*, 23–8).

[98] *CARD* xi. 353.

Leinster to allow his son to stand for the seat, thereby demonstrating his influence with Ireland's foremost peer and acknowledged Patriot. Nine years later, when factions within the Independent Electors were still divided over whom to endorse at the forthcoming general election, Bradstreet was ready and willing to take the pledge required that year of the candidates, that they accept no place or pension from government as long as they held the seat. The upshot was that he and the sitting MP, Dr Clement, were returned unopposed, thus avoiding the trouble and expense of a contest. Bradstreet held the seat until he was made a judge in 1784.[99]

Another candidate who involved himself in civic affairs and in business ventures approved of by merchants and manufacturers was Redmond Morres. He successfully contested a Dublin seat at the 1773 by-election, and subsequently became known to the Castle as 'A violent Patriot—always against.' In the 1750s he had campaigned to reduce the aldermen's powers, and later supported a quarterage bill. Among numerous business activities he was a subscriber to the Grand Canal scheme, a project dear to the corporation since it promised better access to the capital and an enhanced water supply for the city. Morres was also a vice-president of the Dublin Society, and one of the directors of the Irish silk warehouse. As such, he attracted the favourable attention of the influential weavers' guild, which tried to persuade him to stand for a seat in 1771. In 1773 his return was backed by several of the guilds, the Aldermen of Skinner's Alley, and the Free Citizens.[100] In view of the well-known cost of contesting elections for the city, it was common for guilds, when endorsing particular candidates, to indicate that they would not expect the candidate to bear any expense (such as treating the voters) on their account.[101]

A further way in which prospective candidates could emerge was through an outstanding political record. Nothing touched the Patriot instincts of the Dublin freemen so much as the spectacle of a public figure suffering—or apparently suffering—in the cause of liberty.[102] This explains the otherwise

---

[99] Letter from 'A By-Stander', *FJ*, 17–20 Oct. 1767; meetings of the Independent Electors, *FJ*, 13–15, 17–20 Feb. 1776. Bradstreet's case showed the weakness of the Patriot position: independent MPs often yielded to the lure of office. Cf. Derek Jarrett, 'The Myth of "Patriotism" in Eighteenth-Century English Politics', in J. S. Bromley and E. H. Kossmann (eds.), *Britain and the Netherlands*, v (The Hague, 1975), 120–40.

[100] William Hunt (ed.), *The Irish Parliament 1775* (London, 1907), 38; toast no. 8, weavers' guild dinner, *FJ*, 13–17 Oct. 1767; *FJ*, 14–16 Nov. 1771; Morres's reply to Free Citizens' Society, *FJ*, 7–9 Dec. 1773.

[101] See e.g. declarations of guilds of carpenters, cutlers, and hosiers (*FJ*, 12–14 Nov. 1771); glovers, chandlers, and goldsmiths (*FJ*, 2–5, 7–9 Feb. 1782). The cost of contesting the city without some such arrangement (or even with it) was high: Charles Gardiner to duke of Bedford, 4 Nov. 1760 (PRONI, Bedford corr., T 2915/10/47); *Correspondence of Emily, Duchess of Leinster (1731–1814)*, ed. Brian Fitzgerald (Dublin, 1957), iii. 503–4, 506.

[102] One MP who benefited from this susceptibility was Sir Edward Newenham (1732–1814), younger son of a gentry family in Co. Cork; MP Enniscorthy, 1769–76, Co. Dublin,

surprising presence among the city MPs of Dr William Clement,[103] vice-provost of Trinity College, who succeeded to Lucas's seat in 1771. As MP for the university Clement had sided with Lucas and other Patriots in opposition to the 'unconstitutional' measures of Lord Townshend in the late 1760s; and on this account, it was widely believed, he had fallen foul of Provost Andrews and lost his seat. Accordingly, despite newspaper exhortations to the voters to avoid making 'hasty promises', Dr Clement was being spoken of as the choice of the guilds almost before Lucas had been buried (7 November 1771).[104] His emergence as candidate thus perhaps came closest to the Patriot ideal; and although he did have to face a contest, Clement secured almost three votes for every two that went to his opponent, Benjamin Geale, a merchant whose enterprises ranged from the Hibernian Warehouse to the Grand Canal and the Royal Exchange.[105] (Unfortunately for his prospects, Geale was also an alderman and a banker.)[106] Following Dr Clement's death in 1782, the tenor of his politics was summed up in the archbishop of Dublin's phlegmatic remark: 'The city has not yet fixed on a successor, but doubtless they will endeavour to choose one who will invariably oppose (as usual) the measures of government.'[107]

Lastly, it is necessary to say something about the electorate. It was noted by one commentator during this period that the size of the electorate was not keeping pace with the growth in Dublin's population; the numbers voting in 1773 were much the same as in 1749 (about 3,000).[108] Nor did its composition change significantly. In 1749 the freemen of the guilds represented 79.4 per cent of those who voted; in 1773 the figure was 78.9 per cent. With around four-fifths of the voters, the disposition of the guilds towards the candidates was clearly crucial; furthermore, it appears that half

1776–97; married into the Dublin banking family of Burton. Opposition to Lord Townshend's reforms (1772) cost him his post as collector of the excise for Co. Dublin. The city commons promptly chose him as one of 8 nominees for sheriff, but the aldermen failed to select him (DCA, C1/JSC/3, pp. 172, 180). The Castle regarded him as invariably 'in violent opposition' (Hunt, *The Irish Parliament 1775*, 39). See *DNB*; Coyle, 'Sir Edward Newenham'.

[103] Dr William Clement, below, App. B. See also R. B. McDowell and D. A. Webb, *Trinity College Dublin 1592–1952* (Cambridge, 1982), 42–3, 50.

[104] *FJ*, 5–7, 7–9 Nov. 1771.

[105] Clement, 1,521 votes; Geale, 1,079 (Holmes, *An Alphabetical List of the Freeholders and Freemen who Voted on the Late Election*, 39).

[106] Benjamin Geale, d. 1783; originally an attorney; married a granddaughter of Alderman Daniel Falkiner, becoming a partner in his mercantile business. Sheriff 1758–9, alderman (on Falkiner's death) 1759, lord mayor 1764–5; subsequently a banker. Geale did better when he stood against Morres in 1773, losing by only 86 votes (Holmes, *An Alphabetical List*, 39).

[107] *HMC Lothian MSS*, 408–9. It is thus mistaken to suppose that the city was in government hands until the victory of Henry Grattan in 1790 (Elliott, *Tone*, 81). That is not to suggest that only those in permanent opposition could be regarded as 'Patriots': see Dublin corporation's praise for Speaker John Ponsonby's 'patriotic conduct' (*CARD* xii. 122). Ponsonby had connived at 'Patriot' legislative gains, leading to dismissal from his revenue post (Dickson, *New Foundations*, 138–9).

[108] *FJ*, 17–19 Jan. 1782; Holmes, *An Alphabetical List*, 38–9.

a dozen of the craft guilds showed consistently strong backing for the independent candidates.[109] Much importance, therefore, was attached by candidates to obtaining endorsement from the guilds. Occasionally there were complaints of underhand means being used to acquire such support. In 1767 one observer challenged the means by which Kildare's candidacy was endorsed by Dublin corporation; another asserted that the weavers' pronouncement in favour of John La Touche had been obtained by pressure exerted by the candidate's father, the banker David La Touche.[110] During the actual elections, the role of the sheriffs was still crucial: they determined whether a show of hands would settle the matter, or whether a poll was necessary.[111] They also decided the timing of the poll, the venues, and who was entitled to vote. In such circumstances, it was not uncommon for irregularities to occur,[112] but by the 1770s the Free Citizens' Society was beginning to scrutinize proceedings on behalf of their preferred candidates. After the by-election of 1773 the Free Citizens indicted two unqualified freeholders who had voted for Geale: they were tried and found guilty, sentenced to imprisonment and to stand in the pillory.[113]

All this concerned the official electorate. But others, who lacked formal qualifications, nevertheless frequently found ways of making their views known, and thus can be said to have exerted informal pressure on the proceedings. It was not unknown for crowds to take sides: if there was a contest, the victorious candidate was wise to provide the means to enable the crowd to celebrate his victory, by dispensing drink or coins at the termination of the poll.[114] For the authorities, therefore, it was a matter for gratification if all passed off quietly.

Apart from those who were too poor to aspire to civic freedom and hence a vote, there were those who, whatever their wealth or property, were excluded on religious grounds. Catholics had not been able to vote since 1728, and were in a minority among the Dublin mercantile community, but from the 1760s on they had an organization, the Catholic Committee; and it was occasionally alleged that the Catholic body took sides in electoral contests, and even brought pressure to bear on behalf of particular candidates. In 1767 David La Touche was said to have deployed Catholics to canvass members of the weavers' guild on behalf of his son John. The reason given for their willingness to intervene was that they believed La Touche would not support a quarterage measure.[115]

---

[109] Above, Ch. 4, Table 4.2.
[110] 'A By-Stander', *FJ*, 17–20 Oct. 1767; *The City Spy-Glass*, 20.
[111] As in 1773: see Holmes, *An Alphabetical List*, 4.
[112] There were complaints of the sheriffs' partiality towards Hartley during the 1782 poll (*FJ*, 26–8 Feb., 28 Feb.–2 Mar. 1782).
[113] Holmes, *An Alphabetical List*, 36.   [114] *FJ*, 28 Nov.–1 Dec. 1767.
[115] *The City Spy-Glass*, 20, 30. In England too the politically active exceeded the total electorate: John A. Phillips, 'Popular Politics in Unreformed England', *JMH* 52 (1980), 599–625, at 624.

The by-election of February 1782 took on an even more overtly religious dimension. The choice of the Free Citizens and the 'Independent Electors' had fallen on the Presbyterian merchant, Travers Hartley, who was closely identified with the committee of merchants. His opponent was Alderman Nathaniel Warren, who was alleged to have some support from 'Court-voters'.[116] The run-up to the election coincided with the passage through the Irish parliament of the relief bill that allowed Catholics to buy land.[117] The bill was sponsored by Luke Gardiner, MP for County Dublin, who, though nominally independent, had in 1778 promoted what was certainly a government measure, the act that allowed Catholics to take long leases. On this occasion, the administration was not directly involved, but was probably alive to the possibility that a Catholic relief measure might serve to divide Protestants and thus weaken the call for legislative independence.[118]

At all events, for the first time during a Dublin election, Catholic relief became an issue. The *Freeman's Journal*, by now coming under Castle influence, supported Warren and took a stance as the Catholics' friend, insinuating that Hartley and his supporters (the dissenters, the Free Citizens, and the *Hibernian Journal*) opposed Catholic relief.[119] The *Hibernian Journal* in turn accused its rival of merely pretending to support the Catholics. A correspondent denied that dissenters opposed Catholic relief: on the contrary, northern dissenters supported the bill.[120] Some very recent developments lent substance to that claim. Grattan had recognized the possibility that government might play 'the Catholic card' to divide Protestants, and he had encouraged the Ulster Volunteers at Dungannon on 15 February to pronounce in favour of further Catholic relief, a move endorsed by the synod of Ulster.[121] But this development came too late to prevent the *Freeman's Journal* from presenting the Dublin election in terms that would scarcely have been out of place in the civic disputes of the 1670s: 'The event of this election will determine whether puritanical prerogative is to bear sway over citizens of the established church, Roman Catholics, and other denominations of inhabitants, who do not aim at universal power and religious arbitrary authority.'[122]

As in that period, the main sparring was not between Protestants and Catholics but between Anglicans and dissenters, and there was no sign as yet of any significant backlash against Catholic relief. However, although the question of political rights for Catholics had yet to be raised, the debates on Gardiner's bill witnessed warnings that there were limits beyond which

[116] Letter from 'An Independent Elector', *FJ*, 14–16 Feb. 1782. For Warren, see below, App. B.   [117] 21 & 22 Geo. III, c. 24.
[118] Bartlett, *Fall and Rise of the Irish Nation*, 85–6, 100–1.
[119] 'An Independent Elector', *FJ*, 14–16 Feb. 1782; *FJ*, 16–19 Feb. 1782.
[120] *Hib. Jn.*, 15–18, 20–2 Feb. 1782.
[121] Bartlett, *The Fall and Rise of the Irish Nation*, 101.
[122] *FJ*, 16–19 Feb. 1782.

concessions could not be allowed to go without endangering 'the Protestant constitution', or (as MPs groped for a term to signify the various manifestations of Protestant control in Ireland) a new phrase, 'the Protestants ascendancy' (sic).[123] Henry Flood made the point:

Ninety years ago the question was, whether Popery and arbitrary power should be established in the person of King James, or freedom and the Protestant religion in the person of King William—four-fifths of the inhabitants of Ireland adhered to the cause of King James; they were defeated, and I rejoice in their defeat. The laws that followed this event were not laws of persecution, but of political necessity . . .[124]

---

[123] The speaker was Sir Boyle Roche, quoted in W. J. McCormack, 'Vision and Revision in the Study of Eighteenth-Century Irish Parliamentary Rhetoric', *ECI* 2 (1987), 7–35, at 16. See also Ch. 8 below.

[124] *The Parliamentary Register: Or, History of the Proceedings . . . of the House of Commons of Ireland (Parl. Reg.)*, i. 252.

6

The Indian Summer of Civic Patriotism, 1783–1791

I. The National Context

A period of euphoria followed the winning of legislative independence, and a variety of reform schemes were advanced with a view to consolidating recent commercial and constitutional gains. For a time Ulster led the way in pressing for political reform, but with the onset of an economic depression, by the autumn of 1783 Dublin had regained the initiative, with a campaign for commercial protection and subsequently parliamentary reform.[1] Through the influence of the American revolution, and a renewed interest in Locke's *Two Treatises* and Molyneux's *The Case of Ireland*, appeals to natural rights now became more frequent.[2] And with parliament and the administration resisting calls for change in 1783 and 1784, reformers became more critical of the aristocracy, the established church, and the disposition of British ministers towards Ireland.

Nevertheless, even advanced reformers remained, by and large, tied to conventional Patriot concepts, publicly defending the rights of the king as well as the people, and upholding constitutional balance.[3] The diagnosis was that corruption and interest had altered that balance: the house of commons had succumbed to aristocratic influence, and had lost its 'independency'.[4] Since it remained the monarch's prerogative to appoint

---

[1] The most thorough study of the reform movement is James Kelly, 'The Irish Parliamentary Reform Movement: The Administration and Popular Politics, 1783–5', MA thesis (NUI (UCD), 1981), published in condensed form as *Prelude to Union: Anglo-Irish Politics in the 1780s* (Cork, 1992).

[2] A Dublin aggregate meeting sought rights based on 'the laws of GOD and NATURE' (*DEP*, 22 June 1784). See also Patrick Kelly, 'Perceptions of Locke in Eighteenth Century Ireland', *RIA Proc.* 89C (1989), 17–35, at 27–8.

[3] The Constitutional Society of Dublin (1784) supported 'the rights of the monarch and the people of this imperial, independent kingdom' (William Drennan, *Letters of an Irish Helot, Signed Orellana* (Dublin, 1785), 6); vote of thanks by Tandy to T. Hartley, (*Hib. Jn.*, 21 Apr. 1790). English reformers too invoked a balanced constitution: Paul Langford, *A Polite and Commercial People: England 1717–1783* (Oxford, 1992), 684–5.

[4] 'In order to render your Constitution perfect . . . you aimed at crushing aristocratic influence' (letter from 'Leonidas' [Sir Edward Newenham], *DEP*, 11 May 1784). But the *Hib. Jn.* (26 Apr. 1790) did not condemn influence when exercised by an opposition peer (Lord Charlemont).

ministers, some were ready to appeal to the king over the head of the Irish parliament. (The idea was not fanciful: in England, George III's dismissal of the Fox–North coalition in 1784 was endorsed by the voters, who were prepared to regard the ministry—despite its parliamentary majority—as a corrupt aristocratic oligarchy.)[5] Amid tributes to the role of 'the people' in maintaining balance, efforts were made to add precision to the term. Henry Grattan spoke for many when he argued that 'the populace differ much and should be clearly distinguished from the people'.[6] With certain corps trying to halt the decline in Volunteering by enlisting Catholics, there was some tentative discussion among advanced reformers as to whether an extended franchise might include Catholics, perhaps on a restricted basis. But the question was ducked by the national Volunteer convention in 1783, and by the more radical Dublin-inspired congress in 1784. Evasion was facilitated by the failure of the Catholic Committee to articulate a clear request for political rights. Lacking support from any influential individual (save the earl-bishop of Derry) or institutions of weight, and with British reformers divided in their advice on the subject, the issue quickly dropped out of sight.[7]

Two considerations helped check tendencies to break out of familiar patterns of thought. One was the apparent vitality of the old order everywhere before 1789. Admittedly, in the 1770s the American colonists had invoked natural rights, thrown off the British link, and would shortly adopt a constitution that separated church and state; but the colonies were remote and their future as free states uncertain.[8] In Europe, there were few signs to presage the revolutionary train of events that was to begin in France in 1789. In 1788 Louis XVI displayed a willingness to relax the penal laws against Protestants (thereby, according to critics, breaking his coronation oath);[9] but that was an exercise in regulating privilege. The impact of the French revolution was at first limited; down to 1791 it appeared that the French were merely introducing reforms that would render the French constitution more like that of Britain.[10]

Secondly, in Ireland—and this was an important difference in the

---

[5] 'Seek the renovation of your constitution from the father of his people' (Letter from 'Fitzpatrick', *DEP*, 3 Apr. 1784); 'the people's only resource is to supplicate the Monarch to exercise his prerogative in their favour' (*DEP*, 15 June 1784); Langford, *A Polite and Commercial People*, 559–63.

[6] Quoted in Lecky, *A History of Ireland in the Eighteenth Century*, 207.

[7] McDowell, *Irish Public Opinion*, ch. 6; Bartlett, *The Fall and Rise of the Irish Nation*, ch. 7; James Kelly, 'The Parliamentary Reform Movement of the 1780s and the Catholic Question', *Arch. Hib.* 43 (1988), 95–117, at 97–8.

[8] Figures from the US congress showed that between 1775 and 1784 the US population had dropped from 3,137,000 to 2,389,300 (*DEP*, 27 May 1784).

[9] J. M. Roberts, *The French Revolution* (Oxford, 1978), 39.

[10] Thus when Belfast Whigs in Oct. 1790 praised the French for adopting 'the wise system of a republican government' (cited in Elliott, *Tone*, 119), they meant a constitutional monarchy: France did not become a republic in the modern sense until September 1792.

experience of Irish and American Patriots—'ancient rights' had to all appearances been conceded by government in the period since 1760, beginning with the Dublin city corporation act and culminating in the repeal of the declaratory act, the amending of Poynings' law, and the renunciation by the British parliament of any claim to legislate for Ireland. These concessions were given retrospective significance in the 'Annals of the City of Dublin', a chronology published annually in *Wilson's Dublin Directories*. A number of new items appeared in the 1783 and 1784 editions, including entries for the years 1172, 1177, 1210, 1216, and 1227. These recorded the ('voluntary') submission of several Irish princes to Henry II ('on condition of being governed by the same laws, civil and ecclesiastical, and enjoying the same liberties ... as the people of England' (1172); the designation of Prince John as lord of Ireland (1177); the swearing of allegiance to King John by Irish princes (1210), and the granting of 'Magna Charta' to the Irish by Henry III in 1216 ('eight years prior to the English charter'[11]). Lastly, Henry III's command (1227) that a charter granted to the Irish by John in 1210[12] should be kept inviolably ('which proves, that the Irish were possessed of a charter of liberties, prior to that of Henry III'). These entries, all inspired by Molyneux's claims in *The Case of Ireland*, tended to confirm Ireland's distinct status, with a constitution that was the result of agreement (i.e. not a royal conquest), and a great charter that was not dependent on English parliamentary approval.[13] There could be no more striking indication of the enduring relevance of 'the ancient constitution' for Irish Patriots.[14]

True, British recognition of Ireland's ancient rights had come about only after the people had intervened in political affairs to a remarkable degree; but Patriot ideology was comfortable with the view that the people had a role to play when the constitution was agreed to be in need of regeneration. As Grattan correctly foresaw, these modes of thought helped to ensure that, once it had become apparent that there was no significant support for reform in either the Irish or British parliaments, the impetus for change would tend to die away rather than to gather force.

The other institution that came in for the attention of those who wished

[11] 'The English charter' was apparently that of 1225, regarded as the first English statute (Maitland, *Constitutional History of England*, 16).

[12] Art Cosgrove (ed.), *A New History of Ireland*, ii. *Medieval Ireland, 1169–1534* (Oxford, 1987), 145.

[13] 'Annals of the City of Dublin, Brought Down to the Present Year', in *Wilson's Dublin Directory*, bound with *The Gentleman's and Citizen's Almanack compiled by Samuel Watson, for ... 1784* (Dublin, 1784), 132–9. Cf. Molyneux, *The Case of Ireland*, 28–30, 47–51, 55–7. From 1785 on the (1216) claim that the Irish Magna Carta was older than the English one was dropped from the 'Annals', and there was a partial retreat on the 1227 claims, but the other new entries were retained into the 19th c.

[14] English reformers still valued ancient rights (Butterfield, *George III, Lord North and the People 1779–80*, ch. 8).

to purify the constitution at this time was the established church. Francis Dobbs, a barrister and graduate of Trinity College, who was already known for his Patriot writings, suggested in 1783 that the state church should be remodelled so as to command wider support. He proposed a much simplified liturgy, and a latitudinarian set of articles, based on the ten commandments and the sermon on the mount. The clergy of all denominations might become salaried servants of the state.[15] These proposals for a form of civil religion were not implemented, but that they were made at all is a reminder that, as in Britain, politics and religion were still closely enmeshed. With such schemes in the air, and the power of the papacy in decline, for a time rumours circulated about the possibility of seismic changes in the religious landscape. While elections were being held for the national congress in the autumn of 1784, the reformist *Dublin Evening Post* reported that propertied Catholics in Munster were planning to demonstrate support for reform by converting *en masse* to the established church. ('If other provinces should imitate their example, what a glorious harvest should the friends of constitutional liberty reap, to the confusion of all their enemies.')[16] To Protestants, steeped in assumptions about the link between 'popery' and 'passive obedience and non-resistance', this must have seemed a plausible way for Catholics to demonstrate that they were fit to exercise political rights.

No such dramatic event occurred; nevertheless, it was with a church-related issue that it did look, briefly, as if the parliamentary opposition might succeed later in the decade. This concerned the tithe question, which came to the fore as a result of agrarian disturbances in 1785–6.[17] But, thanks to an able defence by a Munster bishop of the link between church and state, both parliament and the Castle rallied to the church, and here too reform was defeated. Dr Woodward's influential tract, *The Present State of the Church of Ireland* (1786) has been discussed in detail elsewhere. Here it will suffice to note that in his defence of the established church the bishop drew on conventional assumptions about the tendency of the Catholic church towards absolutism and of radical Protestants towards republicanism. What was not conventional, but was symptomatic of growing anxieties about the future of Protestant control in Ireland, was his repeated use of the term 'Protestant ascendancy'. According to Dr Woodward, the maintenance of the established church was essential to Protestant ascendancy—denoting (as has been argued recently) not merely the Protestant constitution in church and state, the link with Britain, and the land settlement, but

---

[15] McDowell, *Irish Public Opinion*, 91.
[16] *DEP*, 7 Oct. 1784; Bartlett, *The Fall and Rise of the Irish Nation*, ch. 7.
[17] James S. Donnelly, Jr., 'The Rightboy Movement, 1785–8', in *Studia Hib.* 17–18 (1977–8), 176–202.

Protestant control in the disturbed areas of Munster, and, ultimately, security of property itself.[18]

II. The Dublin Patriots' Indian Summer, 1783–1790

> The Freemen of Dublin stand above all that shallow trick and mean artifice, which a *certain class* find necessary to adopt, to cover the infamy of measures, which to be known must be detested . . . The Freemen of Dublin are as much superior to them in virtue as in property.—Their resolves are not the hasty ebulitions [*sic*] of pensioners, of placemen, of tasters of wines . . . and all those other appendages of *titled insignificance.*[19]

Dublin's prominence in the various reform initiatives that surfaced in 1783–4 has been widely noted, though the part played by the guilds, corporation, and the freemen has received little attention. Despite some signs of a challenge, political debate and even strategy remained embedded in the civic Patriot tradition, still essentially confessional and corporatist. Never again would public opinion in the capital be so united in its political expression. Politics was still rooted in the idea of community: ministers ruled, but 'opposition' (a term coming into more general use)[20]—including the parliamentary opposition, guilds, Dublin city commons, societies, and, occasionally, the crowd—criticized. That is not to deny that beneath the surface of unanimity lay great divisions, some of an economic and social nature,[21] some religious, especially between Protestants and Catholics, and some political: the aldermen were often at odds with the city commons, and by 1790 even the latter contained a small, cohesive Castle party. But during the 1780s these divisions detracted little from the Patriot consensus.

As in the past, the thrust of Patriot politics in Dublin was directed towards the improvement of trade and industry, defence of the city's chartered rights, and promotion of constitutional 'virtue'. At a time when the established church and the landed class were beginning to show signs of defensiveness, confidence was still the hallmark of the Dublin freemen and their corporate bodies, buoyed up by belief in their own independence, even though certain individual aldermen seemed to be succumbing to the lure of

---

[18] Richard Woodward, *The Present State of the Church of Ireland* (Dublin, 1786), 13–19; see also Leighton, *Catholicism in a Protestant Kingdom*, 60–1; Jacqueline Hill, 'The Meaning and Significance of "Protestant Ascendancy", 1787–1840', in *Ireland Under the Union: Proceedings of the Second Joint Meeting of the Royal Irish Academy and the British Academy* (Oxford, 1989), 1–22; Kelly, 'Eighteenth Century Ascendancy'; W. J. McCormack, *The Dublin Paper War of 1786–1788* (Dublin, 1993), chs. 2–3.

[19] *DEP*, 15 Apr. 1784, commenting on a meeting of Dublin citizens.

[20] See *Hib. Jn.*, 12 Feb. 1790, commenting on the Whig club.

[21] Like the United Irishmen in the 1790s, propertied Patriots had no sympathy for combining journeymen (cf. Smyth, *The Men of No Property*, 83). The opposition press was also hostile, and could be critical even of a pro-opposition crowd (*Hib. Jn.*, 12 Apr., 28 June 1790).

patronage. The importance of urban corporations as a check on monarchical and aristocratic power was still generally acknowledged, although opinions differed as to whether they were now able to fulfil this role effectively without reform of the borough franchise.[22] Of Dublin's importance there could be little doubt, as the city had delivered an unbroken succession of independent MPs since the mid-1760s.

Before considering the final decade of Patriotism's appeal as an ideology to which most sections of the population could pay at least lip-service, it will be worth noting the state of Protestant–Catholic relations in Dublin. The position of Catholics—who remained a minority group in the city's business community—had recently improved as a result of the collapse of the quarterage campaign, and the relaxation of curbs on the purchase of land (though not in parliamentary boroughs). Certain wealthy Catholics had benefited from these changes. Relations with Protestants do not appear to have suffered: the merchants' guild appointed a Catholic to be a trustee of the Royal Exchange (built for merchants in the 1770s). All employers had a common interest in resisting the growing challenge of combinations by workmen. However, there were few intermarriages or multi-denominational business partnerships, which suggests that there was little social *rapprochement*.[23] Willingness to make further concessions depended on the conviction that there was no serious challenge to Protestant control. A correspondent in the now Castle-oriented *Freeman's Journal* in early 1784 urged directorships of the new Bank of Ireland to be opened to Catholics. Such a step, the writer argued, could hardly be dangerous, for although Catholics were numerous, they lacked weight, influence, and power.[24]

Something of the extent and the limitations of co-operation between Dublin Protestants and Catholics can be illustrated by the case of the chamber of commerce, founded in the optimistic atmosphere of February 1783. This body is of interest because it shows that many members of the guilds and corporation were willing to work with Catholics in the commercial sphere, but that mercantile goodwill alone was not sufficient to secure a permanent role for such a body. The chamber's prospects of success initially looked better than those of its predecessor, the committee of merchants (set up in 1761). By the 1780s the failure of the quarterage campaign had removed one obstacle to better relations between free and unfree merchants. When the chamber was first set up, nearly 300 merchants paid a subscription, and this included approximately one-third of the aldermanic board, and about the same proportion of the guild of merchants'

---

[22] Some argued that 'close' boroughs had returned MPs of Grattan's stature (parliamentary report, *Volunteer Evening Post* (*VEP*), 20–3 Mar. 1784).

[23] Dickson, 'Catholics and Trade in Eighteenth-Century Ireland'; Cullen, *Princes & Pirates*, 36. The election of new trustees for the Royal Exchange was vested in the merchants' guild (7 Geo. III, c. 22).

[24] Letter signed 'Hortensius', *FJ*, 20–2 Jan. 1784.

representatives on the city commons, and of the sheriffs' peers. The chamber's membership reflected the fact that most Dublin merchants were Protestants, but in 1783 the elected council of forty-one included at least six Catholics and a Quaker.[25] The first president was Travers Hartley, the Presbyterian merchant shortly to be elected MP for the city in the independent interest.

However, by the end of 1783 support had fallen off considerably, and within five years the chamber's organizing council was reduced to a handful of members; after 1791 meetings ceased altogether. In part this was owing to the effects of a severe economic depression; but it has also been suggested that the chamber's difficulties were political—that by identifying so openly with the parliamentary opposition over issues such as protection and the British commercial propositions, it was too radical for its own survival.[26] Since the chamber's position on these issues was broadly in line with those adopted by the guild of merchants and Dublin corporation,[27] it seems unlikely that its commercial stand alone made very much difference to its fate. What undoubtedly did hamper its work (and this was not a problem shared by corporate bodies) was that it lacked a royal charter or statutory recognition. The possibility that *ad hoc* bodies such as the Volunteer convention would be regarded as the real organs of public opinion had made the Irish parliament sensitive to any unaccredited body claiming to speak for particular interests. In the case of the chamber of commerce, several MPs argued that parliament should not even accept a petition from a body whose title was not recognized at law.[28] Its prospects for success were therefore limited, and, as the national mood turned against reform, within two or three years the chamber's leading supporter among radical reformers, Napper Tandy, was throwing his energies into the guild of merchants, a body whose chartered rights to represent mercantile opinion could hardly be disputed.[29]

The economic depression of 1783 was all the more frustrating because early in the year cloth manufacturers had been looking forward to the opening of new markets in Europe and America. But Portugal continued to resist admitting Irish goods, and within a few months the American market had become glutted. Credit became very tight, and manufacturing industry languished; thousands of artisans were unemployed. By the autumn several concerned bodies, including Dublin corporation, the guild of merchants,

[25] Cullen, *Princes & Pirates*, chs. 3 and 4, esp. 45–6.   [26] Ibid. 49–53.
[27] DPLGC, MS 79, fos. 258, 263; *CARD* xiii. 328, 430–1.
[28] Report of proceedings, Irish house of commons. The petition was accepted on the following day (*VEP*, 22–5, 25–7 Nov. 1783).
[29] In 1776 Tandy was elected to represent the guild on the city commons. His return was challenged, perhaps because he was no longer a merchant, but he was re-elected in 1778 (DCA, C1/JSC/3, p. 343, C1/JSC/4, fo. 72). A founder member, chamber of commerce, he resumed guild activities after 1785, on committees (1786), as warden (1787), and as master (1789, 1790) (DPLGC, MS 79, fos. 268, 278).

and the chamber of commerce, were endorsing the call from Luke Gardiner, MP for County Dublin, for protective duties.[30] Proposals were laid before parliament, but by the end of March 1784 (coinciding with the rejection of the Volunteers' parliamentary reform bill) they had been defeated. In certain opposition newspapers these setbacks prompted questions about the value of the British connection[31]—though such speculation was still constrained by fears that British domination would be replaced by that of France. The *Volunteer's Journal*[32] made such scurrilous attacks on ministers that the administration introduced a libel act, giving greater control over the press. The cost of the official stamp for newspapers was raised, and subsidies began to be used to try to keep the press in line. Several newspapers eventually succumbed to these pressures.[33]

At this time too there was concern among Dublin citizens about a new paving bill, which threatened to raise taxes, abolish rights of Protestant parishioners under the 1774 paving act, and compromise the corporation's independence by increasing the scope of government patronage through a new paving commission.[34] Following a large public meeting at the Tholsel on this issue (5 April), a crowd of several hundred artisans from the Liberties, angered at the rejection of protective duties, invaded the gallery of the house of commons. The administration, rendered nervous by the Gordon riots, demanded action from the lord mayor, who, together with the sheriffs, cleared the gallery. But crowds lingered around College Green, and after some delay the lord mayor at length summoned troops to disperse them.[35] This move was controversial, since citizens were accustomed to regard the use of troops in such cases as a threat to their liberties. Fortunately for the lord mayor (Alderman Thomas Greene), a parliamentary committee censured him for neglect in handling the matter, and this produced a strong public reaction in his favour.[36]

---

[30] DPLGC, MS 79, fo. 258; *CARD* xiii. 328; Cullen, *Princes & Pirates*, 49. Gardiner's estates in Dublin city and county were home to many woollen workers (Kelly, 'The Irish Parliamentary Reform Movement', 148).

[31] See e.g. *DEP*, 1 May 1784. The Castle press seized on such comments so as to portray the reformers as separatists, a charge for which no evidence has been found for this period (Kelly, 'Napper Tandy', 6–7).

[32] This paper, founded 1783, was conducted by a Catholic, Mathew Carey. It was novel for a Catholic paper to back the opposition: in the early 1770s the *Dublin Mercury* (conducted by Peter and James Hoey) had taken a Castle stand (Evans, 'The Ancient Guilds of Dublin', 74).

[33] The *Volunteer's Journal* had ceased publication by 1788, while others (including the *FJ*, but not the *DEP* or *Hib. Jn.*) had abandoned opposition (Inglis, *Freedom of the Press*, 36–7, 49–50).

[34] The 1774 act (13 & 14 Geo. III, c. 22) provided for Protestant parishioners to elect committee members of the paving board; the 1784 act (23 & 24 Geo. III, c. 57) set up a non-elected paving commission. The *DEP* denounced an alderman's appointment to the commission as likely to erode 'the liberty of the subject' (22 May 1784).

[35] *DEP*, 6 Apr. 1784.

[36] *Commons Jn. Ire.* xi. 264–5. For the lord mayor's account see report of the meeting to consider the riot of 5 April (*DEP*, 15 Apr. 1784).

Public concern over the 'insult' to the lord mayor and other current issues was voiced in a way that was seized on in the opposition press. No fewer than seven parishes, all but one (St Michans, north of the river) in or around the textile heartland of the Liberties, took the chance afforded by routine Easter vestry meetings to pass resolutions on these matters.[37] The resolutions were apparently spontaneous, for they varied considerably, with several taking an 'Irish-only' stand on behalf of the textile trades, some extolling the liberty of the press, and some urging protective duties and parliamentary reform. All, however, pledged support for the lord mayor, on grounds similar to those invoked by the St Michan's meeting: 'That it is necessary for the preservation of our liberties (which we will relinquish but with our lives) to support the honour and dignity of our Magistrates whilst they demonstrate a due regard for the public cause.'[38]

It was scarcely novel for vestries to express views on law and order matters.[39] The passing of these resolutions, however, lent some weight to opposition claims that the public at large was behind the reform campaign. For there was a dimension to vestry pronouncements that was lacking in the case of the guilds or the corporation. The latter were the mouthpieces, exclusively, of Protestant opinion: vestries, except when dealing with church-related matters, in principle represented residents irrespective of denomination.[40] And since by the mid-1780s Catholics had obtained some of the rights of citizens, the vestry had acquired new potential as the expression of public opinion. An attempt was even made at this time to have a Catholic appointed to a key parochial office. This occurred in St Michan's parish, which, like most of the parishes in the western half of the city, was largely Catholic, though it also contained some of the most radical Protestants in Dublin.[41] To the consternation of the minister, at the parish's Easter vestry in 1784 a Catholic was nominated for churchwarden. With a Protestant also in nomination, an election was held, with the result that 'Mr Geo. Booker of King Street had the Majority of Protestant Voices and Mr

---

[37] The other parishes were St Nicholas Within, St Nicholas Without, St Werburgh's, St Bride's, St Audeon's, and St Catherine's (*DEP*, 15, 17, 29 Apr., 1 May 1784).

[38] *DEP*, 15 Apr. 1784. A correspondent had urged citizens to assemble in their parishes to adopt non-importation agreements (*FJ*, 6–8 Apr. 1784).

[39] Vestries had a wide range of functions, including allotting parochial taxes and appointing overseers of the poor and constables of the watch (Rowena V. Dudley, 'Dublin's Parishes 1660–1729: The Church of Ireland Parishes and Their Role in the Civic Administration of the City', Ph.D. thesis (2 vols.; TCD, 1995)).

[40] Catholics were formally excluded from parish administration (Dudley, 'Dublin's Parishes 1660–1729', i. 18, 71). A 1726 act (12 Geo. I, c. 9) also prevented them from voting at vestries on church-related matters.

[41] St Michan's parish was at least 75% Catholic (Fagan, 'The Population of Dublin', 141–2). One of its streets was Pill Lane (now Chancery St.), later associated with the United Irishmen. Twenty of 425 identified members of the society resided there, and at least 10 were Protestants (R. B. McDowell, 'The Personnel of the Dublin Society of United Irishmen 1791–4', *IHS* 2 (1940–1), 12–53; Smyth, *Men of No Property*, 153–5).

Rich[d] Dillon[42] of Pill Lane a Roman Catholic was elected by the Majority of Voices—Thus a double return was made.' After the matter was referred for legal review, Dillon resigned and a fresh election (of a Protestant) took place.[43] Subsequently, legislation clarified that Catholics were not eligible to vote at such elections.[44] Thus even at vestry level, the opportunities for Catholics to make their mark on public life were very few.

During the spring of 1784, both in Dublin and elsewhere the main concern in industrial circles continued to be parliament's failure to implement either protective duties or, what was seen as a related issue, parliamentary reform. One response was the readoption in several of the larger towns of non-importation or non-consumption agreements; in Dublin several Volunteer corps and vestries took such action. Certain guilds, too, were critical of the administration and concerned at the state of manufactures.[45] As the Easter quarter assembly of Dublin corporation approached, steps were taken by guild activists, especially Tandy and John Binns of the weavers' guild, to have 'freemen, freeholders and inhabitants' summoned to the Tholsel to deliberate on public issues.[46] The term 'inhabitants' indicated that the meeting was not to be confined to freemen, though the committee of fourteen formed as a result of the meeting was apparently an exclusively Protestant one: it included four members of the corporation and at least three other freemen, including a former master of the merchants' guild.[47] The timing of the meeting, a day ahead of the Easter assembly, suggests that the intention was to give the corporation the benefit of public opinion—a procedure that Lucas had advocated. In fact, the meeting went well beyond this. The committee was instructed to prepare a petition to the king against the press bill and the paving bill, and to prepare resolutions for the promotion of Irish manufactures and parliamentary reform.

On the following day both houses of the corporation adopted an Irish-only consumption resolution.[48] The guild representatives' displeasure with

[42] Richard Dillon, wholesale linen merchant, future United Irishman (from 1785 living just across the river in Bridge St.). In 1797 his house was a venue for those whom a Castle informant called 'the Pill Lane King Killers' (McDowell, 'Personnel of the Dublin Society', 30).

[43] St Michan's parish, vestry minute book, 1777–1800, Representative Church Body (RCB) Library, P 276/4/3, pp. 189, 200. One churchwarden was usually nominated by the minister, the other by the parishioners.

[44] 25 Geo. III, c. 58 (1785), reaffirmed by 33 Geo. III, c. 21 (1793). In 1795 another bid to elect a Catholic (the printer Peter Hoey, Ormond Quay) as a St Michan's churchwarden (McDowell, 'Personnel of the Dublin Society', 35) also failed. By that time the press was reporting the holding of alternative Catholic vestry meetings (*Hib. Jn.*, 18 Mar. 1795).

[45] *DEP*, 8, 11 May 1784; NLI, MS 12125, pp. 309–10; TCD, MS 1447/8/2, p. 287. For non-importation agreements, see Kelly, 'The Irish Parliamentary Reform Movement', chs. 5–6.

[46] *DEP*, 27 Apr. 1784.

[47] The corporation members were Tandy, Richard Hayes (linen draper), Joseph Dickinson (wholesale merchant), all representing the merchants' guild, and John Binns (weavers' guild).

[48] *CARD* xiii. 358–9.

the administration was reflected in a resolution of the city commons not to grant honorary freedom to viceroys and their secretaries except on merit: a snub that was not endorsed by the aldermanic board.[49] The board did, however, agree to a commons' resolution that directed the 'vigilant attention of the people' to the current administration's opposition to any scheme for national improvement. It also approved another commons' resolution, after toning down the language to express 'concern' (the commons' word was 'indignation') at the imprisonment of fellow subjects contrary to law and the constitution: this in response to the government's order for the arrest, two weeks earlier, of the printers of three opposition newspapers.[50]

Some weeks later, Tandy and some guild colleagues, no doubt disappointed at the relatively moderate response of the corporation, again organized a requisition asking the sheriffs to convene an aggregate meeting of Dublin 'freemen, freeholders and inhabitants' to press the parliamentary reform issue by addressing the king and the people. The sheriffs agreed, despite the absence of any really weighty names among the signatories: no alderman signed, and only half a dozen of the guild representatives on the city commons.[51] The meeting, held at the Tholsel, passed resolutions in favour of reform, including one that expressed guarded support for extending 'the Right of Suffrage to our Roman Catholic Brethren, STILL PRESERVING IN ITS FULLEST EXTENT THE PRESENT PROTESTANT GOVERNMENT of this Country'. A committee of nineteen was formed, including Tandy, Binns, one other guild representative on the city commons, and lord mayor elect Alderman James Horan, the merchant who had taken a leading role in the campaign for free trade. The Presbyterian minister, Dr William Bruce[52] (recently recalled to the Strand Street congregation after serving for a time in Lisburn) was appointed to the committee, as was John Keogh[53] and other members of the Catholic Committee. Two weeks later a second meeting agreed to invite sheriffs of counties, cities, and large towns to convene meetings for the purpose of electing delegates to a 'national congress', which would deliberate on measures likely 'to re-establish the Constitution on a pure and permanent basis'.[54]

Analysing these developments, one historian has commented: 'For the

[49] DCA, C1/JSC/5, fo. 129. The new viceroy (the duke of Rutland) was not granted freedom until the following Michaelmas (*CARD* xiii. 385–6).

[50] DCA, C1/JSC/5, fo. 129; *CARD* xiii. 359; Inglis, *Freedom of the Press*, 25–6.

[51] The guild representatives included Tandy and Patrick Ewing (merchants' guild), James Crosbie (smiths), Ralph Mulhern (shoemakers), and Mark Bloxham (chandlers). A sheriffs' peer, Henry Williams, also signed. For the meeting itself (7 June), see *DEP*, 27 May, 10 June 1784.

[52] Dr William Bruce (1757–1841), Arian; often designated 'of Belfast', but born Dublin, educated TCD, served in Strand St., Dublin 1782–90 (*DNB*).

[53] John Keogh (1740–1817), Dublin merchant; prominent member of the Catholic Committee (*DNB*).   [54] *DEP*, 22 June 1784.

first time a non-gentry, urban, part-catholic, part-dissenter group was leading a national political movement.'[55] Certainly these various elements were present, though the choice of venue, and the sheriffs in the chair, plus the presence on the committee of four members of the corporation including the lord mayor elect, indicates how much these developments still owed to the civic Patriot tradition, and to activists, especially Tandy, Binns, and a silk weaver, William Arnold, who were all members of the city commons.[56] However, what is also of interest is the presence on the committee of five barristers, including the radical MP for Lisburn, William Todd Jones. Their participation reinforces the sense that a watershed in Dublin opposition politics was approaching, in which leadership would shift from those with guild backgrounds to professional men, who were less firmly rooted in the corporatist world.[57]

Such changes, however, lay largely in the future, and in the meantime certain activists in Dublin and elsewhere had been attempting, particularly since the spring of 1784, to maintain the pressure for reform by bringing Catholics (still officially banned from bearing arms) into the now declining Volunteer movement. Catholics and lower-class Protestants were recruited into the Liberty corps captained by Tandy, and into the Dublin Irish Brigade.[58] This worried the authorities, who also took alarm at the prospect of the proposed congress. The Volunteer convention had been unwelcome enough, but at least it had been a Protestant and a mainly landed affair. The congress was not only less predictable in its religious composition, but, as the invitation to 'inhabitants' suggested in the case of the Dublin meeting, the custom that such gatherings should be confined to members of recognized orders and corporate bodies was being compromised. As in the case of the Volunteer convention, the idea of a delegate meeting, with elected representatives, threatened the primacy of parliament. Such was the concern that for a time the possibility of a conspiracy, fomented by 'French agents'—supposedly in contact with Tandy, Binns, and the earl-bishop of Derry—was taken seriously by the viceroy.[59] The attorney-general (with some effect) warned sheriffs that meetings held for the purpose of choosing

---

[55] Dickson, *New Foundations*, 165.

[56] The corporation members were Tandy, John Binns, William Arnold, silk weaver, and Alderman James Horan. See also Kelly, 'Napper Tandy', 6–7.

[57] Other barristers included Anthony King, Joseph Pollock, and Edward Houghton. There were tensions between lawyers and guild members in the United Irish movement (McDowell, 'Personnel of the Dublin Society', 16; Rosamond Jacob, *The Rise of the United Irishmen 1791–94* (London, 1937), 73). For similar tensions among Patriots in the Dutch town of Deventer see Wayne P. Te Brake, *Regents and Rebels: The Revolutionary World of an Eighteenth Century Dutch City* (Oxford, 1989), 171.

[58] James Kelly, 'A Secret Return of the Volunteers of Ireland in 1784', *IHS* 26 (1989), 268–92, at 272, 284; *Charlemont MSS i, HMC 12th Rep., App., pt. x*, 117. Some Catholics had been recruited as early as 1782 (*DEP*, 6 Aug. 1782).

[59] No evidence has been found for these rumours (McDowell, *Irish Public Opinion*, 115; Kelly, 'Napper Tandy', 7–8).

delegates to the congress would be illegal, and the Castle (with less effect) urged those newspapers over which it had influence to warn about foreign agents, and the supposed dangers of an alliance between Catholics and dissenters. Volunteer leaders, too, especially Lord Charlemont, did their best to steer the Ulster Volunteers away from pursuing the Catholic question.[60]

If the activists were beginning to press beyond the customary bounds of corporatist and confessional politics, this constituted an implicit challenge to the freemen, the guilds, and the corporation as well as to the landed class. How did they respond? According to press reports, one Dublin freeman did challenge the legality of the second aggregate meeting on 21 June. This was the future Orangeman, John Giffard of the apothecaries' guild, who had recently obtained a government post in the customs. Giffard challenged the sheriffs' authority to summon a meeting of any but freemen and freeholders, but he received no support (save from a revenue officer) and withdrew from the meeting.[61] For their part, during the summer of 1784 the guilds and corporation were slow to pronounce on these matters. However, the ongoing decline of Volunteering in Dublin in the summer and autumn of 1784 suggests that Tandy's recruitment of a more plebeian and denominationally mixed class into the movement was not generally popular with the Protestant business and professional classes.[62] As for Dublin corporation, faced with sometimes violent disturbances from artisans in pursuit of Irish-only agreements, relations with the Castle had improved sufficiently by June and July 1784 for the aldermen to request the viceroy to station guards in the Liberties and at the Tholsel.[63]

By mid-September, in what the *Dublin Evening Post* called 'an insult' to the citizens of Dublin, several public bodies throughout the country had passed resolutions condemning the proposed national congress.[64] This did not deter some thirteen acting or former guild officials from signing a requisition calling on the sheriffs to convene a meeting for the purpose of electing Dublin city delegates to the congress. (Others also signed: of the sixty-one signatures, the Castle reckoned that about one-third were those of Catholics.)[65] When the meeting assembled, the sheriffs were intimidated by the presence of the attorney-general, and adjourned the proceedings before

[60] Moody and Vaughan (eds.), *NHI* iv. 275; Dickson, *New Foundations*, 165.

[61] *DEP*, 22 June 1784. Giffard's raising of the legality issue foreshadowed the attorney-general's intervention. Until 1779 Giffard had still been acting with Tandy and Binns (*FJ*, 21–3 Oct. 1779).

[62] Certain corps refused to drill with the mainly Catholic Liberty corps (Jacob, *The Rise of the United Irishmen*, 41). There is no sign that the Catholic question was raised in either the merchants' or the weavers' guilds, although these were the guilds to which Tandy and Binns belonged.

[63] Monday book 1784–1842, DCA, MR/20, pp. 2–4, 6–7.

[64] *DEP*, 16 Sept. 1784.

[65] Ibid.; Rutland to Sydney, 20 Sept. 1784 (PRO, HO 100/14, fos. 102–5).

elections could take place. Subsequently, a second requisition, signed only by freemen and freeholders, was published.[66] This was more circumspect, making no direct mention of the congress and calling simply for a meeting of 'freemen and freeholders' on 11 October to consider 'a parliamentary reform'. The 182 signatories included eighteen members of the city commons, plus at least one who had formerly held guild office. About 40 per cent (sixty-three) of those whose occupations could be identified were involved in the textile trades. Of the signatories who gave addresses, the overwhelming majority lived in the western half of the city (only 18 per cent lived east of a line running from Capel Street and the Castle to Aungier Street). Those who signed, therefore, were drawn almost entirely from the older industrial areas of the city, and their occupations reflected this (Table 6.1). Although the sheriffs declined to convene this meeting, it did take place (in the weavers' hall on the Coombe) and Dublin delegates to the congress were duly elected.[67]

Under pressure from the authorities, therefore, the activists fell back on those whose right to speak out on public issues could not be challenged: the freemen. And the requisition indicated that there was support in freeman circles for the congress, especially among the textile trades. However, neither of the most recent requisitions had mentioned the issue raised at the June meeting: the extension of the franchise to Catholics. In fact, by the autumn Tandy himself had reconsidered this matter, finding limited support

TABLE 6.1. *Occupations of 152 freemen and 30 freeholders who signed a requisition for a parliamentary reform meeting, 7 October 1784*

Gentry	5
Merchants (excluding textiles)	11
Silk trade	14
Other textile trades	49
Goldsmiths	10
Printers, booksellers	7
Building, furnishing trades	15
Smiths, braziers, ironmongers	17
Food, drink trades	7
Other trades	21
Unidentified	26
TOTAL	182

Sources: DEP, 7 Oct. 1784; Dublin *Directories*; Dublin Heritage Group Freemen Database.

[66] *DEP*, 28 Sept., 7 Oct. 1784. Thirty freeholders and 152 freemen signed the requisition; the Castle organized a counter-petition (HO 100/14, fos. 123–4ᵛ, 127).

[67] *DEP*, 12 Oct. 1784. The meeting was crowded, with an overflow gathering in St Luke's churchyard. The Dublin delegates, Sir Edward Newenham, MP, Co. Dublin, Sir James Stratford Tynte, bt. (high sheriff, Co. Wicklow, 1785), Sir William Fortick (former sheriff, Co. Dublin), George Putland, and John Phepoe were freeholders rather than freemen, probably because no alderman could be prevailed upon to stand. See also map 2 above.

for it even in reforming circles,[68] and having failed to induce Catholic spokesmen to endorse the reform movement openly. By early October he was hoping that the Catholics could be persuaded to renounce aspirations to the parliamentary franchise, in order to smooth the way to reform.[69] Dublin corporation's attitude on the question of voting rights for Catholics was revealed at its Michaelmas assembly held on 15 October 1784, just ten days before the congress held its first meeting. On this occasion the city commons unanimously adopted an address to Lord Charlemont, the Volunteer general, who during the summer had thrown his weight against the idea of votes for Catholics. The address, endorsed by the aldermanic board, praised Charlemont's 'manly and constitutional' answer to the Belfast Volunteers:

While we admire the spirit and moderation of that answer, we concur with your lordship in declaring that as the interests of our country are our grand objects, so we will pursue them by constitutional means alone, having the utmost good will to our fellow subjects of the Roman Catholic persuasion, we rejoice in the late privileges which an enlightened legislature has extended to them, but we never can consent to any measure which may weaken or endanger the Protestant establishment in church or state.[70]

Several points here are worth noting. Most obviously, there is the indirect warning to the congress not to seek political rights for Catholics. The commitment to pursue Irish interests 'by constitutional means alone' might sound like an option for political means as opposed to violence, but actually indicated that agitation should proceed through existing constitutional channels—parliament, grand juries, corporations, meetings of freemen— rather than through agencies unknown to the constitution. The polite reference to Catholics is noteworthy: no reference here to popery or papists. All in all (and bearing in mind an earlier paragraph in which Dublin was described as 'the first [i.e. oldest] Protestant corporation') the address was designed to reaffirm the corporation's long-standing commitment to the Protestant constitution, and to convey a sense of goodwill towards Catholics—as long as they remained content with their economic privileges and freedom of worship.

The fact that no one in the city commons challenged the address is also significant. The radicals, including Binns and Tandy, were certainly present, for they failed in a bid to prevent the adoption of an address expressing

---

[68] Even Sir Edward Newenham was opposed to political rights for Catholics (Kelly, 'The Parliamentary Reform Movement of the 1780s', 107).

[69] McDowell, *Irish Public Opinion*, 94. It was at this time that the *DEP* speculated about a mass conversion of Catholics (above, beginning of sect. II). The Catholic Committee remained neutral in these clashes between the reformers and the Castle (Bartlett, *The Fall and Rise of the Irish Nation*, 116).

[70] DCA, C1/JSC/5, fos. 145ᵛ–146; *CARD* xiii. 385.

satisfaction with the administration. And when the congress met, delegates agreed to drop the question of Catholic political rights, in the hope of building up more (Protestant) support. Subsequently the smiths' guild endorsed Lord Charlemont's stand, as did the hosiers' guild, though the latter took a somewhat more positive, if still cautious, stand: 'we hope to see our Roman Catholic fellow-subjects possess every privilege that is consistent with a Protestant Government and Constitution'.[71]

There were other signs during 1784 that even the city commons was coming to share some of the government's fears about the nature of the reform campaigns. The Irish-only agreements (endorsed by the corporation) were still producing a good deal of violence, with tarring and feathering punishments being meted out to those who imported English cloth. In July the city commons complained about a riot of 'the lower Order of the People' in which one of the sheriffs had been assaulted. Attitudes towards the clamp-down on the press also softened; in October the commons granted a sum of twenty pounds towards the prosecution of the printer of the *Volunteer's Journal* for libels on the recorder. (This was a rather grudging amount; the aldermen had asked for fifty guineas.)[72]

Did these developments indicate a shift towards a 'Court' or Castle position? The election in 1784, for the first time since the 1760 corporation act, of an alderman (Nathaniel Warren) to represent the city in parliament might seem suggestive.[73] Certainly, there were signs late in 1784 that the more radical newspapers were becoming disillusioned with the caution displayed by corporate bodies. In November the *Dublin Evening Post* published the names of the new Dublin city term grand jury (picked by the sheriff, and usually composed of corporation members), and noted that several of its members depended on the Castle for place or preferment. In the same month, that newspaper ostentatiously welcomed the advent of a new Constitutional Society in Dublin, and called for the setting up of similar clubs all over the city: they would henceforth be 'the palladium of individual security—the barrier against the incursions of tyranny'. The unspoken message was that corporate bodies were faltering in their political duty, and must hand on the defence of constitutional purity to other agencies.[74] This was a new departure: groups like the Free Citizens had been praised in the past, but their role had always been regarded as complementary to that of corporate bodies.

[71] DCA, C1/JSC/5, fos. 140ᵛ–141; *DEP*, 16 Nov. 1784.
[72] DCA, C1/JSC/5, fos. 134ᵛ–135, 145. On the reform campaigns, see Kelly, 'The Irish Parliamentary Reform Movement', ch. 6.
[73] *FJ*, 21–4 Feb. 1784. On Dublin's representation, see above, Ch. 5.
[74] *DEP*, 4, 9, 20 Nov. 1784; n. 3 above. Any connection between this body and a constitutional club mentioned by Charlemont in 1770 (*Charlemont MSS i, HMC 12th Rep., App., pt. x*, 303) is unclear.

However, the suggestion that politics had moved to a new plane was premature. Once the delegate congress had met,[75] and its own reform proposals (lacking a Catholic dimension) had been published without producing any enthusiasm in parliamentary circles, politics went on very much as before. It was as if the question of enfranchising Catholics had never been raised. As for Alderman Warren (who was elected unopposed), although he was not the most radical member of the board, neither was he what the *Dublin Evening Post* called a 'Castle alderman'. He had been the most popular candidate in the shrieval elections in 1773; during his mayoral year (1782–3) he had been widely praised for his efforts to revive trade and help the unemployed; he had been a delegate at the Volunteer convention in 1783, and his election notices indicated that he was ready to receive his constituents' instructions. Any latent Castle tendencies were therefore well concealed, and his parliamentary record was at first satisfactory enough.[76]

In fact, the entire aldermanic board was still ready, on occasion, to adopt an opposition stance. One sign of this was to be found in the very address to the viceroy that Tandy and Binns had attempted to defeat in October 1784. That address did express confidence in the viceroy, but it also called for reform of parliamentary representation, and a satisfactory Anglo-Irish commercial arrangement. In 1785 both aldermen and city commons opposed the government-backed commercial propositions. Another significant sign in that year was a statement by a number of sheriffs' peers to the effect that, in the event of being elected aldermen, they would not accept a place from government.[77]

But the most striking indication that opposition had not lost its appeal (in the city commons, at any rate) was the enormous popularity of Tandy—once he had shelved the issue of votes for Catholics. This can be judged by the ballots that took place annually at Easter for eight freemen, usually members of the commons, to be put in nomination for sheriff (the aldermen picked two from the eight). At Easter 1785 for the first time since his election to the commons Tandy came top in the ballot (the aldermen failed to select him on that or subsequent occasions); as late as 1790 he was still receiving more votes than any other candidate. In his guild, too, he was held in esteem; his son was admitted to freedom in 1787 without the usual fine,

---

[75] The congress was a moderate affair (McDowell, *Irish Public Opinion*, 106–10; Kelly, 'The Irish Parliamentary Reform Movement', ch. 8).

[76] *CARD* xii. 251–2; xiii. 327–8; election notice (*FJ*, 30 Dec. 1783–1 Jan. 1784); report of cooks' guild meeting (*FJ*, 10–13 Jan. 1784). Warren voted with Hartley, the other city MP, against Foster's libel act, but accepted a commissionership under the police act, 1786 (below), and backed the Castle over the regency issue (DCA, C1/JSC/6, fos. 106ᵛ–107; *DEP*, 13 Apr. 1784, 17 Feb. 1789).

[77] *CARD* xiii. 383–4, 430–1; DCA, C1/JSC/5, fo. 185. Parliamentary reform had Court as well as opposition overtones: Prime Minister Pitt unsuccessfully introduced a reform bill into the British parliament in 1785 (John Cannon, *Parliamentary Reform 1640–1832* (Cambridge, 1972), 86–90).

because of the guild's strong sense of 'the public conduct and patriotic principles of his father'.[78] The guilds, therefore, still showed strong opposition tendencies; had they not done so, the great controversy about to break out over the Dublin police act would have been much more muted.

In order to appreciate the extraordinary heat generated by this issue, which was to dominate Dublin politics for years to come, two aspects of eighteenth-century political culture in England and Ireland should be recalled: the cherished importance of common law, and the dread of anything resembling an armed police force under central government control. The former was generally believed to guarantee civil liberties; the latter was associated with Continental 'despotism', and with memories of Cromwellian military rule and 'arbitrary' Stuart government. The system of policing that had evolved from the common law tradition involved locally chosen, unarmed, often elderly, unpaid or poorly paid constables or watchmen. It was not particularly efficient, but it posed no threat to civil liberties. It also fitted in well with the civic republican tradition, which extolled the ideal of the self-governing citizen.[79]

Such was the system in force all over England and Ireland, a system that had scarcely begun to be questioned until the authorities faced the shock of the Gordon riots in 1780. Not only did those London riots cause great loss of life and injury as well as damage to property, they proved extremely difficult to bring under control. The constables were completely ineffective, and the troops at first fared not much better, being obliged to act under the direction of civilian magistrates. It was only when the king permitted this rule to be relaxed that the riots were brought to an end. Subsequently, as MPs began to discuss possible remedies, the term 'police' (the word itself was French, and in English had hitherto referred only to the general regulation or government of a country or town, not to a body of men) began to be heard. In 1785 Pitt introduced a bill into the British parliament that would have created a full-time, properly paid police force for metropolitan London, responsible to commissioners appointed by government. Although the bill provided for the old watch to remain, and the new police were not to carry arms, the outcry against it in the city and in parliament was such that it was withdrawn.[80]

In Ireland, although there had been nothing on the scale of the Gordon riots, concern was growing about the state of public order in the capital, which by the late 1770s was frequently disturbed by labour disputes and clashes between citizens and soldiers. In 1778 the corporation centralized

---

[78] DCA, C1/JSC/5, fo. 160ᵛ; C1/JSC/6, fo. 156; DPLGC, MS 79, fos. 269–70.

[79] See Stanley H. Palmer, *Police and Protest in England and Ireland 1780–1850* (Cambridge, 1988), pp. xviii, 13–15, 24, 61.

[80] Ibid. 18, 30, 69–70, 86–7, 89–91. The Dublin paving bill had been a police measure in the old sense (*DEP*, 6 Apr. 1784, *FJ*, 10–13 Apr. 1784).

the watch by grouping the parishes into six wards, each under an aldermanic guardian, but with little effect.[81] Concern was expressed not just by government and MPs, but by vestries and corporate bodies; in June 1783 the guild of merchants instructed its representatives to work for an act to improve the Dublin watch. The disturbances of 1784 confirmed the problem. It is safe to say, however, that the government's proposals, embodied in a bill in 1786, offended just about every hallowed assumption on the subject.[82]

In the first place, the new body was modelled on the Paris police, a force whose name, *gens d'armes*, highlighted a key difference between British and Continental ideas of policing. It was to be a salaried, armed and uniformed body, under the control of the state, although a sop was thrown to the corporation in that the commissioners would be chosen from among the civic magistrates. Besides crime prevention, the duties of the new, exclusively Protestant, force were to include licensing trade, suppressing disturbances and popular amusements, removing prostitutes from the streets, rounding up beggars, and regulating traffic. Journeymen, apprentices and servants drinking or gaming at unseasonable hours were to be detained. The intention was apparently to employ the police as a semi-bureaucratic arm of the state, and to impose greater discipline on the lower classes.[83] Despite strenuous opposition from the city commons, guilds, freeholders, and opposition MPs, the bill became law in May 1786.[84]

Although this was not the first statutory encroachment on Dublin corporation's powers, it proved by far the most controversial. It was condemned by the parliamentary opposition as a measure of 'absolute monarchy' contrary to 'our free constitution'; it was 'foreign' and 'unconstitutional'; a similar measure had been rejected for London: to impose it on Dublin was to treat the Irish capital with contempt. The city commons resolved in March 1786 that the bill contained clauses 'highly repugnant to the Principles of the Constitution as established by Magna Charta, and militating against the chartered Rights of the Citizens of Dublin'. St Michan's parish invoked the balanced constitution against the measure: it was calculated 'to erect on the ruins of the Democratic part of [the] Constitution a monstrous & oppressive Aristocracy, no less injurious

[81] Palmer, *Police and Protest*, 81.

[82] DPLGC, MS 79, fo. 257. In 1777 the St Bride's parishioners had called for watchmen to be able-bodied and 'well armed', but under parish control (St Bride's vestry minute book 1742–1780, RCB, P 327/3/2, pp. 493–4).

[83] Palmer, *Police and Protest*, 99–100, 119–20. No opposition MP criticized the Protestant nature of the force: ibid. 113.

[84] 26 Geo. III, c. 24. See DCA, C1/JSC/6, fos. 5–6; DPLGC, MS 79, fos. 268, 272, 275; St Michan's vestry minute book 1777–1800, RCB, P 276/4/3, p. 243; Henry F. Berry, 'Records of the Feltmakers' Company of Dublin, 1787–1841: Their Loss and Recovery', *JRSAI* 41 (1911), 26–45, at 35–6.

to the ... rights of our beloved sovereign than derogatory to the ... privileges of his People'.[85]

What most upset members of the city commons and the guilds, however, was the prospect of the aldermen participating in the new system, as the bill intended they should. Not only would this expose individuals to the temptation of government places, it would seriously compromise the independence of Dublin corporation in general. Although the 1760 act had curbed some of the aldermen's powers, the board still had great weight in corporation affairs; among other things, its assent was necessary for any measure to become an act of assembly. As the bill progressed through parliament, these fears were given substance by the board's failure to support the city commons in denouncing the measure. At a post assembly held to consider the bill in March 1786, this dereliction of duty was deplored by the commons; two weeks earlier, the latter had unanimously affirmed its belief that a majority of the aldermen had already sacrificed their independence to government in the hope of immediate or future appointments. The word 'corruption', little used of municipal politics since the reforms of 1760, began to fly about again, in condemnation of the supposed unholy alliance between the aldermen and the government.[86] The measure proved no more acceptable once it had become law. It remained the target of criticism on the grounds of its corrupting nature, expense for the citizen (special taxes were set aside to pay for it) and—a judgement endorsed by a modern study—its ineffectiveness in combating crime and disorder.[87]

In the campaign against the new system, the city commons' first priority was to preserve the corporation's independence of government patronage. One of its weapons was a moral one. The commons' own standing rules, dating from 1772, stipulated that none of its members could be elected to any place of profit in the corporation, or employed in any of the city works. That rule was taken seriously; guild representatives resigned their seats on appointment to any corporation post.[88] As noted above, in 1785 several sheriffs' peers had signed a pledge not to accept any government place or pension if they were elected to the aldermanic board. In 1786 it emerged that signing this pledge had not deterred Alderman Richard Moncrieffe from accepting the post of divisional justice for the Rotunda ward of the city under the police act. Summoned before the city commons to explain his conduct, Moncrieffe denied that there was any conflict between his pledge

[85] Palmer, *Police and Protest*, 101; DCA, C1/JSC/6, fo. 5; RCB, P 276/4/3, p. 243.

[86] DCA, C1/JSC/6, fos. 3ᵛ, 5–6. Aldermen James, Rose, and Warren were the first police commissioners.

[87] Ibid. fos. 123, 138; weavers' guild minute book 1755–1809 (RSAI), entries for 1 Jan. 1791, 1 Apr. 1793; TCD, MS 1447/8/2, p. 332; NA, M 2925, fos. 57–8, 64–6, 78; Palmer, *Police and Protest*, 124.

[88] See DCA, C1/JSC/6, fo. 42ᵛ; *CARD* xii. 447; xiv. 279–80; xvi. 40.

and the office he now held, and indicated that he had no intention of resigning it (nor did he do so). Despite this setback, sheriffs' peers continued to give a verbal pledge to remain independent should they be elected to the aldermanic board.[89]

The other weapon at the commons' disposal was its role in selecting the civic magistrates. Under the 1760 corporation act, the commons had a veto over the election of lord mayor, and also filled vacancies (caused by death or resignation) on the board from among four sheriffs' peers nominated by the aldermen. The timing of vacancies on the board was obviously unpredictable, but the mayoral election came up every year. Usually the lower house simply endorsed the aldermen's choice for lord mayor, but in 1788 the indefatigable Tandy led a challenge to the confirmation of Alderman John Rose, on the grounds that he was a police commissioner. A ballot was held, and the challenge almost succeeded—Rose was endorsed by just 65 votes to 55.[90]

During the next two years the campaign gathered strength from the manifest inadequacies of the new system. The police failed to prevent large-scale rioting on two occasions in 1787, and an attempt to suppress May Day disturbances in 1789 ended ignominiously with the police having to be rescued by the army.[91] The regency crisis (November 1788–February 1789), and the possibility of the parliamentary opposition coming to power, put new heart into the Dublin opposition. By this time, criticism of the new police was apparently having some effect even on the aldermen. In May 1789 Alderman John Exshaw unexpectedly became the most senior member of the board, and thus next in line to be lord mayor. He took the calculated step of resigning his post as divisional justice before the meeting at which he was, as expected, chosen to be chief magistrate for the ensuing year. He was said to have described the police establishment as 'repugnant to the spirit of the Constitution', and odious to the citizens in general.[92] At Michaelmas, his inauguration as lord mayor inspired the city commons to resolve to keep up the campaign, pledging themselves in particular not to vote for any person 'to be Chief Magistrate of, or Representative in Parliament for this City, who holds Place or Employment in an Establishment so justly, and so universally Odious to the Public in general'.[93] The reference to parliament was pertinent, for a general election was due in 1790—and one of the sitting MPs, Alderman Warren, had become a police commissioner. A long debate

---

[89] DCA, C1/JSC/6, fos. 22–3ᵛ, 49ᵛ.

[90] Coughlan, *Napper Tandy*, 14.

[91] Palmer, *Police and Protest*, 122, 124.

[92] DPLGC, MS 79, fo. 276; DCA, C1/JSC/6, fo. 114. Exshaw (d. 1827), a prosperous printer and bookseller (alderman 1782, lord mayor 1789–90), may have been looking ahead to the general election (1790), in which he and Alderman Henry Gore Sankey, with Castle backing, unsuccessfully contested Dublin city (Spencer Bernard papers, PRONI, T 2627/6/2/7).

[93] DCA, C1/JSC/6, fo. 123; goldsmiths' guild minutes 1779–1807, NLI, n 6056 P 6782, pp. 154–5.

took place on this section of the resolution, but an amendment to omit it was lost by 38 votes to 78, and the whole was carried with only one negative vote. The board, however, negatived the resolution, as well as one in January 1790 calling for the repeal of the police act: thereby confirming the city commons' suspicions that the board's independence had indeed been compromised.[94]

It could therefore hardly have come as a surprise when, at the Easter assembly held on 16 April 1790, the city commons refused to approve Alderman William James as lord mayor elect, for he was a police commissioner.[95] The next two names sent down from the board were those of the other two commissioners, and they too were rejected. Eventually, having rejected another five names, the commons moved on to other business before their proceedings were terminated by the lord mayor. Thereupon, standing on their rights under the 1760 act, the lower house agreed to take the highly unusual step of holding a separate meeting to carry out its own election of a lord mayor.[96] Next day, at a well-attended meeting, members of the commons resolved that, since the board had failed to send down the name of an acceptable candidate, it was their duty under the 1760 act to proceed to an election: and one of the more junior aldermen, Henry Howison, a long-term associate of Tandy's, was elected as lord mayor by 85 votes to 29.[97] A committee was nominated to take Howison's name to the privy council, as required by law: its members included Tandy and Binns, as well as John Chambers, the future United Irishman. For its part, the board submitted the name of Alderman James.[98]

The privy council at first refused to endorse either candidate and returned the matter to the corporation. But at a meeting in May the city commons again rejected Alderman James, by 74 votes to 51, and again held a separate meeting at which Howison was elected by 77 votes to 14. (In the meantime the opposition had been strengthened by the outcome of the general election in Dublin: all but two of the guilds had decided to ask two members of the newly formed parliamentary Whig party,[99] Henry Grattan and Lord Henry Fitzgerald, to stand for the city: the Whigs were opposed to the police act,

[94] DCA, C1/JSC/6, fos. 123^v, 138. In 1790 anti-police feeling was to force Warren to withdraw from the general election.

[95] William James, d. 1807 (alderman 1783, lord mayor 1793–4) had also given offence during the disturbances of 1784 by over-energetic use of his powers as a magistrate (Inglis, *Freedom of the Press*, 29).

[96] DCA, C1/JSC/6, fos. 154^v, 163.

[97] Henry Howison, merchant, d. 1817; alderman 1783, lord mayor 1790–1. Activist for free trade (1779), parliamentary reform (1784). With Tandy, he had tried to find a more radical candidate than Alderman Warren for the 1784 by-election (*FJ*, 21–3 Oct. 1779; 10–13, 15–17 Jan. 1784).   [98] DCA, C1/JSC/6, fos. 164–5.

[99] *CARD* xiv. 520–3; *Hib. Jn.*, 5, 20, 27, 29 Jan., 24 Feb., 1 Mar. 1790. The duke of Leinster, Grattan, and other independent MPs formed the party in 1789 after the regency crisis. Associated with it was the Whig Club of Ireland (June 1789), which sought a place bill, tithe reform, and reform of the Dublin police (Moody and Vaughan (eds.), *NHI* iv. 285–6).

and Grattan and Fitzgerald were duly returned on 12 May, defeating two aldermanic candidates.)[100] But the opposition did not have everything its own way. On this occasion twenty-five of the city commons registered a protest against the rejection of Alderman James, arguing that no lawful cause had been shown against him.[101] The first to sign it was John Giffard: evidently there was by now a Castle party in the city commons.[102] Again the privy council returned the matter to the corporation, and again (in June) the lower house refused to approve Alderman James.[103]

By this time there were fears that the campaign—which had received the endorsement of eighteen of the twenty-five guilds[104]—was causing such exasperation to the aldermen and to the Castle that prosecutions might be started against guilds or individuals who publicly upheld the city commons' stand. For the city Patriots, however, the very basis of political liberty appeared to be at stake. As the merchants' guild put it, the city commons' aim was to prevent 'the first local Corporation in the Kingdom from being under the controul and direction of the Minister'. The smiths' guild expressed the fear that Dublin was likely to become 'an Aldermanick borough'. The city commons passed resolutions upholding its own role in mayoral elections and defending the rights of 'the People' and the guilds to instruct their corporation representatives and MPs.[105] On 24 June the commons held another meeting without the board, and again, by a majority of 67 votes to 3, reaffirmed approval for Howison: for a third time two names were sent to the privy council. Both sides now prepared to defend their respective positions. Alderman James had already petitioned the privy council in his own behalf, and the city commons retained two leading Whig MPs, the barristers J. P. Curran and George Ponsonby, to put their case. Curran took his stand on the British constitution, and warned the privy council against following the example of James II by stripping corporate bodies of their rights. But on 9 July a decision was given in favour of Alderman James.[106]

The opposition leaders in the city commons were not prepared to accept this outcome, and at the next corporation meeting they won support (by 75 votes to 33) for a resolution asserting that the viceroy and privy council, by approving as lord mayor elect an alderman who had not been endorsed by the lower house, were acting illegally. It was further decided to oppose

[100] For Fitzgerald see below, App. B. The claim that the result represented the first victory for 'independence' in the city since Lucas's death (Grattan, *Memoirs*, iii. 463) was sheer hyperbole (above, Ch. 5).   [101] DCA, C1/JSC/6, fos. 166–70.
[102] At the Castle's suggestion Giffard had recently taken over *Faulkner's Dublin Journal*; he had supported government both in the *FDJ* and in the corporation during the regency crisis (DCA, C1/JSC/6, fo. 106ᵛ).   [103] Ibid. fos. 172ᵛ–173.
[104] *The Speeches of John Philpot Curran, Before the Privy Council, on the Petitions of Alderman James and Alderman Howison* (Dublin, 1791), 3.
[105] DPLGC, MS 79, fo. 285; NA, M 2925, fos. 65–6; DCA, C1/JSC/6, fo. 174.
[106] DCA, C1/JSC/6, fos. 175ᵛ–176; *Speeches of John Philpot Curran*, 30–1.

Alderman James's exercise of the mayoral office by all legal means available; withholding his salary as lord mayor; requesting guild officers to have no dealings with him; retaking the Mansion House into the corporation's possession, and urging tradesmen to give the corporation no further credit. It was also agreed to hold a public meeting on the matter, and to petition the king in the name of the citizens of Dublin, detailing the ways in which their rights had been infringed, and beseeching him to remove from his councils 'the Advisers and Promoters of those baneful Measures, which have destroyed the Confidence the People should have in their Governors and Magistrates'.[107]

Within three weeks, however, Alderman James had reconsidered his position and had resigned as lord mayor elect. At a special meeting of the corporation on 5 August, the board proceeded to send down Alderman Howison's name to the city commons. By 97 votes to 6 the commons signified their approval of this belated conversion to the man of their choice, and when the privy council approved the election, the 1790 mayoral dispute was over.[108] At its height it had distracted the corporation and guilds, drawn in opposition MPs, the Aldermen of Skinner's Alley, and the recently formed Whig Club,[109] and threatened to paralyse local government in the city. It thus came close to rivalling that earlier opposition triumph in the annals of Dublin corporation, the famous mayoral dispute of 1711–14. But whereas that occasion had represented a victory for the aldermen against the government, this was a victory for the city commons against the aldermen and government combined. There could scarcely have been a clearer vindication of the rights won by the lower house in 1760, and Tandy—who was currently senior master of the guild of merchants—was the hero of the hour. He likened the episode to the worst constitutional crises of the Stuarts; and the opposition press applauded 'the patriot Commoners'.[110]

In its final stages the dispute had soured relations between the city opposition and the Castle. Since 1785, when parliament had rejected the British commercial propositions, these relations had been reasonably cordial, at least as far as commercial issues were concerned. In January 1790 the guild of merchants had voted freedom to John Fitzgibbon (recently

---

[107] DCA, C1/JSC/6, fos. 177–80.

[108] Ibid. fo. 186ᵛ. Government supporters acknowledged the strength of the city commons' legal case (*Kenyon MSS, HMC 14th Rep., App., pt. iv*, 530–1).

[109] The Whig Club asserted that 'where corporate rights are attacked, it is not unbecoming the Peers of the realm to . . . consider themselves not merely as hereditary Judges but (what they value more infinitely) as hereditary Freemen' (*The Whig Club, Attacked and Defended* (Dublin, 1790), 24, 31). See also *Hib. Jn.*, 9 July 1790.

[110] *Hib. Jn.*, 21 Apr. 1790; DPLGC, MS 79, fo. 286; Milne, 'Irish Municipal Corporations', 102. In view of Tandy's triumph, it is difficult to agree with Smyth that 'Tandy's career as a city politician peaked in 1784' (*The Men of No Property*, 135).

promoted to be lord chancellor) for his 'liberality of principle', and his dispatch in expediting justice in commercial cases. In an address to Fitzgibbon at that time the guild had looked forward to improvements in 'the law of merchants' as a result of Fitzgibbon's tenure of office. But on 12 July, three days after the privy council sided with the aldermen, the guild voted to expunge the address from its records.[111]

Heartened by victory in the dispute, the various opposition forces in Dublin returned to their original preoccupation: the new police establishment. If its constitutional dangers had been, for the moment, averted, it remained a grievance in its cost, its ineffectiveness in combating crime, and in its very nature. By January 1791, resolutions were being passed in the merchants' guild and city commons expressing determination to work for the repeal of the act.[112] Unknown to them, events were to unfold during 1791 that would, within little more than a year, shatter the unity of the Patriot opposition, and change the course of Irish history.

[111] DPLGC, MS 79, fos. 279–80, 285.
[112] Ibid. fos. 287–8; DCA, C1/JSC/6, fo. 201; *CARD* xiv. 530–2.

PART 2

Patriots Divided: The Phoney War,
1792–1814

Introduction

During the 1790s the *ancien régime* in Europe was everywhere challenged by the ideology and example of the French revolution, powerfully reinforced by the armies of revolutionary France herself. That the privileged orders should have reacted, on the whole, defensively, is not surprising— though under the pressure of events, odd things happened. One of the reasons why the old regime collapsed so fast in France was that some privileged men actually embraced change, appearing positively eager to renounce the rights of their order in favour of the rights of citizens.[1] No doubt utopian overtones in the political climate helped account for this, but the phenomenon also raises questions about the nature of the *ancien régime*, which is often thought to have been essentially static. In Great Britain and Ireland, for instance, the 'unreformed' political system proved apparently impervious to change in the second half of the eighteenth century. No significant measures of parliamentary reform were obtained, despite the efforts of the London and county reform movements and of Prime Minister Pitt himself in the 1780s. The Volunteers and other reformers in Ireland at the same period were no more successful.

In fact, the old order was more dynamic than is sometimes supposed. Dublin was a case in point. Down to the mid-eighteenth century Dublin's civic élite, a merchant patriciate of relatively small numbers, had constituted a local oligarchy. By 1790 the guilds had obtained greater powers in their relations with the city corporation, and the role of the city commons was much enhanced. As for the freemen, they had lost exclusive trading privileges, but had carved out a political role for themselves independent of the aldermen and of the Castle, especially in respect of parliamentary representation, but also over particular issues such as the new police. No doubt they often looked to an opposition element in the aristocracy for support, but in defending corporate rights they had their own priorities, and could draw on powerful ideologies, including ancient rights, civic republicanism, and corporatism. Accordingly, a body of around 3,000 merchants, master craftsmen, and shopkeepers had been elevated on to the civic and national political stage. Something of the significance of this becomes clear

---

[1] Cf. Gail Bossenga, 'From *Corps* to Citizenship: The *Bureaux des Finances* before the French Revolution', *JMH* 58 (1986), 610–42. Lord Charlemont recorded something similar when at the Volunteer convention (1783) landed delegates vied to renounce claims to nomination boroughs: he noted that the keenest to renounce such privileges had the weakest claims to them (*Charlemont MSS* i, HMC *12th Rep.*, App., pt. x, 124–5).

when it is recalled that there were only about 5,000 Protestant landowners in the entire country.

Relations between the landed élite and the bourgeoisie in eighteenth-century Ireland have not been much explored, but it has been argued above that while the Dublin freemen took pride in their status as citizens, and could be critical of the aristocracy, they nevertheless identified to a considerable extent with the gentry and their values. This was apparent in matters of social conduct, with 'citizens' such as Charles Lucas and James Napper Tandy being drawn in to the practice of duelling.[2] Moreover, as the decades passed, it ceased to be a matter for congratulation that the citizens' origins lay in trade rather than in (aristocratic) 'plunder'. In politics, the freemen embraced a quasi-aristocratic role in helping to maintain a constitutional balance, the main purpose of which was to check arbitrary royal power; and they enthusiastically embraced Volunteering, which, while certainly consistent with civic traditions, also enabled tradesmen to put on uniform and emulate the gentry. These developments had lasting effects, helping to perpetuate a sense of caste among the civic élite: in 1836 the chief secretary, Lord Morpeth, commented that the Dublin merchants with whom he had just dined at a corporation function, though of less commercial weight than their London counterparts, more closely resembled viceregal aides-de-camp in their bearing.[3] In such ways, it can be argued that the reforms of the mid-century had served not to weaken but to strengthen the aristocracy by broadening its base.[4]

Meanwhile, changes were taking place that were beginning to produce the first outlines of a society based on class differences rather than the old society of orders. Since the 1750s the gulf between masters and journeymen had been growing, and it was becoming much less common for apprentices to live with their masters. The guilds were losing their primary function as regulators of trade. A gap between popular and élite culture was emerging. The last riding of the franchises in which something like the full civic hierarchy was displayed to public view took place in 1782, when, in addition to the circuit made by the lord mayor and city regalia, journeymen from several guilds paraded through the city 'according to triennial custom'. But by this time even the opposition press was inclined to criticize the journeymen component for encouraging idleness and excess.[5] Well before the event was due to take place again in August 1785 both houses of the corporation agreed to place notices warning that participation by journeymen was likely to interrupt work and create 'a general dissipation among

[2] Grattan, *Memoirs*, i. 89; James Kelly, 'Napper Tandy', 12–13, 19; id., *That Damn'd Thing Called Honour: Duelling in Ireland 1570–1860* (Cork, 1995).

[3] R. B. McDowell, *Public Opinion and Government Policy in Ireland 1801–46* (London, 1952), 41.

[4] Cf. Armand Arriaza, 'Mousnier and Barber: The Theoretical Underpinning of the "Society of Orders" in Early Modern Europe', *P. & P.* 89 (1980), 39–57, at 56.

[5] *DEP* 17, 20 Aug. 1782.

the lower class of people'.[6] The corporation also became more critical of 'the mob'. Despite the unpopularity of the new police system of 1786, it was widely recognized that some reform was necessary to check the rising street disorders of the 1770s and 1780s. It has been argued that the last appearance of the crowd in its capacity as representative of the community came with the Fitzwilliam riots in 1795; but the era had already effectively passed, since on that occasion only a minority even of the city commons was in harmony with the crowd's wishes (for full Catholic emancipation).[7]

What of religion? Lucas had always been ready to attack Protestant churchmen for failing to uphold liberty, and such were the close links between church and state in eighteenth-century Ireland and Britain that any opposition movement was likely to contain an anticlerical dimension. The appeal of the Methodists in the second half of the century indicated some dissatisfaction with the performance of the established church even among the propertied classes.[8] But, as has been pointed out elsewhere,[9] none of this indicated more positive attitudes towards Roman Catholicism. As the penal laws began to be dismantled from the 1770s on, the corporation and merchants' guild provided new inducements for Catholics to join the established church by admitting conformists to freedom on favourable terms. And repeal of the sacramental test in 1780 removed any legal basis for discriminating against Protestant dissenters in urban corporations,[10] thus serving to consolidate the Protestant, as opposed to the merely Anglican, nature of the élite.

These changes had considerable, if neglected, significance for Catholics, and especially for urban Catholics. Certainly, several penal laws were repealed in the 1770s and 1780s, notably those relating to land, education, and freedom of worship. On the face of it, therefore, it appears perverse for the Catholic Society of Dublin, towards the end of 1791, to have complained of 'new penal statutes' recently enacted against Catholics.[11] Yet it is not difficult to see their point. From the 1770s new opportunities had been created for propertied Protestants to take part in public life, while the door had been kept firmly closed to Catholics. The role for Protestant parishioners introduced by the first paving act of 1774; the court of

---

[6] DCA, C1/JSC/5, fo. 164ᵛ; *CARD* xiii. 422. Despite (or because of) these precautions, the usually festive occasion turned out badly in 1785. When the lord mayor and his entourage reached the Coombe, where by custom a ritual attempt to take the civic sword was staged, disturbances arose, troops were called, and three people were killed (*DEP*, 13 Aug. 1785).

[7] Smyth, *The Men of No Property*, 149; below, Ch. 9. Before the 1790s, when the Catholic question was rarely to the fore, the crowd and large sections of corporation opinion were more likely to be in harmony.

[8] Cole, *A History of Methodism in Dublin*, 53.

[9] Leighton, *Catholicism in a Protestant Kingdom*, 51–3.

[10] Protestant dissenter relief act (19 & 20 Geo. III, c. 6).

[11] Declaration of the Catholic Society of Dublin, 21 Oct. 1791, in *Transactions of the General Committee of the Roman Catholics of Ireland During the Year 1791* (Dublin, 1792), 11–15, at 12.

directors of the Bank of Ireland (founded 1782); the new police of 1786; these openings were all reserved, directly or indirectly, for Protestants. Moreover, at vestry level legislation of 1785 had removed doubts as to whether Catholics were entitled to vote in elections for churchwarden by confirming that they were not.[12] Thus, although the distinction between (free) Protestants and (unfree) Catholics no longer had much significance in the commercial sphere, in terms of citizenship confessionalism had actually been reinforced.[13] The link, so important to the old order, between rights and functions had been broken, but for Catholic tradesmen any role in civic life was virtually confined to participation in the (declining) chamber of commerce.

The revolutionary challenge, therefore, when it arrived in the 1790s, found a city that had undergone very extensive change in the previous fifty years. Dublin had become less oligarchical, but, if anything, more aristocratic, and more confessional—in the broad Protestant sense of that term. These changes meant that it was not simply a matter of how the landed élite would respond to the challenge: the reaction of the Protestant freemen was also of crucial importance. They had prided themselves on their status as citizens; they had boasted of their commitment to liberty; they had endorsed the (hitherto limited) relaxation of the penal laws. But they were also strongly attached to their corporate rights and privileges, and down to this period there had been little reason to question the assumption that these privileges were intrinsically and necessarily Protestant.

The extension of a wide range of political rights to Catholics in the 1790s accordingly led most freemen to rally to the Protestant constitution. Yet in certain respects the underlying issue of the relations between Protestants and Catholics in the post-penal-law era was not engaged during this period. In part, this was because the main counter-revolutionary target—as identified by Edmund Burke—was not Catholics, but Painites, Jacobins, deists: radicals of all kinds. Secondly, although many political rights were given, some could not be exercised in the absence of further reform, and the political climate from the mid-1790s was not conducive either to institutional reform or to full 'Catholic emancipation'. To that extent defence of the Protestant constitution remained largely inseparable from counter-revolutionary loyalism. New political fissures opened: but they occurred as much between Protestants as between Protestants and Catholics. In that sense, the years 1791 to 1815 represented a period of phoney war, not belonging wholly to the Protestant world of the eighteenth century, nor to the sectarian one of the nineteenth.

[12] Above, Ch. 6; T. K. Whitaker, 'Origins and Consolidation, 1783–1826', in F. S. L. Lyons (ed.), *Bicentenary Essays. Bank of Ireland 1783–1983* (Dublin, 1983), 11–29, at 19–20; 25 Geo. III, c. 58.
[13] Cf. Louis Cullen, 'Catholics Under the Penal Laws', in *ECI* 1 (1986), 23–36, at 24–5.

7

The Economic and Social Background in Dublin after the Quarterage Dispute, c.1780–1814

I. Population and Employment

During this period Dublin city continued its apparently inexorable growth: in 1778, 154,000 population; in 1798, 180,000; and in 1821, 224,000. However, the Protestant proportion continued to fall. A recent estimate settles for about 30 per cent (c.54,000) by 1798;[1] but this may be too low, since there is no agreement as to when Protestant numbers began their absolute decline. David Dickson has suggested that they continued to rise into the late eighteenth or early nineteenth centuries, which would mean that they came to exceed 66,763, which was his estimate for the 1760s. On the other hand, Patrick Fagan has argued that Protestant numbers peaked at c.75,000 as early as the 1730s, thereafter declining to c.58,000 by 1766, and then levelling off to end the century at around 54,000. His estimates allow explicitly for suburban drift, but even taking this into account it is difficult to accept that Protestant numbers in the city would have fallen by 20 per cent between 1733 and 1766. The size of town populations in this period is notoriously difficult to determine with any precision, but Dickson's projection of a growth in Protestant numbers until towards the end of the eighteenth century appears most compatible with what is known of Dublin's economic and political history at that time.[2]

The extent of suburban drift is not easy to measure before the Victorian period. During the eighteenth century the Dublin *Directories* tended to list only city addresses for merchants and substantial traders, irrespective of where they actually resided. However, other evidence (below, Ch. 9) suggests that already by the 1790s several aldermen had residences outside the circular road that bounded the city, and it appears that by then it was becoming quite common for the wealthy to combine a city business with a suburban residence, a phenomenon that was not reflected to any extent in the *Directories* until the mid-1830s.

---

[1] Fagan, 'Population of Dublin', 148–9.
[2] Dickson, 'Demographic Implications of Dublin's Growth', 182; Fagan, 'Population of Dublin', 149. See also map 3 above.

Whatever the absolute numbers of Protestants, emigration was being reported by the 1780s. Silk weavers (a trade with particularly strong Protestant connections) were the first to go in any numbers; during the depression of 1783 many hundreds were said to be emigrating to America with their families.[3] The rebellion of 1798 brought a temporary influx of Protestants to the capital, but the act of union prompted another exodus, though this time of landed gentry rather than the artisan classes, and in a gradual trickle rather than a flood. However, emigration became more difficult during the war with France, and it was not until after the return of peace in 1815 that another major round of departures began. Meanwhile, migration to the city from rural areas, together with high fertility rates, was rapidly swelling the Catholic element in the population, which more than doubled in the course of the eighteenth century.

The effect of these developments was to put pressure on the middling ranks of Dublin society, especially the disproportionately Protestant artisan class, while greatly augmenting the ranks of the mainly Catholic labouring poor. Visitors' perceptions of the city began to change accordingly. In 1779 Philip Luckombe had commented on Dublin's poor, but he noticed that they appeared to have work. He had also been struck by signs of the presence of the middling orders; the lifestyle of the merchants, he thought, was comparable to that in London; and nearly every parish in the city had its Protestant schools, supported by charitable donations (indeed, he reported that by some estimates Protestants still made up half the city's population, though others put the proportion as low as one-third).[4] Twenty-five years later in 1804, an anonymous English visitor compared Dublin unfavourably with London in terms of the state of the poorer classes: the worst parishes in London seemed a paradise compared with the worst areas in Dublin for vice, filth, and wretchedness. And for that writer, exaggerating to make the point, the middling orders had vanished altogether: 'Everything in Dublin is pomp or poverty, splendour or squalid wretchedness. No decent comforts of the middle ranks unite, as in London, the magnificence and the misery.'[5] This impression was doubtless reinforced by the middle-class suburban drift noted by Fagan.

The textile industries were the index of Dublin's prosperity, providing employment for several thousand people. Well before the end of the eighteenth century they were showing signs of contraction, partly through the impact of foreign (especially English) competition. This was already being complained of in 1773 when a house of commons committee heard evidence on the state of Irish manufactures.[6] In the woollen industry

---

[3] Kerby A. Miller, *Emigrants and Exiles: Ireland and the Irish Exodus to North America* (Oxford, 1985), 175.
[4] Philip Luckombe, *A Tour Through Ireland*, 2nd. edn. (London, 1783), 7, 14–19.
[5] Anon., *Ireland in 1804* (London, 1806; repr. Dublin, 1980), 20, 66.
[6] McDowell, *Ireland in the Age of Imperialism*, 313.

manufacturers in the north of England began to gain advantages of scale and cost as a result of mechanization, powered by water and later by steam, from the 1760s onwards. With the breakdown of guild control over Dublin trade, by the 1780s a class of retailers without a manufacturing base had arisen. The guilds themselves were affected by these developments. By the end of the century four of the five representatives of the weavers' and dyers' guilds on the city commons were merchants, clothiers, or drapers rather than weavers and dyers. In the weavers' guild, the number of free brothers fell from 382 in 1759 to 303 in 1789 and to 269 in 1821.[7]

Against this background, the question of protection was raised, revealing (significantly) that northern linen manufacturers were opposed to tariffs, which might harm linen in the British market. Support for protection gave added zest to the boycott of English goods that formed part of the free trade campaign in 1779. As already noted, in 1784 Dublin artisans staged attacks on importers and retailers of English goods, and associations were formed in Dublin and elsewhere to promote the exclusive use of Irish-made goods. When the parliamentary committee reported in 1784, its chairman, Luke Gardiner, MP for County Dublin, emerged as the first in a line of protectionists who recognized that Ireland's special needs made unqualified *laissez-faire* inappropiate. Gardiner indicated that in general he supported the arguments of Adam Smith; but the people must be employed.[8] It was not until 1794, however, that the principle of a high protective tariff for Irish manufactures was accepted, and soon afterwards the act of union introduced a projected time-scale—originally designed to culminate in the year 1821—for the complete phasing out of protective duties between Ireland and Great Britain. In the meantime, Dublin textile manufactures were prominent among those who supported electoral reform in the 1780s and the United Irishmen in the 1790s.[9]

In addition to protection, manufacturers also sought financial aid from the Irish parliament to help fend off English competition. In the 1780s grants were given to support a new mechanized cotton manufacture in the Dublin region. Such use of state funds was not entirely new; nor (though they encouraged enterprise) were state-aided projects invariably successful. Robert Brooke's ill-fated cotton manufactory at Prosperous, County Kildare, which received disproportionate state funding, was dealt a severe blow when Brooke went bankrupt in 1786.[10]

---

[7] *Wilson's Dublin Directory for . . . 1798* (Dublin, 1798), 152; RSAI, weavers' guild, book of brothers 1746–64; book of brothers 1767–92; book of brothers 1792–1820. The 1821 figure may be misleading: F. O'Neill, *The Stain Removed, and Corporation Explained. Being an Alphabetical List of the Freemen & Freeholders of the City of Dublin . . . Who Voted at the Late Election* ([Dublin], 1820) indicates that of 265 free weavers in 1820, forty had left Dublin without trace (pp. 47–79).

[8] McDowell, *Ireland in the Age of Imperialism*, 313–14.

[9] Cullen, *Economic History of Ireland Since 1600*, 97; id., *Princes & Pirates*, 54; Moody and Vaughan (eds.), *NHI*, iv. 369; above, Ch. 6.

[10] Warburton, Whitelaw, Walsh, *History of the City of Dublin*, ii. 973–4.

Down to the end of the Napoleonic wars the effects of English competition on Dublin textile industries were kept in check, partly because Irish protective tariffs remained in force (a 10 per cent tariff on woollen imports was still in operation in 1813) and partly because the war increased demand in the form of government contracts, some of which went to Irish manufacturers.[11] Down to 1815, therefore, although depressions in trade occurred from time to time, a good deal of optimism remained. This was reflected in continued investment in the cotton industry in the Dublin region. In 1806 new cotton-spinning machinery was installed in the Temple mills at Celbridge, County Kildare; and in 1808 new machinery was put into the Greenmount mill at Harold's Cross on the outskirts of the city. The latter was to be acquired in 1816 by a branch of the Quaker Pim family, which had for some years been importers of raw cotton from New York. In all, before the end of the war there were over a dozen mills in the Dublin region, mostly using water power for spinning yarn, which was then supplied to some sixty manufacturers who in turn gave employment to up to 1,600 Dublin weavers. The weaving side of the industry had benefited in the 1780s from the introduction of the flying shuttle.[12]

While cotton was expanding, the long-established woollen and silk industries were shrinking. However, even here confidence had not entirely disappeared, to judge by developments in the finishing and retailing areas. In 1814 a heated tenter house for the benefit of woollen weavers was erected by private subscription in the Liberties. And in the following year the stationers' guild thanked the lord mayor for help in providing the Liberties with a new market for woollen sales. The silk industry suffered its first serious depression in 1783; as in the case of wool, the industry was affected by competition from the mechanized sector of the industry based in the English midlands and north: both in Dublin and London the older, guild-organized branch of the industry was undermined by this challenge. Changing fashions—especially the growing preference for cotton—posed an additional problem.[13] The response to falling demand was similar to that in the woollen industry. In the mid-1790s journeymen silk-weavers addressed the nobility, gentry, and the public, urging them to buy Irish-made silks. Subsequently, imports of raw silk were interrupted by Napoleon's Continental blockade, but the outbreak of the peninsula war in 1808 created the possibility of obtaining raw silk from Spain.[14]

---

[11] An order for 60,000 army greatcoats was reported in *FJ*, 11 Jan. 1813.

[12] *DEP*, 11 Mar. 1806; Warburton, Whitelaw, Walsh, *History of the City of Dublin*, ii. 975–6; Richard S. Harrison, 'Dublin Quakers in Business 1800–1850', M.Litt. thesis (2 vols.; TCD, 1987), i. 167–8; ii. 387. It has been argued that the Irish cotton industry grew faster than the English, 1800–25 (Frank Geary, 'Counting the Cost of the Union', paper delivered to the Ir. Ec. & Soc. Hist. Soc. conference, UCD, 1993).

[13] *FJ*, 26 Oct. 1814; 16 Oct. 1815; Warburton, Whitelaw, Walsh, *History of the City of Dublin*, ii. 977–8; petition of journeymen hosiers, *Parl. Reg.*, xiii (Dublin, 1793), 158.

[14] *FDJ*, 16 July 1795; *FJ*, 13 July 1808, 8, 13 Sept. (letter from 'A'), 4 Oct. 1810.

Other economic difficulties in the pre-1815 period included mounting levels of taxation (another effect of the war), which in 1810 combined with a depression in the textile trades to produce the most sustained demand for repeal of the union before Daniel O'Connell took up the question in the 1830s and 1840s.[15]

It would be a mistake, however, to emphasize unduly the economic difficulties of the war years, or to imply that English manufacturers had everything their own way. In brewing the home product was holding its own against English imports, and Guinness's porter was beginning to break into the English market. New service industries were emerging, notably those dealing in insurance. The first major Irish company, the Hibernian Insurance Company (offering marine and fire cover) was founded in 1771. From the 1780s onwards new companies proliferated; the amount of property insured (against fire) reached a peak in 1810, when the stamp duty was raised.[16] Several older trades flourished. The building industry was buoyant, for within the limits of the circular road the city was still being filled in, especially on the eastern side. The great Georgian squares— Fitzwilliam and Merrion in the south-east, and Mountjoy in the north-east—were taking shape in the 1790s, and the surrounding streets were still being laid out in the 1830s. Important public buildings were going up, including Kilmainham gaol (*c.*1800); the fever hospital in Cork Street (1802); the King's Inns (completed in 1802); and the Royal College of Surgeons (1806). The General Post Office in Sackville Street was built between 1814 and 1818. And while wages for the unskilled and semi-skilled had been falling since the 1770s, for skilled tradesmen wages held up well during the wartime period; evidence from the building trades indicates that wage agreements, reached between the journeymen and the employers in the favourable conditions of the 1780s, remained in force until 1816–17.[17]

Finally, it was during this period that the natural limitations of Dublin port began to be tackled. After some resistance from Dublin corporation, the ballast board was reconstituted by statute in 1786, placing all powers concerning the river and the bay in 'the corporation for preserving and improving the port of Dublin', comprising the lord mayor, sheriffs, and three aldermen, plus seventeen other representatives of trade and navigation. The completion of the Great South Wall (1795) and especially the North Bull Wall (1823) surmounted the silting problems posed by the Dublin bar, and helped to make the port safer. In time, these developments were to

[15] Below, Ch. 10.
[16] Patrick Lynch and John Vaizey, *Guinness's Brewery in the Irish Economy 1759–1876* (Cambridge, 1960), 83–4, 123–4; Harrison, 'Dublin Quakers in Business', ii. 309–10, 314.
[17] Craig, *Dublin 1660–1860*, 192–3; Dickson, 'Demographic Implications of Dublin's Growth', 184–5; Fergus D'Arcy, 'Dublin, 1800–60', paper read at Dublin Historical Association, Mar. 1983.

transform Dublin's potential as a port, symbolized by the opening of James Gandon's splendid new Custom House in 1791.[18]

II. *The Guilds after the Failure of the Quarterage Campaign,* 1780–1814

By the 1780s any remaining guild aspirations to act as general regulators of trade had been checked by legislative action (and inaction). Parliament's failure to pass a statutory quarterage measure was reinforced by a clause in the combination act of 1780, which freed every manufacturer ('as well journeyman as master') to take unlimited numbers of apprentices, 'whether such master or apprentice be protestant or papist, any statute, usage, custom, charter, bye-law, order or regulation to the contrary notwithstanding'.[19] Consequently, certain guilds that had reaffirmed control of trade in the 1760s were obliged to review their position. In 1784 the stationers dropped their by-law that claimed quarterage from the non-free, while in 1791 the apothecaries agreed (in effect) to bypass the guild by co-operating with the non-free to set up a hall to regulate the trade. In 1792 the saddlers dropped most of their regulations concerning quality of materials, as well as some obsolete and unenforceable laws such as the prohibition on keeping more than two shops without the master's consent, and the obligation not to intrude on the arts of other brethren.[20] In some guilds vestiges of the quarter brother system lingered into the 1780s, and there were still occasional tensions between free and unfree traders, but the loss of the guilds' principal function rendered it increasingly difficult to collect quarterage fees even from freemen.[21]

However, the requirement that apprentices be enrolled in the guilds was reaffirmed, at least in the case of the saddlers, the stationers, and the goldsmiths.[22] And there were other signs that some sort of role in the regulation of trade persisted for certain guilds, even if not all the employers were freemen. In 1792 the weavers' guild was petitioned successfully by manufacturers of 'single stuffs' for an adjustment of prices in the trade, the

---

[18] 26 Geo. III, c. 19; Geoffrey Corry, 'The Dublin Bar—the Obstacle to the Improvement of the Port of Dublin', *Dublin Hist. Rec.* 23 (1970), 137–52.

[19] 19 & 20 Geo. III, c. 19 (*The Statutes at Large*, xi. 552). It was alleged that restrictions on employing apprentices made Catholics sympathetic to combinations (*Commons Jn. Ire.* 1779–82, x, App., p. cxiii). The prohibition (in 8 Anne, c. 3) on Catholics keeping no more than two apprentices was not repealed until 1792 (32 Geo. III, c. 21).

[20] Wall, *Catholic Ireland in the Eighteenth Century*, 72; NLI, MS 81, fo. 75; Apothecaries' hall, transactions 1747–95, pp. 256–8.

[21] NLI, MS 12126, pp. 234–45; petition of several skinners of Dublin ('Non-freemen'), *Commons Jn. Ire.* 1779–82, x. 158–9; goldsmiths' guild, minutes 1779–1807, NLI, n 6056 p 6782, pp. 11, 72, 86.

[22] NLI, MS 81, fos. 67–99; MS 12133, p. 27 (adopted 6 Apr. 1813); goldsmiths' guild, apprentices' book (details of the period 1767–1823 are missing from NLI reel, n 6062 p 6788, but are held in the Assay Office).

new rates being entered in the hall books.[23] In 1799 'the freemen and employers of journeymen painters' rejected a request from the journeymen for a rise in wages, and warned that no one would be employed who was dissatisfied with existing wages.[24] Also in 1799, the smiths' guild approved new prices for the trade, entering them in the 'book of rates', and proceeded to review prices of material used by glaziers. Three years later journeymen glaziers, who were described as forming a 'considerable portion' of the brethren, petitioned the guild for a reduction in their hours of work, claiming that they worked for two hours longer than others in the building trades. After hearing legal opinion, the guild declined to act, on the grounds that to do so would be to interfere with 'the custom of the city'; but in 1810 the journeymen petitioned again, addressing 'the Gentlemen Employers conducting the Glazing & Painting Trade in . . . Dublin', and on that occasion were successful: the names of consenting employers were recorded in the guild books.[25] Such indications of the survival of guild regulation, decades after it had been shown to be unenforceable at law, probably suggests that in certain trades the employers continued to be strongly identified with the guilds. The smiths' guild, in fact, retained sufficient confidence and buoyancy in numbers to contemplate the building of a new hall in 1800.[26] As already noted, the building trades had continued to flourish during the war years.

Thus for at least some of the guilds the failure of the quarterage campaign and the rise of a more active political role for the freemen did not lead to any collapse of interest in trading matters. What about the size and composition of the freeman body? In the absence of firm figures, the numbers of freemen voting at elections (Table 7.3) are of interest. They rose only slightly between the 1760s and 1806. Assuming a turn-out of *c*.75 per cent, this suggests that total freemen numbers rose by only some 200–300 beyond their 1749 figure (*c*.3,000), which would be consistent with a Protestant population that had largely ceased to grow.[27] Table 7.1 provides some insights into admissions to freedom of the city (which was a necessary step to full guild freedom) in a number of periods between 1780 and 1822.

These figures show that there was a good deal of fluctuation over the entire period; and that there was neither a collapse in admissions, nor was freedom opened to all and sundry. Some of the variation may be explained by higher levels of admission in election years; 1790, 1802, and 1820 witnessed hotly contested parliamentary elections in the city. The marked drop in admissions, 1810–12, probably reflected the impact of the

---

[23] RSAI, weavers' guild, minute book 1755–1809, entry for 2 July 1792.
[24] NLI, MS 12126, p. 148.   [25] NA, M 2926, fos. 115–16, 130, 150.
[26] Ibid. fo. 119. No hall was built.
[27] Catholics were permitted by law to be freemen from 1793, but as none were admitted to freedom of the city, these figures relate solely to Protestants: below, Ch. 8.

TABLE 7.1. *Admissions to civic freedom in five 3-year periods*

	1780–2		1790–2		1800–2		1810–12		1820–2	
	No.	%	No.	%	No.	%	No.	%	No.	%
Members of:										
Craft guilds	249	81.1	517	77.9	406	67.6	203	73.3	240	51.9
Merchants' guild	58	18.9	147	22.1	195	32.4	74	26.7	222	48.1
TOTAL	307	99.9	664	100.0	601	100.0	277	100.0	462*	100.0
How admitted:										
Birth	99	32.2	282	42.4	297	49.4	89	32.1	151	32.7
Service	157	51.1	181	27.3	143	23.8	68	24.5	96	20.8
Special grace	51	16.6	201	30.3	161	26.8	120	43.3	215	46.5
TOTAL	307	99.9	664	100.0	601	100.0	277	99.9	462*	100.0

* Some entries under letter F missing from *Alphabetical List*: total should perhaps be *c.*490.
Source: *An Alphabetical List of the Freemen of the City of Dublin, 1774–1823* ([Dublin], n.d.)
(NLI, ILB 94133 d 2).

depression of 1810. As for composition, although here too there was some fluctuation, the general trend was for the merchants' guild to increase its share of new freedoms at the expense of the craft guilds: the connection with manufacturing trade was being diluted. Particularly significant are the figures showing by what right admission was granted. At the beginning of the period admissions by service (i.e. following apprenticeship to a freeman) represented half of all admissions, but by the early 1820s they were down to only 20 per cent. That is what might be expected in view of the guilds' declining links with trade; but clearly apprenticeship had not entirely vanished as a route to freedom even at the end of this period.

Admissions by birth initially showed some tendency to increase as a proportion of the whole, but finished the period at much the same level as in the 1780s. Following the failure of the quarterage campaign Dublin corporation had ceased to insist that freedom should be granted only to those following their guild's trades (the last reminder came in 1772).[28] Relaxation of this rule had important implications, easing the path to freedom for sons who did not follow their fathers' trades. In such cases, it was the acquisition of a parliamentary vote that made freedom attractive: given the existing state of the franchise, this might be one of the only ways in which those outside the business (or landed) world could obtain a vote. One freeman's son who took advantage of that privilege was Theobald Wolfe Tone, who in 1789 had recently qualified as a barrister. With a general election only months away, he applied for and was granted freedom of the

[28] *CARD* xii. 556.

saddlers' guild by birth (his father Peter Tone was a former coachmaker and freeman of the guild).[29]

The last category of admissions, by special grace, showed a fairly marked rising tendency for most of the period, finishing up at not much under half of all admissions. In the past, those who applied for freedom by special grace would have fallen into a few well-defined categories (see Ch. 1); but with the corporation becoming more easy-going about admitting non-tradesmen, the scope became wider—though always at a cost. In 1773 the aldermen had almost doubled the fine payable on admission by special grace from £5 to £8 for the merchants' guild and from £2 to £4 for the craft guilds. Applications for admission by grace declined sharply, though in the optimistic climate of the early 1780s after free trade was conceded they resumed their earlier levels. However, the high cost of such freedoms became a grievance for the reformers among the freemen, who wanted a low fine so as to increase the number of voters. In 1782 the city commons, orchestrated by Tandy and John Binns, complained about the high cost of admission by grace, but nothing was done, prompting a concerted protest by the guilds towards the end of the decade. By the turn of the century fines had been reduced to £4 (merchants) and £2 (craft guilds), at which level they remained until they were drastically reduced, to £1 for the merchants' guild and 10s. for the craft guilds, in 1821.[30]

The easing of the requirement that freemen be practising tradesmen posed problems in certain trades where strict control was still aspired to. Various solutions were found. The goldsmiths reaffirmed that only practising tradesmen would be admitted to the guild by grace, though they too continued to admit freemen by birth irrespective of their calling. In the case of the surgeons (who were granted a charter of incorporation as the Royal College of Surgeons in 1784), and the apothecaries (who in 1791 gained statutory powers as a medical licensing corporation) professional associations emerged, open to Catholics as well as Protestants.[31] A gap grew up between the guild—now free to admit non-practising tradesmen—and the profession.[32] This also occurred in the brewers and maltsters' guild: by 1813 the number of freemen was growing, but there was a significant non-brewer element among them. Some time before the 1830s, regulation of the trade appears to have passed to a Dublin Brewers' Society. Similarly, a company of bookbinders and one of booksellers emerged in the second half

---

[29] Saddlers' guild, admission lists 1776–92 (NLI, MS 82, 12 Oct. 1789); *An Alphabetical List of the Freemen of the City of Dublin, 1774–1823* ([Dublin], n. d.). For Peter Tone, see Elliott, *Wolfe Tone*, 9–12.

[30] *CARD* xiii. 526–35; *DEP*, 1, 6 Nov. 1788; DCA, Fr/B/1803/3, Fr/B/1821/2.

[31] Goldsmiths' minute book 1779–1807, NLI, n 6056 p 6782, p. 321; McWalter, *History of the Worshipful Company of Apothecaries*, 80.

[32] The apothecaries' guild retained some regulatory functions (Apothecaries' hall, transactions 1796–1837, p. 79).

TABLE 7.2. *Occupations of 74 freemen of the bricklayers' guild who voted for representatives on the city commons, 1813 guild elections*

	No.	%
Following the guild's trades (bricklayers, plasterers)	43	58.1
Allied trades (architects, measurers, painters, carpenters, builders, sash-makers)	11	13.5
Other trades (publicans, coal factors, cutlers, hosiers)	4	5.4
Professions (barristers, attorneys)	9	12.1
Clerks	2	2.7
Unidentified	5	8.1
TOTAL	74	99.9

Source: *Freeman's Journal*, 4 Nov. 1813.

of the eighteenth century, with an existence distinct from that of the stationers' faculty of St Luke's guild.[33]

Some idea of the nature and extent of the changes discussed above on the composition of one guild can be gained in respect of seventy-four freemen of the bricklayers' and plasterers' guild who voted in the election for guild representatives on the city commons in 1813. Their occupations and addresses were conveniently listed in a press report. Table 7.2 shows that the bulk of members were still following the appropriate trades. Moreover, only one lived outside the city or the Liberties.

If the available evidence suggests that there was no very marked rise in the overall size of the freeman body during this period, what was happening to individual guilds? Since so many of the records are missing, it is impossible to provide a complete answer, but turn-out at elections sheds some light on the matter. The parliamentary elections of 1761, 1773, and 1806 saw broadly similar numbers of freemen voting, but there were significant changes in the turn-out for different guilds (Table 7.3).

The figures in Table 7.3 can be no more than a rough guide to guild size, since turn-out of voters varied, and rarely amounted to more than about 75 per cent of guild members. However, when the guilds are grouped according to their trades, as in Table 7.3, certain patterns are suggested. Those engaged in manufacturing textiles and clothing (1–5) displayed some fluctuations, but by 1806 most showed generally downward trends. The same was true of guilds that processed cattle products (6–12); here the butchers and the tanners seemed to be in marked decline. Guilds that

[33] GMD, brewers' minute book 1804–31 (entry for 2 Feb. 1813); Lynch and Vaizey, *Guinness's Brewery*, 98; Pollard, *Dublin's Trade in Books*, 168.

TABLE 7.3. *Freemen voters at the elections of 1761, 1773, and 1806, by guild*

	1761	1773		1806	
	No.	No.	% change	No.	% change
1. Weavers	229	230	+0.4	214	−6.9
2. Tailors	124	146	+17.7	121	−17.2
3. Hosiers	57	50	−12.3	52	+4.0
4. Hatters	52	51	−2.0	41	−19.6
5. Sheermen	45	79	+75.6	46	−41.8
6. Saddlers	120	140	+16.6	130	−7.2
7. Butchers	104	69	−33.7	46	−33.3
8. Chandlers	80	56	−30.0	57	+1.8
9. Shoemakers	75	83	+10.7	80	−3.7
10. Tanners	45	24	−46.7	14	−41.7
11. Skinners, glovers	36	38	+5.6	33	−13.2
12. Curriers	20	19	−5.0	16	−15.8
13. Carpenters	209	233	+11.5	192	−17.6
14. Smiths	149	170	+14.1	175	+2.9
15. Bricklayers	72	50	−30.6	70	+40.0
16. Joiners	68	87	+27.9	69	−20.7
17. Coopers	53	46	−13.3	38	−17.4
18. Cooks	30	35	+16.7	54	+54.3
19. Bakers	16	14	−12.5	13	−7.2
20. Brewers	9	5	−44.5	28	+460.0
21. Merchants	516	465	−9.9	629	+35.3
22. Cutlers, painter-stainers, stationers	96	121	+26.0	147	+21.5
23. Barbers	88	99	+12.5	77	−22.3
24. Goldsmiths	75	80	+6.7	74	−7.5
25. Apothecaries	18	13	−27.8	50	+284.6
TOTAL	2,386	2,403		2,466	

Sources: An Alphabetical List of the Freemen and Freeholders that Polled at the Election of Members to Represent the City of Dublin (1761) (Dublin, 1761); Holmes, An Alphabetical List of the Freeholders and Freemen (1773); The Poll for Electing Two Members to Represent the City of Dublin in the Imperial Parliament (1806) (Dublin, n.d.).

catered for the building, woodworking, and metal trades (13–17) showed rather more positive signs; the bricklayers recovered well from a dip in 1773, and the smiths (as noted above) were positively buoyant. Certain guilds catering for the food and drink trades (18–20) were also growing; however, the tendency of the brewers' guild to admit non-brewers or maltsters in some numbers has already been noted. A final, miscellaneous group (21–5) contained several buoyant guilds: St Luke's (stationers, etc.), the merchants, and the apothecaries.

One other indicator of the state of the guilds reinforces the conclusion suggested by the statistics given above—that the connection with trade, though declining in this period, remained important. On the eve of the act of union over two-thirds of the sixty-five craft guild representatives on the city

TABLE 7.4. *Occupations of craft guild representatives, Dublin city commons, in selected years*

	1788		1798		1808		1818	
	No.	%	No.	%	No.	%	No.	%
Following guild's trades	52	80.0	42	64.7	45	69.2	40	61.5
Allied trades	5	7.7	12	18.5	12	18.5	7	10.8
Other trades	0	0.0	2	3.1	5	7.7	7	10.8
Unidentified	8	12.3	9	13.8	3	4.6	11	16.9
TOTAL	65	100.0	65	100.1	65	100.0	65	100.0

Sources: *Watson's Gentleman's and Citizen's Almanack*, for 1788, 1798, 1808, 1818.

commons were following their guilds' trades (as the corporation reform act of 1760 required them to do): and only two followed trades completely unconnected with their guild. By 1818 some further slippage had occurred, but still not very much (Table 7.4).

The decline of the guilds as regulators of trade was also affected by changing relations between employers and journeymen. During the 1770s industrial combinations had begun to cause serious concern. In the past, parliament had acted occasionally to curb such activities, and there now appeared a flurry of anti-combination acts that set out penalties for combination in designated trades: tailors and shipwrights (1772); bakers (1779), and the slaughtering, curing, and coopering trades (1780).[34] It is hardly coincidental that those singled out included the food and leather trades in which Catholic participation had traditionally been high, and which had proved least amenable to guild control.[35] In the case of the tailors and shipwrights, the power of regulating wages was given to magistrates at quarter sessions. Following a parliamentary inquiry at which employers complained of rising wage costs (relative to those in England), 1780 saw the passage of a general combination act, which outlawed all forms of journeymen's clubs and societies.[36]

This legislative onslaught on combination reflected the employers' determination to obtain greater control over the journeymen in the wake of the successful campaign for free trade. Journeymen had played their part in that campaign, but once the object had been attained a more tractable workforce was desirable. The combination acts followed a period in which the journeymen had had some success in ensuring that the prosperity of the 1750s and 1760s extended to them. It was clearly in their interests to

[34] 11 & 12 Geo. III, c. 33; 19 & 20 Geo. III, c. 24; 19 & 20 Geo. III, c. 36.
[35] Doyle, 'The Dublin Guilds', 10.
[36] 19 & 20 Geo. III, c. 19; *Commons Jn. Ire. 1779–82*, x, 120, App., pp. cxi–cxviii.

maintain customary guild controls on wages and admission of apprentices: these had been the subject of most disputes between journeymen and masters from the 1720s to the 1770s.[37] While industry was booming, employers could afford to increase the wages of a relatively small pool of highly skilled labour. But as the period of expansion passed, and combination continued to spread, such restrictions became increasingly irksome to employers. Besides, perceptions of the economy were changing. A new science of political economy was growing up, claiming to provide insights into the conditions likely to maximize prosperity and economic progress, and monopolistic practices were coming in for criticism.[38]

If the new economic thinking was inimical to the principle of guild control of trade, it also provided grounds for employers to circumvent guild restrictions on the employment of labour. From 1780 onwards this changing outlook had parliamentary backing, and the results were soon apparent in the labour disputes of the 1780s and early 1790s. The standard complaint of the journeymen was that employers were using cheap rural labour.[39] Master tailors and bakers were said to have openly advertised for such labour so as to avoid paying good wages to properly trained Dublin journeymen.[40] Significantly, these were trades in which combination had been judged serious enough to justify specific anti-combination legislation in the 1770s. But whereas in earlier decades employers had been induced to accept that the number of apprentices should be restricted, and that journeymen should not have to work with 'foreigners' (i.e. those who had not served an apprenticeship in Dublin), at the end of the century the protests of the Dublin journeymen, who doubtless felt that custom and justice were on their side, were unavailing. The lack of official sympathy for them was demonstrated by a case in 1806 in which several carpenters were charged with combination. The recorder of Dublin alleged that it was notorious that men could be recruited in the country to work for two shillings a day less than the Dublin rate. The carpenters, he conceded, were not among those trades that could apply to quarter sessions for wage increases; yet they actually earned more than tailors, who did have that option. Was it any wonder, he asked, rhetorically, that workmen were coming to Dublin from Scotland to do the work Dublin workmen should be doing, or that master cabinet-makers could get work done in Liverpool at cheaper rates than in Dublin?[41]

The breakdown of guild control plus the demographic changes noted

---

[37] Doyle, 'The Dublin Guilds', 9–10.   [38] Above, Ch. 4.

[39] See *FDJ*, 15 Dec. 1792; *Hib. Jn.*, 18 Nov. 1793.

[40] For a notice placed by master tailors, offering work to journeymen tailors ('from all parts'), see *DEP*, 3 June 1784.

[41] *FDJ*, 6 Sept. 1806. The prisoners were found guilty on the evidence of a rule book, taken to be a sign of combination.

above affected the religious composition of Dublin's industrial and commercial classes. The Dublin Catholic middle class, though still smaller than its Protestant counterpart, by now contained many wealthy individuals. And with Protestant artisans taking to emigration, and (Protestant) employers increasingly willing to take on non-guild and Catholic labour, the artisan classes and the journeymen's clubs were acquiring a more Catholic complexion.

Would the admission of Catholics to the guilds in significant numbers have stemmed their decline as regulators of trade? In view of the fact that employers in general, Catholic and Protestant, were increasingly reluctant to make use of guild powers to regulate trade, it seems unlikely that, even if Catholics had been admitted to full guild privileges, the retreat from guild control would have been reversed. Yet among both journeymen and (some) employers the idea of a body representing masters and men to regulate the trade continued to appeal. In the bricklayers' and plasterers' guild—one of those industries with plenty of work in the early 1800s—a campaign was launched in 1813 to revive the guild's claims to control the work of all in the trade. The move was led by a former master, Benjamin Pemberton, who argued that combination arose from the breakdown of guild regulation, and that the guild charters contained full authority for reviving guild control. Such a move, he suggested, would help to defeat combination and prevent frauds upon the public through the use of unskilled labour. It would have other benefits, too: a guildhall could be built and journeymen encouraged to resort to it rather than to public houses. However, Pemberton's plan required a willingness to admit Catholics to freedom, and on this issue opposition was mobilized within the guild, effectively blocking the initiative.[42] But as late as the 1830s nostalgia for the principle of guild control remained strong among artisans in the building and decorating trades; and during the 1840s a concerted attempt (again, ultimately unsuccessful) was made to revive the guilds.[43]

The lingering appeal of guild ideals helps explain why, despite the fact that solidarity between masters and men was breaking down, class tensions remained largely latent during this period. Admittedly, during the 1790s the absence of a significant economic dimension in the United Irishmen's reform plans meant that there was nothing to focus journeymen's grievances and channel them towards class conflict.[44] Neither in Ireland nor in England did the radicals of the 1790s build on Tom Paine's ideas, contained in some of his later works, for social reconstruction:[45] though for a generation

---

[42] See Benjamin Pemberton, *A Letter to William Walker, Esq., Recorder of the City of Dublin, on the Primary Cause of Combination Among the Tradesmen of Dublin* (Dublin, 1814), and reports in *FJ*, Oct.–Nov. 1813.

[43] Hill, 'Artisans, Sectarianism and Politics in Dublin', 18; see also below, Ch. 11.

[44] Cf. McDowell, *Irish Public Opinion*, 216; Smyth, *The Men of No Property*, 83.

[45] Thomas Paine, *Rights of Man* (Harmondsworth, 1984), pt. 2, ch. 5.

steeped in the ideals of civic republicanism the extension of citizenship would have effects far beyond the narrowly political sphere. But in any case it is clear that for all their resort to combination, the Dublin journeymen still hoped, by appealing to the higher classes and to parliament, to win back employers to a sense of traditional obligations. In other words, they had not yet ceased to think of society as held together by ties of dependency and obligation that transcended social divisions. They were in fact seeking to defend the high wage levels achieved some decades earlier; and they were still far from seeing themselves as the 'poor operatives', the victims of decades of chronic industrial decline, which is how Dublin journeymen referred to themselves in the 1830s and 1840s.[46]

---

[46] Open letter of the trades' committee to Daniel O'Connell, *FJ*, 18 Jan. 1838, quoted in F. A. D'Arcy, 'The Artisans of Dublin and Daniel O'Connell, 1830–47: An Unquiet Liaison', *IHS* 17 (1970), 221–43, at 221.

8

'Protestant Ascendancy', Challenge and Definition, 1791–1793

The excitement generated by the French revolution sparked off a wide-ranging debate about all aspects of the *ancien régime*: the institutions of hereditary monarchy and aristocracy; religious establishments; corporate and prescriptive rights. Champions of 'the rights of man' had only limited success in winning over members of the privileged orders in Britain and Ireland to their views, but they did force their opponents to formulate defences for the existing system.

In Britain, any upsurge of constitutional debate was bound to focus, to a greater or lesser extent, on the revolution of 1688–9. It was a sermon preached in 1789 by the Arian minister Dr Richard Price for the Society for Commemorating the Revolution in Great Britain on its festival day (the anniversary of William III's birthday) that prompted Edmund Burke to write his *Reflections on the Revolution in France* (1790).[1] Price had contended that the revolution had given the English people the right to choose and cashier their governors. Burke denied any such discontinuity; for him, existing institutions had evolved gradually over many centuries and were better suited to national needs than any abstract plan of government. As for the rights of man, Burke insisted that men had duties as well as rights, and that they had a duty to their predecessors and to posterity to cherish what they had inherited.[2]

The other main protagonist in the debate, Tom Paine, argued that Burke was investing the constitution as a whole with a 'divine right' quality once attributed to the monarchy alone; and that the effect of his argument was to deprive contemporaries of any political rights at all. He rejected monarchical, aristocratic, and corporate privileges, tracing them to the same source, the Norman conquest: 'William the Conqueror and his descendants parcelled out the country . . . and bribed one part of it by what they called Charters, to hold the other parts of it the better subjected to their will.'[3]

---

[1] *The Correspondence of Edmund Burke*, vi, ed. Alfred Cobban and Robert A. Smith (Cambridge, 1967), 81.
[2] *Reflections on the Revolution in France*, in *Works*, ii. 277–518, at 290–306, 330–1, 363–9.
[3] Thomas Paine, *Rights of Man: Being an Answer to Mr Burke's Attack on the French Revolution*, pt. 1 (Dublin, 1791), 9–11, 57.

Significantly, therefore, it was now the champions of the status quo who were contending for the antiquity of the constitution, while the radicals claimed that natural rights superseded any appeals to prescription. The debate raged fairly freely until 1793–4, when the government, invoking the interests of national security (for Britain was by now at war with revolutionary France) began a clampdown on the reform clubs that had sprung up in London and elsewhere in the wake of the revolution.

In Ireland too the debate was under way by 1791; both the *Reflections* and the *Rights of Man* were published in Dublin editions.[4] A Dublin newpaper entitled *The Rights of Irishmen* appeared in 1791. But the regime in Ireland almost at once found itself under attack not merely from radicals but from Burke, the leading protagonist of counter-revolution. In order to appreciate how the British and Irish defenders of the *ancien régime* found themselves at odds it will be necessary, first, to return to the evolution of British thought on the Catholic question.

I. *The Attack on Confessionalism: The British and Imperial Context*

> All our English Protestant colonies [in N. America] revolted . . . and it so happened that Popish Canada was the only place which preserved its fidelity; the only place in which France got no footing; the only peopled colony which now remains to Great Britain.[5]

It has already been noted that 'the growth of toleration' can be a misleading way to describe the effects on Protestants in Britain and Ireland of the Enlightenment, the effective ending of the Jacobite claim to the throne, and the diminution of papal power in the 1760s and 1770s. For if 'toleration' implied a willingness to commend Catholicism as a valid religion, such a position was rare even among 'enlightened' Protestants down to the 1790s. What had begun to change in the British ruling élite was the perception of Catholics as a serious danger to church and state. Even so, the relaxation of the penal laws was a spasmodic process, in which the main considerations were military and strategic. Not until the 1780s did any British political connection (the Foxite Whigs) adopt a pro-Catholic stance on ideological grounds.[6]

The result was that when the French revolution broke out there were wide variations in the rights enjoyed by Catholics in different parts of the empire.

---

[4] The *Reflections* was well received in Ireland (*Burke Corr.* vi. 192–3). So was the *Rights of Man* (David Dickson, 'Paine and Ireland', in Dickson, Keogh, Whelan (eds.), *The United Irishmen*, 135–50).

[5] Edmund Burke, *Letter to Sir Hercules Langrishe, Bart. M.P. on the Subject of the Roman Catholics of Ireland* (1792), in Burke, *Works*, iii. 298–344, at 342.

[6] Haydon, 'Anti-Catholicism in Eighteenth Century England', 210–14, 292–3; Leighton, *Catholicism in a Protestant Kingdom*, 51–4.

Catholics in territory recently captured from France, with predominantly Catholic populations, were the best off: those in Quebec enjoyed legal freedom to worship, could serve on governors' councils, and their church's property was secure. In the West Indian island of Grenada Catholics were even permitted to vote. Nearer home, Irish Catholics were relatively advantaged, with the right (since 1782) to worship, buy and sell land, and conduct schools. In England and Scotland freedom of worship was still withheld, though the penalties for saying Mass were not enforced.[7]

It was against this background, and in the aftermath of the revolutionary assault on the privileges of the Catholic church in France, that a private member's bill came before the British parliament in February 1791 seeking to legalize worship for those English Catholics who were prepared to deny the pope's power to absolve his followers from their civil allegiance to the crown. During the debates, no serious reservations were expressed about the measure. Particularly striking was the relaxed attitude of both houses towards the waning power of the pope. Burke made MPs laugh by comparing popes to Roman emperors, their temporal power now dead and gone. As for Catholicism at home, Lord Rawdon remarked, 'we, at present, contemplate the Roman Catholic religion, in this country, as what was once great, and an object of apprehension; but we view it with that tranquil emotion with which we contemplate a ruin!'[8]

There was general support for the Enlightenment principle that the only legitimate ground for withholding freedom of worship was danger to the state. The point was made that English Catholics were not asking for political power, simply for relief from penalties which, although fallen into disuse, remained on the statute book. The case of Ireland was cited as demonstrating, through the continuing peaceable demeanour of the Catholics, how safe it was to concede such a right, even in a country with a Catholic majority. There was also a sense that Britain must not be seen to fall behind the practice of revolutionary France in these matters. Yet, for all the air of complacency, some reservations were expressed. Prime Minister Pitt was anxious to have a clause in the bill obliging Catholics to avow that no priest or other human agency could absolve sins.[9] However, the bill passed, removing the penalties for attending Mass. Some rather ambiguous clauses in the act extended the rights of the laity to educate their children.

---

[7] John Garner, 'The Enfranchisement of Roman Catholics in the Maritimes', *CHR* 34 (1953), 203–18.

[8] *Parl. Hist. Eng.* xxviii, cols. 1262–9, 1364–76; xxix, col. 666.

[9] Ibid. xxviii, cols. 1264–6, 1268, 1365–6; xxix, cols. 115–17. Pitt had already urged English Catholics to seek opinions from Catholic universities on the compatibility of Catholic doctrine and civil allegiance (Bartlett, *The Fall and Rise of the Irish Nation*, 122). The oath imposed by the 1793 Irish relief act (33 Geo. III, c. 21) required Catholics to deny that sins could be forgiven 'at the mere will' of any pope or priest.

English Catholics were also admitted to the legal profession. But there was no question of political rights being granted.[10]

The fact that the changes conceded in this act were so limited should not obscure the importance of the shift in attitudes it reflected. Its real significance emerged more clearly in comparison with the fate of a motion brought forward by Fox in the following year (May 1792) to repeal certain penal laws that affected Unitarians. The response, led by Burke, was largely hostile, on the grounds that Unitarians were supporters of the French revolution; and the house of commons voted against the motion, by more than two to one. Admittedly, by this time the French revolution had taken a more serious turn—France had declared war on Austria—but the point about parliament's willingness to indulge the Catholics but not the (Protestant) Unitarians was that the former could now be regarded as loyal and peaceable subjects, whose Trinitarian orthodoxy marked them out as conservatives in theological and political terms, while the latter were regarded as a serious threat to all establishments.[11]

Until 1791 the government's willingness to depart from Protestant confessionalism, whether at home or in the overseas empire, had been justified on essentially pragmatic grounds. It was Burke who, in his paper 'Thoughts on French Affairs' (December 1791), elevated the matter into a principle of statecraft. Comparing the French revolution with the Reformation in the sense that the protagonists of both sought to export their ideals beyond 'natural' boundaries, Burke reflected on what he took to be the evils arising from such a missionary spirit:

Europe was for a long time divided into two great factions, under the name of Catholic and Protestant, which not only often alienated state from state, but also divided almost every state within itself. The warm parties in each state were more affectionately attached to those of their own doctrinal interest in some other country, than to their fellow-citizens, or to their natural government, when they or either of them happened to be of a different persuasion. These factions, wherever they prevailed, if they did not absolutely destroy, at least weakened and distracted, the locality of patriotism . . . These principles of internal as well as external division and coalition are but just now extinguished . . .[12]

The goal of religious uniformity, then, was renounced, and the idea of an international Protestant (or Catholic) interest rejected and consigned to the past. Instead, Burke commended allegiance to 'natural governments', by which he evidently meant those resting on long-settled and dynastic foundations, with an order of nobility and an established church—Protestant

---

[10] See Bernard Ward, *The Dawn of the Catholic Revival in England 1781–1803*, (2 vols.; London, 1909), i. 296–314.
[11] *Parl. Hist. Eng.* xxix, cols. 1394–5, 1403. Cf. Clark, *English Society*, 344.
[12] Burke, 'Thoughts on French Affairs' (published posthumously). Shown to ministers in the winter of 1791–2, though without attracting any response (*Works*, iii. 345–93, at 350–1; *Burke Corr.* vii. 81).

or Catholic, as the case might be, but with toleration for the other (Trinitarian) churches. The point was given a local and historical dimension in Burke's controversial *Letter to Sir Hercules Langrishe* (February 1792), in which Burke attacked the view that the 1688 revolution had guaranteed 'that the state should be protestant without *any qualification of the term*'. The king of England, Burke asserted, had an obligation to be 'of the Christian religion', but the nature of the established church depended on the law of the land 'for the time being'.[13]

Before the 1790s, a proposition so much at odds with popular perceptions of the constitution might have been ignored: Burke had long been suspected of holding unorthodox opinions on the Catholic question.[14] But as the new hero of counter-revolution (a cause in which London and Rome found themselves on the same side) Burke's views took on greater importance. Among many others, George III expressed his admiration for the *Reflections*; and as Burke drew further away from his Foxite Whig colleagues, his relations with the government became closer.[15] Their views on the Irish Catholic question, which came before ministers in the autumn of 1791, began in some degree to converge.

The minister whose views were particularly important was W. W. Grenville. He had been the author, earlier in 1791, of the Canada constitution act, which conferred political rights, in a representative system, upon Canadian Catholics as well as Protestants. That act has been described as the first deliberate attempt by government to reproduce British political institutions in a colonial setting.[16] In official eyes the old colonial representative system had been found wanting at the time of the American revolution, chiefly because the forces of 'democracy' had not been balanced by the forces of 'aristocracy'. Hence the importance attached to the Canada act's provision for upper chambers or legislative councils: their members were to be chosen for life, but it was intended that their descendants should obtain hereditary titles. Although this last intention was never acted on, it bears out Pitt's claim that the purpose of the act was to give the Canadians 'all the advantages of the British Constitution'.[17] What this suggests is that, fifteen years after the American revolution, and a year after the French constitutent assembly had abolished the titles and status of hereditary

---

[13] 'Thoughts on French Affairs', 353; *Letter to Sir Hercules Langrishe* (*Works*, iii. 308, 310). Cf. Leighton, *Catholicism in a Protestant Kingdom*, 141–2.

[14] Paine, a former friend, insinuated that Burke's discovery of the 'divine right' of the prescriptive constitution had shortened 'his journey to Rome' (*Rights of Man*, pt. 1, p. 11). For a more sensitive analysis see Conor Cruise O'Brien, *The Great Melody: A Thematic Biography and Commented Anthology of Edmund Burke* (London, 1992), ch. 1.

[15] *Burke Corr.* vi. pp. xiv, xix–xx; O'Brien, *The Great Melody*, 398–9, 428–9.

[16] NA, Westmorland correspondence, letterbook I. 70; letterbook III. 66; Ward, *Colonial Self-Government*, 14–17.

[17] Ward, *Colonial Self-Government*, 17; Peter Jupp, *Lord Grenville 1759–1834* (Oxford, 1985), 94–5; *Parl. Hist. Eng.* xxviii, col. 1377.

nobility, the government remained convinced—perhaps even more convinced—that the British balance of monarchy, aristocracy, and democracy was the only foundation for order and stability. The novelty was that this formula was being applied to a largely Catholic population. And such was the faith in the superiority of the constitution that it was asserted that the Canadian Catholics would come to see that 'the English laws were best'.[18] In taking this stand, ministers were close to Burke's prescription for the Irish Catholics: that timely concessions to deferential, propertied Catholics would actually reinforce aristocratic values and demonstrate the superiority of the British over the new French constitution.[19]

Only months after the passing of this act, the government was faced with the need to respond to developments in Ireland. Heartened by the English Catholic measure in February 1791, the Catholic Committee decided to petition for further (unspecified) relief. In July their spokesmen approached Grattan, but he simply referred them to the chief secretary, who in turn indicated that the matter was one for the British government.[20] Simultaneously, Dublin Castle was warning of the danger of a possible *rapprochement* between the Catholics and the radical wing of the Protestant dissenters.[21] This prospect was also stressed by Burke's son, Richard, whom the Catholic Committee had appointed as its agent and who was fiercely dedicated to promoting his father's causes. He was granted a series of meetings with ministers in the last quarter of 1791, at which he urged the wisdom of conceding a range of political rights, including the right to vote, that went well beyond what English Catholics had just received.[22]

Against this background, the government's shift of policy on the Catholic question at the end of 1791 comes into clearer focus. Certainly, in communicating the change to Dublin Castle—that, in the government's view, the principle of total exclusion of Catholics from political rights in Ireland should cease—the danger of a 'levelling' alliance between Catholics and dissenters was stressed. But references to the Catholics as 'loyal & faithful subjects', and as 'moderate men', alongside some rather pointed allusions to the growing importance and independence of the Irish parliament, hinted at a sea change in government attitudes.[23] That is not to suggest that ministers had come to share Burke's 'Catholic' view of Irish

---

[18] The speaker was Pitt (*Parl. Hist. Eng.* xxix, col. 113).

[19] *Burke Corr.* vi. 464–5; vii. 40–1.

[20] The most thorough account is to be found in Bartlett, *The Fall and Rise of the Irish Nation*, ch. 8; see also Malcomson, *John Foster*, 411.

[21] The Castle's worries were heightened by the impact, especially on Belfast Volunteers, of Tone's *An Argument on Behalf of the Catholics of Ireland* (Aug. 1791), which sought to allay doubts about the Catholics' fitness for liberty. However, the prospect of an interdenominational alliance turned out to be exaggerated (Bartlett, *The Fall and Rise of the Irish Nation*, 126–7, 133).

[22] *Burke Corr.* vi. 429–30, 463–4, 468–9.

[23] NA, Westmorland corr., letterbook I. 3–5, 67–8.

history;[24] Pitt expressly denied any contact with Burke senior on the issue. Nevertheless, correspondence from the British ministers contains some echoes of Burke's approach to the subject, with references to 'former Animosities [between Protestants and Catholics], the original Grounds of which seem no longer to exist'; to the numerical majority of Catholics in Ireland; and to their loyalty.[25]

II. The Irish Reaction

> The great Patriot Napper Tandy has lost his consequence & Influence
> by his Flirtation with the Catholics. I hope we shall not share the same
> Fate, for as we cannot sham sick and avoid the Common Council, the
> former Scene of his Glory, as he did, we may not escape so well.[26]

In Ireland, public opinion was unprepared for any significant official shift on the Catholic question. Recent research has shown that even the most radical Irish Protestants, such as joined the United Irishmen in 1791–2, were by no means all of one mind on the subject.[27] After all, Irish Catholics already enjoyed most of the rights just granted to English Catholics, and the question had not been seriously agitated since the mid-1780s, when William Drennan had concluded that the Catholics were not yet fit for political rights. It was only five years since the bishop of Cloyne had fended off a legislative attack on tithes by predicating the importance of the established church to 'Protestant ascendancy', or Protestant control in Ireland. His claims for the church had not gone unchallenged, but there had been no attack on Protestant ascendancy. Moreover (*pace* Burke), the bishop had placed his defence of the church in the familiar context of an international Protestant interest. Having discussed (and rejected) possible modifications of the tithe system in Ireland, Dr Woodward had pointed out that even in England, where there could be little reason to fear the growth of popery, there was no disposition to adopt such innovations 'as must ruin in *the Sister Country* that Protestant interest, of which she is the Protectress, even in the remotest nations in Europe'. Accordingly, the bishop concluded that Ireland, with its strong Catholic presence, was not a good case on which to try 'hazardous *experiments* on the Protestant interest'.[28]

What must have appeared to statesmen in London as a position reflecting both self-confidence and prudence, therefore, took on a quite different

---

[24] As set out in the *Letter to Sir Hercules Langrishe* (*Works*, iii. 320–1), and discussed in O'Brien, *The Great Melody*, 480–1.

[25] NA, Westmorland corr., letterbook I. 5–7, 153.

[26] Westmorland to ? Pitt, post-20 Jan. 1792, ibid. letterbook II. 17.

[27] W. H. Crawford, 'The Belfast Middle Classes in the Late Eighteenth Century'; Louis M. Cullen , 'The Internal Politics of the United Irishmen', both in Dickson, Keogh, Whelan (eds.), *The United Irishmen*, 62–73, at 70–1; 176–96, at 179–81.

[28] Woodward, *The Present State of the Church of Ireland*, 84.

complexion in Ireland. Although Ireland might superficially resemble Canada, with a Catholic majority and a Protestant minority divided between Anglicans and dissenters, there the similarities ended. The Catholics of Quebec were already an establishment when they were incorporated into the empire. Their property was not confiscated, and their church was accorded some of the rights of an established church. But Irish Catholics had experienced confiscation; their church had been proscribed, and they were obliged to pay tithes to the established church. The failure of their seventeenth-century efforts to overturn this condition still featured in the Protestant liturgical calendar. For its part, the Church of Ireland not only enjoyed established status, but in tracing its own descent directly from St Patrick it yielded nothing to the Church of England or the Roman Catholic church in respect of antiquity and apostolicity. And whereas two centuries earlier the Church of Ireland had been in effect an English importation, by this time the clergy as well as the laity were overwhelmingly Irish.[29] In these circumstances, the tendency to see popery as an enduring danger to the established church had persisted; whereas in England, particularly since the American revolution, churchmen had developed a greater fear of heterodox Protestant dissent.[30]

In this context, the hostile reaction of Irish ministers towards the proposed new Catholic policy in the winter of 1791–2 may be re-evaluated. It has typically been presented as a reactionary stand, at odds with a more enlightened spirit supposed to have arisen at the time of the Volunteers.[31] But Irish public opinion, except in some radical circles, had not become more enlightened on the Catholic question; or, to be more precise, public opinion had accepted freedom of worship and the repeal of discriminatory land laws, but the question of political rights was so sensitive that it had yet to be openly debated. In the autumn of 1791 the viceroy had been confident that he could win over 'our leading Friends' to support the limited changes extended to English Catholics. But the combination of raised demands (now rumoured to be backed by the British government, perhaps planning to play 'a Catholic game'), plus a more assertive tone in certain Catholic quarters, produced alarm—tending towards intransigence—in Protestant circles. It was natural, therefore, for the viceroy to warn of the dangers of outstripping Protestant opinion, and to remind the British ministers of their historic reliance on Protestants to maintain stability in Ireland.[32] But the ministers, although prepared to make some short-term concessions to

---

[29] Of the bishops, however, just over half of those appointed 1750–1800 were English (Donald Harman Akenson, *The Church of Ireland: Ecclesiastical Reform and Revolution, 1800–1885* (New Haven, 1971), 12.

[30] Leighton, *Catholicism in a Protestant Kingdom*, ch. 3; Clark, *English Society*, 216–35.

[31] Lecky, *History of Ireland in the Eighteenth Century*, 241.

[32] NA, Westmorland corr., letterbook I. 34–41, 94–5; III. 31–2, 35, 40. See also Bartlett, *The Fall and Rise of the Irish Nation*, 134–40.

Protestant feeling, insisted that the implementation of its policy should not
be held up indefinitely.

If the new policy posed a challenge to the Irish cabinet, its implications for
the parliamentary opposition were even more serious. Although as recently
as July 1791 Grattan had failed to respond when approached by the
Catholic Committee, and even in December other opposition groups were
still discounting the possibility of action, once it became known that the
British government was prepared to move then there was a strong incentive
for the parliamentary opposition to modify its position. Failure to do so
would place a future Catholic electorate wholly in the government's debt.
Yet so sensitive was the issue that opposition MPs were slow to move:
Grattan, for instance, only committed himself at the time of the Catholic
petition for the franchise in February 1792.[33]

The opposition in Ireland, moreover, was not confined to parliament.
Corporations and grand juries—the 'popular' element in the constitution—
had become accustomed in recent decades to acting as constitutional
guardians; and these bodies, whose members did not have to contemplate
the prospect of facing a future Catholic electorate, were not disposed to
abandon long-held positions. In January 1792 Dublin corporation addressed
the king, praying that he would preserve the 'Protestant ascendancy'. The
corporation also instructed the city MPs, Henry Grattan and Lord Henry
Fitzgerald, to oppose any measure that might 'shake the security of property
or subvert the Protestant ascendancy in our happy Constitution'.[34]

Dublin corporation and guilds did contain members who had joined the
United Irishmen and who supported political rights for Catholics;[35] these
included Tandy, who had become secretary to the Dublin Society of United
Irishmen set up in November 1791. But despite Tandy's enormous
popularity in the city commons on account of his exertions against the
controversial new police, in this matter he exercised no more influence than
he had done in 1784: and his decision to stay away from the meeting in
question must be judged to have been a prudent one.[36] The address in
defence of Protestant ascendancy—which, after an unsuccessful challenge,
was accepted by the sheriffs and commons unanimously—simply restated
the traditional position, last set out in 1784.[37] Edmund Burke's insinuation,
which has been repeated in recent times,[38] that Castle influence was behind

[33] NA, Westmorland corr., letterbook II. 39–40; Malcomson, *John Foster*, 411–12.
[34] Copies of the address to the MPs were sent out to chief magistrates of towns and sheriffs
of counties (*CARD* xiv. 241–4), and handbills were prepared for distribution in the city (NA,
Rebellion papers, 620/19/48). [35] Below, Ch. 9.
[36] '[Tandy's] Catholic Declarations have compleatly ruined him in the City' (Westmorland
to Pitt, 24 Feb. 1792, NA, Westmorland corr., letterbook II. 43); see also the quotation at n. 26
above. [37] Above, Ch. 6.
[38] *Letter to Richard Burke, Esq.*, in *Works*, vi. 61–80, at 64; McCormack, *Ascendancy and
Tradition*, 74–5.

the address, contained, possibly, an element of truth. William Cope, the wealthy silk merchant who introduced it, claimed long afterwards that he had acted at the prompting of John Lees, head of the Irish Post Office. However, even if the claim was reliable (and Cope had no record as a Castle agent),[39] 'Castle influence' would scarcely have recommended the address to the city commons. The committee that drew up the address included, besides two police commissioners and John Giffard on the Castle side, one of the most popular opposition aldermen (Henry Howison), and the Presbyterian, Alderman William Alexander: it was therefore broadly representative of all shades of opinion on the corporation. In fact it appears that the city commons, and also the opposition press, remained largely preoccupied with the police issue, and failed to accord the address much importance.[40] The term 'Protestant ascendancy', denoting Protestant control in its broadest sense, had been in the public domain for several years, and had yet to become controversial.[41]

Nor did the address betray any new hostility towards Catholics, who had still made no explicit requests for political rights. On the contrary, the address spoke of 'our Roman Catholic brethren'; and the assumption was the familiar one—since Catholics already enjoyed as many rights as were compatible with the security of the constitution, they should rest content with their lot.

This outlook, however, was rapidly becoming unrealistic. The Catholic Committee had learned, through Richard Burke, that the British government was prepared to make concessions beyond anything it had hitherto thought prudent to ask. Despite the introduction on 25 January 1792 of a private bill by Sir Hercules Langrishe (with tacit government support) to grant the Irish Catholics the concessions recently made to English Catholics, the Committee, urged on by Richard Burke, decided to petition parliament specifically for admission to the bar, the county magistracy, grand and petty juries, and for a limited participation in the county franchise.[42] Attempts were made to reassure Protestants on controversial points of imputed Catholic doctrine, such as not keeping faith with heretics.[43] But while Langrishe's bill, giving admission to the legal profession, and lifting remaining restrictions on Catholic education, passed the Irish parliament

---

[39] The claim was made when Cope, whose business had been thriving in 1792, was in straitened circumstances and looking to government for relief (Joseph W. Hammond, 'Mr William Cope's Petition, 1804', *Dublin Hist. Rec.* 6 (1943), 25–38; Jacqueline Hill, 'The Politics of Dublin Corporation, 1760–92', in Dickson, Keogh, Whelan (eds.) *The United Irishmen*, 88–101, at 89–90, 99–100). The Castle stressed the opposition credentials of the activists (NA, O.P. 30/3/2).

[40] Hill, 'The Politics of Dublin Corporation', 98–9.

[41] For studies on the origins of the term, see above, Ch. 6, n. 18.

[42] Bartlett, *The Fall and Rise of the Irish Nation*, 142–3.

[43] See *An Address from the General Committee of Roman Catholics, to their Protestant Fellow Subjects* (Dublin, 1792).

without difficulty[44]—Westmorland had gone to considerable lengths to reassure Protestants that the government had no designs against them, and had encouraged the publication of deferential Catholic addresses—the Catholic petition was rejected by a huge majority, 208 to 25.

Already, however, there were signs that the old unanimity among MPs on the Catholic question was breaking down. In the debate on the ill-fated Catholic petition Grattan asked MPs to reflect on whether they were wise to entrust their future security to Protestant ascendancy, a system that could not ensure good government. If Ireland was not to remain subject to 'a Ministerial and an Aristocrate Ascendancy' Protestants must acquire new strength by progressively adopting the Catholic body.[45] In other words, Protestant ascendancy must be so defined as to allow for Catholics gaining at least some political rights. However, Grattan did not condemn Protestant ascendancy; that task fell, appropriately, to Edmund Burke.

Burke had long been a supporter of the interests of Irish Catholics, and there can be no doubt that he was particularly concerned at this time to see them given the opportunity to help strengthen the forces of counter-revolution. What was more striking than his eloquent defence of Catholic loyalty, however, was his denigration of Irish Protestants, whom he portrayed in the *Letter to Sir Hercules Langrishe* (February 1792) as an oppressive colonial garrison, their ancestors implementing the penal laws in a spirit of 'national hatred and scorn towards a conquered people'.[46] During the spring of 1792 Burke addressed a letter to his son, in which he reflected at some length on the term 'Protestant ascendancy', alleging that Dublin corporation and Dublin Castle had given the term a new meaning:

A word has been lately struck in the mint of the Castle of Dublin; thence it was conveyed to the Tholsel, or city hall, where, having passed the touch of the corporation . . . it soon became current in parliament . . . The word is *Ascendency*. . . . If Protestant ascendancy means the proscription from citizenship of by far the major part of the people of any country, then Protestant ascendancy is a bad thing; and it ought to have no existence.[47]

Burke's anger at the resistance shown in Irish political circles—especially that displayed by plebeian Protestants[48]—to Catholic political rights was understandable, but it led him to make claims that were wide of the mark. The Castle and Dublin corporation had not given a new meaning to 'Protestant ascendancy'. They had used the term, just as Dr Woodward had

---

[44] 32 Geo. III, c. 21.

[45] McCormack, *Ascendancy and Tradition*, 84–5.

[46] *Works*, iii. 320–1. Similar, if milder, sentiments were expressed in Burke's *Letter to a Peer of Ireland* (1782), which caused little stir: Burke was then a less prominent figure (*Works*, iii. 282–97, at 296).

[47] *Letter to Richard Burke, Esq*, (*Works*, vi. 64, 66).

[48] Cf. Leighton, *Catholicism in a Protestant Kingdom*, 34–5.

done, on the hitherto scarcely challenged assumption that Protestant control was fundamental to good government and the protection of British interests in Ireland. It was the British government, by its unexpected new policy, that was mainly responsible for dissolving the public consensus and rendering Protestant ascendancy itself contentious. The fact was that long residence in England had left Burke out of touch with Irish opinion and insensitive to the persistent vitality there of values that were being questioned in British parliamentary circles; and he might usefully have remembered the precept that he himself had commended to the over-hasty French reformers: 'Time is required to produce that union of minds which alone can produce all the good we aim at.'[49]

Already, however, the threat to Protestant ascendancy posed by recent developments had prompted its defenders to do what had not hitherto been necessary: attempt a definition of the term. In February 1792 the MP Richard Sheridan gave his view:

by Protestant ascendancy he meant, a Protestant king, to whom only being Protestant we owed allegiance; a Protestant house of peers ... and a Protestant house of commons, elected and deputed by Protestant constituents; in short a Protestant legislative, a Protestant judicial, and a Protestant executive, in all and each of their varieties, degrees, and gradations.[50]

And so far was Sheridan, a veteran opposition figure,[51] from conceiving that such a position was unreasonable that he urged Irish Catholics to put their faith in the wisdom and liberality of Irish Protestants, rather than looking to 'foreign or ministerial negociation'. Such statements, however, angered those who, like Burke, approved of the principle of Catholic political rights; and they began to use the term 'Protestant ascendancy' in a pejorative way.[52]

For their part, the Catholics were disappointed at the limited concessions of 1792. Buoyed up by intimations of government goodwill, and stung by suggestions that the petition for the franchise had emanated from a small, unrepresentative group, they decided to hold a delegate convention. But such an announcement from the hitherto cautious Catholics caused alarm. In September 1792 Dublin corporation held a special meeting to consider the Catholic Committee's plan. From this meeting emanated a *Letter to the Protestants of Ireland*, which marked a significant development in the defence of the Irish *ancien régime*.[53]

---

[49] *Reflections on the Revolution in France* (*Works*, ii. 439).

[50] Quoted in McCormack, *Ascendancy and Tradition*, 76. The definition was echoed in the corporation's *Letter to the Protestants of Ireland*, below.

[51] Richard Sheridan (related to playwright R. B. Sheridan); member of the Free Citizens Society, 1770s (McDowell, *Irish Public Opinion*, 43).

[52] Hill, 'The Meaning and Significance of "Protestant Ascendancy" ', 1.

[53] *Vindication of the Cause of the Catholics of Ireland, Adopted ... by the General Committee ... December 7, 1792* (Dublin, 1793), 6–7; CARD xiv. 284–7.

The *Letter to the Protestants* began by reaffirming support for the 'liberal and enlightened' policy of recent times, which allowed 'our Roman Catholic fellow subjects' to enjoy freedom of worship, security of property, and 'the highest degree of personal liberty'. However, the letter went on, 'experience has taught us, that without the ruin of the Protestant establishment, the Catholic cannot be allowed the smallest influence in the state'. Reviewing the Catholics' intention 'to proceed upon the plan of the French democracy to elect a representation of their own', the *Letter to the Protestants* went on to state the corporation's view of the relative position of Protestants and Catholics in Ireland:

One hundred years are just elapsed, since the question was tried upon an appeal to heaven, whether this country should become a Popish kingdom, governed by an arbitrary and unconstitutional Popish tyrant, and dependant upon France, or enjoy the blessings of a free Protestant government, a Protestant monarchy limited by the constitution, and an intimate connection with the free empire of Britain. The great ruler of all things decided in favour of our ancestors, he gave them victory and Ireland became a Protestant nation enjoying a British constitution.

To the claim that the king and parliament would grant them political rights if the Catholics made their wishes clearly known, the corporation replied 'we tell them, that the Protestants of Ireland would not be compelled by any authority whatever to abandon that political situation, which their forefathers won with their swords, and which is therefore their birthright, or to surrender their religion at the footstool of Popery'.[54]

The *Letter to the Protestants* needs to be considered in the context of the renewed debate about the glorious revolution. Just as Dr Price's assertions about 1688 had inspired Burke to write the *Reflections*, so Burke's reinterpretation of the revolution may be said to have coloured the *Letter to the Protestants*. For the corporation's insistence that the revolution in Ireland had produced an inherently Protestant constitution ran directly counter to what Burke had argued in his *Letter to Sir Hercules Langrishe*. Thus, while the *Letter to the Protestants* would have had little appeal for Dr Price—who had not invoked the revolution in order to defend the status quo—it also cut across Burke's attempt to take the Protestantism out of the revolution, or at any rate to render it a matter of mere contingency.

If even Burke was too radical for the corporation, this might suggest that the *Letter to the Protestants* was a very reactionary document indeed. Yet to dismiss it as simply archaic would be a mistake. For one thing, while it contained echoes of Bishop King's providentialism, there were even stronger echoes of Locke, especially in the description of the revolution as the

---

[54] CARD xiv. 285–6.

outcome of 'an appeal to heaven'.[55] The Irish Williamite revolution had always lent itself more readily than the English one to a Lockian interpretation. But as noted in Chapter 2, quite quickly the dominant English view of the revolution—that there had been no dissolution of government—began to be incorporated into Irish political language. Of course it was not forgotten that the Irish revolution had not been bloodless, but events in Ireland (and Scotland) came to appear relatively marginal. Even after the American revolution had prompted new interest in Locke's political ideas, there had been little incentive to apply them to the Irish Williamite revolution.[56] In 1782, Henry Flood had reminded parliament that the penal laws ('laws . . . of political necessity') had followed the military defeat of the Irish Jacobites, but his description had lacked the bite of a Lockian 'appeal to heaven'.[57] By adding this dimension, the corporation was attempting to put the Protestant constitution beyond the reach of legislative change. And by casting its own members among the heirs of those whom Providence had favoured following a Lockian dissolution, the corporation signalled that the political nation consisted of more than just landowners. The *Letter to the Protestants* contained its own commitment to equality—not indeed to that of the United Irishmen, but to a species of Protestant equality derived via Locke and Lucas from natural law, contract, and the right of resistance:

Every Irish Protestant has an interest in the government of this kingdom, he is born a member of the state and with a capacity for filling its offices, this capacity he derives from that constitution which his ancestors acquired when they overthrew the Popish tyrant, it is guaranteed by that constitution, it is secured by the law, he is in possession of it, and we know of no power under heaven authorized to alienate this our most valuable inheritance.[58]

Thus both the authorities and the Catholics were being warned not to ignore the Protestant citizenry, whose gains since mid-century (as Burke recognized) had secured them a real place in the political system.

Inevitably there were attempts to discredit the *Letter*. Grattan claimed that it was the work of the Castle's 'city agents': without them, the city would be moderate.[59] He meant, in particular, John Giffard. But Giffard's

---

[55] For Locke, government being a trust, if the trust were broken then the government was dissolved, and, lacking an earthly tribunal, the people could 'Appeal to Heaven': take up arms to seek a God-given judgement (*Two Treatises of Government*, ed. Peter Laslett (Cambridge, 1988), 385–6, 426–7).

[56] See Robert Eccleshall, 'Anglican Political Thought in the Century After the Revolution of 1688', in G. D. Boyce, R. Eccleshall, V. Geoghegan (eds.), *Political Thought in Ireland Since the Seventeenth Century* (London, 1993), 36–72, at 48–58; J. G. A. Pocock, 'The Fourth English Civil War', *Government and Opposition*, 23 (1988), 151–66; Kelly, 'Perceptions of Locke in Eighteenth Century Ireland', 25–8.   [57] *Parl. Reg.* i. 252.

[58] *CARD* xiv. 286. Cf. Lucas, 'It is the wisdom of our Policy . . . to exclude no Man from the highest Offices and Ranks in the State' (*A Third Address to the . . . Lord Mayor, [etc].*, 38–9).   [59] *Parl. Reg.* xiii. 10.

links with the Castle were well known, and had never earned him support before. The fact was that the admission of Catholics to political rights posed an even more immediate challenge to the citizens than to the landed élite. It is not surprising that those who lacked one of the badges of superiority under the existing system—landed property—should cling particularly strongly to another—religious affiliation.[60]

The *Letter to the Protestants* was not an isolated instance of opposition to the more assertive tone of Catholic pronouncements. During the summer assizes many grand juries, reflecting local Protestant landed opinion, passed resolutions of a similar tendency.[61] In view of the status and prestige of Dublin corporation in Patriot politics, however, the *Letter to the Protestants* assumed the nature and purpose of a rallying cry to the Protestant nation, defined in highly inclusive terms, against the tendency of Catholic aspirations and government policy.

III. The Fragmentation of the Patriots

During 1792 the structure of Patriot politics in Dublin began to break up under the combined pressures of radical ideology, French example, and, above all, the transformation of the Catholic question. The corporation, the guilds, Dublin Volunteer corps, and political societies such as the Aldermen of Skinner's Alley[62] were all affected. To the scorn of their more conservative critics in the corporation, the Volunteers—their numbers now much depleted—found themselves divided over whether to take part in the usual celebrations of Williamite anniversaries,[63] or whether to celebrate the storming of the Bastille. Some Volunteers, wearing green cockades, took the latter course; others turned out as usual for the Williamite anniversaries.[64] The traditionalists urged the guilds to return supporters of Protestant ascendancy at the triennial elections for representatives to the city commons (November 1792). One reformist newspaper reported unprecedented efforts by the Castle to influence the outcome of the elections, but still expressed satisfaction at the results; and certainly some reformers and even radicals were returned.[65]

Meanwhile, by the autumn of 1792 the challenge posed by France to the rest of Europe had become far more formidable. After a disastrous start to

---

[60] Cf. Leighton, *Catholicism in a Protestant Kingdom*, 34. Many Dutch guildsmen defected from the Patriots in opposition to political rights for Catholics in the 1780s (Te Brake, *Regents and Rebels*, 95–104, 116–17).

[61] Moody and Vaughan (eds.), *NHI* iv. 315–16. [62] Below, sect. IV.

[63] In 1791 the Catholic Society of Dublin had complained of 'the celebration of festivals memorable only, as they denote the aera, and the events, from which we date our bondage' (*Declaration of the Catholic Society of Dublin* (Dublin, 1791), 12).

[64] *FDJ*, 6 Nov. 1792.

[65] Ibid. 8 Nov. 1792; *DEP*, 10 Nov. 1792. The names of those elected are given in *CARD* xiv. 547–8. See also Ch. 9 below.

the war against Austria and Prussia, the revolutionary government set up the convention, abolished the monarchy, and rallied its forces. The invading armies were repulsed, and in November 1792 the convention offered aid to subject peoples wishing to be free. The king's execution followed in January 1793, and war was declared on Britain in February.

These developments produced more tensions in Dublin. Volunteering began to revive in the summer of 1792. By December plans had been made for electing officers for the 'first national battalion', modelled on the French national guard; and uniforms were being made up under the direction of Thomas Bacon, a United Irishman who represented the tailors' guild on the city commons. Ministers responded (8 December) by banning Volunteer assemblies.[66] On 14 December the Dublin Society of United Irishmen issued an address to Volunteers ('Citizen-Soldiers, to arms!') rejecting the proposed government-controlled militia and calling for another Volunteer convention.[67] The declaration, couched in radical utopian terms,[68] self-consciously renounced the familiar world of corporate privilege:

we address you without any authority save that of reason . . . Here we sit, without mace or beadle, neither a mystery, nor a craft, nor a corporation. In four words lies all our power—Universal Emancipation and Representative Legislature; yet we are confident that on the pivot of this principle, a convention—*still less, a society, still less, a single man, would be able, first to move, and then to raise the world.*[69]

On the same day, Dublin corporation was summoned to a post assembly (about 100 members of both houses signed the necessary requisition). The assembly reaffirmed loyalty to the king, and expressed determination to suppress 'unlawful assemblies'. Dublin freemen were reminded of their oath, obliging them to be true to the king, to keep the peace and to know no gatherings or conspiracies against the king.[70] Apparently there was concern in corporation circles that the freemen in general might be caught up by the tide of utopian rhetoric emanating from the United Irishmen.

For their part, the Catholics continued to pursue the political rights that had appeared so tantalizingly close at the start of the year. The controversial Catholic convention met in December 1792, and decided to bypass the authorities in Dublin and go straight to the king with a new, though deferential, request for political rights. The delegates received a gracious

[66] *Autobiograpy of Archibald Hamilton Rowan*, ed. W. H. Drummond (Shannon, 1972), p. viii; R. B. McDowell (ed.), 'Proceedings of the Dublin Society of United Irishmen', *Anal. Hib.* 17 (1949), 3–143, at 42.
[67] The author was William Drennan.
[68] In the USA in the 1790s a radical utopian language complemented more familiar biblical millennialism (Bloch, *Visionary Republic*, ch. 8). The United Irishmen used both languages (Kevin Whelan, 'The United Irishmen, the Enlightenment and Popular Culture', in Dickson, Keogh, Whelan (eds.), *The United Irishmen*, 269–96).
[69] Quoted in Jacob, *The Rise of the United Irishmen*, 151.
[70] DCA, C1/JSC/7, fos. 55–6ᵛ.

reception from George III, and found the British ministers polite and still sympathetic, although reluctant to be specific about precisely what rights might be conceded. The response among Dublin Protestants to these moves was predictably mixed. In December 1792 the United Irishmen sent a deputation to the Catholic Committee urging it to demand unqualified repeal of the remaining penal laws (the deputation was, however, coolly received).[71] A meeting of freemen and freeholders, held at the Royal Exchange in January 1793 to commend parliamentary reform, passed a resolution, with only one dissenting voice, in favour of Catholic 'liberty'— on the grounds of its importance to liberty in general.[72] More cautious views were also expressed. On the eve of the 1793 parliamentary session the *Freeman's Journal*, conducted by the government informer, Francis Higgins, urged Catholics not to abandon their political aspirations but to refrain from pressing them at present. Otherwise they might appear to be putting undue pressure on parliament, at a time when 'republicans and levellers' were openly deriding the constitution.[73]

The British government, however, had already taken its decision. In January, Dundas renewed the subject with the viceroy, outlining the proposed concessions. Irish Catholics were to obtain a whole range of civil and political rights, including the right to bear arms, to hold certain naval and military commissions, to enter the lower levels of the public service, to take degrees at Dublin university, become members of guilds and corporations, and to vote in parliamentary elections. Only the higher public, judicial, and military offices would remain closed to them, plus access to parliament itself. On this occasion, the viceroy was inclined to acquiesce, on the grounds that the government's shift on the Catholic question a year earlier had had a demoralizing effect on Irish Protestants, who consequently (he thought) would accept the proposals, in the hope of attaching Catholics to the constitution and saving it from any revolutionary challenge. The bill, which came before the Irish parliament in February as a government measure, duly passed, although several speakers in both houses expressed serious reservations, even, in some cases, while voting in support.[74] (The pressure on MPs, particularly members of the opposition and those from

[71] Moody and Vaughan (eds.), *NHI* iv. 316–18, 326.

[72] *Hib. Jn.*, 23 Jan. 1793. The meeting was chaired by one of the sheriffs, Henry Hutton of Winetavern St., tanner, d. 1808 (alderman, 1796, lord mayor 1803–4), a Presbyterian and colleague of Tandy's. The radical *Hib. Jn.* called the attendance 'numerous and respectable', but Dr Patrick Duigenan claimed that only about 100 people, half of them Catholics, attended (*Parl. Reg.* xiii. 132).

[73] *FJ*, 2–8 Jan. 1793. For a hostile account of Higgins's role in the 1790s see W. J. Fitzpatrick, *'The Sham Squire' and the Informers of 1798; With Jottings About Ireland a Century Ago*, new edn. (Dublin, 1895).

[74] 33 Geo. III, c. 21. See Moody and Vaughan (eds.) *NHI* iv. 318; Malcomson, *John Foster*, 416–17.

strongly Catholic areas, not to appear to lag behind the government on this issue has already been noted.)

It is worth re-emphasizing that Catholics were being given political rights as part of a counter-revolutionary strategy, in the expectation that this would reinforce their habitual deference. The concessions were not accompanied by constitutional change, such as parliamentary reform. In other words, Catholics were being admitted, on the same terms as Protestants, to some of the benefits of a political system still based on privilege. But would matters work out as ministers expected? It was one thing to contemplate giving political rights to English Catholics, few in number and strongly landed in composition—though they were not granted the vote until 1829. It was one thing to give such rights to French-Canadian Catholics, who outnumbered Canadian Protestants, but who already enjoyed the status of an establishment. It was arguably a different matter to extend such rights to Irish Catholics, whose large numbers, weak landed element, rising middle class, and long proscription from power made their exercise of political privileges far more unpredictable. After all, Wolfe Tone and the United Irishmen had cast the Catholics not as upholders of privilege but as participants in its destruction.

In this respect it should be borne in mind that the Irish Catholics were, for the most part, an unknown quantity. The experience of the past century had fostered a closed culture, obliging their spokesmen to present their case in terms that would appeal to Protestants.[75] Accordingly, Protestants, buoyed up by belief in their own civil and religious rectitude, were apt to regard them as malleable material, to be fashioned according to Protestant interests. Hence the variety of opinions on how Catholics were likely to exercise political privileges. Some saw them as propping up the existing system. Others saw them as supporters of the rights of man. Either way, it was assumed, they would be following a Protestant lead. Yet another element, anxious at the upsurge of agrarian disturbances, feared an assault on the land system and the established church: such pessimists thought their fears had come true in 1798.

Ambiguity, then, was present in the Catholic political rights issue from the outset; and a great deal would depend on how the concessions worked in practice. In view of the unprecedented ferment unleashed by the French revolution, and the fact that the new Catholic policy had been initiated from outside, there was an obvious danger that it would produce a Protestant backlash. Such a danger was not uniformly spread; the landed élite produced staunch defenders of Protestant ascendancy, but in general the gentry's interests were not as directly threatened as those of certain other groups. Land ownership was still largely in Protestant hands, and the government had not proposed that Catholics be admitted to parliament. At

[75] Leighton, *Catholicism in a Protestant Kingdom*, 102–9.

urban level, the change in Catholic status proved most controversial not in towns (such as Belfast) where Protestants were still in a comfortable majority, nor where they had never been numerous (Galway), but where numbers were more evenly balanced, or where what has been described as a 'critical mass' of Protestants existed (such as Dublin, Cork, Waterford, and Clonmel).[76] In such cases the reforms raised a real possibility that control of corporations could pass from Protestants to Catholics.

In Dublin, the admission of Catholics to guilds and the corporation was a matter for the existing Protestant members of those bodies. This gave new significance to a problem about which the Catholics themselves only began to speak openly in 1791:

The *liberty of Ireland to those of our communion is a calamity*, and their misfortunes seem likely to increase, as the country shall improve in prosperity and freedom. They may look with envy to the subjects of an arbitrary Monarch, and contrast that government in which one great tyrant ravages the land, with the thousand inferior despots whom at every instant they must encounter. . . . We are satisfied that the mere repeal of the laws against us will prove but feebly beneficial, unless the act be sanctioned by the concurrence of our Protestant brethren, and those jealousies removed by which the social intercourse of private life is interrupted.[77]

The tone of this statement, though strong, was measured and detached. A year later, when Catholic hopes for political rights had first been raised and then dashed, Catholics were goaded into wholesale denunciations of Dublin corporation for its defence of Protestant ascendancy. At a Catholic meeting held in Dublin to consider the corporation's *Letter to the Protestants of Ireland* the merchant Randal McDonnell delivered a stinging rebuke:

As a trader of this city I shall say it [civic freedom] must first become an object of the ambition of *respectable* Protestant and Presbyterian traders, of whom, though I see some in their lists, they are comparatively few indeed . . . Till this becomes the case, the corporation need not fear . . . to be besieged or assailed by the Catholics. We have opportunities enough already to waste our time, and lavish our money. We have examples enough of excess, of intemperance, and improvidence. We have roads enough open to us to bankruptcy and ruin. *Our* cause is the cause of our country. *Our* object is the relief of our oppressed and miserable peasantry, and to raise our body from its present degraded state in our native country.[78]

If these last remarks could be construed as a challenge, points raised by other speakers sounded more like defiance. Without the Catholics, said

---

[76] Dickson, ' "Centres of Motion" ', 109–10.

[77] *Declaration of the Catholic Society of Dublin* (21 Oct. 1791), in *Transactions of the General Committee of the Roman Catholics of Ireland, During the Year 1791* (Dublin, 1792), 11–15, at 12.

[78] *Proceedings at the Catholic Meeting of Dublin, Duly Convened on . . . October 31, 1792 . . . with the Letter of the Corporation of Dublin to the Protestants of Ireland* (Dublin, 1792), 13.

another merchant, Ireland had no claim to be called a nation—'we have three millions'. A Dr Thomas Ryan spoke of the Catholics as having been a wretched, debilitated people for six hundred years. He described members of the corporation as 'vultures who cling to their country in order to feed on its bowels'. The *Letter to the Protestants*, he said, had spoken of the Williamite victories as an appeal to heaven; in the subsequent violation of the Treaty of Limerick he saw an appeal to hell. And what did Protestants actually possess? An unrepresentative house of commons, a marketable peerage, an English episcopacy, and a set of rotten boroughs! Protestants were too weak to achieve real improvement in Ireland, yet they refused to receive the strength that Catholics could bring.[79]

These remarks indicated that Catholics, or urban Catholics at any rate, were not the blank slate that many Protestants took them to be. The Vatican's new significance as a counter-revolutionary force; the government's conversion to political rights for Catholics; and Burke's denigration of Irish Protestants, offered Catholics new respectability and an unaccustomed freedom to speak openly about their situation. The sentiments contained in these speeches are thus of considerable interest. The opposition outlook, for instance, and the telling reference to Catholic numbers in relation to the term 'nation', cast doubt on whether these Catholics were likely to support the status quo. A distinctive view of the past (centuries of oppression, the sense of grievance over the Treaty of Limerick) stands out, so different from Dublin corporation's complacency concerning the enlightened but partial repeal of the penal laws, and its insistence on the providential rights conferred on Protestants by the Williamite victories. But of particular significance is the resentment directed against the corporation itself ('our oppressors') in contrast to repeated statements of goodwill to 'the Protestants of Ireland', which apparently meant those who now looked for a lead to Henry Grattan.[80]

Six months later, following the change in the law, the Dublin guilds were faced with the prospect of Catholic applications, as a first step towards freedom of the city. For, despite the bravado, it quickly emerged that Catholic tradesmen were not indifferent to the allure of civic freedom. Certain Catholics attempted to smooth the way to guild admission by seeking to enrol as quarter brothers before the act came into effect.[81] Since admission was a matter for the guilds themselves, the response to Catholic applicants might be expected to reflect the divisions already noted in corporate circles; and the scope for varying reactions was increased by the

[79] Ibid. 17–20, 23.   [80] Speech of John Keogh, ibid. 36–7.

[81] In July 1792 John O'Neill, Michael Boylan, Anthony Dempsey, Thomas Smyth, and Michael Stapleton were admitted as quarter brothers of St Luke's guild (cutlers, painter-stainers, stationers). After the relief act O'Neill and Dempsey were among the painters admitted as freemen of the guild, with some Catholic stationers (NLI, MS 12126, pp. 69, 76).

need for Catholics to apply by special grace, since few of them were qualified by birth or service.

Certainly, guild reactions varied considerably. In one case (the stationers' guild, whose master was the United Irishman John Chambers)[82] the guild amended its by-laws to remove the ban on Catholic freedom, and even elected a Catholic[83] as warden in 1794—though this was later overturned on legal advice. As befitted the master's political outlook, five of the ten Catholics admitted in 1793 were United Irishmen.[84] The tailors' guild took a more cavalier approach and simply ignored its own by-law confining membership to Protestants (as the relief act entitled it to do). This guild displayed a particularly generous spirit, admitting six Catholics shortly after the relief act passed, and allowing them to exercise equal rights in all guild activities, including the most sensitive political right of voting for guild representatives on the city commons. In all, at least six guilds, nearly one-quarter of the whole, have been identified as admitting some Catholics in 1793; the stationers, smiths, apothecaries, carpenters, and tailors—even the prestigious merchants' guild, with thirty-one representatives on the city commons, having first rejected over thirty applicants in July on a very close ballot, subsequently relented and admitted eleven of them in October.[85]

Other guilds, however, reacted much more defensively. The barber-surgeons, shoemakers, and cooks rejected all their Catholic applicants; though the barbers did review their by-laws to allow for the possibility of Catholic admissions. And even where Catholics were admitted, the new members remained less than fully free, because they had not been made free of the city, and consequently, according to municipal by-laws, were ineligible to exercise full guild privileges or to obtain a parliamentary vote. Certain guilds raised the fee payable by applicants for admission by special grace. The apothecaries admitted two Catholics, but turned down four others, including two United Irishmen.[86] In the corporation itself, only one

---

[82] John Chambers (1754–1837), printer; b. Dublin, married into a Catholic family (Fitzsimons); founder member, Dublin Society of United Irishmen. Master of St Luke's guild 1793–4 (NLI, MS 12126, p. 80); representative on city commons 1789–98. Charged with high treason, May 1798, banished, later emigrated to America (M. Pollard, 'John Chambers, Printer and United Irishman', *The Irish Book*, 3 (1964), 1–22).

[83] John O'Neill, painter (NLI, MS 12126, pp. 88, 91). The relief act required guild officers to take the oaths of supremacy and allegiance, and the declaration against popery.

[84] Patrick Byrne, Richard Cross, Peter Hoey (booksellers), Thomas McDonnell (stationer), and Jeremiah Sullivan (paper-maker) (McDowell, 'The Personnel of the Dublin Society of United Irishmen'). By contrast, none of the five Catholics admitted to the smiths' guild in July 1793 were United Irishmen (NA, M 2925, f. 89).

[85] *Hib. Jn.*, 17 July, 16, 28 Oct. 1793; Jacqueline Hill, 'The Politics of Privilege: Dublin Corporation and the Catholic Question, 1792–1823', *Maynooth Review*, 7 (1982), 17–36, at 23–5.

[86] The United Irishmen were Charles Ryan and Edmond Dillon (Transactions 1747–95, Apothecaries' hall, pp. 273–4). For the barbers, see TCD, MS 1447/8/3, pp. 9–10.

Catholic merchant, Valentine O'Connor,[87] obtained aldermanic backing; and when his application was sent down for approval to the city commons it was rejected by 66 votes to 29.[88] Even in the most well-disposed guilds, Catholic admissions dried up quickly after 1794, by which time the political climate had become still more defensive; and there was little that radical guild members, who were the principal champions of Catholic membership, could achieve.

Since admissions were decided by ballot, guild members did not have to explain the reasons for their vote. However, some were all too anxious to justify their stand. In the merchants' guild, Sir Edward Newenham, Tandy's former colleague, said that he welcomed the chance to declare his views on the application of two Catholic merchants, Edward Byrne[89] and Valentine O'Connor. Both, he conceded, were merchants of very respectable character, men of property and virtue: but he would not give them such power as would put the guild into their hands. If Catholics obtained the ascendancy in the guild they could elect the city commons and ultimately the lord mayor and sheriffs, which would enable them to oust the Protestants. He counselled delay until it was seen how Catholics would exercise the freehold franchise.[90] Thus, while there was evidence of much goodwill towards Catholics, this was tempered by a strong sense of caution, doubtless reinforced by the presence of United Irishmen among those Catholics who had been admitted, which helped to keep the number of Catholic admissions small, and their influence limited.

For the Catholic middle class this outcome was naturally disappointing. It quickly quelled the euphoric mood that had greeted the passing of the relief act, when Catholics had agreed to abandon their own meetings in order to merge in the general body of citizens.[91] Just as the Catholic Society of Dublin had warned in 1791, changes in the law alone had not proved sufficient to guarantee the exercise of political rights; and it had become clear that Catholics depended for their civic status not on the government, nor on parliament, but on the corporation and the guilds. By the end of 1793 urban Catholics were considering how to pursue the exercise of their rights. Some were prepared to trust to the passage of time; some looked to

---

[87] Valentine O'Connor (1744–1814), merchant; member of the first council of the Dublin chamber of commerce.

[88] DCA, C1/JSC/7, fo. 88ᵛ. Purported details of the ostensibly secret ballot were published (NA, Thomas Braughall papers, 620/34/50; *DEP*, 2, 5 Nov. 1793). It appears that representatives of nine guilds, mainly those associated with the strongly Catholic food and leather trades (the bakers, butchers, saddlers, shoemakers, cooks, tanners, bricklayers, curriers, and joiners) all voted against admission; the two hosiers both voted in favour, and the remaining representatives, and the sheriffs' peers, were divided.

[89] Edward Byrne, d. 1804, sugar merchant, of Mullinahack, Co. Dublin.

[90] *FDJ*, 16 July 1793.

[91] A skeleton body remained in existence (Deirdre Lindsay, 'The Fitzwilliam Episode Revisited', in Dickson, Keogh, Whelan (eds.), *The United Irishmen*, 197–208, at 198.

legal remedies; and some to a radical reform of parliament, a goal they shared with the United Irishmen.[92]

IV. *The New Political Alignments of 1792–1793*

Since mid-century Dublin politics had operated on the premiss of a court–opposition configuration, which had been sustained by a number of shared values. These included the belief that sovereignty was divided (this justified both royal and local rights); the idea of constitutional balance; and the retention of political rights in Protestant hands. There were differences of emphasis; even differences of principle over the new police system, and parliamentary reform. But those who questioned the underlying values were unrepresentative and wielded little influence.

Between 1791 and 1793 this broad consensus was shattered by the combined effects of the government's shift on the Catholic question, and the new radicalism. Two broad tendencies emerged from the upheavals; one reformist—including many Whigs and United Irishmen (the latter for the most part not yet committed separatists)—the other anxious to preserve the status quo. Although political rights for Catholics had not formed part of the Whig Club's original agenda, during 1792 several Whig groups shifted on this question, and in 1793 they also took up parliamentary reform. Henry Grattan was strongly identified with the new outlook.[93] Thus the Whigs came to have much in common with the United Irishmen, who already stood for parliamentary reform and political rights for Catholics: their opponents viewed both as part of a single political continuum.[94]

On the other side—inevitably, in view of the importance of Protestant control in the Irish *ancien régime*—traditionalists found themselves associated with 'Protestant ascendancy', which during 1792 had ceased to be a neutral description of the status quo, becoming instead a rallying cry and even a collective noun.[95] Supporters were to be found in parliament, the established church, the corporation, and the guilds. There were also sympathizers in the Castle, which has led some historians to dismiss them as a Castle party.[96] This scarcely does justice to those who held such views, despite the fact that since 1788 one notable activist, John Giffard of the city commons, had been receiving Castle subventions for his newspaper, *Faulkner's Dublin Journal*, which expounded views close to those of government on issues such as policing and patronage. Giffard was also a

[92] Hill, 'The Politics of Privilege', 27–9. An act was passed 'for giving relief in proceedings upon writs of mandamus, for the admission of freemen into corporations' (33 Geo. III, c. 38), but the difficulty of proving a *right* of admission meant it had little effect (below, Ch. 11).

[93] McDowell, *Irish Public Opinion*, 187–8.

[94] See 'Associations', in *FJ*, 19–21 Mar. 1793.

[95] Thus Tone in July 1792 referred to meetings of 'the Protestant ascendancy' (McCormack, *Ascendancy and Tradition*, 71).

[96] See e.g. Lecky, *History of Ireland in the Eighteenth Century*, 248.

channel for communicating secret reports on the United Irishmen to the Castle. But he could not be relied on to follow a government line, as ministers were to find in future.[97] Certain traditionalists also supported the revived movement for the 'reformation of manners', aimed at bringing 'civility' to the lower orders. This had been gaining ground in corporate circles since the late 1780s, culminating in 1792 in the formation of the Association for Discountenancing Vice and Promoting the Practice of the Christian Religion.[98]

Neither the reformers nor the traditionalists were parties in the modern sense, although on the reformist side the Whig Club, the Friends of the Constitution, and the United Irishmen provided institutional dimensions that had no real counterpart on the other side. Their respective strengths on Dublin corporation will be examined in Chapter 9; meanwhile, the shattering effect of the upheavals of 1792–3 can be seen in the fate of the oldest and most prestigious of Dublin political societies, the Aldermen of Skinner's Alley. Claiming to date from the era of Jacobite adversity, the society attracted the cream of Dublin's Protestant business community, particularly those with corporation connections, as well as members of the gentry. Although it has been portrayed as an unvarying vehicle of militant Protestantism,[99] during the 1770s and 1780s it had a marked opposition bias. In 1790 most of its members took the opposition side in the mayoral dispute, and as late as March 1792 the society dined with other Dublin reformers—Whigs, United Irishmen, and members of the Catholic Committee—and toasted the hope that the glorious revolution in France might be realized in Ireland.[100] But the controversy over the Catholic question, and the solicitor-general's attack on Tandy, one of the society's stalwarts, produced a change of mood. In June 1792 James McMahon, a United Irishman, was expelled for showing disrespect to King William's memory and to Protestant ascendancy.[101] Radicals made an attempt to have the expulsion overturned, but the spy Thomas Collins, a member both of

[97] Inglis, *Freedom of the Press in Ireland*, 58, 60–1; below, Ch. 9. Giffard's undoubted importance in countering radicalism in the 1790s led to him being credited (wrongly) with coining the phrase 'Protestant ascendancy' (*Recollections of Jonah Barrington*, 154).

[98] See Joseph Liechty, 'Irish Evangelicalism, Trinity College Dublin, and the Mission of the Church of Ireland at the End of the Eighteenth Century', Ph.D. thesis (NUI (Maynooth), 1987), 96–101. For earlier initiatives see above, Ch. 3; for English counterparts see M. J. D. Roberts, 'The Society for the Suppression of Vice and its Early Critics, 1802–1812', *Hist. Jn.* 26 (1983), 159–76.

[99] Most modern accounts draw on Barrington's essay, itself influenced by the events of the 1790s (*Recollections of Jonah Barrington*, 154–60).

[100] *Hib. Jn.*, 9 July 1790; NA, Rebellion papers, 620/19/69. Members of the society had to be freemen or freeholders of Dublin.

[101] James McMahon, Aungier St., apothecary (*FDJ*, 2–5 June, 30 June–3 July 1792). Barrington's colourful account (*Recollections*, 158–60) implies that McMahon was a Catholic: if so, on admission to the apothecaries' guild (1790) he had taken the oaths and declaration against popery (Transactions 1747–95, Apothecaries' hall, p. 253).

the Skinner's Alley society and of the United Irishmen, worked on the anxieties of those whom the radicals called 'the old-fashioned Protestants' to such effect that only a handful of the 150 members who attended the meeting in question were prepared to defend McMahon. According to Collins, Tandy did not dare to turn up.[102]

Subsequently, something of the old spirit returned, for in September 1793 when the city sheriffs-elect (one of whom was John Giffard) were proposed for membership their applications were blocked. This time the society split, and for a time two sections, one radical, the other conservative, continued to meet, each claiming to represent the spirit of the original members. The radical wing—closely identified with the Dublin United Irishmen, by now in decline as a public organization—appears to have retained the allegiance of many of the members, if not the officers; about 100 attended a meeting in October 1793 to condemn the officers and set up a new committee. However, the radical wing does not seem to have survived long. By December 1793 the *Hibernian Journal* was criticizing the Aldermen of Skinner's Alley for their 'Protestant Ascendancy' outlook.[103]

These broad divisions were reflected in the press. Although the climate for reformist newspapers became increasingly difficult during 1793, the *Hibernian Journal*, the *Dublin Evening Post*, and the *Morning Post* all took a reformist stand. 'Ascendancy' supporters were served by *Faulkner's*. But the conservative forces were divided among themselves; Lucas's old paper, the *Freeman's Journal*, now in receipt of Castle money, was hostile to Whigs and United Irishmen, but in line with the British government's outlook welcomed the admission of Catholics to political rights as likely to promote stability in Ireland.[104]

The seriousness of these divisions among Protestants was duly reflected in the charges and counter-charges that appeared in the satire and political comment of the day. Both sides saw the other as responsible not merely for political divisions, but also for wider social and economic ills, including the commercial depression that affected Dublin in the spring and early summer of 1793.[105] Having themselves performed an about-face on the Catholic question, the opposition newspapers charged the ascendancy party with 'prejudice'; and, in their opposition to Catholic admission to civic freedom, with being 'monopolists'. Fears for the church, and for possible revolution, made good targets for ridicule.[106]

---

[102] McDowell (ed.), 'Proceedings of the Dublin Society of United Irishmen', 15–16, 27. McMahon was unlucky to have belonged to the same guild as John Giffard, the recipient of Collins' secret reports on the United Irishmen.

[103] McDowell (ed.), 'Proceedings of the Dublin Society of United Irishmen', 87–91; *Hib. Jn.*, 9 Dec. 1793.

[104] *FJ*, 20–3 Apr. 1793. See also Inglis, *Freedom of the Press in Ireland*, 57–62, 75–88.

[105] See *The Drennan Letters*, ed. D. A. Chart (Belfast, 1931), 158; *FJ*, 11–14 May 1793.

[106] *Hib Jn.*, 24 July, 11, 23 Oct. 1793; see also 'Protestant Ascendancy: Or, Rebellion Detected', ibid., 14 Mar. 1792.

However, the 'old-fashioned Protestants' also had a persuasive case. In an increasingly counter-revolutionary climate they had the advantage of defending the status quo and traditional values associated with the church and the social order. Giffard's paper printed a letter from the ghost of Swift to the people of the Liberties, urging them to shun the fellows in green coats who told them they were slaves; prosperity would be gained through hard work, not revolutionary ideas.[107] A political poem of 1792 invoked St Patrick as one whose original mission to Ireland had been to preach co-operation and banish strife: 'unite, you conquer—but divide, you die!' For a time, the poet implied, these counsels had been heeded and reason and prosperity reigned; but in latter times a monster called 'party' had arisen: and the poet lamented that snake-banishing St Patrick, before departing for heaven, had not crushed its hydra head. The poem was dedicated to Henry Grattan, who, together with his Whig colleagues, was censured for disregarding Dublin corporation's fears for the integrity of the Protestant constitution.[108]

A similar perspective, though not featuring St Patrick, was adopted by 'Candidus Redintegratus' (probably the MP for Dublin University, Dr Arthur Browne).[109] Faced with a reform movement that was veering into utopianism and republicanism, Candidus delivered a swingeing attack not just on those extremes, but on the entire opposition Patriot tradition: its suspicion of government; its reliance on 'unconstitutional' bodies such as the Volunteers; its (professed) hostility to accepting government places; and the habit of instructing MPs. The new Whigs, he alleged, were 'professional Patriots', who condemned an unfettered royal prerogative, yet who had been ready to grant the prince of Wales unlimited power as regent in 1788. In fact, they were paving the way for a return to the 1640s. Above all, Candidus attacked Grattan. His hostility to tithes was a dereliction of duty on the part of an episcopal Protestant. The established church really was in danger, both from Catholics and from heterodox dissent. Appealing to James Harrington himself in defence of church establishments and tithes, Candidus defended the Church of Ireland and the British constitution as providing more real liberty than any other system.[110]

---

[107] *FDJ*, 13 Dec. 1792.

[108] *The Expulsion, or, Tycho Tickled, an Irregular Poem* (Dublin, 1792).

[109] Arthur Browne (?1756–1805), regius professor of civil and canon law, TCD; MP, Dublin University 1783–1802 (*DNB*). Defended tithes in 1788, but usually supported the opposition, though the description 'keen nationalist' (McDowell, *Irish Public Opinion*, 116) hardly fits. For his worries over the utopian rhetoric of the 1790s see *Parl. Reg.* xv. 315–16.

[110] Candidus Redintegratus, *Free Thoughts on the Measures of Opposition, Civil and Religious . . . with a Modest Plea for the Rights and Ascendancy of Episcopal Protestantism* (Dublin, 1792).

9

The Constitution Defended:
Opposition to Rebellion,
1792–1798

Recent research has modified the received picture of the evolution of revolutionary thinking in Ireland during the 1790s. According to that picture, such ideas only assumed formidable proportions from the mid-1790s when the United Irishmen, persecuted by government and despairing of reform, moved towards alliance with France and separation from Britain.[1] Historians now emphasize the presence, almost from the outset, of a more radical and secretive element within the movement,[2] but it has also emerged that others were contemplating revolution in Ireland during the 1790s. The Defenders, a mainly Catholic, oath-bound secret society, were already spreading widely in 1792. Their political horizons had been extended by the excitement surrounding the pursuit of Catholic political rights; expectations of the demise of the existing order were heightened by French revolutionary rhetoric and example. By the winter of 1792–3 they were preparing for insurrection.[3] This evidence sets in fresh context the counter-revolutionary efforts of government and local authorities, which began in 1792 and continued until after Emmet's rebellion of 1803. For Dublin corporation, the task of countering revolutionary tendencies and maintaining law and order was a role that conformed well with its historic self-image, and it proved to be perfectly compatible with a traditional 'opposition' stand over issues such as the legislative union with Britain.

I. Opposition to Rebellion

The Rightboy activities of the mid-1780s had scared the authorities, who responded with a tumultuous risings act in 1787.[4] For some years the countryside remained quiet, but early in 1791 disturbances broke out again in the Dundalk region, where the perpetrators were known as Defenders.

[1] See e.g. J. C. Beckett, *The Making of Modern Ireland 1603–1923* (London, 1969), 252.
[2] Nancy J. Curtin, 'The Transformation of the Society of United Irishmen into a Mass-Based Revolutionary Organisation, 1794–6', *IHS* 24 (1985), 463–92, at 469–70; Cullen, 'The Internal Politics of the United Irishmen', 181–92.
[3] Marianne Elliott, *Partners in Revolution: The United Irishmen and France* (New Haven, 1982), 40–3; Smyth, *The Men of No Property*, 50–1.
[4] 27 Geo. III, c. 15.

Historians are not entirely agreed about the genesis of the Defenders, but it appears that they had originated in County Armagh in the mid-1780s, largely as a result of the destabilizing effects of the erosion of the penal laws. In this region certain Protestants, organized as 'Peep O'Day Boys', took it upon themselves to enforce the penal laws relating to arms by dawn raids on Catholic houses. The Defenders represented a response to such attacks, but they had other goals: the regulation of rents, reducing tithes, and the reduction of dues to Catholic priests.[5]

Although they had earlier attracted some Protestant support, the Defenders remained an essentially Catholic movement, and by 1792 they were spreading widely in south Ulster and north Leinster, and into Connaught. In such areas Defender raids for arms on Protestant homes produced panic and fears of 'massacre' during the winter of 1792–3. Such fears may be understood not only in terms of the official cult of commemorating 1641 (which in any case was in decline),[6] but in the light of what had just been achieved in France by direct peasant action, afterwards legitimized by the National Assembly: the abolition of tithes and feudal tenures.[7] What made the Defenders more formidable than most of their predecessors was the fact that they were as much a political as an agrarian movement, having absorbed some of the ideology of the political opposition, by this time in a state of unprecedented ferment. The mixture of traditional agrarian and Catholic grievances with new revolutionary slogans produced a heady compound, made all the more explosive by the expectations aroused in 1792 by the activities of the Catholic Committee.[8]

In these conditions traditional goals readily acquired apocalyptic overtones. Before the end of 1792 expectations were spreading of the impending abolition of various dues, including tithes. According to the viceroy, there was no general disaffection towards landlords, but there were rumours that arms were being purchased, and that tithes would not be paid after Christmas. Several Defenders, captured in County Meath after laying an ambush to rescue one of their leaders, admitted to having acted in the expectation of 'an equal distribution of property', 'assistance from France', 'the conditions of Limerick', and 'to destroy the Protestant religion'.[9] 'Assistance from France' may be assessed in the context of traditional

[5] See David W. Miller, 'The Armagh Troubles, 1784–95', in Samuel Clark and James S. Donnelly, jun., *Irish Peasants: Violence & Political Unrest 1780–1914* (Manchester, 1983), 155–91; Elliott, *Partners in Revolution*, 40–2; L. M. Cullen, 'The Political Structures of the Defenders', in Hugh Gough and David Dickson (eds.), *Ireland and the French Revolution* (Dublin, 1990), 117–38; Smyth, *The Men of No Property*, ch. 2.
[6] Barnard, 'The Uses of 23 October 1641'; Jacqueline Hill, '1641 and the Quest for Catholic Emancipation, 1691–1829', in Brian Mac Cuarta (ed.), *Ulster 1641: Aspects of the Rising* (Belfast, 1993), 159–71, at 167.
[7] William Doyle, *Origins of the French Revolution* (Oxford, 1980), 205–6.
[8] Elliott, *Partners in Revolution*, 42; Smyth, *The Men of No Property*, 50–1.
[9] Elliott, *Partners in Revolution*, 43.

Jacobite attitudes as well as the new pledge from revolutionary France to help peoples struggling to be free. 'The conditions of Limerick' suggests that the Defenders were familiar with the recently revived controversy about the 1691 treaty of Limerick.[10] As for the destruction of Protestantism, an edition of *Pastorini's Prophecies*, foretelling such an event, had been published in Dublin in 1790.[11] Given the importance of Protestantism in the existing order, religion was bound to loom large in populist expectations of revolutionary change.

Against a background of worsening international relations, ideological turmoil, Defenders raiding for arms in the countryside, armed Volunteers parading in Dublin, and the Catholic Committee holding a convention to press for political rights, towards the end of 1792 more conservative Protestants were becoming distinctly anxious. Looking back on that period, the loyalist Sir Richard Musgrave recalled the mood of the capital: 'the City was like a great shell, fraught with various combustibles, and ready to explode on the application of a match'. In common with the authorities, Musgrave dismissed the possibility that the Defenders themselves were capable of initiating revolutionary action. He suspected that the Catholic Committee was behind the disturbances.[12] This was, no doubt, a mistaken view, though one not entirely discounted in recent writing.[13] However, in the light of what is now known of Defender activities, the allegation that a revolution was in prospect was not far-fetched. Moreover, it is known that contacts existed between members of the Catholic Committee and Defenders, and between United Irishmen and Defenders—although it has been suggested that, in the case of the United Irishmen, what appeared to be sedition was little more than bravado.[14]

At all events, in December 1792 the government took steps to forestall the possibility of a rising. A proclamation was issued against the Dublin Volunteers, and magistrates were ordered to patrol the streets at night. In the same month an arms bill was passed, unopposed, to encourage disarming, and to prevent the purchase of arms without licence.[15] When the Dublin United Irishmen responded by urging the Volunteers to arm in

---

[10] The Treaty of Limerick's terms only became really contentious after the prospect of a Jacobite restoration had receded: Connolly, *Religion, Law, and Power*, 233; Arthur Browne, *A Brief Review of the Question, Whether the Articles of Limerick have been Violated?* (Dublin, 1788).

[11] [Charles Walmesley], *The General History of the Christian Church, From her Birth to her Final Triumphant State in Heaven, Chiefly Deduced from the Apocalypse of St John the Apostle, by Signor Pastorini* (1771) (Dublin, 1790). Walmesley (1722–97) was a vicar apostolic in England (*DNB*).

[12] Richard Musgrave, *Memoirs of the Different Rebellions in Ireland, From the Arrival of the English*, 2nd edn. (Dublin, 1801), 81–90, 117.

[13] Smyth, *The Men of No Property*, 50–1.

[14] Cullen, 'The Political Structures of the Defenders', 127; Elliott, *Partners in Revolution*, 43–4.   [15] 33 Geo. III, c. 2; Musgrave, *Memoirs*, 117.

Ireland's defence and to demand parliamentary reform and political rights for Catholics, the government prosecuted Archibald Hamilton Rowan and the proprietor of the *Northern Star* for printing the address.[16] The city magistrates, occasionally aided by regular troops, set about enforcing the proclamation banning the assembly of persons under arms. This brought them into direct conflict with those Dublin Volunteers who were prepared to defy the proclamation, and also with the Dublin populace—'the mob' (by now predominantly Catholic in composition), which backed the Volunteers.[17]

The outbreak of war between Britain and France in February 1793 provided the authorities with a further incentive to try to quell the Defenders and those believed to be encouraging them. Exemplary sentences were passed on convicted Defenders at the spring assizes. Certain prominent United Irishmen were imprisoned for questioning the authority of a secret committee of the house of lords to examine witnesses under oath. Tandy, who had been seriously compromised by his contacts with Defenders, was charged with having been sworn a member of that society. He fled the country rather than face charges of high treason. A convention act was passed, which outlawed assemblies purporting to represent the people.[18] However, the Castle was instructed to proceed with the year-old plan to extend political rights to Catholics; and (as already noted) the 1793 relief act granted Catholics a wide range of political rights.

These measures put pressure on the United Irishmen, many of whose members still expected to achieve reforms by constitutional means. But the country remained disturbed, partly as a result of the militia act of April 1793, designed to provide a force for home defence under government control.[19] The 1793 relief act had legalized the recruitment of Catholics into the armed forces, and they duly came to form the bulk of the militia rank-and-file (the officers were mostly Protestants). It was notorious that during the American war the militia had been posted abroad, and popular hostility to such a prospect produced widespread riots during the summer of 1793. The Defenders were not slow to exploit this unrest.[20]

It is not known precisely when the city of Dublin first acquired a Defender presence. During the winter of 1792–3 Defenders were active in the northern part of County Meath, only some thirty miles from the capital. In January 1793 it was reported that Defenders were raiding farms in the Balbriggan area, even closer to the city. Rural immigration to Dublin was on

---

[16] Elliott, *Partners in Revolution*, 46. Archibald Hamilton Rowan (1751–1834); born London, but settled in Ireland. Sentenced to two years' imprisonment in 1794, but escaped to France and the United States (*DNB*).   [17] Musgrave, *Memoirs*, 119.
[18] 33 Geo. III, c. 29; Musgrave, *Memoirs*, 102–3, 121.
[19] 33 Geo. III, c. 22.
[20] Thomas Bartlett, 'An End to Moral Economy: The Irish Militia Disturbances of 1793', *P. & P.* 99 (1983), 41–64; Elliott, *Partners in Revolution*, 44–5.

the increase during the early 1790s, boosted by economic depression; and the discovery in March 1793 of pikes in Suffolk Street, close to College Green and parliament, suggests that the Defenders were already organizing there.[21] This lends a certain credibility to Musgrave's assertion that a rising was planned for the winter of 1792–3, the signal for which was to be the demolition of the statue of King William in College Green. Certainly, spies reported talk in Catholic circles about pulling down the statue—though in view of its importance as a symbol of the existing order the attack might have been intended for symbolic rather than military purposes.[22] From the outset the statue had been a target for Jacobites, and had suffered so many assaults earlier in the century that it had been raised and railed off to afford some protection. More recently, especially since parliament and the Castle had ceased public commemorations of 1641, Williamite anniversaries had assumed greater importance in the capital; but since 1792 certain Dublin Volunteers had pointedly refused to celebrate William's birthday according to custom.[23]

The clamp-down by the authorities, in conjunction with the measure of Catholic relief, put a check on Defender activities. But two years later, when Catholic expectations were once more at a high pitch—this time for complete political equality with Protestants—Defenders were again active in the city, swearing in recruits among tradesmen and soldiers: their numbers reached an estimated 4,000. The recruits included a number of Protestants, although according to Musgrave some of them turned informers on discovering that they had joined an organization whose members expected that the revolution would involve the downfall of Protestantism.[24]

The policing of the city continued to be a function of the new police system, supplemented where necessary by regular troops. By 1793 police duties were already rendering magistrates unpopular with the mob, and when the time came to elect the civic officials for 1793–4 two of those chosen by the corporation were men who had already demonstrated their ability to stand firm in unpopular causes. The nomination as lord mayor elect of Alderman William James, police commissioner, raised some hackles in the city commons, but his name was approved by a majority. As an unarmed magistrate he had not shrunk from confronting the Dublin Rangers, a Volunteer corps that had been parading illegally earlier in the year.[25]

[21] *FJ*, 24–6 Jan. 1793; Musgrave, *Memoirs*, 121.

[22] Musgrave, *Memoirs*, 117; McDowell (ed.), 'Proceedings of the Dublin Society of United Irishmen', 38. Secret societies continued to target the statue (id., *Public Opinion and Government Policy in Ireland*, 63–4).

[23] Above, Ch. 8. The last viceroy to go in state to Christ Church to commemorate 1641 was the duke of Rutland in 1784 (Hill, '1641 and the Quest for Catholic Emancipation', 167).

[24] Smyth, *The Men of No Property*, 149; Musgrave, *Memoirs*, 139–42.

[25] DCA, C1/JSC/7, fos. 73–4; CARD xiv. 304; *FJ*, 11–13 Apr. 1793; Musgrave, *Memoirs*, 119.

The other significant choice, for one of the two sheriffs elect, was John Giffard, the apothecaries' guild representative whose links with the Castle and indifference to public opinion had been demonstrated on several occasions. Through his subsidized newspaper, *Faulkner's Dublin Journal*, he had sided with the Castle over the mayoral dispute in 1790, when he had insulted the opposition MP John Philpot Curran, one of the counsel for the city commons: a duel had ensued. By 1792 Giffard was acting as a go-between for the Castle and the spy Thomas Collins, the first of the Castle's systematic informers.[26] It has been implied that Giffard's selection as sheriff was a Castle choice.[27] No doubt the Castle was satisfied to have Giffard occupying the position; but he had been a freeman of the city since 1768 and a guild representative since 1775, yet only once before had he won sufficient votes to be nominated for sheriff, and that had been in 1781 when he was still acting with the opposition.[28] Both these choices suggest that, faced with the threat of insurrection, most corporation members were prepared to put aside their differences and place civic authority in the hands of energetic magistrates. During 1794 Giffard was duly active against radicals of all kinds. As sheriff, he picked—some said packed—the jury that convicted Hamilton Rowan (January); conducted the raid (with Police Commissioner Warren) on the tailors' hall that put an end to the public phase of the Dublin United Irishmen (May); and intimidated citizens celebrating the acquittal of William Drennan on a charge of seditious libel (June).[29] But his habitual truculence—he allegedly libelled the duke of Leinster, Ireland's premier peer—ensured that he remained a controversial figure, and at the end of his year of office the usual vote of thanks to outgoing officers was opposed in the city commons by almost half the members present.[30]

The government policies of coercion and conciliation had a calming effect on Dublin during the remainder of 1793 and 1794. So too did the operation of the militia act, which absorbed such numbers of journeymen in the capital that doubts arose as to whether the silk industry would be able to meet demand. But the formation of reading clubs with Painite overtones went on,[31] and in 1795 Dublin was once more brought to a pitch of excitement by the Fitzwilliam episode.

---

[26] Inglis, *Freedom of the Press in Ireland*, 57–9; McDowell (ed.), 'Proceedings of the Dublin Society of United Irishmen', 3.

[27] Inglis, *Freedom of the Press in Ireland*, 58–9.

[28] *CARD* xiii. 175; Thrift, 'Roll of Freemen', NLI, MS 77.

[29] Smyth, *The Men of No Property*, 146–7; Inglis, *Freedom of the Press in Ireland*, 59; McDowell (ed.), 'Proceedings of the Dublin Society of United Irishmen', 127–9.

[30] *Hib. Jn.*, 15 Nov. 1793; DCA, C1/JSC/7, fo. 123. Certain guild representatives were instructed to oppose thanks to Giffard (NLI, MS 12126, p. 89; NA, M 2925, fo. 91). The merchants' guild also allegedly refused to grant him freedom as an outgoing sheriff (DPLGC, MS 79, fo. 305; *FJ*, 14 Oct. 1794). Giffard even annoyed his own guild, despite having received its thanks (Transactions 1747–95, Apothecaries' hall, pp. 280, 283–4).

[31] *FJ*, 18 Sept. 1794; Smyth, *The Men of No Property*, 147.

244   *Part 2. The Phoney War, 1792–1814*

The extensive political rights granted to Catholics in 1793 had turned out to be disappointing in practice, particularly when measured against heightened expectations. In Dublin, several Catholics had been admitted to the first stage of freedom, but as in most southern towns with sizeable Protestant minorities they had not progressed further; partly because the Protestant freemen stood to be swamped if Catholics were admitted in any numbers, but also because the times were so unsettled. The upshot was Catholic frustration at the prospect of prolonged exclusion from civic status. Among the means of redress under consideration by 1794 was the removal of what remained of the penal laws, or 'Catholic emancipation',[32] as it was coming to be called.

The appointment of a Whig viceroy, Earl Fitzwilliam, in January 1795 accordingly sent the hopes of Catholics and their supporters soaring. Even before Fitzwilliam's arrival rumours were circulating that he would act to remove remaining Catholic disabilities. Fitzwilliam himself was sympathetic towards the Catholics and quickly became convinced that failure to act would have serious consequences. But his authority to act in the matter had been reserved to the British government, and ministers became alarmed at the speed with which he was moving and his abrupt dismissal of certain key members of the Irish administration. After an unfortunate delay, the British cabinet instructed Fitzwilliam not to commit himself to a Catholic relief bill, already introduced by Grattan into the house of commons. The viceroy resigned, and left Ireland on 25 March. Not only did this virtually end the bill's chances of passing, it also ended the Whig opposition's brief spell in power.[33] The outcry from the Catholic leaders, the Whigs, and the radical press, was considerable. On the arrival of the new viceroy, the earl of Camden, in late March, Dublin was the scene of rioting orchestrated by United Irishmen that lasted for days. Popular anger was directed at those members of the Irish administration, such as the lord chancellor, John Fitzgibbon, who were judged responsible for the recent turn of events, and who now came back to office.[34]

The corporation's response to this episode was predictably mixed. Fitzwilliam's appointment had been welcomed by the corporation, and by the merchants' guild, but that was largely a matter of form.[35] A more telling indication of civic sentiment emerged from a post assembly, summoned in mid-March by corporation members opposed to Catholic relief. (The relief

---

[32] The genesis of the term would repay study. Musgrave thought it was deliberately used in the 1790s to win British sympathy (*Memoirs*, 119).

[33] Moody and Vaughan (eds.), *NHI* iv. 340–6; Lindsay, 'The Fitzwilliam Episode Revisited'.

[34] For a lively account of the riot, by Fitzgibbon's sister, see Constantia Maxwell, *Dublin Under the Georges 1714–1830*, Sackville Library edn. (Dublin, 1979), 30; also Smyth, *The Men of No Property*, 149–50.

[35] *CARD* xiv. 390–1; DPLGC, MS 79, fo. 305.

bill was before parliament, but Fitzwilliam had already resigned). In the city commons, a bid to have the meeting adjourned was narrowly defeated by 40 votes to 33, and a committee proceeded to draw up petitions to the king and parliament against the bill. Although the references to Catholics ('our Roman Catholic fellow subjects') were polite, it was stated that the bill's object—to admit Catholics to parliament—would constitute a threat to civil and religious liberty, and to 'the Protestant religion as established by law'. However, a radical minority of about nineteen members attacked both petitions, challenging every paragraph with wrecking amendments, and, after being defeated on every point, entering a formal protest on the journals of the house. This deplored the day's proceedings for letting loose 'all those passions which tend to destroy the Peace, the Happiness, and the Union of the Irish Nation'.[36]

Among those who signed the protest was to be found, not surprisingly, the city commons' complement of United Irishmen—with the sole exception of Patrick McLaughlin, who, as a sheriffs' peer, was the most senior, in civic terms, of the United Irishmen in the corporation. That accounted for nine of the signatures.[37] The other ten, though not United Irishmen, included some long-standing colleagues of Tandy's, such as John Binns. Altogether the nineteen protesters represented nine different guilds, of which five were associated with the textile trades (the tailors, weavers, glovers, hosiers, and sheermen and dyers). At the other extreme some forty members (dwindling to about thirty towards the end) consistently backed the petitions: John Giffard acted as a teller for that group. Leaving aside both these elements, however, it appears that only just over half the members of the city commons (73 out of 128) had attended the meeting at all; and a dozen of them had left as soon as the first vote not to adjourn was taken. Although some members may have been kept away on business, Friday was the corporation's usual meeting day; and on such an issue, it was unlikely that apathy would affect attendance. More likely, many members were reluctant to take a stand on such a potentially divisive issue; on previous sensitive occasions the ostensible secrecy of the ballot had failed to prevent the publication of details of the voting.[38]

Partly as a result of economic distress in the west of Ireland, and partly because of Defender activities in Ulster and Leinster, the country continued to be disturbed during the summer and autumn of 1795. One effect was the formation of defensive loyalist societies. In County Armagh clashes broke out again between Defenders and Peep O'Day Boys, culminating on 21

---

[36] For the meeting, see *CARD* xiv. 537–42; DCA, C1/JSC/7, fos. 138–41ᵛ.

[37] Patrick Ewing, John Dawson, Henry Jackson, James Tandy (merchants' guild); Thomas Bacon, William Bell, Abraham Creighton (tailors' guild); George Binns (smiths' guild), John Chambers (stationers' guild). Cf. McDowell, 'Personnel of the Dublin Society'.

[38] Above, Ch. 8, n. 88.

September in 'the battle of the Diamond', near Loughgall, in which several lives were lost. Following this incident, an 'Orange society' was set up by local Protestant farmers and artisans for their own defence. It was designed to facilitate participation by the gentry, though for some time the propertied classes were reluctant to identify with a society whose early activities, such as intimidation of local Catholics (the 'Armagh outrages'), flouted the law, and brought the term 'Orange' into disrepute.[39]

Meanwhile, in Dublin, following repeated attempts by the city commons, guilds, and the parliamentary opposition to restore policing to citizen control, a police act was passed in June 1795, removing the powers that government had temporarily exercised over the appointment of magistrates, and replacing authority in corporation hands. The new system was to be headed by magistrates nominated by the aldermen, and elected by the city commons, subject to viceregal approval. A force of fifty uniformed but unarmed men would work with night watchmen provided by the parishes.[40] The debates on this and earlier bills to overturn the 1786 police act afforded opportunities for the guilds to reiterate their opposition to the centralized system. Scarcely had the reforms been implemented when in late August several Defenders were arrested in the city. News of the arrests produced alarm, particularly in the outlying suburbs that were beyond the scope of whatever surveillance the watch could provide.[41] As yet, no steps had been taken by government to embody the yeomanry.

Against this background, the inhabitants of the Mountpleasant/Ranelagh area beyond the circular road on the southern outskirts of the city decided to combine for mutual defence. Further out to the south-west a Rathfarnham association was formed for the same purpose. To the north of the city, similar action was taken by the inhabitants of the village of Baldoyle.[42] One of the features of these suburban associations was the prominence of aldermen and other senior corporation personnel among the membership— their participation highlighting the process of suburban drift. The Rathfarnham association, for instance, had the support of Alderman John Exshaw, Jacob Poole and Lundy Foot (sheriffs' peers), and Nathaniel Hone (merchants' guild representative on the city commons). In the city itself, a meeting was held on 7 October 1795 to found the Association for the

---

[39] The standard work on the Orange Order is Hereward Senior, *Orangeism in Ireland and Britain, 1795–1836* (London, 1966). See also Miller, 'The Armagh Troubles', and Cullen, 'The Political Structures of the Defenders', who argues that electoral feuds were pivotal in the early establishment of the Order (pp. 119–20).

[40] 35 Geo. III, c. 36; *CARD* xiv. 532–3; *FDJ*, 30 June 1795. The act was, no doubt, a palliative for Dublin Protestants, who had been working for reform, but hardly 'a growing Protestant reaction against the rising tide of liberalism' (Palmer, *Police and Protest*, 134–5): it marked a partial return to traditional Patriot ideas about policing (above, Ch. 6).

[41] TCD, MS 1447/8/2, p. 332; NLI, MS 12126, p. 75; DPLGC, MS 79, fo. 307; *FDJ* 1, 3 Sept. 1795. [42] Musgrave, *Memoirs*, 146; *FDJ*, 3 Oct. 1795.

Protection of Property and the Constitution in the District of the Metropolis. The lord mayor lent his support, as did members of the nobility and gentry, the corporation, and the Castle. The Defender presence in Dublin was singled out as indicating the need for such a body, and a secret committee was set up to receive confidential information about 'Defenders and Jacobins'.[43] Such moves were not confined to Ireland; similar associations had been in formation in England since 1792, as part of the counter-revolutionary movement there.[44]

Further arrests of Defenders took place in Dublin during the autumn of 1795, and the loyalist associations remained in being through the winter, though by the spring of 1796 their activities appear to have died down. The historian of Orangeism has portrayed them as forerunners of the Orange Order in Dublin, which were abandoned in face of government hostility and in the expectation of the formation of the yeomanry.[45] In some respects these associations did foreshadow the Orange Order. Members attested their loyalty to the king, the constitution, and the laws of Ireland. Early members included the Giffards, John and his son Ambrose Hardinge,[46] who were among the first Dublin Orangemen when a lodge was founded in the capital in 1797. By contrast, Catholics and radical Protestants were conspicuously absent from the names published in connection with the associations. These bodies therefore had much in common with that other society, described by Jonah Barrington as 'the first Orange association ever formed', the Aldermen of Skinner's Alley, from whom the radicals had departed at the time of the split of 1793. By 1795 the traditionalists had rallied under a new governor, Dr Patrick Duigenan (another pillar of the first Dublin Orange lodge), and new members were being enrolled.[47]

This, however, raises a question. If by the mid-1790s Dublin boasted so many proto-Orange societies, what need was there for an Orange lodge in the capital at all? If armed associations worried the Castle, there was always the Skinner's Alley society. The latter shared the Orange Order's willingness to recruit Protestants from a variety of social backgrounds, and it also took sides in electoral contests, a role sometimes played by Orange lodges.[48] Perhaps these bodies were too public? But the Orange Order itself, with its love of display on important anniversaries, did not place undue emphasis on

---

[43] *FDJ*, 24 Sept., 3, 8, 15 Oct. 1795.

[44] See Robert R. Dozier, *For King, Constitution and Country: The English Loyalists and the French Revolution* (Lexington, Ky., 1983).

[45] Senior, *Orangeism in Ireland and Britain*, 76.

[46] *FDJ*, 15 Oct. 1795. For Ambrose Giffard see *DNB*.

[47] *Recollections of Jonah Barrington*, 155; *FDJ*, 5, 27 Oct. 1795; above, Ch. 8. Patrick Duigenan (1735–1816), regius professor of feudal and English law, TCD, 1776–1816; judge of the consistorial court of Dublin; MP, Old Leighlin 1790–8, Armagh 1798–1816 (*DNB*). His speeches against political rights for Catholics won him the civic freedom of Dublin, 1793 (*CARD* xiv. 316), but his unionism later divided him from the corporation.

[48] *Recollections of Jonah Barrington*, 156; *Hib. Jn.*, 24 July 1797. See also n. 39 above.

secrecy. There was, however, one significant respect in which these bodies differed from the Orange Order. Neither the armed associations nor the Aldermen of Skinner's Alley could be depended on to exclude Protestants who, whatever their attachment to church and king, might harbour sentiments on the Catholic question of a Burkean kind. And such members there were. The chairman at the first meeting of the Association for the Protection of Property was Lord Mountjoy, the former Luke Gardiner, a champion of Catholic rights. The second Arthur Guinness (1768–1855), who held similar views, also took part.[49] As for the 'reformed' Aldermen of Skinner's Alley, Barrington (himself recruited to the society by Dr Duigenan) expressed it well: 'In the year 1795, I saw that the people were likely to grow too strong for the Crown, and therefore, became at once, not indeed an *ultra*, but one in whom loyalty absorbed almost every other consideration.'[50] That was the point: these bodies exuded a loyalist spirit, highlighting the dangers posed by Jacobins and other radicals to stability and property but otherwise keen, like their counterparts in England, to rally supporters of order regardless of their political views. The Orange Order, too, was loyalist and anti-radical; but it was also uniquely dedicated to resisting political rights for Catholics.[51]

In 1795 the foundation of the first Dublin Orange lodge still lay ahead; at the other political extreme, radicals could look to the United Irishmen as an institutional expression of their views. Dublin freemen were well represented in the society: fifty-eight have been identified, comprising almost half (44%) of the 130 members identified by McDowell as Protestants[52]— though most were young men who had only recently taken out their freedom.[53] But the Fitzwilliam episode highlighted the weakness of the radical minority in civic affairs. Even in 1791 and 1792 there were no more than eleven United Irishmen in the city commons, dropping to ten after Tandy's flight in 1793.[54] On the other hand, they suffered little attrition

---

[49] *FDJ*, 15 Oct. 1795. The second Arthur Guinness shared the views of his father (1725–1803) on the Catholic question: see *CARD* xiv. 542 (where the first Arthur is named); Lynch and Vaizey, *Guinness's Brewery*, 73, 142.

[50] *Recollections of Jonah Barrington*, 154.

[51] See rules of the Orange Society, 1798 (Senior, *Orangeism in Ireland and Britain*, 298–301).

[52] McDowell, 'Personnel of the Dublin Society', 15. The following should be added to those identified by McDowell as freemen or corporation members (guilds and dates of admission to freedom in brackets): William Arnold (weaver, 1759), Edward Brooks (dyer, 1770), William Cole (shoemaker, 1768), Thomas Collins, John Dawson, George Tandy, James Napper Tandy (merchants, 1769, 1760, 1767, 1760); Theobald Wolfe Tone (saddler, 1790). See Thrift, 'Roll of freemen', NLI, MSS 76–9. Dickson suggests that *c*.200 United Irishmen were Protestants (' "Centres of Motion" ', 116).

[53] Thirty-five of the fifty-eight (60%) had taken out their freedom in 1786 or later.

[54] In addition to the seven common councilmen noted by McDowell, the following United Irishmen were members of the city commons in 1791: John Chambers, George Binns, John Dawson, James Napper Tandy (*CARD* xiv. 545–6).

during what was a strongly counter-revolutionary decade. All were re-elected by their guilds in late 1792, and all but three of them were returned at the next election in 1795. Moreover, one of the three, Patrick Ewing, was subsequently chosen by the merchants' guild to fill a vacancy on the commons, despite the efforts of Francis Higgins, proprietor of the *Freeman's Journal*, sometime master of the hosiers' guild, and Castle informant, to have him kept out.[55] Higgins also tried and failed to keep out another activist from the original United Irishmen, who was new to the city commons in 1798: the lace manufacturer James Riddall.[56]

These members, then, owed their presence on the city commons to guild support. Some of them were obviously extremely popular: John Chambers was re-elected by the stationers' faculty of St Luke's guild in 1795 by 98 votes to 1. In fact St Luke's had some of the hallmarks of a radical guild, deploring Fitzwilliam's departure in 1795 as 'a National Calamity'. On the other hand, part of Chambers' appeal probably sprang from the fact that he was an assiduous upholder of guild rights, using his term as master (1793–4) to pursue arrears of quarterage owed by freemen. And within the same guild, the cutlers' faculty gave a similar endorsement to a man of quite different views, the cutler Joseph Pemberton. He had acted with Giffard as teller on the majority side in the debate on the anti-emancipation petitions in 1795—yet he too received a massive vote when he came up for re-election later that year.[57]

Some United Irishmen were obliged to compromise in order to obtain re-election. In 1792 the smiths' guild instructed its representatives to oppose the extension of the vote to Catholics. Arguably those instructions were nullified by the 1793 relief act: at any rate, they did not prevent George Binns from voting with the pro-Catholic minority on the city commons in March 1795, or from signing the protest. But some months later, up for re-election, he and the other candidates were asked to take a pledge to maintain 'the Protestant ascendancy': having taken it, he was duly re-elected. Once elected, further compromises may have been necessary. In October 1793 Binns and another United Irishman, William Bell, found themselves serving with Giffard on a corporation committee set up to encourage 'able men, both landsmen and seamen, to enlist in his majesty's service'.[58] All this points to the limits of radical influence in corporate

---

[55] *CARD* xiv. 547–8; xv. 532–3; Francis Higgins to Edward Cooke, 30 Sept. 1796 (NA, Rebellion papers, 620/18/14). Ewing was serving on a corporation committee by Jan. 1797 (*CARD* xv. 2).

[56] McDowell, 'Personnel of the Dublin Society', 46. James Riddall, d. 1831; sheriff 1809–10, city sword-bearer 1817–31.

[57] NLI, MS 12126, pp. 96–8, 102. Joseph Pemberton, Capel St., cutler, d. 1816; sheriff 1796–7, alderman 1798, lord mayor 1806–7.

[58] NA, M 2925, fos. 81, 95–6; *CARD* xiv. 336.

circles. Individual United Irishmen might be held in esteem,[59] and opposition causes, such as the police issue (in St Luke's guild, even Catholic emancipation) might find support;[60] but, once Britain had become involved in the war, the weight of corporate traditions must have made it difficult to resist rallying behind the war effort.

The radicals also failed to rise in the civic hierarchy. Although three United Irishmen were among the eight nominees for sheriff in 1792,[61] during the remainder of the decade none of them even made it to the nomination stage. Nominations for sheriff were determined by ballot in the city commons; in selecting nominees for promotion to the aldermanic board, the aldermen tended to favour political moderates. United Irishmen were not selected (and McLaughlin was the only sheriffs' peer available to be selected), but neither was Giffard. In 1796 Francis Higgins fretted over what he saw as a 'Presbyter party' in the corporation, orchestrated by Alderman William Alexander,[62] himself a Presbyterian. Higgins drew Dublin Castle's attention to the fact that three of the four nominees selected by the aldermen for a vacancy on the board in September 1796 were Presbyterians: the commons chose one of them, Henry Hutton, to fill the post.[63] Hutton was not a United Irishman, though in his capacity as sheriff he had presided over a radical reform meeting in 1793.

Higgins' concern about Alderman Alexander's efforts to promote Presbyterians did not spring primarily from doubts about their loyalty, though he was soon warning the Castle that Presbyterian meeting houses in the city were omitting the usual prayers for the king and royal family. Already thoughts were turning to the impending general election, due in 1797. The matter was of particular interest, for it had become apparent since 1792, and especially since 1795, that many of those who had voted for Grattan and Lord Henry Fitzgerald in 1790 were opposed to the new Whig policy on the Catholic question. Higgins believed that Alexander planned to throw the Presbyterians behind one of the candidates defeated in 1790, Alderman Henry Gore Sankey. Others, too, were thinking ahead. The freeman who received most votes for sheriff to serve during the election year was Joseph Pemberton, who, together with Giffard, had co-ordinated the

---

[59] There was much sympathy for the popular Rowan when his prison sentence was announced in 1794 (see NA, M 2925, fo. 90). The *FJ* derided 'little potwalloping parties' in the guilds for preparing addresses to him. But some guild members opposed any show of sympathy (*FJ*, 27 Mar, 29 Apr. 1794).

[60] St Luke's guild (NLI, MS 12126, pp. 96–7); St Loy's guild (NA, M 2925, fos. 79–80); Barber-surgeons' guild (TCD, MS 1447/8/2, p. 332); RSAI, corporation of weavers, minute book 1755–1809 (1 Apr. 1793).

[61] Patrick Ewing, Napper Tandy, and Henry Jackson (*CARD* xiv. 266).

[62] William Alexander, jun., d. 1822; sheriff 1776–7, alderman 1779, lord mayor 1787–8.

[63] Higgins to Cooke, 14 Sept. 1796 (NA, Rebellion papers, 620/18/14; *CARD* xiv. 469–70. At least three of the twelve sheriffs in office 1787–93 were Presbyterians: Brent Neville, Benjamin Gault (merchants), Henry Hutton (tanners' guild).

majority in the city commons for the anti-emancipation petitions in 1795. His nomination and election as sheriff indicated that the ultra Protestants were looking ahead to the general election.[64] And it was hardly a coincidence that the first Dublin Orange lodge was founded in June 1797, shortly before the election.[65]

By that time the country had become quite seriously disturbed. Much of Ulster had been proclaimed, and in May 1797 parts of Leinster were also proclaimed.[66] Also in May, a secret committee of the house of lords uncovered evidence of United Irish links with France, and the society was declared illegal. Following the defeat of a reform bill, a number of Whigs, including Grattan, seceded from parliament; Grattan went on to announce that he would not contest the election as long as the house of commons remained unreformed.[67] That was an invitation to his constituents not to vote at the election. Such an option was discussed in radical Catholic circles, along with the possibility of running the former MP, Travers Hartley, or even Lord Edward Fitzgerald.

None of the aldermen proved capable of attracting strong support, even in Dublin corporation itself, and the possibility of ministerial candidates began to be discussed.[68] That would give the city representation a different complexion from that of the last thirty years, but in view of the dangerous situation at home and abroad the usual inhibitions about supporting place-holding candidates were much weaker. An approach was made to the speaker of the house of commons, John Foster, whose services to trade and 'independent' stance on the Catholic question (that is, his hostility to the British government's policy) had overcome his earlier unpopularity. But he declined to stand, in view of the probable expense.[69] Instead, the attorney-general Arthur Wolfe, who had a similar record on the Catholic question,

[64] Higgins to Cooke, 14 Sept. 1796, 18 Jan. 1797 (NA, Rebellion papers, 620/18/14); *CARD* xiv. 440–1.

[65] Senior, *Orangeism in Ireland and Britain*, 63, 75. The first Dublin Orange lodge has been dated to 4 June 1796 (R. M. Sibbett, *Orangeism in Ireland and Throughout the Empire*, 2nd edn. (2 vols.; London, [1939]), i. 328), but Senior relies on Lt.-Col. William Verner, whose brother founded the Dublin lodge (*Report from the Select Committee [on] . . . Orange Lodges, Associations or Societies in Ireland*, 9–10, HC 1835 (377), xv). The composition of Dublin Orange lodges awaits examination, but freemen were well represented (Sibbett, *Orangeism*, i. 328; NA, 620/51/202).

[66] An insurrection act (36 Geo. III, c. 20) permitted curfews and arms searches in proclaimed districts.

[67] *The Address of the Rt. Hon. Henry Grattan, to his Constituents . . . on his Retiring from the Parliament of Ireland*, 2nd edn. (London, 1797), 11. Around this time Fox temporarily withdrew from the British commons.

[68] Higgins to Cooke, 8, 11, 15 July 1797 (NA, Rebellion papers, 620/18/14); *FJ*, 4 July 1797.

[69] John Foster (1740–1828); chancellor of the exchequer, 1784–5, speaker of the commons, 1785–1800; chancellor of the Irish exchequer, 1804–6, 1807–11. Won civic thanks (1793) for opposing Catholic political rights, for efforts to open the East India trade to Irish merchants, and for seeking a review of the navigation acts (*CARD* xiv. 342–3; *FJ*, 11 Feb. 1794). See also Malcomson, *John Foster*, 32, 49, 68–9, 161.

having been dismissed by Fitzwilliam in 1795, succumbed to the allure of representing the most prestigious constituency in Ireland.[70] A second candidate was found in the banker John Claudius Beresford, a younger son of the chief revenue commissioner. Beresford junior was on good terms with the merchants' guild for having bowed to mercantile pressure over proposed statutory regulation of the coal trade.[71] Foster, Wolfe, and Beresford might all be called 'ministerial Patriots':[72] their offices did not prevent them occasionally opposing government.

In the end, despite Higgins' worry about Presbyterian or even Painite candidates, most of the guilds lined up behind Beresford and Wolfe, who were returned unopposed, their backers taking care to pay polite tributes to Grattan.[73] The election itself was a low-key affair. There was no talk of reform; what the city needed, according to the Aldermen of Skinner's Alley, was two 'Protestant' candidates who would support 'the lawful prerogative of the Crown, and . . . the just privileges of the People'.[74] This was standard Patriot rhetoric—though in the period since the end of the Jacobite threat it would not have been necessary to add the word 'Protestant'—and not yet anachronistic. Grattan himself still talked as if royal absolutism and clericalism were the main dangers: he invoked the memory of Hampden and the spirit of resistance to the Stuarts, and urged ministers, in their struggle against 'Democracy', not to ally with 'Priestcraft'. The fact was, as in America, that the loyalists and many of their critics shared a common ideological heritage.[75]

As for the United Irishmen, despite setbacks in Ulster, down to the start of 1798 their leaders still retained much self-confidence, largely as a result of reports from France that the desired military assistance was in preparation, as part of plans for an invasion of England. But through a network of spies and informers the government was aware of French preparations. In February 1798 several United Irishmen were arrested in Kent; they had been in touch with members of the nascent republican movement in Britain in the hope of co-ordinating revolutionary activity in England, Scotland, and

---

[70] Arthur Wolfe, 1st Viscount Kilwarden, below, App. B. Won civic thanks (1796) for opposing Catholic emancipation and for services to trade (*CARD* xiv. 435–6). His election for Dublin city cost him £2,000 in small sums (Malcomson, *John Foster*, 161).

[71] DPLGC, MS 79, fo. 313. For John Claudius Beresford see G. C. Bolton, *The Passing of the Irish Act of Union: A Study in Parliamentary Politics* (Oxford, 1966), 31 n. 4; G. L. Barrow, 'Some Dublin Private Banks', *Dublin Hist. Rec.* 25 (1971), 38–53, at 44–5; below, App. B.

[72] Cf. Malcomson, *John Foster*, 32.

[73] See *FJ*, 15 July, 1 Aug. 1797; *The Address of . . . Henry Grattan, to his Constituents*, 45. For guild choices, see *FJ*, 13, 18, 20, 22, 27, 29 July 1797. Demoralization in the radical stationers' guild was such that few turned up to a meeting to consider whom to support (*FJ*, 25 July 1797).   [74] *Hib. Jn.*, 24 July 1797.

[75] *The Address of . . . Henry Grattan, to his Constituents*, 12, 15, 19, 22; Janice Potter, *The Liberty We Seek: Loyalist Ideology in Colonial New York and Massachusetts* (Cambridge, Mass., 1983), ch. 5, at p. 85.

Ireland. On 12 March, by means of information received from Thomas Reynolds,[76] certain members of the Leinster executive were arrested at Oliver Bond's house in Dublin.[77] The remaining leaders, of whom Lord Edward Fitzgerald was the most prominent, were still unable to agree on a schedule for a rising, but that scarcely affected the widespread popular conviction that a rising and a French landing were imminent.

By mid-May, the leaders still at large were being censured by their followers for inactivity. About this time, the Sheares brothers, acting without the sanction of the executive, decided to proceed with their plan for a rising, to begin in Dublin. The executive, still hoping for French assistance, toyed with June as a likely date. When Lord Edward and the Sheares brothers were arrested on 19 and 21 May, what remained of the United Irish leadership decided to take action, apparently on the lines of Lord Edward's plan for Dublin to be taken with the help of insurgents from the surrounding counties.[78]

II. Dublin and the Rebellion

In Dublin, where the rising was planned to start, by the spring of 1798 there were several thousand United Irishmen, most of them supplied with pikes.[79] On the government side, relatively few regular troops were stationed there, and the approaches to the city were not fortified. In these circumstances, a great deal would depend on the disposition of the citizens themselves. The summer of 1796 had seen an attempt (suppressed by government) to revive the moribund association movement. The Castle's informant, Higgins, was glad that the proposed meeting had been suppressed, 'for a Mob would have followed them, to call out "The Protestant Ascendancy Club etc." '; in his view the associations had been 'unnecessarily intolerant against the admission of respectable Roman Catholics'. Higgins also reported a proposal by the popular outgoing lord mayor, Alderman William Worthington,[80] for the formation of a citizens' army. Higgins urged government to become involved if this idea was to be of any practical use,

---

[76] See Thomas Reynolds, jun., *The Life of Thomas Reynolds* (2 vols.; London, 1839); Fitzpatrick, 'The Sham Squire', 227–46; Hammond, 'Mr William Cope's Petition', 26–31. In terms that recalled the tradition of 1641, the corporation granted Reynolds civic freedom for having averted 'a general massacre' of loyal Dublin citizens (*CARD* xv. 75–6).

[77] One of those who escaped on 12 Mar. was John Chambers: he had attended guild meetings down to Apr. 1797 (NLI, MS 12126, p. 117).

[78] See Elliott, *Partners in Revolution*, 194–201; Thomas Graham, ' "An Union of Power"? The United Irish Organisation: 1795–1798', in Dickson, Keogh, Whelan (eds.), *The United Irishmen*, 244–55, at 250–4.

[79] Roger Wells, *Insurrection: The British Experience 1795–1803* (Gloucester, 1983), 134–5, suggests 5,000; Graham, ' "An Union of Power"?' argues for 10,000 (p. 251).

[80] Sir William Worthington, d. 1814, dyer; alderman 1788, lord mayor 1795–6. Sometimes in opposition, and a moderate on the Catholic question. Knighted for encouragement to the yeomanry in 1796 (*CARD* xiv. 473–4).

warning of the danger of the revival of Volunteering ('which cost you dear before').[81] In fact, the government was on the point of embodying the yeomanry, and the upshot was, as Higgins had recommended, that Dublin corporation enlisted the support of churchwardens to encourage enrolment in yeomanry corps. The target was to raise a troop of infantry and one of cavalry for each of the four police wards of the city.[82] Although there were some protests at vestry meetings and (according to Higgins) from the Catholic Committee,[83] the response was generally favourable. By the end of 1796 some 3,000 mainly Protestant volunteers had joined yeomanry corps; 'sufficient', according to John Lees, head of the Irish Post Office, 'to bring back the Spirit of old Fred. of Prussia from his Grave'.[84] Catholics also came forward, particularly after the Bantry Bay scare at the end of the year. Constantia Maxwell has described the result:

There were students' corps, lawyers' corps, merchants corps, and even a corps formed of elderly gentlemen living in the fashionable Merrion Square. These used to parade on fine evenings . . . on every side of the Square, drinking tea and playing whist afterwards. But when nights were wet or damp they patrolled through the streets in a long file of sedan chairs with their muskets hanging out of the windows 'ready to deploy and fire upon any rebel enemy to Church or State who should dare to oppose their progress and manœuvres'.[85]

Besides all these there was also at least one street corps, the French Street[86] Association, organized by ex-sheriff Humphry Minchin and his brother-in-law Major Henry Charles Sirr. Sirr, a former army officer, was appointed by the Castle in November 1796 to take charge of security in the city, and it was he who led the counter-offensive against the United Irishmen during 1797 and 1798.[87]

Despite all these precautions, Dublin was disturbed in the early months of 1798, especially in the Thomas Street area on the western side of the city, where sentinels occasionally came under fire. As more Leinster counties

---

[81] Higgins to Cooke, 14 Sept. 1796 (NA, 620/18/14). For the need to avoid any revival of Volunteering, see also *Beresford Corr.* ii. 128.

[82] Act for regulating yeomanry corps, 37 Geo. III, c. 2; *CARD* xiv. 471–3; Musgrave, *Memoirs*, 159.

[83] Higgins also reported that the United Irishmen were alleging that a legislative union was to be proposed, and Catholic political rights withdrawn (Higgins to Cooke, 11, 13 Oct. 1796, NA, 620/18/14).

[84] J[ohn] L[ees] to Auckland, 26 Dec. 1796, PRONI, Sneyd papers, T 3229/2/12.

[85] Maxwell, *Dublin Under the Georges*, 35.

[86] Now Upper Mercer St., off Cuffe St., west of St Stephen's Green.

[87] Henry Charles Sirr (1764–1841), son of Major Joseph Sirr, a former town major of Dublin. Boyhood friend of Tandy's son James. Left the army as captain, 1791, became a wine merchant; merchants' guild representative, 1793, in Tandy's place. Appointed acting town major, 1796, and town major, 1798–1826. Sheriffs' peer 1807–41. Arrested Lord Edward Fitzgerald and Robert Emmet (*DNB*; Joseph W. Hammond, 'Town Major Henry Charles Sirr', *Dublin Hist. Rec.* 4 (1941), 14–33, 58–75).

were proclaimed, the city became a refuge for country people fleeing from military repression. In March, following the arrest of the Leinster leaders, Fitzgibbon (now Lord Clare) was hissed in the streets, and 2,000 yeomanry turned out to parade in a show of strength. In April, the lord mayor ordered all householders in the city and Liberties to display lists of any strangers lodging with them.[88] In the same month, the city commons gained the approval of the aldermen for calling on the freemen of the guilds to arm themselves as required by their oaths. The call was echoed in the merchants' guild.[89]

In mid-May came the discovery of arms and cannon in the city, and the arrest of most of the remaining leaders. A proclamation in the possession of the Sheares brothers, to have been published after the rising, confirmed that a Dublin outbreak (known to the authorities for some days previously) was at hand. This discovery nerved Lord Camden to authorize magistrates and yeomanry to undertake a limited search for arms, which took place on 22 May. Several houses in Thomas Street, where Lord Edward had been captured, were ransacked, suspects were flogged, and large quantities of arms discovered. But on 23 May, just as the authorities were congratulating themselves on having forestalled a rising, came news that a rising was planned for that very night, with men from the surrounding counties poised to march on the city.[90]

Amid considerable confusion, the yeomanry were called out, most of them to be deployed in Smithfield to guard against an attack from the north. The City of Cork militia, with their two battalion guns, were positioned in St Stephen's Green to resist any onslaught from the south. As darkness fell, tension was heightened by the failure of the lamplighters to do their job, until forced to do so by a party of yeomanry. In the event, considerable numbers of men entered the city from the north, but as their leader, Samuel Neilson, contemplated an attempt to rescue Lord Edward, he was recognized and intercepted by Tresham Gregg, the gaoler of Newgate. Bereft of their leader, the rebels melted away. On 24 May Commander-in-Chief General Lake imposed a curfew on Dublin. The lord mayor ordered all arms to be registered, and householders to post new lists on their doors of all inhabitants. Several executions took place, among them members of the yeomanry who were suspected of complicity with the rebels. Their places were more than filled by a new spate of volunteers, bringing the yeomanry up to about 6,000. Even the Irish Whigs, hitherto strong critics of the government, rallied to the authorities.

---

[88] Musgrave, *Memoirs*, 203–5; Thomas Pakenham, *The Year of Liberty: The Story of the Great Irish Rebellion of 1798* (London, 1969), 47.

[89] DCA, C1/JSC/8, fos. 77ᵛ–8; *CARD* xv. 45; DPLGC, MS 79, fo. 316.

[90] Musgrave, *Memoirs*, 205–10; Pakenham, *Year of Liberty*, 95–100; Graham, ' "An Union of Power"?', 249–53.

During the following week, the roads out of Dublin were in the hands of the rebels, but the city itself was fairly quiet. However, loyalist fears were kept at a high pitch by the revelations of a servant of the lord mayor, who confessed to an alleged plot in which Catholic servants were to kill their masters.[91] At the end of the week, government troops under Sir James Duff reoccupied Kildare town and the Curragh, and reopened communications between Dublin and the south of Ireland; and despite later scares, occasioned by the effective action of the rebels at New Ross in June, and the belated arrival of a French force in August, prospects for the capture of Dublin receded.[92]

After the rebellion, Dublin corporation, with its four regiments of yeomanry, was singled out by Sir Richard Musgrave for its firmness and loyalty. The corporation certainly took the view that the yeomanry had been crucial to the defeat of the rebellion, and this view was endorsed by Lord Camden: 'To the yeomanry of Dublin is owing the salvation of the metropolis and therein the salvation of the country.'[93] This, no doubt, was to exaggerate the yeomanry's achievement. Had the rebels not lost some potential as a result of arms raids and arrests of key leaders before and during the rising, the yeomanry's task might have been harder and the outcome, conceivably, different. Under the circumstances, some of the Dublin United Irishmen preferred to wait for the French to arrive, or joined the rebels outside the city. Nevertheless, whatever weight is attached to these different considerations, it is apparent from recent assessments that the rebels' failure to take Dublin was 'one key cause of the insurrection's course and collapse'.[94]

---

[91] Musgrave, *Memoirs*, 211–22, 286–9; Pakenham, *Year of Liberty*, 100–3.

[92] Musgrave, *Memoirs*, 293–4. One casualty in Kildare town was John Giffard's son William (1781–98), a lieutenant of the 82nd regiment, killed when rebels stopped the Limerick mail coach on 23 May. His father, serving as a captain in the Dublin city militia under Sir James Duff, took part in the subsequent massacre of some 350 surrendering rebels at the Curragh (Pakenham, *Year of Liberty*, 163–4; Bartlett, *Fall and Rise of the Irish Nation*, 236). Giffard's nephew, Captain Daniel Ryan, had been mortally wounded during the capture of Lord Edward Fitzgerald (*Correspondence of Charles, First Marquis Cornwallis*, ed. Charles Ross, 2nd. edn. (3 vols.; London, 1859), ii. 346).

[93] Musgrave, *Memoirs*, 293–4; *CARD* xv. 53–4.

[94] Wells, *Insurrection*, 134; Graham, ' "An Union of Power"?', 254–5.

10

The Constitution Defended:
Opposition to Union, 1798–1814

I. The Proposals for Union

when I warn you of the universal disgust, nay, horror, that Dublin . . .
[has] at the idea of the Union, I do not do it with any idea that my
opinion would have a weight in turning Government from their design,
but from a wish that they should know what they have to contend
with . . .[1]

The rebellion had scarcely been quelled when a new question arose to
agitate the country: the government proposal for a legislative union between
Great Britain and Ireland. It has already been seen that by the 1750s the idea
of a union on libertarian grounds had lost any appeal it may once have had
for the tradesmen of Dublin, who had come to associate regular meetings of
the Irish parliament with increasing prosperity. Periodic scares about the
introduction of a union were responsible for manifestations of the
'purposive crowd', as in 1759 and 1779,[2] for the subject was raised
occasionally from mid-century on by writers and statesmen in Ireland and
England as a remedy for a range of perceived economic, social, and political
problems. A union, it was claimed, would provide a means of regulating
Irish commerce with Britain's overseas empire (this issue came to the fore
following the granting of free trade, and especially after the failure of Pitt's
commercial propositions in 1784–5); it would guarantee property, prosperity, and the link with Britain, and foster a sense of unity between all classes
of Irish people.[3]

However, the rise of the Volunteers in the late 1770s saw anti-union
sentiments being taken up more widely. From the British government's
viewpoint, the regency crisis of 1788–9 confirmed the danger inherent in the
Irish constitution of 1782 that Ireland might seek to take an independent
course over a matter as crucial as who wielded royal authority. Against a

---

[1] J. C. Beresford to Castlereagh, 19 Dec. 1798, *Memoirs and Correspondence of Viscount
Castlereagh . . . Edited by his Brother, Charles Vane, Marquess of Londonderry* (4 vols.;
London, 1848–9), ii. 51.
[2] Above, Ch. 4; Smyth, *The Men of No Property*, 131–3.
[3] Kelly, 'Origins of the Act of Union', 249–63; McDowell, *Irish Public Opinion*, 243–5;
Malcomson, *John Foster*, 49–60.

background of worsening international relations, fears of loss of control over Ireland surfaced again late in 1792, and Pitt indicated to the viceroy that he was contemplating the possibility of a union in the event of the failure of his policy of strengthening the existing order by granting political rights to Catholics. Some even suspected the government's endorsement of Catholic claims in 1792 to be a deliberate ploy to divide Protestants and bring about a union.[4]

To the British government the rising of 1798 revealed starkly how unstable Ireland had become; and the possibility of instability persisting, with all the attendant risks of renewed invasion attempts by the French, highlighted the urgency of resolving the problem. Moreover, following the partial extension of political rights to Catholics the idea of a legislative union as a protective measure for Protestants had found some support among Irish politicians, including the lord chancellor, Lord Clare. The 1798 rising had further weakened Protestant morale. Against this background, the government began to sound out Irish politicians on the subject of union in the autumn of 1798. The response was not particularly encouraging. In the Irish cabinet, John Beresford and Archbishop Agar backed the idea; Lord Clare was in favour of the principle, but doubtful about the timing; while the speaker, John Foster, and the chancellor of the exchequer, Sir John Parnell, were both implacably opposed.[5]

The reaction in Dublin to the proposal, when these soundings became publicly known towards the end of 1798, was predictably and vehemently hostile. The city became, in the words of the historian of the union, 'the focal point of anti-unionism'.[6] For the Protestant merchants and tradesmen who composed the bulk of the freeman body, the integrity of the Irish parliament was bound up with a whole range of important issues: industrial and commercial prosperity, a virtuous constitution, the prestige of a capital city. Moreover, it was Dublin opinion that had been vigilant, during several decades, to detect and condemn talk of union, from whatever quarter. And if Protestants in general were demoralized as a result of the rising and the disturbances that preceded it, that scarcely applied to Dublin Protestants, who remained convinced that the armed citizens themselves, rather than the regular army, had defeated the plans for a rising in the capital and thus had helped to thwart the entire project.

The Castle was expecting opposition from the city, but hoped that this might be countered through the good offices of a few key individuals.

---

[4] Lecky, *History of Ireland in the Eighteenth Century*, 242.

[5] Bolton, *Passing of the Irish Act of Union*, 13; Malcomson, *John Foster*, 363, 389, 418.

[6] Bolton, *Passing of the Irish Act of Union*, 130. Rumours of Pitt's intentions reached Dublin in 1797 via Valentine Lawless (below, Ch. 14, n. 40). But the scare was premature, and the response to an anti-union meeting (Royal Exchange), chaired by Lawless, was muted (*FJ*, 1 Aug. 1797).

George Ogle,[7] who had succeeded Arthur Wolfe as MP for the city in July 1798, was well disposed towards a union, as was Alderman William James, whose energy as a magistrate during the troubled 1790s had won him much respect. Lord Castlereagh, the chief secretary, believed that the latter 'has great weight, not only in the Corporation, but particularly in the Orange lodges; he is eager for the question, considering the Prince of Wales and the Opposition as pledged to the Catholics'.[8]

It swiftly transpired that the Castle's faith in these individuals, and in the prospect that fear of Catholics would neutralize Protestant hostility to the proposal, was misplaced. The utmost the unionists were able to achieve was to dissuade certain unofficial vehicles of Dublin Protestant opinion, such as the Aldermen of Skinner's Alley and the Orange lodges, from condemning the proposal out of hand. According to the anti-unionist J. C. Beresford, the other MP for the city, these bodies were averse to the measure, the former particularly so. Even Dr Duigenan, himself a unionist, and never one to fear unpopularity, was shaken by the degree of hostility in loyalist circles. It proved impossible in December 1798 to prevent the Dublin bar, and a meeting of merchants and bankers (including some Catholics and Presbyterians as well as Anglicans), from voicing condemnation.[9] Nor, despite the efforts of Alderman James, could Dublin corporation and the guilds be dissuaded from speaking out. Union was denounced at three post assemblies and at the usual quarterly meeting of the corporation at the end of 1798, the board of aldermen supporting the city commons: 'Resolved unanimously, that having boldly defended the Constitution in King, Lords, and Commons, against the open and secret abettors of Rebellion, we are determined steadily to oppose any attempt that may be made to surrender the free legislation [*sic*] of this kingdom by uniting it with the legislature of Great Britain.'[10] Down to this point, opposition had largely been confined to the (mainly Protestant) middle classes; but when the Irish parliament failed to endorse union in January 1799, the (mainly Catholic) mob broke the windows of those citizens who failed to celebrate the victory. It was even reported that the United Irishmen were reviving on the strength of the issue.[11]

Through the first half of 1799 the Castle laboured to gain supporters among the aldermen, and by July Castlereagh was cautiously optimistic, reporting a hesitation to live up to former anti-union declarations. A modest success was achieved when the board voted to tone down an address from

---

[7] George Ogle (1742–1814), below, App. B, and *DNB*. Returned unopposed for Dublin city in 1798 on Wolfe's promotion to chief justice, when the public was still struck by his apparently prophetic warning to Luke Gardiner (Lord Mountjoy), sponsor of several Catholic relief bills, who had recently been killed by the rebels at New Ross (*Cornwallis Corr.* ii. 272).

[8] *Cornwallis Corr.* ii. 446–7.

[9] Ibid. ii. 41–3, 47–8, 50–3, 81; Bolton, *Passing of the Irish Act of Union*, 75–82.

[10] *CARD* xv. 80–2, 92–5.   [11] *Castlereagh Corr.* ii. 51, 79–81.

the city commons accompanying a grant of freedom to William Saurin,[12] who was leading the barristers' resistance to union. However, Saurin was granted his freedom. By this time the Castle's principal hope lay in the Presbyterian Alderman William Alexander, who had built up a party of supporters on the board some years earlier.[13] But when the city commons pressed again for anti-union resolutions at the Michaelmas 1799 meeting of the corporation, the aldermen assented, by a majority of 7 to 2. Alexander's influence was of no avail, and Alderman James actually voted with the majority.[14] This showed the limits of Castle influence, even where the board was concerned.

There were, of course, a number of special factors that contributed to the hostility with which the union proposals were greeted in Dublin. These included the self-interest of lawyers, whose career prospects might be blighted by a union; the fears of merchants and manufacturers that the abolition of protection would expose them to even greater English competition; the traditional loyalties of the freemen, for whom, in addition to economic interests, the Irish parliament confirmed the principle of local self-government. The freemen's views were represented most directly by the guilds. At least seventeen of the twenty-five guilds are known to have passed anti-union resolutions during 1799 and 1800.[15]

Two things stand out about these resolutions. First, the widespread identification between the preservation of the Irish parliament and economic prosperity.[16] This conviction sprang in part from recognition of the measures taken in the Irish parliament to protect trade and industry. But beyond this, the guilds took it for granted, just as in Molyneux's day, that England and Ireland were commercial and industrial rivals. The tailors' guild remarked that 'the selfish principle predominates in all commercial states', and the smiths' guild elaborated the point: 'we should abandon all hope of national improvement for ever, if thrown upon the foreign mercy of a foreign legislature.'[17] There was little indication here that the guilds had imbibed the new economic thinking, which since mid-century had been

---

[12] William Saurin (1757–1839), called to the bar, 1780; turned down post of solicitor-general in 1798 on account of the union. For orchestrating opposition to union among the Irish bar he was stripped of his silk gown. Later (1807–22) attorney-general (see *DNB*).

[13] *CARD* xv. 115; *Castlereagh Corr.* ii. 353–4; above, Ch. 9.

[14] *CARD* xv. 118; *Castlereagh Corr.* ii. 431.

[15] For the resolutions of sixteen guilds see W. J. Battersby's *The Fall and Rise of Ireland, or, the Repealer's Manual*, 2nd edn. (Dublin, 1834), 331–51. For the hatters, see Berry, 'The Records of the Feltmakers' Company', 36. Guilds that do not appear to have passed such resolutions were the bakers, cooks, brewers, curriers, tanners, glovers, apothecaries, and dyers. But these were all among the smallest guilds (below, Table 12.3), and it may be that in some cases their resolutions were not printed.

[16] The merchants, hosiers, butchers, smiths, weavers, goldsmiths, tailors, and carpenters all stressed the adverse commercial implications of union (Battersby, *Fall and Rise of Ireland*, 331, 333, 340, 346, 349).

[17] Ibid. 340, 346; see also the weavers' resolutions, 340.

moving away from the mercantilist view that wealth and trade had fixed and finite limits, and hence that any improvement in one country must inevitably be at the expense of others. The guilds therefore lagged behind Irish statesmen such as John Foster, who, while always anxious to drive a hard bargain on behalf of Irish interests, deprecated 'the mistaken policy of treating the two Countries as rivals'.[18]

Secondly, despite some appearances to the contrary, the anti-union arguments employed in these guild resolutions were Patriot rather than nationalist ones. The hosiers' guild, admittedly, invoked 'the national will' and 'the general will' in opposition to the union. But 'the general will', as popularized by Rousseau, did not imply a simple majority will. Rather, the concept had contractual and anti-oligarchical overtones, as well as a moral dimension, much as natural rights had had for Lucas.[19] The hosiers went on to assert that Great Britain and Ireland 'are two independent nations', while the smiths and the carpenters described Britain, or at least the British parliament, as 'foreign'.[20] However, since these guilds did not reject the crown, it must be presumed that their thinking remained in line with that of Molyneux, Lucas, and Grattan: two parliaments independent of each other, but under the same monarch, and with the crown still enjoying the right to appoint ministers. More frequently invoked were unassailable privileges or 'birthrights': a blend of common law and contractual rights. As St. Luke's guild put it: 'Resolved, That as a free and independent corporation of the city of Dublin, we behold with abhorrence and detestation the vile attempt which is made, by every species of corruption, to deprive us of our glorious constitution, our birth-rights, and our liberties, which we are bound by our oaths to defend.'[21] Such rights did not depend on the weight of numbers. In any case, union had its attractions for Catholics. Accordingly, although certain resolutions welcomed the anti-union stand adopted by Dublin Catholics, there was no suggestion that the views of the majority had to be taken into account. It was the freemen, together with the 'independent' landed gentry, whose views mattered: that is, members of the privileged— and still mainly Protestant—classes. Thus Lucas's old guild, the barbers: 'Resolved unanimously, That the establishment of Ireland's independence, achieved by the manly and patriotic exertions of a resident Irish parliament in 1782, secures to the people of this land, the full and free enjoyment of their political rights, the benefits of which none but freemen can estimate, and which freemen ought not to surrender.'[22] And other resolutions had a decidedly loyalist flavour: thus the stationers' guild argued that the Irish

---

[18] Malcomson, *John Foster*, 369.

[19] Rosenfeld, 'Rousseau's Unanimous Contract and the Doctrine of Popular Sovereignty'.

[20] Battersby, *Fall and Rise of Ireland*, 333–4, 340, 349.

[21] Ibid. 341; also resolutions of the butchers and joiners, 334–5.

[22] Resolutions of merchants, stationers, hosiers, and barbers (ibid. 336, 338–9, 341, 343–4).

parliament was quite adequate to defeat 'the designs of the foreign and domestic enemies of our king and happy Constitution'.[23]

Several guild resolutions followed Molyneux in suggesting that any threat to the Irish parliament threatened the rights of the crown, on the assumption that the summoning of parliaments was an inherent part of the royal prerogative. Thus the carpenters' guild warned, 'we consider the advisers of this measure enemies to our country, and betrayers of the rights of our Sovereign and his family.' The hosiers, for all their appeal to 'the national will', used similar language: 'any man who shall prove instrumental to the measure of an Union, will be an enemy to his king, the people of Ireland, and the interests of the empire'. There was also evidence of the influence of more recent developments in Patriot thinking, particularly in the view expressed in 1800 by several guilds that MPs were merely delegates, who accordingly lacked the authority 'to annihilate the perpetual franchises of their constituents'.[24] Thus both the economic and constitutional thinking contained in these resolutions fitted into a Patriot pattern. The absence of references to the Williamite revolution, which had loomed so large in constitutional debate only a few years before, may seem surprising; but the debate had shifted away from the Protestant nature of the constitution to Irish parliamentary rights, for which the settlement of 1782–3, confirming 'the ancient constitution', provided the relevant context.

Meanwhile, following the Irish parliament's unenthusiastic response to the union proposal in January 1799, the Castle had been busy trying to win greater parliamentary support. The inducements were the usual ones offered by eighteenth-century governments, though on a far greater scale: pensions, offices, and titles, as well as compensation for boroughs that stood to lose their representation. By the start of 1800 these overtures, and the evident commitment of government to a union, were making an impact on MPs. Government approaches to Catholic leaders, too, had an effect. The expectation that a union would facilitate the abolition of the remaining penal laws made Catholics generally favourable, and this was reflected in the votes of MPs from the south and west where Catholic voters were concentrated.[25]

Moreover, during the parliamentary debates on the union, brought forward again in February 1800, ministers were heartened by unexpected divisions among the opponents of the measure. Paradoxically, these were in part occasioned by Henry Grattan's re-entry on the political scene. Since 1798, when he had been removed from the Irish privy council on account of

[23] NLI, MS 12126, p. 144.

[24] Battersby, *Fall and Rise of Ireland*, 333, 344, 349.

[25] Bolton, *Passing of the Irish Act of Union*, 109, 153–4; Bartlett, *Fall and Rise of the Irish Nation*, 246–67.

unfounded allegations that he was a sworn United Irishman, Grattan had been in poor health and not active in politics. But in January 1800 he was elected MP for Wicklow town. His eloquence in defence of the integrity of the Irish parliament was undeniable, but his reappearance in the house of commons and his emphasis on the need for action on Catholic emancipation had a divisive effect on those opponents of union who considered him, and the Catholics, to be little better than rebels. One of the leading opponents of union, Speaker John Foster, was outraged when handbills circulating in the city linked his name with Grattan's.[26] All this helped to make the government's majority more certain. The union resolutions passed both houses of the Irish parliament in March 1800 and received the royal assent in August.[27]

These developments took place in the teeth of persistent opposition in the capital. Dublin corporation spoke out against the measure on three occasions during January and February 1800, while the guild of merchants, in a much-admired resolution, expressed its members' revulsion at the means employed by government to gain a pro-union majority:

Resolved, That we look with horror and disgust at the arts practiced with unblushing effrontery, to defraud us of a constitution which was acquired by so much virtue, and maintained with so much glory. We cannot think that a measure supported by the annihilation of all honourable feeling, and propped up by the most audacious traffics, can be either useful or permanent. It is to us equal, whether it be the result of fraud or force; in either case it is tyranny, and tyranny never had in any country, or in any age, a righteous claim to submission.[28]

And on this occasion the loyalist Aldermen of Skinner's Alley also spoke out, deploring 'wicked' attempts on the liberties of fellow citizens, and pointedly indicating that its members could see no benefit in a union.[29]

In the face of near unanimity in corporate circles, it took some temerity to speak out in favour of union. But one member was prepared to take such an unpopular stand, and even to record a formal protest against the corporation's proceedings: John Giffard. His protest, entered in the city commons' journal in April 1800, recorded that he had stood in 'almost single opposition' to the commons' views on the union. Giffard gave four reasons for differing from his fellow members: the danger facing Protestants since the 'guards and fences which the wisdom of our Ancestors had placed round the Protestant religion have been removed'; the likelihood of Ireland

---

[26] 'Green ribbands are sold with this motto—Grattan and Foster the Friends of Ireland—this makes the speaker mad' (Cooke to Lord Auckland, 18 Jan. 1800, PRONI, Sneyd Papers, T 3229/2/51; same to same, 20 Jan. 1800, T 3229/2/52; John Beresford to Auckland, 20 Jan. 1800, T. 3229/2/53). See also *Cornwallis Corr.* iii. 166.

[27] 40 Geo. III, c. 38.

[28] *CARD* xv. 127–8, 136–8; Battersby, *Fall and Rise of Ireland*, 338.

[29] *FJ*, 15 Feb. 1800.

falling under French control unless protected by a union; the calming effect a union would have on Irish life; and its role in encouraging British investment in Ireland, which would promote prosperity and the inculcation of 'British manners and British principles amongst our common Irish'. His ultimate goals—security for Irish Protestantism, the link with Britain, and Irish prosperity—were broadly similar to those of his fellow members; where Giffard stood out was in his conviction that these goals could no longer be achieved by Irish Protestants and the Irish parliament alone.[30]

Once again, it would be wrong to see Giffard as a government stooge. On the union, his views coincided with government's; but his protest revealed his own agenda, above all in the importance it attached to the defence of Protestantism. It is more appropriate to see him as one of a new breed of Irish Protestants, able to shed Patriot assumptions in favour of a vision based on union with Britain and the professionalization of the police and administration[31]—developments considered necessary to protect Protestants in the new era following the virtual abandonment of the penal laws. The fact that Giffard had so few supporters in corporate circles testifies to the high morale of Dublin Protestants and to the powerful influence that Patriot assumptions still wielded over them. If Giffard was able to break out of those habits of thought this probably had something to do with his personal circumstances. He had lost two near relatives during the 1798 rising; besides, since his own constitutional 'birthright' owed little to birth itself, he was probably more open than others to considering new ways of protecting his constitutional privileges.

II. The Union in Operation

While Dublin was firmly opposed to a union, outside the capital public opinion was far more divided, and Dubliners were left without effective allies. On the eve of the final parliamentary debates on the question, handbills were circulated in the city urging the yeomanry, Orangemen, and Catholics to unite and save the Irish parliament. Some MPs suffered physical attacks: one of the ringleaders in the disturbances, a custom-house officer and member of the yeomanry, was arrested. Cavalry were brought in to patrol the streets. However, the guilds and corporation had stressed that the measure should be resisted only by legal means,[32] and once the act had been passed, overt opposition died down. The government displayed some nervousness during the actual transition to union on 1 January 1801. A sharp eye was kept on the Orangemen—three Dublin lodges had defied the grand lodge to register their hostility to union—but the capital was full of

---

[30] DCA, C1/JSC/8, fos. 135ᵛ–136ᵛ; *CARD* xv. 519–20.
[31] Palmer has pointed out that those in favour of the centralizing police act of 1808 were also in favour of the union (*Police and Protest*, 155).
[32] *Cornwallis Corr.* iii. 167–8, 180–1; NLI, MS 12126, p. 153.

troops, and the event passed off quietly.[33] During the next few years the union apparently ceased to be controversial in the capital, and historians have generally agreed that hostility died away very quickly.[34] But in fact Dublin opinion, and notably that represented by the freemen, remained unreconciled; opposition to union was to be periodically and publicly recorded down to the early 1830s.

The first significant manifestation of anti-union sentiment appeared, not surprisingly, after the fall of the ministry that had introduced the measure, following the death of Pitt in January 1806. (Since opposition to union did not extend to support for rebellion, Emmet's rebellion of 1803 called forth only condemnation in corporate circles.)[35] In February 1806 St Luke's guild was convened by requisition, and appointed a committee to prepare a petition to parliament for the repeal of the union. The shoemakers' guild took a more forthright line in April, rejoicing in the dismissal of the ministers responsible for the union, and resolving to pursue with other 'constitutional bodies' the propriety of applying for a restoration of 'our just and alienated rights'. The hosiers' guild, too, called for the restoration of the constitution of 1782.[36] The change of ministry brought to power several English Whigs who had been in opposition at the time of the union. As ministers, they did not shrink from impugning the means employed to carry it. Fox, for instance, who now became secretary for foreign affairs, made scathing references to Irish sinecures created at the time of the union by means of what 'the world called bribes'.[37] And at the general election of November 1806 Henry Grattan headed the poll for Dublin city. Repeal of the union was not mentioned, but no one had forgotten Grattan's championing of the Irish parliament.[38] However, the new ministry fell in March 1807, and in the spring of 1808, against a background of rising prices, higher wartime taxation, and another centralizing police measure, several Dublin guilds again passed resolutions urging repeal of the union. Speaking in the house of commons in April 1808, Sir John Newport, MP for Waterford city, expressed his disappointment with the effects of the union on Ireland.[39]

A city commons debate on the union in April 1808 afforded an opportunity for the guild representatives to reflect on the condition of

---

[33] Bolton, *Passing of the Irish Act of Union*, 189; *Castlereagh Corr.* iv. 13–14; Senior, *Orangeism in Ireland and Britain*, 133, 137.
[34] Moody & Vaughan (eds.), *NHI* iv. 370–3; Beckett, *The Anglo-Irish Tradition*, 84–6.
[35] Address to Attorney-General Standish O'Grady (*CARD* xv. 325–7).
[36] NLI, MS 12126, pp. 204–5; *FJ*, 3 Apr. 1806; retrospective report in *FJ*, 1 Sept. 1810. The weavers also debated the issue (*FDJ*, 11 Mar. 1806).
[37] *FJ*, 19 June 1806.   [38] See *FJ*, 16, 29 May, 2 June, 5 Nov. 1806.
[39] The glovers, tailors, smiths, and stationers (*DEP*, 26 Mar., 26, 30 Apr. 1808; NLI, MS 12126, p. 225). The police act (48 Geo. III, c. 140) enabled government to appoint most police magistrates (Palmer, *Police and Protest*, 152–5). For Newport, see report from *Globe* (*DEP*, 3 May 1808).

Ireland seven years after the measure had come into effect. In a widely reported speech, William Patterson of the cooks' guild argued that the supposed economic benefits of the union had not materialized. English capital had not appeared, although the warehouses, he complained, were crammed with English goods, underselling Irish-made articles and threatening the future of Irish industry. Dublin, he admitted, was still expanding; he saw new squares and rows of tiny houses being built: but the town houses of the gentry were now filled with retired merchants, while the Liberties, the industrial heartland of Dublin, were deserted. Nor would he allow that rising demand for agricultural produce meant that the union had brought benefits for Irish farmers or the rural poor. At the end of the debate the city commons resolved by 49 votes to 32 to reaffirm its anti-union resolution of 26 May 1800, though a proposal for a committee to petition for repeal was rejected.[40]

In 1808 there were still doubts over whether to pursue repeal of the union. But two years later, at the corporation's Easter assembly in 1810, John Willis[41] of the glovers' guild introduced a resolution for repeal of the union that passed the city commons, though it failed to obtain the support of the board of aldermen. In July, by 45 votes to 15, the commons reiterated support for repeal, appealing to 'our Countrymen and Fellow Citizens to come forward in Corporate Bodies and in County and in Grand Jury Meetings to Demand a Restoration of that Constitution which is our birthright and of which we have been despoiled by fraud and Corruption'.[42] On this occasion the aldermen agreed to the setting up of a committee to promote the objects of the resolution, and endorsed resolutions encouraging the consumption of Irish-made goods. Moreover, between August and October 1810 at least twelve of the twenty-five guilds declared their support for repeal. Certain Dublin parishes took up the question, and the *Freeman's Journal*—which in line with government policy had welcomed union in 1801—threw its weight behind the campaign. Once again, the corporation found itself in good standing with the populace: in October 1810 the incoming lord mayor, Alderman Nathaniel Hone, was given the popular distinction of having the horses taken out of the shafts of his carriage, which was then pulled by the crowd.[43]

[40] *DEP*, 5 May 1808; DCA, C1/JSC/9, fo. 116. William Patterson, Club House, College Green, representative of cooks' guild, 1808–14.

[41] John (Jack) Willis of Trinity St., glover and breeches maker; representative of glovers' guild from 1787; supporter of Catholic claims.

[42] DCA, C1/JSC/9, fos. 185, 190ᵛ–191; *FDJ*, 5 May 1810; *CARD* xvi. 223–4. The unionist minority included John Giffard and William McAuley (merchants' guild), who argued that it was either a union or the pikes of the United Irishmen; in any case union would bring prosperity (*FDJ*, 21 July 1810).

[43] *FJ*, 2 Oct. 1810. The guilds included the hosiers, stationers, barbers, tailors, smiths, hatters, dyers, shoemakers, chandlers, joiners, saddlers, and goldsmiths (ibid., 29, 31 Aug., 1, 4, 7, 11, 17 Sept., 10, 19, 20, 25 Oct. 1810). For parishes see *FJ*, 29, 31 Aug. 1810; & 17 Sept. 1810 for the *FJ*'s assessment of its own role in the repeal movement.

Two developments had brought this on. One was a sharp economic depression, beginning in England, by this time suffering the effects of Napoleon's economic blockade. English textiles were shunted on to the Dublin market, swamping Irish products, and English merchants with bases in Dublin were said to be supplying even Irish regiments with English-made cloth. Castle officials reported severe distress among woollen and cotton workers. The other cause was the Irish budget of July 1810. John Foster, who had come to terms with the union sufficiently to accept the post of chancellor of the Irish exchequer, was attempting to meet the requirements of the rising Irish national debt in part by increasing the window tax by 50 per cent. This was a wartime tax, levied on buildings with more than seven windows, and a high proportion of it fell on Dublin.[44]

Against this background, discontent among the citizens mounted to a climax during the summer of 1810, inducing the chief secretary to review the state of the army in case of trouble.[45] On 18 September an 'aggregate' meeting of freemen and freeholders was held in order to petition for repeal of the union. Sir James Riddall, veteran United Irishman, now one of the city sheriffs, took the chair, and Robert Shaw, one of the city MPs, was in attendance.[46] (The other sheriff, Sir Edward Stanley, refused to comply with the requisition on the grounds that it was unlikely to achieve its objects and was calculated to excite the public mind.) The beadles of the guilds were appointed to keep order, and it passed off peacefully. The meeting agreed to appoint a committee, which contained several Catholics, including Daniel O'Connell,[47] to prepare petitions to the king and parliament for repeal. The petition to parliament contained expressions of warm attachment to the British connection and to the principles of the British constitution, but asserted that an Irish parliament was necessary to safeguard Irish interests.[48]

Guild meetings at which repeal resolutions were passed continued to be held into October, and once again at the Michaelmas assembly of the corporation the city commons attempted to pursue the question, requesting the aldermanic board to send down to them for consideration the report of the committee on the union, set up in July. But the aldermen replied bluntly

[44] Ibid., 12, 13 July 1810; William Wellesley Pole to Richard Ryder, 5 July 1810, PRONI, Harrowby Papers, T 3228/5/8; F. J. Holden, 'Property Taxes in Old Dublin', *Dublin Hist. Rec.* 13 (1953), 133–7, at 136–7.

[45] The Castle was also anxious about the Dublin Catholics, one of whose leaders, John Keogh, had allegedly spoken warmly of Wolfe Tone (Pole to Ryder, 23 July 1810, PRONI, T 3228/5/14).

[46] *FJ*, 14, 19 Sept. 1810. For Shaw, see below, App. B; for Riddall, who with his brother sheriff Sir Edward Stanley was knighted on the occasion of the king's jubilee in October 1809, see Ch. 9 above.

[47] Daniel O'Connell (1775–1847), below, App. B; Oliver MacDonagh, *O'Connell: The Life of Daniel O'Connell 1775–1847* (London, 1991), 102–4.

[48] *FJ*, 19 Sept. 1810.

that the report on the union 'has been disposed of', and as the commons attempted to pass their own repeal resolutions, the lord mayor entered the commons' chamber and dissolved the assembly.[49]

For its part, Dublin Castle had been careful to take no overt action against the incipient repeal movement; in fact, the aggregate meeting passed a vote of thanks to the viceroy. But behind the scenes officials were labouring to dampen down the campaign.[50] This was widely suspected. In a public letter to the guild of merchants, 'An old merchant' urged the guild to choose its representatives for the forthcoming city commons elections (November 1810) carefully; the government, he alleged, was anxious to weaken Dublin corporation and destroy its independence. According to him, patronage associated with the new police act and the paving board already afforded government the means of influencing the aldermen. It was therefore vital for the guild representatives to preserve their independence so as to ensure that Dublin corporation as a whole remained independent no matter how 'corrupt' the aldermen might become. In the city commons, the silversmith Samuel Neville alleged that every government pensioner and placeman had been brought into play, and that treason and rebellion were imputed to the repealers.[51]

Repeal of the union thus became a contentious issue in certain guilds, with at least one guild (the shoemakers) imposing a repeal pledge for city commons' candidates at the November elections. In the smiths' guild a leading anti-unionist candidate felt obliged to refute attacks on his character, including the charge that he was a papist, and had failed to pay his quarterage fees. In the guild of merchants a resolution was carried unanimously, expressing determination to resist the undue influence hitherto exercised by the board of aldermen over the guild's choice of representatives for the commons: apparently it had become common practice for the board to circulate a printed list of those they wished to see elected. After the elections the *Freeman's Journal* reported that anti-unionist candidates had generally been successful.[52]

But before confrontation between the guilds and the aldermen could come to a head, the momentum of the repeal movement suddenly evaporated. At a post assembly of the corporation on 9 November to consider petitioning for repeal, both the board and the commons agreed not to pursue the matter, though they failed to agree on a mutually acceptable

[49] DCA, C1/JSC/9, fos. 199^{r-v}; meetings of guilds of joiners, saddlers, and goldsmiths, *FJ*, 19, 20, 25 Oct. 1810; goldsmiths' guild, minute book 1807–24, NLI, n 6058 p 6784, pp. 112–15; barber-surgeons' minute book 1792–1826, TCD, MS 1447/8/3, p. 111.

[50] *FJ*, 19 Sept. 1810; Pole to Ryder, 6 Aug. 1810, PRONI, T 3228/5/16; see also 'The unionists' in *FJ*, 31 Oct. 1810, and the *FJ*'s allegations (2 Nov. 1810) of Castle influence in the carpenters' guild elections.

[51] *FJ*, 11 Oct. 1810; Dublin corporation meeting, ibid., 23 Oct. 1810.

[52] Ibid., 17, 19, 20 Oct., 2, 6, 9, 16 Nov. 1810.

form of wording.[53] No further guild or parish repeal meetings were held in 1810, and the question was not revived for several years.

There were a number of reasons for this collapse. As early as August, government measures to alleviate the industrial crisis, notably a loan to assist public credit, were said to be having a good effect, and by October the silk trade was reviving. Also in October, certain MPs who had talked of pressing for repeal of the union were drawing back. In Dublin, it was reported to the Castle at the end of October that both propertied people and the lower orders were inclined to drop the subject.[54] For the city commons and guilds, however, the crucial event had nothing to do with the economy, Castle pressures, or aldermanic influence. Towards the end of October 1810 George III, now in his seventies, and almost completely blind, once again fell victim to the hereditary disease that had raised the question of a regency in 1788. On that occasion, he had recovered; this time an act of parliament was passed to make the prince of Wales regent, with effect from February 1811. Since the monarch remained, in a real sense, the head of government, this constituted a political crisis; all the more serious because the king had become a symbol of resistance to the threat from Napoleonic France. In these circumstances, the city commons, whose resolutions had frequently emphasized loyalty to the monarch, was not disposed to press for repeal, though it was determined to record its continued commitment to the restoration of the Irish parliament.[55] Thus the movement died away without causing so much as a ripple in parliament.

The recurrent anti-union protests emanating from the guilds and the city commons between 1806 and 1810 indicated that the Dublin Protestant business community was by no means reconciled to the loss of the Irish parliament. Economic distress and high wartime taxation helped to bring latent anti-unionism out into the open. However, despite forebodings on the economic front, there was little sense as yet of Dublin as a city whose main industries were in irreversible decline. Dublin and London (the 'sister metropolis')[56] were still seen very much as equals. The real significance of the repeal campaign at this time lay in the freemen's continuing confidence in the role of corporate bodies, with their overwhelmingly Protestant membership, as champions of Irish liberties.

As in 1799 and 1800, Catholic support—such as it was—for the anti-union cause was welcomed, and Catholics were represented on the

---

[53] The city commons wanted it to be recorded that the matter was merely postponed (DCA, C1/JSC/9, fo. 200; *FJ*, 10 Nov. 1810).

[54] Pole to Ryder, 6 Aug. 1810, PRONI, T 3228/5/16; same to same, 20 Oct. 1810, T 3228/5/23; 'Information about the movements of disaffected persons in Dublin, 26–7 Oct. 1810', T 3228/6/20.

[55] Report of Daniel Hutton's speech (*FJ*, 10 Nov. 1810). The commons mourned the calamity that had befallen the royal family (C1/JSC/9, fo. 200).

[56] *FJ*, 4 Jan. 1809.

committee set up by the aggregate repeal meeting in 1810.[57] Moreover, two of the chief repealers on the city commons were in favour of Catholic emancipation, though they did not dwell on the matter.[58] But there were also many who were strongly opposed to further concessions; and any attempt to act on the call from the *Evening Herald*—for corporate bodies to campaign for emancipation as well as repeal, and to urge Catholics to join the movement[59]—would have been extremely divisive. However, there was little incentive to link the two issues. The Catholic question was in abeyance for most of the first post-union decade, for the king remained implacably hostile to full emancipation. In these circumstances, O'Connell was prepared to state that he would endorse repeal of the union even if it meant prolonging the existence of the remaining penal laws.[60] In other words, even Catholics were prepared to make public statements that connived at the perpetuation of the Irish *ancien régime*.

III. The Dublin Freemen and Politics during the Phoney War, 1795–1814

Following the act of union, continuity remained the dominant theme of Dublin politics. Parliamentary election contests operated along lines established in Charles Lucas's day half a century earlier. The (Protestant) freemen still constituted the great majority of the voters—85 per cent at the 1806 election—and candidates continued to tour the guildhalls to put their case.[61] Political debate was still dominated by familiar opposition rhetoric, with 'independence' being the qualification most widely claimed by and for candidates, and candidates frequently appealing to the independence of the voters. In certain contexts the term simply meant 'public-spirited', but as in the past it could also convey a variety of more precise meanings. It usually indicated independence of government, but it might also mean independence of the mob,[62] as well as financial independence[63]—the necessary wealth to

[57] The committee of nine included at least three Catholics: Daniel O'Connell; Randal McDonnell, d. 1821, of Allen's Court, Mullinahack, Co. Dublin (wealthiest Catholic in Dublin); Nicholas Mahon (below, Ch. 14, n. 15). The Protestants included four members of the city commons: Thomas Abbott, silk manufacturer, sheriffs' peer, lord mayor of Dublin, 1825–6; William Ferrall, dyers' guild; Robert Harty (hosiers' guild, below, App. B); Daniel Hutton, Mary St., builder, carpenters' guild (*FJ*, 19 Sept. 1810).

[58] Notably John Willis and William Patterson, above, nn. 40 and 41; see e.g. *DEP*, 5 May 1808.   [59] 'Repeal of the Union', reprinted in *FJ*, 31 Aug. 1810.

[60] Speech at aggregate repeal meeting, *FJ*, 19 Sept. 1810. For this reason, it is important not to exaggerate what has been described as the 'interdenominational anti-Unionism of 1810' (MacDonagh, *O'Connell*, 103).

[61] *Recollections of Jonah Barrington*, 178–9.

[62] Henry Grattan's speech to merchants' guild, *FJ*, 10 Nov. 1806.

[63] John La Touche was praised for his 'independence of fortune' and 'of sentiment', (Anon.), *Letter to the Independent Citizens of Dublin, From a Member of the Guild of Merchants* (Dublin, 1802), 19. Jonah Barrington proclaimed his own independence by pledging that if elected he would accept no government pension or employment (*FDJ*, 22 July 1802).

resist the temptations of corruption. Occasionally, the phrase 'national independence', referring to the constitution of 1782, was used. Alternatively, or in addition, candidates might appeal for support on the basis of their personal or family record and their devotion to the commercial and industrial interests of Dublin.[64]

The persistence of traditional political values, reinforced by pressures for counter-revolutionary cohesion, worked against any tendency to campaign on sectional, class-based, or reformist issues. The reluctance of candidates to take up such issues was striking. Thus, when Henry Grattan contested his old Dublin seat in 1806, he was already a leading parliamentary exponent of Catholic emancipation, and might have been expected to explain his position on this matter to the city electorate—which, since 1793, had included a small number of Catholic freeholders. But he did not depart from the prevailing pattern. It was not (as will be argued) that there were no issues underlying electoral contests; but during this period traditional assumptions about the desirability of a non-party approach meant that divisive matters were relegated to the background. Indeed, the small number of contested elections between the union and the end of the war—only the 1802 and 1806 elections were contested, and the two MPs elected in 1806 both served until 1820—testifies to the fact that electoral contests were not considered essential to the political process: they revealed divisions within a supposedly united electorate whose role it was to act as a check on government.

It is difficult to determine how disadvantageous it was for a candidate to have links with government, since there were always circumstances in which a Patriot could justify being in office. Certainly, in an era of war and rebellion, such links were acceptable in the interests of counter-revolutionary solidarity. The two MPs who had been returned unopposed in 1797, J. C. Beresford and Arthur Wolfe, both held official posts, as did George Ogle, who replaced Wolfe in 1798. By the time of the 1802 election the threat of rebellion had receded, and both Beresford and Ogle were attacked by one critic for having government support;[65] Beresford (who had in fact resigned his posts in protest at the union) was re-elected, but Ogle lost to John La Touche,[66] whose wealth and consequent independence were stressed by his supporters. La Touche, like Beresford, had strong local and commercial ties, while Ogle was a Wexford man. But it is possible that the crucial issue in that election was neither government backing nor local ties, but the Catholic question. While both Beresford and Ogle were intimately connected with the Orange Order, Ogle had become identified in the public mind with a

---

[64] *DEP*, recommending Henry Grattan, 18 Oct. 1806; statements of George Ogle and John La Touche at the 1802 poll, *FDJ*, 22 July 1802.

[65] *Letter to the Independent Citizens of Dublin*, 9–10.

[66] John La Touche, jun. (below, App. B).

notably anti-Catholic variety of Protestant ascendancy, which may have damaged him in some quarters. Beresford's father commented, 'it was the papists and rebels who brought in Latouche, not for his sake, but in opposition to Ogle, who [*sic*] they hate of all men'.[67]

Henry Grattan, who in turn took La Touche's seat in 1806, was charged by his other opponent, the Dublin banker Robert Shaw,[68] with having government backing: the ministry of all the talents had recently restored him to the Irish privy council and had offered him a ministerial post, though he turned the latter down.[69] Moreover, although he had a Dublin background, Grattan was not a commercial man. Yet he comfortably headed the poll.[70] This suggests that something else was working in his favour. Election addresses themselves shed little light on the subject, but other sources point to two underlying issues of importance to the voters: the act of union (which continued to be resented), and loyalty to king and (Protestant) constitution (which continued to militate against any active pursuit of Catholic emancipation).

On the union, no candidate so much as presented himself for election without being able to claim, or have it claimed on his behalf, that he had opposed the introduction of the union.[71] Grattan's success at the polls arose largely from the fact that his name was synonymous with the constitution of 1782.[72] That is not to say that Grattan was given a specific mandate to seek repeal. The union was widely unpopular with Dubliners, but the only electoral contests of the period took place in 1802 and 1806, when discussion of possible repeal had scarcely begun.

The issue of loyalty, in an era of war and rebellion, was equally important. In 1802 the candidates' record during and after the 1798

[67] Beresford to Auckland, 12 Aug. 1802, PRONI, Sneyd Papers, T 3229/2/72. La Touche beat Ogle by 392 votes. Catholic (freehold) voters alone could not have turned the scale: only 270 of some 3,000 voters were freeholders, and not all were Catholics. Ogle was challenged to a duel by a Catholic merchant in 1802 for allegedly claiming that Catholics did not keep oaths (*FDJ*, 19 Jan. 1802), and 'George Ogle and Protestant Ascendancy' became a common toast among ultra Protestants (dinner for Ogle's birthday; cooks' guild dinner, Dublin, ibid., 19 Oct. 1809, 28 July 1814); above, n. 7.

[68] Robert Shaw (1774–1849), below, App. B; *Cornwallis Corr.* iii. 80, n. 1. With the election of Beresford in 1797 and Shaw in 1804, the voters' prejudice against bankers (above, Ch. 5) had evidently evaporated.

[69] For Shaw's attack, see his election address, *FDJ*, 6 Nov. 1806.

[70] *The Poll for Electing Two Members to Represent the City of Dublin in the Imperial Parliament . . . 1806* (Dublin, n.d.), 73. For 19th-c. election results see B. M. Walker (ed.), *Parliamentary Election Results in Ireland, 1801–1922* (Dublin, 1978).

[71] For the election of 1802, see *FDJ*, 22 July 1802; of 1804, see Shaw's election address, ibid., 8 Mar. 1804; of 1806, see *DEP*'s verdict on Grattan, 18 Oct. 1806. Beresford, Ogle, Grattan, La Touche, and Shaw had all voted against union on 6 Feb. 1800 (in Ogle's case, in deference to his constituents' wishes). In La Touche's case, the fact that the head of the family, David La Touche, had voted for union was held against him in 1802 (speech of John Kelly, city commons, *FDJ*, 23 Jan. 1802).

[72] See *DEP*'s eulogy on Grattan, 18 Oct. 1806; shoemakers' guild debate (ibid., 6 Nov. 1806, supplement).

rebellion was canvassed by their respective critics and supporters. At guild and corporation elections, too, the issue cropped up repeatedly. In 1807 *Faulkner's Dublin Journal* was satisfied that all the candidates for the merchants' guild elections to the city commons had established their loyalty to king and constitution.[73] This conservative climate placed those who wished to complete the process of Catholic emancipation at a serious disadvantage. During the 1790s, the main supporters of emancipation, apart from the Catholics themselves, had been United Irishmen. Subsequently, the rebellion of 1798, the concordat between Napoleon and the papacy in 1801, and George III's well-known hostility, all hampered the cause, with supporters in any case divided over the issue of a government veto on episcopal appointments.[74] Emancipation was rarely discussed in parliament while the war lasted; outside parliament, opponents had merely to raise the question of loyalty to throw supporters on to the defensive.

The lead in reaffirming loyalty to king and constitution was taken with great éclat by John Giffard, both in the corporation and through the *FDJ*, which paid fulsome tributes to George III and praised the British constitution as the best in the world. The 'tyranny of France' was contrasted with 'the liberty of Britons'.[75] In these circumstances, the question of Catholic emancipation itself rarely needed to be addressed directly. In contrast with their stand on the union, on the issue of the Protestant constitution Giffard and the *FDJ* were going with the tide of opinion in the corporation and guilds. The corporation had never deviated from its policy of opposition to Catholic political rights, although since 1795 a minority had publicly taken a different view, asserting that the monarch desired 'the Cordial and hearty Union of all Classes of his Subjects of this Kingdom'.[76] But the king's opposition to complete equality for Catholics served to reinforce claims that only Protestants could be fully loyal to the constitution; and the pro-emancipation group on the corporation failed to achieve more than minority status.

Despite the conservatism of this period, some subtle changes were creeping into the debate on the Catholic question. Under the impact of the admission of Catholics to certain political rights, and of Burke's attack on Protestant ascendancy, terms such as 'bigotry' were beginning to be used in new ways. During the 1802 parliamentary election campaign, the anonym-

---

[73] Resolutions of chandlers' guild to support Beresford and Ogle (*FDJ*, 7 Jan. 1802); speeches of John Giffard, John Kelly, in Dublin corporation (ibid., 23 Jan. 1802); *FDJ*, 10 Nov. 1807.

[74] A too-progressive position on the Catholic question led to the resignation of Pitt and other ministers in 1801, and the downfall of the ministry of all the talents in 1807: W. E. Vaughan (ed.), *A New History of Ireland*, v. *Ireland Under the Union, 1: 1801–1870* (Oxford, 1989), 34–5.

[75] *FDJ*, 1 Jan. 1801, 2 Jan. 1802; Giffard's speech in city commons, ibid., 18 Oct. 1806.

[76] DCA, C1/JSC/7, fo. 141.

ous author of *The City Candidates; Or a Plumper for John Claudius Beresford* (Dublin, 1802) urged voters to support Beresford on the grounds that he was a '*Sound Orange*'; not 'bigotted' against the Roman Catholic, but preferring the Protestant because the laws gave him a preference. Here 'bigotry' was being used in the standard enlightenment way: it was acceptable to make distinctions between Catholics and Protestants as long as these were made on civil and Erastian (i.e. not theological) grounds. However, the equally anonymous author of the *Letter to the Independent Citizens of Dublin, from a Member of the Guild of Merchants* (Dublin, 1802), adopted a Burkean position in support of John La Touche. Having rehearsed the usual arguments against Beresford and Ogle for having Castle support, and having stressed the pro-Catholic La Touche's virtue and wealth, the author went on to claim that an 'intolerant' and 'unforgiving' Protestant was an incongruous character—'his bigotry is not sanctioned by his creed'. The writer concluded by arguing that if the Dublin voters elected La Touche, they would prove themselves worthy of enjoying a constitution that was 'the envy and admiration of the World'. This was coming close to the view that exclusion of Catholics from political rights, even on Erastian grounds, was wrong.[77]

Subtle developments of this kind, however, did little to modify the inherent conservatism of this period, in which it is difficult to distinguish the views of ultra Protestants and Orangemen (such as Giffard) from those of Dublin Protestants in general. It is worth making the attempt, however, if only to show that Giffard's influence on Dublin politics, even where he was in tune with the prevailing outlook, was limited. This can be illustrated by examining the outcome of contested parliamentary elections. In 1802 Giffard and the *FDJ* supported Beresford and Ogle; Beresford and La Touche were returned. In 1806 they opposed Henry Grattan, and endorsed only Robert Shaw: unlike La Touche, Shaw had been willing to present the corporation's petition against Catholic emancipation to parliament in 1805.[78] Both Shaw and Grattan were elected.

A development on the eve of the poll in 1806 suggested that the image of the Orange Order was not entirely favourable in Dublin, even in Protestant circles. The poll took place only two weeks after the annual celebrations to mark King William's birthday on 4 November. And it was in that year that a new Whig viceroy failed to take part in the usual procession to the statue in College Green. The implication, that the state was beginning to distance itself from Williamite anniversaries, was not lost on either the Grattanites or

[77] *The City Candidates*, 16; *Letter to the Independent Citizens of Dublin*, 8–9, 12–13, 19–22. For similar changes in England, see Robert Hole, *Pulpits, Politics and Public Order in England 1760–1832* (Cambridge, 1989), 120–1.
[78] See the partisan comments in reporting a shoemakers' guild meeting; speeches by Giffard in city commons (*FDJ*, 21, 23 Jan. 1802, 18 Oct. 1806).

the supporters of Orangeism. The *Freeman's Journal*, now Grattanite in politics, came out on 8 November with a report, apparently calculated to damage Shaw's chances, that his supporters were requested to attend the hustings wearing Orange cockades. The *FDJ* replied with a denial from Shaw's committee, asserting that the report was a gross and malicious falsehood.[79] This exchange lends weight to the point that opposition to Catholic claims during this period did not necessarily mean support for the Orange Order. However, a significant minority of the voters (22.5%) followed the *FDJ*'s lead by refusing to vote for either Grattan or La Touche (the two candidates perceived to be friendly to Catholic claims) and plumping for Shaw. At the other extreme, freemen from three guilds, the brewers (71.4%), the hosiers (69.2%), and the apothecaries (60%) voted decisively for the pro-emancipation candidates, with very few members of these guilds plumping for Shaw (7.1%, 7.7%, and 14% respectively).[80]

Thus from 1795 onwards, and for the duration of the war, debate on the Catholic question was in general subordinated to the overriding issue of loyalty to the existing constitution. Although Orangemen took the lead in articulating the virtues of the constitution, it is difficult to measure their influence, because the probity of the constitution was so widely endorsed. Accordingly, on the rare occasions when Catholic emancipation was raised in parliament, its opponents had no need to raise theological issues, or to go beyond conventional Erastian formulae: 'and we most humbly submit that if the demands contained in said petition were acceded to, all the fences and securities of our excellent constitution in church and state established by Protestant legislators from the time of the Reformation to the reign of his present majesty would be destroyed and annihilated'.[81]

IV. A More British Identity?

In England, Scotland, and Wales the protracted wars against revolutionary and Napoleonic France marked a crucial phase in the evolution of a stronger sense of British identity. Linda Colley has shown that the threat of invasion and the unprecedented degree of recruitment into the armed forces fostered a shared sense of patriotic endeavour and pride in Britain's constitutional monarchy and in her military and naval successes. She has also contended that these developments were by and large the result of popular rather than government-led initiatives.[82] Although the subject has been little studied, it is apparent that such tendencies were also present in

---

[79] Jacqueline Hill, 'National Festivals, the State and "Protestant Ascendancy" in Ireland 1790–1829', *IHS* 24 (1984), 30–51, at 40; *FJ*, 8, 10, 12 Nov. 1806; *FDJ*, 11, 13 Nov. 1806.

[80] Calculated from *The Poll for Electing Two Members . . . 1806*. The stationers' faculty of St Luke's (John Chambers' old guild) also supported Catholic claims, dining with O'Connell in 1812 (*FJ*, 20 Oct. 1812).

[81] Dublin corporation, petition to parliament, Apr. 1805 (*CARD* xv. 405).

[82] Colley, *Britons*, esp. chs. 5–7.

Ireland. Even among Catholics, where popular sympathies might be expected to lie with France, those anxious to secure full political equality could scarcely forbear to use one of the main arguments in favour of emancipation: that Catholics were playing an important part in the British military effort.[83] After the death of Admiral Nelson at the battle of Trafalgar in 1805, the pro-Catholic *Dublin Evening Post* indicated that all the letters it had received on the subject registered warmth for the dead hero. The committee established to erect a monument in Nelson's memory included leading Catholic merchants, such as Randal McDonnell, Denis Thomas O'Brien, and Valentine O'Connor.[84] In the case of the duke of Wellington, it was liberal Protestants and Catholics, including Daniel O'Connell, who, after Wellington's government had granted Catholic emancipation in 1829, kept up the pressure for the completion of the Wellington testimonial, set on foot in 1813.[85]

As far as royalty was concerned, for Catholics George III was the monarch who had approved the virtual dismantling of the penal laws, yet who from the mid-1790s represented a major obstacle to full emancipation; while the prince of Wales, on becoming regent in 1811, disappointed the hopes placed in him by repudiating his youthful Foxite inclinations. But the pro-Catholic press took great interest in the regent's popular daughter and heir, Princess Charlotte, and strongly sided with his wife, Princess Caroline, in her public squabbles with her husband.[86] Nor did Catholics remain entirely aloof from the upsurge of patriotic and monarchical symbols that characterized the war years. The Sons of the Shamrock was a charitable society that prided itself on a membership drawn from all religious persuasions in Ireland. Its feast day was St Patrick's Day. On 17 March 1812 the president of the society, Edmond Jones, expressed his disappointment at the most recent setback to the cause of Catholic emancipation. When a toast to the prince regent was proposed, there was some disapproval—someone suggested cynically that it might as well be drunk to the accompaniment of 'The Protestant Boys'—but this was overruled in favour of the playing of what was becoming known in Britain as 'the

[83] A Catholic freeman of the bricklayers' guild expressed his anger that, having fought under Nelson and others, for which he had been granted the freedom of London, he had been told by an alderman (Charles Thorp) in his native city that he was not entitled to vote in the guild's elections: *FJ*, 2 Nov. 1813. See also Bartlett, *Fall and Rise of the Irish Nation*, 309–10.

[84] *Nelson's Pillar. A Description of the Pillar, with a List of the Subscribers* (Dublin, 1846), 9; Patrick Henchy, 'Nelson's Pillar', *Dublin Hist. Rec.* 10 (1948), 53–63, at 53–4. Watty Cox's *Irish Magazine* may have been untypical in proclaiming its utter indifference to the 'English' victory at Trafalgar (ibid. 59).

[85] P. F. Garnett, 'The Wellington Testimonial', *Dublin Hist. Rec.* 13 (1952), 48–61, at 55–6. In fact, the memorial was still incomplete when Wellington died in 1852.

[86] See *DEP*, 28 Mar. 1812, 30 Mar. 1813, 30 July 1814; below, Ch. 12. For the cults of Charlotte (d. in childbirth, 1817) and Caroline (d. 1821) see Colley, *Britons*, 265–73.

national anthem', 'God Save the King'.[87] In this way, supporters of Catholic emancipation were emulating the radicals campaigning for parliamentary reform in England, whose tactics have been described by Linda Colley: 'Behaving so ostentatiously as loyal Britons was a way of challenging the official description of such activities as seditious.'[88]

But if Catholics were not immune from the patriotic British fervour of these years, it was Protestants who embraced it most fully, and none more than the ultra-Protestant element on Dublin corporation. It was Lord Mayor James Vance, an Orangeman, who convened the meeting to organize a monument to commemorate Nelson's death and victory in 1805; and Nelson's pillar in Dublin, which opened to the public in 1809, was one of the earliest completed monuments to Nelson's memory in the United Kingdom.[89] It was John Giffard, sheriffs' peer, also an Orangeman, who proposed that a jubilee should be held in Dublin in 1809 to mark the onset of George III's fiftieth year on the throne (Giffard managed to convince friends and foes that the very idea for the jubilee, celebrated throughout the United Kingdom and in parts of the empire, had originated with him).[90] Dublin corporation took up the suggestion, and its members organized the event, taking much satisfaction in the fact that Dublin was ahead of London in deciding to mark the occasion. The opposition press, in common with its counterparts in Britain, was at first sceptical, but came round when it transpired that the idea had struck a popular chord.[91] The Dublin celebrations, announced weeks ahead, were to be on an unprecedented scale: all the public buildings and mail coaches decorated with transparencies,[92] a firework display, and a grand ball at the Rotunda.

Inevitably, in view of its inspiration, planning, and execution, the event had a Protestant flavour. Celebrations commenced with a procession of the viceroy and other officials, the corporation, nobility, and gentry, to Christ Church cathedral for a service of thanksgiving. Some 600 attended the dinner at the Rotunda, again, mostly drawn from the official élite, the corporation, nobility, and gentry; very few Catholics were present. To that

---

[87] *DEP*, 26 Mar. 1812. 'God Save the King', first sung publicly in 1745, became popular in Britain in the late 18th c. (Colley, *Britons*, 44, 209). It was beginning to be sung in Dublin by the 1790s (Theatre Royal, *FDJ*, 13 Dec. 1792), and became widely acceptable: in the 1820s liberals welcomed it as a 'non-party' tune (inauguration of new lord mayor, *FJ*, 1 Oct. 1822).

[88] Colley, *Britons*, 337.

[89] Nelson's victory was marked by the singing after Dublin theatre performances of 'Rule Britannia' (1740: became popular in England, Wales, and Scotland in the early 19th. c.: Colley, *Britons*, 338–9). The Dublin monument opened on the anniverary of Nelson's death, 21 Oct. 1809 (*Nelson's Pillar*, 12–14; *CARD*, xv. 438).

[90] The real originator of the jubilee idea—the first such royal event of its kind—was apparently Mrs Biggs, a widow from the Welsh borders (Colley, *Britons*, 217–18), who in 1809 urged the idea on many influential people. For Giffard see *FDJ*, 9 Sept., 28 Oct. 1809, *DEP*, 26 Oct. 1809.

[91] *FDJ*, 14 Sept.– 28 Oct. 1809; *DEP*, 19, 30 Sept., 3, 5, 10, 17, 21, 24, 26, 28, 31 Oct. 1809.   [92] Pictures or other devices created with lights.

extent it was an expression of *ancien-régime* Dublin. However, in claiming that the sponsors intended the event to be exclusive, the opposition press was wide of the mark. Giffard himself had stressed early on that all classes of the king's subjects should join in, and even the *Dublin Evening Post*, a week before the event, was forced to admit that the public was almost completely preoccupied with it.[93] In fact there were plenty of features that transcended a narrow sectarian spirit: the emphasis on promotion of Irish-made goods; the raising of a fund to free debtors and relieve the poor; and, not least, the focus on the king, who was presented as a (non-partisan) paragon of domestic and constitutional virtues. Transparencies showed him surrounded by his wife and (thirteen) children, very much 'The Father of his People'. 'His people' were pre-eminently free: in his realms, ran the message on specially printed 'jubilee ribbands', there were no slaves.[94] All this was meant to explain why, amid the wreck of European monarchies, George III had triumphantly survived; and he was shown presiding over the defeat of French tyranny.

Five years later Giffard was keen to repeat this success by proposing that Dublin should hold a jubilee to celebrate the centenary of the house of Hanover in August 1814.[95] This occasion had the makings of an even greater triumph. Napoleon had been defeated, and it was intended to combine the Hanoverian celebrations with those for peace. But other omens were less favourable. The regent had replaced his father as head of state, and could scarcely be celebrated as a paragon of domestic virtues. The viceroy was absent, owing to a bereavement. The exodus of nobility and gentry from the capital had continued, so that the celebratory dinner was less well attended and less glittering than in 1809. Worse still for the ultra Protestants, although the Catholic question had made little progress, the Orange Order had been forced to answer criticisms about its allegedly conditional loyalty. Still, so long as Orangemen had defenders of the calibre of Chief Secretary Robert Peel, there was little cause for serious concern.[96] As for the festivities themselves, they were not at all negligible; featuring a procession to the cathedral by soldiers, corporation, and guild members, and some 4,000 children from parish and other charitable schools. The prince regent authorized the board of ordnance to make available fireworks on a scale unknown in Ireland, and the corporation had the hedges around St Stephen's Green levelled so that the public might have a better view.[97]

---

[93] *DEP*, 10, 21 Oct. 1809; *FDJ*, 16, 19 Sept. 1809.

[94] *FDJ*, 21, 24, 26 Oct. 1809; *CARD* xvi. 189. There were still slaves in the king's realms, but the slave trade had been abolished in 1807.

[95] *FDJ*, 22 Jan. 1814, and for details, ibid., 26, 28 July, 2, 9, 13, 16 Aug. 1814. For the celebrations in Britain, see Colley, *Britons*, 216.

[96] *FDJ*, 21, 23 July 1814. For the 'conditional' aspect of early Orange loyalty see *Report from the Select Committee [on] Orange Lodges*, 36, 95–7, App. 3, p. 4, HC 1835 (377), xv.

[97] *FDJ*, 9 Aug. 1814; *DEP*, 28 July 1814.

It is worth stressing that while the ultra Protestants were particularly anxious to demonstrate the vitality of Protestant institutions in church and state, these festivities could not have attracted such support had they not also been expressions of civic pride that went beyond any particular group. The politicization of the civic calendar, involving the celebration of royal birthdays and marriages, as well as military victories, had affected urban corporations throughout Britain and Ireland during the eighteenth century. It has been noted that the more successful a town felt itself to be, the more inclined it was to seize on royal anniversaries as an occasion for demonstrating civic achievement.[98] Dublin was no exception to this pattern.

If developments of this kind were fostering a stronger British identity, it should not be supposed that a sense of Irish identity was thereby jettisoned. This was apparent, for instance, in the tributes paid to the then Sir Arthur Wellesley, following his victories against the French in Portugal in 1809. Wellesley had been serving as chief secretary in Ireland since 1807, with periods of leave to take part in the war on the Continent. Along with several other Irish corporations, Dublin presented a congratulatory address to Wellesley, in which much was made of his return to Ireland ('his native country'): this at a time when the common council of London was critical of Wellesley's conduct.[99] Later, in the very address (May 1814) in which St Luke's guild linked the duke's victories with those of 'The Black Prince of England', Wellington was singled out as 'our Illustrious Countryman'. During the jubilee celebrations for George III, depictions of naval and military victories were complemented by figures of Hibernia and Britannia. And in the official ode composed for the occasion, Erin and Albion stood side by side against Gallia.[100]

Did any of this constitute a more positive attitude towards the act of union? It must be re-emphasized that during this period Dublin was not a unionist city. Catholics, disillusioned over the failure of union to bring emancipation, shared the antipathy of Protestants, among whom only a minority could be described as unionists. There is no sign of any significant weakening of regret for the loss of the Irish parliament. However, there can be little doubt that the Continental victories, as well as the cult of monarchy, served as a distraction from its loss. That at any rate was the view of the chief secretary in October 1810, as he strove to contain the Dublin repeal movement: 'Lord Wellington's success has been of great use to us here.'[101]

Moreover, the continual stress on the war effort as one designed to

[98] Rogers, *Whigs and Cities*, 354–8; Colley, *Britons*, 224.
[99] *CARD* xvi. 124–5, 242.
[100] NLI, MS 12127, pp. 15–16; *FDJ*, 26, 28 Oct. 1809.
[101] Pole to Ryder, 20 Oct. 1810, PRONI, Harrowby Papers, T 3228/5/23.

establish liberty as opposed to despotism probably helped to reorient local pride, if not to acceptance of union, at any rate to a greater acceptance of Ireland's partnership in 'the British empire'.[102] The latter was a concept that had come into vogue in Britain only at a time when the American colonies, which gave the term much of its meaning, were on the point of being lost. In Ireland, during the 1780s and 1790s, most Patriots had taken it for granted that for 'the British empire' to flourish the Irish parliament must retain its independence.[103] By 1814, the union notwithstanding, there was a greater sense that the empire was something to take pride in. After all, what had produced the vaunted 'British' victories if not the combined efforts of soldiers and sailors from all the king's dominions? The corporation's granting of honorary freedoms during the war years illustrates the point. Of five generals and admirals who were granted honorary freedom at the Michaelmas assembly in 1806,[104] Sir David Baird was a Scot; William Carr Beresford was Irish; Sir John Stuart was an American loyalist; and Sir Home Rigg Popham had been born in Morocco, where his father was consul. Only Sir Samuel Hood was English.

---

[102] For the popularizing of the term in Britain, see Richard Koebner, *Empire*, Universal Library edn. (New York, 1965), 234–7.   [103] Ibid. ch. 6.
[104] *CARD* xv. 488. See also *DNB*.

PART 3

From Patriots to Unionists, 1815–1840

Introduction

The main event of this period was the remarkable turn taken by the Catholic emancipation campaign in the 1820s, notably the mobilization of Catholics to vote for emancipation candidates, regardless of their landlords' politics. By 1829 the ensuing electoral successes had induced government to give way.[1] The Dublin corporate bodies had, in general, shown no inclination to back calls for emancipation; but even if they had been more favourably disposed, the tactics of the 1820s, which saw the emergence of the Catholic Association as a powerful body drawing in the masses, would have offended their sense of proper political procedures. As it was, the battle lines in the city were already drawn at the start of the decade, symbolized by a highly contentious by-election in 1820.

Once the issue was resolved, however, with Catholics entitled to sit in parliament and to enter all but a handful of government posts, many Protestants hoped for a new start, and especially for a respite from agitation. After all, its supporters had argued that emancipation would take the Catholic question out of politics. No doubt that was an unrealistic prospect. The events of the 1790s had shown that in the absence of reform, mere legal entitlements did not necessarily enable Catholics to exercise political rights. But what disturbed even those Protestants who had supported emancipation was the fact that the Catholic leader, Daniel O'Connell, went straight on to outline a reform programme that included repeal of the union, without waiting to test the reaction of his former Protestant supporters. The subsequent loss of much Protestant support for reform during the 1830s meant that post-emancipation Irish politics became more, rather than less, divided on sectarian lines. For emancipation had been granted without any of the usual safeguards, such as a veto over key church appointments, which might reassure Protestants that their own constitutional rights were secure. As Catholics exulted in their achievements and in their numbers, among Protestants a sense of seige—never entirely absent—was heightened. It became more, rather than less common, to seek religious explanations for the rapid political flux.

Dublin corporation had petitioned against further concessions to Catholics, but both the corporation and the guilds contained sizeable minorities that took the Catholic side. Moreover, in the immediate aftermath of emancipation, when the issue of parliamentary reform took

---

[1] Catholic relief act, 10 Geo. IV, c. 7 ('Catholic emancipation').

centre stage, some 40 per cent of the Dublin freemen voted for reform candidates to represent the city in parliament.[2] But the freemen's willingness to vote for reforming candidates was severely dented by O'Connell's decision in 1832 to stand himself as a candidate for Dublin on a repeal platform, and the tendency to align behind Conservative candidates grew even stronger as the decade progressed. Paradoxically, there can be little doubt that O'Connell's decision to contest the Dublin seat as a repealer was taken partly in the knowledge that there was still considerable antipathy to the union among the Dublin freemen. That antipathy was real; but the emergence of repeal as a serious political issue under Catholic auspices effectively put paid to the freemen's willingness to oppose the union publicly. Nevertheless, it was to take the protracted battle over municipal reform in the later 1830s to draw Dublin corporation towards a more positive unionist position.

[2] Below, Ch. 13.

11

The Economic and Social Background, 1815–1840

I. The Dublin Economy

In certain respects, this twenty-five year period was the most difficult and traumatic of the entire nineteenth century. More extensive poverty, and larger numbers living in deplorable housing conditions may have been present later in the century,[1] but it was in these decades that the reality of the decay of Dublin's eighteenth-century industrial economy became generally apparent, setting off a wide-ranging debate about causes and remedies. A spirit of enterprise was not lacking, but some of its most characteristic offshoots, such as developments in steam navigation and the commencement of railway building, were more likely to have contributed to the cause of industrial decline than its cure. For it was during this period that improvements in communications helped to bring Ireland (particularly the eastern parts of the country) more closely into the orbit of the British economy, thereby not merely intensifying the challenge of competition but exposing Dublin to the cyclical pattern of boom and slump that emerged in post-war industrial Britain.

By the time of the 1841 census Dublin had ceased to be 'the second city of the empire', having been overtaken by Glasgow and Liverpool; two decades later Dublin ranked only fifth in a league of United Kingdom cities.[2] Although the population continued to grow, its relative size declined, even within Ireland. Belfast did not overtake Dublin until the end of the century, but already during this period the northern city was becoming an important regional capital, thanks largely to the linen industry, now concentrating in that area and being transformed by factory production. Dublin's share of linen exports was already declining in the later eighteenth century, but still made up almost half the total as late as 1816. By 1828, however, the Dublin linen hall off North King Street had ceased to be used as a market.[3]

At the same time, Dublin's status as a financial centre was being

---

[1] Mary E. Daly, *Dublin the Deposed Capital: A Social and Economic History 1860–1914* (Cork, 1985), chs. 4, 9.
[2] Fergus D'Arcy, 'An Age of Distress and Reform: 1800–1860', in Art Cosgrove (ed.), *Dublin Through the Ages* (Dublin, 1988), 93–112, at 98. See also map 4 above.
[3] Maxwell, *Dublin Under the Georges*, 218.

undermined, for provincial wholesalers were bypassing Dublin merchants and dealing directly with British manufacturers. Provincial banks sprang up following an act of 1821 that modified the Bank of Ireland's powers,[4] and by contrast with the role of the Bank of England in the English provinces, the Bank of Ireland remained a predominantly Dublin bank.

The city might have taken these setbacks in its stride, had manufacturing industry held up, or even maintained the slow pace of decline of the previous quarter-century. In the woollen industry, for instance, between 1800 and 1822 the number of master-manufacturers fell by half, yet employment declined only by just over a quarter. But after the war there occurred a series of economic depressions: 1815–17, 1822, 1825–6, and the worst of the entire century, 1838–42, which had a devasting effect on certain branches of Dublin's textile industries. Most of these depressions were set off by slumps in Britain, and the later ones were exacerbated by the ending of protective duties after 1824. During the 1825 slump, English woollens were dumped on the Irish market at rock-bottom prices. Imports of woollen cloth doubled within ten years, and by 1838, on the eve of the next severe depression, the Irish woollen industry was supplying only 14 per cent of the Irish market. The value of cloth production in the Dublin area fell by more than half between 1822 and 1837.[5] By the time of the 1841 census, just over 200 people were returned as working in the woollen trades, with a further 600 describing themselves as winders, warpers, and weavers without specifying any particular branch of trade; half a century earlier the industry had provided work for about 5,000.[6]

The pattern was very similar in the silk industry, save that specialization in branches such as poplin and tabinet helped to maintain some investment and an export trade into the second half of the century. The 1841 census recorded fewer than 600 people in the various branches of the industry, which represented a drop of some 3,000 since 1815.[7] The travel writers, Mr and Mrs Hall, found some 600–700 silk weavers in Dublin in the early 1840s, mostly heads of families earning 10–25s. a week. The Halls were enthusiastic about the firm of Atkinson in College Green, which had introduced Jacquard looms and was employing up to 200 people in the manufacture of poplin, mostly for export to England and Scotland.[8] But the

---

[4] 1 & 2 Geo. IV, c. 72; Dickson, 'The Place of Dublin', 188.

[5] Evidence of Mr Willans, woollen manufacturer of Dublin and Leeds, in *Second Report of the Commissioners [on] . . . a General System of Railways for Ireland*, 7–8, HC 1837–8, xxxv. See also David O'Toole, 'The Employment Crisis of 1826', in Dickson (ed.), *The Gorgeous Mask*, 157–71.

[6] Warburton, Whitelaw, Walsh, *History of the City of Dublin*, ii. 983; *Census of Ireland . . . 1841*, City of Dublin, table vi, 22, HC 1843, xxiv.

[7] 'Silk trade', *FJ*, 23 May 1815; *Census of Ireland . . . 1841*, City of Dublin, table vi, p. 22, HC 1843, xxiv.

[8] S. C. and A. M. Hall, *Ireland: Its Scenery, Character, etc.* (3 vols.; London, 1841–3), ii. 330–1.

scope for such initiatives in the silk industry was limited. Dublin's aristocratic clientele was by now much depleted; silks had long gone out of fashion for formal occasions; and the industry was exposed to British and Continental competition after the end of protection in 1824.

Neither the linen nor the cotton industry proved able to fill the employment gap left by the decline in wool and silk. Linen weaving had never been extensive in Dublin, and was affected by the general propensity from the 1820s onwards for the industry to concentrate in the Belfast area. As for cotton, although the export of calicoes (mainly to America) held up well, and investment continued, the total number of factories had declined by 1839. In the Pim's Harold's Cross mill power looms were installed during the 1830s, but by 1839 the labour force of spinners and weavers had been reduced from some 300 to around 100. It was a sign of Dublin's relative backwardness that in 1836 only one-fifth of the steam engines in use in Ireland were in Dublin; Belfast boasted one-third.[9]

These contractions in the textile trades had repercussions for the entire labour market. The failure of the cotton industry to maintain its early promise meant less work for cotton spinners. And changing fashions and the reduction in aristocratic custom undermined employment in a range of subsidiary textile trades that had traditionally given work to women, as ribbon-weavers, embroiderers, lace-workers, and makers of silk stockings. Textile workers comprised by far the most numerous element among the artisans admitted to the Mendicity Institution in the mid-1820s.[10]

In the face of these recurring difficulties many manufacturers went out of business. With prices falling, those who remained had little choice but to reduce wages or employ even more cheap, rural, or unskilled labour. The Dublin journeymen, increasingly well organized—by 1840 at least thirty-nine separate trades had journeymen's organizations, or unions—resisted these changes; and during the 1820s and 1830s the city became notorious for labour troubles, as the unions pursued their aims of limiting apprentices, making union membership compulsory, and obtaining a minimum wage. Employers and other workers were intimidated, sometimes with violence, and certain employers began to carry arms. Not until the early 1840s, when concerted efforts were made to promote the consumption of Irish manufactures, and the repeal campaign was revived, did labour violence die down, as the trade-unionists returned to earlier practices of appealing for support to public opinion.[11]

[9] Harrison, 'Dublin Quakers in Business', ii. 405–8; T. W. Freeman, *Pre-Famine Ireland: A Study in Historical Geography* (Manchester, 1957), 91.

[10] 'Public Distress', *FJ*, 3 Jan. 1822; *Poor Inquiry (Ireland)*, app. C, pt. II, Report on the City of Dublin, 35–6, HC 1836. xxx.

[11] F. A. D'Arcy, 'Dublin Artisan Activity, Opinion and Organisation, 1820–1850', MA thesis (NUI (UCD), 1968), 2; id., 'The Artisans of Dublin and Daniel O'Connell', 240–1.

The spread of labour organizations represented one response on the part of journeymen to declining living standards and rising unemployment. Emigration also increased. In the silk industry this had begun as early as the 1780s; there were high levels again from 1815 onwards. At times of acute distress—bread prices reached uprecedented heights in 1817–18—artisans appealed for relief to the corporation, or the Castle, or the general public. In 1817 the government made relief funds available, both for Ireland and Britain. But none of this, nor the establishment of *ad-hoc* relief committees (some highly organized—unemployment registers were kept by certain parish relief committees in 1817) was adequate to meet the scale of the problem in the post-war period. Nor could the burgeoning charitable institutions, most of them, such as the Molyneux Asylum (1815), and the Mendicity Institution (1818), established by private initiative, cope with the scale of poverty and distress.[12] By the 1830s proposals for the establishment of a state system of poor relief were being widely canvassed, and (although the scheme itself was highly controversial) in 1838 the new centralized system of English poor law, based on workhouse relief, was extended to Ireland.[13]

During this period, too, population growth and migration were compounding problems of overcrowding in several of the poorer areas of Dublin. The 1841 census revealed that almost half (46.8%) of all Dublin families lived in the fourth or lowest class of accommodation (mostly crowded into single rooms in tenement buildings) while a further 24.8 per cent lived in third-class accommodation, consisting of houses with two to four rooms. The degree of congestion in certain parishes, such as St Michan's, exceeded that in the most congested parts of London.[14]

In this harsh economic climate numerous remedies were proposed, from the establishment of savings banks to the reduction of taxes. But of all the panaceas the most popular was that known by the 1840s as the 'Irish manufacture' movement. Efforts to induce the public to buy Irish-made goods in preference to cheaper but imported (which in practice usually meant British) products went back to the early eighteenth century, when Swift had taken up the cause.[15] In those days, textiles were the main targets for such campaigns. The guilds and the city corporation, whose very ethos was the protection of Irish goods, had lent support.[16] The king's jubilee of 1809 had seen more publicity for the cause. By this time, industries other than textiles were experiencing difficulties; the printing, cutlery, jewellery,

---

[12] *FJ*, 24, 28 Dec. 1816, 9 Jan., 3 May 1817; Lewis, *History and Topography of Dublin*, 153–5; Vaughan (ed.), *NHI* v. 136.   [13] 1 & 2 Vict., c. 56.

[14] D'Arcy, 'An Age of Distress and Reform', 102.

[15] Jonathan Swift, *A Proposal for the Universal Use of Irish Manufacture* (Dublin, 1720).

[16] Above, ch. 6; DPLGC, MS 79, fo. 314.

and coach-building trades were all facing competition from British imports.[17]

In 1810, with unemployment in the Liberties rife, and support for repeal of the union growing, workers in the woollen industry appealed to the public to give a preference to Irish goods, and recommended that non-consumption agreements, as in the 1770s and 1780s, be resumed. Dublin corporation was not unsympathetic. But the Irish manufacture resolutions of the aldermen, endorsed by the city commons, were loosely worded, and fell well short of non-consumption commitments. Moreover, while the hosiers' guild explicitly endorsed Irish manufacture as well as repeal, other pro-repeal guilds were slower to link the two issues. For the guilds were less closely identified with manufacturing than in the past—merchants and retailers had grown in numbers and importance—and it was the working classes, notably cutlers, Liberty weavers, and woollen workers, who showed the greatest commitment to the cause.[18]

If Protestant employers, as represented by the corporation and guilds, were growing less warm in support of Irish manufacture, the cause had obvious populist appeal in Dublin; and this was recognized early on by O'Connell, who in 1813 induced the Catholic Board to support the principle.[19] Much later, in 1840–1, a full-scale Irish manufacture movement grew up during a particularly severe industrial depression exacerbated by harvest failure. In the autumn of 1840 Fr. Matthew Flanagan, parish priest of St Nicholas Without, set up a board of trade, with provision for representation from employers, workers, and consumers. The board administered a pledge to consume Irish manufactures, a precedent that was followed in several towns in Leinster and Munster. Markets were organized for the exclusive sale of Irish-made goods. For a short time the movement obtained a very positive response, and achieved some success in creating employment. In order to win the widest possible support, topics of a political or religious nature were excluded, and at first the board proved capable of attracting Protestant artisans, despite the fact that it was led by a Catholic priest. But as it emerged that the movement had no effective strategies for dealing with the underlying problems of the economy—lack of risk capital and a largely unskilled labour force—support declined and the call for repeal once again came to the fore. In the autumn of 1841 O'Connell took steps to bring what was left of the movement under the umbrella of repeal. By now Protestant tradesmen were wary of repeal

[17] Richard Cargill Cole, *Irish Booksellers and English Writers 1740–1800* (London, 1986), 148–55; *FJ*, 31 Oct. 1810.

[18] *FJ*, 12, 13 July, 4 Oct. 1810; *CARD* xvi. 225–6. For the hosiers, see *FJ*, 29 Aug. 1810; for other guilds that supported repeal see above, Ch. 10.

[19] *FJ*, 6, 12 July 1813.

because of its O'Connellite and Catholic overtones, and this development effectively put an end to co-operation from them.[20]

Not all Dublin industries fared badly during these years. As in the wartime period, there was still much work for the building industry. The growing confidence of the Catholic community began to be expressed in church building in the 1810s and 1820s, producing St Michan's (1811–14), the Pro-Cathedral (1815), and the Carmelite church in Whitefriar Street (1825). After Catholic emancipation, church building really took off: churches dating from the 1830s included St Andrew's, Westland Row; the Franciscan church, Merchant's Quay; St Paul's, Arran Quay, and the Jesuit church in Upper Gardiner Street. Members of the Church of Ireland, their numbers already declining, did not require new churches, except where migration was taking place towards the edge of the city and the suburbs; but most of the existing city churches were extensively repaired in the 1830s with money from the ecclesiastical commissioners. Methodist chapels, too, were springing up during this period, including those in Cork Street, Abbey Street, and Langrishe Place.[21]

Other building enterprises included new docks and warehouses for Dublin port in the 1820s, though not before the dangers of Dublin Bay had prompted merchants to explore alternative port facilities at Dun Laoghaire (renamed Kingstown after George IV's visit in 1821), some 5 miles to the south east. Extensive new wharfs, piers, and quays were constructed there between 1816 and 1820, and Kingstown became the destination for the mail packet service from Holyhead and Liverpool. But by that time the silting problems of Dublin port itself had been overcome, and despite the gloomy forecasts of the chamber of commerce, Dublin was still Ireland's greatest port, although with a considerable excess of imports over exports. In 1824 the Dublin and Liverpool Steam Navigation Company, established with Irish Quaker capital, was set up to operate the Dublin–Liverpool route, producing a dramatic fall in the journey time from several days for sailing vessels to 14 hours.[22] In the short term these initiatives made industrial problems worse, by facilitating the import of British goods: but even in this period there were Irish industries, such as Guinness's, that took advantage of improved communications to increase their exports to Britain. The period of most spectacular development for Guinness's still lay ahead, for despite growing sales in Britain and in the rest of Ireland, the Dublin market (where the bulk of sales still took place) was depressed, and total output did not recover to pre-1816 levels until 1833.[23]

[20] A valuable short study is C. D. A. Leighton, *The Irish Manufacture Movement 1840–1843* (Maynooth Historical Series, 7; Maynooth, 1987).

[21] See Lewis, *History and Topography of Dublin*, 127–45.

[22] Ibid. 80–3, 186–8; Report of the Council of the Chamber of Commerce of Dublin (4 Dec. 1821), NA, 1064/1/1, 17–18; Harrison, 'Dublin Quakers in Business', i. 183–4. The Quaker company amalgamated with the City of Dublin Steam Packet Company in 1825 (ibid. i. 184).

[23] Lynch and Vaizey, *Guinness's Brewery*, 124, 260 (appendix).

Railway transport, too, began in the 1830s; the first line, linking Dublin and Kingstown, opened in 1834. It was soon carrying some 4,000 passengers a day. Construction of railway stations resulted in more work for the building industry. There were also signs of new industrial development in the gas works, chemical works, and coach works (to supply the Dublin to Kingstown line), situated near the south quays, and other small factories scattered through the city, including vinegar works, chemical works, breweries, and glass factories. In other words, despite the prevailing picture of distress and depression, stemming from the decline of Dublin's eighteenth-century industrial base, the foundations were being laid in this period for future growth.[24]

Finally, Dublin in the early nineteenth century was becoming more dependent on rural Ireland. In part, this was owing to immigration from the countryside. By 1841 over a quarter of Dublin residents had been born outside the city or county, and the proportion was growing. Newcomers tended to congregate in the western areas of the city, often moving in as longer-established and better-off residents moved to the more fashionable eastern side. To service these new residents, supplies of turf for fuel—coal was notoriously expensive—began to be imported at the end of the eighteenth century via the two great canals that linked Dublin with the midlands.[25] At the same time, as aristocratic customers dwindled, Dubliners became more aware of the capital's economic dependence on the rest of Ireland, and, in particular, on the prosperity of Irish farmers. In 1815, an impassioned speech to the city commons by Thomas Abbott, silk manufacturer, helped persuade the corporation to moderate its opposition to the corn laws, in the interests of Irish farmers. Farmers, manufacturers, and tradesmen, Abbott argued, were all links in one chain.[26]

II. Social Developments

Eighteenth-century Dublin, like the rest of Irish society, had been dominated by the aristocracy. The fact that Dublin was a great commercial and industrial city, in which contemporaries could speak of 'these commercial, manufacturing and enlightened times',[27] had proved perfectly compatible with aristocratic pre-eminence, even in the regulation of trade, industry, and banking. Aristocrats and gentry headed the list of trustees of the linen manufacture. They superintended the Irish silk warehouse in Parliament Street and were prominent members of the Dublin Society. They rubbed shoulders with merchants in masonic lodges,[28] and became honorary

---

[24] Freeman, *Pre-Famine Ireland*, 165.
[25] Daly, *Dublin the Deposed Capital*, 4; Dickson, 'The Place of Dublin', 186.
[26] *FJ*, 11 Mar. 1815. By 1839 the corporation was opposed to repeal of the corn laws (*CARD* xvii. 61; xix. 371).   [27] McDowell, *Ireland in the Age of Imperialism*, 62.
[28] Terence de Vere White, 'The Freemasons', in T. D. Williams (ed.), *Secret Societies in Ireland* (Dublin, 1973), 46–57, at 48–9.

members of guilds. On the political front, they had thrown themselves into reforming clubs and societies. In 1784 the congress that adopted resolutions in favour of parliamentary reform included a peer, several baronets, and other members of the gentry. The Dublin Society of United Irishmen was under the chairmanship of a peer's brother in 1791. Such importance was attached to their support for the Patriot interest that the representation of Dublin city in parliament in the 1770s and again in the 1790s had fallen to members of the titled Fitzgerald family, whose head was the duke of Leinster. This was not something unique to Dublin or Ireland, but could be matched in Britain and elsewhere.

The social domination of Dublin by the aristocracy did not come to an abrupt end with the transfer of parliamentary representation to London after the union. In the immediate post-union period there were newly ennobled peers who owed their titles to support for government over the union, and who were not entitled to sit in parliament. The exodus was a gradual one, becoming really marked only after the end of the war in 1815, by which time the relative cost of living in Dublin was rising. By the 1820s the aristocratic presence in the capital had dwindled to insignificance (although most of the peers and gentry had removed not to London but to their estates elsewhere in Ireland). The number of resident peers dropped from 249 before the union to thirty-four by 1821, while of 300 MPs with town houses before 1800 only five remained by 1821.[29]

This withdrawal had far-reaching consequences for Dublin. As the aristocracy departed, their place at Castle balls and levees was taken by merchants and the professional classes, who now emerged as the tone-setters for Dublin society. (At first, this meant Protestants: Catholics were rarely invited to Castle functions before the 1820s.) The number of merchants recorded in Dublin *Directories* increased from 840 in 1752 to nearly 5,000 in 1815; and by 1841 there were some 700 medical practitioners and almost 2,000 lawyers in the city.[30] Shortly after the end of the war the social effects of these changes were commented on. The relish for public amusement had diminished; only one theatre remained operational; and the propensity for gambling had declined—even in domestic circles, apparently, the card-table rarely made an appearance: 'The character of the people of Dublin seems to have undergone a complete change. It was once gay, convivial, and in some degree dissipated; it is now more serious, prudent, and religious; but it still maintains its reputation for unfeigned benevolence and genuine charity.'[31]

[29] 'The Union' (*FJ*, 24 Jan. 1817); Craig, *Dublin 1660–1860*, 274; Maxwell, *Dublin Under the Georges*, 113.

[30] Rosemary ffolliott and Donal F. Begley, 'Guide to Irish Directories', in Donal F. Begley, *Irish Genealogy: A Record Finder* (Dublin, 1981), 75–106, at 77.

[31] Warburton, Whitelaw, Walsh, *History of the City of Dublin*, ii. 1169.

Other changes of a related kind were taking place. The yeomanry were disbanded and the military presence was greatly reduced. There was less crime in the city, the 1808 police act having increased the size of the watch by half, leaving Dublin far more heavily policed than London. From 1825 the streets were better lit, after two companies obtained permission to provide gas lighting for the city. The prostitutes, whom Philip Luckombe had found so ubiquitous in 1779, had lost their aristocratic clientele and were more or less confined to the quays leading from the barracks to the city centre. And the sedan chairs, so much a part of aristocratic Dublin, had disappeared by the 1820s.[32]

This was a city in which organized attempts to reform religion and manners, which had sprung up from time to time since the late seventeenth century, could at last find a more congenial atmosphere. The aims of organizations such as the Association for Discountenancing Vice[33] had received the weighty endorsement of Edmund Burke, who was to assert in 1796 that manners were more important than laws. But it was not until the 1820s and 1830s, when the peers themselves had virtually disappeared from Dublin but their values still showed signs of persisting, that a new round of moral campaigns was launched: to abolish duelling, to end cruelty to animals, and greatest of all, to promote temperance.[34]

If religion was taken more seriously in early nineteenth-century Dublin, this was not simply because middle-class values had risen to the surface, nor because of the post-war retreat into religious orthodoxy. It was also a reflection of the fact that the old relations between Protestants and Catholics were breaking down, and it was not yet clear what would replace them. Eighteenth-century Dublin had been a Protestant city, less because of numbers—although at the beginning of the century the balance was on the Protestant side—than because it was dominated by the mainly Protestant aristocracy and gentry, by the Protestant corporation and guilds, and by Protestant churches: at least, those that were in the public eye were Protestant: for reasons of prudence, Catholic chapels had kept to alleys and back lanes.[35] In 1815, despite the relaxation of most of the penal laws, this world was still virtually intact. There were scarcely any Catholics in government posts, few in the guilds, none on Dublin corporation, and less than 10 per cent among the Dublin voters.[36] Nevertheless, the legal basis for

---

[32] D. A. Chart, *Ireland from the Union to Catholic Emancipation* (London, 1910), 294–6; Luckombe, *A Tour Through Ireland*, 15–16, 18.

[33] Above, Ch. 8.

[34] J. B. M'Crea, *Duelling: Being the Enlargement of a Discourse on a Late Fatal Event* (Dublin, 1830); Shevawn Lynam, *Humanity Dick Martin 'King of Connemara' 1754–1834* (Dublin, 1989); Elizabeth Malcolm, *'Ireland Sober, Ireland Free': Drink and Temperance in Nineteenth-Century Ireland* (Dublin, 1986), ch. 2.

[35] Nuala Burke, ' "A Hidden Church?" The Structure of Catholic Dublin in the Mid-Eighteenth Century', *Arch. Hib.* 32 (1974), 81–92.   [36] Below, Ch. 12.

Protestant ascendancy had been largely removed, and governments had been forced to take the question of numbers more seriously during the unprecedented wartime mobilization. One sign of this was the introduction of an official census of population.

In Ireland, once numbers began to assume political importance there was bound to be a heightened interest in the relative weight of Protestants and Catholics. Although religious affiliation was not brought within the scope of the official census for several decades, certain contemporaries attempted estimates. In 1798 the Reverend James Whitelaw, rector of St Catherine's parish, undertook a census of Dublin that is still considered generally reliable. To his disappointment he was unable to conduct a religious census beyond his own parish, finding this a matter of 'extreme delicacy' in such troubled times.[37] In 1804 Thomas Newenham gave his view that Protestants made up about two-fifths of Dublin city's population; if so, they numbered *c*.72,000.[38] This was almost certainly too high (as he conceded); a more realistic estimate for 1814 put the Protestant proportion at about one-third, *c*.60,200. The commissioners of public instruction in 1835 calculated the Protestant numbers to be 66,211 (26.4%); this figure also was too high, since it included a small, disproportionately Protestant suburban element. The first official census to include religious affiliation in 1861 showed that Dublin city, excluding suburbs, contained 58,259 Protestants (22.9%).[39]

Dublin's Protestant community in this period, therefore, was declining from its eighteenth-century peak,[40] but numbers had not yet dropped by very much. In denominational terms, this was still an overwhelmingly Church of Ireland population. The commissioners of public instruction in 1835 underestimated the number of dissenters in their conclusion that 94.8 per cent of Dublin Protestants belonged to the established church, but another estimate put the proportion of dissenters at only some 4 per cent (about 8,000) of the total Dublin population in the early nineteenth century.[41] From 1841 onwards the census contained data about occupation, and from 1871 that data was also broken down by religious affiliation. Although they belong to a period some decades after the period in question here, the 1871 figures are of some interest in revealing that nearly one-third (31.8%) of Dublin Protestant males worked in public service and professional occupations, and over one-quarter (27.1%) in skilled trades. A further 12.1 per cent were engaged in dealing and retailing; 4.5 per cent

---

[37] Fagan, 'The Population of Dublin', 146.

[38] Thomas Newenham, *A Statistical and Historical Inquiry into the Progress and Magnitude of the Population of Ireland* (London, 1805), 305.

[39] Fagan, 'The Population of Dublin', 147; W. E. Vaughan and A. J. Fitzpatrick, *Irish Historical Statistics: Population, 1821–1971* (Dublin, 1978), 51.

[40] See above, Ch. 7.   [41] Fagan, 'The Population of Dublin', 147 n. 102.

were domestic servants. Even in the 1870s, then, there was still a significant artisan element in the Protestant community. In the pre-famine period it was probably even greater.[42] As for the employer class, one contemporary asserted in 1846 that 'it was a notorious fact that the employers of Dublin were for the most part Protestants'.[43]

Protestant tradesmen, shopkeepers, and merchants suffered from the same economic difficulties that affected Dublin in general during the post-war period. The condition of the silk-weavers, for instance—a trade strongly identified with Protestants—was noted by a parliamentary com-missioner: 'a body of able and skilful tradesmen with large families looking to them for support . . . reduced to the necessity of depending for their supply of the necessaries of life on the bounty of their friends, or on the unprofitable charity of the public'.[44] But in the severe depression of 1838–42 the Protestant gentry displayed little concern for the tradesmen's plight, and by 1840 a section of the Protestant community had begun to perceive itself in class terms, as the 'operatives', who were prepared to organize separately from members of other classes, and to take part in the Irish manufacture movement alongside Catholics—at least until the movement was brought under the umbrella of O'Connellite repeal.[45]

III. The Freemen and the Guilds

The relief act of 1793 had brought no real change to the composition of the Dublin freeman body, which remained (with a handful of exceptions) exclusively Protestant, though not exclusively Anglican. Few of the Catholics admitted to the guilds immediately after the act survived to see the return of peace. In St Luke's guild only five of the ten Catholic freemen were still on the guild books in 1810. The counter-revolutionary climate from the mid-1790s militated against further Catholic admissions, though towards the end of the war John Giffard began to utter warnings on the subject again.[46] In any case, Dublin corporation did not admit Catholics to civic freedom. After the war a precedent was set when O'Connell secured a writ of mandamus to compel the corporation to admit to civic freedom John Cole, a hosier who possessed the necessary qualifications. Following the contentious 1820 by-election, Catholics were urged to follow this example and obtain parliamentary votes. But the cost of resorting to law; the fact that few Catholics could qualify by birth or service; and the difficulty of

---

[42] Hill, 'Artisans, Sectarianism and Politics in Dublin', 14.

[43] Thomas Arkins, a Catholic master tailor, quoted in F. A. D'Arcy, 'The Trade Unions of Dublin and the Attempted Revival of the Guilds', *JRSAI* 101 (1971), 113–27, at 120.

[44] Hill, 'Artisans, Sectarianism and Politics in Dublin', 16.

[45] For discussion of religion, class, and the Irish manufacture movement, see Leighton, *The Irish Manufacture Movement*, 20–1, 25–32.

[46] NLI, MS 12126, pp. 252–8; corporation meeting (*FDJ*, 22 Jan. 1814).

establishing a right of admission all combined to mean that such action was open to very few.[47]

An estimate by parliamentary commissioners of total freemen numbers in 1830 put the number of freemen at about 3,500, of which it was thought that perhaps 1,000 (or 28%) lived beyond a 7-mile radius of the city centre. Both the total and the non-resident element seem on the high side: the commissioners had had to estimate the numbers for four guilds, the weavers, tanners, glovers, and coopers, and the real total was probably between 3,000 and 3,500.[48] Non-residents at this period fell into several distinct categories. There were Dublin tradesmen or merchants who had migrated or retired out of the city, often to the suburbs. Others had been admitted as the sons of freemen: they might or might not follow their guild's trades, and might or might not be Dublin residents. Then there were the strictly honorary freemen, who had been admitted because the guilds wished to distinguish them. The new rules of 1672 had stipulated that freemen should be resident 'for the most part';[49] and in practice, it seems, most of those who actually voted in Dublin elections were residents. A sample of the freemen who voted at the 1820 by-election suggests that 86 per cent were residents of the city, 4 per cent lived in the suburbs and County Dublin, and only 10 per cent lived elsewhere.[50]

Until the 1832 reform act,[51] which made £10 householders eligible for the vote, the freemen constituted the great majority of the Dublin city electorate. Exact figures are not available, but poll book data for the 1806 and 1820 elections indicates that freemen represented respectively 85.2 and 89.6 per cent of those who voted.[52] Shortly after the reform act, which required all voters to be registered and to reside within 7 statute miles of the usual place of election, the number of registered freemen dropped to just under 2,000, or 28.1 per cent of the newly enlarged electorate. By 1841, when 3,121 freemen were registered, their proportion of the electorate had fallen to 25.4 per cent.[53]

[47] For the Cole case, see FJ, 28 Jan. 1818; for the right of admission issue see Rex v. Corporation of Dublin, in Espine Batty (ed.), Reports of Cases Argued and Determined in the Court of King's Bench in Ireland from ... 1825 to 1826 (Dublin, 1828), 628–39. Three Catholics gained admission to the smiths' guild by mandamus (Municipal Corporations (Ireland), app. to report on the city of Dublin, pt. II, p. 279, HC 1836, xxiv).
[48] Parliamentary Representation, Ireland (Boundary Reports). Report on the County of the City of Dublin, 52, HC 1831–2 (519), xliii.   [49] CARD i. 64.
[50] Sample based on 1 in 8 names of the freemen voters for both candidates in the election, giving a sample of 235 out of a gross poll of 1,879 (12.5%). Source: F. O'Neill, The Stain Removed, and Corporation Juggling Explained. Being an Alphabetical List of the Freemen & Freeholders of the City of Dublin ... Who Voted at the Late Election ([Dublin], 1820).
[51] Representation of the people (Ireland) act (1832), 2 & 3 Will. IV, c. 88.
[52] Calculated from The Poll for Electing Two Members to Represent the City of Dublin in ... Parliament ... 1806 (Dublin, n.d.); O'Neill, The Stain Removed.
[53] A Return of the Electors Registered in ... Ireland, County of the city of Dublin, 8, HC 1833 (177), xxvii; Returns of the Number of Electors . . . Qualified to Vote at Any Election . . . Before the 1st of May 1841, 7, HC 1841 (108), xx. See also below, Ch. 14.

For the guilds themselves, the post-war period was a very difficult one. Admission costs were high (partly because of government stamp duties) and freemen became still more reluctant to pay quarterage fees.[54] Even in this period, guild records show the occasional admission of a quarter brother,[55] but quarterage payments no longer had any commercial relevance. However, they did represent a principal source of guild income, all the more important at a time when there were unprecedented demands for charitable relief from freemen and their dependents. A small but significant number of freemen emigrated.[56] The link with trade was further eroded, partly because of the continued admission of those who did not follow the guilds' trades, but also because the depressed state of the economy forced freemen to take up other work. By 1833 the bricklayers' guild, most of whose members had followed the trade in 1813, contained only a minority (21.1%) who were doing so, though a further 16.3 per cent were qualified, but had emigrated or were in other employment.[57]

Another way of measuring the link with trade is to consider the guild representatives on the city commons. Technically (under the 1760 reform act) they were supposed to be following their guilds' trades, but the erosion of this principle was already underway by the 1790s,[58] and the process, though still a slow one, went further in this period (Table 11.1).

Down to the eve of municipal reform in 1840 certain guilds were exemplary in selecting only members following the appropriate trades to

TABLE 11.1. *Occupations of craft guild representatives, Dublin city commons, in selected years*

	1818		1828		1838	
	No.	%	No.	%	No.	%
Following guild's trades	40	61.5	34	52.3	32	49.2
Allied trades	7	10.8	8	12.3	5	7.7
Other trades	5	7.7	5	7.7	8	12.3
Professions, salaried	2	3.1	4	6.2	7	10.8
Unidentified	11	16.9	14	21.5	13	20.0
TOTAL	65	100.0	65	100.0	65	100.0

Source: Dublin *Directories*, 1818–38.

[54] See e.g. NLI, MS 12127, pp. 48–51; NLI, MS 80, pp. 149–51, 153–4; DCA, G3/1, p. 402.

[55] NLI, MS 12127, p. 14.

[56] Of the 200 freemen of St Luke's guild in 1825, fourteen (7%) were recorded as being in England or America (ibid. 260–7).

[57] *Municipal Corporations (Ireland)*, app. to report on the city of Dublin, pt. II, p. 279, HC 1836, xxiv.

[58] *Third Report from the Select Committee on Fictitious Votes (Ireland)*, 57, HC 1837 (480), xi, pt. II. See also above, Ch. 7, Table 7.4.

represent them. These included the saddlers, whose control over the trade at least until the 1790s has already been noted, and the apothecaries (John Giffard's guild). St Luke's also showed a high degree of consistency in this respect: its three faculties were invariably represented by a cutler, a painter-stainer, and a stationer.[59] And when a section of the St Luke's brethren formed a Brunswick (ultra Protestant) club in 1829, they confined membership strictly to those following the guild's trades.[60] The hosiers' guild, too, rarely chose any but hosiers for the city commons.

Not all guilds, however, were so strict. Table 11.1 shows that by 1838 about one-quarter of the craft guild places on the city commons, affecting half the guilds,[61] had fallen into the hands of professionals, those on salaries, and others unconnected with the guilds' trades. Even in the goldsmiths' guild some representatives in the 1820s and 1830s are difficult to identify as practising tradesmen. The first lawyer to appear among the craft guild representatives was apparently Richard Guinness,[62] a member of the brewing family, who was elected by the brewers' guild in 1810. By 1838 craft guild representatives included a doctor, a solicitor, an attorney, two auctioneers, a land agent, and a captain on half pay.

These developments gave an added edge to Catholic resentment at the corporation's anti-Catholic stance as the struggles over emancipation and then municipal reform intensified in the 1820s and 1830s. Protestant ascendancy was harder to accept when in local terms it meant the ascendancy of those who no longer fulfilled the conditions that had originally underpinned privilege. At least professional men possessed some status and respectability; greater resentment was expressed towards those freemen who were coming down in the world. The contentious 1820 by-election produced a palpable sense of indignation at a state of affairs that allowed the likes of clerks, tax-collectors, and letter-carriers to vote by virtue of being freemen, while respectable Catholics had to make do (if qualified) with the freehold franchise.[63] No doubt critics exaggerated these tendencies; but they had some basis in fact.[64]

With the main exception of the goldsmiths' guild, intervention in the regulation of trade occurred less and less frequently in the post-war period. In 1824 St George's guild (of chandlers and soap-boilers) agreed to call a

---

[59] For a charge (1828) that one St Luke's representative was no longer following his trade see NLI, MS 12127, pp. 360–5.

[60] St Luke's guild Brunswick club minute book 1828–32 (NLI, MS 12136).

[61] The smiths, barber-surgeons, carpenters, shoemakers, tanners, glovers, weavers, sheer-men, coopers, feltmakers, bricklayers, and curriers.

[62] Richard Guinness (1755–1829), barrister; represented brewers' guild on city commons, 1811–22.

[63] See *The Temple of Fame: Or, A Tribute to the Supporters of the Independence of their Native City. Humbly Dedicated to Them by 'A True Blue'*, 2nd edn. (Dublin, 1820), *passim*; O'Neill, *The Stain Removed*, 4–7.   [64] Below, Ch. 14, esp. n. 73.

meeting when a noted firm of soap- and candlemakers was accused of causing a nuisance in its manufacturing process. The following year St George's summoned meetings of the guild and the trade in general to consider the grievances of working tallow chandlers and soap-boilers. As late as 1833 the guild was still influential in the trade.[65] In 1828 the feltmakers' guild advised the public that, on account of the rise in the price of materials, it would be impossible to sell hats at former prices. In 1826 the smiths' guild set up a committee to ascertain its rights to regulate its various faculties, though this initiative was not, apparently, followed up.[66] But such instances were rare. Even had there been a will on the part of Protestant master craftsmen to revitalize the guilds, of which there were only limited signs, the failure to admit Catholics in any numbers, and the rise of trade unions—which from 1824–5 had the legal right to organize and bargain about wages and hours—reduced the guilds' potential, at best, to that of employers' organizations. However, as the bond provided by trade diminished, complaints arose from the brethren themselves of the decay of the fraternal guild spirit.[67]

On the relation of unions to the guilds, the Webbs were doubtless correct to dismiss the idea of any 'organic connection' between the Protestant guilds, abolished in the 1840s, and the mainly Catholic trade unions.[68] The difference was not simply one of religion—certain unions were themselves organized on sectarian lines[69]—but of composition. In general, the trade unions confined their membership to journeymen, while by the 1800s the guilds contained relatively few journeymen.[70] However, historically the guilds had been inclusive bodies, and there is no doubt that the influence of guild procedures, conventions, and sense of historical origins was strong. In one of the printers' unions, the fine for those from outside the city to join the union was 17*s*. 6*d*., precisely the sum payable after 1824 in St Luke's guild, with its stationers' and printers' faculty, for freemen admitted by grace. One of the bricklayers' unions not only admitted employers, of whom one, Benjamin Pemberton, was a former master of the bricklayers' and plasterers' guild, but incorporated much of the guild structure, even down to appointing beadles (Pemberton had notoriously been in favour of

---

[65] NLI, MS 80, pp. 113, 123; *The Correspondence of Daniel O'Connell*, ed. Maurice R. O'Connell (8 vols.; Dublin, 1972–80), v (letter 1946).

[66] Berry, 'The Records of the Feltmakers' Company of Dublin', 33; DCA, G3/1, p. 194.

[67] TCD, MS 1447/8/4, p. 21.

[68] Sidney and Beatrice Webb, *The History of Trade Unionism* (London, 1894), 13–14.

[69] Hill, 'Artisans, Sectarianism and Politics in Dublin', 18–19.

[70] In the printers' society of Dublin, those who became master printers ceased to be members (*Second Report from the Select Committee on Combinations of Workmen*, 100, HC 1837–8 (646), viii); while the bricklayers' guild was reported to have had only seven (6.7%) working journeymen out of 104 members in 1833 (*Municipal Corporations (Ireland)*, App. to report on the city of Dublin, pt. II, p. 279, HC 1836, xxiv).

reviving the guilds through the admission of Catholics).[71] One of the house-painters' unions called itself after St Luke, following the precedent of the painters' faculty in St Luke's guild. Certain other unions claimed origins that turned out to be in line with those of the guild representing their trade.[72] Guild procedures were also copied by umbrella organizations such as the O'Connellite Dublin Trades Political Union in the 1830s, which made provision for professional men to be enrolled 'by grace especial'.[73] All this testifies to the continued prestige of guild ideals, and suggests a nostalgia for the corporate world-view that was to manifest itself strongly in the attempted but unsuccessful revival of the guilds by the mainly Catholic Dublin artisans in the mid-1840s.[74]

[71] NLI, MS 12127, p. 253; *Second Report . . . on Combinations of Workmen*, 102, HC 1837–8 (646), viii; Bricklayers' characteristic and charitable record book, NA, MS 1097/1/1.

[72] *Second Report . . . on Combinations of Workmen*, 158, HC 1837–8 (646), viii. In 1838 a member claimed that the plasterers' society was about 175 years old, placing its origins in the 1660s (the bricklayers' and plasterers' guild charter dated from 1670: ibid. 126).

[73] Report of Trades Political Union meeting (*Dublin Evening Mail*, 26 Oct. 1831); F. A. D'Arcy, 'The National Trades Political Union and Daniel O'Connell 1830–1848', *Eire-Ireland*, 17 (1982), 7–16.

[74] The attempted revival prompted legislation (9 & 10 Vict., c. 76) (1846) to formally abolish the power of Irish guilds to regulate trade (the goldsmiths' guild was excepted). See also D'Arcy, 'The Trade Unions of Dublin and the Attempted Revival of the Guilds'.

12

Security Versus Conciliation,
1815–1822

I. The Catholic Question

For almost fifteen years after 1815 Irish political life was dominated by the Catholic question. It is difficult to arrive at a balanced view of Dublin civic politics in this period without noting how exceptional Irish Catholic politics were in being geared to the promotion of liberal, if not democratic, goals. The prevailing climate of post-war Europe, reacting against the excesses of the revolutionary era, was highly conservative. Although occasionally tempered by pragmatic concerns, the dominant principles of the Vienna peace settlement were those of legitimism and confessionalism; and for over a decade after 1815, the leading European Catholic intellectuals, including de Maistre and the young Lammenais, endorsed the demand for authority in church and state. The papacy played its part: in 1814 Pius VII, released at last from French custody, returned triumphantly to Rome, and the church proceeded to revive its traditional claims. The Index was resurrected; in Catholic countries the church reasserted and exercised its claims to control education; the Jesuit order was restored to papal favour; even the Inquisition was reintroduced in Spain, and in Rome. Viewing the Catholic church as an ally in strengthening the forces of conservatism, the British government actively encouraged the revival of papal power in Europe.[1]

In Britain, where the establishment had suffered no defeat, the authorities had more reason than most to feel that two decades of war had vindicated existing constitutional arrangements. But the experience of war had also raised demands for reform. The continued progress of urbanization and industrial wealth was showing up anomalies in the system of parliamentary representation; while the growth of Protestant dissent, and the accession of some five million Catholics to the United Kingdom as a result of the Irish act of union highlighted the problem of obtaining the widest possible consent in what remained a confessional state.[2]

With the return of peace, it was not clear which of these causes would rise

---

[1] Matthias Buschkühl, *Great Britain and the Holy See 1746–1870* (Dublin, 1982), 55, 58–9; Donal Kerr, 'Under the Union Flag: The Catholic Church in Ireland, 1800–1870', in *Ireland After the Union* (Oxford, 1989), 23–43.

[2] Clark, *English Society*, 353–9.

to the top of the reformers' political agenda. In the immediate post-war years, parliamentary reform acquired a large following, generating petitions and mass meetings. But in the prevailing political climate a populist cause was not likely to recommend itself to an aristocratic parliament. Suspicion of anything of a demotic nature was compounded by industrial unrest, and by the first stirrings of public antipathy towards the prince regent, who was casting round for ways of divorcing Princess Caroline. By 1819 wartime restrictions on public meetings and freedom of the press had been reimposed, and even the Whigs had hastened to line up behind the establishment.

Conversely, neither the Protestant dissenters' nor the Catholics' cause contained a significant populist element: not until 1824 did the revived Catholic Association begin to enrol the Irish Catholic masses in support of emancipation. Accordingly, public debate on these questions could take place in a more relaxed manner. Following the clampdown on reform meetings, the Whig clergyman and founder of the *Edinburgh Review*, Sydney Smith, wrote to the Whig leader, Lord Grey, 'I entirely agree with you that mere force alone without some attempt at conciliation will not do . . . What I want to see the State do is to lessen in these sad times some of their [*sic*] numerous enemies. Why not do something for the Catholics and scratch them off the list?'[3]

By putting the Catholic question at the top of his political agenda, Smith was giving pride of place to what was essentially an Irish issue. The numbers of English Catholics were small, their leaders deferential. Irish Catholics, despite their superior political rights (English Catholics did not obtain the vote until 1829), had a greater sense of grievance. This sprang from their large, and growing, numbers; from frustration over continued exclusion from areas of Irish life, such as corporations, for which they had been legally eligible since 1793; from the barriers to career prospects that faced barristers and others; and from the knowledge that Catholics had played a full part in the recent war. Moreover, during the pre-union negotiations, Catholic leaders had been given to understand that a union would facilitate the removal of their remaining disabilities.

But while many MPs could agree on the desirability of some sort of 'conciliation' of Catholics, the granting of full equality still presented serious difficulties. Utilitarian arguments had become more common in British political debate,[4] but much of the Erastian ideological legacy of the past remained intact. This can be illustrated most clearly by reference to the contentious veto question, which bedevilled the pursuit of emancipation from 1808 until the early 1820s. In 1799, when prospects for Catholic

---

[3] *Selected Letters of Sydney Smith.* ed. Nowell C. Smith (Oxford, 1981), 93, letter 348.
[4] Hole, *Pulpits, Politics and Public Order in England*, 249–50; Gregory Claeys, 'The French Revolution Debate and British Political Thought', *Hist. Pol. Thought*, 11 (1990), 59–80, at 80.

emancipation seemed bright, the Irish hierarchy had expressed a willingness to accept some state control over the church, including a veto over episcopal appointments, such as the government had exercised in repect of Catholic bishops in Quebec,[5] and was common elsewhere.

However, a decade later the dimming of hopes for emancipation, and the spectacle of a British ministry once again allying itself with popular anti-Catholicism, combined to give the matter a different complexion. Since the Stuarts had ceased to nominate to Irish sees in the 1760s the right of nomination had passed to Rome; but in practice Irish Catholics, both clerical and lay, had gained considerable influence in church appointments. This influence was threatened by the prospect of ministers, guided by local advisers who might hold ultra-Protestant views, exercising power in church affairs; and in 1808 the hierarchy formally repudiated the veto proposals in a move that won the approval of lay Catholic activists. But this development was seriously embarrassing for the friends of emancipation in parliament, where a veto was still regarded as a necessary and reasonable security in return for further concessions. Accordingly, a veto continued to feature in parliamentary discussion of emancipation, and when in 1821 an emancipation bill finally passed the house of commons (it was defeated in the lords), it contained provisions for a veto on the appointment of bishops and deans. Moreover, W. C. Plunket, who had introduced the bill, could see no hope of emancipation succeeding in future without some similar security.[6]

On the veto question, therefore, Irish Catholic activists were parting company with their Whig champions in parliament. Daniel O'Connell, who emerged as the leading Catholic spokesman in the post-war era, was moving towards a position which, by the late 1820s, would be called 'liberal', in a political sense.[7] He criticized the principle of legitimism; he condemned the revival of the Inquisition; by 1818 he was contending that civil and religious liberty constituted a universal human right. His personal religious views—despite, or perhaps because of, a lapse into Deism in the 1790s—were those of a devout Catholic; but for him Catholicism was an inherently liberal religion.[8]

O'Connell, however, could not detach himself entirely from the powerful

[5] The Quebec chapter's nomination for bishop in 1764 was vetoed by the governor. Subsequently the Erastian principle in Quebec appears to have operated through state payment of the bishop's stipend rather than directly through a veto (Somers, 'The Legal Status of the Bishop of Quebec').

[6] See C. D. A. Leighton, 'Gallicanism and the Veto Controversy: Church, State and Catholic Community in Early Nineteenth-Century Ireland', in Comerford, Cullen, Hill & Lennon (eds.), *Religion, Conflict and Coexistence in Ireland*, 135–58; *O'Connell Corr.* ii, letter 954a.

[7] The arrival of the term in its political sense was heralded by the formation of 'liberal clubs' under the direction of the Catholic Association in 1828 (*O'Connell Corr.* iii, letter 1473, n. 3).

[8] Ibid. ii, letters 813a, 858; Maurice R. O'Connell, *Daniel O'Connell: The Man and His Politics* (Dublin, 1990), 34; MacDonagh, *O'Connell*, 41–4; O'Connell's address to the Catholics of Ireland, *FDJ*, 4 Jan. 1819.

forces of tradition that persisted even in post-war Britain. During one uncharacteristically pessimistic phase he admitted to his wife that his fellow Catholics saw little hope of emancipation unless the French Bourbons brought pressure to bear on the government—a proposition that would not have seemed out of place two centuries earlier.[9] 1820 saw him pursuing the age-old tactic of exploiting divisions between the new king and queen in the hope that the queen would use her prerogative to appoint him her attorney-general for Ireland, thus bypassing the statutory barriers on Catholics holding such offices. In 1827 he made discreet overtures to the heir to the throne, the duke of Clarence, promising Catholic loyalty and attachment to the dynasty.[10]

O'Connell, then, was not above deploying monarchical and dynastic strategies in pursuit of his goal, and this highlights the ambiguity inherent in the emancipation campaign. On the one hand, emancipation was still presented in Burkean fashion as likely to reinforce traditional values.[11] On the other hand, O'Connell himself was increasingly apt to refer to it as a 'right',[12] a proposition that was still controversial in the 1820s, and would seem even more alarming when backed by mass enrolments in the Catholic Association. Thus among many Protestants, the campaign fostered both conventional fears of popery—the prospect that Catholics would prove too yielding to the resurgent claims of Rome—as well as newer worries about the radical potential of Irish Catholicism. Either way, Protestant control seemed threatened. In particular, critics asked, if the Catholics were really ready to participate fully in a Protestant constitution without seeking to undermine it, why did they refuse to accept the veto, designed to protect the Erastian nature of the church establishment? Admission to parliament would give Catholics the power to influence the affairs of the established church: yet they would brook no interference by the state in the affairs of their own church.[13]

II. The Battle for Metropolitan Opinion: Parliamentary Representation

> let them dismiss their demagogues and renounce their seditious measures—let them learn from the mottos of their Guilds, to love the Brotherhood, fear God, and honour the King;—this done, he was bold

---

[9] *O'Connell Corr.* ii, letter 1033.

[10] Ibid. ii, letters 869, 873–81, 883–6, 888, 905; iii, letter 1359.

[11] Mary O'Connell to O'Connell, 7 Feb. 1824, ibid. iii, letter 1091.

[12] Speech at a public dinner at Tralee, Co. Kerry, *c.*1818, quoted in O'Connell, *Daniel O'Connell*, 34; *O'Connell Corr.* iii, letter 1364.

[13] See Jacqueline Hill, 'The Legal Profession and the Defence of the *Ancien Régime* in Ireland, 1790–1840', in Daire Hogan & W. N. Osborough (eds.), *Bretons, Serjeants and Attorneys: Studies in the History of the Irish Legal Profession* (Dublin, 1990), 181–209, at 197–201.

to assert, the Common Council would gladly open their arms to receive them; this not done, they need never expect to be freemen of the Ancient, Loyal Protestant City of Dublin.[14]

Faced with the task of convincing Protestants that the extension of full political rights to Catholics was compatible with the maintenance of civil and religious liberty, spokesmen for the Irish Catholics in the post-war period could draw little comfort from the prevailing authoritarian outlook of the Catholic church. When O'Connell claimed, in 1819, that the finest examples of religious freedom were to be found in Catholic states, John Giffard's old paper, the *Dublin Journal*, was not slow to draw attention to what that paper described as his 'remarkable assertions'.[15]

There was little point, therefore, in Catholics appealing to the Vatican or the current crop of European thinkers in order to substantiate their claims. The proposition that Catholics would not abuse admission to parliament by seeking to weaken the established church, or undermine the sovereignty of the civil power, would have to receive endorsement from other quarters. Hence the importance of Irish Protestants. Since they would be the first to bear the brunt of any discrepancy between Catholic claims and Catholic conduct, their concurrence would be particularly welcome.

No Irish city ranked higher than Dublin in terms of the weight attached to the public expression of its views. Its sheer size and status as the Irish capital; its ancient corporate traditions and Patriot credentials; the open nature of its parliamentary constituency, and the adherence of the great majority of the freemen to the established church; all this meant that it was particularly desirable for the Catholic leaders to have metropolitan opinion on their side. This helps explain why, as the Catholic cause revived in the post-war years, the battle for Dublin Protestant opinion became so intense and so bitter.

As the war drew to a close, it is apparent from the speech cited at the head of this section that even the ultra Protestants in Dublin corporation had not completely ruled out the prospect of some sort of Catholic advancement within the existing system. But equally, it was being firmly signalled that progress would have to be at a Protestant pace and on Protestant terms. Such a prospect was naturally uncongenial to O'Connell, who was impatient to proceed to full emancipation and to see Catholics playing the part in Irish life warranted by their numbers. The status quo must have seemed all the more anomalous in view of the continued erosion (through

[14] John Giffard, speech in Dublin city commons on the subject of admitting Catholics to civic freedom (*FDJ*, 22 Jan. 1814).
[15] O'Connell to the Catholics of Ireland, 1 Jan. 1819 (address and comments, ibid., 4, 6, 18 Jan. 1819). Giffard had succumbed to government pressure to sever his links with the paper in 1816, but some traces of his views remained (Inglis, *Freedom of the Press*, 148, 179–80).

emigration) of the Protestant middle-class presence, if not to any great extent in Dublin, then elsewhere in southern Ireland.[16] However, immediately after the return of peace, the emancipation campaign was in some disarray, partly because of divisions in Ireland over the veto, and partly because it had not yet become clear which of the main reform issues would come to the fore in British parliamentary politics. Late in 1817 the Catholic Board suspended its meetings while parliamentary reform temporarily held centre stage. But a year later O'Connell became convinced that the complexion of British politics was altering in favour of emancipation. He accordingly composed the first in what became for a time an annual series, a public letter 'to the Catholics of Ireland'—which was nevertheless directed as much at Protestant as at Catholic opinion. He argued that there could now be no reason not to grant emancipation. The war was over; there was no Stuart pretender; the pope was no longer in the hands of the national enemy. He made his controversial claim about the 'perfect liberality' of the Catholic religion.[17]

But while the ultra-Protestant press might demolish such claims to its own satisfaction, the prospect of a new campaign for emancipation was bound to be disquieting. Not only was there now entrenched in Dublin Castle a supporter of emancipation (Charles Grant, chief secretary, 1818–21), but the lord mayor, Alderman Thomas McKenny,[18] a member of the pro-Catholic hosiers' guild, was also sympathetic to Catholic claims. He proved willing, much to the outrage of Giffard and his allies, to accede to the request of several Protestant peers, including the duke of Leinster, to sanction the holding of a public meeting of Protestants in Dublin to petition for emancipation (the initiative had come from O'Connell). The meeting, held on 11 February 1819, judged emancipation to be 'highly conducive to the tranquillity of Ireland'.[19] This seemed to confirm one of O'Connell's assertions in his 'Letter to the Catholics': that Irish Protestants were becoming more favourably disposed to Catholic claims.[20]

Although ultra Protestants quickly organized a counter-petition, the very fact that such a meeting had been held represented a setback for the opponents of emancipation.[21] According to Giffard, 'the world was turned

---

[16] Miller, 'No Middle Ground'.

[17] *O'Connell Corr.* ii, letter 754, n. 1; *FDJ*, 4, 6, Jan. 1819.

[18] Thomas McKenny (1770–1849), hosier; chosen sheriff 1805, but excused after 300 guinea fine; alderman 1811, lord mayor 1818–19, made bt. 1831.

[19] *FJ*, 20 Feb. 1819. McKenny's stance won popularity with Catholics and liberal Protestants: an engraving (*CARD* xvii. facing p. 480) shows him holding the requisition for the meeting. Cf. MacDonagh, *O'Connell*, 164–5.   [20] *FDJ*, 6 Jan. 1819.

[21] As noted in *FJ*, 11 Feb. 1819. The *FJ*'s generous estimate (12 Feb.) was that up to 3,000 Protestants had attended the meeting, in the Rotunda. John Giffard attempted to pack it with ultra Protestants, and a group led by Alderman William Archer (d. 1830; lord mayor 1811–12, treasurer, Dublin corporation, 1818–28) tried unsuccessfully to persuade the meeting to leave the matter to parliament (*DEP* report, in *FJ*, 26 Feb. 1819).

upside down'.[22] The meeting had highlighted the existence of divisions on the issue in civic circles, and constituted a snub to the corporation, the official mouthpiece of Dublin Protestant opinion.[23] All this meant that when, the following year, a vacancy appeared in Dublin city's parliamentary representation, the ultra Protestants were determined to field a candidate sympathetic to their views.

It was a measure of the relatively poor prospects for emancipation before this period that Dublin Protestants had enjoyed the freedom, not merely to differ from each other on the subject, but, to a remarkable degree and for long periods of time, to ignore it altogether. It was still being ignored, for instance, at the general election held in March 1820. On that occasion, the two sitting MPs, Henry Grattan and Robert Shaw, who together had represented the city for over thirteen years and were entering their fourth consecutive unopposed election, had issued the usual noncommittal election addresses. Shaw's supporters felt obliged to defend his role as a supporter of the government. The candidates were questioned by constituents on a range of subjects, including the level of Dublin taxes, tithes, and the future of the lord-lieutenancy. Nostalgic references were made to the constitution of 1782. But, to judge by the coverage in the *Freeman's Journal*, a newspaper well disposed towards Catholic claims, the issue of emancipation was not raised at all.[24]

It was the death on 4 June 1820, shortly before his seventy-fourth birthday, of the veteran Patriot Henry Grattan that precipitated emancipation into the forefront of Dublin electoral politics. Grattan's death removed the one politician whose prestige in relation to the still lamented Irish parliament was such that, despite his prominence in the cause of emancipation—which was never mentioned in his election literature—the ultra Protestants had not put up a candidate to oppose him. In fact, for some years neither of the city MPs had been popular with the ultra Protestants, for Shaw had disappointed them by taking a conciliatory line on emancipation when the issue had arisen in 1811–12.[25] Within days of the news of the vacancy reaching Dublin, an opponent of emancipation, Thomas Ellis,[26] governor of the Aldermen of Skinner's Alley, had declared

[22] Report of Dublin corporation meeting (*FJ*, 20 Feb. 1819).

[23] On 22 Jan. Giffard's resolution asking the lord mayor not to hold the meeting was carried in the city commons by 44 : 13; the corporation also decided to petition against Catholic claims (*CARD* xvii. 255–6; *FJ*, 23 Jan. 1819; *FDJ*, 27 Jan. 1819).

[24] *FJ*, 11, 17, 18 Mar. 1820.

[25] Report of proceedings, house of commons, 7 Mar. 1811 (*DEP*, 12 Mar. 1811); report of Dublin corporation meeting (*FJ*, 18 July 1812).

[26] For Ellis, a Master in Chancery, see below, App. B. Even before the election, his eligibility for parliament while holding his legal post had been queried in the Whig *Edinburgh Review* (*FJ*, 19 June 1820). Afterwards, to the anger of Dublin corporate bodies, a clause was added to the Irish court of chancery bill to exclude such office holders from parliament, but it was defeated in the lords (DPLGC, MS 79, fos. 342, 344; *CARD* xvii. 317–19; *FJ*, 5, 8, 17, 29 July 1820; *Hansard*, NS ii, cols. 569–74).

his intention to stand, and had been described by a speaker at a Catholic meeting as 'the advocate of intolerance'. The same speaker urged the 'Independent Electors' and the Catholic freeholders to rally behind the former MP's son, Henry Grattan, junior.[27]

When the first election addresses of the two candidates were published, they contained little beyond conventional expressions of commitment to the city of Dublin and the interests of Ireland. But it quickly emerged that the Catholic question would be the only important issue, and passions soon ran high. The supporters of Ellis were charged by their opponents with 'bigotry', and Ellis himself was accused of being a sworn Orangeman.[28] At a corporation meeting held to decide whom to endorse, both candidates were given a hearing. Taking his stand on the values of the old Whigs, Ellis emphasized his attachment to the principles of 1688: civil and religious liberty in the traditional Protestant sense. Grattan chose instead to invoke the memory of 1782, and he condemned Ellis for opposing the claims of a majority of his countrymen. By thus bracketing together the spirit of 1782 and the issue of emancipation, Grattan evidently hoped to persuade his audience that commitment to the one implied commitment to the other. But by a large majority (63 : 11) the city commons reaffirmed its traditional position by voting to support Ellis. Several of the guilds followed suit, prompting the *Freeman's Journal* to remind voters that guild pledges before the 1806 election had been a poor indicator of how the votes had actually been cast.[29]

As guild after guild held pre-election meetings the polarization between the candidates grew more marked.[30] At a meeting of the coopers' guild Ellis was hissed when he sneered at the applause that greeted the arrival of his opponent, saying that he had learned to distinguish the praise of freemen from the uproar of a mob. Ellis also charged Grattan's supporters with threatening an economic boycott of those who voted against their candidate, a tactic defended by Grattan at a meeting of the smiths' guild. The Grattanites, in turn, charged Ellis and his supporters with using undue influence—even physical violence—to secure favourable guild pledges of support. Both candidates charged the other with fomenting religious discord; and Ellis went as far as to imply that Grattan and his supporters were the remnants of a 'disaffected' party that had disgraced the country by

[27] The speaker was Nicholas Purcell O'Gorman (*FJ*, 9 June 1820). For Henry Grattan, jun., see below, App. B.
[28] *FJ*, 12, 13 June 1820; 'An Independent', 'R' (ibid., 15, 19 June 1820).
[29] *CARD* xvii. 317; *FJ*, 20, 22 June 1820.
[30] St Loy's guild, transactions 1811–35, DCA, G3/1, 88–9; GMD, brewers' guild, minute book 1804–31, entry for 24 June 1820; reports of guild meetings (*FJ*, 22, 23, 24, 26 June 1820).

precipitating the 1798 rebellion.[31] At the poll, held during the last week of June, Ellis—though clearly unpopular with the mob—established an early lead, which he never lost. The final result showed Ellis with 1,094 votes, Grattan with 785.[32]

To the pro-emancipation side the outcome of this election came as a major blow. To see the seat held for so long by the venerable Patriot fall into the hands of the 'degenerate Orange faction' (as the *Freeman's Journal* put it), just when the prospects in Britain for emancipation looked better than for some time, was galling. The *Freeman* had hinted throughout the campaign that Ellis's supporters were an unrepresentative minority; now they had triumphed.[33] And Ellis had scored another victory, beyond the obvious one at the polls. By repeatedly stressing the need for loyalty to the existing constitution in church and state, and by raising the spectre of the '98 rebellion, he had driven his opponent, with his talk of 'Liberty, Toleration and Concord' on to the defensive, and forced Grattan's supporters to preface their electoral pledges with statements of their attachment to king and constitution.[34]

The Grattanites reacted bitterly to their defeat. Ellis's supporters were castigated, held up as corrupt men motivated by a monopolistic clinging to place and profit; and the names of his supporters who held civic or government posts were published. The corporation, the city grand jury, and the guild of merchants emerged as special targets for wrath because they provided the employment that had (allegedly) induced voters to betray the candidate who had the real interests of Ireland at heart. The craft guilds were accused of not keeping proper records of those entitled to vote; and the guild of merchants was alleged to have drafted in 'many' voters from remote parts of the country to vote for Ellis.[35]

Were any of these charges justified? To some extent it is possible to test their validity, since poll book and other data survives for the 1820 election. First, however, the point must be made that this election showed up the pro-emancipation side not only as on the defensive in argument, but ill-organized and ineffective at turning out their supporters.[36] After the election it emerged that up to 1,000 freemen had failed to vote at all (Table

---

[31] Reports of meetings of coopers' and smiths' guilds (*FJ*, 22, 23, 24 June 1820); Robert Willard (shoemakers' guild) to proprietor, *FJ*; signed statement by fifteen freemen of the smiths' guild (*FJ*, 24, 26 June 1820).

[32] These results differ slightly from Walker's (*Parliamentary Election Results*, 34: Ellis, 1137: Grattan, 789), but are calculated from an unusually detailed poll book (O'Neill, *The Stain Removed*). [33] *FJ*, 20 June, 13 July 1820.

[34] See Ellis's speech to coopers' guild meeting; his election address; Grattan's election address; statement by fifteen freemen of the smiths' guild (*FJ*, 22, 23, 24, 26 June 1820).

[35] O'Neill, *The Stain Removed*, 3–7, 11; *The Temple of Fame*, 3–16; George Ness, *A Letter to Henry Brougham, Esq. M.P. Containing an Account of the Conduct . . . of the Guild of Merchants of Dublin* (Dublin, 1824), 31.

[36] The *FJ* itself hinted at such deficiencies (20 June 1820).

12.1), as well as perhaps around 200 freeholders, the majority of whom, it can be assumed, were Catholics.[37] Beside this degree of abstentionism, the charges of 'corporation juggling' levelled against Ellis's supporters paled into insignificance.

Analysis of those who did vote (Table 12.2) revealed few striking differences between the two sides, beyond the predictable finding that freeholders

TABLE 12.1. *Dublin city by-election, June 1820, by turn-out*

Qualification	Voted		Qualified but did not vote		Total	
	No.	%	No.	%	No.	%
Freeholders	161	44.6	c.200[a]	55.4	c.361	100.0
Freemen:						
merchants' guild	428	61.2	271	38.8	699	100.0
craft guilds	1,256	63.3	728	36.7	1,984	100.0
Others[b]	34	10.4	293	89.6	327	100.0
TOTAL	1,879	55.7	1,492	44.3	3,371	100.0

[a] Present author's estimate, based on difference between numbers voting in 1806 and 1820. The number of freeholders became much greater in the 1820s (below, Ch. 13).

[b] Free of the city corporation only; mostly honorary freemen and non-residents.

Source: Compiled from F. O'Neill, *The Stain Removed, and Corporation Juggling, Explained. Being an Alphabetical List of the Freemen & Freeholders . . . Who Voted at the Late Election. And Also, a List of Those who Remained Neutral on that Occasion* ([Dublin], 1820).

TABLE 12.2. *Dublin city by-election, June 1820, votes cast, by qualification*

	Grattan voters		Ellis voters		Total	
	No.	%	No.	%	No.	%
Freeholders	127	78.9	34	21.1	161	100.0
Freemen:						
merchants' guild	118	27.6	310	72.4	428	100.0
craft guilds	532	42.4	724	57.6	1,256	100.0
Others	8	23.5	26	76.4	34	100.0
TOTAL	785		1,094		1,879	

Source: As Table 12.1.

[37] The figure (999) for non-voting freemen represents all those recorded as 'neutrals' (excluding 172 made free since the election) in O'Neill, *The Stain Removed*, 47–79. Freemen voting in 1820 (1,684) were far fewer than in 1806 (2,466: *The Poll . . . for Electing Two Members to Represent the City of Dublin . . . 1806*, 73), which bears out claims that many hundreds of freemen and freeholders had failed to vote (*FJ*, 30 June 1820). The figure of 1,879 freemen voting in 1820 (*Boundary Reports*, report on the county of the city of Dublin, 52, HC 1831–2 (519) xliii) is too high by c.200.

voted overwhelmingly for Grattan, while members of the merchants' guild[38] voted almost as consistently for Ellis.

Of the three guilds that had demonstrated the strongest pro-Catholic tendencies at the last contested election in 1806, the hosiers and brewers were consistent in preferring Grattan, though the brewers' turn-out, at only 50 per cent, was among the lowest (Table 12.3). The other previously liberal guild, the apothecaries, now gave a majority of votes to Ellis. Among the craft guilds, no clear voting pattern emerged among occupational groups, save that guilds in the building, woodworking, and metal trades (bricklayers, carpenters, coopers, joiners, and smiths) uniformly favoured Ellis. In the textile and clothing guilds, the weavers and tailors voted predominantly for Ellis, while the sheermen, hosiers, and hatters preferred Grattan. One generalization that can be made relates to the size of guild (Table 12.3). Of

TABLE 12.3. *Dublin city by-election, June 1820, by guild size, turn-out, and votes cast* (*E = Ellis, G = Grattan*)

Guild	Size	Turn-out		Majority votes cast		
		No.	%		No.	%
Merchants	699	428	61.2	E	310	72.4
Weavers	265	138	51.2	E	82	59.4
Carpenters	219	118	53.9	E	70	59.3
Cutlers, etc.	177	100	56.5	E	61	61.0
Smiths	174	129	74.1	E	82	63.6
Saddlers	111	77	69.4	E	44	57.1
Shoemakers	104	79	76.0	E	54	68.4
Tailors	101	83	82.2	E	65	78.3
Chandlers	89	56	62.9	E	34	60.7
Goldsmiths	81	55	67.9	G	32	58.2
Bricklayers	76	51	67.1	E	29	56.9
Barbers	68	42	61.8	E	27	64.3
Joiners	65	41	63.1	E	24	58.5
Apothecaries	61	34	55.7	E	22	64.7
Hosiers	60	46	76.7	G	34	73.9
Cooks	52	31	59.6	E	20	64.5
Sheermen, dyers	50	29	58.0	G	22	75.9
Hatters	46	35	76.1	G	21	60.0
Coopers	38	30	78.9	E	20	66.7
Brewers	36	18	50.0	G	12	66.7
Glovers, skinners	31	23	74.2	G	12	52.2
Butchers	27	20	74.1	G	13	65.0
Tanners	23	8	34.8	G	6	75.0
Bakers	18	7	38.9	G	5	71.4
Curriers	12	6	50.0	E	6	100.0

Source: As Table 12.1.

[38] The merchants' guild voters as a proportion of all freemen voting remained the same (25.5%) in 1820 as in 1806 (25.4%).

the fourteen largest guilds, from the apothecaries (61) to the merchants (699), with a median size of 102.5, all but the goldsmiths (81) voted predominantly for Ellis. Among the eleven smallest guilds, from the curriers (12) to the hosiers (60), with a median size of 36, all but three guilds (the curriers, coopers, and cooks) preferred Grattan. Whether the smaller guilds were naturally more sympathetic to their Catholic neighbours, or whether, lacking what has been described as a 'critical mass'[39] of Protestants in particular trades, they were less confident and perhaps more vulnerable to trade boycotts are questions that cannot be determined within the present limits of knowledge.[40]

Turning to the voters as individuals, if date of admission to freedom may be taken as an indicator of age (Table 12.4), Ellis's supporters were somewhat younger than Grattan's. The question of civic employment is more difficult to assess fairly, in part because the victorious side published no corresponding lists of Grattan's supporters in public employment (if any). Some 113 Ellis voters were identified by one anonymous commentator as possessing a corporation or government office—past, present, or in anticipation.[41] Putting such data in the context of the election result, it appears that 19 (13.8%) of a random sample of 137 Ellis voters enjoyed some sort of public employment or contract. If the same proportion held good for all Ellis's 1,094 voters, it would have affected about 151 of them; a figure not to be dismissed, though insignificant compared with the many hundreds of voters who failed to vote at all.

TABLE 12.4. *Dublin city by-election, June 1820, sample freeman voters,[a] by date of civic freedom*

	Grattan voters		Ellis voters		Total in sample
	No.	%	No.	%	
Before 1793	17	22.7	18	13.7	35
1793–1806	25	33.3	43	32.8	68
After 1806	25	33.3	59	45.0	84
Not ascertained	8	10.7	11	8.4	19
TOTAL	75	100.0	131	99.9	206

[a] Random sample of 1 in 8 voters for Grattan, and 1 in 8 voters for Ellis, yielding 235 names, of which 206 were freemen.

Sources: As Table 12.1; *An Alphabetical List of the Freemen of the City of Dublin, 1774–1823* ([Dublin], n.d.).

[39] See Dickson, ' "Centres of Motion" ', 109.

[40] The voters in some of the smallest guilds had lost links with the trade almost entirely. None of the eight 'tanners' followed the trade, and only one of the six 'curriers'. By contrast, most of the seven members of the bakers' guild who voted followed some branch of the trade.

[41] *The Temple of Fame, passim.*

However, the most revealing picture emerged when the voters were examined to see whether their allegiance had changed since the last contested election in 1806 (Table 12.5). Of a random sample of 98 voters for Grattan, 44 (44.9%) had voted in 1806, while 53 (38.7%) of a sample of 137 voters for Ellis had voted in 1806. On that occasion, Giffard and his allies had urged voters to support only Robert Shaw: both Grattan and La Touche were too much identified with emancipation to find favour with Giffard.[42] Thus in 1806 strong supporters of emancipation might vote for Grattan or La Touche, or both; convinced opponents of that measure would plump for Shaw; as it turned out, emancipation was not a major issue at that election, and a majority cross-voted.

Table 12.5 reveals that among the sample of Grattan's supporters in 1820 over 60 per cent of those who had voted in 1806 had on that occasion supported his father, or La Touche, or both; only 9 per cent had plumped for Shaw. But less than one-third of Ellis's supporters who had voted in 1806 had plumped for Shaw; almost one-third had voted for the emancipation candidates alone. Ellis's supporters, therefore, were much more likely than Grattan's to have changed sides since the last contested election: indeed, if the sample here is representative, then no fewer than 352 of Ellis's 1,094 voters had given a pro-emancipation vote in 1806.

Had Ellis's supporters changed their allegiance for fear of losing public employment? Here the data compiled by the disappointed Grattanites is particularly instructive. Table 12.6 shows the 17 sample Ellis voters who, at the 1806 election, had not given Shaw even one vote. They had thus

TABLE 12.5. *Dublin city by-election, June 1820, sample voters[a] by voting record, 1806 general election*

	Grattan voters		Ellis voters		Total in sample
	No.	%	No.	%	
Voted only for pro-emancipation candidate(s)	27	61.4	17	32.1	44
Voted only for ultra-Protestant candidate	4	9.1	16	30.2	20
Cross-voted	13	29.5	20	37.7	33
TOTAL	44	100.0	53	100.0	97

[a] Random sample as Table 12.4, of which 97 had voted in 1806.

Sources: As Table 12.1; *The Poll for Electing Two Members to Represent the City of Dublin in . . . 1806* (Dublin, n.d.).

[42] Giffard's city commons speech (*FDJ*, 18 Oct. 1806); also Ch. 10 above.

markedly failed on that occasion to vote for the candidate with ultra-Protestant approval. The picture that emerges of them is one of men who, by 1820, were middle-aged or elderly; almost one-third had received their freedom before 1793. A large majority had obtained freedom by birth or service. Over three-quarters had addresses in the city, the rest living in the suburbs or in counties bordering on the city. Only one of them, according to Ellis's detractor's information, had a civic or Castle post.

Analysis of Ellis's supporters who had cross-voted in 1806 reveals a similar pattern: 30 per cent had received their freedom before 1793; a majority, if only a bare majority, had gained freedom by birth or service; 80 per cent were city residents. None of them held public posts or contracts. Taken as a whole, only one voter in these two categories had such a post, far fewer than Ellis's supporters in general.

Those of Ellis's voters who had voted only for Shaw in 1806, however, presented a significantly different picture. Only one member of this group had received his freedom before 1793; over 37 per cent were members of the merchants' guild; a high proportion had been admitted to freedom by grace; and no fewer than five had corporation or Castle employment. The Shaw supporters of 1806, therefore, exemplified two of the most characteristic charges levelled against Ellis's supporters in 1820: they were disproportionately identified with the merchants' guild, and with public employment. But

TABLE 12.6. *Dublin city by-election, June 1820: sample voters for Ellis who had also voted in 1806 (by guild, qualification, date of civic freedom, address, and public employment)*

	Guild				Date of civic freedom			
	Mcht.	Craft	n/a	Total	pre-1792	1793–1806	n/a	Total
For Grattan/ La Touche	5	10	2	17	5	10	2	17
Cross-voters	5	15	0	20	6	12	2	20
For Shaw	6	9	1	16	1	14	1	16

	Qualification					Address				Public office/ contract
	Birth	Serv.	GE	n/a	Total	City	Sub.	Other	n/a	Total	
For Grattan/ La Touche	6	7	2	2	17	13	1	3	0	17	1
Cross-voters	6	5	7	2	20	16	1	3	0	20	0
For Shaw	7	1	7	1	16	12	2	1	1	16	5

Note: Mcht. = Merchant; n/a = not ascertained; Serv. = Service; GE = Grace especial; Sub. = Suburbs.

Sources: As Table 12.5 (Ellis voters only: total in sample, 53); Anon. *The Temple of Fame: Or, a Tribute to the Supporters of the Independence of their Native City. Humbly Dedicated to Them by 'A True Blue'*, 2nd edn. (Dublin, 1820).

these charges did not fit those who had switched sides, or had moved to Ellis from a previously neutral position. It therefore appears that there was a kernel of truth in the charges made against the Ellis voters; but the charges applied to a section of his supporters, and not the majority.

Comparing the two elections, it appears that in 1806, when emancipation was not generally perceived as a major issue, a relatively small number of voters (650, or 22.5%) followed the ultra-Protestant lead and plumped for Shaw. Their characteristics were those denounced by the Grattanites in 1820: disproportionately identified with the merchants' guild, enjoying an undue share of public patronage—if their offices or contracts were already in existence by 1806—and depending quite heavily on admission to freedom by special grace. (It may also be significant that almost all in this group had gained their freedom since 1793, the year in which Catholics acquired the right to vote.) The great majority of such voters displayed their consistency by voting for Ellis in 1820. But in 1820 this element was completely swamped by the addition of considerable numbers of those who in 1806 had either not voted for the ultra-Protestant candidate at all, or who had cross-voted. Since there is no evidence that these voters enjoyed significant corporation employment or contracts, how is the tide of support for Ellis to be explained?

Here it must be remembered that in 1820 the voters faced, for the first time in Dublin electoral politics, an inescapable choice between a pro- and an anti-emancipation candidate. No other serious issue had surfaced, and the only way to avoid a choice, and a public choice at that, was by failing to vote. Significantly, large numbers of voters abstained, thus reflecting, it may be suggested, widespread disillusion and apathy. Years of returning Henry Grattan, senior, to the London parliament had done nothing to hinder the progressive strengthening of the unpopular act of union; and what was Grattan's son likely to achieve where his father had failed? In any case, the issue of the union had scarcely arisen during the campaign.[43] Since 1801 hostility to the union had served as a unifying factor among the Dublin electors: almost everyone could agree on deploring the loss of the Irish parliament. Emancipation, by contrast, could not fail to be deeply divisive. Looking no further than the political implications, it was apparent that given the Catholic majority in the population, if the freemen supported emancipation they facilitated the approach of Catholic domination in the parliamentary representation, and ultimately, in the Irish corporations and guilds. And this at a time when Catholics were openly reluctant to accept Erastian securities designed to provide safeguards against an international Catholic church more assertive in its claims than at any time since the mid-eighteenth century.

---

[43] The union was criticized by James Grattan, the candidate's brother (meeting of Dublin grocers, *FJ*, 28 June 1820).

If on the other hand the freemen voted against emancipation they risked incurring the hostility of Catholics, some of whom were now adopting the principle of the trade boycott against their political opponents.[44] Moreover, no matter how committed they might consider themselves to be to the original Whig principles of civil and religious liberty, if they opposed emancipation they now stood publicly branded as bigots, lacking in patriotism and charity towards their fellow Irishmen. In these circumstances, it is not surprising that so many voters—including Catholics—preferred not to vote at all rather than take part in such a damaging contest. As for those who did respond to the challenge, the most likely explanation for Ellis's victory appears to be the obvious one: when forced to make a choice, most of the freemen who voted displayed their commitment to traditional Patriot values by supporting the Protestant constitution in church and state.

III. The Battle for Metropolitan Opinion: The Cult of King William

The founding of a gentlemen's lodge in the capital in 1797, quickly followed by others, marked the consolidation of Dublin's leading role in the Williamite cult that was to become so central to the Orange Order. Demographic and historical reasons had much to do with this. Dublin still contained the largest concentration of Protestants in Ireland, the great majority of them members of the established church. (As late as the 1830s Dublin's Church of Ireland population alone was larger than the entire population of Belfast.) Ever since its erection under civic auspices in 1701 the statue of King William in College Green had been the focus for Williamite commemorations, and the annual celebration of the royal birthday on 4 November had grown into a great ceremony usually attended by the viceroy and other dignitaries. The Dublin Volunteers had added extra glamour. But since the 1790s, when Protestants became divided over the extension of political rights to Catholics, these anniversaries had ceased to be occasions for the reaffirmation of shared Protestant values.[45] For upholders of the status quo Williamite symbols represented everything they had escaped from under the Stuarts;[46] while liberal Protestants and

---

[44] This election witnessed for the first time non-guild and largely Catholic trade groups (without votes) holding meetings to try to affect the outcome. The Dublin grocers (followed by the vintners and bakers) pledged to give preference in commercial dealings to merchants who had endorsed Grattan (*FJ*, 28, 29 June 1820).

[45] Hill, 'National Festivals, the State and "Protestant Ascendancy" '. The Grand Lodge of Ireland met in Dublin by 1798, and by the 1830s it was a matter of course for the assistant grand secretary (who communicated with local lodges) to be a Dublin resident (*Report [on]* . . . *Orange Lodges*, 19, 84, HC 1835 (377), xv).

[46] In the ultra-Protestant *Warder* (31 Mar. 1821) 'Somniator' recounted a recent nightmare: the statue of King William had turned into King James, the Bible was trampled underfoot, a procession of the host was *en route* to Christ Church, and Trinity College had become a palace of the Inquisition.

Catholics, loth to abandon the prestigious tradition entirely, strove to present William as a prince 'whose whole life was one continued struggle to establish religious toleration'.[47] Nevertheless, by the early years of the new century Williamite anniversaries in the capital had become mainly the preserve of Orangemen and the lower orders of Protestants.

It is appropriate to remember at this point that the Catholics' pursuit of emancipation was concerned only in part with the removal of remaining political restrictions. Equally important was the desire to activate rights that they had enjoyed, in principle, for nearly thirty years, such as civic freedom;[48] and in general to attain a role in Irish life consistent with Catholic property and numbers. Similarly, celebrations of Williamite anniversaries did not merely imply hostility to the principle of full legal equality. They also signified resistance to any Catholic aspirations that threatened Protestant ascendancy, or Protestant control, and they were directed as much at local Protestant opinion and at the government as at the Catholics themselves. Hence, if emancipation was to be obtained, it was desirable, perhaps imperative, that the cult be displaced from its position in the public domain.

The withdrawal of the Whig viceroy, the duke of Bedford, from participation in the annual procession to mark King William's birthday in 1806 thus marked a significant setback for the defenders of the status quo. His successors did not resume the custom, and this left a void that could not adequately be filled by the ringing of church bells or assemblies of yeomanry. Following the viceroy's lead, Dublin corporation, too, drew back from public display on 4 November, settling instead for a civic dinner.[49] Nevertheless, as long as the war lasted, it was not to be expected that the authorities would discountenance Williamite anniversaries entirely. After all, the parallels between the wars of the 1690s and the 1790s were obvious, and in so far as Williamite anniversaries represented the celebration of earlier defeats of the French—a dimension emphasized in the loyalist press—they played a part in maintaining wartime morale. Thus the celebration of those anniversaries continued to be regarded with official tolerance, despite the disturbances that from time to time occurred in Dublin and elsewhere. Flags were flown at the Castle to mark 4 November; the guns at the Phoenix Park were fired; the duke of Richmond (viceroy,

[47] *FJ*, 16 July 1821.

[48] One town where the reforms of 1793 had already given the corporation a predominantly Catholic complexion was Galway, where Protestants were few (Martin Coen, *The Wardenship of Galway* (Galway, 1984), 46–7).

[49] Hill, 'National Festivals, the State and "Protestant Ascendancy" ', 40–1. *DEP* (5 Nov. 1807) noted with approval that the lord mayor and corporation, 'with much true patriotism and good sense, declined appearing on the occasion'. The subject remains unexplored, but there are signs that as 4 Nov. fell out of official favour, conservative Protestants made more of 5 Nov. (still marked in the liturgy of the united established church).

1807–13) was prepared to drink to the 'glorious, pious and immortal memory of King William'; and Robert Peel (chief secretary, 1812–18) retained much sympathy with ultra-Protestant values.[50]

Once the war was over, such official indulgence could no longer be taken for granted. The Catholic contribution to the war effort seemed to call, if not for outright emancipation, then at least for a spirit of goodwill that sat uncomfortably beside periodic reminders of former defeats at Protestant hands—for once the anti-French dimension had receded, and in the absence of any threat from absolute monarchy, it was difficult to interpret these anniversaries in any other light. In keeping with this spirit, the Irish administration began, cautiously, to indicate its confidence in Catholics; in 1816 a Catholic was appointed to the revenue board in Dublin.[51] Meanwhile, although the Orange Order had dropped its original secret articles and the clause in its oath that made loyalty to the king conditional on his being Protestant, its growing presence in Britain, particularly in the army, was a cause of concern in parliament. Attempts were made in 1815 and 1816 to obtain an inquiry into Orange societies, and in 1816 several MPs called for them to be suppressed.[52] Nothing was done, but the Order remained an object of suspicion.

Against this background, in 1816 the *Freeman's Journal* began to call for a ban on the public celebration of Williamite anniversaries in Dublin, on the grounds that they were divisive and caused disturbances. Implicitly, this represented a call for action by Dublin Castle, which had regained some initiative in the policing of the capital through the appointment of two-thirds of the divisional justices under the 1808 Dublin police magistrates act.[53] (Dublin corporation appointed the rest, and the chief magistrate of police, who hired the watchmen, was required to be an alderman.) Accordingly, the successors of the duke of Richmond and Peel came under some pressure from the pro-emancipation press to distance themselves completely from the cult. The first administrator who seemed likely to comply with these hints was Peel's successor as chief secretary, the Scot Charles Grant. Grant's appointment in August 1818 was followed within weeks by the inauguration as lord mayor (according to seniority) of Alderman Thomas McKenny—who in 1819 was to chair the Protestant meeting in support of emancipation.[54] At the customary civic dinner for the viceroy to mark the inauguration, McKenny, wishing to dispense with the customary toast to King William's memory and the playing of what were

---

[50] Hill, 'National Festivals, the State and "Protestant Ascendancy" ', 37–45.
[51] *FJ*, 7 Mar. 1816.
[52] *FJ*, 13 July 1815, 9 May 1816; Senior, *Orangeism in Ireland and Britain*, 151–63, 192.
[53] 48 Geo. III, c. 140.
[54] The *FJ* reported approvingly (1 Oct. 1818) that the usual orange and purple 'party' colours would not be displayed on his coach during the inaugural procession, only the civic colours of scarlet and yellow.

now labelled 'party' tunes, clashed with members of Giffard's party. A few days later, at Sheriff White's dinner for the new lord mayor, Grant's name was hissed.[55] For the first time since the short-lived 'Talents' ministry of 1806–7, the ultra Protestants found themselves out of sympathy with the administration; and this proved merely the start of a more serious cooling of relations between that party and government over the next five years.

It was not mere chance that this confrontation over Williamite toasts and anniversaries coincided with brighter prospects for emancipation in British politics, following the 1818 general election. The issue remained to the fore in Dublin during 1819, for the holding of the Protestant pro-emancipation meeting provoked opponents of the measure to organize a counter-petition. That move backfired when its sponsors, heedless of official sensitivities about the presence of Orangeism in the army, allowed the petition to be left at the barracks for signature. A regimental order was issued, warning soldiers that interference in political matters constituted a violation of duty, and reminding officers that they should try to prevent their men from attending Orange lodges.[56] These developments were encouraging to the conductors of the pro-emancipation press; and the subsequent disappointment over the election of Thomas Ellis as MP for the city in 1820 was correspondingly severe.

Following the election, the pro-emancipation press continued to snipe at the ultra Protestants, and in particular to highlight their links with the Orange Order. In July 1820 the *Freeman's Journal* carried a letter from a Limerick freeholder, claiming that since Ellis's victory a deputation from a Dublin Orange lodge in Werburgh Street had visited Limerick to invite any local Orangemen who could afford it to apply for freedom of Dublin corporation, so as to swell the number of votes for their party.[57] In October, the incoming lord mayor, Alderman King,[58] was criticized for displaying orange colours on his state carriage, together with a medal that was said to bear the likeness of King William and the words 'glorious and immortal memory'. But a call from the *Freeman's Journal* for the magistrates to curb the celebrations expected for William's birthday on 4 November produced no noticeable response.[59]

---

[55] *FJ*, 3, 8 Oct. 1818. Robert White, partner in Hawkes, Mosley & Co., army hatters, Grafton St., sheriff 1818–19. The tunes included 'Croppies Lie Down', alleged to have been played at every civic feast since 1798 (Jeremiah Single (pseud.), *McKenny's Feast, an Ode* (Dublin, 1818), 3–4).   [56] *FJ*, 25, 26 Feb., 1, 8 Mar. 1819.

[57] *FJ*, 28 July 1820.

[58] Abraham Bradley King (1773–1838); king's stationer; sometime deputy grand master of the Orange Order, alderman 1805, lord mayor 1812–13, 1820–1, created bt. 1821. Popular in civic circles as mayor for his munificence and for asserting in person the corporation's right to present petitions at the bar of the house of commons. His second mayoralty arose out of a dispute (settled by the privy council) between the two houses of the corporation over the city finances (*CARD* xvi. 415; xvii. 512–19, 541–2).

[59] *FJ*, 2, 3 Oct., 3 Nov. 1820.

It was at this period that the hosiers' guild took an initiative that was to bear fruit in 1821. In December 1820 the guild addressed George IV, now king in his own right, referring to the distressed condition of Ireland, alluding (delicately) to the fact that many benefits supposed to flow from the union had not materialized, and suggesting that nothing was more calculated to strengthen the bond between Ireland and Britain than a visit, or periodic visits, from the king. Early in the new year the corporation was able to report a gracious response to this appeal.[60]

The news that George IV intended to visit Ireland was greeted in Dublin with general enthusiasm. The ultra Protestants in particular had reason for complacency. It was well known that the king had long since abandoned the Whigs, and had embraced essentially the same conventional position on the constitution as his father. The ultras had therefore sided with him during the constitutional crisis that threatened to arise from his divorce proceedings against his estranged wife, Princess Caroline, in 1819–20.[61] As recently as December 1820, following the abandoning of the divorce case, certain ultra Protestants had taken part in a meeting to express loyalty to the king; and the corporation, too, had presented a loyal address.[62] The Catholics were less happily placed. In common with Whig politicians in England, O'Connell and other leading Irish Catholics had publicly taken the queen's side over the divorce; and from November 1820 until the summer of 1821 O'Connell was pursuing the possibility of his appointment as the queen's attorney-general in Ireland. Not until June 1821 did the Catholics begin to plan a meeting to address the king.[63]

It was therefore from a position of some strength that in the city commons, Sir Edward Stanley,[64] a prominent supporter of the late John Giffard, expressed the magnanimous hope that the royal visit would unite Protestant and Catholic, rich and poor.[65] An opportunity for the corporation to display a conciliatory spirit soon arose. The Williamite summer anniversary season was approaching, and the Orange Order had recently

---

[60] *FJ*, 28 Dec. 1820; *CARD* xvii. 360. A meeting of citizens reinforced the invitation (*FJ*, 29 Jan. 1821).

[61] The prince and his wife had lived apart almost from the outset of their marriage in 1795. On George III's death in Jan. 1820 Caroline returned to become queen, but George IV began divorce proceedings in the house of lords on the grounds of her adultery. Amid popular sympathy for the queen and damaging press publicity, the attempt was abandoned in Nov. 1820, but Caroline died suddenly on 7 Aug. 1821 (Colley, *Britons*, 265–8).

[62] Report of Co. Dublin meeting to address the king (*FJ*, 1 Jan. 1821); *CARD* xvii. 349–50; address of St Luke's guild to the king (NLI, MS 12127, pp. 160–4). A liberal guild, the glovers, addressed the queen via the duke of Leinster (*Autobiography of Archibald Hamilton Rowan*, 398–9).

[63] Above, n. 10; *O'Connell Corr.* ii, letter 907; *FJ*, 5, 6 July 1821.

[64] Sir Edward Stanley, sheriff 1809–10 (knighted on occasion of George III's jubilee); sheriffs' peer 1810–41; deputy barrack master to Dublin city; wine and provision supplier to Dublin Castle.

[65] *FJ*, 5 Mar. 1821. Giffard had died, aged 73, on 5 May 1819 (*Gent's Mag.*, 98 (1819), 484).

suffered a setback when in June 1821 the heir to the throne, the duke of York, reacted to further hostile questions in parliament concerning the Order by resigning as grand master of British Orange lodges. In these circumstances, support grew in the corporation and outside it for the lord mayor to ban the ceremonial dressing of the statue on 12 July. Although Alderman King was himself an Orangeman, he announced his willingness to comply with this groundswell of opinion by banning the ceremony. The welcome given to the ban in the pro-emancipation press was tempered by a certain scepticism about its probable effect, which turned out to be only too well founded. According to press reports, at the very moment when the lord mayor was explaining the ban to members of the Werburgh Street Orange lodge, the deed itself was being accomplished by a group of journeymen tailors. Liberal Protestants and Catholics were outraged, and Alderman King showed his displeasure by resigning from the Order.[66]

The incident had put the lord mayor in the wrong, and given a handle to the Catholics, who were quick to point out that soldiers had been among those taking part in the Orange celebrations on 12 July. For a time, it looked as if co-operation between Catholics and Dublin corporation in respect of the royal visit would prove abortive. However, some were prepared to concede that the lord mayor had been well intentioned, and his resignation from the Order was appreciated. According to the *Freeman's Journal* O'Connell even looked back nostalgically to the day when (he claimed) Protestants and Catholics had marched 'arm in arm' round the statue.[67] At all events, meetings began to take place between the lord mayor and Catholic representatives to make arrangements for the visit. In the city commons another of Giffard's supporters, Robert Sutter,[68] attempted to dissociate the corporation from the lord mayor's eirenic moves. But this attempt failed. At a public meeting chaired by the lord mayor it was agreed that a committee of thirty-two stewards (sixteen Protestants and sixteen Catholics) should be appointed to make the arrangments for a 'coronation dinner' to coincide with the anniversary of the Hanoverian succession (1 August). In a remarkable gesture (as a sign 'of our mutual confidence and good will') the Catholic stewards would be nominated by Protestants, and vice versa. Not surprisingly, most of the Protestants nominated were liberals, but several of them were corporation members, and at least one had a record of opposing emancipation.[69]

[66] Senior, *Orangeism in Ireland and Britain*, 173–4; *FJ*, 11 July 1821; *Patriot* report, in *FJ*, 16 July; Catholic meeting report, *FJ*, 14 July 1821.   [67] *FJ*, 14, 16, 18 July 1821.

[68] Robert Sutter, admitted free of brewers' guild by grace as a practising brewer (GMD, Brewers' guild, minute book 1804–31, entry for 28 Jan. 1810); representative of brewers' guild 1811–22, merchants' guild 1823–41, made inspector of pipe-water collectors, 1824 (*CARD* xviii. 68).

[69] Report of Dublin corporation meeting, *FJ*, 21 July 1821. The opponent of emancipation was Alderman Archer, n. 21 above (*FJ*, 31 July 1821).

The dinner itself, which took place shortly before the king's arrival, turned out to be a model of harmony. Some 400 Catholics and Protestants attended, the lord mayor presided, and the Catholic earl of Fingall was vice-president. Among the toasts, the duke of Wellington (the 'conquering hero') and the memory of Nelson figured prominently. No Orange tunes or toasts intruded; although the air 'St Patrick's Day'—which ultra Protestants associated with Catholic claims—was played. And as a follow-up, the citizens were urged to attend vestry meetings to prepare for the visit and to promote the use of Irish-made goods for the occasion.[70] Thus in terms of real interdenominational co-operation at civic level, some progress had been made since the royal celebrations of 1809 and 1814, when the organization had been entirely Protestant. The *Freeman's Journal* commented 'These things look indeed as if we should at last be ONE PEOPLE.'[71]

The same spirit pervaded the king's visit itself. The crowds were large and enthusiastic; expressions of loyalty emanated from all sides. The king's evident desire to 'conciliate' the Catholics (the term 'conciliation' in this context now came into vogue) was manifested in his reception of the Catholic bishops wearing their robes, and by the installation of the earl of Fingall as one of the Knights of St Patrick.[72] There were even plans to raise subscriptions to build a royal palace as an inducement for further visits, 'to which', O'Connell hypothesized, 'not alone the rank around him could contribute, but . . . every peasant could from his cottage contribute his humble mite'.[73] Not until the occasion of the civic dinner did a note of controversy creep into press reports. During the evening, well after the king and his host the lord mayor had left, the presiding alderman (Beresford) came under some pressure from representatives of the craft guilds to toast 'the glorious memory'. In the *Freeman's Journal*'s words, the request was refused, on the grounds 'that to grant it would be to break a solemn compact, which the nation, and the illustrious Guest who had been but a few hours before in that room, had so highly approved'.[74] At that point, Alderman Darley,[75] an Orangeman and head of the Dublin police, proposed the toast himself.

Following his return to England, the king reiterated his support for

[70] *FJ*, 2, 4, 16 Aug. 1821. The activists at the vestry meetings were mostly Protestants. On the significance of the tune 'St Patrick's Day' see Hill, 'National Festivals, the State and "Protestant Ascendancy" ', 43–8.   [71] *FJ*, 31 July 1821.

[72] *FJ*, 4, 15, 16, 21, 22, 24, 25, 29 Aug. 1821.

[73] *FJ*, 22 Aug. 1821. For the palace scheme see also ibid., 31 Aug., 11 Sept. 1821. Catholics and Protestants served on the organizing committee; by 1822 the plans were being pruned for lack of funds (*FJ*, 26 April 1822).   [74] *FJ*, 25, 27 Aug. 1821.

[75] Frederick Darley, architect, d. 1841; sheriff 1798–9, alderman 1800, lord mayor 1808–9; head of Dublin police from 1814; brother-in-law of the 2nd Arthur Guinness. His buildings (including the merchants' guildhall, 1821) are noted in Craig, *Dublin*, 298. His defiance on this occasion became the theme of ballads and satires: e.g. *Judy's Lamentation on the Departure of His Majesty from Dublin* [1821], NLI, JP 4268.

'conciliation', news of which was conveyed in a ministerial letter, widely publicized in pro-emancipation circles.[76] But only a month later, the toast was proposed in public again; this time by the incoming lord mayor (Alderman Sir John Kingston James)[77] at a Mansion House dinner for the viceroy. The outcry that greeted this latest sign of intransigence was not confined to Ireland. English newspapers, including *The Times*, condemned the lord mayor for disregarding the king's exhortations and for fostering 'party discord'. With the anniversary of King William's birthday imminent, the lord mayor and police magistrates decided to ban the dressing of the statue. But once again rank-and-file Orangemen got the better of them.[78] With the magistrates apparently unable to enforce a ban, during the winter of 1821–2 the supporters of conciliation took heart from two appointments of ministers favourable to Catholic claims: Marquis Wellesley as lord-lieutenant, and W. C. Plunket as attorney-general in place of the ultra Protestant, William Saurin. In these circumstances, Catholics showed signs of becoming even more ardent monarchists than Protestants, with O'Connell insisting that Ireland celebrate the second anniversary of the king's accession to the throne (29 January 1822).[79]

One effect of these appointments was to prompt fresh efforts by sympathetic Protestants, the first since the end of the war, to induce the guilds—of their own volition—to admit Catholics. The most important of these initiatives occurred in the merchants' guild. In January 1822 George Ness,[80] a Scottish merchant who had worked in Dublin for over thirty years, gave notice that he intended to propose the names of twenty Catholic merchants, residents of Dublin, for admission to the guild by special grace. His stated aim was 'to give effect to the existing laws, to promote conciliation and His Majesty's paternal Recommendation'. Attendance at the meeting was unusually large (a sign that the outcome was not a foregone conclusion) and included at least two MPs.[81] Nearly 300 members took part in the final ballot on the applications.

During the debates, those in favour of admission dwelled chiefly on the ministerial letter. Until recently, they conceded, opponents could feel that

[76] Lord Sidmouth to the viceroy, 3 Sept. 1821 (*FJ*, 5 Sept. 1821).

[77] Sir John Kingston James, bt. (1784–1869), wholesale wine and West India merchant (son of Francis James, merchant); sheriff 1811–12, alderman 1817, lord mayor 1821–2, 1840–1; treasurer, Dublin corporation, 1828–41; created bt. on occasion of king's visit.

[78] *FJ*, 2, 10 Oct., 3, 5 Nov. 1821. The deed was carried out after careful planning by Dublin Orange lodges (NA, CSORP, 1821/26, 1821/304).

[79] *FJ*, 16 Jan. 1822. Richard Wellesley, 1st Marquis Wellesley, viceroy 1821–8. William Conyngham Plunket, attorney-general 1822–7 (*DNB*).

[80] Ness had come to Dublin in 1788, serving an apprenticeship in the firm of La Touche (merchants' guild report, *FJ*, 23, 24 Apr. 1822).

[81] Thomas Ellis, MP Dublin city; James Grattan, MP Co. Wicklow. For the meeting, see DPLGC, MS 79, fos. 348–9; *FJ*, 11, 15, 16 Jan. 1822. A bid to admit Catholics to the coopers' guild came to nothing (*FJ*, 17 Jan. 1822).

they enjoyed the support of higher powers: this was now no longer the case. However, the viceroy, although approached beforehand by Ness, had refused to lend his own authority to the initiative;[82] and this argument made little impression on the opponents of admission, who drew attention to the disturbed state of the country. The south of Ireland, they asserted, was effectively in a state of rebellion: a more appropriate time to admit Catholics to the exercise of political power in the towns would be when king and parliament had unequivocally endorsed emancipation, and when the country was peaceful. Meanwhile, asked Thomas Ellis, MP, rhetorically, 'were the merchants of Dublin to be intimidated like the landholders of Munster?'[83] After more speeches, Robert Sutter proposed an adjournment, *sine die*. The subsequent ballot recorded 240 in favour of adjournment, and 59 against. The qualities of the individual Catholic merchants themselves were not touched on; indeed, opponents were careful to stress that they bore the Catholics no hostility. The debate was conducted solely in terms of the wider political implications of admission.

Following another unsuccessful attempt to raise the question in April, Ness repeated his bid for Catholic admission in October. The tenor of the debate was much the same. One opponent of admission remarked, 'Surely Mr Ness could not expect them to commit an act of suicide upon themselves, by the transfer of such political power, the object of which was to influence the elective franchise . . .'[84] And even Henry Grattan, junior, while acknowledging Ness's good intentions, gave his view that the initiative was not timely. He moved a successful amendment to the effect that no disrespect was intended to the respectable Catholic merchants concerned, but that it was not expedient to grant them their freedom at present.[85] Again, however, the price exacted for this stand was a high one. Until 1822 several prominent Dublin Catholic merchants were still at loggerheads with O'Connell over the question of the veto. Following the failure of these attempts to effect admission to the guilds, opposition in these quarters to O'Connell's hardline rejection of a veto disappeared.[86]

Wellesley's appointment as viceroy also prompted an unprecedented campaign for an effective ban on the public celebration of Williamite anniversaries in Dublin. In the summer of 1822 the Catholics themselves,

[82] Ness's correspondence with the chief secretary was published (*Warder*, 19 Jan. 1822); see also Ness, *A Letter to Henry Brougham*, 12–13. Ness had failed to persuade the duke of Leinster to propose or second his motion (Ness to Leinster, 10 Jan. 1822, Leinster papers, PRONI, D 3078/3/14/3).

[83] *FJ*, 15 Jan. 1822. The 1821 potato crop had failed, and a wave of agrarian unrest in Munster (with millenarian and anti-tithe overtones) led in Feb. 1822 to the passing of an insurrection act and the suspension of habeas corpus (3 Geo. IV, c. 1 & 2); Vaughan (ed.), *NHI* v. 81–3.

[84] *FJ*, 16, 23 Apr., 7, 15 Oct. 1822; DPLGC, MS 79, fos. 350–1.

[85] Grattan later claimed that both he and James Grattan had voted for Ness's motion ('Union', in *FJ*, 20 Nov. 1822).   [86] Hill, 'The Politics of Privilege', 34.

who had hitherto remained prudently in the background, entered the fray. O'Connell addressed an open letter to the viceroy, the burden of which was that Wellesley's reputation would stand or fall by his conduct in respect of the celebrations on 12 July. He urged the viceroy to dismiss civic magistrates who failed to prevent a breach of the peace. But interference by the state in matters that fell within the corporation's purview was still a sensitive issue, and the publication of this letter probably did more harm than good to the cause of securing an effective ban on Orange celebrations in Dublin. O'Connell himself later tacitly admitted that the letter had alienated Wellesley. At all events, the outcome was not significantly different from previous years. On 12 July the statue was decorated, and the usual disturbances took place, giving rise to protests in parliament itself, and more calls for official action.[87]

Three months later Alderman Fleming,[88] who was liberal in his sympathies, took office as lord mayor, and on this occasion the viceroy sought and obtained the attorney-general's opinion that the chief magistrate had the authority to ban the dressing of the statue. The lord mayor's proclamation in advance of 4 November turned out to be the most effective action to date. The police succeeded in preventing the dressing of the statue, although they failed to stop Orangemen gathering in numbers in College Green, firing guns and celebrating until early the next morning. According to the *Freeman's Journal*, hapless passers-by were forced to salute the statue—'Down on your knees to King William—a groan for the Lord Mayor—and Damn the Pope.'[89]

Resentment against the lord mayor's action was not confined to the artisan-class Orangemen who in recent years had preserved the tradition of dressing the statue. On 2 November nearly fifty members of the city commons assembled in response to a circular, and by 45 votes to 2 passed a resolution censuring the lord mayor for his proclamation. Since the sheriffs were not present, this did not constitute a valid meeting of the lower house, but it indicated the strength of feeling on the matter. A separate issue, then before the public, was calculated to intensify the sense of alienation from a lord mayor whose action had exposed him to the charge that he was a pawn of the administration. Early in November, revelations in a Dublin court pointed to the existence of a widely diffused, oath-bound Ribbon society, whose members were organized in lodges and who were, allegedly, preparing for the destruction of Protestantism in line with the prophecies of

---

[87] O'Connell to Marquis Wellesley (*FJ*, 11 July 1822); NA, CSORP, 1822/1359; parliamentary reports, *FJ*, 11, 12, 13, 20, 22, 23 July, 2 Aug. 1822; *O'Connell Corr.* ii, letter 982.

[88] John Smith Fleming, card manufacturer; sheriff 1814–15, alderman 1816, lord mayor 1822–3.

[89] NA, CSORP, 1822/1359; *FJ*, 1, 4, 6 Nov. 1822.

Pastorini. Six Dublin Ribbonmen were eventually sentenced to transportation for administering illegal oaths.[90]

At the forthcoming guild elections for representatives on the city commons, passions ran high in the guild of merchants, where determined and successful efforts were made to return among the guild's thirty-one representatives Robert Sutter, whose part in the move to censure the lord mayor had incurred the displeasure of the liberal brewers' guild, which duly dropped him as one of its own representatives.[91] A speech by the master of the merchants' guild, Alderman Nugent,[92] reflects the almost apocalyptic atmosphere that had arisen as a result of the estrangement between the ultra Protestants and the administration, as the political climate began to change in favour of the Catholics:

We must defeat the conspiracy of a certain Junto in this City, who are determined to put us down, aye, and the Government too is putting us down rather than rising [*sic*] us up, and in this they are supported by time-serving men who readily change their politics with every change of Government. *The time is not now far distant when the Government*, when every Protestant will *require and be happy to obtain the assistance* of such men as the independent, the loyal Robert Sutter . . . [here looking at Alderman King] We once had a Protestant Board of Aldermen, of whose loyalty we could boast . . . now we have liberal conceders, philanthropic legislators, and disinterested peace-makers, who has [*sic*] endeavoured, by armed force, to smother our annual demonstrations of loyalty to the Protestant House of Brunswick; but is there a man who does not bewail the day the Statue was not dressed? . . . These are quere [*sic*] times, they cannot last long—there must be a change some way or other.[93]

The change, which came about more quickly than Alderman Nugent could have imagined, arose from incidents that occurred during the viceroy's first state visit to the Theatre Royal on 14 December 1822. The visit had been publicized beforehand and the cream of society was expected to be present. From the outset a section of the audience was clearly determined to demonstrate its disenchantment with the administration. Scurrilous leaflets were distributed, bearing insulting remarks about the 'Ex-governor of the Bantams' (Wellesley, a former governor-general of India, was a small man). There were catcalls and groans for the 'knave of clubs' (the lord mayor was a manufacturer of playing cards). The performance (of Goldsmith's *She Stoops to Conquer*) however, had got as far as the fifth act,

---

[90] *FJ*, 4, 6, 14 Nov. 1822.

[91] Report of brewers' guild meeting, *FJ*, 11 Nov. 1822. Sutter claimed that the guild dropped him after a deputation of publicans threatened to withhold their custom (speech at merchants' guild, *FJ*, 18 Nov. 1822).

[92] Edmond Nugent, cloth merchant; sheriff 1806–7, alderman 1819, lord mayor 1827–8, knighted 1828. By 1828 Nugent was on dining terms with O'Connell and unpopular in the city commons (DCA, C1/JSC/11, fo. 190).

[93] Report of merchants' guild meeting (*FJ*, 18 Nov. 1822).

when actors, appearing on stage with tankards, were exhorted from the audience to toast the 'Glorious Memory'. This interruption was ignored, but a bottle was thrown at the stage. Shortly afterwards, as the band played 'St Patrick's Day', and Wellesley was seen to mark time, part of a watchman's rattle was thrown at the viceregal box. The viceroy was not hit, but his secretary promptly ordered the arrest of those responsible.[94]

The incident, though trivial in itself, had far-reaching consequences. The viceroy was disposed to treat it seriously ('this awful and calamitous occasion') as an attempt to injure or even assassinate him. Public excitement was intense. The Catholic leaders, reacting with understandable speed, announced a meeting to express their abhorrence of 'the recent daring outrage offered to the representative of our beloved Sovereign'.[95] Other citizens and public institutions, including the corporation and certain guilds, hastened to follow suit. One theme at such meetings, much stressed by liberal Protestants and Catholics, was the responsibility of Orangemen for the disturbances, and the need for government to suppress all secret societies, both Ribbon and Orange. Criticism, too, was levelled at the police, whose conduct during the disturbances had been lax, and at the corporation, since Frederick Darley, head of the police, was an alderman. Above all, the Catholic spokesmen seized the opportunity to hammer home their theme that loyalty was not the prerogative of Protestants alone. They also took the chance to praise the viceroy's achievements 'for the glory of the British empire'—achievements that had been mocked in the theatre handbills.[96] More important, however, than the reaction in Ireland was press opinion in England, which would indicate the probable parliamentary response. Although some newspapers were inclined to treat it more lightly than others, the English press generally deplored the incident. Significantly, the Whig press singled out the corporation for rebuke: 'We have long witnessed with pain the disgraceful proceedings of the fanatics of the Corporation of Dublin, but so flagrant a departure from decency as was displayed on the occasion alluded to was more than we anticipated . . .'[97]

For their part, the Dublin magistrates puzzled over whether to charge those arrested with riot or treason. On 23 December, three prisoners, a carpenter, a printer, and a man with 'respectable connections' (all later identified as Orangemen) were committed on capital charges, and three

[94] *FJ*, 11, 16, 17 Dec. 1822. For a semi-serious account (written from the perpetrators' standpoint) implicating *agents provocateurs*, see *X O Fish O! A Patched, Vamp'd, Future, Old, Revived Bran-New Poem* (Dublin, 1823).

[95] Reply from viceroy to Dublin corporation's address (*CARD* xvii. 496); requisition for a Catholic meeting (*FJ*, 16 Dec. 1922).

[96] For the corporation and guild meetings (cooks, merchants, smiths, and barbers), see *CARD* xvii. 494–5, *FJ*, 18, 20, 23, 28 Dec. 1822; for parish and public meetings, ibid., 20, 21, 23, 24, 28 Dec. 1822, 1 Jan. 1823.

[97] Extract from *Morning Chronicle*, reprinted in *FJ*, 21 Dec. 1822. For other English press views see also *FJ*, 20, 27 Dec. 1822, 1 Jan. 1823.

others were charged with causing a riot. However, to the chagrin of the attorney-general, on 2 January 1823 a city grand jury (empanelled by Sheriff Charles Thorp,[98] whose Orange sympathies had already made him an object of suspicion in certain quarters) found that there was no case to answer. When the crown subsequently brought a prosecution of its own against the prisoners, the jury failed to agree, and the case was lost.[99] But although those directly concerned escaped punishment, the implications for the Orange Order, and also for the corporation, were serious. Only six months earlier, the prime minister, Lord Liverpool, had defended the rights of those who wished to hold public ceremonies to mark Williamite anniversaries. Now the attorney-general had stated in court that the Irish administration, the cabinet, and the king himself, had all approved the viceroy's view that the dressing of the statue should be discontinued. The ban had become official, at the highest level.[100]

From all this, the Orange Order in Dublin had emerged with much discredit. At best, it seemed to be loutish, and obsessed with rituals now widely deemed to be divisive; at worst, it could be seen as seeking to overawe the government by violent or even murderous means. The following July, troops were posted to prevent the dressing of the statue, and parliament strengthened the laws against oath-bound associations. Two years later the unlawful societies (Ireland) act suppressed all large political organizations, Orange and Catholic.[101] Although the Orange Order was reconstituted in 1825 on the lines of a friendly society, it aroused little enthusiasm among Orangemen. Not until the autumn of 1828, when the act lapsed, was the Orange Order restored on its old foundation, with the customary oaths and signs.[102]

The public celebration of Williamite anniversaries in Dublin never recovered from this setback, which effectively marked the end of the period when the lower classes of Protestants, despite their status as a numerical minority, could periodically assert their dominance in the capital city. As for the corporation, it had been castigated in the English press; and the conduct of Sheriff Thorp, in empanelling an 'Orange' jury, became the subject of a

---

[98] Charles Thorp, jun., plasterer, sheriff 1822–3, sheriffs' peer 1823–41. Allegedly, he was related to the prisoners (O'Connell Corr. ii, letter 982). The fall-out from the 'bottle riot' blighted his civic career prospects: in 1839 the corporation awarded him £300 compensation for his expenses at the 1823 parliamentary inquiry (CARD xix. 243, 367).

[99] FJ, 19, 24 Dec. 1822, 3 Jan., 10 Feb. 1823. Several policemen were sacked for not stopping disturbances earlier on 14 Dec. (FJ, 18 Dec. 1822).

[100] FJ, 2 Aug. 1822; FJ supplement, 7 Feb. 1823. Even the corporation supported the ban (DCA, C1/JSC/11, fo. 56; CARD xviii. 34).

[101] 4 Geo. IV, c. 87; 6 Geo. IV, c. 4. Public celebrations of Williamite anniversaries also ended about this time in Cork city; see correspondence between Cork magistrates and the viceroy, DEP, 1 July 1823.

[102] Senior, Orangeism in Ireland and Britain, 207, 218–19.

parliamentary inquiry in 1823.[103] The chief beneficiaries were the Catholics, who were able to organize the emancipation campaign in Dublin from 1824 to 1828 free of the irritation of the Order and the periodic public assertions of exclusive Protestant loyalty. O'Connell's jubilation at the unexpected turn of events was reflected in a letter to his wife, a week after the theatre incident: 'You may imagine what a curious revolution it is in Dublin when the Catholics are admitted to be the only genuine loyalists. For the first time has this truth reached the Castle . . . If we had hired at large wages the Orangemen, they would not have done our business half so well . . .'[104]

---

[103] See *Papers Relating to a Riot at Dublin Theatre on the 14th December 1822*, HC 1823 (165), vi; *Minutes of Evidence, Taken Before the Committee of the Whole House, From May 2, to May 27, on the Conduct of the Sheriff of the City of Dublin, in Relation to [the Dublin Theatre Riot]*, HC 1823 (308), vi. The latter inquiry heard allegations about the influence of a quasi-Orange 'amicable society' in the city commons (p. 46), influencing the choice of sheriff. It was probably similar to a faction headed by John Giffard, said to influence the selection of aldermen (*FJ*, 30 Mar. 1816).

[104] *O'Connell Corr.* ii, letter 982.

13

The Ancien régime *Defended,*
1822–1832

I. *The Inseparability of Religion and Politics*

The Freemen of Dublin maintained, that the Reformation, the Revolution, and the Act of Settlement, formed a consummate whole, unequalled in perfection . . . and if the rest of Ireland was inundated by sedition, Dublin would still be a refuge for those who lingered [*sic*] after British law, and sought for British protection.[1]

By the end of 1822 the late John Giffard's party in the Dublin city commons was in disarray. In part, this stemmed from the increasing dislike in official circles for the cult of King William in general and for the Orange Order in particular. Giffard's supporters had links with both. But they were not alone in having such connections, and the problem was not simply one of a poor public image. The real difficulty lay in the apparent bankruptcy of the strategy proclaimed by Giffard as far back as 1800. Central to that strategy, as formulated by the earl of Clare and others, was the conviction that, following the relaxation of the penal laws, the maintenance of Protestant control in Ireland would best be secured through union with Great Britain. A union would safeguard the established church and the British link, turn the Irish Catholics into a minority, and secure Protestant ascendancy. The necessary price to be paid was the surrender of the Irish parliament; yet that sacrifice would be worth making, not only for the supposed political benefits, but because a union was expected to encourage British investment and boost prosperity, thus helping to reconcile the Catholic majority to the status quo.

For some twenty years this had been the refrain, first of Giffard alone, later backed by his small band of unionist supporters in the city commons, in marked contrast to the general anti-union spirit of that body.[2] By 1822, however, apart from anything else, the state of the country was raising serious questions about the benefits of union. The south and west of Ireland gripped by famine and fever; agrarian and anti-tithe disturbances on the increase; chronic industrial depression in Dublin; and worst of all, as far as ultra Protestants were concerned, a dangerous tendency on the part of the

[1] Speech by John Semple, sheriffs' peer, at civic dinner (*Warder*, 17 Jan. 1824).
[2] Above, Ch. 10.

administration to indulge Catholics and their Protestant supporters, rather than upholding those Protestants who, in their own eyes, represented the only real loyalists in Ireland.

In these circumstances, the unionists faltered. Their commitment to Protestant ascendancy, in its national and local manifestations, was as strong as ever, but their belief in union as the guarantee of ascendancy and the solution to Ireland's other problems was being severely tested. After Giffard's death in 1819 his supporter John Semple[3] continued to eulogize the union in the city commons, but a more notorious adherent, Robert Sutter, added his voice to the call for repeal of the union that sounded again in corporate circles during 1822. In October 1822 the merchants' and glovers' guilds adopted repeal resolutions, as did the city commons—the latter with only one dissenting voice. Speakers noted the decay of trade, the condition of the people, and the resulting danger to the British connection. At the aldermanic board, the resolution was lost only by the narrow margin of 7 votes to 9.[4] Another former Giffard supporter, Alderman Nugent, master of the guild of merchants, now referred to the union as 'that fatal act', and he called on the lord mayor to convene a public meeting to petition for repeal. The city MPs came under pressure to take a stand. Shaw agreed that the union had been damaging, though he believed that repeal was impracticable; Ellis took much the same view. Alderman King stood out as resisting repeal resolutions in the merchants' guild in 1822; but otherwise for the time being the ultra-Protestant unionists tended to fade back into the general body of Dublin freemen who had always deplored the abolition of the Irish parliament.[5]

Criticizing the union and calling for its repeal afforded some relief to all those freemen who were concerned about the country's prospects and for the increasingly uncertain future of Protestant control. An immediate task was to reaffirm the necessity for parliament to remain an exclusively Protestant preserve. And, despite recent setbacks, this was far from being a lost cause. It still had the backing of articulate advocates in government, notably the lord chancellor, Lord Eldon, and members of the royal family, including the heir to the throne, the duke of York, and his brother the duke of Cumberland.[6] George IV himself became more rather than less hostile to full emancipation as the decade passed. Moreover, another ally was

---

[3] John Semple, plasterer; chosen sheriff 1797, but excused after fine; appointed first Dublin city architect, 1823; sheriffs' peer 1797–1841 (*CARD* xviii. 46, 502).

[4] DCA, C1/JSC/11, fo. 34; DPLGC, MS 79, pp. 351–2; *FJ*, 14, 15, 19, 21 Oct. 1822.

[5] *FJ*, 15 Oct., 4 Nov. 1822. Repeal activity in civic circles had been encouraged by a report that Lucius Concannon, Irish-born MP for Winchelsea, intended to move for repeal in parliament; in the event, he did not (*FJ*, 20 July 1822; report of glovers' guild meeting, ibid., 14 Oct. 1822).

[6] The corporation's anti-emancipation sentiments were expressed to or through these personnel (*CARD* xviii. 138, 217–19, 351).

appearing. By the 1820s there were signs in the Church of Ireland of the preoccupation with the Catholic challenge that was to be so characteristic of the nineteenth century. This highlighted the common ground between the established church and the Dublin corporate bodies.

The Church of Ireland shared with the Irish corporations a particularly exposed position as the confessional state came under attack in the 1820s. Superficially, there was little sign of this. The Church of Ireland was still, officially, 'the national church', its connection with the state guaranteed 'for ever' by the act of union. But in fact its position was precarious. Its status had been weakened by concessions to dissenters, especially the repeal of the sacramental test in 1780, which removed the main distinction—in the eyes of the state—between the established church and Protestant dissent in Ireland. The wide range of political rights extended to Catholics in 1792 and 1793 suggested that here too the state made little distinction between an Irish Protestant and an Irish Catholic. In England, by contrast, where the test and corporation acts still remained on the statute book, where Catholics had no vote, and where the established church was strong in numerical terms, the privileged status of Anglicans and their church appeared much more secure.

Other forces, too, were combining to weaken the established church. One was the growing confidence of the Irish Catholic church, aided by the relaxation of the penal laws and the resurgence of the papacy as a bastion of order and authority in post-war Europe. The early 1800s had seen the breakdown of the eighteenth-century consensus among Irish Anglicans and 'enlightened' Catholics that the pre-Norman church in Ireland had been effectively free from Roman authority. In an age where many still looked to the past for validation, this was an issue of more than antiquarian importance. By the 1810s Catholics were reasserting the Roman aspect of early Irish Christianity, and openly dismissing Protestantism as a late arrival.[7] The inexorable rise in population was tending to increase still further the Catholic majority in Ireland, and (partly in response to an upsurge in Protestant evangelical activities) a drive to improve the quality of the popular faith, to render it more obviously a matter of choice rather than of birth, was under way. The danger of proselytism in schools catering for Catholics as well as Protestants was being stressed. And in the 1820s reported miracles attributed to the German Prince Hohenlohe were hailed as likely to strengthen the faith of Catholics and win converts among Protestants. On top of all this, resistance to paying tithes, held in check while wartime agricultural prosperity lasted, was reappearing, spurred on

---

[7] On the background, see Hill, 'Popery and Protestantism', 107, 114–15, 127–8. Politicians clashed over the issue (*Select Committee on Fictitious Votes, 3rd Report*, 144, HC 1837 (480), xi, pt. II).

by the renewed circulation of Pastorini's prophecies foretelling the downfall of Protestantism in 1825.[8]

Within the space of the first post-war decade, therefore, Irish Catholics were beginning to shed their customary deference and were openly challenging the Church of Ireland on spiritual, historical, and utilitarian grounds. The transformation was noted by contemporaries; as late as 1817 it was still possible for Protestant observers to assume that Catholicism was losing its grip in Ireland: by 1825 it was clear that the church was extending its authority.[9]

Against this background, a heightening of sectarian rivalry was inevitable. This was intensified by the possibility during the 1820s that the state would concede Catholic emancipation, thus negating what remained of the Church of Ireland's civil claim to superiority: that its members alone were fully loyal to the constitution. It thus appears to be a matter chiefly of academic interest to establish which church or individual 'began' the era of sectarian controversy that commenced in the early 1820s.[10] Underlying the conflict was the ambiguous status of these two churches in Ireland once the penal laws had been relaxed.

For the Church of Ireland, the career of William Magee[11] affords an insight into the process that culminated in sectarian controversy. As a Fellow of Trinity College, Dublin, during the war years Magee had seen his main task as the defence of Christianity against the threat of rationalism, Deism, and heterodox dissent. In common with pre-Tractarian High-Churchmen in England, he reaffirmed Anglican orthodoxy, emphasizing the truths of revealed religion, and the sacrificial nature of Christ's death. Magee was a defender of the rights of the Irish church and an opponent of Catholic emancipation, but as late as 1821 when as bishop of Raphoe he addressed his diocesan clergy, his preoccupation with Protestant dissent was still to the fore, and that address caused no stir.[12]

However, within months Magee had been appointed to the see of Dublin, and a year after the Raphoe address his *Charge* to the Dublin diocesan clergy struck a new note:

<hr>

[8] *O'Connell Corr.* ii, letter 1045; Fergus O'Ferrall, *Catholic Emancipation: Daniel O'Connell and the Birth of Irish Democracy 1820–30* (Dublin, 1985), 46–7, 61–2, 71–3; Desmond Bowen, *The Protestant Crusade in Ireland, 1800–70* (Dublin, 1978), 63–7, 132.

[9] Bowen, *The Protestant Crusade*, 59–60.

[10] Ibid. 83–98. Bowen's suggestion that 'religious peace' had reigned until the 1820s is corrected in David Hempton and Myrtle Hill, *Evangelical Protestantism in Ulster Society 1740–1890* (London, 1992), ch. 5.

[11] William Magee (1766–1831), b. Enniskillen; FTCD, 1788; bishop of Raphoe, 1819–22; archbishop of Dublin, 1822–31 (*DNB*). For his early views see Liechty, 'Irish Evangelicalism, Trinity College Dublin', 250–312.

[12] Willam Magee, *Discourses and Dissertations on the Scriptural Doctrines of Atonement and Sacrifice*, new edn. (Dublin, 1809); id., *A Charge, Delivered to the Clergy of the Diocese of Raphoe . . . on 17th of October, 1821* (Dublin, 1822).

We, my Reverend Brethren ... are hemmed in by two opposite descriptions of professing Christians: the one, possessing a Church, without what *we* can properly call a Religion; and the other, possessing a Religion without what *we* can properly call a Church: the one so blindly enslaved to a supposed infallible Ecclesiastical authority, as not to seek in the Word of God a reason for the faith they profess; the other, so confident in the infallibility of their individual judgement as to the reasons of their faith, that they deem it their duty to resist all authority in matters of religion.[13]

These comments were widely interpreted by Catholics at the time (and the verdict has been endorsed by later commentators) as 'a declaration of religious war'. Furthermore, they have been evaluated primarily in the context of the evangelical movement.[14] Neither of these approaches does justice to Magee's preoccupations in his *Charge*, or explains why such a change had come about in the thrust of his remarks within the space of only a year: Magee could have jumped on the evangelical bandwagon at any time from the 1790s onwards. A more fruitful approach takes into account the agrarian and anti-tithe disturbances outlined above, which had broken out only in recent months, and posed not a remote but an immediate threat to the local income and mission of the Church of Ireland clergy. A bishop had fled from his diocese under pressure of these events, and Irish tithes had come under attack in parliament.[15] The 1822 *Charge* abounds in references to the clergy 'resisted and oppressed' in 'their property, character and teaching'; 'our order endangered', 'in a state little short of direct persecution'.[16] The circumstances thus mirrored those in 1786–7, when similar pressures had induced the bishop of Cloyne to produce his celebrated pamphlet, deflecting any legislative attack on tithes (as it turned out) for decades to come.[17]

In defending the privileges of the church in 1822, Magee's task was a good deal harder than that facing Woodward in 1786. Both bishops showed an awareness of the Church of Ireland coming under pressure from Catholics as well as dissenters, but the rehabilitation of the papacy in British eyes, and the rise of Burkean and utilitarian arguments in favour of all the

[13] Id., *A Charge Delivered at his Primary Visitation ... on 24th of October, 1822* (Dublin, 1822), 21–2. There are echoes here of Archbishop Ussher's indictment of the Catholic church, '*they* have only the shell without the kernel (sic), and *we* the kernel without the shell' (James Ussher, *An Answer to a Challenge Made by a Iesuite in Ireland*, 3rd edn. (London, 1631), Dedication to King James).

[14] See e.g. *A Church, Not Without Religion; Or, a Few Modest Remarks Upon the Inconsistent Charge of His Grace Doctor Magee ... by W. B. [William John Battersby?] a Catholic Layman* (Dublin, 1822). For later endorsements see *DNB*, and Bowen, *The Protestant Crusade*, 83–4, 89.

[15] The bishop was Richard Mant of Killaloe (Bowen, *The Protestant Crusade*, 85–6). For parliamentary tithe debates see *FJ*, 25, 27 Apr. 1822.

[16] Magee, *A Charge Delivered at his Primary Visitation*, 1, 9, 12.

[17] Above, Ch. 6.

Trinitarian Christian churches meant that for Magee Erastian arguments and appeals to preserve Protestant ascendancy were unlikely to succeed. Instead, he argued that the church's title did not rest on recognition by the state, but on its divine and apostolic foundations. This was hardly a new claim, even for Magee,[18] but it was one on which there had been little need to dwell during the Erastian heyday of the eighteenth century.

However, Magee was not content simply to invoke the divine claims of the established church. In keeping with his previous record, he also stressed its pastoral mission.[19] His two immediate predecessors, for different reasons, had been ineffective pastors; Magee sought to bring order into the chaos he found in the archdiocese, to ensure that there were sufficient churches for the faithful, and that the clergy attended to their duties. In 1825 he told a parliamentary committee that Protestantism in Dublin was flourishing, with crowded churches and improved attendance at holy communion.[20] As the decade went on, and the emancipation struggle neared its climax, Magee's preoccupation with the divine claims of the church grew stronger and more apocalyptic. By 1827 he was asserting that, despite the obstacles it faced in Ireland, the established church would eventually triumph: 'the clouds of ignorance and gross error will pass away, and the sun of righteousness and truth will spread his beams throughout the land'. Two years earlier he had commented, 'in truth, with respect to Ireland, the Reformation may, strictly speaking, be truly said only now to have begun'.[21] If these sentiments seemed to bring him close to evangelicals who wished to take the gospel message to all regardless of denomination, then it is important to recognize that for Magee, it was the Church of Ireland clergy alone who had the right and the duty to preach that message, and only through the church's proper structures.[22] He therefore did not so much give evangelicals a strategy,[23] rather he sought to harness the rising evangelical impulse under the control and authority of the established church.

Dublin corporation, which itself derived some small income from tithes, displayed a similar sense of alarm over the renewed pressure on the church in 1821–2. This was reflected in its address welcoming Magee's appointment and conferring on him the freedom of the city, drawn up before Magee

---

[18] Magee, *A Charge Delivered at his Primary Visitation*, 19–20; Liechty, 'Irish Evangelicalism, Trinity College Dublin', 265–6.

[19] Magee, *A Charge Delivered at his Primary Visitation*, 14–29.

[20] *The Evidence of His Grace the Archbishop of Dublin Before the Select Committee of the House of Lords, on the State of Ireland* (Dublin, 1825), 6–8.

[21] Quoted in Joseph Liechty, 'The Popular Reformation Comes to Ireland: The Case of John Walker and the Church of God, 1804', in Comerford *et al.*, *Religion, Conflict and Coexistence*, 159–87, at 159.

[22] Magee, *A Charge Delivered at his Primary Visitation*, 26–9.

[23] Bowen, *The Protestant Crusade*, 83.

had delivered his controversial *Charge*, but in the knowledge that the new archbishop was a defender of the church's rights. The address praised Magee for his character and learning, and noted that his qualities

never perhaps were . . . so imperatively called for, as at the present unprecedented and alarming crisis, when infidelity has dared to take the most audacious strides, and the church which may in our opinion be called the palladium of the constitution has been assailed by avowed and clandestine enemies with an obstinacy not to be abashed, and a virulence altogether without parallel. At such a period of domestic peril, we look forward with confidence to the aid of your enlightened and vigorous mind in support of our inestimable constitution in church and state . . .[24]

It was common for archbishops of Dublin to be granted honorary freedom: the corporation had long-standing links with the church, symbolised by the installation of each new lord mayor in Christ Church cathedral, and by the custom whereby on certain holy days the lord mayor, sheriffs, and other civic officials attended church in their corporate capacity.[25] But did the corporation have anything in common with Magee beyond the obvious parallels: both were champions of beleaguered Protestant privilege? The difficulty is to discover what religion meant in civic life at this period. It is comparatively easy to pick out figures in the civic hierarchy who had gained reputations for piety or evangelical commitment: they included Aldermen William James, John Cash, and Sir John Kingston James, who all filled the mayoral office between the 1790s and the 1820s. There were also some Methodists, including William McAuley, a merchants' guild representative.[26] But they were only individuals, and the corporation had made no move in its official capacity to endorse (or condemn) any evangelical strategy. More telling than any number of pious aldermen is an address, dating from 1827, in the records of the guild of St George (of tallow-chandlers, soap-boilers, and wax-light makers)—a guild that retained some role in the regulation of trade into the 1830s.[27] It is of interest not least because it had nothing directly to do with religion, but concerned the most mundane of matters, the collection from members of quarterage fees, an important source of guild income.

On this occasion, it appears that the guild representatives on the city commons had succeeded in inducing certain recalcitrant brethren to pay these fees, and this earned them an address of thanks from the master and

---

[24] *CARD* xvii. 489–90.

[25] The tradition was still kept up: see e.g. report of Christmas observance at St Werburgh's church, *Warder* (suppl.), 29 Dec. 1832.

[26] Alderman William James (above, Ch. 6), praised for 'active zeal in the cause of religion', 1794 (DPLGC, MS 79, fo. 304); Alderman John Cash (d. 1833), stationer, lord mayor 1813–14, helped form Hibernian Church Missionary Society (*FJ*, 22 July 1814); Alderman Sir John Kingston James (above, Ch. 12), committee member, Hibernian Bible Society. For Hutton, see above, Ch. 8. [27] Above, Ch. 11.

wardens. The address began by thanking the representatives for their efforts, and went on to explain that the money thus collected would enable the guild to redeem its debts,

agreeable to the primitive charter granted to our Father Abraham Genesis chap. 17 which is further expounded on by St Paul to the Galatians Chap. 4 as allegorical of the ransom or price by which the *Lord of Jerusalem on high* purchased the Freedom of admission into his happy City—for the faithful and that we may be enabled to do as well as say 'Thy Will be done in Earth as it is in Heaven' instead of vending Franchises and Indulgences as practiced by that *Licentious Rival* of all *Authorities* for Empire the Corporation of Rome . . .[28]

Rome's false claims to 'empire', robbing the civil power and the laity of their proper rights, was a theme that went back to the Reformation and beyond. Here, however, the theme took on contemporary signficance in that, by describing Christ's death as a 'ransom', it reinforced the Anglican interpretation of the atonement elaborated by Archbishop Magee, whose book on the subject had been warmly welcomed in English High-Church circles. As part of his attack on heterodox dissent Magee had reaffirmed that salvation was not to be obtained through good works, contemplating Christ as a moral exemplar, or even through repentance for sins. Only Christ's death—which was sacrificial in nature—was sufficient to redeem mankind from the bondage of sin and death.[29]

The appeal for the guild of Genesis 17 (1–8, 15–21) and Galatians 4 (22–31) is not hard to find, for the Galatians text takes up the Genesis theme of a 'covenant'—the authorized King James version uses this term rather than 'charter'—between God and Abraham, and deals with it in a corporate metaphor. God had covenanted with Abraham that the children of his lawful wife, the 'freewoman' Sarah, should be free: and Christ's redeeming sacrifice had purchased for them the freedom to enter the heavenly city. The (Anglican) emphasis on the sufficiency of this sacrifice for salvation was then contrasted with the alleged Roman practice of duping Catholics with the doctrine of purgatory so as to delude them into believing that more was necessary. In this way, a routine civic obligation became infused with religious significance, and afforded the opportunity for a restatement of the reasons why Anglicanism was superior to Catholicism, and (by extension) why the brethren should value their status as citizens of 'the most Free Empire in the World'. Since the address was intended only for guild members, there is little reason to suspect that its sentiments were anything other than those that came naturally to men steeped in a corporate, Anglican, and Erastian world-view.

The beliefs outlined here help to dispel the suspicion that in taking up the theme of 'the church in danger' the Dublin corporate bodies were simply

---

[28] NLI, MS 80, pp. 149–50.
[29] Magee, *Discourses on the Atonement*, 17–18.

giving blind support to the divine claims of the established church. It is
necessary to make this point, since in England during the 1820s opposition
to Catholic emancipation was accompanied by a revival of the party label
'Tory'. Even in England this label did not do justice to the underlying
convictions of the opponents of reform,[30] and certainly in respect of the
Dublin corporate bodies the convictions were those of the old Whigs.
According to this view Protestantism was an essential component of the
British constitution, which had already reached an exemplary form.[31]
Unresolved questions about the boundaries between the pope's spiritual and
temporal claims meant that it was too dangerous to admit Catholics to
parliament, where they would have the power to undermine the existing
church settlement. This position had been endorsed by those eighteenth-
century Whigs and Patriots who had regarded the Protestant Erastian state
as a vehicle of progress, containing not merely the prospect of universal
freedom from papal, priestly, and (for some) prelatical tyranny as the
Enlightenment loosened the bonds of superstition and ignorance, but of
economic welfare as the laity were freed to pursue civic virtue and
prosperity. The controversy, since 1808, over the question of a state veto on
episcopal appointments suggested that Irish Catholics had not yet grasped
the importance of the Erastian state as a bulwark against priestly
domination; hence Dublin corporation was at least consistent in deploring
the prospect of conferring political power on those 'who constantly separate
their spiritual rulers from the temporal governors of the state, and assert the
superior dignity and paramount authority of the former'.[32]

    The threat of priestly domination came to seem much more immediate
from the mid-1820s when the Catholic Association began to work through
the priests and others to enrol the masses in the emancipation campaign and
to promote the 'Catholic rent'. The corporation drew attention to 'those
considerable levies of money, which . . . they [the Catholic Association]
have made from his majesty's subjects, by the assumption of an authority,
which even his majesty himself could not constitutionally exercise'.[33] The
Association's strategies were said to subvert the freedom of election; priests
influenced voters 'by the exercise of ecclesiastical power to support such
candidates as they choose, or oppose such as they proscribe'. The king was
warned that 'a confederation of ecclesiastics deriving under the Prince
Bishop of Rome has assumed titles which within your realm, your Majesty

[30] On this point, see John Wolffe, *The Protestant Crusade in Great Britain 1829–1860*
(Oxford, 1991), 22–3.
[31] Cf. the elder Pitt's constitutional eulogy (above, Ch. 5); quotation at beginning of
chapter; St Luke's guild petition, 1829 (NLI, MS 12127, p. 380).
[32] *CARD* xvi. 381.
[33] Ibid. xviii. 181. The barbers' guild attacked priests for levying an 'Illegal Impost' (the
Catholic rent), for opposing the circulation of the Scriptures, and freedom of elections (TCD,
MS 1447/8/4, p. 22).

only should confer, powers derived from the confederation determine suits for goods between man and man, decrees are formally issued, and ... obeyed through terror of midnight visitations, which inflict the vengeance of the confederation with atrocious severity'.[34]

This, of course, represented an obsessive preoccupation with the priests' role in Catholic affairs. All the anti-clericalism in the Whig and Patriot traditions, which in the previous century had occasionally been directed at Anglican clergymen suspected of 'priestcraft', had become focused on the priests. By contrast, and as if to reinforce the point that they held the correct view of church–state relations, certain Church of Ireland clergymen were made much of, to an extent not witnessed since the death of Dean Swift. Those individuals who had spoken out in defence of the constitution were granted the freedom of guilds, honoured with addresses, and their words inscribed on guild books. A few came to play an active part in guild life.[35] There can be little doubt that during the last decade of the emancipation campaign such clergymen played a part in sustaining morale among those freemen—the majority—who opposed the measure.[36] One or two Protestant dissenting clergymen who were active in the anti-emancipation cause were also admitted to civic freedom.[37]

Besides Erastian arguments, other issues were brought forward in the corporation's case against emancipation. One was the question of loyalty. The Catholic Association was accused of fostering hostility to the British connection.[38] Moreover, the corporation detected democratic and even revolutionary tendencies in the emancipation campaign, with the Catholics appealing to 'natural rights'. The response, as in the 1790s, was a Lockian one, spelled out most succinctly by St Luke's guild. Claims based on universal natural rights were spurious, for 'no such *right* exists, society being [a] matter of *Compact*, and none but those who observe all its Conditions are entitled to come within its pale'. It was 'our ancestors' who had 'procured and paid for with their blood', 'those inestimable blessings of

[34] *CARD* xviii. 246, 348. For similar themes, see St Luke's guild petition (NLI, MS 12127, pp. 380–1).

[35] Notably Reverend Sir Harcourt Lees, bt., of Blackrock House (1776–1852), eldest son of Sir John Lees, head of the Irish Post Office. He praised the constitution, attacked emancipation, and was thanked by Dublin corporation, 1820 (*CARD* xvii. 337). He was made free of the merchants', apothecaries', smiths' guilds; active in the Loyal and Benevolent Orange Institution of Ireland, 1825–8 (*DNB*). Other clergy made free in the 1820s included the Reverend Edward Tighe Gregory (b. 1793) curate at St Doloughs, Co. Dublin, active in the smiths' guild; and the Reverend Charles Boyton, FTCD (1799–1844), a future leader of the Protestant Conservative Society.

[36] Though the role of clergymen in corporate affairs was slight compared with that in the reconstituted Orange Order (1828) where fifteen of twenty-five committee members were Church of Ireland clergy (Senior, *Orangeism*, 237).

[37] e.g. Reverend John B. McCrea, evangelical preacher, minister to the Independent congregation at D'Olier St. chapel; admitted to honorary freedom, 1829 (DCA, C1/JSC/11, fos. 209–10).   [38] Petition to parliament (*CARD* xviii. 246–7).

civil and religious freedom' that were now at risk as a result of the mistaken policy of granting Catholics the vote in 1793.[39]

The great symbol of that compact was King William; and it was to William's successor on the throne that the corporation and guilds looked in the last resort to guarantee their rights. Who was more obliged to uphold the Protestant constitution than the monarch who owed his crown to that constitution? If there had been a shift in the Patriot position, it was from contending that the rights of the subject and those of the crown were in a state of balance towards insisting that they were complementary. For the corporation, 'our rights and liberties are so closely interwoven with the royal power, that we could not separate them if we would'. In 1821, George IV had endorsed that sentiment: the two 'must stand or fall together'.[40] The importance attached to the dynasty in the defence of the Protestant constitution was highlighted by the formation of 'Brunswick clubs' in the aftermath of O'Connell's dramatic by-election victory in County Clare in 1828. Dublin corporation welcomed the initiative, and at least one of the guilds (St Luke's) established its own club.[41]

The corporation's case against emancipation during the 1820s thus had several strands. However, Erastian arguments remained central, right down to 1829 when the struggle was finally lost. And it is worth noting that, for all the accolades heaped on clerical champions of the constitution, there were certain religious arguments that the corporation did not use—though some of the guilds were attracted by them. Evangelicalism, for instance, might have seemed an obvious strategy to recommend, if only to counter what the Reverend Sir Harcourt Lees told the smiths' guild was Rome's real goal in the 1820s: converting the British empire in North America to Catholicism.[42] But although an evangelical strategy was endorsed in a much admired report drawn up by the guild of merchants in 1828, it was not mentioned by the city corporation.[43] Neither did the corporation indulge in apocalyptic speculation, nor attack the theology of the Catholic church, even though the 1820s witnessed the resumption of disputation by Protestant and Catholic spokesmen on controversial points of doctrine. The Reverend E. T. Gregory, who became a regular attender at meetings of the smiths' guild, likened Catholicism to Islam, and the merchants' guild

[39] NLI, MS 12127, p. 381; petition to parliament; address to king (*CARD* xviii. 182, 348–9).   [40] *CARD* xvii. 369; xviii. 347.
[41] St Luke's guild, Brunswick club minute book, 1828–32, NLI, MS 12136. For Brunswick clubs see G. I. T. Machin, *The Catholic Question in English Politics 1820 to 1830* (Oxford, 1964), ch. 7; Senior, *Orangeism*, 225–37; Hempton and Hill, *Evangelical Protestantism*, 100–1.   [42] DCA, G3/1, pp. 205–10.
[43] *The Report of the Committee Appointed by the Guild of Merchants, Dublin, to Prepare Petitions to Parliament Against the Demand Called 'Catholic Emancipation'* (Dublin, 1828), 18. A principal author of the report was John Semple (n. 3 above): see *CARD* xviii. 263.

attacked the 'false Deity' that the priests offered to Irish Catholics; but such topics were avoided by the city corporation.[44]

There were several reasons for this. First, it was a key element in the corporation's defence of the constitution that religious faith was not at issue: 'The free and tolerant spirit of the united Protestant Church neither allows nor practices persecution'. It was the political tendencies of Catholicism that were objected to. As noted above, this was a view that still had very considerable support, in Ireland, in Britain, and also on the Continent.[45] There was perhaps another consideration. The corporation still contained a sizeable liberal minority, especially on the aldermanic board, and there was also a Presbyterian presence.[46] If opposition within its own ranks was to be minimized, there was a strong incentive to stick to arguments that commanded the widest possible assent.

In another way too the corporation showed restraint. At its Michaelmas meeting in 1828 the electoral implications for Dublin of the emancipation campaign were reviewed. Ever since the bitterly contested 1820 by-election, when freeholders had comprised less than 10 per cent of the voters, Catholics had begun to register as freeholders in the city in large numbers. In the period 1821–8 (inclusive), at a cost of only a few shillings, 1,829 freeholders had registered while those with the qualifications for freedom of the city and guilds were still being deterred from applying by the cost, which ranged from nine to twelve pounds: only 1,029 freemen were admitted in the same period.[47] There was thus a real possibility that freeholders would outnumber the freemen at the next election. Faced with this prospect, the city commons considered the propriety of admitting applicants solely on the grounds of 'uncompromising Protestant loyalty' and on paying the government stamp duty. The aldermen agreed to set up a committee on the matter, and sent down to the commons a proposal to admit an annexed list of 1,200 Brunswick club members, 'Noblemen and Gentlemen of known Protestant principles, being the only means in our power of preserving the purity of the Representation of the City of Dublin'. Although this was agreed to, at least in principle, in the event it was not carried through.[48] It

[44] *Report of the Committee Appointed by the Guild of Merchants*, 18; DCA, G3/1, pp. 212–13. For disputations, see Bowen, *The Protestant Crusade*, 97–123.

[45] Address to the king (*CARD* xviii. 348). In Europe a notable supporter was Hegel (Goldie, 'The Civil Religion of James Harrington', 199–200).

[46] The corporation's religious composition awaits study, but certain members of the 'Presbyter party' in the 1790s survived into the 1820s, including Alderman Alexander (d. 1822), and Brent Neville, sheriffs' peer (attended meetings until 1825): his son, Brent Neville, jun. (sheriff 1810–11) was a sheriffs' peer from 1811 until the mid-1830s.

[47] *Returns of the Numbers of Persons Registered as Freeholders, Within the Last Eight Years, in Every City and Town . . . in Ireland; Number of Persons Admitted . . . For the Last Eight Years, into the Corporation of the City of Dublin*, 1–19, HC 1829 (253), xxii; *CARD* xviii. 316.

[48] For conflicting evidence on the admission of the Brunswickers, see *CARD* xviii. 313–14, 549. The commons' journal indicates agreement to admit them in principle, but only on an

would have constituted a complete break with past practice; for while the corporation had always claimed and exercised the right to reject applicants for freedom, it had never admitted applicants *en masse*, without individual scrutiny, on any pretext.[49]

II. A New Beginning?

O'Connell's momentous victory at the Clare by-election in 1828 forced ministers to reconsider their position on emancipation. They still did not accept that the question was one of rights, but made a virtue of the argument from expediency.[50] Pressure was applied to George IV to overcome his scruples about the coronation oath; and on 13 April 1829 the royal assent was given to a relief act, which abolished the supremacy oath and the declaration that asserted that the invocation of the saints and the sacrifice of the mass were superstitious and idolatrous. A more acceptable oath was introduced to enable Catholics to sit in parliament and hold higher posts in the public service and the armed forces.[51]

With the act on the statute book, certain sections of Protestant opinion continued to express abhorrence of the measure. The *Dublin Evening Mail* made scathing attacks on the 'apostacy' of ministers and lambasted the duke of Wellington: emancipation had cancelled out his military glory. The *Warder* talked of this 'fatal enactment', and bluntly announced that it would be working for its repeal. In the city commons there were signs of the same inflexible spirit. Judging the act likely to undermine the established church, the commons joined the call for its repeal—though the aldermen were not persuaded to endorse this stand.[52]

None of this boded well for the future of interdenominational relations in the post-emancipation era. However, politics was in a state of flux, and it was to take another three years before the characteristic political features of the 1830s became apparent in Dublin. On the anti-emancipation side, not

individual basis (DCA, C1/JSC/11, fos. 193ᵛ–194ᵛ, 197ᵛ; *CARD* xviii. 522). This is borne out by the freemens' beseeches, which for 1829 contain a batch of about 220 on printed forms for admission to the 'city at large', with the grounds ('the rather for his Loyalty to the King and Constitution') already inserted (DCA, Fr/B/1829). They show that not all the Dublin residents were admitted, and the non-residents, almost half the batch, were all postponed (in effect, rejected).

[49] After 1798 the corporation rejected many who sought freedom by grace for (in effect) having helped quell the rebellion (e.g. DCA, Fr/B 1803/3). After the 1820 by-election the merchants' guild was accused of admitting 500 members at once in the ultra-Protestant interest (Ness, *Letter to Henry Brougham*, 31). But only 222 merchants in all were admitted to *civic* freedom, 1820–2 (inclusive), a figure not much out of line with the numbers admitted two decades earlier (1800–2: 195, calculated from *An Alphabetical List of the Freemen of the City of Dublin, 1774–1823*).

[50] Hole, *Pulpits, Politics and Public Order in England*, 243–4.

[51] 10 Geo. IV, c. 7. The new oath required acceptance of the Protestant succession, the denial of any papal civil power within the realm, and the disavowal of any design to subvert the established church.

[52] *DEM*, 8, 13, 29 Apr. 1829; *Warder*, 25 Apr. 1829; DCA, C1/JSC/11, fo. 239.

even the more hardline elements in the corporate world contented themselves with mere rhetoric. In August 1829, the St Luke's guild Brunswick club changed its name to the 'Independent Club of the Guild of St Luke', signalling that political life went on, and that it still remained necessary to secure the return of reliable officers who would counteract efforts by the 'Roman Catholic and Radical party' to bring Catholics into the guilds. Bracketing 'Roman Catholic' and 'Radical' together reflected O'Connell's claim to be a radical reformer.[53]

But would the reformers or their opponents succeed in setting the political agenda? At the general election held in August 1830 following the death of George IV there were signs of political realignment in Dublin. On 20 July the liberal *Dublin Evening Post* reported approvingly that an influential body of electors planned to invite George Dawson,[54] MP for County Londonderry, to stand for Dublin. Dawson was financial secretary to the treasury and a brother-in-law of Sir Robert Peel; he was known for his effective work for commercial interests. He was also a former opponent of emancipation who had publicly announced a change of heart in 1828. The requisition asking him to stand was signed by several aldermen, including the lord mayor elect, Robert Harty,[55] as well as by other commercial men, both Protestant and Catholic. Among his supporters was Alderman Frederick Darley, head of the Dublin police, another former anti-emancipationist. However, the culture of opposition persisted to the extent that Dawson's backers felt obliged to defend his government post.[56]

Speeches made in Dawson's favour were noteworthy for the importance they attached to the representation of Dublin's commercial interests. But Dawson—who had good prospects of being returned for an English seat—declined to stand, leaving his backers without any very attractive candidate. Convinced liberals might endorse Henry Grattan, junior, one of the sitting MPs; but he and his father had been criticized for failing to promote commerce, and Grattan's campaign was somewhat defensive. He duly lost his seat. The winning candidates, who both had the backing of the corporation,[57] were the other sitting MP, George Moore[58]—a member of

[53] NLI, MS 12136, fos. 78, 81. For Catholic efforts to obtain civic freedom after emancipation see below, Ch. 14. For O'Connell's views, see *O'Connell Corr.* iii, letter 1488, n. 1.

[54] George Robert Dawson (1790–1856), MP Co. Londonderry 1815–30, Harwich 1830–2. Financial secretary to the treasury 1828–30, and Peel's private secretary. His speech (Aug. 1828) announcing conversion to emancipation was thought to herald a ministerial volte-face (Machin, *Catholic Question*, 126–7).   [55] For Harty see below, App. B.

[56] *DEP*, 27, 29 July 1830. The hatters' guild attacked Dawson for being under 'ministerial influence' (ibid., 27 July), and the city commons criticized the requisition (DCA, C1/JSC/11, fo. 255).   [57] *DEP*, 29 July, 5 Aug. 1830; *CARD* xviii. 454.

[58] For Moore, see below, App. B. He and Henry Grattan, jun. had been returned unopposed at the 1826 general election: Ellis had retired, and Robert Shaw withdrew rather than declare firmly for or against emancipation (*DEP*, 13, 15 June 1826).

344 Part 3. Patriots to Unionists, 1815–1840

the Orange Order—and the more moderate Frederick Shaw,[59] son of the former MP for the city, Robert Shaw, and now recorder of Dublin.[60]

Although Shaw, who maintained that he had become reconciled to emancipation before the act passed, claimed that he had received some Catholic support,[61] the prospect of being represented by two 'corporators'[62] was uncongenial to the freeholder element in the electorate and to Whigs generally. Hence, by the time of the next general election, in May 1831, there was a determination to redress the balance. By that time parliamentary reform had moved to the top of the political agenda, following the appointment of the Whig Lord Grey as prime minister in November 1830, and the introduction of a reform bill for England. Reform held obvious dangers for the corporation and the guilds—notably the possibility that extension of the franchise would undermine the freemen's privileges—and most of the freemen, according to the *Dublin Evening Mail*, agreed to support the sitting (anti-reform) candidates. However, reform also had its champions in civic circles. On this occasion Major Sirr joined Alderman Darley to canvass for the reform candidates, Lord Mayor Harty and barrister Louis Perrin.[63] Both sides displayed a high degree of organization. A central committee, composed of Catholics as well as Protestants, was set up to canvass and collect subscriptions for Harty and Perrin; while on the anti-reform side the Royal York club (first active at the 1826 election) set up its own committee to confer with guild officers to secure the return of 'the friends of the constitution'.[64]

The result was a clear victory for the reformers.[65] Predictably, they received the support of the great majority (85%) of the freeholders; more significantly, over one thousand (41%) of the freemen also voted for them.[66] This held out the hope that the emerging two-party political system in Dublin would not simply reflect sectarian divisions. It was unlikely that many Catholics voted for Shaw and Moore; but at least Protestant freemen were to be found on both sides. However, a petition was presented against the result, complaining of bribery and undue government influence (including threats of dismissal) to boost support for the reform candidates.[67]

[59] For Shaw, see below, App. B, and *DNB*.
[60] The voting was Moore, 1,852; Shaw, 1,579; Grattan, 1,014 (Walker, *Parliamentary Election Results*, 42). The *DEP* (12 Aug. 1830) asserted that about 500 freeholders failed to vote.   [61] *DEP*, 12, 14 Aug. 1830.
[62] The term was becoming current in the 1830s (*O'Connell Corr.* iv. 451, *CARD* xix. 246) as corporate privilege came in for scrutiny.
[63] *DEM*, 4 May 1831; *DEP*, 3, 5 May 1831. For Perrin, see below, App. B.
[64] *DEP*, 5 May 1831; *DEM*, 25 Apr., 2 May 1831.
[65] The voting was Harty, 1,943; Perrin, 1,935; Shaw, 1,568; Moore, 1,562 (Walker, *Parliamentary Election Results*, 47).
[66] *FJ*, 8 June 1831, cited in Peter Jupp, 'Urban Politics in Ireland 1801–31', in David Harkness and Mary O'Dowd (eds.), *The Town in Ireland* (Historical Studies, XIII, Belfast, 1981), 103–23, at 116.
[67] Some dismissals were reported to have taken place (*DEP*, 3 May 1831).

A house of commons' committee declared the election invalid; at a fresh election, with a considerably reduced turn-out, victory went to the anti-reformers.[68]

Although these developments were disappointing for the reformers, there was no reason to imagine that they were anything more than a temporary setback. In the weeks before the May election there was much speculation that 'the tired themes of Catholic and Protestant Ascendancy' would be left behind or become superfluous as even former Orangemen were seen to line up behind the reformers.[69] And reform was indeed to triumph during 1832, with the extension of the franchise.[70] Yet far from withering away, the anti-reformers were to grow in strength during the 1830s; and more significantly, they proved capable of effectively monopolizing the Dublin Protestant vote. The explanation for this lay largely in the evolution of Catholic politics.

III. The Repeal Issue Transformed

For many liberal Protestants, Catholic emancipation had been an act of political wisdom as well as one of justice. It would take the Catholic question out of politics, and thus help to safeguard aristocratic and Protestant hegemony, social harmony, and (following British investment), economic prosperity.[71] This expectation, however, was unrealistic. The conditions that had imposed passivity and deference on Irish Catholics in the eighteenth century were losing their force, while the legacy of the old order was such that, even after emancipation, serious imbalances remained between Catholics and Protestants in many areas of Irish life. Inevitably, a major theme of post-emancipation Irish politics would be the redressing of those imbalances; and, inevitably, in view of Catholic numbers, this cause would tend to be identified with the national interest—'the battle of Ireland and of Catholicity', as O'Connell put it. For his part, O'Connell had no intention of relinquishing the political initiative. 'How mistaken men are', he wrote to Edward Dwyer, secretary of the Catholic Association, 'who suppose that the history of the world will be over as soon as we are emancipated! Oh! *that* will be the time *to commence* the struggle for popular rights.'[72]

His early moves in this direction included issuing in May 1829 the so-called 'Address of the Hundred Promises', which outlined a programme of

---

[68] The voting was Shaw, 1,292; Viscount Ingestre, 1,250; David La Touche, 1,053; Michael O'Loghlen, 937; Marcus Costello, 28 (Walker, *Parliamentary Election Results*, 50, where the election date should read 18 Aug. 1831).

[69] *DEP*, 30 Apr., 5, 10 May 1831. Lord Mayor Harty looked forward to none but reformers ever contesting Dublin again (*DEP*, 14 May 1831).

[70] Representation of the people (Ireland) act, 2 & 3 Will. IV, c. 88: the franchise was extended to £10 householders in towns and cities.

[71] See e.g. *O'Connell Corr.* iii, letters 1278, 1289.

[72] Ibid. iv, letters 1536, 1550.

moderate reform, including changes in the tax laws, land law, the grand jury system, and the restoration of the forty-shilling freehold franchise (abolished as part of the emancipation package). Within days of the publication of this programme, however, O'Connell was writing to the Catholics' agent in London: 'Having no object of personal advantage to look for I turn my thoughts exclusively to what I deem useful to Ireland and I am most thoroughly convinced that nothing but "the Repeal of the Union" can permanently serve her interests.' Six months later he indicated in a public letter 'to the People of Ireland' (7 January 1830) that repeal of the union was the most important of all topics, although he intended to refrain from raising it in parliament 'until the combined wish of the Irish people shall demand that repeal in a voice too distinct to be misunderstood'. And in April 1830 repeal was included among the aims of the Society of the Friends of Ireland of All Religious Persuasions, established under O'Connell's aegis.[73]

Repeal of the union was not a new issue for O'Connell. As a young man, unknown in politics, he had spoken out against the union in 1800, and from time to time subsequently had added his voice to those of its Protestant critics. Considerations of prudence and the desire to concentrate on a goal with good prospects of success had ensured that the issue remained in the background during his leadership of the Catholic Association. With emancipation behind him, he was free to turn to repeal; besides, he had to consider how best to channel the raised expectations of his supporters, which in some of the larger towns and cities had separatist overtones.[74] There was also the question of how Protestants would react. O'Connell himself appears to have had few doubts about the disadvantages of the union for all the inhabitants of Ireland—though he was evidently prepared for Catholics to take the initiative in campaigning for repeal even without Protestant support. In 1828 he had written to the liberal Protestant Lord Cloncurry, 'the time is coming when every honest and sensible Irishman should be preparing to compel the Repeal of that measure [the union]. But *we* must do this *alone*. Protestant assistance will be given us when the difficulties are over and that success is approaching.'[75]

In the aftermath of emancipation, the response of liberal Protestants was not encouraging. The short-lived Society of the Friends of Ireland was marked by disputes over repeal, and the question languished until the summer of 1830 when events at home and abroad gave repealers new hope.

---

[73] *O'Connell Corr.* iv, letters 1577, n. 2, 1581, 1682, n. 6; O'Connell 'to the People of Ireland' (*DEM*, 11 Jan. 1830).

[74] MacDonagh, *O'Connell*, 92–3; Thomas Wyse, *Historical Sketch of the Late Catholic Association of Ireland*, (2 vols.; London, 1829), i. 314–23.

[75] *O'Connell Corr.* iii, letter 1489. The young Cloncurry had criticized union, but like most liberal Protestants he declined to pursue repeal in the 1830s (above, Ch. 10, n. 6; *DNB*).

Abroad, the feasibility of more or less peaceful political change was demonstrated by the July revolution in France, and by the Belgian revolution (August–November 1830) against union with the Dutch. O'Connell was heartened by both events, and was soon announcing confidently that repeal of the union with Britain would be obtained within three years.[76] There was still no sign that he envisaged serious Protestant opposition to repeal, although he had recently taken to warning the landed class of the grim alternatives to repeal (poor laws and falling values of land).[77]

In view of these considerations, it might have been expected that O'Connell would endeavour in his public pronouncements to avoid issues likely to inflame Protestant susceptibilities. Yet in the first of a new series of letters addressed 'to the People of Ireland' in September 1830, far from avoiding irritating topics, he seemed to go out of his way to dwell on them. The superiority of the Roman Catholic religion; the recent victory over 'the foul dominion of Protestant ascendancy'; the exemplary conduct of Irish Catholics when in power compared with 'any other people in ancient or modern times'; the bright periods of Irish history, coinciding with the eras of Irish control, contrasted with the 'dark and dismal' periods of English control; all these and similar topics were detailed at some length.[78] Did this spring from sheer insensitivity on O'Connell's part, or was there another explanation?

O'Connell has sometimes been condemned for dwelling too much on Catholic rights at the expense of Irish national rights. Such criticisms show little understanding of the constraints facing a would-be populist leader in early nineteenth-century Ireland. In the wake of the 1798 rising, and during the French wars, the only anti-union movement that would not have been proscribed was a Protestant one: the sort of movement that the Dublin guilds and city commons had been periodically anxious to promote. But, outside Dublin, their efforts had attracted little response; nor, given parliamentary attitudes to the union, was there much chance of success. The campaign for Catholic emancipation, by contrast, not only could be kept alive during the war years, but (thanks to Protestant divisions over the issue) had some prospect of succeeding.

The emancipation campaign, however, had reinforced the process by which Irish Catholics were acquiring a sense of importance and self-esteem primarily through their religion. No leader who wished to mobilize them in the 1830s and 1840s could afford to ignore this, or to ignore the clerical channels for communication with the people that had been so important in

[76] Fourth letter 'to the People of Ireland', 27 Sept. 1830 (*DEM*, 8 Oct. 1830).
[77] *The First Letter of Daniel O'Connell, Esq. on the Repeal of the Union. To the People of Ireland* (6 Sept. 1830), 6.   [78] Ibid. 1–4.

the 1820s.[79] The best that could be done—and this was clearly what O'Connell sought to do—was to acknowledge, and indeed to foster, the sense of Catholic identity, while insisting that Irish Catholicism was of a liberal kind that guaranteed the perfect safety of Protestants, their property, and their religion.

Such a task alone would have been sufficiently demanding. But besides reinforcing Catholics' belief in themselves and in their capacity for political action, it was also necessary to conciliate Protestants, so that they would support, or at least not actively oppose, repeal. In the event, pursuit of the first objective was likely to prejudice the second. During the 1820s, Irish Protestants had been exposed, for the first time for over a century—save briefly in the 1790s—to the spectacle of Catholics speaking candidly on a range of politico-religious topics: bible societies; tithes; the vestry system; education; the 'novelty' of the Protestant religion. Moreover, Catholics had set up an association that collected a 'rent' from members, and in certain respects behaved almost like a local parliament. For many Protestants these developments were deeply disturbing, conjuring up images of militant Catholicism bent (at best) on securing Catholic ascendancy, (at worst) on the extermination of heretics: it was most unfortunate that the transformation of the Catholic Association into a populist movement coincided with the circulation of Pastorini's prophecies foretelling the impending doom of Protestantism. Liberal Protestants, readier to accept that Catholics had real grievances, had been prepared to regard these events with greater equanimity; but it is important to remember the essentially conservative motives that led them to support emancipation, and the hope that it would take the Catholic question out of politics. Yet here was O'Connell, not merely labouring the Catholic question once again, but labouring it in support of an issue with very far-reaching implications—repeal of the union.

In these circumstances it was most unlikely that liberal Protestants, who earlier in the year had still been acting with O'Connell in the Society for the Improvement of Ireland,[80] would follow his lead. Within a week of the founding of O'Connell's Irish Volunteers for the Repeal of the Union (23 October[81] 1830) a meeting was held in Dublin, chaired by the duke of Leinster, to discountenance repeal. From this meeting emanated the Leinster

[79] As the Young Irelanders were to discover in 1848 (Richard Davis, *The Young Ireland Movement* (Dublin, 1987), 152–3).
[80] *DEM*, 20 Jan. 1830. For this society, founded 1828, see *O'Connell Corr.* iv, letter 1672, n. 9.
[81] *DEP*, 26 Oct. 1830. Lack of Protestant comment on the date indicates how much the cult of 1641 had declined. But as recently as 1821 Bishop Magee had defended the Church of Ireland prayerbook (as opposed to the united churches' version), instancing the distinctive prayers 'for the 23rd of October' (*A Charge, Delivered to the Clergy of . . . Raphoe*, 40). For 19th-c. views of 1641 see T. Barnard, '1641: A Bibliographical Essay', in MacCuarta (ed.), *Ulster 1641*, 173–86, at 180–6.

declaration, which reaffirmed support for 'the permanence of the British connection'. Over the following months the declaration received the signatures of at least twenty-three MPs and seventy-five peers. At civic level, the liberal lord mayor Robert Harty refused a request from an O'Connellite deputation to convene a public meeting for repeal.[82]

The coolness of these old allies highlighted the potential importance of Dublin corporation and the guilds. Early in October, O'Connell had expressed his view: 'The Belgic [sic] revolution is more important than the French [i.e. the July revolution]. If the Corporations of Dublin would but now come forward, we would speedily repeal the Union.'[83] What were the prospects for an alliance—on the basis of repeal—between the O'Connellites and the Dublin corporate bodies? As a periodic Dublin resident, O'Connell was naturally aware of the persistent antipathy towards the union among the Dublin freemen, articulated from time to time in guild and city commons' resolutions. Thanks to the freemen, Protestant anti-unionism was not just a matter of historical record but a living tradition.[84] The most recent wave of anti-union sentiment had arisen in 1822, when certain guilds, and the city commons, had adopted repeal resolutions. Since then, the Catholic question had held centre stage; and in the aftermath of emancipation, there were few immediate signs of a return to the subject. There is some evidence that repeal was raised in the joiners' guild in 1829, but at the general election of August 1830 it surfaced only half-heartedly.[85] This apathy was broken on 7 October at the Michaelmas assembly of the smiths' guild, which had a high opinion of its own importance as the second Protestant guild 'for numbers and antiquity' in Ireland. By a small majority, a resolution was passed for repeal petitions to be prepared to both houses of parliament. Trade and manufactures, the resolution asserted, had declined over the last thirty years, and there was no hope of restoring them to their former prosperity except by a repeal of the union.[86]

There was no suggestion in the report of this meeting that the backers of the resolution were working in concert with O'Connell; far from it. The committee appointed to prepare the petitions included several anti-emancipationists, and the guild had not given up hope that the 1829 act might be repealed. The most obvious explanation for the smiths' move is that latent dislike of the union had been activitated by economic adversity (shortly afterwards the city commons set up a committee to inquire into current distresses in the city).[87] A guild meeting later in October endorsed

---

[82] *DEP*, 30 Oct. 1830; *O'Connell Corr.* iv, letters 1721, n. 1, 1739, nn. 5–6.

[83] *O'Connell Corr.* iv, letter 1714.

[84] In their attacks on the union the O'Connellites drew on themes in guild resolutions of 1799–1800, reproduced in Battersby's *The Repealer's Manual*, 331–51.

[85] Speech of William Scott at Dublin corporation (*DEM*, 22 Oct. 1832); *DEP*, 10 Aug. 1830, reporting that Grattan was willing to support repeal.

[86] DCA, G3/1, pp. 323–4, 340.

[87] Address to Thomas Lefroy, 1 Apr. 1830, ibid. 299; DCA, C1/JSC/11, fo. 258[v].

the repeal sentiments, though they were toned down through the intervention of the Reverend E. T. Gregory and Alderman William Hodges.[88]
Early in 1831, when an attempt was made to activate the repeal resolutions,
they were again neutralized by an amendment, moved by Alderman Hodges
and carried by a large majority, calling for a petition to the king, urging him
to hold the imperial parliament in Dublin on a triennial basis.[89]

Despite these appearances, the smiths' readiness to explore alternatives[90]
to the restoration of an Irish parliament did not yet mark a shift towards the
endorsement of unionism. Along with members of the city commons and
several other guilds, over the next two years the smiths continued to attack
the union and to call for its repeal, particularly in 1832 when it appeared
that the parliamentary reform bill would strip freemen of their parliamentary votes.[91] But while these sentiments helped sustain O'Connell's
hopes for a possible alliance, and explain why he supported efforts to save
the freeman franchise,[92] in practice the basis for co-operation did not exist.
For while the O'Connellites hoped that repeal would hasten the removal of
what remained of Protestant ascendancy, guild members still looked to
repeal as a reinforcement of that ascendancy. As the city commons put it in
January 1832, 'inasmuch as the Legislature affords no security to our
religion or vested rights it becomes our duty to endeavour by a Repeal of the
Union to recover the advantages we have lost'.[93]

In fact, imbued as they were with the ingrained assumption that
Protestants 'ought to take the lead in all measures essential to the well-being
of the country', these corporate repealers were apt to ignore the very
existence of O'Connellite repealers. Thus the early months of 1832 saw
members of the city commons calling for repeal both on the usual economic
grounds, and in protest against the reform bill, without adverting at all to
the O'Connellite movement.[94] In their understanding of the dynamics of
post-emancipation Irish politics, then, the corporate repealers lagged behind

[88] William Hodges, ironmonger and smith; sheriff 1827–8; alderman, 1830; lord mayor
1836–7.

[89] DCA, G3/1, pp. 325–6, 331, 338, 340. Before the 1830 general election the prospective
candidate George Dawson was asked whether parliament might be held periodically in Dublin.
Dawson did not stand, so his answer (that it was a matter for the king) was of little moment
(*DEP*, 29 July 1830).

[90] Another alternative to repeal (*CARD* xviii. 492–3) was raised by Jonathan Sisson
(weavers' representative 1828–34) in *Second Letter to the Right Hon. Earl Grey, on the
Necessity of the Appointment of a Board, or Council, at Dublin, for the Internal Interests of
Ireland* (London, 1832).

[91] DCA, G3/1, pp. 408–9; C1/JSC/12, fos. 28, 33–34[v], 50, 55–6, 60[v]; report of corporation
meeting, *DEM*, 8 Aug. 1831. In fact the Irish reform act allowed existing resident freemen to
exercise the parliamentary franchise for life (Hoppen, *Elections, Politics and Society*, 3).

[92] *O'Connell Corr.* iv, letter 1905, n. 5.

[93] DCA, C1/JSC/12, fo. 28.

[94] Reports of Dublin corporation meetings, (*DEM*, 30 Jan., 5 Mar. 1832).

members of the nascent Irish Conservative party,[95] who—although still on occasion willing themselves to threaten government with repeal—condemned repeal out of hand when championed by 'traitors'.[96]

Once the reform act had been passed in the summer of 1832, the risk of alienating liberal Protestants mattered less, and O'Connell could press on with the repeal issue. There were, after all, other Protestants who might be won over. Accordingly, he began to explore prospects for co-operation, on a repeal platform, first with the Dublin Conservatives and subsequently with those he called 'corporate repealers'. His astute election agent, P. V. Fitzpatrick, impressed on him the crucial importance of Dublin if repeal was to make any nation-wide impact at the next election. If O'Connell himself would stand for Dublin, Fitzpatrick argued, it would transform the electoral prospects for repeal.[97] O'Connell was prepared to consider standing, but remained keen that at least one candidate should be a Conservative Protestant. This strategy was undermined when, during the leader's absence in Kerry, the National Political Union—a body that usually deferred to his judgement—nominated Edward Ruthven,[98] a liberal Protestant willing to take a repeal pledge. There still remained hopes that Shaw, one of the sitting Conservative MPs, might be induced to support repeal. But according to O'Connell, who not unnaturally lacked any sympathy with Shaw's scruples, the MP remained opposed to repeal 'upon some fantastic notion of Protestantism . . . a notion which there is no hope of banishing because it is impervious to argument or reasoning'.[99]

Shaw's refusal to entertain support for repeal, however, disappointed others besides O'Connell. During October 1832 several guilds, including the weavers and smiths, indicated that they would support only repealers at the forthcoming election. A subsequent vote in the city commons revealed that over one-third of the members present took the same view.[100] In the light of these developments, Shaw withdrew from the contest:

I find a large portion of my old supporters now in favour of that measure [repeal], as has been evinced in their several corporate meetings within the last few weeks; and I believe that will be found the feeling of a large majority of the new constituency.

---

[95] The term 'conservative' (first used in a political sense *c*.1830) was taken up from 1832 by leaders of the Wellington and Peel party to symbolize a new start after the emancipation and reform conflicts (Robert Blake, *The Conservative Party from Peel to Churchill*, paperback edn. (London, 1972), 6–9). The Dublin-based 'Protestant Conservative Society' emerged (winter 1831–2) from meetings to defend Irish Protestant interests (*DEM*, 21 Nov., 12 Dec. 1831, 29 Feb. 1832; Joseph Spence, 'The Philosophy of Irish Toryism, 1833–52', Ph.D. thesis (Birbeck College, 1991), ch. 2).

[96] *DEM*, 12 Dec. 1831; 13 Jan., 13 June 1832.

[97] W. J. O'Neill Daunt, *Eighty-Five Years of Irish History 1800–1885*, 2nd edn. (2 vols.; London, 1886), i. 247, 249–50; MacDonagh, *O'Connell*, 351–6; *O'Connell Corr.* iv, letters 1914–15. The possibility of contesting Dublin had been in O'Connell's mind since 1831 (ibid. iv, letter 1778).   [98] For Ruthven, see below, App. B.

[99] *O'Connell Corr.* iv, letters 1917, 1921, 1925.

[100] *FJ*, 6, 10, 26 Oct. 1832; *Warder* (suppl.) 13, 20 Oct. 1832; DCA, C1/JSC/12, fo. 60ᵛ.

This causes me no surprise; . . . it is but the fulfilment of what I myself predicted . . . would be the inevitable consequence of the passing of the Irish reform bill, and of the general policy of the present government towards this country.[101]

Cheered by these signs of support for repeal among the guilds—even after the extension of the borough franchise to £10 householders the freemen still constituted over one-quarter of the city electorate—O'Connell then made overtures to a former city sheriff, William Scott[102] of the joiners' guild, who, it was rumoured, might be persuaded to stand as a repealer. Writing to Scott, O'Connell threw in some flattering remarks about the corporation: 'They . . . were in 1782, and later, the best patriots in Ireland. I want to see them so again, and therefore the second candidate for Dublin should be a Corporator.' O'Connell even drank to the memory of King William at a meeting with members of the smiths' guild held at Scott's house.[103] He also attempted to reassure Scott that Protestant fears of Catholic ascendancy were groundless: 'The time is gone by when either Catholic or Protestant could establish an ascendancy.'[104]

But while O'Connell made soothing statements, his supporters made no secret of the link they perceived between repeal and the dismantling of the privileges of the established church. At the National Trades Political Union, members were inclined to be suspicious about the possibility of having to support a corporate repealer for Dublin. Any such candidate, thought John Reynolds,[105] would have to accept the abolition of tithes and the reform of vestry cess; and Richard Barrett[106] argued that the abolition of tithes would be a *sine qua non* for any repealer.[107]

With Ruthven already a declared candidate in the repeal interest, and with the two O'Connellite organizations, the National Political Union and the National Trades Political Union holding repeal meetings,[108] it might seem difficult for the guilds and city commons to continue to ignore the existence of the O'Connellite repealers. Yet in the recorded debates the

[101] *FJ*, 23 Oct. 1832.
[102] William Scott, cabinet maker; sheriff 1829–30, sheriffs' peer 1830–41. Advocated repeal in joiners' guild, 1829, and in city commons, 1832 (*DEM*, 22 Oct. 1832). Expelled from Orange Order for co-operation with O'Connellite repealers (*Warder*, 1 Dec. 1832).
[103] Extract from *Morning Register*, reprinted *DEM*, 23 Nov. 1832.
[104] O'Connell also reminded Scott that he had obtained compensation for the former Orangeman Sir Abraham Bradley King when the latter lost his post as king's stationer in 1830 (*O'Connell Corr.* iv, letter 1929).
[105] John Reynolds (1794–1868), secretary of the National Bank, 1834–41, managing director of the Land Investment Co. of Ireland from 1841; elected to reformed Dublin corporation in 1845; lord mayor 1850; MP Dublin city 1847–52. For his banking career see G. L. Barrow, *The Emergence of the Irish Banking System 1820–1845* (Dublin, 1975).
[106] Richard Barrett (d. 1854), editor and owner of the O'Connellite *Pilot*, founded 1827. A Protestant, Barrett's admission to the liberal brewers' guild (1828) aroused anxiety lest he seek civic freedom (*CARD* xviii. 320).   [107] *FJ*, 2 Nov. 1832.
[108] *DEM*, 7 Sept. 1832; *FJ*, 12, 24 Oct. 1832; see also D'Arcy, 'The National Trades Political Union and Daniel O'Connell', 7–16.

O'Connellite movement was noticed for the most part only indirectly. As before, supporters of repeal continued to dwell on the economy and the role of an Irish parliament in its regeneration. Repeal would also encourage the return of absentee landlords, whose presence would have wide-ranging beneficial effects. A strong subtheme was resentment at the government's recent Irish measures; Catholic emancipation, the reform act, and the proposed scheme of national education—soon to be stigmatized as 'godless' for its failure to provide for religious education. According to B. J. Sisson,[109] who did allude to the O'Connellite repeal campaign, the government was no longer serving Protestant interests, and thus 'nothing could now stem the torrent of Popery and democracy but our Parliament, where the wealth, rank and influence now displayed in a bookseller's parlour would then appear with its illumined force in the senate house, as the legitimate rallying point for the inheritors of the property of the nation'.[110] Sisson also struck an apocalyptic note. England's glory was past: 'she has admitted idolators into the great councils of the nation' and had thus lost her claim as the disposer of human events.[111]

The remedy for Irish ills thus lay in strengthening the Protestant aristocracy and gentry, through the restoration of the Irish parliament, which would offset the democratic tendencies of resurgent Irish Catholicism. The social values inherent in that prescription were perfectly compatible with the outlook of contemporary British Conservatives and Whigs, who in the 1830s continued to uphold the importance of the aristocratic component in government at home and in Britain's dependencies.[112] Yet this remedy for Ireland's problems stood no chance of support in parliamentary circles. In part, this was because it rested on repeal of the union. Contrary to O'Connell's expectations, during the 1830s it emerged that not only the Conservatives but the Whigs and even radicals viewed repeal as tantamount to separation, with all the attendant international dangers.[113] In any case, all the British parties had come to accept the reality of Catholic emancipation: the Whigs were shortly to enter an alliance with the O'Connellites. Consequently the guilds' Protestant ascendancy sentiments seemed too obstinate and unyielding.

Thus the corporate repealers went their own way, disregarding government, disregarding the O'Connellites, lacking any clear lead from the

---

[109] Benjamin J. Sisson, merchants' guild representative 1830–4.

[110] Report of Dublin corporation meeting, *FJ*, 23 Oct. 1832; repeal debates, smiths' guild; 'The repeal question', *DEM*, 26 Oct., 2 Nov. 1832.

[111] *FJ*, 23 Oct. 1832. The corporation's own progress towards an apocalyptic interpretation of events is discussed in Ch. 14 below.

[112] See e.g. policy for Canada (Ward, *Colonial Self-Government*, 39–40).

[113] Urged on by his Dublin constituents, in 1834 O'Connell introduced a repeal motion in the house of commons: it was lost (523 : 38). Only one British MP, James Kennedy, MP, Tiverton, voted for it (*O'Connell Corr.* v, letters 2062, n. 1, 2064, n. 2).

Protestant gentry or clergy. And as far as the election was concerned, they also lacked a candidate, for despite O'Connell's hopes, Scott did not stand. With the election only two weeks away, O'Connell's name was put forward as a second repeal candidate, and the city was placarded with appeals from the NTPU to the freemen to vote for him.[114] Two Conservative candidates, standing on an anti-democratic rather than a unionist platform, emerged in the final days of the campaign.[115] None of the candidates, therefore, really suited the freemen, whose turnout at the polls was comparatively poor. Of those who did vote (less than two-thirds of those entitled to do so), 90 per cent voted for the Conservatives.[116] The sectarian tendency of the new party system had been affirmed.

The election of 1832 thus revealed starkly the dilemma facing the freemen. For the first time since 1800 they had the chance to vote for avowed repeal candidates. Yet, because those candidates also stood, in effect, for further dismantling of Protestant control, the freemen were unwilling to support them. Nevertheless, it was to take some years before any Dublin corporate body was prepared to express a positive view of the union.

---

[114] *DEM*, 14 Dec. 1832.

[115] John Beatty West and Sir George Rich (below, App. B).

[116] Some 1,263 of the 1,967 registered freemen voted: calculated from *A Return of the Electors Registered in . . . Ireland* (County of the City of Dublin), 8, HC 1833 (177), xxvii; *An Alphabetical List of the Constituency of the City of Dublin, with . . . the Votes Given at the Elections of 1832, 1835 and 1837* (Dublin, [1837]).

14

The Corporate World Unravels,
1815–1840

I. Taxation and Representation, 1815–1829

When a member of the city commons asserted in 1808 that Dublin corporation represented the one deliberative assembly 'still authorized by law to take cognizance of the situation of this country, and . . . convey to the foot of the Throne, through . . . Parliament, the sentiments, the wants and the wishes of the Irish People',[1] he was making a large but not untenable claim. The fact that the corporation (like parliament) was still an exclusively Protestant body did not necessarily prejudice its representative capacity in an age when political privileges still rested, for the most part, on inherited rights, confessionalism, and custom, and when the principles of hierarchy and 'virtual' representation still dominated the public domain. Indeed, the success of British forces during the Napoleonic wars was helping to prolong the life of those values.

However, during the 1820s and 1830s it became increasingly apparent that changes in the wider political world were rendering the corporation's role as a representative body and guardian of Patriot values redundant. Decades of administrative reform had reduced the influence of the crown and the threat of royal or ministerial absolutism, thus minimizing the importance of free corporations as a counter to that threat. The growing power of the house of commons meant that it no longer seemed appropriate to invoke the idea of balance. The confessional aspect of the state was severely compromised after 1829, and utilitarian values were becoming more important. Most significant of all was the growing legitimacy of public opinion, not now confined to chartered bodies that could claim ancient rights to address the throne or parliament, but political unions and constituency associations representing the wider borough electorates brought in by the reforms of 1832. And following those reforms, a new party-political system was emerging, in which the old ideal of opposition as a vehicle of supra-party opinion seemed increasingly outmoded.[2]

---

[1] 1 William Patterson, calling for repeal of the union (*DEP*, 5 May 1808).
[2] See Gunn, *Beyond Liberty and Property*, ch. 7; Clark, 'A General Theory of Party, Opposition and Government'; Mark Francis with John Morrow, 'After the Ancient Constitution: Political Theory and English Constitutional Writings, 1765–1832', *History of Political Thought* (*Hist. Pol. Thought*), 9 (1988), 283–302.

These developments, which had implications for municipal corporations throughout Britain and Ireland, ensured that once Catholic emancipation and parliamentary reform had been secured, municipal reform—along with reform of the Church of Ireland and the house of lords—would be high on the reformers' agenda. In this climate, Dublin corporation could at best hope for exemption from the reforms that were introduced for English and Welsh towns in 1835 and for Ireland in 1840. The city of London, with which Dublin was still apt to compare itself,[3] gained exemption from the English measure.[4] A brief comparison will indicate some of the relative advantages and disadvantages enjoyed by the two cities in any campaign to defend their ancient privileges.

To begin with, the city of London was immensely wealthy. Its area of jurisdiction, though small—by the 1830s much of the built-up area, including parliament itself, was outside the corporation's boundaries—was comparatively well run: by contemporary standards, London was one of the best-governed cities in Europe. These features had enabled the city, on the whole, to resist statutory encroachment on its powers. The metropolitan police act of 1829 did not even extend to the area under the corporation's control. Above all, the great majority of resident, rate-paying householders were freemen of the city, and eligible for municipal office. Since most residents were Anglicans or Protestant dissenters, and the latter had long played a full part in civic affairs, there was no serious alienation from the corporation on religious or utilitarian grounds.[5]

Dublin was quite differently placed. Even before the union, merchant capital had been less important in Irish banking than landed capital, and this had weakened the city in its dealings with the Irish parliament. Since the 1750s, statutory bodies had gradually taken over certain civic functions, including street planning, paving, cleaning, and lighting. And it was Dublin, rather than London, that was the testing ground for the first modern police force, set up under the 1786 Dublin police act. Although a degree of corporate control had been restored in the 1790s, it was eroded again by the police act of 1808. At the same time, that act had extended the corporation's responsibility for policing to an 8-mile radius from Dublin Castle, and this was given as one reason for the increase in local taxes so often complained of in the post-war period.

By eighteenth-century urban standards, Dublin had been wealthy, but before the end of the century the decline of the great textile industries had started to erode the foundations of that prosperity. Moreover, during the

---

[3] *CARD* xviii. 85; DCA, C1/JSC/9, fo. 117.

[4] Josef Redlich and Francis W. Hirst, *The History of Local Government in England*, 2nd edn. (London, 1970), 118–19.

[5] George E. Eades, *Historic London* (London, 1966), 237–9; S. K. Ruck and Gerald Rhodes, *The Government of Greater London* (London, 1970), 12–16.

1790s the corporation had incurred heavy debts through its contribution to the war effort—raising its own regiment, and offering bounties to encourage naval recruiting. Income from tolls and customs, due on goods brought into the city for sale, was falling; the Irish parliament had removed tolls from certain goods coming in by canal, which made it harder to collect the rest. The opening of Carlisle bridge in 1795 reduced civic income from ferries. As a result, corporate indebtedness rose. By 1812 retrenching expedients were under discussion, including selling the Mansion House (not, however, actually adopted). A year later, with the civic debt at almost £98,000, a 20 per cent cut in salaries for certain office-holders was agreed.[6] The problems were compounded in 1814 when the treasurer, Alderman John Carleton,[7] defaulted on £44,000 owed to the corporation.[8] (It was around this time, in January 1815, that O'Connell made his gibe about the 'beggarly' corporation of Dublin, which led to the fatal duel with John D'Esterre,[9] a member of the city commons.)

All this raised tensions within the corporation, with the city commons attacking the aldermen who had retained Carleton in office for so many years. It also prompted the last appearance of the commons in its anti-oligarchical role. Certain members, led by John Giffard's party, pressed the aldermen to recognize the right of the city commons to a say in the election of treasurer, citing (a real sign that fear of absolutism was waning) the Jacobite charter of 1687.[10] Dublin residents, still burdened with the wartime window tax (repealed only in 1822),[11] were more concerned about the overall level of local taxes, and questions began to be asked about the services provided in return for taxes paid to the corporation.

At first, such questions concerned the metal main tax, a statutory tax originally imposed in 1809 to enable the corporation to replace the old wooden waterpipes with metal ones.[12] During 1817 and early 1818 several parishes held meetings to complain about deficiencies concerning this tax.[13]

---

[6] *CARD* xiv. 309, 325–6, 367–8, 417–18, 424–5; xvi. 374–5; evidence of Alderman J. C. Beresford, *Second Report from the Select Committee on the Local Taxation of the City of Dublin*, 212–13, HC 1823 (549), vi.

[7] John Carleton, merchant; sheriff 1782–3; alderman, 1787; lord mayor 1792–3; city treasurer 1798–1814; resigned as alderman, 1815.

[8] Report of Dublin corporation meeting, *FJ*, 6 Nov. 1812; address of certain aldermen to lord mayor, etc. of Dublin, *FJ*, 29 Mar. 1819.

[9] John Norcot D'Esterre, d. 1815; provision merchant to Dublin Castle, and half-pay captain from 1810; merchants' guild representative on city commons. For the incident, see MacDonagh, *O'Connell*, 134–8.

[10] *CARD* xvii. 531–3. The Jacobite charter (for summary, see *CARD* i. 73–7) did give rights to the common council and citizens in respect of certain civic appointments.

[11] Alderman Shaw claimed in the house of commons that Dublin alone was liable for one-quarter of this tax (*FJ*, 21 May 1821).

[12] For the metal main tax, see *FJ*, 28, 29 Jan. 1818; *Municipal Corporations (Ireland). App. to Report on the City of Dublin*, pt. II, p. 249, HC 1836, xxiv; P. J. Holden, 'Local Taxation in Dublin, 1812', *Dublin Hist. Rec.* 12 (1951), 114–28, at 117–18.

[13] *FJ*, 27 Sept., 5 Dec. 1817; 14 Feb., 12 Mar. 1818.

According to the inhabitants of James Street in January 1818, after nearly a decade there was little to show for their payments; in breach of statutory requirements, accounts had not been laid before the viceroy, and much of the money had allegedly been misappropriated. The viceroy duly asked the corporation to furnish the metal main and pipe water accounts. They were finally produced in July, whereupon the commissioners of public accounts found that £23,000 of Dublin taxpayers' money was unaccounted for. In April 1818 a meeting of city bond-holders complained that the corporation was defaulting on interest due to them.[14]

By this time the aldermen were looking forward to the easing of the corporation's financial problems when city leases were renewed in the 1820s. But in fact the problems proved to be chronic, stemming from a mixture of increased responsibilities, reduced toll revenues, and the falling value of property. Accordingly, even after the repeal of the window tax in 1822 householders continued to complain about the level of local taxes. Parish committees, formed originally to campaign against the window tax, found plenty to occupy them. These committees, though chaired by Protestant churchwardens, and dominated by Protestants, afforded some limited openings for Catholics to become involved in civic life.[15] Their participation highlighted the exclusive nature of the taxing body. Although some local taxes, for lighting, paving, and water, were statutory charges, others were 'presented' annually by a Dublin city grand jury, whose (Protestant) members, many of them drawn from the ranks of the corporation, were picked by the sheriff. These taxes covered such services as prisons, public works, roads, and bridges.

In 1820 the corporation itself petitioned parliament for 'the more equal assessment or reduction of the local taxes of this city'.[16] In 1822 and 1823 a select committee of the house of commons inquired into the matter. The findings made gloomy reading. The basis on which local taxation rested (ministers' money) had originally been adopted in George I's reign, and since then the value of houses had altered greatly, mostly for the worse. Paving tax returns showed a rise in the number of insolvent houses in Dublin from 880 in 1815 to 4,719 in 1821—the latter figure representing over one-quarter of all houses assessed. Since only solvent houses were liable for grand jury taxes, the burden on them had risen greatly. Other problems were exposed. Part of the metal main taxes had indeed been misapplied; grand jury contracts for services and supplies were rarely

---

[14] Ibid., 27 Jan., 24 Feb., 1 May 1818; 18, 20 July 1819; CARD xvii. 202–3, 243; *Municipal Corporations (Ireland). App. to Report on . . . Dublin*, pt. II, pp. 249–51, HC 1836, xxiv.

[15] These included Nicholas Mahon (c.1746–1841), woollen merchant, one of the few Catholics to serve on public bodies in this period. His nephew and business partner Richard O'Gorman (d. 1867) also spoke at taxation meetings (*FJ*, 14 Feb. 1818; 26, 28 Sept. 1822).

[16] CARD xvii. 314, 358, 438–9.

advertised publicly, and frequently went to those with corporation connections. Grand juries were alleged to have awarded excessively high salaries to public officials. The cumulative result of all this, according to one witness, was that the level of local taxes in Dublin was double that of London. The committee showed some sympathy with the citizens' plight by recommending that, if legislation were to be introduced, the citizens should be given some control over tax levels.[17]

Under increasing pressure from the public, the corporation indicated a willingness to speed up the completion of the metal main works and bring an end to the tax.[18] But at the same time it resolved to pursue the recovery of tolls and customs by statutory means. In 1824 a parliamentary bill for that purpose was prepared, but it met opposition from commercial interests outside corporate circles, and it failed to go beyond a first reading.[19]

In other ways, too, the 1820s turned out to be a bad decade for the corporation and guilds. Hitherto, they had had no serious rivals in their claim to speak for the commercial and industrial interests of the city. The first Dublin chamber of commerce, founded in 1783 and open to Catholics as well as Protestants, had effectively collapsed in 1791. Efforts to re-establish it in 1805–6 had met with a poor response. It was argued above that the chief difficulty that faced such a body in attempting to speak for merchants in general was the prior existence of corporate bodies, whose claims were recognized by the state, and still rested on a strong commercial foundation. However, in the post-war period trade links were becoming weaker: by 1818 only just over two-thirds of the merchants' guild representatives on the city commons could be positively identified as merchants or traders, while among the craft guild representatives the proportion following the appropriate trades was about 60 per cent.[20] This was bound to make the corporate bodies more vulnerable to a renewed challenge to their role as spokesmen for Dublin's commercial interests.

Nevertheless, it was not until the 1820s, when the prestige of Dublin corporate bodies had suffered some serious blows, that a successful challenge was mounted. It came shortly after a controversy arising out of the Dublin by-election of 1820, when Thomas Ellis, Master in Chancery, was elected. After the election a bill was drawn up that would have excluded such office-holders from parliament (the relevant clause was defeated in the

[17] Evidence of John Peters, *Second Report from Select Committee on Local Taxation*, 148–50, HC 1823 (549), vi; committee proceedings report, *FJ*, 9 July 1822. In 1824 a new valuation was introduced by 5 Geo. IV, c. 118.

[18] *FJ*, 17 Dec. 1822; *CARD* xviii. 11. The corporation was later found to have laid a very extensive network of metal pipes (*Municipal Corporations (Ireland). App. to Report on . . . Dublin*, 257, HC 1836, xxiv).

[19] *CARD* xvii. 453; *Reports of the Council of the Chamber of Commerce of Dublin to the Annual Assembly of the Members of the Association* (Dublin, 1821–51), NA 1064/1/1, report dated 1 Mar. 1825, p. 17.

[20] Cullen, *Princes & Pirates*, 53–7; above, Table 11.1.

lords). In a debate on a petition against the bill, comments were made in the merchants' guild that angered several MPs. According to the Whig Sir John Newport, members of the guild ('the chiefs of that wretched Orange faction, who admitted none to be loyal but themselves') had insulted government ministers. The master of the guild narrowly escaped a summons to the bar of the house to explain the affair.[21]

It was against this background, with the guild of merchants clearly out of favour with parliament, that a new bid was made to revive the chamber of commerce as a body to represent the interests of merchants of all religious persuasions. In August 1820 a meeting was held to devise an appropriate constitution; a council was formed, and Dublin merchants came forward in some numbers. By the end of 1821 membership stood at 263.[22] As might be expected in a body whose very existence constituted an implicit challenge to the guild of merchants and, beyond that, to the corporation, the chamber's leading activists tended to be Protestant dissenters, liberal Anglicans, and (to a lesser extent than in the 1780s), Catholics.[23]

The chamber endeavoured to attract merchants of all religious and political persuasions by confining its brief to commercial issues and avoiding crusades against vested corporate interests.[24] But reforms were soon being proposed, as in the butter and coal trades, that cut across long-established corporate rights.[25] In an earlier period, this would have been fatal; but by the 1820s the corporation and guilds no longer enjoyed their former prestige. The chamber quickly established its credentials, dealing with custom-house officials and with the treasury over protective duties, and defending Dublin merchants from new charges imposed following improvements to Dublin docks. It was one of the local bodies to petition against the corporation's attempt to gain statutory backing for its right to levy tolls. These successes helped attract new members and retain existing ones. Significantly—so ingrained was the assumption that authority came from the possession of a royal charter—the council's report for 1822 raised the question of seeking a charter, in order to increase the chamber's authority in dealing with government departments.[26]

---

[21] *FJ*, 17, 29 July 1820.   [22] Cullen, *Princes & Pirates*, 58–60.

[23] The chamber is alleged (ibid. 61–3) to have undergone a marked conservative and even unionist shift in the decade after 1825, partly owing to the influence of Arthur Guinness. But Guinness was a Whig until the mid-1830s (below, sect. II), and the union was not a live issue in Dublin politics, 1825–9. A conservative shift would be in keeping with wider political trends, at least from 1830; but while the merchants' guild existed, the chamber was inevitably going to be on the reforming side of it. The influx of O'Connellites in the 1830s was striking: no fewer than nineteen members of the chamber (1835–6) were future Repealers on the reformed Dublin corporation, and its council worked smoothly with O'Connell as MP for Dublin (*Reports of the . . . Chamber of Commerce*, NA 1064/1/1, reports dated 6 Mar. 1832, 1 Mar. 1836).

[24] NA 1064/1/1, report dated 12 April 1827, p. 35.

[25] The merchants' guild appointed eighty measuring porters to oversee coal weights; the corporation appointed a quality checker for butter (*CARD* xvii. 522–3; xviii. 540–2). Cf. NA 1064/1/1, reports dated 4 Dec. 1821, pp. 5–6; 1 Mar. 1825, pp. 15–17.

[26] NA 1064/1/1, report dated 4 Mar. 1823, p. 5.

For all its determination to maintain neutrality in political matters, the chamber's very success in representing Dublin's commercial interests, and its unavoidable 'anti-corporation' complexion, attracted the attention of those whose interests were primarily political. By the 1830s the chamber, in common with the corporation and the guild of merchants, had its own stock of members who were anything but merchants; including Daniel O'Connell and several of his close associates, Richard Barrett of the *Pilot* newpaper, Pierce Mahony the attorney, and so on.[27]

As if being attacked in parliament, thwarted over its right to tolls, and challenged by the chamber of commerce were not bad enough, the corporation was also facing the first stirrings of a demand for municipal reform from its own citizens, scarcely heard since the reform measure of 1760. The inhabitants of James Street, meeting in 1818 to protest about the metal main tax, called for legislation to identify the corporation with all the inhabitants 'of this once great and flourishing, but now impoverished and almost ruined city, so that the interest of all may, in future, be managed for the common good of all, and not any longer sacrificed to the private views of a few individuals'.[28] In 1822 the select committee on Dublin's taxation showed sympathy for this viewpoint, and other parishes took up the theme. One local taxation activist, John Peters of St Anne's parish, produced a pamphlet accusing the corporation of exclusivity, nepotism, mismanagement of revenue, and excessive display. He claimed that the city's charters were deliberately kept hidden from the citizens in order to conceal the corporation's shortcomings. Echoing Charles Lucas, he called for the revival of the old hundred court so that every citizen might question the corporation about its actions.[29]

Overshadowed as it was by the issue of Catholic emancipation, the question of municipal reform made little headway during the 1820s. And if Peters was at all representative of those whose thoughts were turning in that direction, then the inspiration was still coming from the past. Peters' pamphlet, however, marked a significant stage in the alienation of the citizen from the corporation. In the mid-eighteenth century similar alienation had inspired the great campaign associated with Lucas, culminating in corporate reform and placing Dublin's corporate bodies at the forefront of Patriot politics for decades to come. *The Charter Rights of the City of Dublin* was a sign that the goodwill engendered by that earlier reform had evaporated, and that once again reform was needed to regenerate the corporation. But by the 1820s, although there were freemen

---

[27] Ibid., report dated 6 Mar. 1832.   [28] *FJ*, 27 Jan. 1818.
[29] [John Peters], *The Charter Rights of the City of Dublin; Shewing the Title of the Citizens at Large to the City Estates . . . By a Member of St Anne's Committee on Local Taxation* (Dublin, 1825), 5–9, 14, 22; *Second Report from . . . Committee on Local Taxation*, 147–51, HC 1823 (549), vi.

and even members of the city commons among the reformers,[30] the non-freemen, including Catholics, were also involved: and they had no reason to feel friendly towards the corporation.

II. Municipal Reform and the Catholic Challenge

Judged by utilitarian standards, by the 1830s Dublin corporation's claim to privilege was looking decidedly thin. Its role as the voice of the city's commercial interests had been successfully contested by the chamber of commerce, its treasury was in debt, its charitable activities increasingly marginal[31] in the context of unemployment and underemployment at post-war levels. Even in the field of popular entertainment the great colourful spectacles provided by the triennial processions of the guilds had long since come to an end. None of this, however, held such potentially serious implications for the corporation as its unyielding commitment to Protestant ascendancy, which had attracted censure in parliament during the 1820s, and had been officially discountenanced by the granting of Catholic emancipation in 1829.

The fact that the Irish urban corporations still remained, for the most part, bastions of Protestant privilege rendered them highly objectionable to O'Connell and his supporters, and it was one of their principal aims, once emancipation had been gained, to secure municipal reform. Striving to move the debate away from the chosen ground of his opponents—the necessary connection between religion and politics—in his New Year letter to the people of Ireland (7 January 1830), O'Connell declared himself to be 'a thorough Benthamite'. He outlined his immediate parliamentary goals, which included a measure to reduce 'illegal' tolls, and the extension of civic freedom to all resident householders.[32] This declaration was not calculated to promote the cause of those Catholic merchants who were about to make yet another bid to obtain admission to freedom. According to the *Dublin Evening Mail*, one prominent Catholic merchant, Ignatius Callaghan,[33] personally canvassed the corporation on his own behalf, and drank to the

---

[30] These included a future lord mayor (1835–6), Arthur Morrison, hotelier, of Belleville, Donnybrook; represented cooks' guild on city commons from 1814; chosen sheriff 1824, but excused after fine; alderman, 1829. A monument to him still stands at Donnybrook (*FJ*, 23, 30 Oct. 1822).

[31] Charity and contracts also became more explicitly sectarian. In 1833 the corporation stipulated that tenders for repairs of Drumcondra church were to be sought exclusively from freemen in the building trade, and in 1834 the corporation's almshouse at Clonturk (Drumcondra) was reserved exclusively for Protestant widows (*CARD* xix. 84, 158). This coincided with rising emigration, and complaints from poorer Protestants that their interests were neglected (Charles Boyton, *Speech Delivered … at a Meeting of the Protestant Conservative Society* (Dublin, 1832), 3–6).

[32] *DEM*, 11 Jan. 1830.

[33] Ignatius Callaghan, Fleet St. Turned down for freedom again in July (*DEP*, 20 July 1830). Elected to the reformed Dublin corporation, 1841.

glorious memory of King William. But although the aldermen were divided over his application, the city commons were hostile 'almost to a man', and went on (unsuccessfully) to urge the aldermen to join them in calling for repeal of the emancipation act.[34]

Although both sides had thus taken up their positions by 1830, for the next two years municipal reform took second place to the campaign for parliamentary reform. In many respects the legislation of 1832 was moderate, enabling the aristocracy and gentry to dominate political life for decades to come. But in at least one significant respect it departed from the conservative prescription for constitutional reform laid down by Edmund Burke. By introducing a uniform £10 household franchise for all parliamentary boroughs in place of the diversity that had grown up since medieval times, the Whig government ignored Burke's plea for constitutional change to be piecemeal, rather than systematic, in order to preserve as much as possible of the legacy of the past. Moreover, the principle of representation of corporate bodies was clearly being set aside in favour of the representation of propertied individuals.

On this issue the corporation was at one with the spirit of the *Reflections*, even though its reverence for tradition was cast in anti-Catholic terms that Burke would have deplored. In March 1831 a post assembly of the corporation was held to consider the reform bill, then before parliament. In the city commons a member moved

[that] the preservation of the religion of the state has mainly depended on the corporate vested rights and privileges being held sacred . . . should the proposed plan of reform . . . be carried into effect . . . it will in its effects disfranchise the freemen of Ireland . . . and give the entire and exclusive power of returning the members to the Popish priests and democracy . . .[35]

Despite a temporizing reply from the board of aldermen, the commons persisted, and in April the aldermen agreed to petition parliament against the bill.[36] The eventual passage of the act accordingly represented another defeat for corporate bodies. In voting terms, too, it seriously weakened the freemen. Although the Irish reform act allowed resident Dublin freemen to retain their parliamentary vote, their proportion of the newly expanded electorate dropped from over 60 per cent in 1831 to 28 per cent in 1832 and to 25 per cent by 1841, the last election fought before Dublin corporation passed into Catholic control.[37]

[34] *DEM*, 20, 25 Jan., 1 Feb. 1830; DCA, C1/JSC/11, fo. 239.
[35] DCA, C1/JSC/12, fo. 10.   [36] *CARD* xviii. 503.
[37] Percentages calculated from *Parliamentary Representation, Ireland (Boundary Reports), Report on the County of the City of Dublin*, 52, HC 1831–2 (519), xliii; *A Return of the Electors Registered . . . in Ireland (County of the City of Dublin)*, 8, HC 1833 (177) xxvii; *A Return of the Total Number of Parliamentary Electors . . . Registered . . . in the Years 1835, 1837 and 1841*, 12, HC 1841 (240.–1) xx.

With parliamentary reform out of the way, O'Connell (who from December 1832 was one of the Dublin city MPs) returned to the question of municipal reform. Writing to his political confidants, he had no need to invoke Benthamite values to justify his goal: the breaking down of Protestant control ('If we can get the Corporation monopoly put an end to, we will break a gap in the enemy's fortifications'). Early in 1833 a parliamentary select committee was set up to inquire into the state of municipal corporations in England, Wales, and Ireland; and O'Connell, who was made a member, set about identifying witnesses who would 'prove the entire System of Dublin Corporation abuses'. By April he was satisfied that the committee accepted the need for 'a full reform'. To his agent P. V. Fitzpatrick, still occasionally having discussions with the Dublin Conservatives, he hinted that if the corporation would co-operate, reform might be achieved quickly and be limited in scope; if reform were to be postponed, he argued (correctly, as it turned out), it would be approached on the more sweeping basis envisaged for the English corporations.[38] O'Connell also held out the prospect of a continued role for the Dublin guilds in municipal elections; he even posed as a champion of the craft guilds against the more powerful merchants' guild. He hinted again that the Conservatives should make terms with the Catholics on an anti-union platform, since (he alleged) the government, in its municipal reform policy, appeared to be bent on destroying 'the last but powerful remnant of Protestant ascendancy'. Since this goal reflected O'Connell's own aims more accurately than those of the government, it is not surprising that the Conservatives failed to respond to these overtures.[39]

Nor, despite the continued presence of a substantial liberal minority among its members, was there any sign of Dublin corporation weakening in its commitment to the confessional state. Early in 1836 the corporation was goaded into restating its position in response to an attack from the liberal Protestant Lord Cloncurry,[40] who had described the majority of Irish corporation members as 'insolvent peculators', and 'traders in religious intolerance'. Rebutting these charges, the corporation turned the tables on Cloncurry with a stinging reference to his family's mercantile origins and his own youthful links with the United Irishmen:

And although there are unfortunately to be found not only amongst the members of the Irish Corporations, but in all trading bodies, individuals whose success as tradesmen has not been equal to that of Lord Cloncurry's father; yet there are few

[38] O'Connell to Fitzpatrick, 11 Mar. 1833, *O'Connell Corr.* v, letters 1955a, 1956, 1957, 1963, 1969.
[39] *Second Letter to the People of Ireland* [12 Apr. 1833], in Mary F. Cusack (ed.), *The Speeches and Public Letters of the Liberator* (2 vols.; Dublin, 1875), ii. 388–9; *O'Connell Corr.* v, letters 1957, 1969.
[40] Valentine Browne Lawless, 2nd Baron Cloncurry (1773–1853). United Irishman; imprisoned 1798, 1799–1801 on suspicion of treason (see *DNB*).

amongst them who would accept of Lord Cloncurry's title and estates with the incumbrance of his reputation and character ... the Irish Corporations were established for the maintenance of Protestantism, and the protection of British interests in Ireland, the Irish Corporators are, and have been at all times ... faithful to that trust:—They are the loyal subjects of a legitimate Sovereign ... the inalienable friends of British connexion—the anxious supporters of order and of law—and the unsubdued defenders of our once glorious Constitution in Church and State—true to those principles they are prepared again to take the field in their support, and at the hazard of their lives, defend the Throne—protect the Church— and uphold the Institutions of the United Empire, as they did in 1798, when Lord Cloncurry was in the Tower prisoner for caballing to subvert them.[41]

In passing over (on this occasion) its own earlier origins, the corporation was aligning itself with the Protestant creations of the seventeenth century and displaying its solidarity with corporate interests in general.[42]

The threat of a municipal reform measure became more serious after the publication, in 1835, of the report of a parliamentary commission of inquiry into Irish municipal corporations. The commission, set up in 1833 following the preliminary work of the select committee, was composed of Whigs, who had no sympathy for the Irish corporations, which were in most cases under the control of their political opponents. The report was damning: the corporations were wasteful of public money, provided inadequate services, and with few exceptions were incorrigibly sectarian.[43] Apologists for the corporations complained, with some justice, that they had not been given a fair hearing. In particular, the commissioners had failed to acknowledge the historical circumstances that had made the corporations bastions of Protestantism. But the commissioners were bent on making out a case for reform, rather than presenting a balanced picture;[44] and what damned the corporations was their obvious reluctance to abandon the historic commitment to the confessional state. To Whigs, radicals, and, of course, O'Connellites, such attitudes seemed anomalous in the aftermath of emancipation and parliamentary reform.

However, the magnitude of what was at stake ensured that the struggle over Irish municipal reform would be a protracted one. For, if modelled on the act for England and Wales (1835),[45] Irish municipal reform would have

---

[41] *CARD* xix. 246–7.

[42] The corporation commonly referred to its immemorial origins (ibid. xix, 378).

[43] *Municipal Corporations (Ireland). First Report of the Commissioners*, 16, 21, 36, 38, HC 1835, xxvii. For Dublin see *App. to First Report*, pt. I, pp. 12, 68, 71–2.

[44] Hence the commissioners' charge (often repeated) that the absence of corporation members from the committees of certain commercial bodies proved that they had lost links with trade (*First Report of the Commissioners: App., Report on ... Dublin*, 14, HC 1835, xxvii; Daly, *Dublin the Deposed Capital*, 203). Unrepresentative the corporation undoubtedly was, of Catholic businessmen, and in the 1830s perhaps of liberal Protestants; but the cases mentioned constituted a selective, Whiggish group of Dublin's commercial bodies: no mention was made, for instance, of the trustees of the Royal Exchange, a body closely identified with the merchants' guild. [45] 5 & 6 Will. IV, c. 76.

far greater consequences than any of the constitutional reforms since 1828. Neither the repeal of the English test and corporation acts, Catholic emancipation, parliamentary reform, nor the English municipal reform act had threatened the predominantly Protestant nature of parliament or local government. By contrast, as the government's critics pointed out, the introduction of a uniform civic franchise would have the effect of placing most of the southern Irish corporations in Catholic hands.

This prospect raised several issues, notably the future of the established church, and of the union, which simply did not arise in the case of the other reforms. Accordingly, the opponents of reform mustered strongly, and from 1835 on defeated no fewer than five bills before the sixth was introduced in 1840. All this gave room for opponents to hope that reform might be deferred indefinitely.

What grounds did the defenders of corporate privilege in Ireland have for optimism in the mid-1830s? One source of hope lay in the increasingly organized expression of evangelical Protestantism and anti-Catholicism in Ireland and Britain, which since the late 1820s had developed a more dogmatic and millennial aspect, partly in response to the more assertive tone of post-emancipation Catholic politics. A series of great Protestant meetings in Ireland during 1834 was followed up by similar meetings in England.[46] One such was held at Exeter Hall, London, in June 1835, at which speaker after speaker held forth on the unchanging nature of popery and the dangers to Protestantism posed by government policies. Speakers from Ireland, including the Dublin Anglican minister, R. J. McGhee,[47] and Dr Henry Cooke, leader of the subscribing wing of the Ulster Presbyterians, took a prominent part in this meeting, illustrating the alleged dangers of popery from Irish examples. Their most effective contribution was to publicize the continuing use, in the state-funded Catholic seminary at Maynooth, of Pierre Dens' *Theologia* (first published 1777, and brought out in a new edition in Dublin in 1832), which contained passages relating to the persecution of heretics and the pope's power to dissolve oaths. McGhee and Cooke gave their own summaries of these passages, and succeeded in persuading the meeting that they represented the current teachings of the Catholic church in Ireland. The attendant publicity (as always when the powers claimed by the Catholic church were at issue) forced Catholic spokesmen on to the defensive. Dr Murray, archbishop of Dublin, found himself in the awkward position of defending the work in parts, while discountenancing certain 'obsolete' opinions also present.[48]

---

[46] Gilbert A. Cahill, 'Some Nineteenth Century Roots of the Ulster Problem, 1829–48', *Irish University Review*, 1 (1971), 215–37, at 223–30; Wolffe, *The Protestant Crusade in Great Britain*, 30–1, 77–95.

[47] Robert James McGhee (1789–1872), b. Carlow; founded a theological society, TCD, to study 'polemical divinity', 1830; minister of episcopal free church, Harold's Cross, 1838–46 (Bowen, *Protestant Crusade*, ch. 3).

[48] Donal A. Kerr, *Peel, Priests and Politics* (Oxford, 1982), 232–3, 236–7; *O'Connell Corr.* v, letter 2260a, n. 3.

In such ways Irish spokesmen contributed to the expression of Protestant fears of popery. They did not, of course, create such fears, which were part of the common Protestant heritage in Britain and Ireland. Public opinion was nowhere well prepared for the prospect of O'Connell's mainly Catholic party, in alliance with a reforming Whig government, pursuing measures which, as in the reform of the Church of Ireland, and the establishment of a 'godless' national education system, appeared to represent further departures from the Protestant principles of the constitution. A significant feature of these demonstrations of Protestant feeling was the co-operation of Anglicans and some Protestant dissenters; and in 1839 Dublin corporation conferred honorary freedom not only on the Anglican McGhee, but also on Dr Cooke, praising both for the zeal they had displayed in support of 'our pure religion'. (It is only fair to add that not all the prejudice was on one side: O'Connell, for instance, believed that Protestantism would evaporate without state support.)[49]

Also of value to traditionalists was the formation of Conservative parties in Britain and Ireland as part of the political realignment following emancipation and parliamentary reform. In both countries, 'ultras' as well as more progressive elements united to resist Whig/O'Connellite attempts to reform bastions of Protestant privilege, such as the corporations and the Irish established church. In Ireland, the party's headquarters was in Dublin, its activists drawn from the Dublin professional classes and certain Church of Ireland clergymen: by 1834 many of the nobility and gentry, including former supporters of emancipation, were coming in, and overtures were being made to Protestant dissenters.[50]

The Irish Conservatives' outlook on political affairs, in a number of respects, coincided with that of Dublin corporation. Both were alarmed at the spectacle, apparently unique in Europe, of the convergence in Ireland between popery and 'the democratic mania': as Dr Boyton of the Protestant Conservative Society pointed out, on the Continent 'popery' was usually conservative.[51] (He might have gone on to reflect that what was distinctive about Irish Catholics was that despite constituting a majority of the population, they did not form the religious establishment.) Both regarded O'Connellite agitation as inherently revolutionary and even seditious in its attempts to overturn established laws and institutions.[52] Both were disturbed by O'Connell's attack on the union; even though both contained elements that were occasionally willing, in the early 1830s, to threaten government with a Protestant demand for repeal.[53]

---

[49] *CARD* xix. 344, 370; below, sect. III.

[50] Cahill, 'Some Nineteenth Century Roots', 227.

[51] Speech at Protestant Conservative Society (*Warder* suppl., 2 Mar. 1833); *CARD* xviii. 349.

[52] *Report of the Proceedings at the First Public Meeting of the Irish Metropolitan Conservative Society* (Dublin, [1836]), 4; Dublin corporation address to Baron Smith, 3 Mar. 1834 (*CARD* xix. 135). [53] Below, sect. III.

From the outset of the party's existence there were signs that it was likely to win support in corporate circles. Although poorly prepared for the 1832 general election, the Conservatives had obtained 90 per cent of the freemen votes at the contest in Dublin city; but the turn-out of freemen, at only 64 per cent of those so recently registered, had been poor.[54] At the next general election in 1835, when the threat of municipal reform under O'Connellite auspices had come closer, the convergence between corporate interests and the Conservatives was even stronger. The turn-out of freemen rose to 81 per cent, with 94 per cent of their votes going to the Conservatives.[55] By this time Conservative agents were active in registering voters (which the 1832 reform act had made a requirement for voting) and they were highly visible at election times, often in the company of corporation personnel. It was Conservative funds that financed the expensive election petitions against the return of O'Connell and Ruthven for Dublin city in 1835 (which succeeded) and against O'Connell and Robert Hutton in 1837 (which failed).[56]

On top of all this, and spurred on by an indulgent legal judgment of 1835 concerning the voting rights of resident freemen,[57] the Dublin Conservatives had begun to rummage in the corporation records in order to identify persons who might be qualified for freedom. Freemen by grace had lost their parliamentary votes, but the rights of those qualified by birth or service remained, and in addition the reform act had recognized those qualified by marriage to the daughter of a freeman. The result was that from 1835 to 1839—when a stricter legal decision overturned the previous one— almost two and half times as many new freemen were admitted each year as had been common during the 1820s.[58] These extra numbers were produced by admitting to freedom grandsons, or even great-grandsons, of freemen; others were admitted by service without necessarily having their indentures enrolled with their guild. The O'Connellites, alleging that these were 'fictitious freemen', demanded a parliamentary inquiry, which was conceded in 1837. At the inquiry guild officials confirmed that the Conservatives had

---

[54] Freemen voting (1,263) calculated from *An Alphabetical List of the Constituency of the City of Dublin . . . and the Votes Given at the Elections of 1832, 1835 and 1837* (Dublin [1837]). Poll book records often differ slightly from the totals in the official returns. See also above, Ch. 13.

[55] Calculation of freemen voting (1,620) as in n. 54. After the election and the return of the Whigs to office, Dublin corporation was so much out of sympathy with the new Whig viceroy (the earl of Mulgrave) that it failed to present the usual address (*O'Connell Corr.* vi, letter 2468, n. 1).

[56] Ibid. v, letter 2187, and for the petitions, letters 2216–19, 2221–6, 2229, 2330–4; vi, letters 2451, 2457. For Hutton, see below n. 61.

[57] *CARD* xix. 207; Edward Bullen (ed.), *Five Reports of the Committee of the Precursor Association . . . Upon the Relative State and Nature of the Parliamentary Franchises in the United Kingdom* (Dublin, 1839), *Third Report*, 24–30, app., pp. 55–6.

[58] On average 128 freemen were created annually, 1821–8 (calculated from *Returns of the Number of Persons Registered . . . in Every City and Town . . . in Ireland*, 1–19, HC 1829 (253), xxii. For 1835–8 the figure was 310 (calculated from Bullen (ed.), *Five Reports of . . . Precursor Association*, app., p. 56).

been active in the creation of new freemen, even in some cases paying the necessary admission fines.[59]

Somewhat surprisingly, there still remained individuals who believed that the corporation's political orientation could be turned around. In 1837 the lord mayor, Alderman William Hodges,[60] suggested himself to O'Connell as a (Whig) candidate for Dublin, contending that his candidacy would 'not prove unavailing with the great body of the Corporation'. But in the event O'Connell's running-mate at the 1837 general election was his old ally, the Presbyterian coachmaker Robert Hutton,[61] who was not active in corporate circles: he proved no more popular with the freemen than O'Connell or Ruthven had been.[62]

Of course the corporation was no stranger to partisan politics. During the 1820s it had confirmed its place in the anti-emancipation camp. But opposition to emancipation had to some extent cut across former Court and opposition lines, whereas by the mid-1830s the links with the Conservatives were so close as to suggest that the corporation was becoming little more than a branch of that party. The corporation's opponents had highlighted the link as early as 1832, when they spoke of the 'Conservative or Corporate party'.[63] The corporation and guilds, with their long-standing antipathy to the very idea of party in politics, were slower to use the label; but after the Whigs returned to office in 1835, following a brief Conservative spell in government, even this reluctance died away.[64]

The close identification between the Dublin freemen and the Conservatives must have been galling for O'Connell, who, at a time when he was hopeful of Protestant artisan backing for repeal, had helped to preserve the freemen's parliamentary votes.[65] After all, the Whigs had enjoyed considerable support from Dublin freemen in the 1820s: why was the subsequent Conservative triumph so complete? For instance, how much did it depend on Conservative party funds, and on the bribery that notoriously went on among the freemen of certain boroughs at this period?[66] In keeping with their traditions of constitutional rectitude, the Dublin guilds frowned on

---

[59] *Third Report from the Select Committee on Fictitious Votes, Ireland*, 40, 85, 140–1, HC 1837 (480), xi, pt. II (evidence of G. Archer, Timothy Allen, William Clinton).

[60] Above, Ch. 13, n. 88; *O'Connell Corr.* vi, letter 2435a.

[61] Robert Hutton (1785–1870), below, App. B; Boase, *MEB*; *O'Connell Corr.* vi, letter 2451.

[62] Whether standing as Repealers or Whigs, O'Connell and his running mates never received more than 7% of the freemen vote at any of the Dublin city elections, 1832–41.

[63] Marcus Costello, speech, National Political Union (*DEM*, 7 Sept. 1832).

[64] For the dislike of 'party' see address to W. Gregory, MP (*CARD* xviii. 465). Unable now to call itself 'Whig' (in view of the new connotations of the term), the corporation never adopted 'Tory' (with its 'divine right' overtones) for itself or its preferred parliamentary candidates. The later 1830s saw gradual acceptance of 'Conservative' for candidates and party agents (ibid. xix. 273–4, 337, 345, 392); cf. St Luke's guild's backing, 1837, for 'the Conservative candidates' (NLI, MS 12128, fo. 46).   [65] Above, Ch 13.

[66] Hoppen, *Elections, Politics and Society*, 4–5.

bribery; but it certainly went on.[67] However, there are reasons to suppose that in Dublin its importance in determining party allegiance was limited. First, although the Conservatives doubtless had more money to spend, bribery was also practised by their opponents.[68] Moreover, the sheer number of Dublin voters meant that bribery on a wide scale was impractical. At the 1832 election £3,000 from England was available to the Conservatives to fight the Dublin city and university seats, and in 1837 £2,400 was sent from London to be spent on the city election alone. But with an electorate of over 7,000, rising to over 12,000 in 1841[69] (including 2,000–3,000 freemen), enormous sums would be needed to make much impact. In any case, bribery was most likely to be effective where the voters, besides being few in number, were also poor. There are some signs that the drive to create more freemen between 1835 and 1839 did introduce a poorer element into the Dublin freeman body,[70] though not on the scale claimed by the O'Connellites. Since the Conservatives boasted that the freemen represented 'the great barrier against the progress of democratic principles'[71] they could hardly support the indiscriminate admission of really poor Protestants. Analysis of the 2,288 freemen[72] who voted at the 1841 general election reveals that half were merchants, gentry, or professional men, and over one-third were skilled tradesmen.[73]

---

[67] The city commons condemned bribery among freemen at the election, May 1831 (DCA, C1/JSC/12, fo. 19ᵛ); St Luke's guild resolved (1836) to expel a member for allegedly taking a bribe, as 'unworthy of being a Freeman', though this was not carried through (NLI, MS 12128, fos. 42ʳ⁻ᵛ, 44ʳ⁻ᵛ).

[68] For a case of bribery practised by an O'Connellite freeman (William Stephens, a free hosier, paid a cabinet-maker to vote for Harty and Perrin in 1831) see *O'Connell Corr.* vi, letter 2436. Both Conservatives and Whigs received funds from England to help with election expenses: Hoppen, *Elections, Politics and Society*, 300; Angus Macintyre, *The Liberator: Daniel O'Connell and the Irish Party, 1830–1847* (London, 1965), 96, 124.

[69] Between 1832 and 1850 the actual size of electorates was often at variance with the official size (Hoppen, *Elections, Politics and Society*, 6–7); figures here follow Walker, *Parliamentary Election Results*.

[70] Evidence of W. Clinton, *Third Report . . . on Fictitious Votes, Ireland*, 141, HC 1837 (480), xi, pt. II.

[71] *Suggestions for the Amendment of the Irish Municipal Corporations Reform Bill . . . as Agreed at a Meeting of the Dublin Conservative Registration Society* [31 Mar. 1840] (Dublin, 1840), 16.

[72] Figure calculated from R. Madden, *Mirror of the Dublin Election . . . 1841; Arranged in Street Lists* (Dublin, 1841). It exceeds by 108 that in *FJ*, 22 July 1841, but has been used for occupational analysis, yielding gentry, 31.2%; professionals, 14.1%; merchants, 4.5%; skilled trades, retailing, 39.5%; clerks, 3.5%; others, 2.0%; unidentified, 5.2%.

[73] In the light of these figures, the comment of T. M. Ray, O'Connell's electoral adviser, that 'fully two thirds of all the Freemen who voted in 1837 are merely lodgers and mostly obscure creatures' seems too dismissive: but it was made while the Conservatives were trying (unsuccessfully) to procure the municipal franchise for freemen who had parliamentary votes (*O'Connell Corr.* vi, letter 2689 and n. 1). In fact all but 6% of the Dublin electorate in 1841 met the £10 household qualification (Hoppen, *Elections, Politics and Society*, 12). But the figures do reveal the declining links between the freemen and trade: only 44% of the freemen who voted in 1841 were merchants, skilled artisans, or retailers.

In fact, most of the Conservative party's success with the Dublin freemen was part of a wider pattern, as the dual effects of electoral reform and the O'Connellite challenge combined to weaken the Whigs and give a more sectarian cast to urban politics. Thus there was a broadly similar development in Cork city, where even the residual influence of the great landed Whig magnates—for which there was no counterpart in Dublin— disappeared after 1832.[74] The Dublin city Whigs managed to retain a distinct existence,[75] but—and this completed their discomfiture—they were overshadowed by the towering figure of O'Connell, MP for the city from 1832 to 1835 and again from 1837 to 1841, at the head of his successive national political organizations, targeting the established church, the corporations, and, from time to time, the union. This produced a marked degree of polarization. Dublin corporation put the matter forcefully: 'the Metropolis is the centre where that organized system of sedition is concocted by the enemies of peace and order'.[76] Hence the absence of serious party-political differences between the two houses of the corporation, between the city corporation and the guilds, and between the corporation and other agencies dedicated to the upkeep of Protestant morale, including the Conservative societies, the Aldermen of Skinner's Alley, and the Orange Order.[77] The O'Connellites were never completely without friends in corporate circles,[78] but the drift of former Whigs to the Conservatives was the prevailing pattern. The most spectacular case was that of the brewer Arthur Guinness, who parted from the Whigs in the mid-1830s. His defection was to be of great long-term significance to the Conservative party, and a correspondingly bitter blow to O'Connell.[79]

The rise of the Conservative party fulfilled other functions besides boosting morale among city Protestants. It both speeded, and helped to cushion, the decline of the guilds. By the 1830s there was scarcely even a

---

[74] D'Alton, *Protestant Society and Politics in Cork*, ch. 5. The dukes of Leinster had lost much influence in Dublin when the 2nd duke (W. R. Fitzgerald) failed to take a strong stand against the act of union (*DNB*).

[75] McDowell, *Public Opinion and Government Policy in Ireland*, 161–2.

[76] *CARD* xix. 135.

[77] Irish Protestant Conservative Society, 1831–3; Metropolitan Conservative Society, founded 1836. Despite a second dissolution in 1836, the Orange Order continued active at election times in the Conservative interest (NLI, MS 12128, fo. 48). The Protestant Association of Ireland, founded 1836, also helped with registration (*First Report of the Protestant Association of Ireland* (Dublin, 1836), 10).

[78] These included Hickman Kearney, Abbey St. (d. 1851); elected sheriff 1809, but excused after fine; sheriffs' peer 1809–41; appointed a paving commissioner, 1827 (*O'Connell Corr.* iii, letter 1399; v, letters 2187, 2324); John Veevers, wine merchant; sheriff 1836–7; sheriffs' peer 1837–41 (ibid. vi, letters 2586, 2642).

[79] Lynch and Vaizey, *Guinness's Brewery*, 105–7, 144–5 (also above, Ch. 9, n. 49). To O'Connell, Guinness became 'that miserable old apostate' (*O'Connell Corr.* vi, letter 2651). Another important defector was John David La Touche (1772–1838): *Proceedings at the Election for the City of Dublin . . . 1835* (Dublin, 1835), 36–7. Both men had been treasurers of the O'Connell testimonial in 1829 (*O'Connell Corr.* iv, letter 1549, n. 4).

residual guild role in the regulation of trade. Most of the energies left over from the ceaseless efforts to stave off debt were focused on politics. Yet even the guilds' political role was beginning to be superseded as the freeman element in the electorate declined. For the best part of a century it had been the custom for parliamentary candidates to tour the guildhalls to seek support. But in May 1831 this tradition was abandoned in favour of one large meeting of freemen in the merchants' hall.[80] Subsequently, guilds continued to endorse particular candidates, but as political parties became more widely accepted and the Conservative candidates published election addresses setting out their policies in detail, visits to guildhalls became largely superfluous.[81] Moreover, some of the freemen admitted under Conservative auspices had only weak links with the guilds. This emerged at a corporation meeting in November 1836, when the absence of guild representatives to vouch for the qualifications of candidates for civic freedom was defended on the grounds (suggested, allegedly, 'by a Conservative gentleman') that to insist upon these formalities put obstacles in the way of 'the common cause'. This met with some protests in the city commons, but less because of the effect on corporate traditions than because without such guarantees 'enemies as well as friends' might be admitted.[82]

In 1837 the reformers' case was strengthened by revelations at the select committee on fictitious votes concerning the Dublin Conservatives' role in the creation of new freemen. Witnesses also confirmed the continued exclusion of Catholics, as well (it was now alleged) of liberal Protestants. But the Whig government's ability to command majorities in parliament and carry a municipal reform bill, even with the O'Connellites' support, remained in doubt. Paradoxically, in view of its reforming image, the government continued in office during 1839 and 1840 chiefly through the support of Queen Victoria. In these circumstances the prospects for Irish municipal reform remained uncertain. In an uncharacteristic mood of pessimism, O'Connell, who had staked a great deal on achieving solid gains to reassure his supporters, contemplated his own descent into political obscurity.[83]

In fact, however, by 1838 Peel and other leading Conservatives in Britain—who had originally been prepared to accept complete abolition of the Irish corporations rather than see them fall into Catholic hands[84]—were

---

[80] *DEM*, 4 May 1831. For the origins of the custom see above, Ch. 3.

[81] See e.g. NLI, MS 12128, fo. 29; for election addresses, see *An Alphabetical List of the Constituency of the City of Dublin, with . . . the Votes Given . . . [in] 1832, 1835 and 1837*, pp. vi–vii.

[82] Corporation meeting report, *FJ*, 5 Nov. 1836; DCA, C1/JSC/12, fo. 178ᵛ.

[83] *O'Connell Corr.* vi, letters 2645, 2646, 2648.

[84] G. S. Lefevre, *Peel and O'Connell: A Review of the Irish Policy of Parliament from the Act of Union to the Death of Sir Robert Peel* (London, 1887), 184.

becoming increasingly disturbed at the apparently unending struggle over Irish municipal reform. The Irish Conservatives were anxious to fight on, but they came under growing pressure from their British counterparts who argued that this would jeopardize party unity. Under these pressures, it was the Irish Conservatives who split, with the recorder of Dublin, Frederick Shaw, now MP for the university, leading those who were reluctantly prepared to accept a compromise, while others, headed by the young barrister and professor of political economy at the university, Isaac Butt,[85] stood firm. The ensuing recriminations, which were taken up by rival newspapers, were very bitter.[86]

Dublin corporation's anger with Shaw was reflected in the transfer of its confidence to Butt early in 1839, and in its public denial that it had agreed to the compromises of 1838. The corporation proceeded to petition Conservatives in both houses of parliament, the Protestants of the United Kingdom, and the queen against the bill of 1839. These petitions included many familiar themes. The corporation's privileges rested on immemorial rights, royal charters, and on a contractual understanding of the state, in which rights had been granted in return for loyalty and to promote fundamental and unchanging 'principles of perfect freedom'. Accusations of 'intolerant bigotry' were rejected: the corporation had never desired the exclusion from civil rights of any subject promising undivided allegiance to the sovereign and unequivocal submission to the laws, and it was prepared to make 'great sacrifices', 'if it be true that our freedom, and our Church which gave it birth, are safe in the pledges already exchanged for an admission to civil power'.[87]

Yet even as these themes were being reiterated, the corporation betrayed its consciousness that such arguments were no longer central to contemporary thought ('In believing, as we are compelled to do, that there is any portion of our fellow subjects whose principles dis-entitle them . . . to a participation in our privileges, we know that we are behind the philosophy of the day . . .').[88] The corporation was right. Ever since the 1790s, but especially in the 1820s and 1830s, traditional natural rights arguments and contractualism had been in decline in Britain, along with the ancient constitution. The idea of checks and balances in a mixed government was being set aside in favour of the sovereign (liberal) state, in which, it was

---

[85] Isaac Butt (1813–79), barrister; secretary, Protestant Association of Ireland, 1836; retained by Dublin corporation as counsel against the municipal reform bill, 1839–40. Later a leader of the home rule party: see *DNB*; David Thornley, *Isaac Butt and Home Rule* (London, 1964).

[86] The *Warder* (2 Jan. 1841), with which Butt was associated, backed Butt and 'the Protestant democracy' against the Irish Conservative leaders. The *DEM* backed Shaw (McDowell, *Public Opinion and Government Policy*, 184).

[87] *CARD* xix. 338, 371, 378–9. The Conservative party attempts to secure compromise are outlined in Macintyre, *The Liberator*, 250–4. [88] *CARD* xix. 379.

held, individual liberties, including security of person and property, could be protected adequately through the courts.[89]

The sense that the times were out of sympathy with corporate values might have been cause for despair. But the corporation had not lost hope. After all, for Irish Protestants history abounded with examples of divine intervention ('Shall we put out of view that omnipotent and all disposing power, who has hitherto preserved us and our holy religion, and who assures us, that He will never leave nor forsake those who trust in Him?').[90] Hitherto, the corporation (though not always the guilds) had maintained in its public statements a strict, Lockian adherence to the civil aspects of popery. The truth or falsehood of the Catholic religion, evangelical crusades—these had been avoided. But now, calling the Protestants of the United Kingdom to the defence of the Irish corporations, the cause of Ireland's wretchedness was unequivocally attributed to an unscriptural religion. 'Brethren—We boldly declare unto you the truth—the cause is Popery. That system which the unerring Word of God denounces in terms the most awful and instructive . . . paralyses the energies of the people and produces those disastrous results which we have here alluded to.' And the remedy lay to hand:

in the universal diffusion of Protestant light, and truth, and in the firm establishment of the Protestant Church. Are these most desirable results attainable? They are. Why, then, have they not been effected long before? Because essayed in a Popish way, through the instrumentality of penal enactments. Let us have a government that will adopt a course of national policy, conceived in the spirit of those private Associations whose object is the very one now under consideration—the Protestant-ising of Ireland in Scriptural Principles—and Popery will soon only be known within our borders in the recollection of the evils it has perpetrated.[91]

The sponsors of municipal reform were condemned for working on false assumptions: 'that it is possible to amalgamate the Popish and Protestant population of our towns . . . that a legal juxtaposition of these opposites would lead them to a perfect agreement with each other'. On the contrary, according to the corporation, Irish Protestants learned 'from God's Word that so far are fellowship and union with Papists from being in accordance with His will, that they are directly opposed to it, the dictate of Holy Scripture being, "Come out from thence and be separate." ' Accordingly, Irish Protestants would continue to cherish 'the *Glorious, Pious, and Immortal Memory of the Great and Good King William—the triumphs of Aughrim and the Boyne—the defeat of Popish treachery, and Gunpowder treason*—and all those memorable interpositions of a gracious Providence'.

[89] Francis and Morrow, 'After the Ancient Constitution', 300–2; Claeys, 'The French Revolution Debate and British Political Thought', 78–80.
[90] Address to the Protestants of the U.K., 6 Feb. 1839 (*CARD* xix. 364).
[91] *CARD* xix. 353–4.

Municipal reform might be required: but it should be reform on Protestant lines, which would not break down the barriers 'between truth and falsehood—between idolatry and Christian worship—between Christ and Antichrist'. Since all the evils predicted from granting Catholic emancipation had been realized, there could be no inconsistency in holding firm now. 'Hence, Brethren, our cry is, "No Surrender" ... If our Protestant Corporations must perish ... we will, at least, have the satisfaction of not being consenting parties to their extinction.'[92]

Thus, when faced with the unthinkable prospect of city government passing into Catholic hands, the corporation sought comfort and hope from ideas that could not go out of date, in the sense that they rested on religious and biblical belief: the seventeenth-century legacy of a Protestant people, whose lot it was to dwell and to suffer in an idolatrous land, yet who always remained God's chosen people—as long as they kept their distance from the treacherous Catholics. And because this legacy dated from a period when the Church of Ireland had had strong Calvinist overtones, it was likely to strike a chord not merely among Anglicans but also among Protestant dissenters.[93]

With this appeal to United Kingdom Protestants the corporation had shot its bolt. Other resolutions and petitions were to follow, but they ran on more familiar lines.[94] In fact, the 1839 bill was amended in the lords and thrown out on its return to the commons; but early in 1840 another bill was introduced. At this stage, one of the Irish Conservatives, Serjeant Joseph Jackson, proposed an imaginative amendment, arising from the widely expressed fears that in several Irish towns and cities municipal reform would merely replace Protestant ascendancy with Catholic ascendancy, and Catholic exclusion with Protestant exclusion:

It was his intention when the bill got into committee to propose some amendments, with the view of counteracting the exclusion of protestants ... suppose that in a town there were two roman catholic voters for one protestant voter; to prevent the overwhelming effect of such a majority he should propose that each elector should only have the power of voting for a number equal to one moiety of the town-council ...[95]

Jackson argued that Lord Grey had earlier recommended such a policy for Ireland, as a means of avoiding the exclusive domination by one party. And something like this principle was actually adopted in the Canada union act of 1840, in circumstances where the mainly Catholic French Canadians of Lower Canada still outnumbered the mainly Protestant Anglo-Canadians of

---

[92] Ibid. xix. 360–3, 365.
[93] Cf. Alan Ford, *The Protestant Reformation in Ireland, 1590–1641* (Frankfurt am Main, 1985), 220–1.   [94] *CARD* xix. 381–2, 401–2.
[95] *Hansard*[3], lii. 258–9 (14 Feb. 1840).

Upper Canada: both parts were to have an equal number of seats in the new united parliament.[96] But Peel, leader of the opposition, showed no interest in the proposal, and Lord John Russell, for the government, took the view that Ireland must be governed in the same way as England. The amendment was lost at the committee stage by 102 votes to 35, and on 10 August 1840 the sixth Irish municipal reform bill became law.[97]

Amid the last impassioned pleas for the bill to be defeated, one voice stood out, if only because it spoke as 'The Ghost of Lucas'. On a printed broadsheet, 'Iscariot Shaw' and the rest of the Protestant aristocracy, clergy, and 'literati' were denounced for submitting to a measure that 'with one fell swoop, blasts the summit, the middle, and the foundation of the Constitution'. Complaining that 'the present generation . . . will neither see, hear, nor understand history', the author rehearsed the fate of Irish Protestants under James II, and reminded Dublin corporation that in the last years of Queen Anne's reign it had defeated 'the Pope's scheme' for dismembering the empire by subverting all constitutional and municipal authorities. In those days the corporation had been praised for its stand; now it was being told to submit quietly. The destruction of Protestantism all over Christendom would surely follow, yet no protest was heard from the queen or the people. In view of what was at stake, would 'Protestant legislators of the nineteenth century, still continue to sanction and approve of this wholesale destruction of patents, charters, oaths, honor, and the faith of kings'?[98]

III. From Patriots to Unionists

Despite studied attempts to ignore the O'Connellite repealers, Dublin corporate bodies shared with the Irish Conservatives a sense of alarm at O'Connell's attack on the legislative union, particularly in 1831–2, when the prospect of parliamentary reform led the city commons to forecast the election (by 'the Popish priests and democracy') of eighty to ninety 'republicans of desperate fortunes', who would work with English 'infidels' to repeal the union, separate Ireland from Britain, and eventually pull down the established church.[99] This warning was couched in terms similar to those used by Lucas's critics almost a century earlier, and rested on similar premisses. The link with Britain must not be threatened; no undue popular

---

[96] Hill, 'The Legal Profession and the Defence of the *Ancien Régime*', 207, n. 74. A related idea for protecting the Protestant minority once their political monopoly had gone was Charles Sheridan's scheme (1793) for an additional seat for each county (to be reserved for Catholics), while Protestants filled the other two (*An Essay Upon the True Principles of Civil Liberty . . . in Which is Also Discussed the Roman Catholic Claim to the Elective Franchise in Ireland* (London, 1793), 127–31, 140–1).   [97] 3 & 4 Vict., c. 108.

[98] *Experimental and Historical Reflections on the Bill Now Before Parliament for the Establishment of Popery, Misnamed 'The Irish Municipal Reform Bill'* (signed 'The Ghost of Lucas'). (CULBC, Hib. O. 840. 3).   [99] DCA, C1/JSC/12, fo. 10.

influence must be allowed to 'unbalance' the constitution; religion and politics were inseparable (political change threatened the church, and vice versa); and accordingly the establishment was equally at risk from its rationalist critics ('infidels') and from 'papists'.[100]

However, while the Conservatives and corporate bodies could agree on deploring repeal when raised by the O'Connellites,[101] on the issue itself they were much less consistent, for both contained elements that were highly critical of the union. Thus in 1832 the Conservative *Dublin Evening Mail* displayed some sympathy with Protestant repealers. According to that paper, ever since the granting of Catholic emancipation Protestant institutions had lacked the proper protection due from government, and this made it understandable that Protestants might seek repeal as the lesser of two evils. Bringing the landed class back to Ireland and removing Catholic MPs from the British house of commons might actually strengthen Protestantism in both countries. A strong attack on repeal was launched in the Protestant Conservative Society in January 1833; but in 1834 the union again came in for some criticism at the Protestant meetings that helped to rally the gentry to the Conservative cause.[102] For its part, the corporate world contained many who were prepared to commend repeal, at least down to the 1832 general election when O'Connell's candidacy and victory at the polls in Dublin city weakened their position.

In short, the issue of repeal raised mixed feelings among O'Connell's Protestant critics during the 1830s, and it featured as only one element in their condemnation of him. For the most part the attack continued on lines laid down by those who had defended eighteenth-century oligarchy and the confessional state. But the advance of popery, together with a sense of being abandoned by the authorities, also prompted a return to even earlier casts of mind. Long before Dublin corporation talked of 'No Surrender', the slogan had appeared on Orange flags celebrating the return for the Dublin university seats in 1832 of two Conservative candidates, Frederick Shaw and Thomas Lefroy. Long before the corporation warned that Protestants might have to flee the country if municipal reform were carried, clergymen were recalling the fires of Smithfield.[103] And well before the corporation described the Catholic church as anti-Christian, the point was being made in

---

[100] Above, Ch. 3, sect. IV.

[101] *DEM*, 29 Mar., 25 Oct. 1830.

[102] *DEM*, 1 Feb., 28 Sept., 1832; Speech of R. J. Orpen at Protestant Conservative Society, ibid., 16 Jan. 1833; *An Authentic Report of the Proceedings at the Meeting of the Protestants of Ireland, Held on . . . the 14th of August, 1834* (Dublin [1834]), speech by Colonel Irwin, 92–3.

[103] *Warder* (suppl.), 22 Dec. 1832; address to Conservative MPs, 6 Feb. 1839 (*CARD* xix. 350); speech of Revd. M. Beresford (*An Authentic Report of the . . . Meeting of the Protestants of Ireland . . . 1834*, 90).

the *Dublin Evening Mail* and by certain Dublin clergymen from the
evangelical wing of the Church of Ireland.[104]

In these circumstances there was little to foster a positive attachment to
the legislative union among those Protestant Dubliners who down to the
early 1830s had been its most vocal critics. Economic troubles continued to
cause distress, and the Whig government continued to arouse suspicion. The
city corporation refrained, in general, from commenting on the union; but
its few references betrayed a lingering sense that Dublin had been injured by
the loss of the Irish parliament.[105] In 1834, with O'Connell about to raise
repeal in the house of commons, the corporation took the opportunity of a
parliamentary petition to distance itself from the O'Connellites with a
highly disingenuous claim that it had never called for repeal;[106] but even
this hinted at Dublin's loss:

since the enactment of the Legislative Union of the two Islands in 1800, the general
interests of the City of Dublin . . . have borne great declension of property . . .
though your petitioners as individual residents of Dublin and as a Corporate body
. . . have largely participated in the general loss, yet they have never murmured, nor
in any instance expressed a desire to sever the Legislative connexion in which they
willingly believed the general prosperity of the Empire was bound up.[107]

From 1835 O'Connell was in alliance with the Whigs, and not pressing
the repeal issue. But by 1839 his threatened revival of the campaign gave the
corporation additional ammunition in its efforts to stave off municipal
reform. 'Popish Corporations' would lead to the destruction of the church,
the university, and to repeal of the union; at which point 'the complete
ascendancy of Popery in this country [will] be established'. Yet even here the
corporation could not refrain from invoking a happier, pre-union era, with
a pointed reference to London's exemption from the English act: 'Had
Ireland retained her Legislature, there is no doubt that the Corporation of
Dublin would have been so excepted, they respectfully claim the same need
of justice from the Imperial Parliament.'[108]

But Dublin was not exempted from the Irish municipal reform bill that
became law on 10 August 1840, although in other respects the act fell well
short of O'Connell's hopes. In contrast to the English act of 1835, which
had granted the municipal vote to all ratepayers, the Irish measure not only

---

[104] 'National Sins and Punishments', *DEM*, 17 Feb. 1832. The clergymen included
Reverend Tresham Dames Gregg (1800–81), BA (TCD) 1826, appointed chaplain to Swift's
Alley free church, 1837, and thus, like McGhee, part of the 'voluntary' system within the
established church.
[105] See e.g. address to William IV, 20 Jan. 1832 (*CARD* xix. 13).
[106] This was strictly correct, but at times between 1800 and 1832 the city commons and
several guilds had called for repeal (above, Chs. 10, 13).
[107] Petition for a ship canal between Kingstown and Dublin port (*CARD* xix. 132).
[108] *CARD* xix. 349, 406.

swept away most of the Irish corporations (fifty-eight were dissolved) but restricted the franchise in the remaining ten to £10 householders. Moreover, thanks to Conservative peers, the freemen's parliamentary franchise was preserved, although they obtained no special privileges concerning the municipal franchise.[109] O'Connell, who had established the Loyal National Repeal Association in July 1840, gave notice that he would work to achieve a 'Repeal Common Council' in Dublin.[110] There was plenty of time to prepare for the contest, since the first elections for the reformed corporations were not due to take place until the autumn of 1841.

Meanwhile, the Whig government had been steadily losing support in and out of parliament. When the general election was eventually held in July 1841, it confirmed what had been apparent for some time; that the Conservatives represented a strong force in politics and were set to form the next government. The undeniable importance of anti-Catholic feeling in this shift gave some credibility to O'Connell's claim that the advent of a Conservative government would threaten recent Catholic gains, and (less plausibly) even herald the reintroduction of penal laws. Such prospects would be all the more intolerable in view of what he took to be the imminent triumph of international Catholicism:

There never was a period when the continent of Europe presented more material for hopes and fears. Prussia and Hanover are the props of Protestantism in Europe and as that has ceased to be a religion and is now merely either political or indifferent, or infidel, if these powers were subverted or even checked the increase of Catholics would probably be enormous . . .[111]

Accordingly, O'Connell was determined to mobilize Catholic Ireland against the Conservatives. Through the Repeal Association and local registration committees he and his supporters prepared for the coming general election. But even in Ireland the Conservatives did well, winning more seats than the Whigs (though fewer than the Whigs and Repealers combined), and Peel duly took office.[112] The party's Irish triumph was sealed by the recapture of the two Dublin city seats.[113] This represented a serious setback for the O'Connellites, and there was an immediate and predictable search for scapegoats. The freemen stood out as one group that had voted overwhelmingly for the Conservatives,[114] and they were at once

---

[109] *Hansard*³, lv. 166–7. The peers intervened to preserve the parliamentary, not the municipal franchise, as suggested in Macintyre, *The Liberator*, 258.

[110] *Pilot*, 10 Aug. 1840.

[111] O'Connell to Fitzpatrick, 21 Aug. 1839 (*O'Connell Corr.* vi, letter 2657).

[112] The result was Conservatives 43, Whigs 42, Repealers 20 (105 seats): Moody, Martin, Byrne (eds.), *NHI* ix. 638.

[113] The voting was John Beatty West (C) 3,860; Edward Grogan (C), 3,839; Daniel O'Connell (R), 3,692; Robert Hutton (Whig), 3,662 (Walker, *Parliamentary Election Results*, 70).

[114] Though not always unconditionally: the weavers' guild asked the Conservatives for a pledge to back Irish-made goods (*DEM*, 21 June 1841).

blamed for the Dublin result. The *Freeman's Journal* complained: 'The freemen of the city are, as a class, houseless, penniless paupers, on whom the now defunct Corporation conferred the "freedom" that they might make them subservient to their own dishonest purposes . . .' The question of bribery was raised again, with allegations that the freemen represented the only corruptible class of voters in Dublin.[115]

These charges were, by and large, ill-founded. Admittedly, one result of the Conservative drive to manufacture new freemen had been to increase slightly the proportion of freemen in the electorate, from 23 per cent in 1837 to 25 per cent in 1841. And it was undoubtedly the case that the freemen had voted overwhelmingly for the Conservatives, who received 90 per cent of the freemen votes. But there was nothing new in this. In 1832 90 per cent of freemen votes had gone to the Conservatives when freemen comprised 28 per cent of the electorate; but O'Connell and Ruthven had won by a huge majority. The real cause of the Conservative victory in 1841 was to be found not in the behaviour of the freemen, but of the non-freemen: the freeholders and £10 householders who in 1832 had provided only 38 per cent of the Conservative votes. In 1841 this figure rose to 47 per cent. Or, from a different perspective, in 1832 the Conservatives received 18 per cent of the non-freemen votes; in 1841 they received 34 per cent, a figure that was quite close to the proportion of Protestants (c.37 per cent)[116] in the non-freemen electorate. Moreover, had the freeholders and house-holders turned out strongly for the election the outcome would have been different. Again the contrast with 1832 was striking: on that occasion 79 per cent of the non-freemen voters had voted, but in 1841 the figure was down to only 58 per cent. A turn-out of even 61 per cent would have retained the seat for O'Connell and Hutton.

The return to power of the Conservatives in Britain and the revival of the O'Connellite repeal movement combined to produce a significant change in the corporation's attitude to the legislative union. Shortly after the election, in an address to the new Conservative viceroy, Earl De Grey, the corporation gave its first unequivocal public blessing to the union:

We beg leave to express the high sense we entertain of her Majesty's most gracious regard for the prosperity and welfare of this country in having selected for that exalted situation a Nobleman so distinguished for his attachment to the principles of the British Constitution, and who we are persuaded will in the exercise of the

---

[115] *FJ*, 12, 22 July 1841. The charge was taken up by later writers: see e.g. Lefevre, *Peel and O'Connell*, 207; R. B. O'Brien, *Two Centuries of Irish History, 1691–1870*, 2nd edn. (London, 1907), 377.

[116] Assuming that c.53% of the Dublin city electorate was Protestant (figure for 1842: Hoppen, *Elections, Politics and Society*, 37) then since all the freemen were Protestant, the proportion of Protestants among the non-freemen electorate was c.37%. Voting analysis for 1832 is based on poll book data; that for 1841 on details in *FJ*, 22 July 1841.

authority vested in him not only maintain unimpaired, but still more strongly cement, the union so happily subsisting between this country and Great Britain.[117]

However, the corporation's first positive endorsement of the union was also to be its last. Already the O'Connellites were preparing for the forthcoming elections under the municipal act; and in view of their defeat at the general election they were all the more determined to succeed. Their opponents were pessimistic, having made the gloomy prediction that with a £10 household franchise Conservative candidates would stand a chance of being returned in only three of the fifteen municipal wards.[118]

In the event, the O'Connellites left nothing to chance. They ran a well-organized and highly centralized campaign, closely supervised by O'Connell himself, who kept excitement at a high pitch by playing on fears of what the new Conservative government was likely to mean for Irish Catholicism. The process of getting on to the burgess roll also kept tension high, for the act stipulated that for the first elections the churchwardens were to make out the roll. That gave the Conservatives an in-built advantage. Moreover, in order to exercise the franchise burgesses were required to have paid all their local taxes; this prompted complaints that provision for paying the taxes was inadequate.[119] Notwithstanding these difficulties, the elections produced the expected result, with thirty-six Repealers and eleven Whigs winning twelve of the fifteen wards. A broadly sectarian pattern was discernible; all but one of the thirteen Conservatives elected were Protestants; all but two of the Repealers were Catholics, and only the Whigs (five Catholics and six Protestants) displayed a real denominational mix.[120] On 1 November 1841 Daniel O'Connell was triumphantly elected as the first Catholic lord mayor of Dublin since Terence McDermott in 1689.

For all the dire predictions, life under a Catholic-controlled corporation proved to be much less cataclysmic than many Protestants had feared. Not only did most municipal functions, such as paving, cleaning, and lighting, remain in the hands of government-appointed boards, but the recapture of the city seats by the Conservatives in 1841 turned out to mark a long-term shift. With the exception of the 1847 general election when alienation of some freemen from the sitting MP W. H. Gregory allowed in the repealer John Reynolds,[121] the Conservatives were to monopolize the city represent-ation until 1865. This testified to the enduring presence of a Protestant

---

[117] *CARD* xix. 437–8. The address's significance may be judged by the scorn heaped on it by O'Connell (Repeal Assoc. meeting, *FJ*, 17 Sept. 1841).

[118] *FJ*, 28 July 1841; *Warder*, 24 July 1841.

[119] *FJ*, 1, 4 Sept. 1841; O'Connell's speech, Repeal Assoc. meeting, ibid., 24 Aug. 1841; memorials to viceroy, Sept. 1841 (NA, CSORP, A 9754; A 11846).

[120] Jacqueline Hill, 'The Role of Dublin in the Irish National Movement, 1840–48', Ph.D. thesis (University of Leeds, 1973), table 5.1 (p. 206).

[121] Ead., 'The Protestant Response to Repeal: The Case of the Dublin Working Class', in F. S. L. Lyons and R. A. J. Hawkins (eds.), *Ireland Under the Union: Varieties of Tension* (Oxford, 1980), 35–68, at 51.

business and professional class in the city,[122] as well as to continuing—but not unconditional—support for the Conservatives from the freemen. Moreover, aware of the value of Protestant goodwill, the Catholic majority on the reformed corporation was generous in its victory. Early on, Lord Mayor O'Connell announced his wish to be succeeded in office by a Protestant; and thereafter an intermittent system of denominational rotation operated, often contentiously, for another forty years. O'Connell even took up Serjeant Jackson's proposal for a guaranteed bloc of seats—he suggested one-third—for the Protestant minority (the offer was turned down).[123]

If Protestants were reassured by these gestures towards power-sharing, some of their other fears turned out to be only too well founded. In 1843 Dublin corporation set the pattern for other southern Irish corporations when it debated O'Connell's motion for repeal of the union, and throughout the decade the corporation continued to provide important support for the O'Connellite repeal movement.[124] Still, for those who could not accept the new dispensation, there was no need to flee the country. If they could afford it, all they had to do was to move the few miles out of the city—beyond the corporation's jurisdiction—to Rathmines, Monkstown, or some other mainly Protestant suburb. The concentration of Protestants in such districts was such that in the years before 1914 the constituency of Dublin County South was the only one outside Ulster (apart from Dublin University) to return a run of Unionist MPs.[125]

In the 1840s there was still some distance for the freemen in general to go before they could take a fully positive view of the union. They remained preoccupied with the wreck of so many of the values they had cherished, and had not yet lost hope of a change in fortune. The state of mind of some is captured in a request from the officers of the joiners' guild to the Aldermen of Skinner's Alley, in September 1843. The Aldermen were asked to take into safe keeping the joiners' charter, municipal reform having rendered the guilds' role in civic affairs redundant. Although the O'Connellite repeal campaign was then at its height, the campaign was mentioned only obliquely. However, the potential for a unionist role is apparent, and the letter is worth quoting in full:

Most Noble Governor & Gentlemen
    Times and circumstances not dissimilar from those which first called your Loyal and distinguished Body into existence having again unhappily recurred through the

---

[122] The 1901 census showed that over half Dublin's doctors and over one-third of the merchants and bankers were Protestants (Hoppen, *Elections, Politics and Society*, 330).

[123] W. J. O'Neill Daunt, *Personal Recollections of the Late Daniel O'Connell, M.P.* (2 vols.; London, 1848), ii. 89; Daly, *Dublin the Deposed Capital*, 209–11, 214.

[124] Hill, 'The Role of Dublin in the Irish National Movement', ch. 5.

[125] Patrick Buckland, *Irish Unionism, i. The Anglo-Irish and the New Ireland 1885–1922* (2 vols; Dublin, 1972), 21.

Transfer of the Corporations into the hands of Treasonable Popish Demagogues, thereby depriving the Protestant Freemen of their rights and privileges conferred from time to time upon them by the Monarchs of these realms for their proved and devoted loyalty to the British Throne, and committing them to the hands of men known only as disaffected, disloyal and rebellious, which passing events now fully prove

We the Master, Wardens, and Brethren of the late Corporation of Joiners have unanimously resolved that your Ancient and Loyal Body be requested to take into your safe Custody the Ancient Charter[126] of our truly Protestant Guild, which our present individuality alone prevents the keeping of it ourselves, that precious boon delivered to us by the great & good King William of Glorious Memory, and in doing so permits us to say, that being long accustomed to regard it with veneration and esteem, we now part with it not without a feeling of sadness, yet fully satisfied that with you it will remain uncontaminated by the touch of Popery, and should Providence in his wise dispensation be pleased to grant us a restoration to our right position we feel confident that this certificate of our Protestantism and our Freedom will be returned pure and untarnished as we hand it to you this day,

In conclusion we would most earnestly pray for the happiness of each Member of your Fraternity, and that to the Aldermen of Skinner's Ally [*sic*] may be granted the glorious privilege (once enjoyed by their faithful Ancestors) of witnessing the total abandonment of hollow expediency, a return to sound and holy principles, and to the real ascendancy of Bible Protestantism in Church and State.

And with great respect and esteem

We remain most noble Governor & Aldermen

Your sincere friends, & brother Protestants

The Members of the late Corporation of Joiners,

Signed on behalf of the Corporation, J. J. Brownlow, Master, G. Mahon, J. Wright, Wardens.[127]

---

[126] The joiners' charter dated from 1700; representation on the city commons was authorized in 1702 (*CARD* vi. 273–4).

[127] Undated letter, with minute of visit from a deputation from the guild, 4 Sept. 1843 (Aldermen of Skinner's Alley, minute book 1841–63 (RIA, MS 23 H 52, pp. 42–7). The joiners' request was granted (ibid. 42–7).

Conclusion

During the eighteenth century Dublin Protestants from the mercantile, manufacturing, and artisan classes took their place among those who considered themselves to be Patriots. Since their numbers—to speak only of the freemen, who enjoyed the formal political qualification of a parliamentary vote—fell not far short of the entire landowning body, it is clear that no rounded picture of Protestant Patriotism can be obtained without taking account of their contribution.

What did the Dublin freemen bring to Irish Patriotism? In the first place, they set a precedent for challenging oligarchy. That challenge grew out of the contradictions inherent in Dublin civic life: as freemen numbers grew, the right of political participation became ever more widespread, but power was still concentrated in very few hands. The capital having given the lead in the 1740s, successive decades witnessed a more assertive mood among other Protestants outside the landed élite, the growth of an independent interest, and the willingness of the Volunteers to take an independent line, even if that at times clashed with parliament's views.

The arrival on the political scene of the Dublin freemen also enhanced the standing of parliamentary Patriots. Once it had become apparent during the 1750s and 1760s that several of the guilds were consistently behind opposition causes, government began to take Patriot MPs more seriously. It is difficult to overstate the importance of this. Research on voting patterns in England has recently confirmed how very exceptional anything like consistent partisan loyalty was before the great reform act of 1832.[1] From the mid-1760s, Dublin's representation was invariably in Patriot hands, and Patriot leaders, such as Henry Grattan, could aspire to a Dublin seat in order to enhance their status. Dublin's impact was reinforced once the octennial act had been passed in 1768: had Ireland enjoyed regular general elections as England had done since 1694, there can be little doubt that the freemen's impact on Irish politics would have been manifested even earlier. Admittedly, party organization in support of the independent or Patriot candidates was weak—at least compared with what appeared after 1832—but even so, such bodies as the Society of Free Citizens fulfilled the same sort of functions in Dublin as the Independent Electors of Westminster did in London.

If resistance to oligarchy supplied a principal motive for the politicization

---

[1] John A. Phillips and Charles Wetherell, 'The Great Reform Act of 1832 and the Political Modernization of England', *AHR* 100 (1995), 411–36, at 421–6.

of the freemen, it was not sufficient to explain the enduring commitment to Patriot causes, which outlasted municipal reform in 1760. One of the keys to that lasting support was Dublin Patriotism's potent ideological blend of ancient rights, Protestant libertarianism, and constitutional balance—all within the context of a widely held faith in urban corporations as bulwarks against royal absolutism. That faith was shared by English Whigs and Patriots: but in Ireland it took on a special significance, because Irish corporations also had a historic role as bastions of Protestantism and the link with England.

For all their apparent modernity in challenging oligarchy and espousing a consistently partisan position, the freemen had become active in a political world that was still remote from the liberal assumptions of the nineteenth century. Quite apart from the confessional issue, politics was still very much the preserve of the aristocracy and gentry. Entering that preserve inevitably highlighted the aristocratic dimension of the freemen's role. Historically, it had been the function of aristocracies both to uphold (through their frontier exploits and other military activities) and to curb royal power. The Dublin freemen, under the inspirational leadership of Charles Lucas, inherited this dual mandate. Who could doubt their commitment to checking royal power through support for a more autonomous Irish parliament, a citizen's watch, and efforts to curtail Castle patronage? Yet who could doubt the pride they took in their historic defence of the city against the king's enemies, a role that was comprehended both in their participation in the Volunteer movement and in their opposition to rebellion in the 1790s?

The Dublin freemen were also peculiarly attached to their corporate privileges. That was hardly surprising, since it was only their chartered, corporate rights that gave them a formal voice in politics at all. Down to the 1770s, through the quarterage campaign, they strove to shore up the economic function—the regulation of all tradesmen—that had underpinned those rights. By the 1780s, when the failure of the campaign had become clear, their political role seemed to provide a new justification for their privileges. But in the aftermath of the French revolution privilege itself came under the spotlight, and the exercise of rights divorced from functions was called in question. Civic freedom was by this time increasingly a matter of birth rather than of calling. It also remained a Protestant preserve at a time when government was anxious to foster the counter-revolutionary potential of Irish Catholicism.

The confessional aspect is one of the key issues concerning Patriotism, and here too the civic sphere affords new insights. Liberty, as held up to the freemen by Charles Lucas and his supporters, was not a merely secular vision. Indebted as it was to the neo-Harringtonian and Whiggish tradition, liberty meant, among other things, the conditions in which 'true religion' could flourish. And among those conditions—in order to counter the papal and priestly *imperium*—was the Erastian state, headed by a prince whose

Protestantism constituted a guarantee that the principle of lay supremacy over the church would be safeguarded. 'Popery', in the sense of papal claims, and freedom appeared to be incompatible. Anxieties on this score did not abate with the effective ending of the Jacobite claim to the throne in the 1760s: they continued to be voiced by Protestants well into the nineteenth century, reinforcing the case for the necessary link between religion and politics, and explaining why the freemen, although opposed to absolutism, were not anti-monarchical.

Viewed from this perspective, it becomes easier to see why the relaxation of the penal laws concerning land and education in the 1770s and 1780s could be accepted with relative equanimity, while in the 1790s the prospect of Catholics exercising political rights posed major problems. No doubt the hostility of the freemen was reinforced by the fact that Protestantism necessarily meant more to them, in terms of élite status, than it did to the gentry, whose status was bolstered by the possession of land. John Giffard, the arch-exponent of 'Protestant ascendancy' on the Dublin city commons for almost three decades, had been deprived of a landed inheritance through the accident of a family feud. Consequently, he had to rely on Protestantism; and he and his sons did their best to ensure that religion would remain integral to élite status. That is not to suggest that commitment to Protestantism was simply a matter of self-interest. Clearly the defence of privilege came into it; but as the evangelical revival showed, religious commitment was quite capable of flourishing in the absence of state support. Some of the most powerful traditions available to Irish Protestants stressed that it was when they seemed most forsaken that divine providence would come to their aid.

No doubt too it was significant that in the towns of Leinster, Munster, and Connaught the admission of Catholics to civic freedom was likely to swamp the Protestant freemen. Landowners, for their part, were cushioned by the exclusion of Catholics from parliament. Arguably, had Irish Protestantism really matched the popular image of it—an essentially landed class—the principle of political rights for Catholics would have been easier to accept. But for the freemen, considerations of ideology, status, and numbers combined to produce such resistance that it would require municipal reform before urban Catholics could exercise the rights extended to them in the 1790s.

Finally, the world of Dublin civic politics was a crucible for some of the most characteristic developments of the nineteenth century. Although the Orange Order had originated in County Armagh, its early and rapid growth in Dublin (still a largely unexplored subject) owed less to the gentry than to members of the university and the corporation;[2] and Dublin freemen gave

[2] Evidence of Lt.-Col. Verner, *Report [on] . . . Orange Lodges*, 9, 14, 19, HC 1835 (377), xv.

the Order its first set of rules. On the nationalist side, almost half the known Protestant members of the Dublin Society of United Irishmen in its early phase (1791–4) were freemen. Why certain freemen were able to overcome their suspicion of Catholics exercising political rights is a question that requires further study. Euphoria generated by the French revolution and the attendant reverses suffered by the papacy probably had something to do with it; but why should these matters have carried weight with some freemen and not the majority? Social factors may have been important, as in the case of John Chambers, who (unusually) had married into a Catholic family.[3] Some of the United Irishmen, clearly, had little or no connection with the guilds of which they were free, as the case of Wolfe Tone shows. For him freedom (by birth) was simply a stepping-stone to a parliamentary vote. But other prominent United Irishmen, such as Napper Tandy, took the world of the guilds and the corporation very seriously, as is shown by their record of corporate activities well into the 1790s. Freemen were also among those who continued to propagate United Irish values after they had emigrated,[4] thus helping to transform the Irish-American Patriotism of the eighteenth century into the nationalism characteristic of the nineteenth.

But perhaps the most important legacy of the Dublin freemen to nineteenth-century Irish politics lay in their support for Irish parliamentary rights. Although that theme had featured in the writings of Molyneux and Swift, and had found champions from time to time in parliament itself, it can be argued that it was the Dublin civic Patriots of the second half of the eighteenth century who gave the issue its prominence on the Patriot agenda. After all, for both Molyneux and Swift the preferred constitutional option was for union with England: only the apparent unattainability of that object turned them towards the defence of local parliamentary rights. Even in Lucas's thought, at least during his period of exile in the 1750s, there was a residual unionist element. But the freemen represented a class of Protestants for whom the presence of a parliament in Dublin offered opportunities for influence that was unlikely ever to be matched in a London body. In their opposition to union they therefore became spokesmen for all those in Dublin's population—Protestant and Catholic—who had no more prospect than they did of exercising real influence on a parliament across the Irish sea.

When Daniel O'Connell began to give priority to repeal of the union in the 1830s one of the attractions was that (thanks to Dublin corporation and the guilds) the cause had respectable and still lively Protestant backing, which could be expected to impress government. Naturally, therefore, O'Connell emphasized continuity with the Patriot tradition.[5] He spoke of

---

[3] Pollard, 'John Chambers, Printer and United Irishman', 1.
[4] Doyle, *Ireland, Irishmen and Revolutionary America*, 198–200.
[5] Kevin B. Nowlan, 'The Meaning of Repeal in Irish History', in G. A. Hayes-McCoy (ed.), *Historical Studies IV* (London, 1963), 1–17.

1782, of 'king, lords, and commons', and of the importance of retaining the link with Britain. The emphasis on continuity has seemed the more convincing because of the tendency of later commentators to take it for granted that defence of Irish parliamentary rights was the very essence of the Patriot tradition.

What undermines the idea of continuity is not simply that by the 1830s the age of absolutism was giving way to one of liberalism, in which the need to maintain constitutional balance between the rights of king, lords, and commons seemed less and less compelling. Like the *ancien régime* in Europe, the old order in Britain and Ireland had also been corporatist, aristocratic, and confessional. It was because the O'Connellite repealers were (inevitably) dedicated to the overturning of those values that the Dublin freemen were, as a body, unable to join them. On the contrary, once the Catholics, with their newly significant weapon of numbers, had embraced repeal, a unionist course was bound to hold attractions for the civic Patriots. It offered a guarantee of sorts for their church, and breathed new life into their loyalist traditions. For repeal under O'Connellite auspices constituted a challenge not simply to Irish Protestants, but to the British authorities, for whom in the nineteenth century union seemed necessary to domestic and imperial security, and who badly needed Irish allies if the union were to survive with any credibility. Nevertheless, the freemen had come to unionism reluctantly and late, and their support was never to be unconditional.

Appendix A. Dublin Guilds and the Trades they Served

(in order of precedence in the city corporation)

MERCHANTS, or guild of Holy Trinity (royal charter, 1451).[1]
Merchants, woollen drapers, linen drapers, ironmongers, grocers, mercers, tobacconists, haberdashers, druggists, timber merchants.[2]

TAILORS, or guild of St John the Baptist (royal charter, 1418).
Tailors, hosiers (until 1688).

SMITHS, or guild of St Loy (royal charter, 1474).
Smiths, glaziers, braziers, embroiderers, founders, trunk-makers, pattern-makers, pewterers, pin-makers, tinplate-workers, wire-drawers, wire-workers,[3] also (in 1688) ironmongers, girdlers.

BARBER-SURGEONS, or guild of St Mary Magdelene (royal charter, 1446).
Barbers (joined with surgeons by royal charter, 1577), wigmakers, apothecaries (until 1747).

BAKERS, or guild of SS Clement and Anne (royal charter, 1478).
Bakers.

BUTCHERS, or guild of the Blessed Virgin Mary (Dublin corporation charter, 1569).
Butchers.

CARPENTERS, or guild of the Blessed Virgin Mary of the House of St Thomas the Martyr (royal charter, 1508).
Carpenters, millers, masons, heliers (tilers), boxmakers, distillers, joiners (until 1700), plumbers, trunkmakers, turners, coopers (down to 1666), bricklayers and plasterers (before 1670).

SHOEMAKERS, or guild of the Blessed Virgin Mary[4] (royal charter, 1465).
Shoemakers.

SADDLERS, or guild of the Blessed Virgin Mary (Dublin corporation charter, 1558).
Saddlers, upholders (upholsterers), coach- and coach-harness makers, bridle-cutters, wheelwrights, collar-makers, rope-makers.[5]

COOKS AND VINTNERS, or guild of St James the Apostle (royal charter, 1444).
Cooks (joined with vintners by royal charter, 1565).

Source: Except where stated, DHDG.
[1] Most of the guilds incorporated before the 1660s claimed earlier origins than the date of the charters instanced here. The merchants' guild was the oldest, claiming to have been in existence as early as the 1190s (see *DHDG*, 11–31, at 23).
[2] Statement by members of the guild (1769), DCA, C1/JSC/3, p. 6.
[3] Guinness, 'Dublin Trade Gilds', 146.
[4] Some sources (*DHDG*, 26 n. 2) give St Michael the Archangel.
[5] NLI, MS 81, printed list of trades, 1816, inside front cover.

TANNERS, or guild of St Nicholas (royal charter, 1688).
   Tanners, curriers (until 1695).
TALLOW CHANDLERS, or guild of St George (Dublin corporation charter, 1583).
   Tallow-chandlers, soap-boilers, wax-light makers.
GLOVERS AND SKINNERS, or guild of St Mary (royal charter, 1476).
   Glovers, skinners.
WEAVERS, or guild of the Blessed Virgin Mary (royal charter, 1446).
   Weavers, combers (added 1697).
SHEERMEN AND DYERS, or guild of St Nicholas (no charter, but sheermen present in
   city commons from 1660, dyers from 1717).
   Sheermen (removed superfluous nap from cloth), dyers.
GOLDSMITHS, or guild of All Saints (royal charter, 1637).
   Goldsmiths, silversmiths, watchmakers, clockmakers.
COOPERS, or guild of St Patrick (royal charter, 1666).
   Coopers.
FELTMAKERS (patron saint not known: royal charter, 1667).
   Feltmakers, hatters.
CUTLERS, PAINTER-STAINERS, STATIONERS, or guild of St Luke (royal charter, 1670).
   Cutlers, painter-stainers, stationers.
BRICKLAYERS AND PLASTERERS, or guild of St Bartholomew (royal charter, 1670).
   Bricklayers, plasterers.
HOSIERS AND KNITTERS, or guild of St George (royal charter, 1688).
   Hosiers, knitters.
CURRIERS (patron saint not known: royal charter, 1695).
   Curriers.
BREWERS AND MALTSTERS, or guild of St Andrew (royal charter, 1696).
   Brewers, maltsters.
JOINERS, CEYLERS AND WAINSCOTTERS, or guild of the Blessed Virgin Mary (royal
   charter, 1700).
   Joiners, ceylers (ceiling-makers), wainscotters.
APOTHECARIES, or guild of St Luke the Evangelist (royal charter, 1747).
   Apothecaries.

Appendix B.
Dublin City MPs, 1660–1841

BERESFORD, JOHN CLAUDIUS (1766–1846), banker, b. Dublin; son of John Beresford, chief revenue commissioner. BA (TCD), 1787. Inspector-general of imports and exports; registrar of tobacco (resigned both posts, Jan. 1799, in protest against the union). General secretary of Orange lodges, 1799–1800. Elected sheriff, 1807, but excused after fine; alderman, 1808; lord mayor, 1814–15. MP Swords, 1790–7, Dublin city, 1797–1804, Co. Waterford, 1806–11.

BRADSTREET, Sir SAMUEL, 3rd. bt. (?1735–91), justice of king's bench. Son of Sir Simon Bradstreet, 1st bt. (who unsuccessfully contested Dublin city by-election, 1737). Attended TCD; called to the bar, 1758. Recorder of Dublin, 1766–84. Appointed justice of king's bench, 1784. MP Dublin city, 1776–84.

BURTON, BENJAMIN, d. 1728, banker, of Dublin and Burton Hall, Co. Carlow. Sheriff 1694–5; alderman; lord mayor, 1706–7. MP Dublin city, 1703–27.

BURTON, Sir CHARLES, d. 1775. Younger son of Benjamin Burton (q.v.). Sheriff, 1733–4; alderman, 1748; lord mayor, 1752–3. His daughter married Sir Edward Newenham (Ch. 5). MP Dublin city, 1749–60.

BURTON, SAMUEL, d. 1733, banker. Eldest son of Benjamin Burton (q.v.). Selected sheriff, 1728, but excused after fine; alderman, 1728 (on his father's death). MP Dublin city, 1727–33.

CLEMENT, Dr WILLIAM (1707–82), vice-provost of TCD, b. Carrickmacross, Co. Monaghan. Son of Thomas Clement. BA (TCD), 1726; FTCD, 1733; vice-provost, 1753–82. MP Dublin University, 1761–8, Dublin city, 1771–82.

COOKE, Sir SAMUEL, d. 1758, brewer. Son of Sir Samuel Cooke (lord mayor, 1712–14). Sheriff, 1730–1; alderman, 1732; lord mayor, 1740–1. MP Dublin city, 1749–58.

COOTE, THOMAS, of Coote Hill, Cavan. Recorder of Dublin, 1690–3. MP Dublin city, 1692–3.

CREAGH, Sir MICHAEL, merchant, Bridge St. Paymaster-general of James II's forces in Ireland. Created alderman by James II, 1687; lord mayor, 1688–9. MP Dublin city, 1689.

DAVIES, Sir WILLIAM, chief justice, king's bench, b. Dublin. Son of Sir Paul Davies (d. 1672), secretary of state (Ireland); brother of Sir John Davies, secretary of state (Ireland), 1678–89. Recorder of Dublin (on recommendation of General Monck), 1661–72, 1672–80; clerk of the Tholsel, 1665–?; prime serjeant, 1675–81, chief justice, king's bench, 1681–7. Married a daughter of Archbp. Michael Boyle. MP Dublin city, 1661–6.

DUNN, Col. JAMES. Sheriff, 1740–1; alderman, 1746–58. MP Dublin city, 1758–60.

ELLIS, THOMAS (1774–?1832), of Merrion Square. Eldest son of Richard Ellis of Youghal. Entered TCD, 1790; called to the bar, 1796; Master in Chancery, 1806–32. Governor of Aldermen of Skinner's Alley, 1819–23. MP Dublin city, 1820–6.

FITZGERALD, Lord HENRY. A younger son of James, 1st duke of Leinster; brother of William, 2nd duke (q.v.), and of Lord Edward (d. 1798). MP Dublin city, 1790–7, Co. Kildare, 1807–13.

FITZGERALD, WILLIAM ROBERT, 2nd duke of Leinster (1749–1804). Eldest surviving son of James, 1st duke. Marquis of Kildare, 1766; 2nd duke, 1773–1804. Master of the rolls, 1788. MP Dublin city, 1767–73.

FORSTER, JOHN (1667–1720). Recorder of Dublin, 1701–14; solicitor-general, 1709–10; attorney-general, 1710–11; lord chief justice, common pleas, 1714–20. Speaker, Irish house of commons, 1710–13. MP Dublin city, 1703–14.

FRENCH, HUMPHREY, d. 1736, brewer. Sheriff, 1711–12; alderman, 1727; lord mayor, 1732–3. MP Dublin city, 1733–6.

GRATTAN, HENRY (1746–1820), b. Dublin. Son of James Grattan (q.v.) and Mary, daughter of Chief Justice Thomas Marlay, but disinherited. BA (TCD), 1767; called to the bar, 1772. Entered parliament as MP for Charlemont, 1775. MP Dublin city, 1790–7, Wicklow town, 1800, Malton (England), 1805–6, Dublin city, 1806–20.

GRATTAN, HENRY, jun. (1789–1859), of The Abbey, Celbridge, Co. Kildare. Son of Henry Grattan (q.v.). BA (TCD), 1808. Married Mary, daughter of Philip Whitfield Harvey, 1826, becoming proprietor (1826–30) of the *Freeman's Journal*. MP Dublin city, 1826–30, Co. Meath, 1831–52.

GRATTAN, JAMES (?1710–66), recorder of Dublin. Born Cavan, son of Henry Grattan. BA (TCD), 1731; called to the bar, 1739; recorder of Dublin, 1756–66. MP Dublin city, 1761–6.

GROGAN, EDWARD (1802–91), of Harcourt St., barrister. Son of John Grogan of Dublin, barrister. BA (TCD), 1823; called to the bar, 1840; created bt. 1859. MP Dublin city, 1841–65.

HAMILTON, GEORGE ALEXANDER (1802–71), b. Co. Down. BA (TCD), 1821; LL B, 1851. Active in Protestant Conservative Society, 1832. Financial secretary to the treasury, 1852, 1858–9; permanent secretary, 1859. MP Dublin city, 1836–7, Dublin University, 1843–59.

HANDCOCK, Sir WILLIAM, d. 1701, b. Co. Westmeath. Son of William Handcock. Entered TCD, 1671. Recorder of Dublin, 1695–1701. MP Dublin city, 1695–9.

HARTLEY, TRAVERS, merchant, of Bride St. Merchants' guild representative on city commons, 1762; founder member and first president, Dublin chamber of commerce, 1783. MP Dublin city, 1782–90.

HARTY, Sir ROBERT WAY., bt. (1779–1832), hosier, of Merrion Square and Prospect House, Roebuck, Co. Dublin. Sheriff, 1811–12; alderman, 1822; lord mayor, 1830–1. Created bt., 1831. Returned as MP Dublin city, May 1831, but unseated on petition, Aug. 1831.

HOWARD, WILLIAM, d. 1728, KC. A younger son of Dr Ralph Howard (1638–1710) of Shelton, Co. Wicklow, regius professor of physic, TCD; brother of Robert Howard, bishop of Elphin. Educated England (?); KC, 1725. Free of merchants' guild. MP Dublin city, 1727–8.

HUTTON, ROBERT (1785–1870), coach builder. MP Dublin city, 1837–41.

INGESTRE, Viscount (Henry John Chetwynd Talbot, 18th earl of Shrewsbury) (1802–68). MP Hertford, 1830–1, Armagh city, 1831, Dublin city, 1831–2, S. Staffs., 1837–49.

LA TOUCHE, JAMES DIGGES (?1707–63), cloth merchant. Son of David Digues La

Touche (d. 1745), cloth merchant and banker. Representative of merchants' guild on city commons, 1738–44. Returned as MP for Dublin city at the by-election of 1749, but unseated on petition, 1750.

LA TOUCHE, JOHN, jun., (?1774–1820), of Merrion Square. Son of John La Touche, banker (who contested Dublin city at the 1767 by-election); nephew of David La Touche, first governor, Bank of Ireland. BA (TCD), 1795. MP Harristown, 1797–1800, Dublin city, 1802–6, Co. Leitrim, 1807–20.

LUCAS, CHARLES (1713–71), apothecary, b. Co. Clare. Son of Benjamin Lucas. MD (TCD), 1761. Representative of barber-surgeons' guild on city commons, 1741–4, 1762–5. Fled into exile after being condemned by the Irish parliament as an enemy to his country, following his controversial campaigning for the 1749 by-election; pardoned by George III. MP Dublin city, 1761–71.

McDERMOTT, TERENCE. Created alderman by James II, 1687; lord mayor, 1689–90. MP Dublin city, 1689.

MITCHEL, Sir MICHAEL. Sheriff, 1683–4; alderman, 1686; lord mayor, 1691–3. MP Dublin city, 1692–3.

MOORE, GEORGE OGLE, b. ?1779, Co. Wexford. Son of John Moore, Co. Wexford; nephew and heir of George Ogle (q.v.). BA (TCD), 1797; called to the bar, 1800. Deputy registrar of deeds, 1802–31; registrar of deeds, 1831–46. MP Dublin city, 1826–31.

MORRES, REDMOND, KC, b. ?1712, of Newtown, Co. Waterford. Son of Francis Morres. LL D (TCD), 1756. MP Thomastown, 1755–60, Newtown, 1761–8, Dublin city, 1773–6.

O'CONNELL, DANIEL (1775–1847), barrister. Alderman (under municipal reform act), 1841–7; lord mayor, 1841–2. Represented many constituencies in the imperial parliament, 1829–47. MP Dublin city, 1832–5, 1837–41.

OGLE, GEORGE (1742–1814), of Bellevue, Co. Wexford. Only son of George Ogle (d. 1746), and grandson of Samuel Ogle of Northumberland (commissioner of the revenue for Ireland). Long history of opposition before accepting registrarship of deeds, 1784; governor of Wexford, 1796. Grand master of Orange lodges, 1801. MP Co. Wexford, 1768–96, Dublin city, 1798–1802.

PEARSON, NATHANIEL, d. 1749. Sheriff, 1721–2; alderman, 1724; lord mayor, 1730–1. MP Dublin city, 1737–49.

PERRIN, LOUIS, KC (1782–1864), of Granby Row, judge of king's bench. Son of Jean Baptiste Perrin, teacher. BA (TCD), 1801; called to the bar, 1806. Attorney-general, 1835; judge of king's bench, 1835. Returned MP for Dublin city, May 1831, but unseated on petition (Aug. 1831). MP Monaghan, 1832–5, Cashel, 1835.

ROGERSON, Sir JOHN, d. 1724. Alderman by 1686; lord mayor, 1693–4. MP Dublin city, 1695–9.

ROGERSON, Sir JOHN, d. 1741, chief justice, king's bench. BA (TCD), 1694; called to the bar, 1701. Recorder of Dublin, 1714–27; solicitor general, 1714–20; attorney-general, 1720–7; chief justice, king's bench, 1727. MP Dublin city, 1715–27.

RUTHVEN, EDWARD SOUTHWELL (1772–1836). Born Edward Trotter, son of Reverend Edward Trotter, Co. Down. Took name Ruthven, 1800. MP Downpatrick, 1806–7, 1830–2, Dublin city, 1832–5 (unseated on petition, 1836).

SHAW, FREDERICK, 3rd. bt. (1799–1876). Younger son of Robert Shaw (q.v.). BA (?Oxford), 1819; called to the Irish bar, 1822; LL D, 1841. Recorder of Dundalk, 1826–8; recorder of Dublin, 1828–76. MP Dublin city, 1830–2, Dublin University, 1832–48.

SHAW, ROBERT, 1st bt. (1774–1849), banker. Son of Robert Shaw, flour merchant, of Fleet St. BA (TCD), 1792. Elected sheriff, 1797, but excused after fine; alderman, 1808, lord mayor, 1815–16. Founded Shaw's bank, 1805, incorporated as the Royal Bank of Ireland, 1836. Created bt. 1821. MP Bannow, 1799–1800, St Johnstown, Longford, 1800, Dublin city (following Beresford's resignation), 1804–26.

SMITH, WILLIAM, Alderman. Mayor, 1642–7, lord mayor, 1663–5, 1675–6. MP Dublin city, 1661–6.

SOMERVILLE, JAMES, d. 1748, merchant. Son of Alderman Thomas Somerville. Sheriff, 1720–1; alderman, 1729; lord mayor, 1736–7. MP Dublin city, 1729–48.

STOYTE, JOHN, d. 1728. Sheriff, 1701–2; alderman, 1703; lord mayor, 1715–16. MP Dublin city, 1728.

WARREN, NATHANIEL, d. 1796, brewer. Sheriff, 1773–4; alderman, 1775; lord mayor, 1782–3. Police commissioner, 1786; superintendent magistrate of police, 1795. MP Dublin city, 1784–90.

WEST, JOHN BEATTY, KC (1791–1841), of St Stephen's Green and Mount Anville, Co. Dublin. Son of Francis West, QC. BA (TCD), 1812; called to the bar, 1815. MP Dublin city, 1835–7, 1841.

WOLFE, ARTHUR, 1st Viscount Kilwarden (1739–1803). 5th son of John Wolfe, Forenaughts, Co. Kildare. BA (TCD), 1760; called to the bar, 1766, KC, 1778; solicitor-general, 1787–9; attorney-general, 1789–98; chief justice, king's bench, 1798. Created Viscount Kilwarden, 1800. Killed in Emmet's rebellion. MP Dublin city, 1797–8.

Principal sources:

Frederic Boase, *Modern English Biography* (2 vols.; Truro, 1892–1901); *CARD*; *Commons Jn. Ire.*; *DNB*; Moody, Martin, Byrne (eds.), *NHI*, ix; Constantine J. Smyth, *Chronicle of the Law Officers of Ireland* (London, 1839); R. G. Thorne, *The House of Commons 1790–1820* (5 vols.; London, 1986).

Appendix C. Recorders of Dublin, 1660–1841

BARNEWALL, Sir JOHN, recorder, 1687–9; baron of the exchequer, 1688–90.

BRADSTREET, Sir SAMUEL, recorder, 1766–84 (see App. B).

COOTE, THOMAS, recorder, 1690–3 (see App. B).

DAVIES, Sir WILLIAM, recorder, 1661–72, 1672–80 (see App. B).

DILLON, GERARD, prime serjeant, 1687–90; recorder, 1689–90.

DONNELLAN, NEHEMIAH, d. 1696. Prime serjeant, 1693–5; recorder, 1693–5; baron of the exchequer, 1695–6.

FORSTER, JOHN, recorder, 1701–14 (see App. B).

GEORGE, DENIS, d. 1821; recorder, 1785–94; baron of the exchequer, 1794–1821.

GREENE, Sir JONAS, d. 1828. Son of Richard Greene, merchant. BA (TCD), 1787; called to the bar, 1790; recorder, 1821–8. Knighted, 1821.

GRATTAN, JAMES, recorder, 1756–66 (see App. B).

HANDCOCK, WILLIAM, recorder, 1695–1701 (see App. B).

HUSSEY, DUDLEY, d. 1785; recorder, 1784–5.

LEIGHTON, Sir ELLIS, d. 1685; younger son of Alexander Leighton. Colonel in royalist army, 1640s; secretary to James, duke of York. LL D (Cambridge), 1665. Secretary to Lord Berkeley, viceroy; recorder, 1672.

MORGAN, THOMAS, b. ?1709. Entered TCD, 1726; called to the bar, 1733. Recorder, 1749–56(?).

ROGERSON, Sir JOHN, recorder, 1714–27 (see App. B).

RYVES, Sir RICHARD (?1643–95), baron of the exchequer, 1692–5. Son of Charles Ryves. Entered TCD, 1657; LL D, 1690; recorder, 1680–7, 1690.

SHAW, FREDERICK, recorder, 1828–76 (see App. B).

STANNARD, EATON (?1685–1757). Son of Reverend Robert Stannard. BA (TCD), 1706; called to the bar, 1714. Recorder, 1733–49; prime serjeant, 1754–7.

STOYTE, FRANCIS, d. 1733. Son of John Stoyte, MP (App. B). BA (TCD), 1715, recorder, 1727–33.

WALKER, WILLIAM (?1757–1820), b. Dublin. Son of Matthew Walker, merchant. Entered TCD, 1773; called to the bar, 1779; recorder, 1794–1820.

Sources: as App. B. also *CARD* iv. 197; v. 13, 17, 190, 193, 450, 495, 511; vi. 34, 103, 253, 504; vii. 388; viii. 92; ix. 310; x. 211; xi. 334; xiii. 355, 455; xiv. 364; xvii. 351; xviii. 255.

Select Bibliography

Primary Sources

1. Manuscript Sources

Apothecaries' Hall, 95 Merrion Sq., Dublin
Transactions of the corporation of apothecaries, 1747–95, 1796–1837.

Assay Office, Dublin Castle (read on microfilm in NLI. N 6056–8 p 6782–4; n 6062 p 6788).
Company of goldsmiths, apprentices enrolment books, 1752–67.
Attendance book, 1818–35.
Book of freemen, 1807–40.
Touch books, 1788–99, 1795–1802.

Dublin Corporation Archives, City Assembly House, South William St.
Book of oaths. MR/32.
Freedom beseeches. Fr/B/1660–1765, 1803/39.
Freedom bonds. Fr/Bond/1674–1759.
Journals of sheriffs and commons. C1/JSC/1–13.
Monday books, 1658–1842. MR/18–20.
Recorders' book. MR/25.
Transactions of the corporation of smiths, 1811–35. G3/1.

Dublin Heritage Group, Clondalkin Public Library
Freemen of Dublin, database.

Dublin Public Libraries, Gilbert Collection, Pearse St., Dublin
Charters and documents of the guild of Holy Trinity or merchants' guild of Dublin, 1438–1824. Transcribed for J. T. Gilbert, 2 vols. MSS 78–9.
Charters and documents of the guild of tailors, Dublin, 1296–1753. Transcribed for J. T. Gilbert. MS 80.
Charters and documents of the Dublin corporation of cutlers, painter-stainers and stationers, also of the Dublin guild of bricklayers. Transcribed for J. T. Gilbert. MS 81.

Guinness Museum, Dublin
Minute books of the corporation of brewers and maltsters, 1750–1802, 1804–31.

Marsh's Library, Dublin
An abstract of the numbers of Protestants, and papists, able to bear arms in the city of Dublin, and Liberties thereof [*c.*1690]. MS Z 2.1.7 (39).
Roll of numbers 'before November 1690'. MS Z 2.1.7 (40).

National Archives, Bishop St., Dublin
Thomas Braughall papers. MS 620/34/50.
Bricklayers' characteristic and charitable record book. MS 1097/1/1.
Calendar of official papers, 1790–1831, 2 vols.

Chief secretary's office, registered papers.

Rebellion papers. MS 620.

Reports of the Council of the Chamber of Commerce to the Annual Assembly of the Members of the Association (Dublin, 1821–51). MS 1064/1/1.

Lists of freemen of the goldsmiths' guild, *c.*1600–1800. Thrift Abstracts, 1427–8.

Transactions of the guild of St Loy, 1766–1811 (extracts, by Charles T. Keatinge, 1901). 2 notebooks, plus index. M 2925–7.

Transcripts of the original record book of the guild of feltmakers, Dublin, then in the Record Office, Four Courts, Dublin, by John J. Webb. 2 notebooks, 1668–1732, 1732–71. M 6118 a–b

Westmorland correspondence, 1789–1808. Letterbooks I–III.

National Library of Ireland, Kildare St., Dublin

Ainsworth reports, ix. Reports on private collections, no. 208: records at Apothecaries' Hall.

The book of bye laws of the corporation of saddlers, upholders, coach makers, etc. (1767). MS 81.

Admission lists, corporation of saddlers 1776–92. MS 82.

Corporation of chandlers, etc., Dublin, record book, 1814–40. MS 80.

EVANS, EDWARD, 'The Ancient Guilds of Dublin'. TS of 10 articles published in the *Evening Telegraph*, 1894–5. MS 738.

GUINNESS, HENRY SEYMOUR, 'Dublin Trade Guilds', a collection of his own and others' work, published and unpublished (n.d.). MS 680.

THRIFT, GERTRUDE (compiler), 'Roll of Freemen, City of Dublin, 1468–85, 1575–1774'. 4 vols. MSS 76–9.

Records of the corporation of cutlers, etc., or guild of St Luke:
By-laws, 1670. MS 12121.
Members' names, 1676–1724. MS 12122.
Transactions, 1696–1841. MSS 12123–8.
Lists, pictures, and accounts. MS 12130.
Apprentices enrolment books 1740–1830. MS 12131.
Quarterage accounts 1787–1841. MS 12132.
By-laws, 1788–1818. MS 12133.
Guild of St Luke, Brunswick club, minute book, 1828–32. MS 12136

Public Record Office, London

Home office papers: Ireland, correspondence and papers. HO 100/12–14.

Public Record Office of Northern Ireland, Belfast

Harrowby papers. T 3228/1/65–6; T 3228/2/9; T 3228/5/8–23 (originals held by Harrowby MSS Trust, Sandon Hall, Stafford).

Leinster papers. D 3078/3/14, 1–19. Read on microfilm in St Patrick's College, Maynooth. MIC 541, Reel 17.

Henry Pelham papers. T 2863/1/40; T 2863/1/6.

Sneyd papers. T 3229/2/12; T 3229/2/51–3; T 3229/2/72 (originals held in Keele University Library).

Spencer Bernard papers. T 2627/6/2/7.

Wilmot papers. T 3019/1421.

Representative Church Body Library, Braemor Park, Dublin

St Bride's parish, Dublin, vestry minute book, 1742–80. P 327/3/2.

St Michan's parish, Dublin, vestry minute book, 1777–1800. P 276/4/3.

Royal Irish Academy, Dublin
The booke of St Anne's guild, Dublin. MS 12/D/1.
Records of the Aldermen of Skinner's Alley:
    Book of members, c.1813–58. MS 23.H.51.
    Minute book, 1814–63. MS 23.H.52.
    Correspondence book, 1841–50. MS 23.H.53.

Royal Society of Antiquaries of Ireland, Dublin
Records of the corporation of weavers:
    Lists of brethren, 1746–1837 (3 vols.).
    Masters' account book, 1691–1714.
    Minute books, 1734–56, 1755–92.
    Quarter brother books, 1707–64 (3 vols.).

Trinity College, Dublin
Hutchinson papers. MSS 8556–8/74–5.
Records of the guild of barber-surgeons:
    Oaths of allegiance, etc. (1837). MS 1447/4/3.
    Minute books, 1757–92, 1792–1826, 1826–41. MS 1447/8/2–4.

2. Printed Sources

Calendars, source compilations and printed correspondence
BEDFORD, JOHN, *Correspondence of John, Fourth Duke of Bedford: With an Introduction by Lord John Russell* (2 vols.; London, 1842–3).
BERESFORD, JOHN, *The Correspondence of the Right Hon. John Beresford . . . Edited, with Notes, by his Grandson, the Right Hon. William Beresford* (2 vols.; London, 1854).
BOYLE, ROGER, *A Collection of the State Letters of the Right Honourable Roger Boyle, the First Earl of Orrery*, ed. Thomas Morrice (2 vols.; Dublin, 1743).
BURKE, EDMUND, *The Correspondence of Edmund Burke*, vi, ed. Alfred Cobban and Robert A. Smith (Cambridge, 1967); vii, ed. P. J. Marshall and John A. Woods (Cambridge and Chicago, 1968).
Calendar of State Papers, Domestic Series, 1671 [–1700].
Calendar of State Papers Relating to Ireland, 1666–9 [–69–70].
Calendar of Treasury Papers, 1556/7–1696.
CAPEL, ARTHUR, earl of Essex, *Letters Written by His Excellency Arthur Capel, Earl of Essex, Lord Lieutenant of Ireland, in the Year 1675* (London, 1770).
CASTLEREAGH, VISCOUNT, *Memoirs and Correspondence of Viscount Castlereagh . . . Edited by his Brother, Charles Vane, Marquess of Londonderry* (4 vols.; London, 1848–9).
CORNWALLIS, CHARLES, *Correspondence of Charles, First Marquis Cornwallis*, ed. Charles Ross, 2nd edn. (3 vols.; London, 1859).
DRENNAN, WILLIAM, *The Drennan Letters*, ed. D. A. Chart (Belfast, 1931).
Eighteenth Century Irish Official Papers in Great Britain. Private Collections, i (Belfast, 1973); ii, compiled by A. P. W. Malcomson (Belfast, 1990).
GILBERT, JOHN T and R. M. (eds.), *Calendar of Ancient Records of Dublin, in Possession of the Municipal Corporation of that City* (19 vols.; Dublin, 1889–1944).

Historical Manuscripts Commission.
  Buccleuch & Queensberry MSS, II, i (London, 1903)
  Charlemont MSS, i. 12th Rep., Appendix, x (London, 1891)
  Emly MSS. 8th Rep., Appendix i (Darlington, 1881)
  Finch MSS, ii (London, 1922)
  Hastings MSS, ii (London, 1930)
  Kenyon MSS. 14th Rep., Appendix, iv (London, 1894)
  Lothian MSS (London, 1905)
  Ormond MSS, NS, iv, vi, vii (London, 1906–12)
  Portland MSS, v, vii (Norwich, 1899; London, 1901)
  Stopford-Sackville MSS. 9th Rep., Appendix, iii (London, 1884)
LEINSTER, Duchess of, *Letters of Lady Louisa Conolly and William, Marquis of Kildare*, ed. Brian Fitzgerald (Dublin, 1957): Vol. iii of *Correspondence of Emily, Duchess of Leinster (1731–1814)*.
MCDOWELL, R. B. (ed.), 'Proceedings of the Dublin Society of United Irishmen', *Anal. Hib.* 17 (1949), 3–143.
O'CONNELL, DANIEL, *The Correspondence of Daniel O'Connell*, ed. Maurice R. O'Connell (8 vols.; Dublin, 1972–80).
SCULLY, DENYS, *The Catholic Question in Ireland & England 1798–1822: The Papers of Denys Scully*, ed. Brian MacDermot (Dublin, 1988).
SMITH, SYDNEY, *Selected Letters of Sydney Smith*, ed. Nowell C. Smith (Oxford, 1981).

Parliamentary papers. Debates, speeches, journals, members:
Cobbett's Parliamentary History of England, v (1688–1702) (London, 1809).
GRATTAN, HENRY, *The Speeches of the Right Hon. Henry Grattan; To Which is Added his Letter on the Union, With a Commentary on his Career and Character by Daniel Owen Madden*, 2nd edn. (Dublin, 1853).
The Parliamentary History of England, From the Earliest Period to the Year 1803, cont. as *The Parliamentary Debates From the Year 1803 to the Present Time* (41 vols.; London, 1804–20).
Hansard's Parliamentary Debates, 3rd ser. (London, 1831–40).
The Parliamentary Register: Or, History of the Proceedings and Debates of the House of Commons of Ireland, 1781–97 (17 vols.; Dublin, 1782–1801).
Journals of the House of Commons of the Kingdom of Ireland, 1613–1800 (19 vols.; Dublin, 1796–1800).
HUNT, WILLIAM (ed.), *The Irish Parliament 1775* (London, 1907).

Parliamentary papers. Poll books, etc.:
An Alphabetical List of the Constituency of the City of Dublin, With the Residence, Qualification, and Profession of Each Voter, and the Votes Given at the Elections of 1832, 1835 and 1837 (Dublin [1837]).
An Alphabetical List of the Freemen of the City of Dublin, 1774–1823 ([Dublin], n.d.).
An Alphabetical List of the Freemen and Freeholders of the City of Dublin, Who Polled at the Election for Members of Parliament (Dublin, 1750).
An Alphabetical List of the Freemen and Freeholders that Polled at the Election of Members to Represent the City of Dublin in Parliament (Dublin, 1761).
HOLMES, HENRY, *An Alphabetical List of the Freeholders and Freemen, Who Voted*

on the Late Election . . . Compiled from the Original Poll Book. Also, a Succinct Account of the Elections for Said City from 1749 to 1773 Inclusive [Dublin, 1774].

MADDEN, RICHARD, *Mirror of the Dublin Election . . . 1841; Arranged in Street Lists* (Dublin, 1841).

O'NEILL, F, *The Stain Removed, and Corporation Juggling Explained. Being an Alphabetical List of the Freemen & Freeholders . . . With their Residences and Occupations, Who Voted at the Late Election. And Also, a List of Those Who Remained Neutral on that Occasion* ([Dublin], 1820).

The Poll for Electing Two Members to Represent the City of Dublin in the Imperial Parliament . . . 1806 (Dublin, n.d.).

Proceedings at the Election for the City of Dublin . . . 1835 . . . to Which is Added, a List of the Voters (Dublin, 1835).

Two Alphabetical Lists of the Freeholders and Freemen Who Voted on the Late Election of a Member . . . in the Room of James Grattan, Esq., Deceased (Dublin, 1768).

Parliamentary papers. Reports etc.:

Electors, Ireland. A Return of the Electors Registered . . . in Ireland. HC 1833 (177), xxvii.

Fictitious Votes (Ireland). Third Report from the Select Committee. HC 1837 (480) xi, Pt. II.

First [and Second] Report From the Select Committee on the Local Taxation of the City of Dublin. HC 1823 (356 & 549), vi.

Minutes of Evidence, Taken Before the Committee of the Whole House . . . on the Conduct of the Sheriff of Dublin, in Relation to [the Dublin Theatre Riot]. HC 1823 (308), vi.

Municipal Corporations (Ireland). Appendix to Report on the City of Dublin, Pt. II. HC 1836, xxiv.

Number of Persons Admitted by Birth, Service and Grace Especial . . . into the Corporation of Dublin [1821–9]. HC 1829 (253), xxii.

Papers Relating to a Riot at Dublin Theatre, on the 14th December 1822. HC 1823 (165), vi.

Parliamentary Representation, Ireland (Boundary Reports). Report on the County of the City of Dublin. HC 1831–2 (519), xliii.

Poor Inquiry (Ireland). Appendix C, Pt. II, Report on the City of Dublin. HC 1836, xxx.

Registration of Electors (Ireland). A Return of the Total Numbers of Parliamentary Electors . . . Registered . . . in Ireland . . . in the Years . . . 1835, 1837 and 1841. HC 1841 (240.–1), xx.

Report of the Commissioners Appointed to Take the Census of Ireland for the Year 1841. HC 1843, xxiv.

Report From the Select Committee Appointed to Inquire into the Nature, Character, Extent and Tendency of Orange Lodges, Associations or Societies in Ireland. HC 1835 (377), xv.

Returns of the Number of Electors . . . Qualified to Vote at any Election Which may Take Place Before the 1st of May 1841. HC 1841 (108), xx.

Returns of the Number of Persons Registered as Freeholders, Within the Last Eight Years, in Every City and Town . . . in Ireland. HC 1829 (253), xxii.

Second Report of the Commissioners Appointed to Consider and Recommend a General System of Railways for Ireland. HC 1837–8, xxxv.

Second Report from the Select Committee on Combinations of Workmen. HC 1837–8 (646), viii.

Parliamentary papers. Statutes:

MERITON, G., *An Exact Abridgment of All the Publick Printed Irish Statutes Now in Force . . . Together With an Abridgment of Such English Statutes Now in Force . . . Relating to the Kingdom of Ireland* (Dublin, 1724).

The Statutes at Large, Passed in the Parliaments Held in Ireland (20 vols.; Dublin, 1765–1801).

A Collection of the Public General Statutes, Passed in the Forty–Second Year of . . . King George the Third [to the] Third and Fourth Year . . . of Queen Victoria (Dublin, 1802–40).

Newspapers, directories

The Apologist: Or, The Alderman's Journal, I–XII. (CULBC, Hib. 3. 748. 1 [16]).

The Censor, Or, The Citizens Journal

The Censor Extraordinary

The Church Monitor, I–II (CULBC, Hib. 3. 748. 1 [48]).

Dublin Evening Mail

Dublin Evening Post

Faulkner's Dublin Journal

The Freeman's Journal

The Gentleman's and Citizen's Almanack, by John [later Samuel] Watson

The Gentleman's Magazine

Hibernian Journal

Volunteer Evening Post

The Volunteer's Journal; Or Irish Herald

The Warder

The Whigg Monitor, I (CULBC, Hib. 3. 748. 1 [44]).

Works of Reference

BATTY, ESPINE (ed.), *Reports of Cases Argued and Determined in the Court of King's Bench in Ireland From . . . 1825 to 1826* (Dublin, 1828).

BOASE, FREDERIC, *Modern English Biography* (2 vols.; Truro, 1892–1901).

BURTCHAELL, GEORGE, and SADLEIR, THOMAS (eds.). *Alumni Dublinenses* (London, 1924).

CLARK, MARY, and REFAUSSÉ, RAYMOND. *Directory of Historic Dublin Guilds* (Dublin, 1993).

Dictionary of National Biography.

MOODY, T. W., MARTIN, F. X., BYRNE F. J. (eds.), *A New History of Ireland*, ix. *Maps, Genealogies, Lists* (Oxford, 1984).

SMYTH, CONSTANTINE J., *Chronicle of the Law Officers of Ireland* (London, 1839).

WALKER, B. M. (ed.), *Parliamentary Election Results in Ireland, 1801–1922* (Dublin, 1978).

Other Contemporary Works

ANON. *Advice to the Freemen and Freeholders of the City of Dublin: In their Choice of a Representative in the Ensuing Election* (n.p., 1733).

ANON. *The Alderman's Guide: Or, a New Pattern for a Lord-Mayor. A Ballad Written by a Craftsman of the City of Dublin*, CULBC, Hib. 3. 730. 1 (25).

—— *An Appeal to the People of Ireland . . . By a Member of the Incorporated Society for Promoting English Protestant Schools in Ireland* (Dublin, 1749).

—— *Astrea's Congratulation. An Ode upon Alderman Humphry French Being Elected Representative for the City of Dublin* [1733], CULBC, Hib. 3. 730. 1 (118).

—— *The City Candidates; Or, a Plumper for John Claudius Beresford* (Dublin, 1802).

—— *The City Spy-Glass: Or, Candidates Mirrour. Wherein the Merits and Pretensions of the Several Candidates are Freely Considered, and Impartially Examined. By a Son of Candour* (Dublin, 1767).

—— *A Critical Review of the Liberties of British Subjects. With a Comparative View of the Proceedings of the H—e of C——s of I——d, Against an Unfortunate Exile of that Country. By a Gentleman of the Middle Temple*, 2nd edn. (London, 1750).

—— *A Fuller Account of the Proceedings at Guild-Hall on Monday, the 2nd of April 1744* (Dublin, 1744).

—— *Ireland in 1804* (London, 1806; repr. Dublin, 1980).

—— *Judy's Lamentation on the Departure of His Majesty from Dublin, Being a Sequel to Paddy's Keenan* [Dublin, 1821].

—— *A Letter to the Citizens of Dublin. By a Farmer* (Dublin, 1766).

—— *A Letter to the Fool* (n.p. [1753]), CULBC, Hib. 1. 679. 1 (74).

—— *Letter to the Independent Citizens of Dublin, from a Member of the Guild of Merchants* (Dublin, 1802).

—— *A Letter to the Right Honourable James, Earl of Kildare, on the Present Posture of Affairs*, 2nd edn. (Dublin, 1754).

—— *A Little More Advice to the People of Dublin* (n.p., 1733), CULBC, Hib. 3. 730. 1 (108).

—— *A New Ballad to be Sung by the C—t Party on the Seventeenth Day of December, 1754*, CULBC, Hib. 1. 679. 1 (87).

—— *A Political Catechism; Serving to Instruct Those That Have Made the Protestation Concerning the Power and Priviledges of Parliament; Taken out of His Majesty's Answer to the 19 Proposition* [sic], in *State Tracts*, pt.1, 447–53.

—— *Queries on the Government of this City, Humbly Offered to Public Impartial Consideration* (Dublin, 1760).

—— *Queries Humbly Offered to the Consideration of the Wise and Just Patriots of Ireland* (n.p., 1749), CULBC, Hib. 3. 748. 1 (27).

—— *To the Right Honourable the Lord Mayor of the City of Dublin. The Counter Address of a Free Citizen* (Dublin, 1766).

—— *A Short but Interesting Address to the Citizens of Dublin* (Dublin, 1767).

—— *The Temple of Fame: Or, a Tribute to the Supporters of the Independence of Their Native City. Humbly Dedicated to Them by 'A True Blue'*, 2nd edn. (Dublin, 1820).

—— *A True Account of a Plot Lately Discovered in Ireland, for Fireing the City of Dublin, and Putting all the Protestants to the Sword* (Dublin, 1690), NLI, Thorpe P 12/24.

—— *Vindication of the Cause of the Catholics of Ireland, Adopted . . . by the General Committee . . . December 7, 1792* (Dublin, 1793).

—— *The Whig Club, Attacked and Defended . . . Addressed to the People of Ireland* (Dublin, 1790).

—— *A Word to the Wise, Or . . . Lucas is the Man* (n.p., 1748), CULBC, Hib. 3. 748. 1 (4).

—— *X O Fish O! A Patched, Vamp'd, Future, Old, Revived Bran-New Poem, Descriptive of Some Recent Important Transactions* (Dublin, 1823).

ANT. CONSTITUTION (pseud.). *A Short and Easy Method of Reducing the Exorbitant Pride and Arrogance of the City of Dublin* (Dublin, 1748).

BARBER, A. F., and CITIZEN [Charles Lucas], *A Second Letter to the Free Citizens of Dublin* (Dublin, 1747).

—— *A Third Letter to the Free-Citizens of Dublin* (Dublin, 1747).

BARNARD, JOHN. *A Speech Made in the House of Commons in England, By Sir John Bernard* [sic], *One of the Aldermen of London, in Support of a Bill for Repealing the Aldermen's Negative* (Dublin, 1749)

BARRINGTON, JONAH, *Recollections of Jonah Barrington*, Every Irishman's Library edn. (Dublin, n.d.).

BATTERSBY, W. J., *The Fall and Rise of Ireland, or the Repealer's Manual*, 2nd edn. (Dublin, 1834).

BLOUNT, CHARLES, *The Miscellaneous Works of Charles Blount, Esq.* (2 vols.; n.p., 1695).

[BOLINGBROKE, HENRY ST JOHN, VISCOUNT BOLINGBROKE], *The Freeholder's Political Catechism* (London, 1733), in id., *A Collection of Political Tracts* (Dublin, 1748), 199–213.

BRITANNICUS [Charles Lucas], *A Free-Man's Answer to the Free-Holder's Address. To the Merchants, Traders, and Others, the Citizens and Free-Men of the City of Dublin* (n.p., 1748).

A BRITON. *The History of the Dublin Election* (London, 1753).

[BROOKE, HENRY], *A First [to Tenth] Letter from the Farmer to the Free and Independent Electors of the City of Dublin* (Dublin, 1749).

—— *An Occasional Letter from the Farmer, to the Free-Men of Dublin* (Dublin, 1749).

[?BROWNE, ARTHUR], *Free Thoughts on the Measures of Opposition, Civil and Religious, from the Commencement of the Last Parliament to the Present Period; With a Modest Plea for the Rights and Ascendency of Episcopal Protestantism . . . by Candidus Redintegratus* (Dublin, 1792).

BULLEN, EDWARD (ed.), *Five Reports of the Committee of the Precursor Association . . . Upon the Relative State and Nature of the Parliamentary Franchises in the United Kingdom* (Dublin, 1839).

[BURGH, JAMES], *Political Disquisitions: Or an Enquiry into Public Errors, Defects and Abuses* (3 vols.; London, 1774).

BURKE, EDMUND, *The Works of Edmund Burke* (6 vols.; London, 1884–99).

Catholic Committee, *An Address from the General Committee of Roman Catholics to their Protestant Fellow Subjects* (Dublin, 1792).

—— *Transactions of the General Committee of the Roman Catholics of Ireland During the Year 1791* (Dublin, 1792).

Catholic Meeting, *Proceedings at the Catholic Meeting of Dublin . . . October 31,*

1792 . . . *With the Letter of the Corporation of Dublin, to the Protestants of Ireland* (Dublin, 1792).

Catholic Society, *Declaration of the Catholic Society of Dublin* [1791], in *Transactions of the General Committee of the Roman Catholics of Ireland.*

A CITIZEN, *A Letter to the Lord Mayor, Sheriffs, Commons and Citizens of the City of Dublin* (Dublin, 1740).

—— [J. D. La Touche], *A Letter to the Commons of the City of Dublin*, 2nd edn. (Dublin, 1743).

—— *A Second Letter to the Commons of the City of Dublin* (Dublin, 1743).

Common Council, *The Standing Rules and Orders of the Commons of the Common-Council of the City of Dublin* (Dublin, 1772).

—— *The Resolutions of the Common Council of the City of Dublin, for Maintaining the Freedom of Elections in the Said City* [1713], NLI, Thorpe P 12/73.

Commons of Dublin, *The Answer of Several of the Commons of the City of Dublin, to a Scandalous Libel, Entituled, The Resolutions of the Common-Council of the City of Dublin*, NLI, Thorpe P 12/74.

CUNNINGHAM, T. (ed.), *Magna Charta Libertatum Civitatis Waterford* (Dublin, 1752).

CURRAN, JOHN PHILPOT, *The Speeches of John Philpot Curran, Before the Privy Council, on the Petitions of Alderman James and Alderman Howison* (Dublin, 1791).

DALRYMPLE, JOHN, *Memoirs of Great Britain and Ireland* (4 vols.; Dublin, 1773).

DAUNT, WILLIAM JOSEPH O'NEILL, *Eighty-Five Years of Irish History 1800–1885*, 2nd edn. (2 vols.; London, 1886).

—— *Personal Recollections of the Late Daniel O'Connell, M.P.* (2 vols.; London, 1848).

DAVEY, SAMUEL, *A View of the Conduct and Writings of Mr Charles Lucas. Being an Answer to Some Passages in the Eighteenth Address of C. Lucas . . . Reflecting on the Late Sir Samuel Cooke* (Dublin, 1749).

DAVIES, JOHN, *A Discoverie of the True Causes why Ireland was Never Entirely Subdued, Nor Brought Under the Obedience of the Crowne of England* (1612), in id., *The Complete Prose Works*, ed. Alexander B. Grosart (2 vols.; n.p., 1876), ii. 1–168.

DRENNAN, WILLIAM, *Letters of an Irish Helot, Signed Orellana* (Dublin, 1785).

FREE BRITON, *A Free-Briton's Advice to the Free Citizens of Dublin* (Dublin, 1748).

FREE CITIZEN [Charles Lucas], *Faction Unmasked: Or, a Short Sketch of the History of the Several Parties that Prevailed in the City of Dublin, Since the Year 1748, to the Present Time* (Dublin, 1767).

FREE CITIZENS, *The Case of the Free-Citizens of Dublin* [Dublin, 1750], CULBC, Hib. 3. 748. 1 (46).

—— *The Free-Citizens Address to Sir Samuel Cooke, Bart. For his Unshakeable Attachment to the True Interest of Ireland this Session of Parliament* (London, 1754).

FREE ELECTORS, *The Free-Electors Address to Colonel Dunn. With his Answer* (Dublin, 1761).

FREE WEAVER, *An Appeal to the Lovers of Truth and Liberty. By a Free Weaver* (n.p., [1761]), CULBC, Hib. 3. 748. 1 (54).

A FREEMAN, BARBER AND CITIZEN OF DUBLIN [Charles Lucas], *A Miror for a Mock-Patriot: Or, the Cork Surgeon Display'd: In a Letter to Himself*, i (Dublin, 1749).

GALE, PETER, *An Inquiry into the Ancient Corporate System of Ireland, and Suggestions for its Immediate Restoration and General Extension* (London, 1834).

[GAST, JOHN], *A Letter to the Tradesmen, Farmers, and the Rest of the Good People of Ireland, by L. B. Haberdasher and Citizen of Dublin*, 2nd edn. (Dublin, 1754).

—— *A Second Letter to the Tradesmen, [etc.]* (Dublin, 1754).

GHOST OF LUCAS, *Experimental and Historical Reflections on the Bill Now Before Parliament for the Establishment of Popery, Misnamed 'The Irish Municipal Reform Bill', by the Ghost of Lucas* (1840), CULBC, Hib. 0. 840. 3.

GRATTAN, HENRY, *The Address of the Rt. Hon. Henry Grattan, to his Constituents (the Citizens of Dublin) on his Retiring from the Parliament of Ireland*, 2nd edn. (London, 1797).

—— *Memoirs of the Life and Times of the Rt. Hon. Henry Grattan, by his Son, Henry Grattan, M.P.* (5 vols.; London, 1839–46).

[GRATTAN, JAMES], *A Second Letter to a Member of the Honourable House of Commons of Ireland. Containing a Scheme for Regulating the Corporation of the City of Dublin* (Dublin, 1760).

Guild of Merchants, *The Report of the Committee Appointed by the Guild of Merchants, Dublin, to Prepare Petitions to Parliament Against the Demand Called 'Catholic Emancipation'* (Dublin, 1828).

HALL, S. C. and A. M., *Ireland: Its Scenery, Character, Etc.* (3 vols.; London, 1841–3).

HARRINGTON, JAMES, *The Oceana and Other Works of James Harrington, with an Account of his Life by John Toland* (London, 1700).

HARRIS, WALTER, *The History of the Life and Reign of William-Henry . . . King of England, Scotland, France and Ireland* (Dublin, 1749).

—— 'William King, D.D.', in id. (ed.), *The Works of Sir James Ware Concerning Ireland. Revised and Improved* (3 vols.; Dublin, 1739).

HERBERT, J. D., *Irish Varieties for the Last Fifty Years* (London, 1836).

[HILLSBOROUGH, EARL OF], *A Proposal for Uniting the Kingdoms of Great Britain and Ireland* (London & Dublin, 1751).

HUME, DAVID, *Essays and Treatises on Several Subjects*, new edn. (2 vols.; Dublin, 1779).

HUNT, THOMAS, *A Defence of the Charter and Municipal Rights of the City of London* (London [1682]).

Incorporated Society in Dublin for Promoting English Protestant Schools in Ireland, *A Protestant Catechism; Shewing the Principal Errors of the Church of Rome* (Dublin, 1740).

Irish Metropolitan Conservative Society, *Report of the Proceedings at the First Public Meeting of the Irish Metropolitan Conservative Society* (Dublin, [1836]).

KING, WILLIAM, *The State of the Protestants of Ireland Under the Late King James's Government* (London, 1691; 4th edn., 1692).

HIBERNICUS [J. D. La Touche], *A Freeholder's Address to the Merchants, Traders and Others . . . of the City of Dublin* (Dublin, 1748).

LELAND, THOMAS, *The History of Ireland from the Invasion of Henry II* (3 vols.; London, 1773).

LEWIS, SAMUEL, *A History and Topography of Dublin City and County* [1837] (Dublin and Cork, 1980).

LITTEN, ANTHONY [Sir Richard Cox], *The Cork Surgeon's Antidote, Against the Dublin Apothecary's Poyson*, i–vii (Dublin, 1749).

LOCKE, JOHN, *Two Treatises of Government*, ed. Peter Laslett (Cambridge, 1988).

LUCAS, CHARLES, *An Address to the Free Electors of the City of Dublin* [1761], CULBC, Hib. 3. 748. 1 (56).

—— *An Answer to the Counter Address of a Pretended Free Citizen. Humbly Addressed to the Right Honourable Sir James Taylor, Knt. Lord Mayor of the City of Dublin. By a True Citizen* (Dublin, 1766).

—— *An Appeal to the Commons and Citizens of London. By Charles Lucas, the Last Free Citizen of Dublin* (London, 1756).

—— *The British Free-Holder's Political Catechism: Addressed . . . to the Free Citizens, and Free-Holders of the City of Dublin* (Dublin, 1748).

—— *The Complaints of Dublin: Humbly Offered to His Excellency William, Earl of Harrington, Lord Lieutenant General . . . of Ireland* (Dublin, 1747).

—— *Divelina Libera: An Apology for the Civil Rights and Liberties of the Commons and Citizens of Dublin* (Dublin, 1744).

—— *A [First to Eighteenth] Address to the Free-Citizens and Free-Holders of the City of Dublin* (Dublin, 1749).

—— *The Great Charter of the Liberties of the City of Dublin. Transcribed and Translated into English . . . Addressed to His Majesty and Presented to His Lords Justices of Ireland* (Dublin, 1749).

—— *The Liberties and Customs of Dublin Asserted and Demonstrated Upon the Principles of Law, Justice, and Good Policy; With a Comparative View of the Constitutions of London and Dublin. And Some Considerations on the Customs of Intrusion and Quarterage*, 2nd edn. (Dublin, 1768).

—— *A Mirror for Courts-Martial*, 3rd edn. (Dublin, 1768).

—— *The Political Constitutions of Great-Britain and Ireland, Asserted and Vindicated; The Connection and Common Interest of Both Kingdoms, Demonstrated* (2 vols.; London, 1751).

—— *A Remonstrance Against Certain Infringements on the Rights and Liberties of the Commons and Citizens of Dublin* (Dublin, 1743).

—— *To the Right Honourable the Lord Mayor, Sheriffs . . . of the City of Dublin, the Memorial of Charles Lucas, M.D.* (n.p., n.d.), CULBC, Hib. 3. 748. 1 (48).

—— *The Rights and Privileges of Parlements Asserted Upon Constitutional Principles; Against the Modern Anti-Constitutional Clames of Chief Governors* (Dublin, 1770).

—— *A Second Address to the Right Hon. the Lord Mayor, the Aldermen, Sheriffs, Commons, Citizens, and Freeholders of . . . Dublin* (Dublin, 1766).

LUCIUS SEVERUS PUBLICOLA (pseud.), *To the Freemen . . . of the City of Kilkenny . . . From . . . A Tribune of the People in Dublin* (Dublin, 1748).

LUCKOMBE, PHILIP, *A Tour Through Ireland*, 2nd. edn. (London, 1783).

M'CREA, J. B., *Protestant Poor a Conservative Element of Society; Being a Sermon Preached in Ebenezer Church, Dublin* (Dublin, [1825]).

MAGEE, WILLIAM, *A Charge Delivered at his Primary Visitation* (Dublin, 1822).

—— *A Charge, Delivered to the Clergy of the Diocese of Raphoe, at the Primary Visitation of that Diocese* (Dublin, 1822).

—— *A Charge Delivered at his Triennial and Metropolitan Visitation* (Dublin, 1827).

—— *The Evidence of His Grace the Archbishop of Dublin Before the Select Committee of the House of Lords, on the State of Ireland* (Dublin, 1825).

MARVEL, ANDREW, *An Account of the Growth of Popery, and Arbitrary Government in England* (n.p., 1677).

MERCHANTS, *To the King's Most Excellent Majesty. The Most Humble Address of the Merchants, Traders, [Etc.] of the City of Dublin* (Dublin, 1753).

MOLYNEUX, WILLIAM, *The Case of Ireland's Being Bound by Acts of Parliament in England, Stated*, ed. J. G. Simms (Dublin, 1977).

MUSGRAVE, RICHARD, *Memoirs of the Different Rebellions in Ireland, From the Arrival of the English*, 2nd edn. (Dublin, 1801).

NELSON, HENRY, *Poem on the Procession of the Journeymen Smiths on May the First, 1729* (Dublin, 1729).

Nelson's Pillar, *A Description of the Pillar, With a List of the Subscribers. To Which is Added, the Amount of the Funds . . . Published by Order of the Committee* (Dublin, 1846).

NESS, GEORGE, *A Letter to Henry Brougham, Esq. M.P., Containing an Account of the Conduct and Proceedings of the Guild of Merchants of Dublin, so far as they Relate to the Admission of Roman Catholics; the Dressing of the Statue of King William, and the Riot at the Theatre-Royal* (Dublin, 1824).

NEWENHAM, THOMAS, *A Statistical and Historical Inquiry into the Progress and Magnitude of the Population of Ireland* (London, 1805).

O'CONNELL, DANIEL, *The [First to Third] Letter of Daniel O'Connell, Esq., on the Repeal of the Union. To the People of Ireland*, RIA HP vol. 1493.

—— *Second Letter to the People of Ireland [12 April 1833]*, in *The Speeches and Public Letters of the Liberator*, ed. M. F. Cusack (2 vols.; Dublin, 1875).

'O'G.', 'The Life of Dr Charles Lucas', *Dublin Penny Journal*, 1 (1832), 389–91.

PAINE, THOMAS, *Rights of Man: Being an Answer to Mr Burke's Attack on the French Revolution*, pt. 1 (Dublin, 1791; New York and London, 1984).

PEMBERTON, BENJAMIN, *A Letter to William Walker, Esq., Recorder of the City of Dublin, on the Primary Cause of Combination Among the Tradesmen of Dublin* (Dublin, 1814).

[PETERS, JOHN], *The Charter Rights of the City of Dublin: Shewing the Title of the Citizens at Large to the City Estates . . . By a Member of St Anne's Committee on Local Taxation* (Dublin, 1825).

PHILO-HIBERNICUS, *His Letter of Advice to the Free-Men, and Free-Holders of the City of Dublin: With a Word to the Five Candidates* (Dublin, 1748).

[POLLOCK, JOSEPH], *Letters of Owen Roe O'Nial* (Dublin, 1779).

Protestant Association, *First Report of the Protestant Association of Ireland* (Dublin, 1836).

REYNOLDS, THOMAS, jun., *The Life of Thomas Reynolds* (2 vols.; London, 1839).

ROWAN, ARCHIBALD HAMILTON, *Autobiography of Archibald Hamilton Rowan*, ed. William Hamilton Drummond (Dublin, 1840; repr., Shannon, 1972).

SHERIDAN, CHARLES FRANCIS, *An Essay Upon the True Principles of Civil Liberty, and of Free Government* (London, 1793).

SINGLE, JEREMIAH (pseud.), *M'Kenny's Feast, An Ode by Jeremiah Single, Bell-Man and Poet-Laureat to the City of Dublin* (Dublin, 1818).

SISSON, JONATHAN, *Second Letter to the Right Hon. Earl Grey, on the Necessity of the Appointment of a Board, or Council, at Dublin, for the Internal Interests of Ireland* (London, 1832).

State Tracts: Being a Collection of Several Treatises Relating to the Government. Privately Printed in the Reign of K. Charles II (London, 1693).

[SWIFT, JONATHAN], *Fraud Detected, Or, the Hibernian Patriot. Containing all the Drapier's Letters* (Dublin, 1725).

—— *A Proposal for the Universal Use of Irish Manufactures* (Dublin, 1720).

—— *The Prose Works of Jonathan Swift, D.D.*, ed. Temple Scott (12 vols.; London, 1902–11).

TEMPLE, JOHN, *The Irish Rebellion: Or, An History . . . of the General Rebellion Raised Within the Kingdom of Ireland* (London, 1646).

[TONE, THEOBALD WOLFE], *An Argument on Behalf of the Catholics of Ireland* (Dublin, 1791).

—— *Life of Theobald Wolfe Tone . . . Written by Himself and Continued by his Son: With . . . Fragments of his Diary* (2 vols.; Washington, 1826).

W.B. [?WILLIAM JOHN BATTERSBY], *A Church, Not Without Religion; Or, A Few Modest Remarks upon the Inconsistent Charge of His Grace Doctor Magee . . . by W. B. a Catholic Layman* (Dublin, 1822).

[WALMESLEY, CHARLES], *The General History of the Christian Church, From her Birth to her Final Triumphant State in Heaven, Chiefly Deduced from the Apocalypse of St John the Apostle, by Signor Pastorini* (Dublin, 1790).

WALSH, JOHN EDWARD, *Rakes and Ruffians: The Underworld of Georgian Dublin* (Dublin, 1979: first published as *Ireland Sixty Years Ago* [1847]).

WARBURTON, JOHN, WHITELAW, JAMES, WALSH, ROBERT, *A History of the City of Dublin* (2 vols.; London, 1818).

WARE, JAMES, *The Antiquities and History of Ireland, by the Right Honourable Sir James Ware, Knt. Now First Published in One Volume in English* (Dublin, 1705).

WHITTY, ROBERT, *A Letter to the Free-Citizens of Dublin* (Dublin, 1749), CULBC, Hib. 3. 748. 1 (45).

WILKES, JOHN (ed.), *The Political Controversy, or Magazine. Of Ministerial and Anti-Ministerial Essays* (London, 1762).

WOODWARD, RICHARD, *The Present State of the Church of Ireland* (Dublin, 1786).

WYSE, THOMAS, *Historical Sketch of the Late Catholic Association of Ireland* (2 vols.; London, 1829).

Modern Works

AALEN, F. H. A., and Whelan, Kevin (eds.), *Dublin City and County: From Prehistory to Present* (Dublin, 1992).

ARRIAZA, ARMAND, 'Mousnier and Barber: The Theoretical Underpinning of the "Society of Orders" in Early Modern Europe', *P. & P.* 89 (1980), 39–57.

BAILYN, BERNARD, *The Origins of American Politics* (New York, 1968).

BARNARD, T. C., 'Crises of Identity among Irish Protestants 1641–1685', *P. & P.* 127 (1990), 39–83.

—— *Cromwellian Ireland* (Oxford, 1975).

—— 'Lawyers and the Law in Later Seventeenth-Century Ireland', *IHS* 28 (1993), 256–82.

—— 'Reforming Irish Manners: The Religious Societies in Dublin during the 1690s', *Hist. Jn.* 35 (1992), 805–38.

—— 'The Uses of 23 October 1641 and Irish Protestant Celebrations', *EHR* 106 (1991), 889–920.

BARROW, G. L., *The Emergence of the Irish Banking System 1820–1845* (Dublin, 1975).

—— 'Some Dublin Private Banks', *Dublin Hist. Rec.* 25 (1971), 38–53.

BARROW, LENNOX, 'Riding the Franchises'; 'The Franchises of Dublin', *Dublin Hist. Rec.* 33 (1979–80), 135–8; 36 (1982–3), 68–80.

BARTLETT, THOMAS, *The Fall and Rise of the Irish Nation: The Catholic Question 1690–1830* (Dublin, 1992).

—— 'The Townshend Viceroyalty, 1767–72', in Bartlett and Hayton (eds.), *Penal Era and Golden Age*, 88–112.

—— and HAYTON, D. W. (eds.), *Penal Era and Golden Age: Essays in Irish History, 1690–1800* (Belfast, 1979).

BECKETT, J. C., *The Anglo-Irish Tradition* (London, 1976).

—— *The Cavalier Duke. A Life of James Butler—1st Duke of Ormaond 1610–1688* (Belfast, 1990).

—— *Confrontations: Studies in Irish History* (London, 1972).

—— *Protestant Dissent in Ireland 1687–1780* (London, 1948).

BEDDARD, ROBERT (ed.), *The Revolutions of 1688* (Oxford, 1991).

BENNETT, DOUGLAS, *The Company of Goldsmiths of Dublin 1637–1987* (Dublin, 1987).

BERRY, HENRY F., 'The Ancient Company of Barber-Surgeons, or Gild of St Mary Magdalene, Dublin', *JRSAI* 33 (1903), 217–38.

—— 'The Goldsmiths' Company of Dublin', *JRSAI* 31 (1901), 119–33.

—— 'The Merchant Tailors' Gild—That of St John the Baptist, Dublin, 1418–1841', *JRSAI* 48 (1918), 19–64.

—— 'The Records of the Dublin Gild of Merchants, Known as the Gild of Holy Trinity, 1438–1671', *JRSAI* 30 (1900), 44–68.

—— 'The Records of the Feltmakers' Company of Dublin, 1787–1841: Their Loss and Recovery', *JRSAI* 41 (1911), 26–45.

BEST, G. F. A., 'The Protestant Constitution and its Supporters, 1800–1829', *TRHS*, 5th ser., 8 (1958), 105–27.

BLACK, ANTONY, *Guilds and Civil Society in European Political Thought from the Twelfth Century to the Present* (London, 1984).

BLACK, JEREMY, 'The Crown, Hanover and the Shift in British Foreign Policy in the 1760s', in id. (ed.), *Knights Errant and True Englishmen: British Foreign Policy 1600–1800* (Edinburgh, 1989).

BLAKE, ROBERT, *The Conservative Party from Peel to Churchill* (London, 1972).

BLOCH, RUTH, *Visionary Republic: Millennial Themes in American Thought, 1756–1800* (Cambridge, 1985).

BOLTON, G. C., *The Passing of the Irish Act of Union: A Study in Parliamentary Politics* (Oxford, 1966).

BOTTIGHEIMER, KARL S., 'The Restoration Land Settlement in Ireland: A Structural View', *IHS* 18 (1972), 1–21.

BOWEN, DESMOND, *The Protestant Crusade in Ireland, 1800–70* (Dublin and Montreal, 1978).

BOYCE, D. G., ECCLESHALL, R., GEOGHEGAN, V. (eds.), *Political Thought in Ireland Since the Seventeenth Century* (London and New York, 1993).

BOYD, ANDREW, *The Rise of the Irish Trade Unions 1729–1970* (Tralee, 1972).

BROPHY, IMELDA, 'Women in the Workforce', in Dickson (ed.), *The Gorgeous Mask*, 51–63.

BROWNING, REED, *Political and Constitutional Ideas of the Court Whigs* (Baton Rouge, La., and London, 1982).

BUCKLAND, PATRICK, *Irish Unionism*, i. *The Anglo-Irish and the New Ireland 1885–1922* (Dublin and New York, 1972).

BURGESS, GLENN, 'The Divine Right of Kings Revisited', *EHR* 107 (1992), 837–61.

BURKE, NUALA, 'A Hidden Church? The Structure of Catholic Dublin in the Mid-Eighteenth Century', *Arch. Hib.* 32 (1974), 81–92.

BURNS, ROBERT E., *Irish Parliamentary Politics in the Eighteenth Century* (2 vols.; Washington, 1990).

BUSCHKÜHL, MATTHIAS, *Great Britain and the Holy See 1746–1870* (Dublin, 1982).

BUTEL, P., and CULLEN, L. M. (eds.), *Cities and Merchants: French and Irish Perspectives on Urban Development, 1500–1900* (Dublin, 1986).

BUTTERFIELD, H., *George III, Lord North and the People 1779–80* (London, 1949).

CAHILL, GILBERT, 'Some Nineteenth Century Roots of the Ulster Problem, 1829–48', *Irish University Review*, 1 (1971), 215–37.

CALDICOTT, C. E. J., GOUGH, H., PITTION, J-P. (eds.), *The Huguenots and Ireland: Anatomy of an Emigration* (Dun Laoghaire, 1987).

CARON, IVANHOE, 'La Nomination des évêques catholiques de Quebec sous le régime anglais', *Memoires de la Société Royale du Canada*, sect. 1, 3rd. ser., 26 (1932), 1–44.

CHAMPION, J. A. I., *The Pillars of Priestcraft Shaken: The Church of England and its Enemies, 1660–1730* (Cambridge, 1992).

CHART, D. A., *Ireland from the Union to Catholic Emancipation* (London, 1910).

CLAEYS, GREGORY, 'The French Revolution Debate and British Political Thought', *Hist. Pol. Thought*, 11 (1990), 59–80.

CLARK, J. C. D., *English Society 1688–1832: Ideology, Social Structure and Political Practice During the Ancien Regime* (Cambridge, 1985).

—— 'A General Theory of Party, Opposition and Government, 1688–1832', *Hist. Jn.* 23 (1980), 295–325.

CLARKE, HOWARD B., 'The 1192 Charter of Liberties and the Beginnings of Dublin's Municipal Life', *Dublin Hist. Rec.* 46 (1993), 5–14.

COLE, RICHARD CARGILL, *Irish Booksellers and English Writers 1740–1800* (London and New Jersey, 1986).

COLE, R. LEE, *A History of Methodism in Dublin* (Dublin, 1932).

COLLEY, LINDA, *Britons: Forging the Nation 1707–1837* (New Haven and London, 1992).

—— *In Defiance of Oligarchy. The Tory Party 1714–60* (Cambridge, 1985).

—— 'Radical Patriotism in Eighteenth-Century England', in Samuels (ed.), *Patriotism*, i. 169–87.

COMERFORD, R. V., CULLEN, MARY, HILL, JACQUELINE, LENNON, COLM (eds.), *Religion, Conflict and Coexistence in Ireland: Essays Presented to Monsignor Patrick J. Corish* (Dublin, 1990).

CONNOLLY, S. J., *Religion, Law, and Power: The Making of Protestant Ireland 1660–1760* (Oxford, 1992).

CORFIELD, P. J., *The Impact of English Towns 1700–1800* (Oxford, 1982).

CORRY, GEOFFREY, 'The Dublin Bar—The Obstacle to the Improvement of the Port of Dublin', *Dublin Hist. Rec.* 23 (1970), 137–52.

COSGROVE, ART (ed.), *Dublin Through the Ages* (Dublin, 1988).

COUGHLAN, RUPERT J., *Napper Tandy* (Dublin, 1976).

COYLE, EUGENE A., 'Sir Edward Newenham—The 18th Century Dublin Radical', *Dublin Hist. Rec.* 46 (1993), 15–30.

CRAIG, MAURICE, *Dublin 1660–1860: A Social and Architectural History* (Dublin, 1969).

CRUICKSHANKS, EVELINE, and BLACK, JEREMY (eds.), *The Jacobite Challenge* (Edinburgh, 1988).

CULLEN, L. M., 'The Dublin Merchant Community in the Eighteenth Century', in Butel and Cullen (eds.), *Cities and Merchants*, 195–209.

—— *An Economic History of Ireland Since 1660* (London, 1972).

—— 'The Growth of Dublin 1600–1900: Character and Heritage', in Aalen and Whelan (eds.), *Dublin City and County*, 251–78.

—— 'The Internal Politics of the United Irishmen', in Dickson, Keogh, Whelan (eds.), *The United Irishmen*, 176–96.

—— 'The Political Structures of the Defenders', in Hugh Gough and David Dickson (eds.), *Ireland and the French Revolution* (Dublin, 1990), 117–38.

—— *Princes & Pirates: The Dublin Chamber of Commerce, 1783–1983* (Dublin, 1983).

Culture et Pratique Politiques en France et en Irlande xvie-xviiie siecle. Actes du Colloque de Marseille, 28 Septembre-2 Octobre 1988 (Paris, 1990).

CUMMINS, SEAMUS, 'Extra-Parliamentary Agitation in Dublin in the 1760s', in Comerford, etc. (eds.), *Religion, Conflict and Coexistence*, 118–34.

CUNNINGHAM, HUGH, 'The Language of Patriotism', in Samuel (ed.), *Patriotism*, i. 57–89.

CURTIN, NANCY J., 'The Transformation of the Society of United Irishmen into a Mass-Based Revolutionary Organisation, 1794–6', *IHS* 24 (1985), 463–92.

D'ALTON, IAN, *Protestant Society and Politics in Cork 1812–1844* (Cork, 1980).

DALY, MARY E., *Dublin the Deposed Capital: A Social and Economic History 1860–1914* (Cork, 1985).

D'ARCY, FERGUS, 'An Age of Distress and Reform: 1800–1860', in Cosgrove (ed.), *Dublin Through the Ages*, 93–112.

—— 'The Artisans of Dublin and Daniel O'Connell, 1830–47: An Unquiet Liaison', *IHS* 17 (1970), 221–43.

—— 'The National Trades Political Union and Daniel O'Connell 1830–1848', *Éire-Ireland*, 17 (1982), 7–16.

—— 'The Trade Unions of Dublin and the Attempted Revival of the Guilds', *JRSAI* 101 (1971), 113–27.

DE KREY, GARY STUART, *A Fractured Society: The Politics of London in the First Age of Party, 1688–1715* (Oxford, 1985).

DE VRIES, JAN, *European Urbanization 1500–1800* (London, 1984).

DEVINE, T. M., and DICKSON, DAVID (eds.), *Ireland and Scotland 1600–1850: Parallels and Contrasts in Economic and Social Development* (Edinburgh, 1983).

DICKSON, DAVID, 'Catholics and Trade in Eighteenth-Century Ireland: An Old Debate Revisited', in Power and Whelan (eds.), *Endurance and Emergence*, 85–100.

—— ' "Centres of Motion": Irish Cities and the Origins of Popular Politics', in *Culture et Pratiques Politiques*, 101–22.

—— 'The Demographic Implications of Dublin's Growth, 1650–1850', in Richard Lawson and Robert Lee (eds.), *Urban Population Development in Western Europe from the Late-Eighteenth to the Early-Twentieth Century* (Liverpool, 1989), 178–89.

—— 'Huguenots in the Urban Economy of Eighteenth-Century Dublin and Cork', in Caldicott, etc. (eds.), *The Huguenots and Ireland*, 321–32.

—— *New Foundations: Ireland 1660–1800* (Dublin, 1987).

—— 'Paine and Ireland', in Dickson, etc. (eds.), *The United Irishmen*, 135–50.

—— 'The Place of Dublin in the Eighteenth-Century Irish Economy', in Devine and Dickson (eds.), *Ireland and Scotland 1600–1850*, 177–92.

—— and ENGLISH, RICHARD, 'The La Touche Dynasty', in Dickson (ed.), *The Gorgeous Mask*, 17–29.

—— (ed.), *The Gorgeous Mask: Dublin 1700–1850* (Dublin, 1987).

—— KEOGH, DÁIRE, and WHELAN, KEVIN (eds.). *The United Irishmen: Republicanism, Radicalism and Rebellion* (Dublin, 1993).

DIXON, F. E, 'The Dublin Tailors and their Hall', *Dublin Hist. Rec.* 22 (1968), 147–59.

DONNELLY, JAMES S., Jun., 'The Rightboy Movement, 1785–8', *Studia Hib.* 17–18 (1977–8), 176–202.

DONOVAN, ROBERT KENT, 'The Military Origins of the Catholic Relief Programme of 1778', *Hist. Jn.* 28 (1985), 79–102.

DOOLITTLE, I. G., 'Walpole's City Elections Act (1725)', *EHR* 97 (1982), 504–29.

DOWNIE, J. A., *Jonathan Swift, Political Writer* (London, 1984).

DOYLE, DAVID NOEL, *Ireland, Irishmen and Revolutionary America, 1760–1820* (Dublin and Cork, 1981).

DOYLE, MEL, 'The Dublin Guilds and Journeymen's Clubs', *Saothar*, 3 (1977), 6–14.

DOYLE, WILLIAM, *The Old European Order 1660–1800* (Oxford, 1978).

DUBY, GEORGES, *The Three Orders: Feudal Society Imagined* (Chicago and London, 1980).

EADES, GEORGE E., *Historic London* (London, 1966).

ECCLESHALL, ROBERT, 'Anglican Political Thought in the Century After the Revolution of 1688', in Boyce, etc. (eds.), *Political Thought in Ireland*, 36–72.

EDWARDS, R. DUDLEY, 'The Beginnings of Municipal Government in Dublin', *Dublin Hist. Rec.* 1 (1938–9), 2–10.

ELLIOTT, MARIANNE, *Partners in Revolution: The United Irishmen and France* (New Haven and London, 1982).

—— *Wolfe Tone: Prophet of Irish Independence* (New Haven and London, 1989).

FAGAN, PATRICK, 'The Population of Dublin in the Eighteenth Century with Particular Reference to the Proportions of Protestants and Catholics', *ECI* 6 (1991), 121–56.

—— *The Second City: Portrait of Dublin 1700–1760* (Dublin, 1986).

FITZPATRICK, W. J., *'The Sham Squire' and the Informers of 1798; With Jottings about Ireland a Century Ago*, new edn. (Dublin, 1895).

FORD, ALAN, *The Protestant Reformation in Ireland, 1590–1641* (Frankfurt am Main, 1985).

FOSTER, ROY, *Modern Ireland 1600–1972* (London, 1988).

FRANCIS, MARK, with MORROW, JOHN, 'After the Ancient Constitution: Political Theory and English Constitutional Writings, 1765–1832', *Hist. Pol. Thought*, 9 (1988), 283–302.

FROUDE, JAMES ANTHONY, *The English in Ireland in the Eighteenth Century* (3 vols.; London, 1872–4).

GARNER, JOHN, 'The Enfranchisement of Roman Catholics in the Maritimes', *CHR*, 34 (1953), 203–18.

GARNETT, P. F., 'The Wellington Testimonial', *Dublin Hist. Rec.* 13 (1952), 48–61.

GILBERT, JOHN T., *A History of the City of Dublin* (3 vols.; Dublin, 1854–9).

GILLESPIE, RAYMOND, 'The Irish Protestants and James II, 1688–90', *IHS* 28 (1992), 124–33.

GOLDIE, MARK, 'The Civil Religion of James Harrington', in Pagden (ed.), *The Languages of Political Theory*, 197–222.

—— 'The Political Thought of the Anglican Revolution', in Beddard (ed.), *The Revolutions of 1688*, 102–36.

GOLDSMITH, M. M., 'Faction Detected: Ideological Consequences of Robert Walpole's Decline and Fall', *History*, 44 (1979), 1–19.

GOODBODY, OLIVE, 'Anthony Sharp, Wool Merchant, 1643–1707 and the Quaker Community in Dublin', *Friends Hist. Soc. Jn.* 48 (1956), 38–50.

GOUBERT, PIERRE, *The Ancien Régime: French Society 1600–1750* (London, 1973).

GOUGH, J. W., *Fundamental Law in English Constitutional History* (Oxford, 1955).

GRAHAM, THOMAS, ' "An Union of Power"? The United Irish Organisation: 1795–1798', in Dickson, etc. (eds.), *The United Irishmen*, 244–55.

GUINNESS, HENRY S., 'Dublin Trade Gilds', *JRSAI* 52 (1922), 143–63.

GUNN, J. A. W., *Beyond Liberty and Property: The Process of Self-Recognition in Eighteenth Century Political Thought* (Kingston and Montreal, 1983).

HAMMOND, JOSEPH W., 'Mr William Cope's Petition, 1804', *Dublin Hist. Rec.* 6 (1943), 25–38.

—— 'Town Major Henry Charles Sirr', pts. 1 and 2, *Dublin Hist. Rec.* 4 (1941), 14–33, 58–75.

HARRIS, TIM, *Politics Under the Later Stuarts: Party Conflict in a Divided Society 1660–1715* (London and New York, 1993).

HAYTON, DAVID, 'Anglo-Irish Attitudes: Changing Perceptions of National Identity among the Protestant Ascendancy in Ireland, ca. 1690–1750', in John Yolton and Leslie Ellen Brown (eds.), *Studies in Eighteenth Century Culture*, 17 (1987), 145–57.

—— 'The Crisis in Ireland and the Disintegration of Queen Anne's Last Ministry', *IHS* 22 (1981), 193–215.

—— 'Walpole and Ireland', in Jeremy Black (ed.), *Britain in the Age of Walpole* (London, 1984).

HEMPTON, DAVID, and HILL, MYRTLE, *Evangelical Protestantism in Ulster Society 1740–1890* (London and New York, 1992).

HENCHY, PATRICK, 'Nelson's Pillar', *Dublin Hist. Rec.* 10 (1948), 53–63.

HILL, JACQUELINE, 'Artisans, Sectarianism and Politics in Dublin, 1829–48', *Saothar*, 7 (1981), 12–27.

—— 'Corporate Values in Hanoverian Edinburgh and Dublin', in S. Connolly, R. Houston, and R. J. Morris, (eds.), *Conflict, Identity and Economic Development, Ireland and Scotland, 1600–1939* (Preston, 1995), 114–24.

—— 'Ireland Without Union: Molyneux and his Legacy', in Robertson (ed.), *A Union for Empire*, 271–96.

—— 'The Legal Profession and the Defence of the *Ancien Regime* in Ireland, 1790–1840', in Daire Hogan and W. N. Osborough (eds.), *Brehons, Serjeants and Attorneys: Studies in the History of the Irish Legal Profession* (Dublin, 1990), 181–209.

—— 'The Meaning and Significance of "Protestant Ascendancy", 1787–1840', in *Ireland After the Union: Proceedings of the Second Joint Meeting of the Royal Irish Academy and the British Academy, London, 1986* (Oxford, 1989), 1–22.

—— 'National Festivals, the State and "Protestant Ascendancy" in Ireland, 1790–1829', *IHS* 24 (1984), 30–51.

—— 'The Politics of Dublin Corporation: 1760–92', in Dickson, etc. (eds.), *The United Irishmen*, 88–101.

—— 'The Politics of Privilege: Dublin Corporation and the Catholic Question, 1792–1823', *Maynooth Review*, 7 (1982), 17–36.

—— 'Popery and Protestantism, Civil and Religious Liberty: The Disputed Lessons of Irish History, 1690–1812', *P. & P.* 118 (1988), 96–129.

—— 'The Protestant Response to Repeal: The Case of the Dublin Working Class', in F. S. L. Lyons and R. A. J. Hawkins (eds.), *Ireland Under the Union: Varieties of Tension* (Oxford, 1980), 35–68.

—— 'Religious Toleration and the Relaxation of the Penal Laws: An Imperial Perspective, 1763–1780', *Arch. Hib.*, 44 (1989), 98–109.

—— '1641 and the Quest for Catholic Emancipation, 1691–1829', in MacCuarta (ed.), *Ulster 1641*, 159–71.

HOLDEN, P. J., 'Local Taxation in Dublin, 1812', *Dublin Hist. Rec.* 12 (1951), 114–28, cont. in 13 (1953), 133–7.

HOLE, ROBERT, *Pulpits, Politics and Public Order in England, 1760–1832* (Cambridge, 1989).

HOPPEN, K. THEODORE, *Elections, Politics and Society in Ireland 1832–1885* (Oxford, 1984).

HUTTON, RONALD, *Charles II King of England, Scotland, and Ireland* (Oxford and New York, 1991).

HYLTON, R. P., 'Dublin's Huguenot Communities: Trials, Development, and Triumph, 1662–1701', *Hug. Soc. Proc.* 24 (1985), 221–31.

INGLIS, BRIAN, *The Freedom of the Press in Ireland 1784–1841* (London, 1954).

JACOB, ROSAMOND, *The Rise of the United Irishmen 1791–94* (London, 1937).

JAMES, F. G., *Ireland in the Empire 1688–1770* (Cambridge, Mass., 1973).

JARRETT, DEREK, 'The Myth of "Patriotism" in Eighteenth-Century English Politics', in J. S. Bromley and E. H. Kossman (eds.), *Britain and the Netherlands*, v (The Hague, 1975), 120–40.

JOHNSTON, E. M., *Great Britain and Ireland, 1760–1800* (Edinburgh, 1963).

JONES, J. R., *The First Whigs: The Politics of the Exclusion Crisis, 1678–1683* (London, 1961).

JUPP, PETER, *Lord Grenville 1759–1834* (Oxford, 1985).

—— 'Urban Politics in Ireland 1801–1831', in David Harkness and Mary O'Dowd (eds.), *The Town in Ireland: Historical Studies, XIII* (Belfast, 1981), 103–23.

KAMENKA, EUGENE (ED.), *Nationalism: The Nature and Evolution of an Idea* (Canberra, 1973).

KELLETT, J. R., 'The Breakdown of Gild and Corporation Control Over the Handicraft and Retail Trade in London', *Econ. Hist. Rev.*, 2nd ser., 10 (1958), 381–94.

KELLY, JAMES, 'Eighteenth-Century Ascendancy: A Commentary', *ECI* 5 (1990), 173–87.

—— ' "The Glorious and Immortal Memory": Commemoration and Protestant Identity in Ireland 1660–1800', *RIA Proc.* 94C (1994). 25–52.

—— 'The Irish Trade Dispute with Portugal, 1780–87', *Studia Hib.* 25 (1989–90), 7–48.

—— 'Napper Tandy: Radical and Republican', in J. Kelly and U. MacGearailt (eds.), *Dublin and Dubliners: Essays in the History and Literature of Dublin City* (Dublin, 1990), 1–24.

—— 'The Origins of the Act of Union: An Examination of Unionist Opinion in Britain and Ireland, 1650–1800', *IHS* 25 (1987), 236–63.

—— 'The Parliamentary Reform Movement of the 1780s and the Catholic Question', *Arch. Hib.* 43 (1988), 95–117.

—— *Prelude to Union: Anglo-Irish Politics in the 1780s* (Cork, 1992).

—— 'A Secret Return of the Volunteers of Ireland in 1784', *IHS* 26 (1989), 268–92.

—— *That Damn'd Thing Called Honour: Duelling in Ireland 1570–1860* (Cork, 1995).

KELLY, PATRICK, 'Ireland and the Glorious Revolution: From Kingdom to Colony', in Beddard (ed.), *The Revolutions of 1688*, 163–90.

—— 'Perceptions of Locke in Eighteenth Century Ireland', *RIA Proc.* 89C (1989), 17–35.

—— 'William Molyneux and the Spirit of Liberty in Eighteenth-Century Ireland', *ECI* 3 (1988), 133–48.

KEMP, BETTY, 'Patriotism, Pledges and the People', in Martin Gilbert (ed.), *A Century of Conflict 1850–1950: Essays for A. J. P. Taylor* (London, 1966), 37–46.

KENYON, J. P., 'The Revolution of 1688: Resistance and Contract', in McKendrick (ed.), *Historical Perspectives*, 43–69.

KING, C. S. (ed.), *A Great Archbishop of Dublin, William King D.D., 1650–1729* (London, 1906).

KOEBNER, RICHARD, *Empire*, Universal Library edn. (New York, 1965).

LANGFORD, PAUL, 'London and the American Revolution', in Stevenson (ed.), *London in the Age of Reform*, 55–78.

—— *A Polite and Commercial People: England 1727–1783* (Oxford, 1992).

LECKY, W. E. H., *A History of Ireland in the Eighteenth Century*, abridged edn. (Chicago and London, 1972).

LEERSSEN, J. T., 'Anglo-Irish Patriotism and its European Context: Notes Towards a Reassessment', *ECI* 3 (1988), 7–24.

LE FANU, T. P., 'A Note on Two Charters of the Smiths' Guild of Dublin', *JRSAI* 60 (1930), 150–64.

LEIGHTON, C. D. A., *Catholicism in a Protestant Kingdom: A Study of the Irish Ancien Régime* (Dublin, 1994).

—— 'Gallicanism and the Veto Controversy: Church, State and Catholic Community in Early Nineteenth Century Ireland', in Comerford, etc. (eds.), *Religion, Conflict and Coexistence*, 135–58.

—— *The Irish Manufacture Movement 1840–1843* (Maynooth Historical Series, 5, Maynooth, 1987).

LENNON, COLM, *The Lords of Dublin in the Age of Reformation* (Dublin, 1989).

LEVACK, BRIAN P., *The Formation of the British State: England, Scotland and the Union 1603–1707* (Oxford, 1987).

LEVIN, JENNIFER, *The Charter Controversy in the City of London, 1660–1688, and its Consequences* (London, 1969).

LIECHTY, JOSEPH, 'The Popular Reformation Comes to Ireland: The Case of John Walker and the Foundation of the Church of God, 1804', in Comerford, etc. (eds.), *Religion, Conflict and Coexistence*, 159–87.

LINDSAY, DEIRDRE, 'The Fitzwilliam Episode Revisited', in Dickson, etc. (eds.), *The United Irishmen*, 197–208.

LUCAS, COLIN, 'The Crowd and Politics Between *Ancien Régime* and Revolution in France', *JMH* 60 (1988), 421–57.

LYDON, JAMES, 'The Medieval City', in Cosgrove (ed.), *Dublin Through the Ages*, 25–45.

LYNCH, PATRICK, and VAIZEY, JOHN, *Guinness's Brewery in the Irish Economy 1759–1876* (Cambridge, 1960).

LYONS, F. S. L. (ed.), *Bicentenary Essays: Bank of Ireland 1783–1983* (Dublin, 1983).

MCBRIDE, IAN, 'William Drennan and the Dissenting Tradition', in Dickson, etc. (eds.), *The United Irishmen*, 49–61.

MCCORMACK, W. J., *Ascendancy and Tradition in Anglo-Irish Literary History from 1789 to 1939* (Oxford, 1985).

MACCUARTA, BRIAN (ed.), *Ulster 1641: Aspects of the Rising* (Belfast, 1993).

MACDONAGH, OLIVER, *O'Connell: The Life of Daniel O'Connell 1775–1847* (London, 1991).

MCDOWELL, R. B, 'Dublin and Belfast—A Comparison', in id. (ed.), *Social Life in Ireland 1800–45* (Cork, 1973), 11–24.

—— *Ireland in the Age of Imperialism and Revolution 1760–1801* (Oxford, 1979).

—— *Irish Public Opinion 1750–1800* (London, 1944).

—— 'The Personnel of the Dublin Society of United Irishmen, 1791–4', *IHS* 2 (1940–1), 12–53.

—— *Public Opinion and Government Policy in Ireland 1801–46* (London, 1952).

MCGUIRE, J. I., 'The Church of Ireland and the "Glorious Revolution" of 1688', in Art Cosgrove and Donal McCartney (eds.), *Studies in Irish History Presented to R. Dudley Edwards* (Dublin, 1979), 137–49.

—— 'Government Attitudes to Religious Non-Conformity in Ireland 1660–1719', in Caldicott, etc. (eds.), *The Huguenots in Ireland*, 255–84.

—— 'The Irish Parliament of 1692', in Bartlett and Hayton (eds.), *Penal Era and Golden Age*, 1–31.

MACHIN, G. I. T., *The Catholic Question in English Politics 1820–1830* (Oxford, 1964).

McKendrick, Neil (ed.), *Historical Perspectives: Studies in English Thought and Society in Honour of J. H. Plumb* (London, 1974).

McNamara, Gerard, 'Crown Versus Municipality: The Struggle for Dublin 1713', *Dublin Hist. Rec.* 39 (1986), 108–17.

McParland, Edward, 'A Note on George II and St Stephen's Green', *ECI* 2 (1987), 187–95.

—— 'Strategy in the Planning of Dublin, 1750–1800', in Butel and Cullen (eds.), *Cities and Merchants*, 97–107.

McWalter, James C., *A History of the Worshipful Company of Apothecaries of the City of Dublin* (Dublin, 1916).

Maitland, F. W., *The Constitutional History of England*, ed. H. A. L. Fisher (Cambridge, 1908).

Malcomson, A. P. W., *John Foster: The Politics of the Anglo-Irish Ascendancy* (Oxford, 1978).

Maxwell, Constantia, *Dublin Under the Georges 1714–1830*, Sackville Library edn. (Dublin, 1979).

Miller, John, 'The Crown and the Borough Charters in the Reign of Charles II', *EHR* 100 (1985), 53–84.

Miller, Kerby A., 'No Middle Ground: The Erosion of the Protestant Middle Class in Southern Ireland during the Pre-Famine Era', *Huntington Library Quarterly*, 49 (1986), 295–306.

Milne, Kenneth, 'The Corporation of Waterford in the Eighteenth Century', in W. Nolan and T. P. Power (eds.), *Waterford: History and Society* (Dublin, 1992), 331–50.

Monks, Patrick J., 'The Aldermen of Skinner's Alley', *Dublin Hist. Rec.* 19 (1963–4), 45–63.

Moody, T. W., Martin, F. X., Byrne, F. J. (eds.), *A New History of Ireland*, iii. *Early Modern Ireland, 1534–1691* (Oxford, 1976).

—— and Vaughan, W. E. (eds.), *A New History of Ireland*, iv. *Eighteenth-Century Ireland, 1691–1800* (Oxford, 1986).

Murphy, Sean, 'Charles Lucas, Catholicism and Nationalism', *ECI* 8 (1993), 83–102.

—— 'Charles Lucas and the Dublin Election of 1748–1749', *Parl. Hist.* 2 (1983), 93–111.

—— 'The Corporation of Dublin 1660–1760', *Dublin Hist. Rec.* 38 (1984), 22–35.

—— 'The Dublin Anti-Union Riot of 3 December 1759', in O'Brien (ed.), *Parliament, Politics and People*, 49–68.

Newman, Gerald, *The Rise of English Nationalism: A Cultural History 1740–1830* (London, 1987).

Nowlan, Kevin B., 'The Meaning of Repeal in Irish History', in G. A. Hayes McCoy (ed.), *Historical Studies IV* (London, 1963), 1–17.

O'Brien, Conor Cruise, *The Great Melody: A Thematic Biography and Commented Anthology of Edmund Burke* (London, 1992).

O'Brien, Gerard, 'The Grattan Mystique', *ECI* 1 (1986), 177–94.

—— (ed.), *Parliament, Politics and People* (Dublin, 1989).

O'Connell, Maurice R., *Daniel O'Connell: The Man and his Politics* (Dublin, 1990).

O'CONNELL, MAURICE R., *Irish Politics and Social Conflict in the Age of the American Revolution* (Philadelphia, 1965).

O'DONOVAN, DECLAN, 'The Money Bill Dispute of 1753', in Bartlett and Hayton (eds.), *Penal Era and Golden Age*, 55–87.

O'FERRALL, FERGUS, *Catholic Emancipation: Daniel O'Connell and the Birth of Irish Democracy 1820–30* (Dublin, 1985).

O'FLAHERTY, EAMON, 'Urban Politics and Municipal Reform in Limerick, 1723–62', *ECI*, 6 (1991), 105–20.

O'GORMAN, FRANK, 'Electoral Deference in "Unreformed" England: 1760–1832', *JMH* 56 (1984), 391–429.

PAGDEN, ANTHONY (ed.), *The Languages of Political Theory in Early-Modern Europe* (Cambridge, 1987).

PAKENHAM, THOMAS, *The Year of Liberty: The Story of the Great Irish Rebellion of 1798* (London, 1969).

PALMER, STANLEY H., *Police and Protest in England and Ireland 1780–1850* (Cambridge, 1988).

PETERS, MARIE, ' "Names and Cant": Party Labels in English Political Propaganda c. 1755–1765', *Parl. Hist.* 3 (1984), 103–27.

PHILLIPS, JOHN A., 'Popular Politics in Unreformed England', *JMH* 52 (1980), 599–625.

—— and WETHERELL, CHARLES, 'The Great Reform Act of 1832 and the Political Modernization of England', *AHR* 100 (1995), 411–36.

PHILLIPSON, NICHOLAS, and SKINNER, QUENTIN (eds.), *Political Discourse in Early Modern Britain* (Cambridge, 1993).

PINCUS, STEVEN, 'The English Debate Over Universal Monarchy', in Robertson (ed.), *A Union for Empire*, 37–62.

POCOCK, J. G. A., *The Ancient Constitution and the Feudal Law* (Cambridge, 1957).

—— 'The Fourth English Civil War: Dissolution, Desertion and Alternative Histories in the Glorious Revolution', *Government and Opposition*, 23 (1988), 151–66.

—— *The Machiavellian Moment: Florentine Political Thought and the Atlantic Republican Tradition* (Princeton and London, 1975).

—— 'The Machiavellian Moment Revisited: A Study in History and Ideology', *JMH* 53 (1981), 49–72.

—— *Virtue, Commerce, and History* (Cambridge, 1985).

POLLARD, M., *Dublin's Trade in Books 1550–1800* (Oxford, 1989).

—— 'John Chambers, Printer and United Irishman', *The Irish Book*, 3 (1964), 1–22.

POPKIN, RICHARD (ed.), *Millenarianism and Messianism in English Literature and Thought 1650–1800* (Leiden and New York, 1988).

POTTER, JANICE, *The Liberty We Seek: Loyalist Ideology in Colonial New York and Massachusetts* (Cambridge, Mass., and London, 1983).

QUANE, MICHAEL, 'The Hibernian Marine School, Dublin', *Dublin Hist. Rec.* 21 (1966–7), 67–78.

—— 'The Royal Hibernian Military School', pts. 1 and 2, *Dublin Hist. Rec.* 18 (1962–3), 15–23, 45–55.

REDLICH, JOSEF, and HIRST, FRANCIS W., *The History of Local Government in England*, 2nd edn. (London, 1970).

ROBBINS, CAROLINE, *The Eighteenth Century Commonwealthman. Studies in the Transmission, Development and Circumstance of English Liberal Thought from the Restoration of Charles II until the War with the Thirteen Colonies* (Cambridge, Mass., 1959).

ROBERTSON, JOHN, 'The Scottish Enlightenment at the Limits of the Civic Tradition', in Istvan Hont and Michael Ignatieff (eds.), *Wealth and Virtue: The Shaping of Political Economy in the Scottish Enlightenment* (Cambridge, 1983), 137–78.

—— (ed.), *A Union for Empire: The Union of 1707 in the History of British Political Thought* (Cambridge, 1995).

ROGERS, NICHOLAS, 'Aristocratic Clientage, Trade and Independency: Popular Politics in Pre-Radical Westminster', *P. & P.* 61 (1973), 70–106.

—— 'Popular Jacobitism in Provincial Context: Eighteenth-Century Bristol and Norwich', in Eveline Cruickshanks and Jeremy Black (eds.), *The Jacobite Challenge* (Edinburgh, 1988), 123–41.

—— 'Resistance to Oligarchy: The City Opposition to Walpole and his Successors, 1725–47', in Stevenson (ed.), *London in the Age of Reform*, 1–29.

—— *Whigs and Cities: Popular Politics in the Age of Walpole and Pitt* (Oxford, 1989).

ROSENFELD, DAVID, 'Rousseau's Unanimous Contract and the Doctrine of Popular Sovereignty', *Hist. Pol. Thought*, 8 (1987), 83–110.

RUCK, S. K., and RHODES, GERALD, *The Government of Greater London* (London, 1970).

RUDÉ, GEORGE, *Wilkes and Liberty: A Social Study of 1763 to 1774* (Oxford, 1965).

SACRET, J. H., 'The Restoration Government and Municipal Corporations', *EHR* 45 (1930), 232–59.

SAGARRA, EDA, 'Frederick II and his Image in Eighteenth Century Dublin', *Hermathena*, 142 (1987), 50–8.

SAMUEL, RAPHAEL (ed.), *Patriotism: The Making and Unmaking of English National Identity* (3 vols.; London, 1989).

SEAWARD, PAUL, *The Restoration, 1660–1688* (London, 1991).

SENIOR, HEREWARD, *Orangeism in Ireland and Britain 1795–1836* (London and Toronto, 1966).

SIBBETT, R. M., *Orangeism in Ireland and Throughout the Empire*, 2nd edn. (2 vols.; London [1939]).

SIMMS, J. G., *Colonial Nationalism, 1698–1776* (Cork, 1976).

—— 'Dublin in 1776', *Dublin Hist. Rec.* 31 (1977–8), 2–13.

—— *Jacobite Ireland 1685–91* (London, 1969).

—— *William Molyneux of Dublin 1656–1698: A Life of the Seventeenth-Century Political Writer and Scientist*, ed. P. H. Kelly (Dublin, 1982).

SKINNER, QUENTIN, *The Foundations of Modern Political Thought* (2 vols.; Cambridge, 1978).

—— 'The Principles and Practice of Opposition: The Case of Bolingbroke versus Walpole', in McKendrick (ed.), *Historical Perspectives*, 93–128.

SMITH, ANTHONY D., *Theories of Nationalism*, 2nd edn. (London, 1983).

SMITH, R. J., *The Gothic Bequest: Medieval Institutions in British Thought, 1688–1863* (Cambridge, 1987).

SMYTH, JIM, *The Men of No Property: Irish Radicals and Popular Politics in the Late Eighteenth Century* (Dublin, 1992).

SMYTH, P. D. H., 'The Volunteers and Parliament, 1779–84', in Bartlett and Hayton (eds.), *Penal Era and Golden Age*, 113–36.

SNELL, K. D. M., *Annals of the Labouring Poor: Social Change and Agrarian England, 1660–1900* (Cambridge, 1985).

SNODDY, OLIVER, 'The Charter of the Guild of St Luke, 1670', *JRSAI* 98 (1968), 79–87.

SOMERS, HUGH J., 'The Legal Status of the Bishop of Quebec', *Catholic Historical Review*, 19 (1933–4), 167–89.

STEVENSON, JOHN (ed.), *London in the Age of Reform* (Oxford, 1977).

STUBBS, WILLIAM COTTER, 'The Weavers' Guild, the Guild of the Blessed Virgin Mary, Dublin, 1446–1840', *JRSAI* 49 (1919), 60–88.

SWIFT, JOHN, *History of the Dublin Bakers and Others* (Dublin [1948]).

TE BRAKE, WAYNE P., *Regents and Rebels: The Revolutionary World of an Eighteenth-Century Dutch City* (Oxford, 1989).

TUVESON, ERNEST LEE, *Redeemer Nation: The Idea of America's Millennial Role* (Chicago and London, 1968).

VAUGHAN, W. E. (ed.), *A New History of Ireland*, v. *Ireland Under the Union, 1. 1801–1870* (Oxford, 1989).

WALKER, MACK, 'Rights and Functions: The Social Categories of Eighteenth-Century German Jurists and Cameralists', *JMH* 50 (1978), 234–51.

WALL, MAUREEN, *Catholic Ireland in the Eighteenth Century: Collected Essays of Maureen Wall*, ed. Gerard O'Brien (Dublin, 1989).

WARD, JOHN MANNING, *Colonial Self-Government: The British Experience 1759–1856* (London, 1976).

WEBB, JOHN J., *The Guilds of Dublin* (Dublin, 1929; London, 1970 repr.).

WEBB, S. AND B., *The History of Trade Unionism* (London, 1894).

WELLS, ROGER, *Insurrection: The British Experience 1795–1803* (Gloucester, 1983).

WESTERN, J. R., *Monarchy and Revolution: The English State in the 1680s* (London, 1972).

WHELAN, KEVIN, 'The United Irishmen, the Enlightenment, and Popular Culture', in Dickson, etc. (eds.), *The United Irishmen*, 269–96.

WHITE, TERENCE DE VERE, 'The Freemasons', in T. D. Williams (ed.), *Secret Societies in Ireland* (Dublin, 1973), 46–57.

WHITESIDE, LESLEY, *A History of the King's Hospital*, 2nd edn. (Dublin, 1985).

WILLMAN, ROBERT, 'The Origins of "Whig" and "Tory" in English Political Language', *Hist. Jn.* 17 (1974), 247–64.

WOOD, NIGEL, *Swift* (Brighton, 1986).

WOLFFE, JOHN, *The Protestant Crusade in Great Britain 1829–1860* (Oxford, 1991).

UNPUBLISHED PAPERS AND THESES

BURKE, NUALA T., 'Dublin 1600–1800: A Study in Urban Morphogenesis', Ph.D. thesis (TCD, 1972).

D'ARCY, F. A., 'Dublin Artisan Activity, Opinion and Organisation, 1820–50', MA thesis (NUI (UCD), 1968).

DUDLEY, ROWENA V., 'Dublin's Parishes 1660–1729: The Church of Ireland Parishes and Their Role in the Civic Administration of the City', Ph.D. thesis (2 vols.; TCD, 1995).

FITZPATRICK, BRENDAN, 'The Municipal Corporation of Dublin 1603–40', Ph.D. thesis (2 vols.; TCD, 1984).

FLANAGAN, CATHERINE M., ' "A Merely Local Dispute"? Partisan Politics and the Dublin Mayoral Dispute of 1709–1715', Ph.D. thesis (Notre Dame, Ind., 1983).

GEARY, FRANK, 'Counting the Cost of the Union. Anglo-Irish Trade and De-Industrialization in Pre-Famine Ireland' (Paper delivered to conference of the Economic and Social History Society of Ireland, UCD, 1993).

HARRISON, RICHARD S., 'Dublin Quakers in Business 1800–1850', M.Litt. thesis (2 vols.; TCD, 1987).

HAYDON, COLIN MARK, 'Anti-Catholicism in Eighteenth Century England c. 1714–c. 1780', D.Phil. thesis (Oxford, 1985).

HAYTON, DAVID, 'Ireland and the English Ministers, 1707–16', D.Phil. thesis (Oxford, 1975).

HILL, JACQUELINE, 'The Role of Dublin in the Irish National Movement, 1840–48', Ph.D. thesis (Leeds, 1973).

KELLY, JAMES J., 'The Irish Parliamentary Reform Movement: The Administration and Popular Politics, 1783–5', MA thesis (NUI (UCD), 1981).

LIECHTY, JOSEPH, 'Irish Evangelicalism, Trinity College Dublin, and the Mission of the Church of Ireland at the End of the Eighteenth Century', Ph.D. thesis (NUI (Maynooth), 1987).

McCOY, JOHN G., 'Court Ideology in Mid-Eighteenth Century Ireland: An Examination of Political Culture', MA thesis (NUI (Maynooth), 1990).

—— 'Local Political Culture in the Hanoverian Empire: The Case of Ireland, 1714–1760', D.Phil. thesis (Oxford, 1993).

MILNE, KENNETH, 'The Irish Municipal Corporations in the Eighteenth Century', Ph.D. thesis (TCD, 1962).

MURPHY, SEAN, 'The Lucas Affair: A Study of Municipal and Electoral Politics in Dublin, 1742–9', MA thesis (NUI (UCD), 1981).

SPENCE, JOSEPH, 'The Philosophy of Irish Toryism, 1833–52', Ph.D. thesis (University of London (Birkbeck College), 1991).

VICTORY, ISOLDE, 'Colonial Nationalism in Ireland, 1692–1725: From Common Law to Natural Right', Ph.D. thesis (TCD, 1984).

Index

Patriots *(cont.)*:
  example of London 96–105
  and exclusion crisis 55–8
  fragmentation of 226–34
  and Hanoverian succession 78–83
  justification of office 132, 271–2
  'ministerial' 252
  new radicalism 234–7
  opposed to union 261–2
  parliamentary reform 166–70
  Protestantism 134–7
  and restoration 45–55
  revolutionary era (1774–82) 138–65
  unionists 376–83
  use of term 56–7, 75, 103–5
  Williamite commemorations 156–8
  see also Court Patriots
patron saints 37
patronage 132, 145, 154, 170–1
  corporation independent of 185–6
Patterson, William 266, 270 n., 355 n.
paving act (1774) 195
paving bill 173, 175, 183 n.
paving board 160, 268
Pearson, Nathaniel 393
Peel, Sir Robert 318, 343, 351 n., 372–3, 376, 379
Peep O'Day Boys 239, 245–6
Pemberton, Benjamin 210, 299–300
Pemberton, Joseph 249, 250–1
penal laws 4, 225, 228, 239, 379, 386
  effects of relaxation 293, 330, 332, 333
  relaxation of 7, 34, 134–5, 158, 195, 213–15, 231, 244, 264, 270
Penn, William 155
Percy, Anthony 67
Perrin Louis 344, 370 n., 393
Peters, John 361
Petty, Sir William 3
Phepoe, John 179 n.
philosophy, develoments in 136–7
Phipps, Sir Constantine 71, 72, 74, 77, 157
Pilot, the 361
Pim family 200
Pim's mill 287
pipe-water committee 84
Pitt, William, the elder, earl of Chatham 120, 127 n., 157
  and Brooke 98
  defends Protestant constitution 140
  Patriot appointment 118 n.
  takes office as Patriot 132
Pitt, William, the younger 216, 218
  and Catholic relief 214
  death of 265
  parliamentary reform 193
  policing 183
  resignation 273 n.
  union proposal 257–8

Pitt club 132
Pius VII, Pope 301
plantations 44–5
plasterers' guild, *see* bricklayers' guild
Plunket, W. C. 303, 323
Plunkett, Sir Nicholas 54
Pocock, J. G. A. 4
police act (1786) 182 n., 183–90, 356
police act (1795) 246
police act (1808) 265, 268, 293, 318
police system 42, 193, 195–6, 221, 234, 242, 250, 318
political languages 7–15, 225
political parties 100, 101–5, 154, 354
Pollock, Joseph 177 n.
Ponsonby, George 188
Ponsonby, John 162 n.
Poole, Jacob 246
poor law 288, 347
popery 75, 101, 103, 165, 386
  after emancipation 367, 374–5
  anti-popery agitation 141–2
  as disloyalty 33, 219
  linked with absolutism 88–9, 165, 224
  seen as disloyalty 134
  seen as political 95
Popham, Sir Home Rigg 280
Popish Plot 35, 52 n., 55–6
population 91, 162, 197, 291, 332
  census of 294
  growth 288
  Protestant percentage 26, 33, 37, 197, 293–5
Portugal 151, 172
poundage 44
Poynings' law 38, 89, 116, 126
  amended 152, 168
  change sought 150
Presbyterians 10, 20, 89, 176, 221
  and Anglicans 60
  as candidates 164, 172
  and Catholic emancipation 366
  in corporation 250, 252, 260, 341
  exclusion 100–1
  marriages valid 153 n.
  'new light' 102
  regium donum 100
  and restoration 45, 47
  union proposals 259, 260
Present State of the Church of Ireland, The (Woodward) 169–70, 334
press bill 175
press freedom 110–11, 132, 173, 174, 176, 181, 302
Price, Dr Richard 212, 224
prince regent, *see* George IV
printers 110, 113–14, 132, 176, 181, 288–9, 299